FAIR DEBT COLLECTION PRACTICES ACT

CONTEMPORARY DECISIONS

Volume 1

* * *

A LandMark Publication

Litigator Series

Fair Debt Collection Practices Act
Contemporary Decisions
Volume 1

Published in the United States of America
by LandMark Publications.
www.landmark-publications.org

Publication Date: September 2024;
Subject Heading: Debtor Creditor Law;
Audience: Law Professionals.

Character Set: ISO 8859-1 (Latin-1);
Language Code: EN;
Interior Type: Text; Monochrome.

Help us serve you better.
Write to landmarkpx@live.com with
your requests, comments and suggestions.

ISBN: 979-8330294909

SUMMARY OF CONTENTS

Prologue

Attempting to collect on a time-barred debt does not *per se* violate the FDCPA. *Manuel,* 956 F.3d at 829; *see also Mahmoud v. De Moss Owners Ass'n, Inc.,* 865 F.3d 322, 333 (5th Cir. 2017) (holding it was not a violation of the FDCPA to collect a partially time-barred debt when only a small portion was subject to the statute of limitations); *Holzman v. Malcolm S. Gerald & Assocs., Inc.,* 920 F.3d 1264, 1273-74 (11th Cir. 2019) ("[C]ourts generally have recognized that the FDCPA does not impose a bright-line rule prohibiting debt collectors from attempting to collect on time-barred debt."). But a debt-collector can run afoul of the FDCPA by threatening judicial action while completely failing to mention that a limitations period might affect judicial enforceability. *Manuel,* 956 F.3d at 831 (emphasizing that disclosure of a potential limitations problem "might give a consumer at least some inkling that the debt might be too old to be legally enforceable"). As we have explained:

> When a collection letter creates confusion about a creditor's right to sue, that is illegal. The FDCPA singles out as unlawful the false representation of the character, amount, or legal status of any debt. Whether a debt is legally enforceable is a central fact about the character and legal status of that debt. A misrepresentation about the limitations period amounts to a straightforward violation of § 1692e(2)(A).

Daugherty v. Convergent Outsourcing, Inc., 836 F.3d 507, 512 (5th Cir. 2016) (quotation omitted).

Calogero v. Shows, Cali & Walsh, LLP, 95 F. 4th 951 (5th Cir. 2024)

FOREWORD

THIS CASEBOOK contains a selection of U. S. Court of Appeals decisions that analyze, discuss and interpret provisions of the Fair Debt Collection Practices Act. Volume 1 of the casebook covers the District of Columbia Circuit and the First through the Fifth Circuit Court of Appeals.

In 2018, Huber visited doctors in the Crozer Health Network (Crozer) on four separate occasions. As a result, she incurred the following debts to Crozer: $178 on February 9, $78 on February 22, $83.50 on March 27, and $178 on May 22. Crozer contracted with SAI—a debt collection agency that specializes in medical billing—to collect outstanding bills from Huber and other patients. *See Huber v. Simon's Agency, Inc.*, 84 F. 4th 132 (3rd Cir. 2023).

Whenever Crozer placed a debt with SAI, SAI sent a form collection letter to the debtor. That letter set out an "Account Summary" that provided the debtor with two figures: in one box, the specific debt SAI sought to collect, entitled "Amount," and in another box, a second figure, entitled "Various Other Acc[oun]ts Total Balance." App. 7. By way of example, the fourth such letter Huber received between May and September of 2018—one for each of her debts to Crozer—showed as follows:

The "Account Summary" informed Huber that she owed an "Amount" of $178, while her "Various Other Accounts Total Balance" was listed at $517.50. *Id.*

Huber brought suit against SAI. According to her deposition testimony, Huber was confused after reading the letter as to how much she owed in total: Was it $695.50 (the sum of the "Amount" and "Various Other Accounts Total Balance") or $517.50 (just the "Various Other Accounts Total Balance")? Uncertain which amount was due, she paid neither. Instead, she sent the letter to a financial advisor she had retained to help her "take care of [her] financial situation."

Following discovery, both parties moved for summary judgment on Huber's § 1692e claim, and Huber prevailed.

Claiming that hundreds of other debtors were also subject to this violation, Huber moved to certify a class under Federal Rule of Civil Procedure 23(b)(3). Her proposed class consisted of "all consumers in Clifton Heights, PA (1) who received a [form] Collection letter from the Defendant (2) containing a reference to 'Various Other Accounts[,'] (3) on an obligation owed or allegedly owed to Crozer, (4) during the time period of April 4, 2018 to May 30, 2018." The District Court granted the motion, holding the proposed class satisfied the numerosity, commonality, typicality, and adequacy requirements of Rule 23(a), and the predominance and superiority requirements of Rule 23(b)(3).

The parties stipulated to the statutory damages Huber and the class would receive under the FDCPA if the District Court's rulings were upheld on appeal. Huber would receive $1,000 in statutory damages; the unnamed class members would collectively receive $5,000 in statutory damages to be "distributed on a pro rata basis"; and Huber would also receive a $5,000 service award "for her work in representing the class over the past three years." *Id.* at 52-53. The District Court entered the stipulation as a final appealable order, and SAI timely appealed.

Affirmed in part — SAI's letter is "deceptive" for purposes of § 1692e. On remand, Huber should submit evidence enabling the District Court to estimate "how many class members (or what proportion of them)" have standing.

* * *

To prevail on an FDCPA claim, a plaintiff must establish that: "(1) she is a consumer, (2) the defendant is a debt collector, (3) the defendant's challenged practice involves an attempt to collect a 'debt' as the [FDCPA] defines it, and (4) the defendant has violated a provision of the FDCPA in attempting to collect the debt." *St. Pierre,* 898 F.3d at 358 (quoting *Douglass v. Convergent Outsourcing,* 765 F.3d 299, 303 (3d Cir. 2014)). The first three elements are uncontested here, so the only question for us is whether the District Court correctly determined that SAI's form letter transgresses the FDCPA— specifically, the prohibition on the "use [of] any false, deceptive, or misleading representation or means in connection with the collection of any debt." 15 U.S.C. § 1692e.

Like the District Court, we make that assessment applying the "least sophisticated debtor" standard. *Moyer v. Patenaude & Felix, A.P.C.,* 991 F.3d 466, 470 (3d Cir. 2021) (quoting *Jensen v. Pressler & Pressler,* 791 F.3d 413, 418 (3d Cir. 2015)); *see also Riccio v. Sentry Credit, Inc.,* 954 F.3d 582, 594 (3d Cir. 2020) (en banc). Under that test, we consider "whether a debt collector's statement in a communication to a debtor would *deceive* or *mislead* the least sophisticated debtor." *Jensen,* 791 F.3d at 420. Because the standard is objective, "the specific plaintiff need not prove that *she* was actually confused or misled, only that the objective least sophisticated debtor would be." *Id.* at 419.

Although the least sophisticated debtor test "protects naïve consumers, it also prevents liability for bizarre or idiosyncratic interpretations of collection notices by preserving a quotient of reasonableness and presuming a basic level of understanding and willingness to read with care." *Wilson v. Quadramed Corp.,* 225 F.3d 350, 354-55 (3d Cir. 2000) (quotation omitted). Accordingly, we have held that a collection letter is deceptive when "it can be reasonably read to have two or more different meanings, one of which is inaccurate." *Moyer,* 991 F.3d at 470 (quoting *Wilson,* 225 F.3d at 354).

Here, the District Court correctly observed that the "Account Summary" in SAI's form letter could be reasonably interpreted in two ways because, without further explanation, it sets out both an "Amount" and "Various Other Accounts Total Balance." Thus, a least sophisticated debtor could read the latter as "Various Other Accounts *Total Balance,*" meaning the sum total of her out-standing debt, including the "Amount." Alternatively, a least sophisticated debtor could read it as "*Various Other Accounts* Total Balance," meaning she owes that figure in addition to the "Amount." So as SAI itself acknowledges, "[i]n a vacuum, the Letter could reasonably be read to have the two meanings ascribed by the District Court," Opening Br. 30, and "one of [them] is inaccurate," *Moyer,* 991 F.3d at 470 (quotation omitted). That is the very definition of a "deceptive" communication, in violation of § 1692e.

SAI resists that conclusion by arguing that a debtor in Huber's situation would have deduced the meaning of "Various Other Accounts Total Balance" by comparing the fourth letter she received with the three prior collection letters SAI sent her. *See* Opening Br. 31 ("Each correspondence was about a separate account and the 'Total Balance' identified increased each time by the amount owed for that specific amount.").

That argument highlights the open question whether the least sophisticated debtor standard is "purely objective" or instead "look[s] to what an objective debtor in [the plaintiff's] situation . . . would have thought or done," *Jensen,* 791 F.3d at 422 n.4, but it is not a question to answer today. SAI sent those letters to Huber on May 24, June 14, and July 12, 2018—months before it mailed her its fourth collection letter on September 6, 2018, App. 281-84—and in the intervals between the collection letters, a least sophisticated debtor "may have lost the [prior letters] and forgotten the amount of the debt completely," *Fields v. Wilber L. Firm, P.C.,* 383 F.3d 562, 566 (7th Cir. 2004); *see also Lukawski v. Client Servs., Inc.,* No. 3:12-cv-02082, 2013 WL 4647482, at *3 (M.D. Pa. Aug. 29, 2013) ("[A] least sophisticated consumer, gullible, trusting, and naïve . . . cannot be expected to recall . . . a collection letter received six weeks prior to a current communication."). So even if we look beyond the four corners of SAI's letter, we would not expect a least sophisticated debtor in Huber's position to recall the precise figures in the prior letters, much less understand clearly what amount was due.

In short, whether we examine the fourth collection letter from the perspective of a purely objective least sophisticated debtor or a least sophisticated debtor in Huber's position, SAI's letter is "deceptive" for purposes of § 1692e. We therefore affirm the District Court's grant of summary judgment in Huber's favor on that claim.

* * *

Because Huber has Article III standing, her proposed class action presents a justiciable case or controversy even though some unnamed class members may lack standing. [. . .] On the other hand, the possibility that some unnamed class members lack standing may prevent certification under Federal Rule of Civil Procedure 23.

DC Circuit Decisions

Fair Debt Collection Practices Act

961 F.3d 1185 (2020)

Phyllis FRANK, Individually and on Behalf of All Others Similarly Situated, Appellant
v.
AUTOVEST, LLC, et al., Appellees.

No. 19-7119.

United States Court of Appeals, District of Columbia Circuit.

Argued May 7, 2020.
Decided June 9, 2020.

Frank v. Autovest, LLC, 961 F. 3d 1185 (DC Cir. 2020)

Appeal from the United States District Court for the District of Columbia, (No. 1:17-cv-02773)

Dean Gregory argued the cause and filed the briefs for appellant.

Scott A. King, Dayton, OH, argued the cause for appellees. With him on the brief were Jessica E. Salisbury-Copper, Dayton, OH, and Eric N. Heyer, Washington, DC.

Before: Srinivasan, Chief Judge, and Griffith and Millett, Circuit Judges.

p.1186 GRIFFITH, Circuit Judge.

When Phyllis Frank failed to make her monthly car payments, Autovest, LLC acquired Frank's debt and sued to collect. In the wake of that aborted collection action, Frank sued Autovest and its debt-collection agency under the Fair Debt Collection Practices Act (FDCPA or the "Act"), 15 U.S.C. § 1692 *et seq*. Because Frank did not suffer a concrete injury-in-fact traceable to the alleged statutory violations, she lacks Article III standing. Accordingly, we vacate the district court's order and remand with instructions to dismiss the complaint.

I

Frank purchased a used Chevrolet Impala in May 2011. The dealership immediately assigned its interest in the financing agreement to First Investors Financial Services (FIFS), and Frank understood that she was financing the vehicle with money borrowed from FIFS. *See* Frank Dep. 22:1-7, J.A. 11. Frank fell behind on payments after losing her job and becoming homeless. She defaulted on the loan in 2014 and voluntarily surrendered the vehicle to FIFS in August 2015. Frank's debt changed hands several times, but was ultimately acquired by Autovest. Michael Andrews & Associates ("Andrews"), Autovest's agent for debt collection, mailed Frank a pair of letters explaining that Autovest had purchased her debt and instructing her to submit all future payments to Andrews's office.

In October 2016, Autovest sued Frank in the Superior Court for the District of Columbia to collect the outstanding principal of $8,557.53 plus interest, attorney's fees, and costs. *See* Complaint for Deficiency Balance, *Autovest, LLC v. Phyllis Frank*, No. 2016-CA-007373 (D.C. Super. Oct. 5, 2016), J.A. 59-60. Autovest attached a sworn "Verification of Complaint" signed by Christina Dunn, who identified herself as an "agent/officer/employee of the Plaintiff" with the "authority to verify the attached complaint." J.A. 75. But Dunn was employed by Andrews, not Autovest.

Four months later, the Superior Court issued an order of default. Frank moved to vacate the default and filed a pro se answer. Autovest moved for default judgment in April 2017, relying on an affidavit signed by Glenn E. Deuman. Deuman averred that he was "employed by Autovest, LLC ... as [a] Sr. Technical Product Manager." Deuman Aff. ¶ 1, J.A. 84. Like Dunn, however, Deuman actually worked for Andrews. Autovest also filed a fee affidavit in which its attorney, Robert D. Wagman, explained that his representation of Autovest was "handled on a contingency fee basis." Wagman Aff. ¶ 3, J.A. 98. But Wagman then calculated his fees using the lodestar method, and the motion for default judgment sought only that lodestar amount of $895. *Id.* at ¶¶ 6-7, J.A. 98-99; Defs. Motion for Summary Judgment Ex. p.1187 7 at 4, No. 17-cv-2773 (D.D.C. Feb. 12, 2019), Dkt. No. 34-7.

Frank paid $20 to vacate the default, declined Autovest's offer to enter judgment by consent, and retained counsel. On January 25, 2018, the Superior Court granted Autovest's request to dismiss its collection suit with prejudice.

Frank filed this putative class action against Autovest and Andrews in federal district court in December 2017. Her First Amended Complaint alleges that the Dunn and Deuman affidavits contain "false, deceptive, or misleading representation[s]" under 15 U.S.C. § 1692e. Am. Compl. ¶¶ 56-57, 61-62, 64-65, S.A. 19-21. Frank also characterizes the affidavits as conduct designed to "harass, oppress, or abuse" in violation of section 1692d, *id.* ¶¶ 48-49, 52-53, S.A. 18-19, and as "unfair or unconscionable" debt-collection practices under section 1692f, *id.* at ¶¶ 67 68, S.A. 21. Finally, Frank alleges that Autovest violated the same provisions of the Act by attempting to collect contractually unauthorized contingency fees. *Id.* at ¶¶ 54, 58, 59, 63, 69, S.A. 20-21.

The district court denied Autovest and Andrews's motion to dismiss for failure to state a claim, and the case proceeded to discovery. At her deposition, Frank testified that she "felt [she] was being scammed" when she learned about the collection suit because she had "never heard of Autovest." Frank Dep. 37:3-13, J.A. 17. However, Frank denied "tak[ing] action" or "refrain[ing] from doing anything" because of the representations of employment in the Dunn and Deuman affidavits. *Id.* at 55:17-56:5, 59:17-60:4, J.A. 28-29, 32-33. Likewise, Frank answered "No" when asked whether she undertook or avoided any action or made any payments "as a result of" the Wagman affidavit. *Id.* at 62:13-63:2, J.A. 35-36.

Autovest and Andrews moved for summary judgment, and the district court granted their motion on September 29, 2019. On the section 1692e false-statement claims, the court reasoned that any falsehoods in the Dunn and Deuman affidavits were immaterial—and thus not actionable—because they "had no effect on Frank's ability to respond or to dispute the debt." Mem. Op. at 11, J.A. 192. On the contingency-fee claims, the court concluded that Autovest did not attempt to collect such fees; Wagman merely "referred to his contingency-fee relationship with Autovest." *Id.* at 12, J.A. 193. Frank appealed.

II

Article III requires a concrete and particularized injury-in-fact traceable to the defendant's conduct and redressable by a favorable judicial order. *See Lujan v. Defs. of Wildlife,* 504 U.S. 555, 560-61, 112 S.Ct. 2130, 119 L.Ed.2d 351 (1992). Although the district court did not evaluate Frank's standing, we have "an independent obligation to assure that standing exists." *Summers v. Earth Island Inst.,* 555 U.S. 488, 499, 129 S.Ct. 1142, 173 L.Ed.2d 1 (2009).

Frank satisfied her burden at the pleading stage by including "general factual allegations of injury resulting from the defendant's conduct." *Lujan,* 504 U.S. at 561, 112 S.Ct. 2130. Her complaint says that she "was deceived by the Defendants' false, deceptive and misleading representations"; that she suffered "agitation, annoyance, emotional distress, and undue inconvenience"; and that she "incurred actual damages including... attorney's fees and costs." Am. Compl. ¶¶ 32-34, S.A. 16. But at the summary-judgment stage, the plaintiff must demonstrate standing by "affidavit or other evidence." *Lujan,* 504 U.S. at 561, 112 S.Ct. 2130.

p.1188 Frank hasn't carried that burden. She fails to identify a concrete personal injury traceable to the false representations in the Dunn and Deuman affidavits or the alleged request for contingency fees in the Wagman affidavit. In fact, Frank testified unequivocally that she neither took nor failed to take *any action* because of these statements. *See* Frank Dep. 55:17-56:2, 59:17-60:10, 62:13-63:2, J.A. 28-29, 32-33, 35-36. Nor did Frank testify that she was otherwise confused, misled, or harmed in any relevant way during the collection action by the contested affidavits. And although Frank stated that Autovest's suit caused her stress and inconvenience, *see id.* at 40:13-22, J.A. 19, she never connected those general harms to the affidavits, *see id.* at 64:8-65:22, 67:15-68:11, J.A. 37-40. Because Frank was unaffected by the conduct that underlies her FDCPA claims, she lacks Article III standing.

Frank's counterarguments are unconvincing. First, she points to pocketbook injuries in the form of "court costs and attorney's fees" she incurred "defending Autovest's lawsuit." Frank Reply 9. But the record contains no evidence linking these expenses to the alleged statutory violations. Frank testified that her litigation decisions were driven by unfamiliarity with Autovest, not the contents of the Dunn, Deuman, or Wagman affidavits. *See* Frank Dep. 37:3-13, J.A. 17 (Q: "What made you decide to seek counsel in connection with the collection action?" A: "Because I felt I was being scammed.... I never heard of Autovest."); *see also id.* at 57:2-8, 68:4-11, 70:13-71:13, J.A. 30, 40, 42-43. In short, there's no evidence that the contested statements rendered litigation more expensive or onerous.

Second, Frank argues that she suffered an informational injury when Dunn and Deuman "denied [her] access to truthful information." Frank Reply 10. A plaintiff suffers a cognizable injury if she (1) "has been deprived of information that, on [her] interpretation, a statute requires ... a third party to disclose," and (2) "suffers, by being denied access to that information, the type of harm Congress sought to prevent by requiring disclosure." *Friends of Animals v. Jewell,* 828 F.3d 989, 992 (D.C. Cir. 2016). Frank cannot satisfy the second requirement. Again, she disclaimed detrimental reliance—or any other harm—based on the misrepresentations in the Dunn and Deuman affidavits.

Finally, Frank contends that the alleged FDCPA violations encompass injuries of "the type Congress 'sought to curb,'" and thus that she need not prove "any *additional* harm," such as "[r]eliance on false information." Frank Reply 9 (quoting *Spokeo, Inc. v. Robins,* ___ U.S. ___, 136 S. Ct. 1540, 1549, 1550, 194 L.Ed.2d 635 (2016)). For support, she cites the Act's private right of action, 15 U.S.C. § 1692k, and Congress's recognition that "[a]busive debt collection practices contribute to ... personal bankruptcies, to marital instability, to the loss of jobs, and to invasions of individual privacy," *id.* § 1692(a).

As the Supreme Court clarified in *Spoken,* however, "Article III standing requires a concrete injury even in the context of a statutory violation." 136 S. Ct. at 1549. Congress may "define [new] injuries and articulate [new] chains of causation." *Lujan,* 504 U.S. at 580, 112 S.Ct. 2130 (Kennedy, J., concurring). But "Congress' role in identifying and elevating intangible harms does not mean that a plaintiff automatically satisfies the injury-in-fact requirement whenever a statute grants a person a statutory right and purports to authorize that person to sue to vindicate that right." *Spokeo,* 136 S. Ct. at 1549; *see also Jeffries v. Volume Servs. Am., Inc.,* 928 F.3d 1059, 1063 (D.C. Cir. 2019) ("The concreteness component of injury in fact p.1189 sharply limits when a plaintiff can establish standing based solely on a violation of his statutory rights."). Nothing in the FDCPA suggests that *every* violation of the provisions implicated here—no matter how immaterial the infraction—creates a cognizable injury. *See Hagy v. Demers & Adams,* 882 F.3d 616, 621 (6th Cir. 2018) ("Nowhere in the [FDCPA] does Congress explain why [a violation of 15 U.S.C. § 1692e(11)] *always* creates an Article III injury.").

Nor is it enough for Frank to simply point to the false statements in the Dunn and Deuman affidavits, because "not all inaccuracies cause harm or present any material risk of harm." *Spokeo,* 136 S. Ct. at 1550; *see also Hancock v. Urban Outfitters, Inc.,* 830 F.3d 511, 514 (D.C. Cir. 2016) ("[S]ome statutory violations ... result in no harm, even if they involve[] producing information in a way that violate[s] the law." (internal quotation marks omitted)). A misrepresentation in a debt collector's court affidavit—including a false statement about the affiant's employer—is certainly *capable* of causing a concrete and particularized injury. But Frank has not demonstrated that *these* statements had that effect. Without that showing, Frank lacks standing—even if Autovest and Andrews violated the FDCPA.

Nevertheless, Frank insists that her subjective response to the contested affidavits is irrelevant. All that matters, in her telling, is the affidavits' likely effect on a hypothetical unsophisticated debtor. Frank Br. 10; Oral Arg. Tr. 4:18-22. But this argument confuses standing with the merits. Frank correctly identifies the *substantive* standard that governs her FDCPA claims, which asks whether the debt collector's statement would confuse or mislead the unsophisticated consumer (or in some courts, the *least* sophisticated consumer). *See Jones v. Dufek,* 830 F.3d 523, 525 n.2 (D.C. Cir. 2016) (explaining that although "[t]he term 'unsophisticated' is probably more accurate[,] ... [i]n practice," the formulations "appear to be the same"). Under this standard, "the specific plaintiff need not prove that she was actually confused or misled, only that the objective," unsophisticated debtor would be. *See Jensen v. Pressler & Pressler,* 791 F.3d 413, 419 (3d Cir. 2015); *see also Pollard v. Law Office of Mandy L. Spaulding,* 766 F.3d 98, 103 (1st Cir. 2014) ("[T]he FDCPA does not require that a plaintiff actually be confused.").

We agree with Frank that the FDCPA creates statutory rights and remedies designed to protect the unsophisticated consumer. *Cf. Jones,* 830 F.3d at 525. But Congress's effort to protect plaintiffs cannot relieve them of the requirement to establish Article III standing—including a "concrete *and* particularized" injury-in-fact. *Spokeo,* 136 S. Ct. at 1548 (explaining that a "particularized" injury is "personal" to the plaintiff). "Broad though Congress's powers may be to define and create injuries, they cannot override constitutional limits." *Hagy,* 882 F.3d at 623.

This mismatch between the (objective) merits inquiry and the (subjective) standing inquiry is not unique to the FDCPA, but it can trip up an unsuspecting plaintiff. And case law has not always helped matters. Some courts have characterized the Act as "enlist[ing] the efforts of sophisticated consumers ... as 'private attorneys general' to aid their less sophisticated counterparts, who are unlikely themselves to bring suit under the Act, but who are assumed by the Act to benefit from the deterrent effect of civil actions brought by others." *Jensen,* 791 F.3d at 419 (quoting *Jacobson v. Healthcare Fin. Servs., Inc.,* 516 F.3d 85, 91 (2d Cir. 2008)).

Read too broadly, this view of the FDCPA is incompatible with the Supreme
p.1190 Court's standing jurisprudence. *See Lujan,* 504 U.S. at 577, 112 S.Ct. 2130 (explaining that "a subclass of citizens who suffer no distinctive concrete harm" may not sue to enforce statutory rights). Article III's case-or-controversy requirement remains in effect regardless of the doctrinal test that courts apply to FDCPA claims. And as decisions by our sister circuits indicate, the Act is rife with procedural requirements and substantive prohibitions that do not necessarily trigger concrete injuries when violated. *See Casillas v. Madison Ave. Assocs., Inc.,* 926 F.3d 329, 339 (7th Cir. 2019) (concluding that a debt collector's failure to inform the debtor that a challenge to the debt under section 1692g(a) must be "in writing" did not cause concrete harm); *Hagy,* 882 F.3d at 622 (holding that the plaintiffs lacked standing to bring a claim under section 1692e(11) for failure to disclose debt-collector status because they did not show that "the non-disclosure created a risk of double payment, caused anxiety, or led to any other concrete harm").

After *Spokeo,* a plaintiff must demonstrate a subjective—that is, an actual—personal injury for standing even when his merits argument turns on the perspective of an objective, unsophisticated consumer. On the margin, this rule might hamper the deterrence purpose of the Act by reducing the number of viable civil suits. Still, an FDCPA plaintiff possesses multiple avenues to standing, *see Hagy,* 882 F.3d at 622, and he need not suffer the *same* harm that underlies his statutory claim. For instance, a plaintiff could submit evidence of investigatory injuries—*e.g.,* resources spent uncovering or confirming the truth—rather than outright deception. In short, there's ample room for consumers of all sorts and levels of sophistication to bring FDCPA suits, but under Article III, they must be proper plaintiffs.

III

We vacate the district court's judgment and remand with instructions to dismiss the complaint for lack of jurisdiction.

So ordered.

857 F.3d 939 (2017)

Demetra BAYLOR, Appellant
v.
MITCHELL RUBENSTEIN & ASSOCIATES, P.C., Appellee.

No. 16-7070 Consolidated with 16-7071.

United States Court of Appeals, District of Columbia Circuit.

Argued February 7, 2017.
Decided May 30, 2017.

Baylor v. Mitchell Rubenstein & Associates, PC, 857 F. 3d 939 (DC Cir. 2017)

Appeal from the United States District Court for the District of Columbia, (No. 1:14-cv-02220)

Radi Dennis argued the cause and filed the briefs for appellant/cross-appellee.

Ronald S. Canter, Rockville, MD, argued the cause and filed the briefs for appellee/cross-appellant.

Before: HENDERSON, Circuit Judge, and EDWARDS and SENTELLE, Senior Circuit Judges.

Concurring opinion filed by Circuit Judge HENDERSON.

p.942 EDWARDS, Senior Circuit Judge:

In order to pursue a Master's degree in Computer Graphics, Demetra Baylor ("Appellant") took out six student loans. Several years after her graduation, Mitchell Rubenstein & Associates, P.C. ("Appellee") came calling to collect. At the heart of this case are a number of inconsistencies in letters that Appellee sent Appellant over the course of several months regarding her loans and the amounts that she owed on them, as well as Appellee's failure to direct all of its communications to Appellant's attorney after she retained counsel. In response, Appellant filed suit on December 17, 2013, alleging that Appellee had violated the Fair Debt Collection Practices Act ("FDCPA"), the District of Columbia Consumer Protections Procedures Act ("CPPA"), and the District of Columbia Debt Collection Law ("DCDCL"), statutes which target abusive debt collection and improper trade practices. *See* 15 U.S.C. § 1692(e); D.C. CODE §§ 28-3904, -3814.

Over the course of the next few years, the parties engaged in what the District Court termed a "particularly striking expenditure of effort and resources," generating "excessive, repetitive, and unnecessarily sharp pleadings." Order, Dkt. No. 41, at 2. Nonetheless, all of Appellant's statutory claims were eventually resolved. Appellant accepted Appellee's offer of judgment regarding her FDCPA claim and the District Court, with the aid of a Magistrate Judge, determined the attorney's fees to which she was entitled for this success. Appellee, meanwhile, prevailed in its Motion to Dismiss all of Appellant's CPPA claims and some of her DCDCL claims, the remainder of which were rejected when the District Court subsequently granted Appellee's Motion for Summary Judgment.

A number of orders from this "clutter[ed]... docket" are challenged on appeal. *Id. First,* the parties dispute the District Court's decision to adopt a Magistrate Judge's recommendation that Appellant receive approximately twenty percent of the attorney's fees that she requested. *Second,* Appellant asserts that the District Court erred in finding that Appellee's conduct does not fall within the aegis of the CPPA. *Third,* Appellant also contends that the District Court abused its discretion in failing to credit her objections to a different Magistrate Judge's denial of her Motion to Compel the disclosure of communications between Appellee and an agent of Appellant's creditor on the grounds that these documents were protected by attorney-client privilege. Appellant additionally disputes the District Court's refusal to award her attorney's fees for her efforts in litigating this issue. *Finally,* Appellant argues that the District Court improperly granted Appellee's Motion for Summary Judgment on her DCDCL claims. On this last point, Appellant contends that the District Court failed to appropriately account for evidence demonstrating that Appellee had "willfully violated" the DCDCL and was therefore subject to liability under the statute.

We do not reach the question of whether the District Court abused its discretion in awarding Appellant only a percentage of p.943 the attorney's fees she sought in connection with her FDCPA claim. In addressing this issue, the District Court relied on the standard set forth in Local Civil Rule 72.2 in finding that the Magistrate Judge's proposed disposition was not "clearly erroneous or contrary to law." This was error. Federal Rules of Civil Procedure 54(d)(2)(D) and 72(b)(3) foreclose the District Court from using a "clearly erroneous or contrary to law" standard when evaluating a Magistrate Judge's proposed disposition of a fee request. The correct standard of review is *de novo.* We therefore reverse and remand to allow the trial judge to reconsider this matter in the first instance applying *de novo* review to assess the Magistrate Judge's recommendation. We affirm all of the remaining Orders challenged on appeal.

I. BACKGROUND

On February 21, 2013, Appellee, a law firm whose primary focus is the recovery of consumer debts, sent the first of several letters to Appellant notifying her that her account, which had been assigned file number R80465, "ha[d] been referred to [its] office for collection." Complaint, Dkt. No. 1, Ex. E; *see* Answer, Dkt. No. 28, at 2. It listed the creditor for her debt as Arrowood Indemnity Company and stated that she currently owed $26,471.07, though cautioned that, "[b]ecause of interest, late charges and other charges that may vary from day to day, the amount due on the day you pay may be greater." Complaint, Dkt. No. 1, Ex. E. Following a request for more information regarding both the ownership and amount of this debt from Appellant, Appellee sent a second letter. It provided a new total for the amount that Appellant owed, $31,268, a slight reformulation of the name of Appellant's creditor, Arrowood Indemnity Company/Tuition Guard, and identified her original creditor as Citibank (South Dakota) N.A. Complaint, Dkt. No. 1, Ex. D; *Baylor v. Mitchell Rubenstein & Assocs., P.C.,* 55 F.Supp.3d 43, 46 (D.D.C. 2014).

Appellant retained counsel, who contacted Appellee regarding the provenance of this debt and advised that any "future communication regarding this matter should be directed to [her] firm" rather than to Appellant. Complaint, Dkt. No. 1, Ex. B. The parties then entered into settlement negotiations, during which Appellant informed Appellee that she had additional outstanding loans not referenced in its second letter. Appellee's client referred these new loans to Appellee so that Appellant could settle all of her debt at once. *See Baylor v. Mitchell Rubenstein & Assocs., P.C.,* 174 F.Supp.3d 146, 150 (D.D.C. 2016); Appellee's Statement of Undisputed Facts, Dkt. No. 96 ¶¶ 12-13. On August 22, 2013, Appellee sent another letter to Appellant's home, albeit addressed to her attorney, regarding this second set of loans. Complaint, Dkt. No. 1, Ex. A. It provided a new file number for this debt, R83798, which totaled $27,459.48, and noted that her creditor was Tuitionguard Arrowood Indemnity. *Id.* After Appellant's counsel requested additional information regarding these loans, Appellee stated that Appellant owed "$27,459.48 plus interest from 10/21/11 at the rate of 3.75% until paid" and listed Tuitionguard/Arrowood Indemnity and Student Loan Corp. as the creditor and original creditor, respectively, of this debt. Complaint, Dkt. No. 1, Ex. C.

On December 17, 2013, Appellant filed suit in the District Court. She claimed that the inconsistencies in the communications she had received from Appellee, including, most notably, the variance in the "character and amount" of Appellant's alleged debt and the creditors associated with these loans, as well as Appellee's failure to direct all of its communications to Appellant's counsel after she had retained legal representation, constituted violations of p.944 both the FDCPA and CPPA. Complaint, Joint Appendix ("JA") 26-28, 31-33. She also asserted that these actions were proof that Appellee had both violated various provisions of the DCDCL and "knowingly maintained policies, practices and procedures that were intentionally and willfully inadequate" to meet its obligations under this statute. *Id.* at 29-31.

Appellee moved to dismiss the Complaint. However, while this motion was pending, Appellee extended, and Appellant accepted, an offer of judgment regarding her FDCPA claims. *See Baylor v. Mitchell Rubenstein & Assocs., P.C.,* 77 F.Supp.3d 113, 115 (D.D.C. 2015). A judgment was then entered "in the amount of $1,001.00 plus costs and expenses together with reasonable attorney fees for all claims under the [FDCPA]" by the Clerk of Court. *Id.* Appellant thereafter filed a motion seeking $155,700 in attorney's fees for 346 hours of work at a rate of $450 an hour. *Id.* She was later permitted to amend her requested fees due to subsequent filings in this case. *Id.* at 115-16.

The District Court referred this request to a Magistrate Judge pursuant to Local Civil Rule 72.2. After reviewing the matter, the Magistrate Judge recommended that the hours included in Appellant's initial fee request be reduced by 85% because they were significantly higher than reasonable. *Baylor v. Mitchell Rubenstein & Assocs., P.C.,* 2014 WL 7014280, at *4 (D.D.C. Oct. 24, 2014). She found that certain tasks were not eligible for attorney's fees under the statute; some of the hours requested were expended on Appellant's unsuccessful state law claims or occurred after Appellant had already accepted Appellee's offer of judgment; and Appellant's counsel had failed to "heed the Court's admonition" to moderate the tenor of her filings. *Id.* at *4-5. The Magistrate Judge also determined that a 50% reduction should be applied to Appellant's additional request for fees because Appellant had "again engaged in the tactics against which the Court cautioned, thus expending considerable unproductive activity." *Id.* at *5. The District Court reviewed the Magistrate Judge's Report and

Recommendation to determine if it was "clearly erroneous or contrary to law" and, after determining that it was not, adopted it in its entirety. *Baylor,* 77 F.Supp.3d at 124.

In July 2014, the District Court granted Appellee's Motion to Dismiss all of Appellant's claims under the CPPA and some of her DCDCL claims. Following a contentious discovery process, in which the District Court affirmed a Magistrate Judge's Memorandum Opinion granting in part and denying in part Appellant's Motion to Compel production of certain communications between Appellee and an agent of its client, Appellant's creditor, Appellee filed a Motion for Summary Judgment and Appellant filed a cross-Motion for Partial Summary Judgment. The District Court granted the former and denied the latter.

II. ANALYSIS

A. Standard of Review

This court reviews *de novo* the District Court's decision to grant a motion to dismiss or motion for summary judgment and the "legal question" of whether it "improperly applied [a local rule] in place of the standards prescribed by [the Federal Rules of Civil Procedure]." *Winston & Strawn, LLP v. McLean,* 843 F.3d 503, 506 (D.C. Cir. 2016); *see Nat'l Wildlife Fed'n v. Browner,* 127 F.3d 1126, 1128 (D.C. Cir. 1997). We will, however, generally review discovery orders only for abuse of discretion, unless the District Court applied the wrong legal standard. *United States v. Deloitte LLP,* 610 F.3d 129, 134 (D.C. Cir. 2010).

p.945 *B.* Appellant's Fee Request

Local Civil Rule 72.2(a) permits the District Court to refer "any pretrial motion or matter," with the exception of certain motions and petitions set forth in Local Civil Rule 72.3, to a Magistrate Judge. If any party files written objections to a Magistrate Judge's ruling on such a matter, the District Court "may modify or set aside any portion of [the] order ... found to be clearly erroneous or contrary to law." Local Civil Rule 72.2(c). Because Local Civil Rule 72.3 makes no specific mention of motions for attorney's fees, the District Court assumed that a Magistrate Judge's recommendation on a fee award could be reviewed according to the deferential "clearly erroneous or contrary to law" standard. This was error.

Federal Rule of Civil Procedure 54(d)(2)(D) states that a court "may refer a motion for attorney's fees to a magistrate judge under Rule 72(b) as if it were a dispositive pretrial matter," a process which requires that a district judge "determine de novo any part of the magistrate judge's disposition that has been properly objected to," FED. R. CIV. P. 72(b)(3). The permissive language of Rule 54(d)(2)(D), specifically its use of the word "may," appears to have led the District Court to believe that referral via Local Civil Rule 72.2, with its attendant "clearly erroneous or contrary to law" standard of review, provided a legitimate alternative to the *de novo* review standard set forth in Federal Rules of Civil Procedure 54(d)(2)(D) and 72(b)(3). *See Baylor,* 77 F.Supp.3d at 117 & n.2. This was not an unreasonable mistake, but it was a mistake.

The Federal Magistrates Act permits district courts to draw upon the assistance of Magistrate Judges to resolve "any pretrial matter pending before the court." 28 U.S.C. § 636(b)(1)(A). The power vested in Magistrate Judges to dispose of issues referred to them under this provision depends upon the type of motion at issue. 28 U.S.C. § 636(b)(1)(A) lists eight pretrial motions, including motions for summary judgement and injunctive relief, for which Magistrate Judges may only provide "proposed findings of fact and recommendations for the disposition [of the matter]." *Id.* § 636(b)(1)(B). These recommendations must be reviewed *de novo* by a district court judge if properly objected to by one of the parties. *See id.* § 636(b)(1)(C). For all other pretrial motions, Magistrate Judges are permitted to "hear and determine" the matter, and a district court will only set aside their order where it has been shown that it is "clearly erroneous or contrary to law." *Id.* § 636(b)(1)(A); *see Phinney v. Wentworth Douglas Hosp.*, 199 F.3d 1, 5-6 (1st Cir. 1999).

This differentiation between the degree of authority a Magistrate Judge is permitted to wield over certain motions, and the standard of review which must be applied to the judge's proposed resolution of such matters, is rooted in "[c]onstitutional concerns," specifically the "possible ... objection that only an article III judge may ultimately determine the litigation." 12 CHARLES ALAN WRIGHT ET AL., FEDERAL PRACTICE AND PROCEDURE § 3068.2, p. 367 (3d ed. 2014); *see PowerShare, Inc. v. Syntel, Inc.*, 597 F.3d 10, 13 (1st Cir. 2010).

When Rule 72 was promulgated to "implement the legislative mandate of Section 636(b)(1)," it retained § 631(b)(1)'s basic structure — dividing pretrial motions between issues that a Magistrate Judge could determine and those for which the judge could simply provide recommendations for consideration by the district court. 12 CHARLES ALAN WRIGHT ET AL., FEDERAL PRACTICE AND PROCEDURE § 3068, p. 351 (3d ed. 2014). It adopted a slightly different organizing principle, however. Rather than relying on § 636(b)(1)(A)'s list of eight motions to identify the pretrial p.946 matters that a Magistrate Judge could not "determine," Rule 72 distinguished between motions that were "not dispositive of a party's claim or defense" and those that were. FED. R. CIV. P. 72(a)-(b); *see* 12 CHARLES ALAN WRIGHT ET AL., FEDERAL PRACTICE AND PROCEDURE § 3068.2, p. 366 (3d ed. 2014). Nondispositive matters would be referred to a Magistrate Judge pursuant to Rule 72(a) and a district court would be required to "consider timely objections and modify or set aside any part of [an order issued following such a referral] that [was] clearly erroneous or [was] contrary to law." Dispositive motions, meanwhile, would be referred to a Magistrate Judge via Rule 72(b) and the district court would be required to "determine de novo any part of [a] magistrate judge's [recommendation] that ha[d] been properly objected to." FED. R. CIV. P. 72(b)(3).

In spite of the legal significance of the distinction between dispositive and nondispositive motions it is not immediately apparent from the text of Rule 72 how, precisely, to determine whether a particular type of motion should be deemed to be "dispositive of a party's claim." While most courts agree that the eight motions set forth in § 636(b)(1)(A) are "dispositive," this list has largely been deemed to be illustrative of the matters that could fall within the scope of Rule 72(b), rather than exhaustive. *See Phinney*, 199 F.3d at 5-6; *Massey v. City of Ferndale*, 7 F.3d 506, 508 (6th Cir. 1993).

Prior to the promulgation of Rule 54(d)(2)(D), therefore, courts lacked any specific guidance regarding whether Magistrate Judges had the authority to provide a determination regarding a request for attorney's fees as if it was a nondispositive motion or were instead permitted only to provide a recommendation regarding the disposition of such matters. Faced with this uncertainty, three circuits held that motions for attorney's fees should be treated as dispositive motions and thus subject to *de novo* review by a district court judge if properly objected to. *See Massey,* 7 F.3d at 509-10; *Estate of Conners by Meredith v. O'Connor,* 6 F.3d 656, 659 (9th Cir. 1993); *Ins. Co. of N. Am. v. Bath,* 968 F.2d 20, at *2 (10th Cir. 1992) (Order and Judgment). Two of these courts also held that Magistrate Judges lacked the authority to "determine[]" a fee request because it was a "post-dismissal motion[]" and Rule 72, by its terms, applies only to "pretrial matters." *Massey,* 7 F.3d at 510 (quoting *Bennett v. Gen. Caster Serv. of N. Gordon Co.,* 976 F.2d 995, 998 n.5 (6th Cir. 1992)); *see Estate of Conners by Meredith,* 6 F.3d at 659 n.2.

Rule 54(d)(2)(D) thus took effect at a time when it was by no means certain what, if any, authority Magistrate Judges could wield when evaluating motions for attorney's fees and the degree of oversight district courts were required to provide over such matters. Its purpose, as described by the accompanying Advisory Committee Note, was to "eliminate[] any controversy" regarding a court's ability to treat "motions for attorneys' fees ... as the equivalent of a dispositive pretrial matter that can be referred to a magistrate judge." Advisory Comm. Notes 1993 Amend. The statutory and legal backdrop against which this amendment took place make clear that this Rule was not intended to permit courts to rely upon the standards and procedures associated with dispositive motions *in addition* to those for nondispositive motions. Indeed, providing district courts with the ability to alternate between these different standards would be anathema to the constitutional concerns that underlie the structure of § 636(b)(1) and Rule 72. Rather, Rule 54(d)(2)(D) provided that if a district court wished to refer a motion for attorney's fees to a Magistrate Judge it could do so pursuant to the procedures laid out in Rule 72(b), p.947 which include a requirement that the district court review a Magistrate Judge's recommendation regarding a fee award *de novo* if properly objected to. Thus, in context, it is clear that Rule 54(d)(2)(D)'s use of the permissive verb "may" refers to the permissive nature of the district judge's authority to refer the case to a magistrate, with no effect on the standard of review to be applied if the reference is made.

It is no response that Local Civil Rule 72.2 provides an "alternative[]" to Rule 54(d). *Baylor,* 77 F.Supp.3d at 117 n.2. While Rule 54(d)(2)(D) permits courts to establish by local rule "special procedures to resolve fee-related issues without extensive evidentiary hearings," there is no indication this language was intended to loosen the standard that should be applied to a Magistrate Judge's recommendation after such hearings have been conducted. Therefore, because district courts may not "circumvent the Federal Rules of Civil Procedure by implementing local rules or 'procedures' which do not afford parties rights that they are afforded under the Federal Rules," we join a number of our sister circuits in requiring that motions for attorney's fees be reviewed *de novo* if referred to a Magistrate Judge and properly objected to. *Jackson v. Finnegan, Henderson, Farabow, Garrett & Dunner,* 101 F.3d 145, 151 n.4 (D.C. Cir. 1996) (quoting *Brown v. Crawford Cty.,* 960 F.2d 1002, 1008 (11th Cir. 1992)); *see McCombs v. Meijer, Inc.,* 395 F.3d 346, 360 (6th Cir. 2005); *ClearOne*

Commc'ns, Inc. v. Bowers, 509 Fed.Appx. 798, 804-05 (10th Cir. 2013); *McConnell v. ABC-Amega, Inc.*, 338 Fed.Appx. 24, 26 (2d Cir. 2009); *cf. Rajaratnam v. Moyer*, 47 F.3d 922, 924 & nn.5, 8 (7th Cir. 1995) (finding that motion for attorney's fees referred via 28 U.S.C. § 636(b)(3) required *de novo* review). To the extent that Local Civil Rule 72.2 can be understood to suggest anything to the contrary, it is overruled.

Because we find that the District Court applied the wrong standard when reviewing the Magistrate Judge's Report and Recommendation, we will not reach the parties' claims that the District Court erred in adopting the Magistrate Judge's proposal to award Appellant approximately twenty percent of her requested attorney's fees. Instead, we remand this matter to the District Court so that it can review the Magistrate Judge's Report and Recommendation anew, and *de novo*.

C. Appellant's CPPA Claims

Appellant contends that the District Court erred in dismissing her claim that Appellee's conduct violated the CPPA, which creates an "enforceable right to truthful information from merchants about consumer goods and services that are or would be purchased, leased, or received in the District of Columbia." D.C. CODE § 28-3901(c). We disagree. "In answering questions involving the proper interpretation of D.C. statutes, [we rely] on the construction of these laws by the D.C. Court of Appeals." *Poole v. Kelly*, 954 F.2d 760, 761 (D.C. Cir. 1992) (per curiam). The D.C. Court of Appeals' precedents and the text of the CPPA itself support the District Court's determination that Appellee's conduct does not fall within the aegis of this law.

One of the principal goals of the CPPA is to "assure that a just mechanism exists to remedy all improper trade practices." D.C. CODE § 28-3901(b)(1). To that end, it embraces both an expansive understanding of the conduct which constitutes a "trade practice" — "any act which does or would create, alter, ... make available, provide information about, or, directly or indirectly, solicit or offer for or effectuate, a sale... or transfer, of consumer goods or services", which are "any and all parts of the economic output of society, at any stage or p.948 related or necessary point in the economic process, and includes consumer credit ... and consumer services of all types" — and provides an extensive list of unlawful trade practices. D.C. CODE § 28-3901(a)(6)-(7); *see id.* § 28-3904; *Howard v. Riggs Nat'l Bank*, 432 A.2d 701, 708 (D.C. 1981). These prohibited practices can only be committed by a merchant, an individual who "sell[s]... or transfer[s], either directly or indirectly, consumer goods or services" or who, in the ordinary course of business, "suppl[ies] the goods or services which are or would be the subject matter of a trade practice." D.C. CODE § 28-3901(a)(3); *see DeBerry v. First Gov't Mortg. & Inv'rs Corp.*, 743 A.2d 699, 701 (D.C. 1999).

There is little question, as Appellant notes, that a merchant who provides a consumer with credit, such as the loans at issue in this case, would fall comfortably within the scope of the CPPA. *See DeBerry*, 743 A.2d at 701; *cf. Jones v. Dufek*, 830 F.3d 523, 527-28 (D.C. Cir. 2016). Yet, that is not this case. Instead, we are confronted with a situation in which a debt collector, attempting to recoup funds on behalf of a creditor who did not itself provide Appellant with any credit, can be found liable under the CPPA. We tread carefully in analyzing this issue, as the D.C. Court of

Appeals has explicitly refrained from addressing a related matter. *See Logan v. LaSalle Bank Nat'l Ass'n,* 80 A.3d 1014, 1026-27 (D.C. 2013) (abstaining from determining whether "the CPPA applies to the trade practices of a mortgage loan servicer"). However, our interpretation of that court's precedents suggests that Appellee's conduct does not fall within the bounds of this statute.

The CPPA applies only to consumer-merchant relationships. *See Snowder v. District of Columbia,* 949 A.2d 590, 598-600 (D.C. 2008). However, decisions from the D.C. Court of Appeals indicate that a merchant need only be connected with the "supply side" of a consumer transaction for liability to attach. *See Save Immaculata/Dunblane, Inc. v. Immaculata Preparatory Sch., Inc.,* 514 A.2d 1152, 1159 (D.C. 1986) (quoting *Howard,* 432 A.2d at 709). In this case, it appears that there are two ways in which the interactions between Appellant and Appellee might be viewed to come within the compass of this statute.

First, Appellant suggests that Appellee is connected to the supply side of the transaction in which Appellant first acquired her student loans. *See* Reply Br. for Appellant at 13. In our view, this argument is based on a strained construction of the statute. It is hard to see Appellee as a culpable party on the supply side of the transaction when we know that there was a merchant who initially provided the consumer credit and then subsequently transferred ownership of this debt after it was in default to a new creditor who, without providing Appellant with any "goods or services" to speak of, retained Appellee to collect on these loans. In this situation, it seems implausible to characterize Appellee as someone who sold or transferred consumer goods or services or who supplied the goods or services which are or would be the subject matter of a trade practice. *See Osinubepi-Alao v. Plainview Fin. Servs., Ltd.,* 44 F.Supp.3d 84, 92-93 (D.D.C. 2014) (refusing to apply CPPA to "a licensed attorney [attempting] to collect the debt through litigation" where the attorney was not engaged in the practice of extending credit or selling debt); *Busby v. Capital One, N.A.,* 772 F.Supp.2d 268, 279-80 (D.D.C. 2011) (refusing to apply CPPA to parties that did not sell or give goods or services to plaintiff).

Second, it might be argued that Appellee is a merchant in its own right. Yet, it seems perverse to suggest that the "consumer" of the services it provides — debt collection — is the individual from whom it p.949 is attempting to collect rather than the creditor who retained it. The provisions of the CPPA cited in Appellant's Complaint, D.C. CODE § 28-3904(e) and (f), appear to apply only when a *consumer* is, or could be, misled by a merchant's actions. *See id.* ("It shall be a violation of this chapter, whether or not any consumer is in fact misled [or] deceived ... for any person to... misrepresent as to a material fact which has a tendency to mislead" or "fail to state a material fact if such failure tends to mislead."). The situation here does not fit within the statutory proscription.

In light of the terms of the statute, we are constrained to hold that Appellee's conduct falls outside the scope of the CPPA. Appellant's arguments to the contrary are unpersuasive. Because we find that Appellee's actions did not take place within the context of a consumer-merchant relationship, as required by the CPPA, we need not address Appellant's claim that debt collection is a "trade practice" as defined by this statute.

It is also unnecessary for us to address Appellant's claim that the CPPA permits certain individuals or entities to seek remedies for "the use of a trade practice in violation of a law of the District," including the DCDCL. D.C. CODE § 28-3905(k)(1)(A); *see id.* § 28-3909; Br. for Appellant at 55. It is true that "[a]lthough § 28-3904 makes a host of consumer trade practices unlawful ... [t]he remainder of the statute ... contemplates that procedures and sanctions provided by the [CPPA] will be used to enforce trade practices made unlawful by other statutes." *Atwater v. D.C. Dep't of Consumer & Regulatory Affairs,* 566 A.2d 462, 466 (D.C. 1989). However, Count III of Appellant's Complaint asserts only that Appellee's actions ran counter to two specific provisions of the CPPA itself, D.C. CODE § 28-3904(e)-(f). Complaint, JA 31-33. It makes no mention of Appellee's alleged violations of any other laws as grounds for recovery under this statute.

For the foregoing reasons, we affirm the District Court's decision to dismiss Appellant's CPPA claims.

D. Appellee's Claim of Attorney-Client Privilege

After the District Court granted in part Appellee's Motion to Dismiss, the parties embarked on an "extremely long and contentious discovery process." *Baylor,* 174 F.Supp.3d at 151. Further problems arose when Appellant filed a Motion to Compel production of certain communications between Appellee and Sunrise Credit Services, Inc. ("Sunrise"), the organization which retained Appellee to collect Appellant's debt on her creditor's behalf. Appellee refused to produce these documents, claiming that they were protected by attorney-client privilege. *See Baylor v. Mitchell Rubenstein & Assocs., P.C.,* 130 F.Supp.3d 326, 328 (D.D.C. 2015). The District Court referred this matter to a Magistrate Judge who found that, because Appellant's creditor, Arrowood Indemnity Company ("Arrowood"), had retained "Sunrise for the limited purpose of finding an attorney to help Arrowood collect [Appellant's] debt," Sunrise had "acted as Arrowood's agent for obtaining legal services." *Baylor v. Mitchell Rubenstein & Assocs., P.C.,* 2015 WL 4624090, at *4 (D.D.C. July 31, 2015). The Magistrate Judge, after reviewing the matter, concluded in turn that attorney-client privilege attached to some of the communications that Appellee wished to withhold.

In finding that attorney-client privilege attached to communications between Sunrise and Appellee, the Magistrate Judge looked to both Maryland and D.C. law, and held that both states recognize that attorney-client privilege extends to communications between a client's agent and his attorney. p.950 *See id.* at *1-2; *Baylor,* 130 F.Supp.3d at 330 n.2 (explaining that the court need not resolve a dispute regarding which state's law applied because there were no substantive differences between the two jurisdictions (citing *Cruz v. Am. Airlines,* 356 F.3d 320, 332 (D.C. Cir. 2004))); *see also In re Sealed Case (Medical Records),* 381 F.3d 1205, 1212 (D.C. Cir. 2004) (noting that when an individual asserts "state claims," such as the DCDCL claims at issue here, "state privilege law applies"). We need not address this determination because Appellant does not contest it on appeal.

The arguments advanced by Appellant before this court speak only to the questions of: (1) whether Appellee provided "record evidence" in support of its claims regarding the nature of the relationships between Appellee, Sunrise and Arrowood, Br. for Appellant at 65; and (2) whether two cases, *E.I. du Pont de Nemours & Co. v. Forma-Pack, Inc.,* 351 Md. 396, 718 A.2d 1129 (1998) and *J.H. Marshall &*

Associates., Inc. v. Burleson, 313 A.2d 587 (D.C. 1973), preclude this court from holding that attorney-client privilege could attach to the communications at issue. We find that the District Court did not abuse its discretion in resolving these issues. We are also unpersuaded by Appellant's claim that the District Court abused its discretion in refusing to award her attorney's fees for her efforts in relation to this matter.

The District Court properly found that Appellee had "proffered adequate evidence" to support its assertion that Sunrise served as Arrowood's agent and an attorney-client relationship existed between Appellee and Arrowood. *See Baylor,* 130 F.Supp.3d at 331; *id.* at 330 (noting that "[a]t bottom, most of [Appellant's] objections boil down to her claim that [Appellee] failed to offer evidence sufficient to show an agency relationship between Arrowood and Sunrise"). Appellee offered an affidavit describing the relationship between Arrowood and Sunrise and two "authorizations by Arrowood for Sunrise to retain counsel." *See id.* at 331; Appellee's Opposition to Appellant's Motion to Compel, Dkt. No. 72-2, Ex. 4, at 41-42; Dkt. No. 72-3, Ex. 4, at 64-65; Dkt. No. 73-4, Ex. 5, at ¶¶ 4-5. Although the affidavit is spare, we cannot say that the District Court abused its discretion in holding that the Magistrate Judge's determination that this evidence sufficed to support a finding of attorney-client privilege was not clearly erroneous or contrary to law.

Appellant raises two additional arguments to suggest that attorney-client privilege cannot attach to the disputed communications. *First,* she contends that attorneys engaged in the business of debt collection cannot invoke this privilege. Br. for Appellant at 64 (citing *E.I. du Pont,* 718 A.2d 1129). The precedent she cites in support of this claim, *E.I. du Pont,* is distinguishable from the instant case. In *E.I. du Pont,* the court held that the privilege did not apply to communications between a corporation and a "non-lawyer collection agency" where the corporation had hired this agency only "for the typical business purpose of collecting a debt" even though the agency had subsequently hired an attorney to "litigate the debt collection matter after [the agency's] efforts [to collect on the debt] proved unsuccessful." 718 A.2d at 1141-42. It justified this decision by noting that the agency "may certainly have been [the corporation's] agent for the business purpose of collecting [a] debt" but it was "*not* hired as an agent for purposes of litigation." *Id.* at 1142. Here, however, the Magistrate Judge specifically found that Sunrise was hired only for "the limited purpose of finding an attorney to help Arrowood collect [Appellant's] debt" and never itself attempted to undertake "direct collection p.951 actions" against Appellant. *Baylor,* 2015 WL 4624090, at *3-4. We find that the District Court properly held that the Magistrate Judge was not clearly erroneous in determining that this precedent did not preclude Appellee from claiming that certain of its communications with Sunrise were covered by attorney-client privilege. *See Baylor,* 130 F.Supp.3d at 334-35.

Second, Appellant asserts that Sunrise's actions constitute the unauthorized practice of law and, as such, attorney-client privilege cannot attach to its communications. In support of this claim, Appellant draws upon *J.H. Marshall,* in which the D.C. Court of Appeals held that a collection agency that filed suit to collect on a debt assigned to it by a creditor had engaged in the unauthorized practice of law. 313 A.2d at 590-91. Central to the D.C. Court of Appeals' reasoning in that case was its belief that a collection agency could not "interpose itself between a creditor and an attorney seeking to collect the creditor's claim," *id.* at 595, and a concern that the collection agency in *J.H. Marshall* was "sell[ing] the services of a lawyer, whom it controls and directs, thereby destroying the privity between attorney and client," *id.* at 597. However here the Magistrate Judge specifically held that Sunrise served only to find "an attorney to help Arrowood collect [Appellant's] debt." *Baylor,* 2015 WL 4624090, at *4. The Magistrate Judge made no findings that Sunrise ever attempted to collect on Appellant's debt on its own or otherwise serve as anything other than an "intermediary between Arrowood and [Appellee]." *Id.* at *3. In the absence of additional findings suggesting that Sunrise controlled and directed Appellee's conduct, we hold that the District Court did not abuse its discretion in affirming the Magistrate Judge's determination that Sunrise did not engage in the unauthorized practice of law.

Finally, Appellant claims that the District Court abused its discretion in refusing to award her attorney's fees relating to her Motion to Compel production of communications between Appellee and Sunrise. However, this motion was only partially successful, and Federal Rule of Civil Procedure 37(a)(5)(C) vests the District Court with discretion to "apportion... reasonable expenses," if such a motion is "granted in part and denied in part," as it was here. *See* Order, JA 185. We see no abuse of discretion in the District Court's determination that Appellant's limited success and "unduly contentious and overly lengthy pleadings" did not entitle her to attorney's fees and costs. *Baylor,* 130 F.Supp.3d at 337.

E. Appellant's DCDCL Claims

In her Complaint, Appellant asserted that Appellee's conduct had violated a variety of provisions of the DCDCL, a statute which prohibits creditors and debt collectors from engaging in certain activities such as "collect[ing] any money ... by means of threat [or] coercion." D.C. CODE § 28-3814(c); *see* Complaint, JA 29-31. Only two of these claims survived Appellee's Motion to Dismiss: (1) Appellant's contention that Appellee misrepresented the amount that she owed in its various letters to her, and (2) her argument that Appellee improperly contacted her after she retained counsel. *See Baylor,* 55 F.Supp.3d at 49-53. Following a protracted discovery process, the District Court granted Appellee's Motion for Summary Judgment and denied Appellant's Motion for Partial Summary Judgment regarding these claims. We affirm this decision.

A creditor or debt collector is subject to liability under the DCDCL only when a claimant offers substantial evidence to prove a "willful violation" of the law. *See* D.C. CODE § 28-3814(j)(1). We note, as the p.952 District Court did in the proceeding below, that neither this court nor the D.C. Court of Appeals appears to have set forth the standard for determining what constitutes "willful" conduct. While we can find no fault in the District Court's decision to treat this term as embracing "not only knowing violations of [the DCDCL], but reckless ones as well," we refrain, out of deference to the D.C. Court of Appeals, from specifically adopting this standard when interpreting this statute. *Baylor,* 174 F.Supp.3d at 153 (quoting *Safeco Ins. Co. of Am. v. Burr,* 551 U.S. 47, 57, 127 S.Ct. 2201, 167 L.Ed.2d 1045 (2007)). Instead, we note simply that no definition of willfulness advanced by any party in this litigation suggests that Appellee's conduct can be viewed as a "willful" violation of this law. *See id.* at 153 n.5 (summarizing definitions of "willfulness" advanced by

Appellant in the proceeding below, including her claim that this standard is satisfied if Appellee "knowingly and intentionally committed an act in conscious disregard for the rights of others" or violates the statute "voluntarily with either an intentional disregard of, or plain indifference to, the Act's requirements"); Br. for Appellee at 15 (adopting District Court's interpretation of willfulness).

In reviewing Appellant's contention that the District Court erred in granting Appellee's Motion for Summary Judgment and denying her Partial Motion for Summary Judgment, this court must determine whether a genuine dispute as to any material fact exists when "viewing the evidence in the light most favorable to the non-movant." *Wheeler v. Georgetown Univ. Hosp.,* 812 F.3d 1109, 1113 (D.C. Cir. 2016). We are cognizant that where, as here, we consider cross-motions for summary judgment, we must accord both parties the solicitude owed non-movants. Nevertheless, in this case, in order to resolve the parties' disputes over the DCDCL claims, it will suffice for us to address Appellant's claims in order and assess the evidence in the light most favorable to her. As we explain below, even on these terms, Appellant's claims fail.

1. D.C. CODE § 28-3814(g)(5): Appellee's Contact With Appellant After She Retained Counsel

Section 28-3814(g)(5) of the DCDCL bars "debt collector[s] ... [from using] unfair or unconscionable means to collect or attempt to collect on any claim... [by communicating] with a consumer whenever it appears that the consumer has notified the creditor that he is represented by an attorney and the attorney's name and address are known." Neither party disputes the fact that Appellant received a letter from Appellee after her counsel had informed it to cease contacting Appellant directly. Appellee, however, notes that this letter was addressed to Appellant's counsel, and attributes its appearance at Appellant's doorstep to a "computer error." Declaration of Mitchell Rubenstein, JA 508. In an affidavit attached to Appellee's Motion for Summary Judgment, its president explained that Appellee's computer system had merely "failed to update the address on the letter to reflect [Appellant's counsel's] mailing address." *Id.*

Appellant, meanwhile, argues that Appellee lacked "procedures reasonably calculated to avoid [this] error" and claims that Appellant's explanation for its failure to direct all of its communications to Appellant's counsel in its Motion for Summary Judgment differs from that proffered in its Motion to Dismiss. Appellant's Opposition to Appellee's Motion for Summary Judgment, Dkt. No. 90, at 5; *see* Br. for Appellant at 58. Yet, the record contains evidence that Appellee did, in fact, have procedures which explicitly barred its staff from "contact[ing] or respond[ing] to a consumer if the consumer is represented p.953 by counsel." *Baylor,* 174 F.Supp.3d at 159. Furthermore, as the District Court noted, there is no reason why Appellee cannot offer "an alternative explanation for its conduct" at summary judgment. *See id.* at 158-59 n.9. Because Appellee's assertion that the letter was mistakenly sent to Appellant's home due to a computer error is not controverted by anything in the record, we find that, even assessing the evidence in the light most favorable to Appellant, she has failed to raise a genuine question of material fact as to whether Appellee violated § 28-3814(g)(5) of the DCDCL. *See Johnson v. Perez,* 823 F.3d 701,

705 (D.C. Cir. 2016) (noting that a court "may not ... believe one witness over another ... [but] if one party presents relevant evidence that another party does not call into question factually, the court must accept the uncontroverted fact").

2. D.C. CODE § 28-3814(f)(5): Appellee's Misrepresentations Regarding the Amount that Appellant Owed

D.C. CODE § 28-3814(f)(5) provides that a debt collector may not "use any fraudulent, deceptive, or misleading representation or means to collect or attempt to collect claims ... [via] any false representation or implication of the character, extent, or amount of a claim against a consumer." There is no question that Appellee provided different figures for the amount that Appellant owed on her first and second set of loans in its various letters to her. However, Appellee's president avers that these errors were due to its reliance on Sunrise's representation of the "amount forwarded" for collection from Arrowood. Declaration of Mitchell Rubenstein, JA 506. He stated that during Appellee's fifteen year "relationship with Sunrise.... [he had] found that the 'amount referred' listed in [its] referral form to be [an] accurate statement as to the present balance owed on [an individual's] debt" and that Appellee had not "knowingly failed to include accrued interest" in its February 21 and August 22, 2013 letters "or otherwise misstate the amount" Appellant owed. *Id.* at 506-508.

In response, Appellant puts forth a slew of claims regarding the training Appellee's employees received and the roles which non-attorneys perform in attempting to collect on various debts. *See* Memorandum in Support of Appellant's Motion for Partial Summary Judgment, Dkt. No. 91-1, at 2-6; Opposition to Appellee's Motion for Summary Judgment, Dkt. No. 90, at 5-7; Reply to Opposition to Motion for Partial Summary Judgment, Dkt. No. 103, at 4-16. Only two appear to be relevant to the specific question of whether Appellee willfully misrepresented the amount that Appellant owed: (1) Appellant's claim that Appellee failed to "maintain or implement any practices or procedures to prevent its employees and managing partner from demanding inaccurate amounts in its demand letters" and lacks "*any* procedures relating to the DCDCL," Dkt. No. 103, at 4; *see* Br. for Appellant at 56; and (2) her argument that a conversation between Appellee and Sunrise, in which Appellee asked if it was possible to "make things simple" by applying an interest rate of 3.75% from the date of Appellant's last payment to her debt after Sunrise had informed Appellee the loans had been "accruing interest at 4% since placement," demonstrated that Appellee permitted its employees to falsify the amount of debt owed by the individuals it sent collection letters to. Collection Notes, JA 489-90; Br. for Appellant at 58-59.

The first of these arguments is easily set aside. As the District Court noted, Appellee maintains policies and procedures which state that "[p]rior to the issuance and mailing of any demand letter, a firm attorney must review the file to ensure p.954 that ... [t]he claim amount matches the amount the creditor claims is owed." *Baylor,* 174 F.Supp.3d at 157. Nothing in the record indicates that an attorney did not review the demand letters sent to Appellant, or that more specific policies are required to ensure that the firm's policies are in step with the requirements of the DCDCL.

Appellant's claim that the conversation between Appellee and Sunrise regarding the correct interest rate to be applied surely does not suffice to demonstrate that

Appellee *willfully misrepresented* the amount that Appellant owed. Even assessing this evidence in the light most favorable to Appellant, what she offers by way of argument is not enough to show a willful violation of the law. Indeed, if anything, the interaction appears to demonstrate that Appellee was attempting to bring the interest rate it would relay to Appellant in line with the information it had been provided regarding this debt, rather than conjure an interest rate "on a whim," as Appellant claims. *See* Dkt. No. 84-4, Ex. 3, at 13 (noting that the "interest amount" had been calculated through "8-12-11," that the interest rate was 3.75%, and that the last date Appellant had paid was 10-21-11); Appellee's Opposition to Motion to Compel, Dkt. No. 71, at 4 (describing this document as the "account referral and suit authorization from" Sunrise to Appellee). In other words, the uncontested facts hardly support an inference that Appellee acted to willfully violate the law.

In light of the record before us, and after having reviewed the claims *de novo,* we affirm the District Court's decision to grant Appellee's Motion for Summary Judgment on Appellant's DCDCL claims.

III. CONCLUSION

For the reasons set forth above, we remand the District Court's Order awarding Appellant attorney's fees in relation to her FDCPA claim so that it may review the Magistrate Judge's Report and Recommendation on this matter *de novo.* We affirm all of the other Orders challenged in this appeal.

KAREN LeCRAFT HENDERSON, Circuit Judge, concurring:

It is a time-honored bargaining tactic: make an unreasonable opening offer in an effort to "anchor" the ensuing give-and-take to an artificially high (or low) range of prices. Russell Korobkin, *Aspirations and Settlement,* 88 CORNELL L. REV. 1, 32 (2002). Even if the offer has no basis in reality and is rejected out of hand, it may for psychological reasons yield an artificially high (or low) final price. *Id.* at 32 & nn.151-53 (citing evidence that people "often begin [a negotiation] with a reference value ... and then adjust from that point to arrive at their final determination," even if starting point does "not bear a rational relationship to the item subject to valuation"). That may be fine for selling a car or conducting a business negotiation. But a request for attorney's fees is not a negotiation.

Federal fee-shifting statutes typically authorize the recovery of a reasonable attorney's fee. If a party seeks more than that — making an excessive demand in hopes that the award, although short of the demand, will be artificially high — a district court can impose a sanction to deter future violations and to protect the integrity of its proceedings. In particular, the court has discretion to deny an award altogether or "impose a lesser sanction, such as awarding a fee below what a 'reasonable' fee would have been." *Envtl. Defense Fund, Inc. v. Reilly,* 1 F.3d 1254, 1258 (D.C. Cir. 1993).

I say all this because Radi Dennis, counsel for plaintiff Demetra Baylor, made what I consider a grossly excessive fee request. In Baylor's name, Dennis sought p.955
a total of $221,155 for her work on Baylor's $1,001 settlement and on the fee request

itself.[1] The $221,155 demand was more than five times the $41,990 that a magistrate judge determined to be reasonable. Reviewing for clear error, the district court overruled objections from both sides and awarded Baylor $41,990. The Court today holds, and I agree, that a remand is in order because the district court erred by not reviewing the magistrate's recommendation de novo.[2] Maj. Op. 942-43, 944-47, 954. The Court is careful not to dictate the outcome on remand, Maj. Op. 942-43, 947, and rightly so because of the district court's discretion in fee matters, *Copeland v. Marshall,* 641 F.2d 880, 901 (D.C. Cir. 1980) (en banc). I write separately only because, on reviewing the fee order, I am uncertain whether the district court recognizes just how broad its discretion is. On the extreme facts of this case — and because Dennis is a repeat offender, *see Jones v. Dufek,* 830 F.3d 523, 529 & n.6 (D.C. Cir. 2016) (affirming denial of excessive fee request Dennis made on behalf of another client) — I believe the court's discretion includes awarding a fee substantially below an otherwise reasonable one.

I. BACKGROUND

The Court details many of the facts, Maj. Op. 943-45, but I recount a few more to provide context for Baylor's fee request.

A. DENNIS'S WORK ON THE FDCPA CLAIM AND FEE REQUEST

Baylor attended graduate school, which she financed with student loans. Through an intermediary, one of Baylor's creditors enlisted defendant Mitchell Rubenstein & Associates (MRA), a law firm, to collect on the debt. In February 2013, MRA sent Baylor the first of several letters about the debt. The letters contained minor inadvertent discrepancies about (*inter alia*) the amount Baylor owed. *See* Maj. Op. 943-44. In March 2013, Baylor disputed the debt and retained Dennis for $325 per hour on a contingency basis. *See* Decl. of Radi Dennis ¶ 14 (Mar. 12, 2014).

Dennis almost immediately began researching the viability of a claim under the Fair Debt Collection Practices Act (FDCPA), 15 U.S.C. §§ 1692 *et seq.* According to her billing records, she performed about 30 hours of FDCPA research between April and December 2013. During the same period, she had unfruitful settlement discussions with MRA.

Dennis spent about 56 hours researching, drafting, editing and serving Baylor's complaint against MRA. The complaint — 15 pages long and filed in December 2013 — alleged that MRA had violated the FDCPA and District of Columbia (D.C.) law. Eight pages of the complaint were devoted to factual allegations and other matters common to all counts. Four pages set forth Baylor's D.C. claims, which were ultimately unsuccessful. Only three pages were dedicated exclusively to Baylor's FDCPA claim.

MRA's president authorized a $1,001 offer of judgment on the FDCPA claim in order "to limit the time and expense of litigation."[3] Aff. of Mitchell Rubenstein ¶ 18 (Mar. 25, 2014); *see* FED. R. CIV. P. 68 p.956 ("Offer of Judgment"). MRA's counsel extended the offer to Dennis by certified mail on January 7, 2014. The offer reached Dennis's address on January 17 but she waited until January 29 to open and read it.

In the meantime, on January 14, 2014, MRA moved to dismiss all counts of the complaint. Between January 18 and January 27 — a ten-day period during which she should have known that MRA had offered to settle the FDCPA claim — Dennis wasted more than 87 hours researching and drafting Baylor's opposition to the motion to dismiss. She filed the opposition on January 27.

Dennis finally retrieved the offer of judgment on January 29, 2014. In the two weeks that followed, she spent about 34 hours researching Rule 68. Baylor accepted MRA's offer on February 28. The judgment was for $1,001 "plus costs and expenses together with reasonable attorney fees for all claims under the Fair Debt Collection Practices Act." J. on Offer and Acceptance (Feb. 28, 2014). The reference to "reasonable attorney fees" accorded with the FDCPA's fee-shifting provision, which states in relevant part that, "in the case of any successful [FDCPA] action," a debt collector who has violated the FDCPA "is liable" to the plaintiff for "the costs of the action, together with a reasonable attorney's fee as determined by the court." 15 U.S.C. § 1692k(a)(3).

In Baylor's name, Dennis sought a "lodestar"[4] fee award of $155,700 for her work on the FDCPA claim and on the fee request itself.[5] She based the amount on two assertions: (1) she had spent a total of 346 hours litigating the FDCPA claim and fee motion, including at least 85 hours on the latter; and (2) her rate under the "*Laffey* Matrix"[6] is $450 per hour. She subsequently sought another $40,075 for drafting Baylor's reply to MRA's opposition to the fee motion,[7] bringing the tally to $195,775. And then she sought another $25,380 for 56 hours she allegedly spent responding (and seeking fees on the response) to MRA's five-page motion for sanctions and relief from judgment — a motion the district court denied in a three-page order. In all, then, Dennis sought $221,155 in fees.[8]

p 957 MRA opposed the fee request, urging the district court to deny it *in toto* because it was grossly exaggerated.

B. THE DISTRICT COURT'S FEE ORDER

The district court referred the fee request to a magistrate judge, who recommended awarding a fee but reducing the total to a reasonable amount: $41,990. Reviewing for clear error, the district court overruled both parties' objections to the magistrate's report and recommendation. 77 F.Supp.3d 113, 117-23 (D.D.C. 2015). The court adopted the report and recommendation and thus awarded $41,990, which it considered "quite generous." *Id.* at 121; *see id.* at 115, 124.

In rejecting Baylor's claim for a larger award, the district court deferred to the magistrate judge's view that a "reasonable attorney" in Dennis's shoes would have spent about 93 hours on the FDCPA claim and the fee request. 77 F.Supp.3d at 121. The court saw no clear error in the magistrate's conclusion that Dennis's time beyond 93 hours was (1) attributable to Baylor's D.C. claims, *id.* at 121-22 & n.6, and (2) "wasteful" and "unnecessary" because (*inter alia*) Dennis failed to timely retrieve MRA's offer of judgment, *id.* at 121-23 & n.5.

In rejecting MRA's entreaty to award nothing, the district court acknowledged cases permitting it to "reject[] an award outright" because of an "outrageous" request. 77 F.Supp.3d at 118. Elsewhere the court remarked on the fact that Dennis "sought more than $220,000 in fees for a successful FDCPA claim worth only $1,001.00 to her client." *Id.* at 122. But the court discerned no clear error in the magistrate judge's recommendation against a sanction. *Id.* at 118-19. Because a fee award under the FDCPA "is mandatory in all but the most unusual circumstances," the court was reluctant to deny the fee request in its entirety. *Id.* at 119 (quoting *Carroll v. Wolpoff & Abramson*, 53 F.3d 626, 628 (4th Cir. 1995)). And in light of the already "significant reduction" to $41,990 — a reduction the magistrate judge deemed necessary to make the award reasonable — the court was unpersuaded that any punitive reduction was necessary. *Id.*

Both sides appealed. Baylor claims the award is too low and MRA claims it is too high.

II. ANALYSIS

We and other courts of appeals have held, in several different statutory contexts, that a court may punish an intolerably excessive fee request by denying any award at all. *See, e.g., Envtl. Defense Fund, Inc. v. Reilly*, 1 F.3d 1254, 1258 (D.C. Cir. 1993) (Resource Conservation and Recovery Act, 42 U.S.C. § 6972(e)); *Jordan v. Dep't of Justice*, 691 F.2d 514, 518 & n.37 (D.C. Cir. 1982) (Freedom of Information Act, 5 U.S.C. § 552(a)(4)(E)); *see also, e.g., Scham v. District Courts Trying Criminal Cases*, 148 F.3d 554, 556-59 (5th Cir. 1998) (Civil Rights Attorney's Fees Awards Act, 42 U.S.C. § 1988(b)), *abrogated on other grounds as noted in Bailey v. Mississippi*, 407 F.3d 684, 686-87 (5th Cir. 2005); *Fair Hous. Council v. Landow*, 999 F.2d 92, 96-98 (4th Cir. 1993) (same); *Lewis v. Kendrick*, 944 F.2d 949, 958 (1st Cir. 1991) (same); *Brown v. Stackler*, 612 F.2d 1057, 1059 (7th Cir. 1980) (same). We have also recognized the authority to "impose a lesser sanction, such as awarding a fee below what a 'reasonable' fee would have been in order to discourage fee petitioners from submitting an excessive request." *Reilly*, 1 F.3d at 1258.

The district court was hesitant to deny Baylor's fee request *in toto* because the FDCPA provides for mandatory fee shifting. 77 F.Supp.3d at 119. The concern is understandable but goes only so far. True, the cases listed above involved statutes p.958 under which a court "may" award a fee, 5 U.S.C. § 552(a)(4)(E); 42 U.S.C. §§ 1988(b), 6972(e), whereas the FDCPA provides that a defendant "is liable" for a fee, 15 U.S.C. § 1692k(a). But at least two courts of appeals have suggested the FDCPA permits outright denial in "unusual circumstances." *Carroll*, 53 F.3d at 628 (4th Cir.); *Graziano v. Harrison*, 950 F.2d 107, 114 & n.13 (3d Cir. 1991). And even assuming arguendo that some "reasonable" fee is always required, 15 U.S.C. § 1692k(a)(3), the statutory text does not preclude a court from deciding — consistent with its inherent authority to protect the integrity of its proceedings, *Chambers v. NASCO, Inc.*, 501 U.S. 32, 42-51, 111 S.Ct. 2123, 115 L.Ed.2d 27 (1991) — that a "reasonable" fee in response to an exorbitant request is a nominal amount approaching zero.

I do not dispute that, if one leaves aside the magnitude of the fee request, $41,990 is reasonable — or at least represents a non-reversible determination of reasonableness within the district court's broad discretion. *See Morgan v. District of Columbia*, 824 F.2d 1049, 1066 (D.C. Cir. 1987) ("[W]e are ill-positioned to second guess the [district] court's [fee] determination."). Nor do I contend that the court *must* exercise its discretion to reduce the award for punitive reasons. But in deciding whether or not to do so, the court must start with the correct legal baseline. *See Koon v. United States,* 518 U.S. 81, 100, 116 S.Ct. 2035, 135 L.Ed.2d 392 (1996) ("A district court by definition abuses its discretion when it makes an error of law."). I am not sure the court started with the correct baseline here.

The district court suggested that, in light of the already "significant reduction" to $41,990, it did not need to reduce the award further as a sanction. 77 F.Supp.3d at 119. But the question is not whether an *award of $41,990* is grossly excessive; it is whether a *request of $221,155* is grossly excessive given that a reasonable fee is $41,990. After all, the point is to deter unreasonable *requests:*

> If ... the Court were required to award a reasonable fee when an outrageously unreasonable one has been asked for, claimants would be encouraged to make unreasonable demands, knowing that the only unfavorable consequence of such misconduct would be reduction of their fee to what they should have asked for in the first place. To discourage such greed a severer reaction is needful, and the District Court responded appropriately in [denying an award entirely].

Brown, 612 F.2d at 1059; *see Reilly,* 1 F.3d at 1258 (approving *Brown*'s rationale in our Circuit); *Landow,* 999 F.2d at 98 (forbidding "gamesmanship" of filing excessive request "in the hope that the district court [will] at least award some, preferably high, percentage of the requested fees"); *Lewis,* 944 F.2d at 958 (emphasizing that fee request is "not an opening gambit in negotiations to reach an ultimate result").

None of this is to say that denial or reduction of fees is routine punishment. As the Court explained in *Jordan:*

> Total denial of requested fees as a purely prophylactic measure ... is a stringent sanction, to be reserved for only the most severe of situations, and appropriately invoked only in very limited circumstances. Outright denial may be justified when the party seeking fees declines to proffer any substantiation in the form of affidavits, timesheets or the like, or when the application is grossly and intolerably exaggerated, or manifestly filed in bad faith.

691 F.2d at 518 (footnotes omitted). Still, the sanction is not as rare as hen's teeth. In several of the cases cited above, a fee was denied or reduced as punishment for a grossly excessive request. *Reilly,* 1 F.3d at p.959 1258-60; *Scham,* 148 F.3d at 556-59; *Landow,* 999 F.2d at 96-98; *Lewis,* 944 F.2d at 954-58; *Brown,* 612 F.2d at 1059. In *Reilly,* for example, this Court reduced a fee request for "outrageously excessive time entries," noting especially that the attorney had tried to claim hours that were "about three times what the work should have required." 1 F.3d at 1259-60. Likewise in *Landow,* the Fourth Circuit reversed a fee award in its entirety because the request on which it was based was "outrageously excessive" insofar as it did not carve out hours spent on unsuccessful claims. 999 F.2d at 97-98. And in *Lewis* the First Circuit reversed an award because the lawyers' fee request was intolerably out of sync with the "degree of success [they] obtained" for their client. 944 F.2d at 956, 958 (internal quotation omitted).

The sanction may be "strong medicine," *Lewis,* 944 F.2d at 958; *see Jordan,* 691 F.2d at 518, but an equally strong case can be made for it here. The record suggests that Dennis, desiring an artificially large award, impermissibly treated the $221,155 fee request as an opening bid. *Compare Reilly,* 1 F.3d at 1258; *Landow,* 999 F.2d at 97-98; *Lewis,* 944 F.2d at 958; *Brown,* 612 F.2d at 1059; *see also* Korobkin, *Aspirations and Settlement,* 88 CORNELL L. REV. at 32-33. The hours she reported are difficult to explain any other way. She reported the 87 hours she had spent opposing MRA's motion to dismiss. She claimed those hours even *after* realizing they had been wasted because she did not timely open her mail.[9] She claimed 34 hours for researching Rule 68 when a few hours should have sufficed. She claimed at least 85 hours for the fee motion itself. She claimed *110 hours* — nearly three standard work weeks at a total "discount" price of $40,075 — for replying to MRA's opposition to the fee motion. And she claimed 56 hours for responding (and seeking fees on the response) to MRA's five-page motion for sanctions.

Through Baylor, Dennis sought more than *five times* the amount the magistrate judge thought reasonable and the district court thought "quite generous." 77 F.Supp.3d at 121; *see id.* at 124. In *Reilly* we cut back a request because (*inter alia*) the lawyer tried to claim hours that were "about three times what the work should have required." 1 F.3d at 1259. *A fortiori,* that case counsels a similar result here.

Moreover, Dennis sought nearly *221 times* the $1,001 she recovered for Baylor. The client's "degree of success" is ordinarily a "critical factor" in calculating a fee award. *Hensley v. Eckerhart,* 461 U.S. 424, 436, 103 S.Ct. 1933, 76 L.Ed.2d 40 (1983); *see Goos v. Nat'l Ass'n of Realtors,* 68 F.3d 1380, 1387 (D.C. Cir. 1995). The First Circuit in *Lewis* believed it "inexcusable" that the lawyers there sought "payment ... amounting to 140 times the worth of the injury." 944 F.2d at 956. I believe the same conclusion is warranted here. Dennis spent more time working on fee matters than on tasks essential to Baylor's FDCPA claim. The time she spent on the fee motion (at least 85 hours) and the reply to MRA's fee opposition (110 hours) easily exceeded the time she spent researching the FDCPA (30 hours) and working on Baylor's complaint (56 hours) — the latter of which was devoted in part to D.C. claims that Baylor *lost. See Landow,* 999 F.2d at 97-98 (fee request excessive because it did not discount work on unsuccessful claims). No wonder the district court said of the fee request that "the tail [is] wagging the dog... in this case." 130 F.Supp.3d 326, 337 (D.D.C. 2015).

p.960 In short, Dennis lost sight of the real party in interest. As further proof, recall that she sought the *Laffey* rate of $450 per hour despite having agreed to represent Baylor for $325 per hour. Dennis has not explained the discrepancy, at least not in this Court. Nor can the FDCPA support such a windfall. The fee-shifting provision states that the defendant is liable to the *plaintiff* for a reasonable attorney's fee. 15 U.S.C. § 1692k(a) ("[A]ny debt collector who fails to comply with any provision of this subchapter with respect to any person is liable to *such person....*" (emphasis added)). In other words, the district court is to award Baylor whatever the FDCPA litigation reasonably cost her. And Baylor's contingency agreement with Dennis manifests that, at least for the latter's services, the litigation cost her $325 per hour. *See* Decl. of Radi Dennis ¶ 14 (Mar. 12, 2014). The extra $125 per hour — a good living for most people — is nothing but avarice.

Importantly, such excess in a fee request is not victimless: the money has to come from someone. Here the money comes from MRA. 15 U.S.C. § 1692k(a) ("debt collector ... is liable"). Yes, MRA owes damages, costs and a reasonable attorney's fee. But by law that is all it owes. Assuming $41,990 is a reasonable attorney's fee,[10]

Dennis improperly demanded $179,165 of MRA's money. Thankfully, the tactic did not succeed. If similar demands become the norm, however, they will sow distrust and spawn satellite fee litigation — one of the last things lawyers and judges should be spending their time on. *See Carroll,* 53 F.3d at 628 (noting "systemic costs" of satellite fee litigation, which is "one of the least socially productive types of litigation imaginable" (internal quotation omitted)). For fee-shifting to work properly, a court must be able to depend on counsel for a measured accounting from the outset. Dennis's accounting was nowise measured.

In the event the district court concludes on remand that the fee request was grossly excessive, such that the award needs to be further reduced, the following considerations may aid its calculation. First, for reasons already explained, I think the court should award $325 per hour instead of $450. Second, I think the court may deny Dennis any credit for fee-related pleadings. *See Trichilo v. Sec'y of HHS,* 823 F.2d 702, 708 (2d Cir. 1987) ("If counsel makes inflated or outrageous fee demands, the court could readily deny compensation for time spent in pressing them, since that time would not have been reasonably spent." (internal quotation omitted)). Indeed, I do not think it would be an abuse of discretion to award Dennis the same amount she won for Baylor: $1,001. Steep overbilling ought to come at a steep price.

[1] For simplicity, I round all monetary figures to the nearest dollar and all increments of time to the nearest hour.

[2] I also agree that the district court correctly disposed of Baylor's claims under District of Columbia law. Maj. Op. 947-54. Accordingly, I join the Court's opinion in full.

[3] It did not have the intended effect. *See generally* Maj. Op. 942-54; 174 F.Supp.3d 146 (D.D.C. 2016); 130 F.Supp.3d 326 (D.D.C. 2015); 77 F.Supp.3d 113 (D.D.C. 2015); 55 F.Supp.3d 43 (D.D.C. 2014).

[4] The "lodestar" method of calculating a fee award "looks to the prevailing market rates in the relevant community." *Perdue v. Kenny A.,* 559 U.S. 542, 551, 130 S.Ct. 1662, 176 L.Ed.2d 494 (2010) (internal quotation omitted). It is meant to "produce[] an award that roughly approximates the fee that the prevailing attorney would have received if he or she had been representing a paying client who was billed by the hour in a comparable case." *Id.* (emphasis omitted).

[5] Because Baylor did not succeed on her D.C. claims, she could not seek a fee award on them. *See Brandywine Apartments, LLC v. McCaster,* 964 A.2d 162, 169 (D.C. 2009) ("successful" claim required).

[6] The *Laffey* Matrix provides a "schedule of prevailing rates" for attorneys who litigate in the D.C. area. *Eley v. District of Columbia,* 793 F.3d 97, 100-01 (D.C. Cir. 2015).

[7] Dennis said she had spent more than 110 hours on the reply but was willing to give MRA a "discount." Supplemental Decl. of Radi Dennis ¶ 6(f) (Apr. 1, 2014).

[8] The $221,155 does not include an additional $48,195 that Dennis sought for preparing objections to the magistrate judge's report and recommendation on the fee award. The district court concluded that the additional $48,195 was too attenuated from the FDCPA claim to be reimbursable. Baylor does not appeal that ruling and

MRA does not argue that the additional $48,195 is relevant to whether the earlier request was outrageously excessive. I therefore use $221,155 as an extremely conservative figure for the total fee request.

[9] It is one thing to make a mistake. It is quite another to bill it to someone else, especially when it costs $39,150 (87 × $450).

[10] Lest it be forgotten, I repeat here that Dennis believes $41,990 is unreasonably low. Br. of Appellant 22-48. I have my doubts but acknowledge that the matter is for the district court. *Morgan,* 824 F.2d at 1066. The court may conclude on de novo review of the magistrate judge's report and recommendation that a reasonable fee is higher or lower than $41,990. If it does so, the new number will become the baseline from which the court must decide whether Dennis's request of $221,155 was grossly excessive.

830 F.3d 523 (2016)

Tawanda JONES, Appellant
v.
David Sean DUFEK, Sr. and CACH, LLC, Appellees.

No. 15-7013.

United States Court of Appeals, District of Columbia Circuit.

Argued April 12, 2016.
Decided July 26, 2016.

Jones v. Dufek, 830 F. 3d 523 (DC Cir. 2016)

p.524 Appeal from the United States District Court for the District of Columbia, (No. 1:14-cv-00533)

Radi Dennis argued the cause and filed the briefs for appellant.

Manuel H. Newburger, Austin, TX, argued the cause for appellees. On the brief was Mikhael D. Charnoff.

Before: HENDERSON and KAVANAUGH, Circuit Judges, and RANDOLPH, Senior Circuit Judge.

RANDOLPH, Senior Circuit Judge:

Tawanda Jones owed $1,050.29 to Bank of America. Bank of America sold the debt to CACH, LLC. That company hired the Law Office of David Sean Dufek in San Diego, California, to help it collect on the debt. In 2013, Dufek sent Jones the following letter:

> Dear TAWANDA JONES,
>
> This office has been retained to collect the debt owed by you to CACH, LLC. As of the date of this letter you owe the sum of $1,050.29. Because of interest, late charges and other charges that may vary from day to day the amount due on the day you pay may be greater.
>
> You are hereby advised: Unless you, the consumer, notify this office within thirty days after receipt of this notice that you dispute the validity of this debt or any portion thereof, the debt will be assumed to be valid by this office. If you, the consumer, notify this office in writing within thirty days after receipt of this notice, that the debt or any portion thereof is disputed, this office will obtain verification of the debt or a copy of a judgment against you and a copy of such verification or judgment will be mailed to you by this office. Upon your written request within thirty days after receipt of this notice this office will provide you with the name and address of the original creditor, if different from the current creditor.
>
> Please remit your payment to: David Sean Dufek [Address]
>
> If you would like to make a payment online, please visit our website: [website URL]
>
> Please call our office. The toll free number is [telephone number].

Sincerely,

[Signature]

Attorney David Sean Dufek

Please be advised that we are acting in our capacity as a debt collector and at this time, no attorney with our law firm has personally reviewed the particular circumstances of your account.

Be advised this is an attempt to collect a debt. Any information obtained will be used for that purpose.

The letter appeared entirely on one sheet of letterhead captioned at the top with the words "Law Office of David Sean Dufek." p.525 The text of the letter, as well as the disclaimers below the signature block, were in the same readable font and size.

Jones alleges that this letter was deceptive and violated three statutes: the Fair Debt Collection Practices Act, 15 U.S.C. § 1692 *et seq.*; the District of Columbia Consumer Protection Procedures Act, D.C. CODE § 28-3901 *et seq.*; and the District of Columbia Debt Collection Law, D.C. CODE § 28-3814 *et seq.* She relies on different sections of each of these statutes, but there is one basic argument underlying all of her claims: that the letter falsely implies both that Dufek is meaningfully involved with the case as an attorney and that the creditor is threatening to bring a lawsuit to collect the debt. We disagree. The letter does not threaten any legal action, and the prominent disclaimer made clear that Dufek was acting only in his capacity as a debt collector.

Section 1692e of the Fair Debt Collection Practices Act prohibits debt collectors from using "any false, deceptive, or misleading representation or means in connection with the collection of any debt." 15 U.S.C. § 1692e. One such "representation or means" is a "false representation or implication that any individual is an attorney or that any communication is from an attorney." 15 U.S.C. § 1692e(3). At first glance this section seems inapplicable. Dufek is an attorney, and reporting that fact cannot be a "false representation."[1] *Id.* But courts that have considered this question — ours is not among them — have held that "some degree of attorney involvement is required before a letter will be considered 'from an attorney' within the meaning of the [federal act]." *Miller v. Wolpoff & Abramson, LLP,* 321 F.3d 292, 301 (2d Cir. 2003); *see also Gonzalez v. Kay,* 577 F.3d 600, 604 (5th Cir. 2009). That means that if an attorney is acting only as a debt collector and has not formed a legal opinion about the case, he or she cannot send a letter implying otherwise. In other words, when attorneys attempt to collect a debt, they cannot mislead debtors about their "level of involvement" in the case. *Greco v. Trauner, Cohen & Thomas, LLP,* 412 F.3d 360, 364 (2d Cir. 2005).

The district court decided Jones's claims on a motion for judgment on the pleadings under Rule 12(c), a decision we review *de novo. See Mpoy v. Rhee,* 758 F.3d 285, 287 (D.C. Cir. 2014). Applying a "least sophisticated consumer standard,"[2] the court found that the letter did not misrepresent the extent of Dufek's involvement p.526 in the case, and we agree. *See Jones v. Law Office of David Sean Dufek,* 77 F.Supp.3d 134, 138, 140 (D.D.C. 2015). Dufek was an attorney acting as a debt collector, and the letter said precisely that. No one at his law office had reviewed the case. Again, the letter so stated.

Jones argues that using the title "attorney" in the letterhead and signature block impermissibly implies that an attorney has evaluated the case from a legal standpoint. Appellant Br. 31-32; *see Avila v. Rubin,* 84 F.3d 222, 229 (7th Cir. 1996). This boils down to the argument that under the federal act, attorneys cannot act as debt collectors unless they conceal the fact that they are attorneys. But this is not the theory of the Fair Debt Collection Practices Act. The Act assumes that attorneys may collect debts so long as they do not mislead debtors. *See Greco,* 412 F.3d at 364.

Attorneys who collect debts therefore must not falsely represent or imply that they have formed a legal opinion regarding the debtor's liability. Here, Dufek included a conspicuous disclaimer describing his involvement in the matter. The letter did not threaten any legal action "that [could not] legally be taken or that [was] not intended to be taken." 15 U.S.C. § 1692e(5). The letter made no reference to legal action. *See Brown v. Card Serv. Ctr.,* 464 F.3d 450, 451 (3d Cir. 2006) ("Refusal to cooperate could result in a legal suit being filed for collection of the account."); *Bentley v. Great Lakes Collection Bureau,* 6 F.3d 60, 62 (2d Cir. 1993). The letter did not give any indication about what the creditor might do if Jones failed to pay the debt. It simply said that Jones owed a debt and that she should send her payment to Dufek's office. The only future consequence the letter discussed was the statutorily required disclosure that if Jones did not dispute the debt's validity within thirty days, Dufek's office would presume that it was valid. *See* 15 U.S.C. § 1692g(a)(3).

Here again, Jones falls back on the idea that using the "attorney" title is enough to constitute an implicit threat of legal action. But lawyers do more than just file lawsuits. Sometimes, they try to collect debts, and the Fair Debt Collection Practices Act does not prohibit them from doing so. The fact that an attorney was involved in collecting Jones's debt does not mean that the collection attempt constituted a threat to take legal action.[3]

Jones criticizes the letter's disclaimer for stating only that no attorney had reviewed the case "at this time." Appellant Br. 42. According to Jones, these words imply that at some future time, an attorney may review the case and file a lawsuit. That may be so. But the federal act prohibits only *threats* to take legal action; merely leaving open the possibility of attorney review that could lead to legal action does not fit the bill.

The disclaimer Dufek included is commonly known as a "*Greco* disclaimer," *see, e.g., Luftig v. Sokoloff,* No. 13 CV 4313, 2015 WL 151463, at *1 n.1 (E.D.N.Y. Jan. 13, 2015), because it tracks language the Second Circuit approved in *Greco v. Trauner, Cohen & Thomas, LLP,* 412 F.3d 360 (2d Cir. 2005). The collection letter in *Greco* stated: "At this time, no attorney with this firm has personally reviewed the particular circumstances of your account. However, if you fail to contact this office, our client may consider additional remedies to recover the balance due." 412 F.3d at 361. The Second Circuit held that this p.527 language was sufficient to "make clear ... that the law firm or attorney sending the letter [was] not, at the time of the letter's transmission, acting as an attorney." *Id.* at 364.

Since *Greco,* many circuits have agreed that a prominent and clear disclaimer stating that an attorney is acting as a debt collector is enough, but a hidden or confusing disclaimer is not. *See, e.g., Gonzales v. Arrow Fin. Servs., LLC,* 660 F.3d 1055, 1063 (9th Cir. 2011); *Lesher v. Law Offices of Mitchell N. Kay, PC,* 650 F.3d 993, 1002-03 (3d Cir. 2011); *Gonzalez v. Kay,* 577 F.3d 600, 606 (5th Cir. 2009); *Kistner v. Law*

Offices of Michael P. Margelefsky, LLC, 518 F.3d 433, 439 (6th Cir. 2008). Jones argues that the disclaimer in Dufek's letter was "obscured" because it followed the signature block rather than appearing in the body of the letter. Appellant Br. 14. But there is no relevant difference we perceive between a disclaimer in the body of the letter before the signature block and one after the signature block. Dufek's disclaimer was in the same font and size as the body of the letter, and a portion of it was in bold typeface. *Compare Kistner,* 518 F.3d at 439 ("no disclaimer"); *Gonzalez,* 577 F.3d at 606 ("disclaimer on the back [of the letter]"); *Wilson v. Quadramed Corp.*, 225 F.3d 350, 358 (3d Cir. 2000) (disclaimer in "grey ink on a light shade of grey computer paper, making it difficult to read, and in a type size less than 1/10 [of an inch]"); *see also Campuzano-Burgos v. Midland Credit Mgmt.*, 550 F.3d 294, 299 (3d Cir. 2008) ("Even the least sophisticated debtor is bound to read collection notices in their entirety."). We do not mean to imply that a disclaimer must be in the same font and size as the body of the letter, but the fact that it was in this case further indicates that this disclaimer was not hidden.

Jones's argument focuses on § 1692e(3) and (5) of the federal act, which deal with attorney involvement and threats of legal action. In passing, she invokes several other sections containing general prohibitions against deception, unfairness, and false representations in connection with debt collection.[4] She offers no separate arguments in support of these claims. Instead, she simply says that because the letter falsely implied than an attorney was involved and threatened legal action, the letter was *a fortiori* deceptive and unfair in a general sense. We have held that the letter did not contain any such false implications or threats, so we reject the remainder of her arguments under the federal act.

We dispose of her claims under the District of Columbia statutes on similar grounds. Jones argues that Dufek and CACH violated the D.C. Consumer Protection Act, which protects "any consumer" from misrepresentation, misleading omissions, and other "[u]nlawful trade practices." D.C. CODE § 28-3904. But here too, Jones relies entirely on her allegations that the letter falsely implied that an attorney was involved and that the defendants were threatening a lawsuit. In their briefs, the parties argue at length about certain threshold issues — in particular, whether Jones is a "consumer" or debt collection is a "trade practice." The district court concluded that the D.C. Act did not p.528 apply because "a loan of money is not a purchase or lease of goods or services." *Jones,* 77 F.Supp.3d at 139 (italics omitted). The court's interpretation may be incorrect; the D.C. Act states specifically that "goods and services ... includes consumer credit...." D.C. CODE § 28-3901(a)(7). However, even if the court erred, its mistake was not fatal. The district court's interpretation was only an "additional reason" that Jones's claims under the Consumer Protection Act fail. *Jones,* 77 F.Supp.3d at 139. Even if the Act applied, it would not help Jones because the letter did not falsely imply attorney involvement or threaten a lawsuit. We therefore affirm the district court's dismissal of this claim without reaching the court's interpretation of the scope of the Consumer Protection Act.

The other consumer statute Jones invokes — the D.C. Debt Collection Law — largely mirrors the language of the Fair Debt Collection Practices Act. *Compare* D.C. CODE § 28-3814(f) (prohibiting "any fraudulent, deceptive, or misleading representation or means to collect or attempt to collect claims or to obtain information concerning consumers") *with* 15 U.S.C. § 1692e(10) (prohibiting "any false representation or deceptive means to collect or attempt to collect any debt or to obtain information concerning a consumer"). Jones has not argued that this D.C. law gives her any more protection than the federal act. We therefore affirm the district court's dismissal of Jones's claim under that law as well. The district court discussed the Debt Collection Law only briefly, *see Jones,* 77 F.Supp.3d at 137-38, likely because separate analysis of that law would have been largely redundant. This was entirely proper; a "court is not required to state findings or conclusions when ruling on a motion under Rule 12." FED. R. CIV. P. 52(a)(3).[5]

The district court properly resolved these questions as a matter of law on a motion under Rule 12(c). *See Jones,* 77 F.Supp.3d at 137. We agree that no reasonable juror could find the letter deceptive. *See Anderson v. Liberty Lobby, Inc.,* 477 U.S. 242, 252, 106 S.Ct. 2505, 91 L.Ed.2d 202 (1986); *see also, e.g., Alexander v. City of Chicago,* 994 F.2d 333, 336 (7th Cir. 1993) ("[T]he standard courts apply for summary judgment and for judgment on the pleadings 'appears to be identical.'") (quoting 5A CHARLES A. WRIGHT AND ARTHUR R. MILLER, FEDERAL PRACTICE AND PROCEDURE § 1368 at 530 (1990)). As the Fifth Circuit put it, "There are some letters that, as a matter of law, are not deceptive...." *Gonzalez,* 577 F.3d at 606.

One extraneous matter remains. While their Rule 12(c) motion was awaiting a ruling, the defendants filed a motion for a protective order under Rule 26(c) to stop Jones from issuing "unauthorized discovery requests." A month later, the court denied this motion in a Minute Order. *See* Minute Order denying Motion to Quash, No. 1:14-cv-00533-RJL (D.D.C. Sept. 7, 2014). In response, Jones moved for attorney's fees under Federal Rule of Civil Procedure 26(c)(3). This rule incorporates Rule 37(a)(5) and states that if the court denies a motion for a protective order, the court "must, after giving an opportunity to be heard, require the movant ... to pay" the opposing party's expenses and attorney's fees. Rule 37(a)(5) also states that "the court must not order this payment if the motion was substantially justified or other circumstances make an award of expenses unjust." FED. R. CIV. P. 37(a)(5)(B).

p.529 District courts have "considerable discretion" to manage discovery. *United States v. Philip Morris Inc.,* 347 F.3d 951, 955 (D.C. Cir. 2003). In particular, courts "possess broad discretion to impose sanctions for discovery violations under Rule 37." *Parsi v. Daioleslam,* 778 F.3d 116, 125 (D.C. Cir. 2015). In 1970, Rule 37 was amended and the section for awarding attorney's fees was rephrased in mandatory terms — the court "must" grant attorney's fees under certain conditions and "must not" grant them under others. FED. R. CIV. P. 37(a)(5)(B). The conditions are fairly vague, particularly the catch-all term that the court must not grant fees if doing so would be "unjust." *Id.* The advisory committee explained that this amendment did "not significantly narrow the discretion of the court" to award attorney's fees for discovery violations. FED. R. CIV. P. 37 advisory committee's notes to 1970 amendments; *see Marquis v. Chrysler Corp.,* 577 F.2d 624, 642 (9th Cir. 1978).

The district court did not explicitly deny the motion for attorney's fees. Its failure to award fees may be taken as a denial of the motion. Rule 37(a)(5) states that under certain circumstances, the court "must not order this payment," and that is what the court did. FED. R. CIV. P. 37(a)(5); *see also* FED. R. CIV. P. 52(a)(3). The district court did not abuse its discretion in coming to this decision. Jones's counsel had asked for $29,241 for sixty-five hours of work on this discovery issue.[6] The court had discretion to find that this award would be excessive and therefore "unjust." In upholding the district court's refusal to grant Jones's motion, we are mindful that Rule 26(c)(3) is meant to prevent needless litigation and wasteful discovery disputes. Requiring still further proceedings in this case would not be consistent with that objective.

Accordingly, we affirm the district court's judgment.

So ordered.

[1] Jones has belatedly tried to contest certain historical facts, including whether Dufek himself sent the letter and whether Dufek exists at all. These additional claims largely rehash Jones's main argument that Dufek misrepresented his involvement in the case. To the extent these claims differ from that overarching argument, Jones did not raise them in the district court and we will not consider them now. *See Anglers Conservation Network v. Pritzker,* 809 F.3d 664, 671 n.6 (D.C. Cir. 2016).

[2] In evaluating whether a collection letter is deceptive, some courts have applied a "least sophisticated consumer" standard, *see, e.g., Clomon v. Jackson,* 988 F.2d 1314, 1318 (2d Cir. 1993), and others have applied an "unsophisticated consumer" standard, *see, e.g., Gammon v. GC Servs. Ltd.,* 27 F.3d 1254, 1257 (7th Cir. 1994). The term "unsophisticated" is probably more accurate because the "least sophisticated" consumer is "not merely 'below average,' he is the very last rung on the sophistication ladder," and "would likely not be able to read a collection notice with care (or at all), let alone interpret it in a reasonable fashion." 27 F.3d at 1257. In practice, "least sophisticated" and "unsophisticated" appear to be the same. Under either conception, the basic goal is to prevent debt collectors from deceiving naive consumers, but not to hold collectors liable simply because their letters may be deceptive under "bizarre or idiosyncratic consumer interpretations." *Gonzalez v. Kay,* 577 F.3d 600, 603 (5th Cir. 2009).

[3] Jones also alleged that Dufek misrepresented that he "was authorized to take legal action against consumers in the District of Columbia, because Dufek is a California law firm not licensed to practice law in the District of Columbia." *Jones,* 77 F.Supp.3d at 138. But Dufek's letter said nothing about his intention or authority to file a lawsuit.

[4] In addition to 15 U.S.C. § 1692e(3) and (5), Jones relies on § 1692e(2)(A) (prohibiting "[t]he false representation of ... the character, amount, or legal status of any debt"); § 1692e(10) (prohibiting "[t]he use of any false representation or deceptive means to collect or attempt to collect any debt or to obtain information concerning a consumer"); § 1692j(a) (prohibiting the use of forms that create "the false belief in a consumer that a person other than the creditor of such consumer is participating in the collection of or in an attempt to collect a debt"); and § 1692f (prohibiting "unfair or unconscionable means to collect or attempt to collect any debt").

[5] Because the district court properly found that Jones's claims fail on their merits, it also denied her motion for class certification as moot. *See Thomas v. Knight,* No. 03-7041, 2003 WL 22239653, at *1 (D.C. Cir. Sept. 24, 2003).

[6] Jones's counsel initially asked for $22,761 for fifty-six hours of work, but later increased that figure by nearly 30% for the additional nine hours of work

required to respond to Dufek's opposition to paying attorney's fees. *Compare* Motion for Attorney Fees at 8, No. 1:14-cv-00533-RJL (D.D.C. Sept. 15, 2014), ECF No. 28; *with* Errata Reply to Defendant's Opposition to Motion for Attorney Fees at 7, No. 1:14-cv-00533-RJL (D.D.C. Oct. 14, 2014), ECF No. 31.

FIRST CIRCUIT DECISIONS

Fair Debt Collection Practices Act

981 F.3d 82 (2020)

Jackeline BARBOSA, individually and on behalf of others similarly situated, Plaintiff, Appellant,
Mark Anderson, individually and on behalf of other similarly situated; Douglass Baker, individually and on behalf of others similarly situated, Plaintiffs,
v.
MIDLAND CREDIT MANAGEMENT, INC; Schreiber/Cohen, LLC, Defendants, Appellees,
Lustig, Glaser & Wilson, P.C., Defendant.

No. 19-1896.

United States Court of Appeals, First Circuit.

November 25, 2020.

Barbosa v. Midland Credit Management, Inc., 981 F. 3d 82 (1st Cir. 2020)

Appeal from the United States District Court for the District of Massachusetts, [Hon. Nathaniel M. Gorton, U.S. District Judge].

Charles M. Delbaum, with whom National Consumer Law Center, Kenneth D. Quat, Quat Law Offices, Alexa Rosenbloom, Nadine Cohen, Matt Brooks, and Greater Boston Legal Services were on brief, for appellant.

Cory W. Eichhorn, with whom Gordon P. Katz, Benjamin M. McGovern, and Holland & Knight LLP were on brief, for appellee Midland Credit Management, Inc.

Marissa I. Delinks, with whom Andrew M. Schneiderman and Hinshaw & Culbertson LLP were on brief, for appellee Schreiber/Cohen, LLC.

Before THOMPSON, LIPEZ, and KAYATTA, Circuit Judges.

p.84 THOMPSON, Circuit Judge.

This case dips us briefly into the vast pool of credit card debt collection efforts within the broader debt collection industry. Here's how it works. When a credit card company gives up on collecting an individual account in default (leading it to "charge-off" the debt), it bundles lots of individual accounts together and sells the bundle to a debt collection entity (otherwise known as the debt buyer). Peter A. Holland, The One Hundred Billion Dollar Problem in Small Claims Court: Robo-Signing and Lack of Proof in Debt Buyer Cases, 6 J. Bus. & Tech. L. 259, 264-65 (2011). Buying such bundles of individual consumer debt is a massive and lucrative industry; in 2016, the participating corporate entities disclosed revenue of over $13 billion. Midland Funding, LLC v. Johnson, ___ U.S. ___, 137 S. Ct. 1407, 1416, 197 L.Ed.2d 790 (2017) (Sotomayor, J., dissenting) (citing Consumer Financial Protection Bur., Fair Debt Collection Practices Act: Annual Report 2016, at 8). Some of this revenue is earned by winning default judgments in state small claims courts, where corporate entities who have bought consumer debt often win their gamble that individual consumers will not appear in court to defend against a debt collection action to the tune of "billions of dollars." Id. at 1417 (quoting Holland, supra, at 263).

The debt buyer in this case, Midland Funding LLC, lost this gamble with appellant Jackeline Barbosa, who showed up in court to defend against the debt collection action and won, then chose to go on the offensive in federal court.

HOW WE GOT HERE[1]

A resident of Massachusetts, Barbosa opened a credit card account with Barclays Bank Delaware ("Barclays") in April 2011. The last payment she made on the account was in November 2012. By June 2013 (the last month for which we have a statement from this account), Barbosa was carrying an overdue, unpaid balance of $3,423.24.

In June 2015, Barclays sold this unpaid balance to Midland Funding LLC. To be more precise, Barclays sold Midland Funding a "series of accounts that originated with" it, à la bundling practice we referred to above. Midland Funding is an empty corporate shell entity (meaning it has no employees) which buys charged-off consumer debt from other entities. For example, when Midland Funding bought Barbosa's account from Barclays, her account p.85 was part of a "pool of charged-off accounts."

Midland Credit Management, Inc. ("MCM") manages the accounts purchased by Midland Funding, acting as its servicer and agent. The rights to Barbosa's account were assigned to MCM pursuant to a Servicing Agreement between Midland Funding and MCM. Schreiber/Cohen LLC is the law firm retained by MCM on behalf of Midland Funding to assist in MCM's debt collection efforts, including filing lawsuits against credit card debtors.

In August 2017, Midland Funding, as assignee of Barclays and represented by Schreiber/Cohen, filed a statement of small claim against Barbosa in the Boston Municipal Court, seeking to collect the unpaid credit card account balance plus court costs. The Municipal Court ultimately issued judgment in Barbosa's favor, concluding Midland Funding had not proved it owned the subject debt.

About a year later, Barbosa, along with two other individuals who similarly experienced the credit card collection practices of Midland Funding and MCM, sued MCM and Schreiber/Cohen (as well as one other law firm not involved with Barbosa's account) in federal district court, claiming the corporate entities violated the Fair Debt Collection Practices Act ("FDCPA"), 15 U.S.C. §§ 1692e and 1692f, by attempting to collect the credit card debt in the Massachusetts state court after the statute of limitations for the collection action had expired pursuant to Delaware state law.[2] The plaintiffs also claimed the violation of the FDCPA was a per se violation of Massachusetts General Laws, chapter 93A, § 2.[3],[4]

MCM and Schreiber/Cohen each responded to the complaint with a motion asking the district court to compel arbitration pursuant to the arbitration election provision in each plaintiff's credit card agreement, to strike the class action allegations, to dismiss the complaint for failure to state a claim, and/or to stay the litigation pursuant to a variety of theories. MCM primarily relied on the arbitration provision of the Barclays Cardmember Agreements.[5] While Schreiber/Cohen argued p.86 that the complaint was worthy of dismissal for failure to state a claim on several grounds, it also argued the district court should compel arbitration.

After a hearing, a magistrate judge issued a report and recommendation (an "R&R" to use court lingo) in which she focused primarily on the arbitration provision in the Barclays Cardmember Agreement. The magistrate judge concluded the agreement contained a valid arbitration provision which MCM and Schreiber/Cohen were authorized to enforce and recommended the district judge send the parties off to arbitration. In addition to suggesting the district judge grant the motion to compel arbitration, the R&R also suggested the district judge: (1) strike the class action claim, and (2) dismiss the amended complaint without prejudice. The plaintiffs filed a timely objection to the R&R but the district judge ultimately agreed with the magistrate judge, accepting and adopting her R&R in its entirety using a margin decision and issuing an order dismissing the plaintiffs' claims. Barbosa was the only plaintiff to file a notice of appeal. Her challenge to the district court's order focuses exclusively on the district court's conclusion that MCM and Schreiber/Cohen are authorized to compel Barbosa to arbitrate her claims against them.[6] As we explain below, the legal principles at play here lead us to affirm.

STANDARD OF REVIEW

"We review a district court's denial of a motion to compel arbitration de novo." Nat'l Fed'n of the Blind v. The Container Store, Inc., 904 F.3d 70, 78 (1st Cir. 2018) (citing Kristian v. Comcast Corp., 446 F.3d 25, 31 (1st Cir. 2006)). "In conducting our inquiry, 'we are not wedded to the lower court's rationale, but, rather, may affirm its order on any independent ground made manifest by the record.'" Id. (quoting Campbell v. Gen. Dynamics Gov't Sys. Corp., 407 F.3d 546, 551 (1st Cir. 2005)).

OUR TAKE

The central issue in this appeal is whether MCM and Schreiber/Cohen, two parties who were not signatories to Barbosa's Cardmember Agreement, can force her into arbitration. Barbosa would like us to answer this question with a resounding "no" and the appellees (of course) want us, like the district court, to say "yes."

Before we get into the weeds to resolve this issue, we begin with a general overview of the Federal Arbitration Act and how we generally consider arbitration provisions within contracts. Then we proceed to describe, based on the amended complaint and the documents filed in this case, the undisputed relationship statuses between the entities.

The Federal Arbitration Act, 9 U.S.C. §§ 1-16, has been in place since 1925, long recognized as Congress's solution to the courts' dim view of arbitration, "replac[ing] judicial indisposition to arbitration with a 'national policy favoring [it] and plac[ing] arbitration agreements on equal footing with all other contracts.'" Nat'l Fed'n of the Blind, 904 F.3d at 79 (second and third alterations in original) (quoting Hall St. Assocs., L.L.C. v. Mattel, Inc., 552 U.S. p.87 576, 581, 128 S.Ct. 1396, 170 L.Ed.2d 254 (2008)).

> As enacted, the FAA promotes a liberal federal policy favoring arbitration and guarantees that "[a] written provision in... a contract evidencing a transaction involving commerce to settle by arbitration a controversy thereafter arising out of such contract or transaction ... shall be valid,

> irrevocable, and enforceable, save upon such grounds as exist at law or in equity for the revocation of any contract."

Id. (quoting 9 U.S.C. § 2).

"The FAA allows one party to an arbitration agreement to ask the court to put the litigation on hold and force the other party to arbitrate the disputes." Rivera-Colón v. AT&T Mobility P.R., Inc., 913 F.3d 200, 207 (1st Cir. 2019) (citing 9 U.S.C. § 4); see also 9 U.S.C. § 3. Basically, "[t]he Federal Arbitration Act requires courts to enforce private arbitration agreements." New Prime Inc. v. Oliveira, ___ U.S. ___, 139 S. Ct. 532, 536, 202 L.Ed.2d 536 (2019). The FAA treats these agreements as "contract[s], and courts must enforce arbitration contracts according to their terms." Biller, 961 F.3d at 508 (quoting Henry Schein, Inc. v. Archer & White Sales, Inc., ___ U.S. ___, 139 S. Ct. 524, 529, 202 L.Ed.2d 480 (2019)).

"A party seeking to compel arbitration under the FAA must demonstrate that a valid agreement to arbitrate exists, that the movant is entitled to invoke the arbitration clause, that the other party is bound by that clause, and that the claim asserted comes within the clause's scope." Id. (quoting Dialysis Access Ctr., LLC v. RMS Lifeline, Inc., 638 F.3d 367, 375 (1st Cir. 2011)). (As we will get into soon, the only disputed element in this case is whether the moving parties (here MCM and Schreiber/Cohen) were entitled to enforce the arbitration provision in the Cardmember Agreement.) "If the movant [shows all four elements], the court has to send the dispute to arbitration 'unless the party resisting arbitration specifically challenges the enforceability of the arbitration clause itself ... or claims that the agreement to arbitrate was never concluded.'" Id. (quoting Granite Rock Co. v. Int'l Bhd. of Teamsters, 561 U.S. 287, 301, 130 S.Ct. 2847, 177 L.Ed.2d 567 (2010)). "Those issues, which implicate 'whether or not a dispute is arbitrable,' are typically for the court to decide." Id. (quoting Dialysis Access Ctr., LLC, 638 F.3d at 375).

Barbosa is not challenging either the validity of the arbitration provision or the formation of the Cardmember Agreement in which the arbitration provision sits. Instead, her challenge is narrowly focused on whether MCM and Schreiber/Cohen have the contractual authority to enforce the Agreement's arbitration provision by virtue of their status as non-signatories to the agreement and agents of Midland Funding, to whom Barclays assigned its contractual rights to Barbosa's credit card account.[7]

p.88 There is no doubt that MCM and Schreiber/Cohen's non-signatory status to the Cardmember Agreement is not in and of itself dispositive for this issue. While in general a "contract cannot bind a non-party[,]... 'there are exceptions allowing non-signatories to compel arbitration' and... 'a non-signatory may be bound by or acquire rights under an arbitration agreement under ordinary state-law principles of agency or contract.'" Grand Wireless, Inc. v. Verizon Wireless, Inc., 748 F.3d 1, 9-10 (1st Cir. 2014) (alteration omitted) (quoting Restoration Pres. Masonry, Inc. v. Grove Eur. Ltd., 325 F.3d 54, 62 n.2 (1st Cir. 2003)); see also id. at 10 n.22 (citing with approval several cases from other circuits "acknowledging that non-signatories may have rights under an arbitration contract under certain circumstances.").

Before turning to our analysis of whether MCM and Schreiber/Cohen have the requisite authority to enforce the arbitration provision in the Cardmember Agreement, it will be helpful to lay out the undisputed relationships between the various parties as presented in Barbosa's complaint and in the documents the appellees submitted in support of their motions to compel arbitration, as well as what the various relevant contractual provisions in these supporting documents say. None of the parties are disputing the following:

> • The validity of the Cardmember Agreement as a valid contract between Barbosa, Barclays, and Barclays' assigns or that this contract includes both valid assignment and arbitration provisions.[8]
>
> • Midland Funding is an assignee of Barclays; the express assignment is in the "Bill of Sale" submitted with MCM's motion to compel arbitration as well as reflected in the "Portfolio Level Affidavit of Sale," also submitted in support of the motion.[9]
>
> • MCM is the servicer and agent of Midland Funding; Barbosa admits as much in her complaint ("MCM has been Midland Funding's servicer and agent with respect to collecting charged-off consumer debts acquired by Midland Funding") and MCM submitted a declaration in support of its motion stating:
>
> p.89 MCM is the servicer and authorized agent for Midland Funding and manages the accounts that Midland Funding purchases. Midland Funding is an indirect subsidiary of MCM. Midland Funding has no employees and is a completely passive entity. To that end, MCM fully services accounts owned by Midland Funding and takes any and all actions on those accounts on behalf of Midland Funding.
>
> • Schreiber/Cohen is Midland Funding's agent. In Barbosa's complaint, she alleges Schreiber/Cohen engaged in its debt collection activities "on behalf of Midland Funding and MCM" and, in her briefing, she refers to the law firm as Midland Funding's agent.

So that's what everyone agrees on. The disagreement lies in whether the arbitration provision authorizes MCM and Schreiber/Cohen to elect arbitration and enforce this provision. To that end, the crux of the parties' dispute centers on the following language in the first paragraph of the arbitration provision:

> For purposes of this provision, "you" includes any authorized user on the Account, and any of your agents, beneficiaries or assigns; and "we" or "us" includes our employees, parents, subsidiaries, affiliates, beneficiaries, agents and assigns, and to the extent included in a proceeding in which Barclays is a party, its service providers and marketing partners.

The district court considered and relied on this language, the assignment provision in the Cardmember Agreement, and the actual assignment of rights to Barbosa's account to Midland Funding memorialized in the "Bill of Sale" when it concluded the following:

> (1) Midland Funding now stands in the shoes of Barclays so Midland Funding's affiliates, agents, and assigns, etc. are entitled to invoke the arbitration provision just as Barclays' affiliates, agents, and assigns, etc. could have invoked the provision.
>
> (2) MCM and Schreiber/Cohen fall within the definition of "us" in the language quoted above because both are agents of Midland Funding and, therefore, each has the authority to invoke the arbitration provision.

Barbosa disagrees with both conclusions for reasons which we discuss in turn.[10]

Standing in Barclays' Shoes

Before we can dive into who has the authority to enforce the arbitration provision, we examine the implications of Midland Funding as Barclays' assignee. Barbosa argues the district court got it wrong when it concluded Midland Funding stands in Barclays' shoes such that Midland Funding has all the same rights as Barclays under the Cardmember Agreement. According to Barbosa, to so conclude creates contract provision surplusage, which is against basic principles of contract interpretation, p.90 because Midland Funding can't be both Barclays' assignee and standing in for Barclays itself.

MCM says no way — the principle that an assignee stands in the shoes of an assignor's contractual rights is well-settled and this principle does not result in the definition of "us" being superfluous. Schreiber/Cohen, for its part, read Barbosa's argument slightly differently, pointing out that the district court's consideration of both the assignment provision and the arbitration provision does not result in impermissible surplusage, but instead demonstrates the proper application of the contract interpretation principle of reading the contract as a whole and giving effect to each provision. In her reply brief, Barbosa shifts her argument a little by asserting that, if Midland Funding is considered to stand in for every mention of Barclays within the Cardmember Agreement, then the list of relationships in the arbitration provision's definition of "us" (i.e., "employees, parents, subsidiaries, affiliates, beneficiaries, agents and assigns ...") is superfluous. We agree with the appellees.

As we stated above, there is no dispute the Cardmember Agreement included an assignment provision giving Barclays permission to "at any time assign or sell your Account" and providing that "the person(s) to whom we make any such assignment or sale shall be entitled to all of our rights under this Agreement, to the extent assigned." There is also no dispute Barclays assigned its full contractual rights to Barbosa's credit card account to Midland Funding. A long-standing given in contract law is indeed that an "assignee stands in the shoes of the assignor." MacKenzie v. Flagstar Bank, FSB, 738 F.3d 486, 494 (1st Cir. 2013) (quoting R.I. Hosp. Trust Nat'l Bank v. Ohio Cas. Ins. Co., 789 F.2d 74, 81 (1st Cir. 1986)). In her brief, Barbosa does not provide any support, beyond her blanket assertion, that this conclusion is in conflict with binding contract law. Therefore, contrary to what she asserts, pursuant to the assignment provision and the express assignment of "all" rights to Barbosa's account in the "Bill of Sale," Midland Funding does in fact stand in Barclays' shoes as its assignee and now has all the same rights regarding Barbosa's account as Barclays had when the Cardmember Agreement was formed. And because of that, in the wake of the assignment, Midland Funding becomes, as Barclays once was, the "other" referred to in the arbitration provision, and MCM and Schreiber/Cohen become "agents ... of the other" (recall the arbitration provision kicks off with "[a]t the election of either you or us, any claim, dispute or controversy ("Claim") by either you or us against the other, or against the employees, agents or assigns of the other ..."). So Barbosa's claims against both appellees are within the arbitration clause's sweep.

To so conclude does not, as Barbosa asserts, render any other part of the Cardmember Agreement surplusage. Another well-settled principle of contract law (using the Delaware Supreme Court's words) tells us to "read a contract as a whole and ... give each provision and term effect, so as not to render any part of the contract mere surplusage." Bank of N.Y. Mellon v. Commerzbank Capital Funding Tr. II, 65 A.3d 539, 549 n.30 (Del. 2013) (quoting Kuhn Constr., Inc. v. Diamond State Port Corp., 990 A.2d 393, 396-97 (Del. 2010)). Barbosa does not provide a detailed argument about how this conclusion results in impermissible surplusage. She does express her view that "[a] general assignment of account rights does not override explicit contract language restricting the parties who may enforce an agreement to arbitrate." Barbosa is not wrong on this point but, in our view, the p.91 assignment and arbitration provisions within the Cardmember Agreement are not in conflict, they co-exist; The assignment provision articulates Barclays' authority to assign all its rights to Barbosa's account to another entity, whereas the arbitration provision specifically sets out what kinds of relationships with the account owner are required before an entity related to the account owner can elect arbitration. The bottom line is there is no surplusage resulting from the district court's interpretation of the Cardmember Agreement. As a result of the assignment from Barclays to Midland Funding, the latter is authorized to enforce the contractual rights created by the Cardmember Agreement, including delegating enforcement of the contractual provisions to one or two of its agents to act on its behalf, as we examine next.

Who Can Elect Arbitration

According to Barbosa, MCM and Schreiber/Cohen lack the authority to elect arbitration and enforce the Cardmember Agreement's arbitration provision because these entities do not have a direct relationship with Barclays and do not otherwise fall within any part of the definition of "us" provided in the provision. The relevant part of the arbitration provision states:

> At the election of either you or us, any claim, dispute or controversy ("Claim") by either you or us against the other, or against the employees, agents or assigns of the other, arising from or relating in any way to this Agreement or your Account ... shall be resolved exclusively and finally by binding arbitration.... For purposes of this provision, "you" includes any authorized user on the Account, and any of your agents, beneficiaries or assigns; and "we" or "us" includes our employees, parents, subsidiaries, affiliates, beneficiaries, agents and assigns, and to the extent included in a proceeding in which Barclays is a party, its service providers and marketing partners.

The way Barbosa reads the first part of the definition ("our employees, parents, subsidiaries, affiliates, beneficiaries, agents and assigns"), the arbitration provision does not authorize the agents and affiliates of a Barclays' assignee (e.g., Midland Funding) to enforce this provision, so the only entities with the authority to elect arbitration are — literally — Barclays and Barclays' "employees, parents, subsidiaries, affiliates, beneficiaries, agents and assigns." So, in Barbosa's thinking, Midland Funding could elect arbitration but Midland Funding's agents and assigns, etc. cannot. MCM and Schreiber/Cohen disagree and assert that, because Midland

Funding has the same contractual rights as Barclays, Midland Funding's agents have the authority to enforce the arbitration provision.

The arbitration provision clearly allows the account owner and the account owner's "employees, ... agents and assigns" to elect arbitration and enforce this provision. Because Midland Funding has the same rights as Barclays had to enforce the Cardmember Agreement, Midland Funding's agents fall squarely within the arbitration provision's definition of "us" and may therefore elect arbitration on Midland Funding's behalf. As we stated previously, the record shows MCM acted as an agent of Midland Funding. Barbosa admitted as much in the allegations of her complaint, and MCM provided evidence to this effect in a declaration MCM submitted in support of its motion to compel arbitration.

Turning our attention to Schreiber/Cohen, Barbosa identified this law firm in her complaint as engaging in debt collection activities "on behalf of Midland Funding" and, in her reply brief, referred to this law p.92 firm as Midland Funding's agent. As Schreiber/Cohen argues, they are Midland Funding's agent as a matter of law. See Comm'r v. Banks, 543 U.S. 426, 436, 125 S.Ct. 826, 160 L.Ed.2d 859 (2005) (recognizing "[t]he relationship between client and attorney, regardless of the variations in particular compensation agreements or the amount of skill and effort the attorney contributes, [a]s a quintessential principal-agent relationship") (citing Restatement (Second) of Agency § 1, Comment e (1958) (stating an attorney is an agent under basic principles of agency)). As Midland Funding's legal counsel, Schreiber/Cohen was authorized to act on its behalf and under its direction, including writing and filing motions to enforce the provisions of the contract to which Midland Funding had the proper authority to enforce.

Not so fast, says Barbosa. She places much emphasis on the second clause in the definition at issue — "'we' or 'us' includes our employees, parents, subsidiaries, affiliates, beneficiaries, agents and assigns, *and to the extent included in a proceeding in which Barclays is a party, its service providers and marketing partners*" (emphasis added) — arguing this clause also does not bring either MCM or Schreiber/Cohen within the definition of "us." Barbosa argues this part of the definition is a more specific articulation of to whom the definition applies and so should control the first part of the sentence's general definition.

As Barbosa sees it, even if MCM and Schreiber/Cohen are service providers, Midland Funding (if considered to now be in Barclays' position) is not a party to this litigation because it is not a named defendant. As a result, she says, neither entity is authorized to enforce the arbitration provision based on this clause. MCM and Schreiber/Cohen respond that this "service provider" clause does not need to come into play at all because the first part of the definition ("'we' or 'us' includes our employees, parents, subsidiaries, affiliates, beneficiaries, *agents* and assigns ..." (emphasis added)) expressly gives them authority as Midland Funding's agents. Schreiber/Cohen specifically argues this "service provider" clause is not a more specific part of the definition limiting the first part and doesn't preclude it from enforcing the arbitration provision as Midland Funding's agent. Once again, we think the appellees have the better understanding.

Based on our interpretation of the first part of this definition, this second clause is not applicable to the situation at hand because, as appellees argue, it does not come into play. Even if Midland Funding was a named defendant, the plain language indicates this clause is simply extending the list of entities that may be authorized to elect arbitration and is not intended to limit the first part of the definition listing the entities with this authority.[11],[12]

p.93 Finally, we quickly touch on an alternative ground with respect to MCM's status vis-à-vis Midland Funding which MCM suggests we consider. According to a declaration from MCM, Midland Funding and MCM entered into a Servicing Agreement in which, "to the extent required and/or permitted by applicable law, [MCM] was assigned the rights in and to certain accounts, including the Barbosa Account." Additionally, according to the "Portfolio Level Affidavit of Sale," Barclays "sold, transferred, assigned, conveyed, granted, bargained, set over and delivered" to Midland Funding "*and its successors and assigns,* good and marketable title to the [pool of charged-off accounts] and any unpaid balance free and clear of any encumbrance...." (Emphasis added.) The district court did not expressly take these documents into account but MCM urges us to consider its status as an assignee of Midland Funding as well as of Barclays itself as alternative grounds to affirm the district court's conclusion that MCM has the requisite authority to enforce the arbitration provision. Remember, in our de novo review of this issue, "we are not wedded to the lower court's rationale, but... may affirm its order on any independent ground made manifest by the record.'" Nat'l Fed'n of the Blind, 904 F.3d at 78 (alteration omitted) (quoting Campbell, 407 F.3d at 551).

MCM's declaration indicates that an official assignor/assignee relationship exists between Midland Funding and MCM. Moreover, pursuant to the language in the "Portfolio Level Affidavit of Sale," Barclays apparently specifically contemplated that Midland Funding may engage its own assignees when it exercises its rights with respect to Barbosa's account and assigned the rights to Midland Funding and Midland Funding's assigns. MCM, therefore, acted not only as Midland Funding's agent but also as Midland Funding's assignee, and was authorized on both levels to enforce the arbitration provision.[13]

p.94 WRAPPING UP

Because we conclude MCM and Schreiber/Cohen have the authority to enforce the arbitration provision, we must "send the parties off to arbitrate" Barbosa's claims. Rivera-Colón, 913 F.3d at 208. The district court's order granting MCM and Schreiber/Cohen's motions to compel Barbosa's claims to the arbitration process is affirmed. Each party to bear its own costs.

[1] Heads up: As this "appeal arises from an order on a motion to compel arbitration in connection with a motion to dismiss, ... we draw the relevant facts from 'the complaint and the parties' submissions to the district court' on the motion." Biller v. S-H OpCo Greenwich Bay Manor, LLC, 961 F.3d 502, 505 n.2 (1st Cir. 2020) (quoting Bekele v. Lyft, Inc., 918 F.3d 181, 184 (1st Cir. 2019)).

[2] The Barclays Cardmember Agreement stated that the agreement and Barbosa's account would be governed by Delaware state law and applicable federal law.

[3] Section 2 declares "[u]nfair methods of competition and unfair or deceptive acts or practices in the conduct of any trade or commerce" to be unlawful. Mass. Gen. Laws ch. 93A, § 2.

[4] The plaintiffs also sought class certification under Fed. R. Civ. P. 23. We say little more about this part of the plaintiffs' claims because the district court struck these claims and this decision has not been challenged in this appeal.

[5] The first part of the long arbitration provision in Barbosa's Cardmember Agreement says:

At the election of either you or us, any claim, dispute or controversy ("Claim") by either you or us against the other, or against the employees, agents or assigns of the other, arising from or relating in any way to this Agreement or your Account, or any transaction on your Account including (without limitation) Claims based on contract, tort (including intentional torts), fraud, agency, negligence, statutory or regulatory provisions or any other source of law and (except as specifically provided in this Agreement) Claims regarding the applicability of this arbitration clause or the validity of the entire Agreement, shall be resolved exclusively and finally by binding arbitration under the rules and procedures of the arbitration Administrator selected at the time the Claim is filed. The Administrator selection process is set forth below. For purposes of this provision, "you" includes any authorized user on the Account, and any of your agents, beneficiaries or assigns; and "we" or "us" includes our employees, parents, subsidiaries, affiliates, beneficiaries, agents and assigns, and to the extent included in a proceeding in which Barclays is a party, its service providers and marketing partners. Claims made and remedies sought as part of a class action, private attorney general or other representative action (hereafter all included in the term "class action") are subject to arbitration on an individual basis, on a class or representative basis.

[6] As we mentioned before, Barbosa does not appeal from the part of the order striking the class action claim.

[7] A quick aside about governing law: Barbosa alleged in her complaint that Delaware law governs the Cardmember Agreement and she has argued in all of her papers that Delaware law governs. The appellees do not dispute this principle and, while the Cardmember Agreement expressly states it is governed by Delaware law, the district court applied both Delaware and Massachusetts state law, finding no significant differences between the two states for the issues at hand. Indeed, "[b]ecause arbitration is a creature of contract, 'principles of state contract law control the determination of whether a valid agreement to arbitrate exists'" as well as other principles of contract interpretation. Rivera-Colón, 913 F.3d at 207 (quoting Soto-Fonalledas v. Ritz-Carlton San Juan Hotel Spa & Casino, 640 F.3d 471, 475 (1st Cir. 2011)). While Barbosa has not challenged the validity of either the Cardmember Agreement or the arbitration provision within it, we will look to Delaware state law when we dig into some of the contract law principles at play in this case.

[8] The assignment provision within the Cardmember Agreement reads:

We may at any time assign or sell your Account, any sums due on your Account, this Agreement or our rights or obligations under this Agreement. The person(s) to whom we make any such assignment or sale shall be entitled to all of our rights under this Agreement, to the extent assigned.

The arbitration provision is long, but the first sentence establishes the general authority to elect arbitration:

At the election of either you or us, any claim, dispute or controversy ("Claim") by either you or us against the other, or against the employees, agents or assigns of the other, arising from or relating in any way to this Agreement or your Account ... shall be resolved exclusively and finally by binding arbitration under the rules and procedures of the arbitration Administrator selected at the time the Claim is filed.

[9] The Bill of Sale between Barclays and Midland Funding regarding the Bulk Debt Sale Agreement "assign[ed], convey[ed], grant[ed] and deliver[ed] [to Midland Funding] ... all [Barclays'] rights title and interest ... in and to those certain evidences of debt," including Barbosa's credit card debt.

The Portfolio Level Affidavit of Sale stated that Barclays "sold, transferred, assigned, conveyed, granted, bargained, set over and delivered" to Midland Funding "and its successors and assigns, good and marketable title to the [pool of charged-off accounts] and any unpaid balance free and clear of any encumbrance...."

[10] We take a brief moment to note that all three parties to this appeal rely heavily on decisions from district courts around the country addressing factual scenarios in similar procedural postures. The parties spill quite a bit of ink arguing why these cases are either analogous to — or distinguishable from — the facts at hand here. None of these decisions carry the day because they are, at best, persuasive. See Camreta v. Greene, 563 U.S. 692, 709 n.7, 131 S.Ct. 2020, 179 L.Ed.2d 1118 (2011) (stating that "[a] decision of a federal district court judge is not binding precedent in either a different judicial district, the same judicial district, or even upon the same judge in a different case." (quoting 18 J. Moore et al., Moore's Federal Practice § 134.02[1][d], p. 134-26 (3d ed. 2011))). We are guided instead by the language of the contracts at play here and the applicable general contract principles.

[11] For the first time before us, Barbosa argues another reason MCM and Schreiber/Cohen do not have the authority to enforce the arbitration provision: In the absence of a direct relationship with Barclays, Barclays did not indicate in the Cardmember Agreement that it intended non-signatory, third-party beneficiaries to be able to invoke the mandatory arbitration clause. As Barbosa herself concedes, however, the authority of a non-signatory to enforce a contractual provision can be based on different grounds such as agency or third-party beneficiary principles.

Because we hold MCM and Schreiber/Cohen had the authority to enforce the arbitration provision as agents of Midland Funding and Barbosa is making this third-party-beneficiary argument for the first time before us, we need not reach her arguments on this point.

[12] Barbosa also makes a preemptive argument that the doctrine of equitable estoppel does not prevent her from denying the appellees' right to invoke the arbitration provision. Because the appellees argued this point to the district court, Barbosa was apparently anticipating they would make a similar contention before us in case we disagreed with the district court's conclusion that MCM and Schreiber/Cohen have the authority to enforce the arbitration provision. She was right, they did. The district court dodged the equitable estoppel issue, concluding in a footnote that, because it concluded "MCM ha[d] the right to invoke the arbitration provision, it need not address MCM's argument that the plaintiffs should be equitably

estopped from avoiding arbitration." Our response to Barbosa's preemptive argument is the same as the district court's: We need not address whether Barbosa should be equitably estopped from fighting the appellees' election to arbitrate because we resolved the primary issue in favor of the appellees.

[13] One final issue bears mentioning because the parties have addressed it in their briefs and it was the subject of some interest during oral argument. MCM attempted to convince the district court that Barbosa's arguments against compelling arbitration of her claims are actually questions of arbitrability that fall under the arbitration provision's delegation clause. Among many details, the arbitration provision also states "[c]laims regarding the applicability of this arbitration clause or the validity of the entire Agreement, shall be resolved exclusively and finally by binding arbitration under the rules and procedures of the arbitration Administrator selected at the time the Claim is filed." MCM says this delegation clause clearly handed the decision of whether MCM had the authority to invoke the arbitration provision to an arbitrator. The district court disagreed and reminded MCM that, according to this Court, "questions about whether an arbitration provision binds a party that did not sign the agreement are presumptively for the court to decide." (Citing Kristian v. Comcast Corp., 446 F.3d 25, 39 (1st Cir. 2006)).

Before us, MCM argues that the district court got it wrong on this point because the Cardmember Agreement required the arbitrator, not the court, to decide whether MCM could compel arbitration, and the district court can't ignore that language within the arbitration provision. MCM urges us to consider sending the entire question of whether it has the authority to invoke the arbitration provision to an arbitrator. In her reply, Barbosa of course disagrees and argues the district court got it right.

We have previously acknowledged that "parties may agree to have an arbitrator decide not only the merits of a particular dispute but also gateway questions of arbitrability, such as whether the parties have agreed to arbitrate or whether their agreement covers a particular controversy [but they] must do so... by 'clear and unmistakable' evidence." Biller, 961 F.3d at 509 (quoting Henry Schein, Inc., 139 S. Ct. at 529, 530). We employ a presumption, however, that courts (instead of arbitrators) resolve gateway disputes about whether a particular arbitration clause binds parties in a particular case, especially when the dispute centers on whether "an arbitration contract binds parties that did not sign the agreement." Kristian, 446 F.3d at 39 (citing First Options of Chicago, Inc. v. Kaplan, 514 U.S. 938, 115 S.Ct. 1920, 131 L.Ed.2d 985 (1995)). In our view, the language in the arbitration provision stating that "the applicability of this arbitration clause ... shall be resolved ... by binding arbitration," does not provide the "clear and unmistakable evidence" that the parties intended an arbitrator to determine whether the parties attempting to enforce the arbitration provision had the requisite authority to do so. Biller, 961 F.3d at 509. The district court properly decided this issue.

775 F.3d 109 (2014)

William M. McDERMOTT, Plaintiff, Appellant,
v.
MARCUS, ERRICO, EMMER & BROOKS, P.C., Defendant, Appellee.

No. 13-2181.

United States Court of Appeals, First Circuit.

December 29, 2014.

McDermott v. Marcus, Errico, Emmer & Brooks, PC, 775 F. 3d 109 (1st Cir. 2014)

p.112 Philip H. Cahalin, for appellant.

Stephen J. Duggan and Edmund A. Allcock, with whom Lynch & Lynch and Marcus, Errico, Emmer & Brooks, P.C. were on brief, for appellee.

Before THOMPSON, Circuit Judge, SOUTER, Associate Justice,[*] and STAHL, Circuit Judge.

THOMPSON, Circuit Judge.

We are, once again, called upon to interpret and apply the Massachusetts consumer protection statute, Mass. Gen. Laws ch. 93A ("Chapter 93A"). This case has humble origins: a seemingly-simple dispute over several $25 late fees the Pondview Condominium trustees charged to one of their residents, appellant William McDermott ("McDermott"), after he didn't pay his condominium fees on time. Unable to resolve the matter with McDermott, the trustees hired law firm appellee Marcus, Errico, Emmer and Brooks, P.C. ("MEEB"), to collect from McDermott. Soon enough, what began as a low-stakes disagreement quickly blossomed into wide-ranging litigation in the state and federal courts. We are concerned here with the two-count complaint McDermott filed against MEEB in the federal district court. McDermott alleged that MEEB's collections activities violated both Chapter 93A and the federal Fair Debt Collection Practices Act, 15 U.S.C. § 1692 et seq. ("FDCPA").

A magistrate judge held a bench trial and initially found in McDermott's favor on both counts. She awarded McDermott $10,400 on his Chapter 93A count, and $800 on the FDCPA claim. Both parties p.113 filed motions for reconsideration, following which the magistrate judge reversed in part, finding MEEB not liable under Chapter 93A, and leaving McDermott with only the $800 recovery under the FDCPA.

McDermott's timely appeal followed.

I. BACKGROUND

The magistrate judge[1] issued a 203-page written decision following a six-day bench trial. *See McDermott v. Marcus, Errico, Emmer & Brooks, P.C.*, 911 F.Supp.2d 1 (D.Mass.2012). We have no need to fully detail the extensive factual background in order to decide the narrow issues before us, and we commend the magistrate judge's thorough decision to the reader seeking a full run-down. We need only sketch a rough outline of the goings-on, which we do based on the magistrate judge's factual findings, the vast majority of which are unchallenged on appeal.

McDermott owned two units—104 and 105—at the Pondview Condominiums, a 19-unit condominium in Lynn, Massachusetts. Pondview's trustees (from now on collectively referred to as "Pondview"), as permitted by the condominium documents, required all unit owners to pay monthly assessments for the upkeep of common areas and facilities, along with several other types of monthly fees.[2] Any assessments not paid on time incurred a late payment fee, which acted as a lien against the owner's unit. If Pondview had to turn the matter over to collections, the condominium documents allowed for the assessment of attorney's fees, late charges, and collection costs against the offending owner.

McDermott lost his job in 2004. He fell behind on his condominium fees for both units in July of that year, and the next month he fell behind on the late payment fees, too. In September, McDermott agreed to pay two months of condominium and late fees for unit 105 (but not unit 104) by September 22. Although McDermott ended up making payments for both units by September 22, this did not bring the accounts current because he did not pay all of the late fees.

In the first of a series of unfortunate misunderstandings, McDermott seems to have thought his September payments brought him up-to-date. Compounding his troubles, McDermott paid his October monthly assessment for unit 105 late, triggering another late fee. He fell further behind in December.

On December 18, Pondview sent McDermott a letter detailing how much he owed for unit 105. The letter also told McDermott that, pursuant to the condominium documents, he was being charged $25 late fees for payments received after the 15th of the month during which each of the payments were due.[3] According to Pondview, by the end of 2004 McDermott owed, including late payment fees, $346.62 on unit 105 and $380.33 for unit 104. McDermott, however, let Pondview know that he disagreed with the late fee assessments and would not pay them. By the time March 2005 rolled around, McDermott had not paid condominium fees, loan payback p.114 charges, or late fees for either unit for January, February, and March.

Having apparently decided enough was enough, Pondview brought in MEEB to collect McDermott's debt. MEEB informed McDermott in a March 23, 2005 letter that he owed $1,495.61 on unit 104, an amount it said encompassed collection costs and attorney's fees. A separate letter with the same date told McDermott he owed $1,431.61 on unit 105. McDermott, who does not appear to have lawyered-up by this point, stood by his refusal to pay.

Over the approximately three-and-a-half years between April 2005 and September 2008, MEEB filed nine collection actions in Massachusetts state court against McDermott. McDermott retained counsel somewhere along the way (the exact date is not important here). Five of MEEB's collection suits related to unit 105, and four related to unit 104. Only two reached trial, but MEEB won them both and was awarded attorney's fees to boot.[4]

During the course of its collection activities, and while litigation was ongoing, MEEB repeatedly contacted the mortgagees on each of McDermott's units without his knowledge or consent, informed them of McDermott's delinquencies, and demanded payment directly from them. When asked to do so, the mortgagees accommodated MEEB and paid the amounts requested. They then passed these costs on to McDermott by tacking them onto the outstanding mortgages. Further, MEEB occasionally contacted McDermott directly, despite knowing he was represented by counsel.

Displeased with MEEB's collection activities, McDermott filed suit against the firm in the federal district court for Massachusetts on February 3, 2009. His two-count complaint alleged a variety of violations of federal (the FDCPA) and state (Chapter 93A) law.[5]

Specifically, McDermott took issue with the wording of several collection letters, contending they "were deliberately misleading, sporadic, inconsistent, confusing, and contained numerous errors and double billings." He also alleged MEEB "consistently and deliberately misleadingly, confusingly, and deceptively conflated its legal fees with condominium assessments in most of its communications concerning [his] debts," and made certain "oppressive and extortive" statements to him in violation of the FDCPA. McDermott further complained about MEEB's direct contacts with himself and his mortgagees. McDermott wrapped up his complaint by espousing his theory that MEEB ran up between $54,000 and $59,000 in legal fees "by its deliberate, intentional provocation of a dispute between Pondview and [himself] over $150 in unlawful late fees and by its other, relentless, egregious, unfair, deceptive, false, misleading, oppressive, and abusive violations of the FDCPA."

After trial, the magistrate judge found that although MEEB acted at all times in good faith and that none of its actions were deceptive, it nevertheless committed numerous violations of the FDCPA. The p.115 details of each FDCPA violation are not important for our purposes, other than that the judge found none of them were in bad faith.[6] The magistrate judge further determined that, pursuant to regulations issued by the Massachusetts Attorney General, MEEB's FDCPA violations served as a basis for imposing liability under Chapter 93A, even though MEEB had not committed any unfair or deceptive acts. In other words, she found the FDCPA violations constituted "per se" violations of Chapter 93A. She also found, however, that MEEB did not commit any unfair or deceptive acts that could give rise to Chapter 93A liability independent of the per se violations. Ultimately, the magistrate judge awarded McDermott $800 under the FDCPA, and $10,400 for the Chapter 93A violations.

MEEB subsequently filed a motion for reconsideration pursuant to Fed.R.Civ.P. 59(e).[7] The magistrate judge reviewed a newly-decided case from the Massachusetts Supreme Judicial Court ("SJC") interpreting Chapter 93A, *Klairmont v. Gainsboro Restaurant, Inc.*, 465 Mass. 165, 987 N.E.2d 1247 (2013), determined her finding of per se Chapter 93A violations was incorrect as a matter of law, and vacated the judgment on that count. *See McDermott v. Marcus, Errico, Emmer & Brooks, P.C.*, 969 F.Supp.2d 74 (D.Mass. 2013). She did not disturb her findings with respect to MEEB's FDCPA violations. As a result of the magistrate judge's reconsideration, McDermott saw his recovery slashed from $11,200 to $800.

Unsatisfied with this outcome, McDermott appealed to us.

II. STANDARD OF REVIEW

This case comes to us after a full bench trial, so we review the magistrate judge's factual findings for clear error. *Smith v. F.W. Morse & Co., Inc.,* 76 F.3d 413, 420 (1st Cir.1996). The clear error standard "constrains us from deciding factual issues anew." *Id.* "[W]e may not disturb the [magistrate judge's] record-rooted findings of fact unless on the whole of the evidence we reach the irresistible conclusion that a mistake has been made." *Id.* We afford this deference not just to straight-up findings of fact, but to any inferences drawn from them. *Id.* Similarly, we defer to a magistrate judge's "findings regarding an actor's motivation" where they are "plausible." *Id.* In sum, "we cannot second-guess the court's credibility determination[s]" following a bench trial. *Calderón-Ortega v. United States,* 753 F.3d 250, 253 n. 1 (1st Cir.2014).

In stark contrast to factual findings, we afford no deference to the magistrate judge's legal conclusions, which we review de novo. *United States v. 15 Bosworth Street,* 236 F.3d 50, 53 (1st Cir. 2001); *Smith,* 76 F.3d at 420. And because the magistrate judge granted MEEB's motion for reconsideration on legal grounds only (rather than after, say, a reevaluation of the facts), we review the legal conclusions undergirding that decision de novo, too. *See, e.g., Santiago v. Puerto Rico,* 655 F.3d 61, 67 (1st Cir.2011) (applying de novo review where "the parties' arguments were directed to the underlying substantive issue (the propriety vel non of summary judgment) rather than the procedural issue (the desirability vel non of reconsideration)").

p.116 III. DISCUSSION

McDermott raises several discrete arguments in this appeal. First and foremost, he says the magistrate judge erred when she snatched away his victory on the Chapter 93A count because MEEB's FDCPA violations give rise to per se Chapter 93A liability, without the need of showing that they are unfair or deceptive. Next, he argues that the magistrate judge should have found MEEB violated the FDCPA by charging him excessive legal fees. Last but not least, and predicated upon the assumption that we will conclude MEEB is liable to him under Chapter 93A on some theory, McDermott takes the position that MEEB's violation of Chapter 93A entitles him to an award of multiple damages. Not surprisingly, MEEB disagrees with each of McDermott's arguments and asks us to affirm the magistrate judge's orders.

We address these topics in turn.

A. Chapter 93A Liability

1. The Basics and the Concept of Per Se Liability

This appeal requires us to interpret and apply Massachusetts consumer protection law as embodied in Chapter 93A. More specifically, we are called upon to look at the concept of "per se" Chapter 93A liability. We open with a primer on the statute, discuss the concept of per se violations, and finally address the parties' arguments on appeal.

Because McDermott's Chapter 93A arguments implicate matters of state law, we apply the substantive law of Massachusetts. *See Dykes v. DePuy, Inc.,* 140 F.3d 31,

39 (1st Cir.1998) ("When facing a claim that does not arise under the Constitution or the laws of the United States, a federal court must apply the substantive law of the forum in which it sits ...."); *see also O'Brien v. Skinner,* 414 U.S. 524, 531, 94 S.Ct. 740, 38 L.Ed.2d 702 (1974) (recognizing that it is not the function of a federal court "to construe a state statute contrary to the construction given it by the highest court of a State"). This is so even where we are dealing with "a state-law claim brought under supplemental jurisdiction," such as McDermott's Chapter 93A claim. *Dykes,* 140 F.3d at 39.

The Massachusetts statute at issue here, Chapter 93A, straightforwardly declares that "[u]nfair methods of competition and unfair or deceptive acts or practices in the conduct of any trade or commerce are ... unlawful." Mass. Gen. Laws ch. 93A, § 2(a). "[T]he intent of the legislature" is that a court hearing a Chapter 93A claim will be "guided by the interpretations given by the Federal Trade Commission and the Federal Courts to section 5(a)(1) of the Federal Trade Commission Act (15 U.S.C. [§] 45(a)(1)), as from time to time amended." Mass. Gen. Laws ch. 93A, § 2(b). The statute permits the Massachusetts Attorney General to implement "rules and regulations interpreting the provisions" of Chapter 93A, but these "shall not be inconsistent with the rules, regulations and decisions of the Federal Trade Commission and the Federal Courts interpreting the provisions of the" Federal Trade Commission Act, "as from time to time amended." Mass. Gen. Laws ch. 93A, § 2(c).

Although Chapter 93A broadly prohibits "unfair" and "deceptive" conduct in trade or commerce, the statute does not spell out what specific actions make the grade.[8] Doing so would not be feasible anyway because, as the SJC has observed, "[t]here is no limit to human inventiveness in this field." *Kattar v. Demoulas,* 433 p.117 Mass. 1, 739 N.E.2d 246, 257 (2000) (alteration in original) (internal quotation marks omitted). Thus, whether or not particular conduct violates Chapter 93A is generally determined on a case-by-case basis. *See id.*

Nevertheless, Massachusetts courts have recognized that violations of a limited number of statutes automatically give rise to liability under Chapter 93A. *See, e.g., Polaroid Corp. v. Travelers Indem. Co.,* 414 Mass. 747, 610 N.E.2d 912, 917 (1993) (violation of state unfair claims settlement act, Mass. Gen. Laws ch. 176D, constitutes violation of Chapter 93A); *Reddish v. Bowen,* 66 Mass.App.Ct. 621, 849 N.E.2d 901, 906 (2006) (same with respect to a home improvement contractor's violation of Mass. Gen. Laws ch. 142A). This automatic liability, which the parties refer to as per se liability, could be thought of as a species of strict liability. In the instances where the Massachusetts appellate courts have found per se Chapter 93A liability based on a statutory violation, such conclusion, as we discuss hereafter, was grounded on explicit statutory language.

With respect to unfair claims settlement act violations like those addressed in *Polaroid,* per se Chapter 93A liability arises directly from the consumer protection act itself. Chapter 93A provides that "[a]ny person ... whose rights are affected by another person violating the provisions of clause (9) of section three of chapter one hundred and seventy-six D [i.e., the unfair claims settlement act] may bring an action in the superior court." Mass. Gen. Laws ch. 93A, § 9(1). In accordance with this statutory text, the SJC has recognized that "[a] consumer asserting a claim under [Chapter] 93A, § 9, may recover for violations of [Chapter] 176D, § 3, cl. 9, without regard to whether the violation was unlawful under [Chapter] 93A, § 2, because of the explicit statement to that effect in [Chapter 93A,] § 9." *Polaroid,* 610 N.E.2d at 917. Thus, Chapter 93A itself established that an act that violates the unfair claims settlement act violates Chapter 93A as well. Voilà, per se liability.

But Chapter 93A's language is not the only way to get to per se liability: it may also arise through the text of an independent statute, as in *Reddish.* The statute at issue there, Chapter 142A, regulates home improvement contractors and provides that "[v]iolations of any of the provisions of this chapter shall constitute an unfair or deceptive act under the provisions of [Chapter 93A]." Mass. Gen. Laws ch. 142A, § 17. One of the act's provisions prohibits contractors from committing any "violation of the building laws of the commonwealth." Mass. Gen. Laws ch. 142A, § 17(10). The Massachusetts Appeals Court has applied this plain language to conclude that a home improvement contractor's violation of the Massachusetts building code, thanks to Chapter 142A, § 17(10), "constituted an unfair or deceptive act under [Chapter 93A] by operation of [Chapter 142A,] § 17." *Reddish,* 849 N.E.2d at 908. Thus, *Reddish* points the way along this alternative path (i.e., the text of an independent statute) to per se Chapter 93A liability.

Taken together, these cases demonstrate a recognition by the Massachusetts courts that the Commonwealth's Legislature has decreed that a limited number of certain statutory violations automatically violate the consumer protection act as well. Whether the per se liability comes about through language the Legislature incorporated directly into Chapter 93A referencing another statute (as is the case with Chapter 176D), or whether it arises from the text of an independent statute (keep Chapter 142A in mind), it is a clear directive by the Legislature that a violation of that particular statute constitutes an p.118 automatic violation of Chapter 93A, without the need of showing the act was otherwise "unfair or deceptive" or occurred in "trade or commerce." This concept is critical to our resolution of the arguments on appeal.

2. Per Se Chapter 93A Liability After *Klairmont*

We proceed to the parties' particular arguments about MEEB's per se Chapter 93A liability. The question they have placed before us is narrow: although Chapter 93A is a statute of broad applicability, *Kattar,* 739 N.E.2d at 257, in the wake of what they both consider to be the key case, *Klairmont v. Gainsboro Restaurant, Inc.,* 465 Mass. 165, 987 N.E.2d 1247 (2013), do FDCPA violations give rise to so-called per se liability under Chapter 93A, § 2? Because the parties have relied so extensively on *Klairmont,* an extended discussion of it is required in order to place the parties' arguments in context. And, although the magistrate judge interpreted and applied *Klairmont,* we consider its import de novo. *See Casavant v. Norwegian Cruise Line Ltd.,* 460 Mass. 500, 952 N.E.2d 908, 912 (2011) (finding that "the boundaries of what may qualify for consideration as a [Chapter 93A] violation is a question of law") (internal quotation marks omitted).[9]

Klairmont involved the alleged wrongful death of a college student who, while in the midst of a cell phone conversation, fell down a flight of steps at a bar. 987 N.E.2d at 1251. The stairway, it turned out, was a bad stairway. Not only was the very "presence of the stairs ... obscured with hanging vinyl strips," *id.,* the stairs themselves violated the Massachusetts building code in multiple respects. For example, the stairway was not equipped with a self-closing "fire-rated" door and landing at the top, there were no hand rails, and the riser and tread dimensions did not meet the building code's dimensional requirements. *Id.* at 1253. Furthermore, the defendants[10] had rebuilt the stairs years before the decedent's fall, yet when they did so they "failed to acquire a building permit or to comply with the building code." *Id.* at 1253-54. Moreover, "the defendants knew that building permits and a change in use permit were required, as evidenced by the fact that the defendants filed, and then abandoned, multiple building permit and change in use permit applications." *Id.* at 1254.

The plaintiffs (decedent's parents) brought a Chapter 93A count premised solely on the defendant's noncompliance with the Massachusetts building code.[11] *See id.* at 1252. They grounded their Chapter 93A theory on the interplay between Chapter 93A, § 2 and 940 C.M.R. § 3.16(3)—an Attorney General regulation declaring that a violation of a state statute providing for public health, safety, or welfare is itself a Chapter 93A violation.[12] p.119 *See id.* In essence, the plaintiffs claimed the defendants were liable under Chapter 93A because they knew about the building code violations but failed to do anything about them.

The defendants took a different tack. They argued that 940 C.M.R. § 3.16(3) should not be construed in such a way as to transform every act that violates a statute concerned with public health, safety, or welfare into a Chapter 93A violation because doing so would enshrine Chapter 93A as the "preeminent law of the Commonwealth." *Id.* at 1254 (internal quotation marks omitted). The defendants sought to convince the SJC that it was not enough for the plaintiffs to simply show a building code violation. Instead, the defendants urged, they must prove the defendants' complained-of acts were "unfair or deceptive" before the defendants could run afoul of Chapter 93A. *Id.*

Taking on these arguments, the SJC first noted that the "building code may qualify as a regulation meant for the protection of the public's health, safety, or welfare" that is of concern to 940 C.M.R. § 3.16(3). *Id.* at 1254-55 (internal quotation marks omitted). Thus, in light of the Attorney General regulation, a violation of the building code opens a defendant up to the possibility of Chapter 93A liability. *See id.* at 1255 ("[T]o the extent the defendants contend that as a matter of law, [Chapter 93A] does not apply to claims premised on violations of the building code, we reject the argument.").

Yet, that the building code is embraced by the "unquestionably broad" ambit of 940 C.M.R. § 3.16(3) does not by itself render its violation a per se violation of Chapter 93A.[13] *Id.* The reach of the regulation —emanating as it does from the Attorney General rather than the Legislature—is "bound by the scope of [Chapter] 93A, § 2(a)." *Id.* This means that "under 940 [C.M.R.] § 3.16(3) a violation of a law or regulation ... will be a violation of [Chapter] 93A, § 2(a), only if the conduct leading to the violation is both unfair or deceptive and occurs in trade or commerce." *Id.* By making this pronouncement, the SJC sharply limited the occasions on which an unlawful act will lead to liability under Chapter 93A through operation of the Attorney General's regulations.

The SJC, reiterating that "whether the particular violation or violations qualify as unfair or deceptive conduct is best discerned from the circumstances of each case," *id.* (internal quotation marks omitted), proceeded to review the evidence in the record relevant to the plaintiffs' Chapter 93A claim. First, it concluded the defendants' conduct was unfair and deceptive within the meaning of Chapter 93A because the defendants "consciously violated the building code for more than twenty years, thereby creating hazardous conditions in a place of public assembly where alcohol is served to commercial patrons." *Id.* Next, the SJC concluded the unfair and deceptive conduct occurred in trade or commerce because the victim was the bar's patron at the time of his accident, and because "the defendants knowingly failed p.120 to acquire the required permits in order to avoid the expense of building code compliance to their restaurant and bar business." *Id.* at 1256. Accordingly, the SJC found the defendants' conduct met both prongs of Chapter 93A.

The course of the SJC's analysis in *Klairmont* demonstrates exactly what it meant when it said that 940 C.M.R. § 3.16(3) is "bound" by the scope of Chapter 93A: despite the regulation's broad wording purporting to do so, the Attorney General is not empowered to issue regulations rendering certain statutory violations "per se" Chapter 93A violations. Indeed, the SJC went out of its way to say that the trial judge got it wrong when she said the defendants' building code violations *were* per se violative of Chapter 93A.

The lesson of *Klairmont* may be summed up as so: the Massachusetts Attorney General's regulatory authority to "make rules and regulations interpreting" Chapter 93A, § 2(a), Mass. Gen. Laws ch. 93A, § 2(c), does not extend so far as to permit her to allow a plaintiff to show that a defendant has violated an independent statute in lieu of satisfying Chapter 93A's substantive requirements of showing the complained-of act was *both* unfair and deceptive *and* that it occurred in trade or commerce.

3. Per Se Chapter 93A Liability and the FDCPA

We come now to McDermott's arguments that MEEB's FDCPA violations result in per se Chapter 93A liability. He advances two separate, but related, grounds.

First, using the federal statute as his starting point, McDermott observes the FDCPA states any act that violates its provisions also violates the Federal Trade Commission Act ("FTC Act"). According to McDermott, the FTC Act is Chapter 93A's federal equivalent. By enacting Chapter 93A, he argues, the Massachusetts Legislature grafted federal consumer protection law, including the FDCPA, onto state law. In his view, this means that a violation of the FDCPA violates the FTC Act and, by extension, Chapter 93A.

Second, McDermott focuses on a regulation promulgated by the Massachusetts Attorney General which is similar to the one addressed in *Klairmont,* and which explicitly provides that violations of federal consumer protection law count as Chapter 93A violations. *See* 940 C.M.R. § 3.16(4). The FDCPA, he maintains, is just such a consumer protection law. In McDermott's view, and thanks to this regulation, one who violates the FDCPA necessarily violates Chapter 93A at the same time.

Not so fast, says MEEB. First, it does not contest the magistrate judge's finding that it committed FDCPA violations. But, in its eyes, the SJC's *Klairmont* opinion was explicit that even per se Chapter 93A violations are subject to a "trade or commerce" requirement. In other words, a so-called per se violation is not truly per se, as per se findings satisfy Chapter 93A's first prong only (i.e., that the conduct at issue is unfair or deceptive). A plaintiff (here, McDermott) still has the burden of proving the conduct occurred in the course of trade or commerce. Because all of its interactions with McDermott were related to its representation of Pondview in a private dispute, MEEB did not act in a "business context" with respect to McDermott and, therefore, did not act in "trade or commerce" when it violated the FDCPA. It follows, according to MEEB, that it may not be held liable under Chapter 93A.

Notably, MEEB misunderstands McDermott's arguments as being limited solely to a claim that per se liability arises through the Attorney General regulation, p.121 940 C.M.R. § 3.16(4). As such, MEEB does not respond to McDermott's first argument that per se liability can also come from Chapter 93A's federal equivalent, the FTC Act. Therefore, we will first turn our attention to McDermott's argument that per se liability arises under the Attorney General regulation, 940 C.M.R. § 3.16(4).

i. Attorney General Regulation

In light of our discussion of *Klairmont*, McDermott's argument that per se Chapter 93A liability may be imposed by 940 C.M.R. § 3.16(4) is easily disposed of. Although *Klairmont* involved a different Attorney General regulation, 940 C.M.R. § 3.16(3), the two are substantially similar:

> Without limiting the scope of any other rule, regulation or statute, an act or practice is a violation of [Chapter 93A], § 2 if:
>
> . . .
>
> (3) It fails to comply with existing statutes, rules, regulations or laws, meant for the protection of the public's health, safety or welfare promulgated by the Commonwealth or any political subdivision thereof intended to provide the consumers of this Commonwealth protection; or
>
> (4) It violates the Federal Trade Commission Act, the Federal Consumer Credit Protection Act or other Federal consumer protection statutes within the purview of [Chapter 93A], § 2.

940 C.M.R. § 3.16.

The regulation McDermott relies upon states that conduct which violates a federal consumer protection statute, like the FDCPA, also violates Chapter 93A.[14] For our purposes, the only relevant substantive difference between *Klairmont*'s regulation, 940 C.M.R. § 3.16(3), and McDermott's, 940 C.M.R. § 3.16(4), is the source of law: § 3.16(3) looks to *state* consumer protection law, while § 3.16(4) refers to *federal* consumer protection law. *Compare* 940 C.M.R. § 3.16(3) (referring to Massachusetts statutes "intended to provide the consumers of this Commonwealth protection") *with* 940 C.M.R. § 3.16(4) (referring to "Federal consumer protection statutes within the purview of [Chapter 93A], § 2").

The logic underpinning *Klairmont* is clearly applicable here. We can conceive of no plausible rationale, and none has been suggested to us, for treating these two provisions differently based solely on the origin of the specific consumer protection law with which each is concerned. Indeed, finding *Klairmont*'s reasoning inapplicable to § 3.16(4) would enshrine a distinction without a difference as a matter of Massachusetts law. This we refuse to do.

We, therefore, conclude that just as the scope of § 3.16(3) is bound by the strictures of Chapter 93A, including the requirements of showing unfair and deceptive conduct occurring in trade or commerce, so too is § 3.16(4) limited by those same requirements. Because the Attorney General is not permitted to regulate away these two requirements with respect to Chapter 93A claims based on p.122 violations of state consumer protection law, the Attorney General may not do likewise when the claimed violation arises out of federal consumer protection law. Applying *Klairmont*'s reasoning, we reject McDermott's argument that 940 C.M.R. § 3.16(4) renders MEEB's violations of the FDCPA per se violative of Chapter 93A.

ii. Per Se Liability Through Federal Consumer Protection Law

Reaching this conclusion does not settle the entire matter. Although MEEB seeks to characterize McDermott's liability arguments as premised solely on the Attorney General regulation, McDermott has in fact also argued per se liability arises through Chapter 93A's incorporation of federal consumer protection law into state law. His position is premised on the notion that Massachusetts incorporated federal unfair competition law into state law when it enacted Chapter 93A.

As it turns out, the FTC Act is quite similar to Chapter 93A. Like Chapter 93A, it provides that "unfair or deceptive acts or practices in or affecting commerce[] are... unlawful." 15 U.S.C. § 45(a)(1); *see also* Mass. Gen. Laws ch. 93A, § 2(a) ("[U]nfair or deceptive acts or practices in the conduct of any trade or commerce are hereby declared unlawful."). Chapter 93A's echo of the FTC Act's language, along with the legislative directive that courts interpreting Chapter 93A are to be guided by the federal courts' interpretation of this statute, *see* Mass. Gen. Laws ch. 93A, § 2(b), are important indications that McDermott is on the right track.

Decades ago, the SJC addressed the connection between federal consumer protection law and Chapter 93A. The SJC announced with striking clarity that Massachusetts has "wholly incorporated" the FTC Act, 15 U.S.C. § 45(a)(1), into Chapter 93A. *Slaney v. Westwood Auto, Inc.*, 366 Mass. 688, 322 N.E.2d 768, 773 n. 8 (1975). Chapter 93A, it explained on another occasion, "was enacted in 1967, partly in response to [a Federal Trade Commission] policy to stop unfair practices on a State level before they become interstate problems." *Purity Supreme, Inc. v. Attorney General*, 380 Mass. 762, 407 N.E.2d 297, 301 (1980). To effectuate this underlying motivation, Chapter 93A "incorporates the extensive body of Federal administrative and decisional law under the FTC Act, at least in so far as it relates to definitions of 'unfair' and 'deceptive.'" *Id.* (internal citation omitted). Lest there be any doubt that the SJC has changed its thinking over the years, it recently stated that Chapter 93A "defines unfair acts or practices by reference to interpretations of those terms in the Federal Trade Commission Act, 15 U.S.C. § 45(a)(1) (2006), in which [Chapter] 93A has its roots." *Kraft Power Corp. v. Merrill*, 464 Mass. 145, 981 N.E.2d 671, 683 (2013). It follows that, because Massachusetts has folded the FTC Act into Chapter 93A, unfair or deceptive conduct that violates the FTC Act also violates Chapter 93A.

Having come this far, we turn to the next part of McDermott's argument, which is that per se liability arises through operation of the FDCPA. The FDCPA explicitly provides that a violation of its provisions "shall be deemed an unfair or deceptive act or practice in violation of the FTC Act. 15 U.S.C. § 1692l (a).

At this point, it is helpful to recall our previous discussion of the alternative paths to per se Chapter 93A liability: the text of Chapter 93A itself, or the text of an independent statute. The FDCPA's language we just quoted is substantially similar to Mass. Gen. Laws ch. 142A's provision imposing per se Chapter 93A liability p.123 on home contractors for violations of Chapter 142A. In other words, just as Chapter 142A does with respect to Chapter 93A, the FDCPA establishes that an unfair debt collection act in violation of the FDCPA is a per se violation of the FTC Act. And because Massachusetts has "wholly incorporated" the FTC Act and its interpretation into state consumer protection law, a violation of the FDCPA not only per se violates the FTC Act, it also constitutes a per se Chapter 93A violation.

To drive the point home, we will make one more comparison to state law. Although not cited by either party, Massachusetts has its own unfair debt collection statute, Mass. Gen. Laws ch. 93, § 49, which is entitled "Debt collection in an unfair, deceptive or unreasonable manner." The statute reads as follows:

> [n]o one who is a creditor or an attorney for a creditor, or an assignee of a creditor, of a natural person present or residing in Massachusetts who has incurred a debt primarily for personal, family or household purposes shall collect or attempt to collect such debt in an unfair, deceptive or unreasonable manner.

Mass. Gen. Laws ch. 93, § 49. It goes on to list various actions that shall be "deemed unfair, deceptive or unreasonable." *Id.* Included is a prohibition against a debt collector "communicat[ing] directly with the alleged debtor after notification from an attorney representing such debtor that all further communications relative to the debt should be addressed to [that attorney]." Mass. Gen. Laws ch. 93, § 49(b). Finally, violations of the statute lead to Chapter 93A liability, as "[f]ailure to comply with the provisions of this section shall constitute an unfair or deceptive act or practice under the provisions of chapter ninety-three A." Mass. Gen. Laws ch. 93, § 49, cl. 7.

Here, the magistrate judge found that MEEB violated the FDCPA by, among other things, contacting McDermott despite its awareness that he was represented by counsel. Although McDermott has not advanced any claims under the state debt collection statute, it is clear that this particular FDCPA violation would have violated state debt collection law as well. And, by virtue of Chapter 93's clear language, it would have constituted an "unfair or deceptive act or practice" for Chapter 93A purposes.[15] That MEEB's direct contact of McDermott would have led to per se Chapter 93A liability under the state debt collection statute provides yet another reason for interpreting the similar language in the FTC Act and the FDCPA in the same way.

Summing up, and although our analysis differs markedly from the magistrate judge's, we conclude MEEB's violations of the FDCPA constitute per se Chapter 93A violations by virtue of the unambiguous statutory language in the FDCPA and the FTC Act. The SJC's *Klairmont* opinion does nothing to alter this reasoning, as *Klairmont* determined only that Attorney General regulations are bound by the scope of Chapter 93A. *Klairmont* simply did not address per se Chapter 93A liability arising through an independent statute. The magistrate judge, therefore, committed an error of law when she concluded that *Klairmont* required a separate "trade or commerce" finding in these circumstances. p.124 Accordingly, to the extent that the magistrate judge vacated the judgment in favor of McDermott on his Chapter 93A claim, we reverse.[16]

B. Excessive, Redundant, or Otherwise Unnecessary Attorney's Fees in Violation of the FDCPA

McDermott next argues that the magistrate judge should have found that MEEB violated the FDCPA by charging and attempting to collect from him "excessive, redundant, or otherwise unnecessary attorney fees." Appellant Br. at 23. To get to this conclusion, McDermott first cites several Massachusetts cases for the proposition that charging excessive fees violates Massachusetts law. Working from this premise, he directs our attention to language in the FDCPA which includes in its definition of unfair debt collection practices the "collection of any amount (including any interest, fee, charge, or expense incidental to the principal obligation) unless such amount is expressly authorized by the agreement creating the debt or permitted by law." 15 U.S.C. § 1692f(1).[17]

After setting forth this basic position, McDermott argues MEEB was obligated to prove at trial that its fees were reasonable. McDermott says MEEB is unable to do so because it violated Mass. Gen. Laws ch. 183A, which McDermott contends required it to send pre-suit notices to McDermott's mortgagees. According to McDermott, these notices were intended to allow the mortgagee to make up the mortgagor's deficiency, and therefore avoid a lawsuit. Per McDermott, had MEEB sent out the notices as required, then his mortgagees would have paid the debt in order to avoid suit. Therefore, he urges us to find that MEEB's failure to send out pre-suit notices resulted in MEEB filing unnecessary lawsuits and, by extension, charging him unnecessary fees.

MEEB makes several responses to these arguments. The only one with which we need concern ourselves is MEEB's position that McDermott is attempting to raise a new legal theory on appeal. MEEB says that McDermott's theory at trial was consistent with the allegations in his Verified Complaint that MEEB was responsible for causing an "unreasonable, unfair, unlawful, unexplained, and retroactive change in Pondview's policy for the specific purpose of p.125 precipitating a dispute with McDermott in order to generate legal fees for MEEB." Appellee Br. at 25. Having failed to make those allegations stick, MEEB says McDermott is now impermissibly "attempt[ing] to 'recast' his theory of liability solely under 15 U.S.C. § 1692f, previously having asserted that the alleged underlying conduct violated various other provisions of the FDCPA." *Id.* at 27.

Having reviewed the record, we agree with MEEB that McDermott's 15 U.S.C. § 1692f(1) excessive fees theory has been advanced for the first time on appeal. Following the six-day bench trial, the magistrate judge ordered each side to submit a post-trial brief of no more than 25 pages detailing their legal positions and requests for findings of fact and rulings of law. McDermott filed a 37-page brief, which included a footnote seeking to incorporate by reference all other legal arguments it raised throughout the history of this case. *See* Pl's Post-Trial Brief, Dist. Ct. Docket

Entry 60 at 2. In a docket order, the magistrate judge allowed the oversized brief, with the exception of that footnote. *See* Dist. Ct. Docket Entry 62. McDermott has not appealed this particular ruling, so we will concentrate only on the theories McDermott espoused in his post-trial brief.

From his opening line, McDermott took the position that he proved at trial that MEEB's "main objective" in its activities "was to run up its attorneys fees to Pondview, which Pondview then assessed to McDermott, and which MEEB then collected from McDermott's mortgagees in part." Pl.'s Post-Trial Br. at 1. He went on to reference 15 U.S.C. § 1692f(1), but that reference is in concert with 15 U.S.C. § 1692d, which prohibits debt collectors from "engag[ing] in any conduct the natural consequence of which is to harass, oppress, or abuse any person in connection with the collection of a debt." He then told the magistrate judge that MEEB violated these two statutes when

> it engaged in a convoluted collection procedure which inevitably caused miscommunication, lack of communication, confusion, and acrimony that escalated litigation costs and served as a pretext for MEEB to evade its obligation under 15 U.S.C. § 1692h to apply payments of McDermott's debt as he directed and not to debts he disputed ... and for MEEB to provide McDermott with communications which were illegible, deceptive, and incomprehensible in violation of 15 U.S.C. §§ 1692d, 1692e, and 1692f.

Id. These arguments smack of Chapter 93A claims of unfair and deceptive conduct. Indeed, the title of each and every subsection in McDermott's post-trial brief referred to MEEB's "bad faith."

15 U.S.C. § 1692f(1), however, is aimed at something else entirely. The statute prohibits attempts to collect any amount "unless such amount is expressly authorized by the agreement creating the debt or permitted by law." 15 U.S.C. § 1692f(1). Although McDermott successfully asserted claims that MEEB violated other provisions of the FDCPA, nowhere in his post-trial brief does he take the position that the amount of his debts were not authorized by the condominium agreement.[18] Further, he did not even hint at the multi-step pathway to a § 1692f(1) violation that he advances in this appeal. Instead, following trial McDermott focused his arguments on MEEB's alleged bad faith and p.126 intentional violations of federal and state law.

In this Circuit, "it is a virtually ironclad rule that a party may not advance for the first time on appeal either a new argument or an old argument that depends on a new factual predicate." *Cochran v. Quest Software, Inc.*, 328 F.3d 1, 11 (1st Cir.2003); *see also United States v. Slade*, 980 F.2d 27, 30 (1st Cir.1992) ("It is a bedrock rule that when a party has not presented an argument to the district court, she may not unveil it in the court of appeals."). Our review of the record leaves us with no doubt that McDermott's 15 U.S.C. § 1692f(1) liability theory in this appeal was never raised to the magistrate judge. Accordingly, we will not consider it further.

C. Multiple Damages for Willful or Intentional Conduct

McDermott next says the magistrate judge should have multiplied the damages award thanks to MEEB's knowing violations of Chapter 93A. Chapter 93A, § 9(3) requires a court to double or treble a plaintiff's damages if that court finds a defendant's violation of Chapter 93A was "a willing or knowing violation" of Chapter 93A, § 2.

To get here, McDermott argues that the magistrate judge committed an error of law when she found MEEB was not obligated under Mass. Gen. Laws ch. 183A to send pre-suit notices to McDermott's mortgagees. According to McDermott, had the magistrate judge gotten this legal ruling right, it would have provided a basis for finding that MEEB willfully or intentionally violated Chapter 93A since it was aware of his mortgagees' names and addresses, thereby bringing the damages multiplier into play. Separately, McDermott argues that the magistrate judge clearly erred when she considered the evidence and found MEEB's FDCPA violations (which resulted in per se Chapter 93A liability) were not in bad faith. The judge, he says, should have found MEEB willfully violated Chapter 93A and awarded multiple damages for that reason.

MEEB urges us to affirm the magistrate judge's determination that it did not act in bad faith. MEEB first says the magistrate judge was correct when she determined that MEEB didn't have to send any pre-suit notices under Chapter 183A. Thus, Chapter 183A provides no basis for imposing multiple damages in MEEB's view. With respect to its purported bad faith, MEEB points out that the magistrate judge, in her initial decision, imposed per se Chapter 93A liability only, explicitly finding MEEB had not acted in bad faith or intentionally violated the law. This conclusion, MEEB asserts, was based on the evidence at trial and should not be uprooted on appeal.

We see no basis for reversal on this record.

1. Chapter 183A

The interpretation of Chapter 183A's requirements presents a legal question, which we review de novo. The specific provision upon which McDermott relies, Chapter 183A, § 6(c) contains the following relevant language:

> When any portion of the unit owner's share of the common expenses has been delinquent for at least sixty days ... the organization of unit owners shall send a notice stating the amount of the delinquency to the unit owner by certified and first class mail. The organization of unit owners shall also send a notice stating the amount of the delinquency to the first mortgagee by certified and first class mail, provided, that the first mortgagee has informed the organization of p.127 unit owners of its name and mailing address.

Mass. Gen. Laws ch. 183A, § 6(c).

The key language in this passage is the clear statement establishing that the notice requirement is triggered only if "the first mortgagee has informed the organization of unit owners of its name and mailing address." *Id.* Per the unambiguous statutory language, such notice by the mortgagee essentially allows a mortgagee to "opt in" to the receipt of deficiency notices. While McDermott argues that the evidence shows MEEB was aware of his mortgagee's identity and address, there is no evidence in the record that any mortgagee ever "informed" MEEB of this information, which is required to bring the statute into play.

McDermott, without providing any convincing reason to do so, asks us to simply ignore this requirement and pick and choose to apply only that statutory language which benefits him. But where, as here, a Massachusetts "statute is unambiguous, our function is to enforce the statute according to its terms." *Reading Co-Op. Bank v. Suffolk Constr. Co., Inc.*, 464 Mass. 543, 984 N.E.2d 776, 780 (2013). We therefore decline McDermott's invitation to rewrite the statute to facilitate the outcome he desires.

Accordingly, we conclude from the plain language of the statute that the magistrate judge did not commit an error of law in finding that MEEB was not required to send pre-suit notices to any mortgagee that had not informed MEEB of its name and address. McDermott may not rely on Chapter 183A in an attempt to demonstrate that MEEB acted in bad faith.

2. MEEB's alleged bad faith

McDermott is now left with his argument that the magistrate judge clearly erred when she found that MEEB did not intentionally violate Chapter 93A and that its actions were not motivated by bad faith, and again when she declined to award multiple damages. "Ultimately, [Chapter] 93A ties liability for multiple damages to the degree of the defendant's culpability." *Kattar,* 739 N.E.2d at 259. A reviewing court will only overturn a trial judge's finding in this regard if it was "clearly erroneous." *Id.* (citing *Clegg v. Butler,* 424 Mass. 413, 676 N.E.2d 1134, 1139 (1997)); *see also Smith,* 76 F.3d at 420 (Where a trial judge's finding as to "an actor's motivation" following a bench trial is "plausible, appellate review is at an end."). McDermott faces an uphill climb on this claim, and he is unable to reach the summit.

The magistrate judge had a front-row seat to each witness's testimony on direct and cross-examination over the course of the six-day bench trial. Her 203-page written decision summarized the testimony and set forth her credibility determinations.[19] She concluded MEEB did not conduct itself in such a manner as to intentionally pump up its legal fees, and that it was instead motivated by its desire to zealously represent Pondview's interests. The magistrate judge further noted that in at least one instance, MEEB's incorrect statement about the amount owed by McDermott went in McDermott's favor (i.e., MEEB said he owed less than he really did), which supports her finding that p.128 MEEB was not simply trying to increase its legal fees.

At the end of the day, the magistrate judge found that MEEB acted in good faith, that it did not willfully or knowingly violate Chapter 93A, and that its "conduct was neither unfair nor deceptive." On this record, we are unable to say the magistrate judge's findings were clearly erroneous. And in the absence of intentional or bad faith violations of Chapter 93A, MEEB is not liable for double or treble damages.

IV. CONCLUSION

In light of the foregoing, the magistrate judge's order with respect to MEEB's Rule 59(e) motion to reconsider and/or alter and amend the judgment is hereby reversed to the extent the magistrate judge determined MEEB is not liable under Chapter 93A. We therefore remand this matter to the magistrate judge with instructions to reinstate the original judgment in McDermott's favor on his Chapter 93A count. The magistrate judge's resolution of the parties' Rule 59(e) motions is affirmed in all other respects. The parties shall bear their own costs.

[*] The Hon. David H. Souter, Associate Justice (Ret.) of the Supreme Court of the United States, sitting by designation.

[1] At the outset of the case, the parties mutually agreed to the jurisdiction of a magistrate judge over all proceedings, including trial.

[2] Monthly fees included a loan payback charge, which was "either part of a special assessment or a line item in [Pondview's] budget."

[3] The magistrate judge found that MEEB "was not involved in the decision to impose a $25.00 charge for delinquent loan payback charges or to change any policy to impose late fees."

[4] In one of these cases the state court awarded $14,000 in attorney's fees, approximately half of what MEEB had sought.

[5] McDermott's complaint grounded federal jurisdiction on 28 U.S.C. § 1331, as his was an action "arising under the Constitution, law, or treaties of the United States." He also invoked the federal court's supplemental jurisdiction to decide his state-law-based Chapter 93A claims. Although in an apparent typographical error McDermott's complaint cited the wrong statute for supplemental jurisdiction (the non-existent "28 U.S.C. § 1328" instead of 28 U.S.C. § 1367), MEEB has never asked the federal courts to decline the exercise of supplemental jurisdiction.

[6] The magistrate judge also found some of McDermott's FDCPA claims, having been brought outside of the FDCPA's one year limitations period, were barred as untimely.

[7] McDermott filed one too, but we need not discuss it as McDermott does not appeal its denial.

[8] Neither does the statute define "trade or commerce."

[9] Some years ago, we noted that a violation of the FDCPA is a per se violation of Chapter 93A. *French v. Corporate Receivables, Inc.,* 489 F.3d 402, 403 n. 1 (1st Cir.2007). And before that, we stated that a violation of a federal consumer protection statute "constitutes a per se violation of Chapter 93A, § 2(a)." *Barnes v. Fleet Nat'l Bank, N.A.,* 370 F.3d 164, 176 (1st Cir.2004). These conclusory statements, devoid of substantive analysis or explanation, are not particularly helpful to our analysis here. Further, these cases were decided prior to *Klairmont,* which controls our interpretation of state law.

[10] The bar itself and trustees of the legal entity that owned the real estate on which it was located.

[11] They also brought general negligence claims, but those are not germane here.

[12] The regulation provides that

an act or practice is a violation of [Chapter 93A], § 2 if:

. . .

(3) It fails to comply with existing statutes, rules, regulations or laws, meant for the protection of the public's health, safety, or welfare promulgated by the Commonwealth or any political subdivision thereof intended to provide the consumers of this Commonwealth protection....

940 C.M.R. § 3.16(3).

[13] Indeed, the SJC noted in no uncertain terms that the trial judge "misstated the law when she said that 'the defendants' [b]uilding [c]ode violations were *per se* deceptive and unfair acts or practices.'" *Id.* at 1255 n. 16 (emphasis added).

[14] The parties take it for granted that the FDCPA is a "Federal consumer protection statute[] within the purview of" Chapter 93A, § 2, as required by the Attorney General regulation. 940 C.M.R. § 3.16(4). The district courts that have considered the issue have concluded that it is. *See In re Pharm. Indus. Average Wholesale Price Litig.*, 491 F.Supp.2d 20, 84 (D.Mass.2007); *Dean v. Compass Receivables Mgmt. Corp.*, 148 F.Supp.2d 116, 119 (D.Mass.2001). The correctness of these holdings is confirmed by the text of the FDCPA itself, which sets forth one of its purposes as "to protect consumers against debt collection abuses." 15 U.S.C. § 1692(e). Thus, we agree the FDCPA is a consumer protection statute for the purposes of Chapter 93A.

[15] At first blush, Chapter 93 may not appear to provide for per se Chapter 93A liability because it does not address the trade or commerce requirement. Yet, Chapter 93 applies specifically to debt collectors. And a debt collector's business is, by definition, collecting debts. Although we need not decide the issue here, we would be hard-pressed to imagine why a debt collector who violates Chapter 93 would not be acting in trade or commerce with respect to the particular debtor.

[16] Before moving on, we note MEEB's contention that because certain FDCPA violations found by the magistrate judge occurred out-side of the FDCPA's one-year limitations period, these "untimely" claims can not serve as the basis for Chapter 93A liability. The Massachusetts appellate courts have unambiguously held that a Chapter 93A claim is subject to Chapter 93A's four-year limitations period. *See Fine v. Huygens, DiMella, Shaffer & Assocs.*, 57 Mass.App.Ct. 397, 783 N.E.2d 842, 849 (2003) (A Chapter 93A claim "need only be dismissed if, under [Chapter] 93A's four-year limitations period and the accrual date applicable to the particular [Chapter] 93A claim, it was not timely filed."). We, too, recognized this more than twenty years ago. *See Tagliente v. Himmer*, 949 F.2d 1, 6 (1st Cir.1991) (distinguishing between statute of limitations applicable to claim of fraudulent concealment and Chapter 93A claim based upon the same underlying conduct). MEEB does not argue that any of its FDCPA violations are untimely under Chapter 93A. Accordingly, its statute of limitations defense is without merit.

[17] McDermott also argues that collection of excessive, redundant, and unnecessary fees "wrongfully cause[s] [a] debtor to incur avoidable costs" in violation of 15 U.S.C. § 1692f(5). Appellant Br. at 24. That section, however, renders it unlawful for a debt collector to "[c]aus[e] charges to be made to any person for communications by concealment of the true purpose of the communication." 15 U.S.C. § 1692f(5). McDermott makes no attempt to explain how this section applies to his avoidable costs theory. Accordingly, we do not consider it further.

[18] As the magistrate judge noted in addressing one of McDermott's other arguments, "[i]t is not abusive to collect or charge the costs of an ordinary collection

action where, as here, the condominium documents gave Pondview the ability to charge those costs to [McDermott]." *McDermott,* 911 F.Supp.2d at 77.

[19] The magistrate judge made multiple findings in this regard. For example, she found McDermott's testimony about why he refused to pay certain assessments was "self serving" and "not credible," and that his testimony that he did not receive a letter MEEB sent to him by certified and first-class mail was "not credible" too. The magistrate judge later commented that McDermott's "demeanor ... markedly changed on cross examination."

766 F.3d 98 (2014)

Robbie POLLARD, Plaintiff, Appellee,
v.
LAW OFFICE OF MANDY L. SPAULDING, Defendant, Appellant.

No. 13-2478.

United States Court of Appeals, First Circuit.

September 8, 2014.

Pollard v. Law Office of Mandy L. Spaulding, 766 F. 3d 98 (1st Cir. 2014)

p.100 Scott Douglas Burke, Tory A. Weigand, Alan E. Brown, and Morrison Mahoney LLP on brief for appellant.

Sergei Lemberg and Lemberg Law, LLC on brief for appellee.

Before KAYATTA, BALDOCK[*] and SELYA, Circuit Judges.

SELYA, Circuit Judge.

This is one of the relatively rare occasions on which we have been asked, in a non-class-action setting, to visit the precincts patrolled by the Fair Debt Collection Practices Act (FDCPA), 15 U.S.C. §§ 1692-1692p. Specifically, we are tasked with determining whether a particular collection letter satisfies section 1692g(b) of the FDCPA, which requires that a debt collector's collection activities and communications "not overshadow or be inconsistent with the disclosure of the consumer's right to dispute the debt or request the name and address of the original creditor." *Id.* § 1692g(b). The district court concluded that the collection letter at issue here fell short of this mark.

We hold that, for FDCPA purposes, a collection letter is to be viewed from the perspective of the hypothetical unsophisticated consumer. Applying this standard, we affirm the judgment below.

I. BACKGROUND

The raw facts, memorialized by the parties' pleadings, are undisputed. At some indeterminate point in time, plaintiff-appellee Robbie Pollard, who is a "consumer" within the meaning of 15 U.S.C. § 1692a(3), allegedly incurred a debt of approximately $611.84. The Law Office of Mandy L. Spaulding, the defendant and appellant here, subsequently was retained to collect the debt. In carrying out this assignment, the defendant was operating as a "debt collector" as defined in section 1692a(6).

On October 23, 2012, the defendant sent the plaintiff a collection letter (a copy of which appears as an appendix to this opinion). This letter was typed on the defendant's letterhead over the signature "Mandy L. Spaulding, Esq." The letter explained that the defendant had been retained to collect the monies allegedly owed and was "not inclined to use further resources attempting to collect this debt before filing suit." It further explained that the defendant planned to collect the debt "through whatever legal means are available and without [the plaintiff's] cooperation." It went on to inform the plaintiff that the defendant was "obligated to [its] client to pursue the next logical course of action without delay" and described how the plaintiff could make payments.

Below the signature block, in smaller print, were several paragraphs preceded by the caption "NOTICE OF IMPORTANT RIGHTS." These paragraphs contained the statutorily mandated notice of consumer rights. *See id.* § 1692g(a)(3)-(5).

Following her receipt of this collection letter, the plaintiff contacted the defendant to dispute ownership of the debt and request validation. Approximately one month after the collection letter arrived, the plaintiff sued. In her complaint, she asserted that the defendant had violated p.101 sundry provisions of the FDCPA, including section 1692g. The defendant answered and, several months later, moved for judgment on the pleadings. *See* Fed.R.Civ.P. 12(c). The district court concluded, among other things, that the collection letter violated section 1692g as a matter of law.[1] *See Pollard v. Law Office of Mandy L. Spaulding,* 967 F.Supp.2d 470, 477 (D.Mass.2013). The parties thereafter agreed upon the damages and attorneys' fees recoverable by the plaintiff. A final judgment entered, which preserved the defendant's right to appeal from the ruling that the collection letter transgressed section 1692g. This timely appeal followed.

II. ANALYSIS

Congress enacted the FDCPA to eliminate "the use of abusive, deceptive, and unfair debt collection practices." 15 U.S.C. § 1692(a). The Act not only proscribes certain invidious methods of debt collection but also requires debt collectors to furnish to consumers a notice, commonly called a "validation notice," limning certain rights and information. *See id.* § 1692g(a). Among other things, a debt collector must inform the consumer that she has thirty days from receipt of the validation notice within which to dispute the debt before it is assumed to be valid and that if she disputes the debt, the debt collector will provide her with verification of the debt's validity. *See id.* § 1692g(a)(3)-(4). If the consumer either disputes the debt or requests information concerning the identity of the original creditor within this thirty-day period, the debt collector must suspend collection efforts until it supplies such data. *See id.* § 1692g (b).

Prior to 2006, the FDCPA did not expressly require that the validation notice convey the consumer's rights in a nonconfusing manner. Courts nevertheless glossed the statute with such a requirement and routinely interpreted section 1692g to bar the use of collection letters that overshadow or contradict the validation notice. *See McMurray v. ProCollect, Inc.,* 687 F.3d 665, 668 n. 1 (5th Cir.2012). The Financial Services Regulatory Relief Act of 2006 removed any lingering doubt on this score: it amended the FDCPA to make pellucid that "[a]ny collection activities and communication during the 30-day period may not overshadow or be inconsistent with the disclosure of the consumer's right to dispute the debt or request the name and address of the original creditor." *See* Pub.L. No. 109-351, § 802(c), 120 Stat.1966, 2006-07 (codified at 15 U.S.C. § 1692g(b)).

Against this backdrop, we turn first to a late-blooming issue that implicates our subject-matter jurisdiction. After clearing that hurdle, we address the defendant's other claims of error.

A. Standing.

The defendant argues for the first time in its reply brief that the plaintiff lacks Article III standing. In most cases, an argument advanced so late in the day and in so perfunctory a fashion would be forfeit. *See, e.g., Merrimon v. Unum Life Ins. Co.,* 758 F.3d 46, 51-52 (1st Cir.2014); *McCoy v. Mass. Inst. of Tech.,* 950 F.2d 13, 22 (1st Cir.1991). But there are exceptions to this general rule, and the defendant's lack of standing argument comes within such an exception. After all, whether a plaintiff has Article III standing implicates a federal court's subject-matter jurisdiction and, thus, must be resolved no matter how tardily the question is raised. p.102 *See Merrimon,* 758 F.3d at 51-52; *see also Vander Luitgaren v. Sun Life Assurance Co.,* 765 F.3d 59, 62-63, 2014 WL 4197947, at *2-3 (1st Cir.2014) (comparing constitutional and statutory standing). We turn to that task.

Federal courts are constitutionally empowered to adjudicate only actual cases and controversies. *See* U.S. Const. art. III, § 2; *Hollingsworth v. Perry,* ___ U.S. ___, 133 S.Ct. 2652, 2661, 186 L.Ed.2d 768 (2013). "A case or controversy exists only when the party soliciting federal court jurisdiction (normally, the plaintiff) demonstrates 'such a personal stake in the outcome of the controversy as to assure that concrete adverseness which sharpens the presentation of issues upon which the court so largely depends.'" *Katz v. Pershing, LLC,* 672 F.3d 64, 71 (1st Cir.2012) (quoting *Baker v. Carr,* 369 U.S. 186, 204, 82 S.Ct. 691, 7 L.Ed.2d 663 (1962)). To demonstrate that she has standing, "a plaintiff must establish each part of a familiar triad: injury, causation, and redressability." *Id.* (citing *Lujan v. Defenders of Wildlife,* 504 U.S. 555, 560-61, 112 S.Ct. 2130, 119 L.Ed.2d 351 (1992)).

The defendant suggests that the plaintiff lacks a constitutionally cognizable injury because she was not flummoxed about her statutory rights after reading the collection letter, as evidenced by the fact that she exercised those rights. But this suggestion gives too short shrift to the well-settled proposition that "[t]he ... injury required by Art. III may exist solely by virtue of 'statutes creating legal rights, the invasion of which creates standing.'" *Warth v. Seldin,* 422 U.S. 490, 500, 95 S.Ct. 2197, 45 L.Ed.2d 343 (1975) (quoting *Linda R.S. v. Richard D.,* 410 U.S. 614, 617 n. 3, 93 S.Ct. 1146, 35 L.Ed.2d 536 (1973)); *see Lujan,* 504 U.S. at 578, 112 S.Ct. 2130; *Havens Realty Corp. v. Coleman,* 455 U.S. 363, 373, 102 S.Ct. 1114, 71 L.Ed.2d 214 (1982).

In cases in which a plaintiff's injury stems solely from the violation of a statute, the nature of the right that the statute confers is of paramount concern. *See Warth,* 422 U.S. at 500, 95 S.Ct. 2197; *Merrimon,* 758 F.3d at 52-53; *Tourgeman v. Collins Fin. Servs., Inc.,* 755 F.3d 1109, 1114-15 (9th Cir.2014). This principle is leavened by the corollary principle that Congress cannot confer standing beyond the boundaries of Article III, that is, upon individuals who have not suffered a concrete injury. *See Summers v. Earth Island Inst.,* 555 U.S. 488, 497, 129 S.Ct. 1142, 173 L.Ed.2d 1 (2009). As a result, a plaintiff always must be able to demonstrate that she suffered some "personal and tangible harm." *Hollingsworth,* 133 S.Ct. at 2661.

Section 1692g prohibits debt collectors from sending collection letters that overshadow or are otherwise inconsistent with the required validation notice. Debt collectors who transgress that prohibition are liable to consumers for actual and statutory damages. *See* 15 U.S.C. § 1692k. Refined to bare essence, the FDCPA bestows upon consumers a right not to receive communications that overshadow or are inconsistent with the validation notice. *Cf. Tourgeman,* 755 F.3d at 1113-14, 1115, 1116-17 (characterizing analogous right conferred by section 1692e as the right not to be the target of misleading communications).

The invasion of a statutorily conferred right may, in and of itself, be a sufficient injury to undergird a plaintiff's standing even in the absence of other harm. *See Havens,* 455 U.S. at 373-74, 102 S.Ct. 1114 (holding that plaintiff suffered cognizable injury when defendant violated statutory right to truthful housing information, notwithstanding plaintiff's p.103 lack of any intention to rent or purchase home). That is the case here: the FDCPA does not require that a plaintiff actually be confused. *See Jacobson v. Healthcare Fin. Servs., Inc.,* 516 F.3d 85, 91 (2d Cir.2008). Seen in this light, the absence of confusion is irrelevant to the standing inquiry.

The short of it is that the plaintiff adequately alleged that her personal right was violated when she received the collection letter. That comprised an injury attributable to the defendant's actions—an injury that will be redressed by an award of damages. No more is exigible to confirm the plaintiff's Article III standing.

B. The Merits.

The defendant protests that its collection letter neither overshadows nor contradicts the validation notice.[2] The district court thought otherwise, and we review that court's entry of judgment on the pleadings de novo.[3] *Mass. Nurses Ass'n v. N. Adams Reg'l Hosp.,* 467 F.3d 27, 31 (1st Cir.2006).

This court has not previously had the occasion to consider from whose perspective a collection letter should be viewed for FDCPA purposes. In confronting this question, we are not navigating uncharted waters. Two of our sister circuits have addressed this issue and concluded that a collection letter is to be viewed from the perspective of the hypothetical unsophisticated consumer.[4] *See Peters v. Gen. Serv. Bureau, Inc.,* 277 F.3d 1051, 1055 (8th Cir.2002); *Gammon v. GC Servs. Ltd. P'ship,* 27 F.3d 1254, 1257 (7th Cir.1994). We think that this reading captures the spirit of the statute. Accordingly, we hold that, for FDCPA purposes, a collection letter is to be viewed from the perspective of the hypothetical unsophisticated consumer.

The standard protects "all consumers, including the inexperienced, the untrained and the credulous." *Taylor v. Perrin,* p.104 *Landry, deLaunay & Durand,* 103 F.3d 1232, 1236 (5th Cir.1997); *see Clomon v. Jackson,* 988 F.2d 1314, 1318 (2d Cir.1993). Even so, the standard remains an objective one, which preserves an element of reasonableness. A debt collector will not be held liable based on an individual consumer's chimerical or farfetched reading of a collection letter. *See Taylor,* 103 F.3d at 1236.

With this holding in place, we turn to the question of whether the collection letter sent by the defendant, when viewed through the eyes of the unsophisticated consumer, overshadows or is inconsistent with the validation notice. We note at the outset that, in the section 1692g milieu, courts do not always distinguish between violations based on the overshadowing of a validation notice and violations based on inconsistencies. Overshadowing is a phenomenon that can take diverse forms. Typically, however, overshadowing is based upon the visual characteristics of a collection letter, such as when a letter demands payment in large, attention-grabbing type and relegates the validation notice to fine or otherwise hard-to-read print. *See McMurray,* 687 F.3d at 671; *Bartlett v. Heibl,* 128 F.3d 497, 500 (7th Cir.1997).

Inconsistencies, too, can occur in various shapes and sizes. They may be either literal or apparent. *See, e.g., Peter v. GC Servs. L.P.,* 310 F.3d 344, 349 (5th Cir. 2002); *Bartlett,* 128 F.3d at 500-01. Most frequently, material inconsistencies arise when a collection letter demands immediate payment or payment in a definite period shorter than thirty days. *See, e.g., McMurray,* 687 F.3d at 670; *Peter,* 310 F.3d at 349.

Whether the controversy centers on overshadowing or inconsistency, the inquiry reduces to whether a particular collection letter would confuse the unsophisticated consumer. *See Bartlett,* 128 F.3d at 500-01. This inquiry is to be conducted with a recognition that confusion can occur in a myriad of ways, such as when a letter visually buries the required validation notice, contains logical inconsistencies, fails to explain an apparent inconsistency, or presents some combination of these (or similar) vices. *See id.* In the last analysis, a collection letter is confusing if, after reading it, the unsophisticated consumer would be left unsure of her right to dispute the debt and request information concerning the original creditor. *See Russell v. Equifax A.R.S.,* 74 F.3d 30, 35 (2d Cir. 1996). The emphasis, then, is on practical effect. *See Graziano v. Harrison,* 950 F.2d 107, 111 (3d Cir.1991) (explaining that "statutory notice must not only explicate a debtor's rights; it must do so effectively").

In conducting the requisite inquiry, we examine the entire collection letter. *See Peter,* 310 F.3d at 349; *McStay v. I.C. Sys., Inc.,* 308 F.3d 188, 191 (2d Cir.2002). Doing so, we conclude—as did the court below—that the collection letter in this case is confusing. The letter conveys the message that the defendant is not inclined to do anything other than file a lawsuit and that it plans to pursue such a course of action "without delay." At bottom, the letter seems to threaten immediate litigation. We think that, implicit in this threat, is the idea that litigation can be avoided only if payment is made forthwith. That idea is reinforced by the fact that the letter appears on law firm letterhead and bears the signature of an attorney.

To be sure, the letter does contain the required section 1692g(a) disclosures, including a statement that the consumer may dispute the debt in writing within thirty days. While Congress for some reason did not require that the notice actually explain what the effect of disputing a debt would be (putting the brakes on collection efforts until a proper response is sent by p.105 the debt collector, *see* 15 U.S.C. § 1692g(b)), we have no doubt that a debt collector is not allowed to suggest that the effect of disputing a debt is different than what the FDCPA provides. To give the required notice of a right to dispute the debt while simultaneously and inaccurately disparaging the benefit of the right is to cause the consumer to think that the right to dispute has less benefit than is actually the case.

Here, this is precisely what the unsophisticated consumer would read the letter as doing. The letter clearly and repeatedly implies that debt collection actions are going to proceed forthwith, come what may. Of utmost significance in this regard is the notice of rights itself. Although the notice is arguably legible, it nonetheless contributes greatly to the incipient confusion. Critically, the second sentence of the second paragraph of the notice reads "we further inform you that despite the fact that you have a thirty (30) day period to dispute the debt may not preclude [sic] the filing of legal action against you prior to the expiration of the period."[5] With its hopelessly scrambled syntax, this sentence is easily read as suggesting that a lawsuit is going to proceed without delay whether the consumer disputes the debt or not. The other affirmative statements in the text of the letter to the effect that the writer is "not inclined to use further resources attempting to collect this debt before filing suit" and is going to "pursue the next logical course of action without delay" reinforce this reading.

In this manner, the letter effectively overshadows the disclosed right to dispute by conveying an inaccurate message that exercise of the right does not have an effect that the statute itself says it has. We believe that when Congress required a debt collector to give notice of this right and provided that conduct overshadowing the disclosure of such right shall not be undertaken, it prohibited conduct such as this—conduct that would dupe the unsophisticated consumer into believing that disputing a debt could not forestall a suit.

The defendant vigorously resists the conclusion that its collection letter is confusing. We have examined the defendant's arguments and find them wanting.

To begin, the defendant points out that the thirty-day validation period is not a grace period. This is true as far as it goes, but it does not get the defendant very far. The FDCPA makes plain that a debt collector's right to seek payment coexists with a consumer's right to notice. *See* 15 U.S.C. § 1692g(b) (stating that "[c]ollection activities and communications that do not otherwise violate this subchapter may continue during the 30-day period" unless the consumer exercises her validation rights). The coexistence of these rights "create[s] a breeding ground for claims for unsophisticated-debtor confusion" because consumers are often faced with two seemingly contradictory statements: that they may dispute the debt and that they must pay immediately. *Durkin v. Equifax Check Servs., Inc.*, 406 F.3d 410, 416 (7th Cir.2005).

But the FDCPA pairs a debt collector's right to pursue payment with a corresponding obligation to ensure that its p.106 communications are not confusing. Consequently, when undertaking collection, a debt collector bears the burden of apprising the consumer of her validation rights in an effective manner.

Next, the defendant asseverates that its collection letter is not confusing because it does not contain an express demand for payment within thirty days. In support of this asseveration, the defendant draws upon case law distinguishing between letters that demand payment immediately or within thirty days and letters that contain open-ended demands for payment. As we explain below, this sets up a false dichotomy.

Unexplained demands for payment immediately or within thirty days confuse the unsophisticated consumer because they contain an apparent contradiction that renders her unsure of her rights. *See Peter,* 310 F.3d at 349. Such collection letters can readily be distinguished from those that merely contain "puffery" (such as encouragement to a consumer to "act now") or that do no more than explain the consequences of a failure to pay. Letters of this latter stripe normally are found not to be confusing. *See, e.g., Zemeckis v. Global Credit & Collection Corp.,* 679 F.3d 632, 636

(7th Cir.2012). So, too, open-ended collection letters that demand payment without reference to any temporal framework typically do not violate section 1692g. *See, e.g., Peter,* 310 F.3d at 349-50.

The distinction that the defendant envisions between these two lines of cases does not aid its cause. The collection letter in this case bears more of a resemblance to a demand for immediate payment than to mere open-ended puffery. Although the letter does not demand immediate payment in haec verba, it not so subtly threatens immediate litigation and tells the plaintiff how to make payments. The clear implication is that the plaintiff can stave off suit only by ignoring her validation rights and making payment.

In any event, the defendant places undue weight on the perceived distinction between an express demand for immediate payment and anything short of that. Overshadowing is rarely a black-or-white proposition: there are many shades of gray. It is impossible to catalogue the manifold ways, some subtle and some not, in which a debt collector may attempt to circumnavigate section 1692g. *See Russell,* 74 F.3d at 35; *Miller v. Payco-Gen. Am. Credits, Inc.,* 943 F.2d 482, 485 (4th Cir.1991). Practical effect is what counts, and we are confident that this collection letter—despite the fact that it does not contain an explicit demand for immediate payment—would confuse the unsophisticated consumer as to her rights.

The defendant also contends that the fact that this collection letter was sent by an attorney is irrelevant. In the defendant's view, the source of a letter has no bearing on the clarity of the validation notice. We do not agree.

We share the view of the Third Circuit that "[u]nder the [FDCPA], attorney debt collectors warrant closer scrutiny because their abusive collection practices are more egregious than those of lay collectors." *Campuzano-Burgos v. Midland Credit Mgmt., Inc.,* 550 F.3d 294, 301 (3d Cir.2008) (internal quotation marks omitted). Thus, "[a]n unsophisticated consumer, getting a letter from an attorney, knows the price of poker has just gone up." *Avila,* 84 F.3d at 229 (internal quotation marks omitted). An attorney's imprimatur conveys authority and induces a consumer to act more quickly. *See id.* With this in mind, it would be naive for a court to ignore the source of a collection letter. That the letter in this case was signed by an attorney reinforces the perception p.107 that it threatens immediate litigation.[6]

The defendant complains that the district court should not have faulted it for not including "transitional" language (that is, language explaining the interface between its threat of suit and the plaintiff's rights) in its collection letter. It correctly points out that the FDCPA does not require any such language, and it laments that the court below gratuitously grafted this additional requirement onto the statute. This plaint contains more cry than wool.

A debt collector is, of course, free to demand immediate payment or (sometimes) even to file suit during the thirty-day validation period. But pursuing such a multi-directional course can lead to confusion,[7] and debt collectors remain firmly bound by the FDCPA's command not to overshadow or be inconsistent with the validation notice. *See Ellis v. Solomon & Solomon, P.C.,* 591 F.3d 130, 136-37 (2d Cir.2010). The simplest way for a debt collector to ensure that its payment demand does not create confusion is to provide a brief, lucid explanation of how collector and consumer rights interact during the validation period. Two courts of appeals have gone so far as to offer sample language. *See Savino v. Computer Credit, Inc.,* 164 F.3d 81, 86 (2d Cir.1998); *Bartlett,* 128 F.3d at 501-02.

Although the FDCPA does not require such an explanation, it does require that collection letters not be confusing. A debt collector who chooses to brandish threats of litigation must take pains to ensure that those threats do not obnubilate or undercut the required validation notice. In evaluating whether a collection letter breeds confusion, a district court thus acts well within its proper province in noting that a debt collector could easily have included explanatory language but chose not to do so. So it is here.

Relatedly, the defendant argues that its collection letter contains language sufficient to dispel any confusion. To be specific, it argues that the second sentence of the second paragraph of its validation notice adequately explains the interaction between its right to initiate litigation and the plaintiff's validation rights. But as we already have explained, the sentence itself is unintelligible and, thus, obfuscates more than it clarifies. Moreover, the sentence only reinforces the defendant's intent to file suit forthwith, regardless of whether or not the plaintiff were to seek validation of the debt. That emphasis hardly advances the defendant's argument.

There is one final matter. Judge Baldock's dissent emphasizes that the information conveyed by the defendant's collection letter is true and posits that a mere typographical error should not result in a statutory violation. To buttress his point, Judge Baldock offers an explanation of how the letter can be read so that it does not violate section 1692g.

But it is not a federal judge's ability to parse a collection letter with which we are concerned. Instead, it is the ability of the unsophisticated consumer. Moreover, that the information is accurate does not render it nonconfusing as presented. *See Bartlett,* 128 F.3d at 500-01 (explaining that the failure to clarify an apparent contradiction
p.108 is just as bad as an outright contradiction). That a debt collector may threaten litigation in a nonconfusing manner without violating section 1692g does not resolve this case. Absent the garbled sentence in the second paragraph of the validation notice, the letter here might well have satisfied section 1692g. However, when the garbled sentence is piled on top of the letter's compendium of threats, we continue to believe that the effect on the unsophisticated consumer would be to confuse.

III. CONCLUSION

We need go no further. For the reasons elucidated above, the judgment of the district court is

Affirmed.

BALDOCK, Circuit Judge, dissenting.

As always, Judge Selya's prose is eloquent and his analysis thorough. Regrettably, I cannot join, as I do not believe this letter violated § 1692g.

Defendant's letter did not explicitly demand immediate payment or payment sooner than thirty days, and Defendant included Plaintiff's rights to dispute the debt and to request information on the front of the only page, in legible font. This much is undisputed and, in my view, should settle the debate as it distinguishes virtually all cases detailing § 1692g violations.[8] Nevertheless, this court finds a statutory breach.

The court, as I read it, initially reasons Defendant *implicitly* demanded immediate payment by expressing an intent to litigate immediately. But, the court later admits—as it must—that Defendant could indeed litigate immediately without violating § 1692g. *See Bartlett v. Heibl,* 128 F.3d 497, 501 (7th Cir.1997) ("The debt collector is perfectly free to sue within thirty days."). Going further, Plaintiff herself confesses "[d]ebt collectors are *free to tell consumers* that, absent payment, the collector will file a lawsuit *without delay.*" Resp. Br. at 5 (emphases added); *see also Zemeckis v. Global Credit & Collection Corp.,* 679 F.3d 632, 636-37 (7th Cir.2012) ("Global Credit's repeated threat of legal action ... fails to convert the letter's puffery into a contradictory payment deadline."). So, if debt collectors are free to litigate immediately, and free to tell consumers they will litigate immediately sans payment, how is this letter improper? Plaintiff theorizes collectors "must use transitional or explanatory language" when they threaten prompt litigation, lest the threat negate the disclosure of Plaintiff's rights to dispute and to gather information. Yet the court (rightly) *rejects* this theory: "[T]he FDCPA," it writes, "does not require any such language." Apparently, a litigation threat and a disclosure of consumer rights *can* coexist absent explanation—so long as the letter does not otherwise confuse. So, aside from lawful litigation threats, how would this letter confuse?

The court gives two reasons. First, the court finds significant Defendant's use of law firm letterhead and a lawyer's signature. The statute does not mention this, however, and the court cites no case law directly on point, despite an abundance of p.109 existing § 1692g cases.[9] Second, the court opines that a sentence in the final paragraph of the validation notice is "unintelligible." I do not see it that way. The sentence in question has a single typo.[10] I am not inclined to find a statutory violation based on an insubstantial typo. More importantly, rather than confuse, the sentence merely lays out the same two propositions discussed above: (1) the consumer has "a thirty (30) day period to dispute the debt", *which is true,* and (2) Defendant may still file a lawsuit within this thirty-day window, *which is also true.* Put another way: The aspect of this letter most relied upon to hold a consumer would be confused about her right to dispute the debt is a sentence that *reiterates* a consumer has a right to dispute the debt. I fail to discern the problem.

In conclusion, the letter as a whole is relatively straightforward and does not "overshadow" or contradict the disclosure of consumer rights. Even an unsophisticated consumer would not be confused here. See *Fed. Home Loan Mortg. Corp. v. Lamar,* 503 F.3d 504, 510 (6th Cir.2007) (least sophisticated consumer would read material "carefully" and "in its entirety").

I respectfully dissent.

APPENDIX A

THE LAW OFFICE OF MANDY L. SPAULDING

P.O. Box. 826 North Attleboro, MA 02761 www.mispatficlingiaw.corn

Mandy I., Spaulding (Licensed In MA)

Nicholas M. Amaral (Licensed in MA arid RI)

Telephone: (508) 643-7200

Facsimile: (508) 809-4634

October 23, 2012

Re: File Number: 12912

Original Crecliror: CONFIN FIRST BANK OF DELAW

Original Account Number: XXXXXXXXXXXXXXXX

Amount: $611.84

Dear Robbie Stefanowich:

I have been retained by Debt Management, Inc., successor in interest to and legal title holder of rho above captioned debt. I have been asked by my client to collect from you the entire balance noted above that you owe on your delinquent account.

This is the first letter being sent to you by my of office, following attempts by the original creditor and a collection agency to reach you to resolve this matter. I am not inclined to use further resources attempting to collect this debt before filing suit.

I have been retained to collect this debt through whatever legal means are available and without your cooperation, I am obligated to my client to pursue the next logical course of action without delay.

While payments can always be made by calling our office to set up payments via phone or mailing payments to the above address, you can also make payments via
p.110 our website (above), or Money Gram which is it service available at your local Shaw's or Walmart. For a Money Gram payment you will need a six digit account number which is the File Number listed above followed by as many O's needed to be six digits, anti our receive code which is 6061.

Thank you for your cooperation in this matter.

Very truly yours,

Mandy Spaulding

Mandy L. Spaulding, Esq.

MS/ms

NOTICE OF IMPORTANT RIGHTS

Pursuant in the Fair Debt Collection Practices Act ("FDCPA") (15 U.S.C. § 1692), a consumer debtor is required to be sent the following notice: (1) unless the consumer, within thirty (30) days after receipt of this notice, disputes the validity of the debt or any portion thereof, the debt will be assumed to be valid by the debt collector; (2) if the consumer notifies the debt collector in writing within the thirty-day period that the debt or any portion thereof, is disputed, the debt collector will obtain verification of the debt or a copy of a judgment against the consumer, and copy of such verification or judgment vrill be mailed to the consumer by the debt collector; and (3) upon the consumer's written request within the thirty-day period, the debt collector vidll provide the consumer with the name and address of the original creditor, if different from the current creditor.

The Law Office of Mandy L. Spaulding is acting as a debt collector pursuant to the FDCPA and any information obtained will be used for that purpose. We further inform you that despite the fact that you have a thirty (30) day period to dispute the debt may not preclude the filing of legal action against you prior to the expiration of the period. You have the right to make a written or oral request that telephone calls regarding your debt not be made to you at your place of employment. Any such oral request will be valid for only ten days unless you provide written confirmation of the request postmarked or delivered within seven days of such request. You may terminate this request by writing to the creditor.

[*] Of the Tenth Circuit, sitting by designation.

[1] At the same time, the court ruled on other issues. Those rulings are immaterial here, and it would serve no useful purpose to chronicle them.

[2] Although section 1692g refers to "inconsistencies," the case law typically refers to "contradictions." Because the 2006 amendments to the FDCPA codified existing case law, courts tend to treat those terms interchangeably. *See McMurray,* 687 F.3d at 669 n. 2. We follow this praxis.

[3] The parties agree, so we assume for present purposes (without deciding), that whether a collection letter overshadows or is inconsistent with a validation notice is a question of law. However, there is no consensus on this point. While the weight of authority holds that the question of whether a collection letter overshadows or is inconsistent with a validation notice is one of law, *see, e.g., Fed. Home Loan Mortg. Corp. v. Lamar,* 503 F.3d 504, 508 n. 2 (6th Cir.2007); *Wilson v. Quadramed Corp.,* 225 F.3d 350, 353 n. 2 (3d Cir.2000), at least one court of appeals has concluded that such a question is one of fact to be resolved by a jury, *see Walker v. Nat'l Recovery, Inc.,* 200 F.3d 500, 503 (7th Cir. 1999). Neither party has addressed this split in authority, and we refrain from delving into the issue without the benefit of either briefing or developed argumentation.

[4] A majority of the circuits applies a "least sophisticated consumer" standard. *See, e.g., Fed. Home Loan Mortg. Corp. v. Lamar,* 503 F.3d 504, 509 (6th Cir.2007); *Terran v. Kaplan,* 109 F.3d 1428, 1431-32 (9th Cir.1997); *Russell v. Equifax A.R.S.,* 74 F.3d 30, 34 (2d Cir. 1996); *cf. Chiang v. Verizon New Eng. Inc.,* 595 F.3d 26, 42 (1st Cir.2010) (referencing, though having no occasion to adopt or apply, the least sophisticated consumer standard). Labels aside, there appears to be little difference between this formulation and the "unsophisticated consumer" formulation. *See Avila v. Rubin,* 84 F.3d 222, 227 (7th Cir.1996) ("[T]he unsophisticated consumer standard is a distinction without much of a practical difference in application."). We adopt the unsophisticated consumer formulation to avoid any appearance of wedding the standard to the "very last rung on the sophistication ladder." *Gammon v. GC Servs. Ltd. P'ship,* 27 F.3d 1254, 1257 (7th Cir.1994).

[5] Our dissenting brother makes the point that this sentence is garbled because of what he regards as a typographical error. But the source of the garbling is irrelevant to our inquiry. It is the unsophisticated consumer's perception of the letter, not the debt collector's intent, that controls a determination of whether a collection letter overshadows or contradicts a validation notice. *See Ellis v. Solomon & Solomon, P.C.,* 591 F.3d 130, 135 (2d Cir.2010) ("To recover damages under the FDCPA, a

consumer does not need to show intentional conduct on the part of the debt collector.").

[6] Although the cases on which we rely for this conclusion involve claims under section 1692e, we think that the principles that they articulate have more general application.

[7] One is reminded of the aphorist Stephen Butler Leacock's tale of a man who "flung himself upon his horse and rode madly off in all directions." Stephen Leacock, *Gertrude the Governess: or, Simple Seventeen, in Nonsense Novels* 71, 73 (John Lane 1920) (1911).

[8] *Compare Miller v. Payco-Gen. Am. Credits, Inc.*, 943 F.2d 482, 483 (4th Cir.1991) (violation: form stated "THIS IS A DEMAND FOR IMMEDIATE FULL PAYMENT" in large, red, and bold type, and "PAY US—NOW" with the "NOW" taking up a third of a page), and *Bartlett v. Heibl,* 128 F.3d 497, 503 (7th Cir. 1997) (violation: letter demanded payment or contact "within one week"), *with McMurray v. ProCollect, Inc.,* 687 F.3d 665, 670 (5th Cir.2012) (no violation: "letter contain[ed] no demand for payment, much less a demand for payment within the 30-day statutory contest period").

[9] The court believes § 1692e cases are applicable, but I am not convinced. Unlike § 1692g, several § 1692e claims *explicitly* discuss attorneys and the legal context. *See, e.g.,* § 1692e(3) ("The false representation ... that any communication is from an attorney [violates § 1692e].").

[10] It appears plain to me Defendant simply forgot to delete the word "despite" from the sentence, perhaps after a revision.

714 F.3d 73 (2013)

Jennifer SMITH, Plaintiff, Appellant,
v.
SOLOMON & SOLOMON, P.C.; Julie B. Solomon, Defendants, Appellees.

No. 12-2169.

United States Court of Appeals, First Circuit.

April 24, 2013.

Smith v. Solomon & Solomon, PC, 714 F. 3d 73 (1st Cir. 2013)

p.74 Roger Stanford and Stanford & Schall on brief for appellant.

Julie B. Solomon and Solomon & Solomon, P.C. on brief for appellees.

Before THOMPSON, Circuit Judge, SOUTER,[*] Associate Justice, and STAHL, Circuit Judge.

STAHL, Circuit Judge.

This case requires us to decide whether the Fair Debt Collection Practices Act (FDCPA), 15 U.S.C. § 1692 *et seq.*, controls the choice of venue in a post-judgment enforcement action to recover a debt under Massachusetts trustee process law. We conclude that it does not.

The facts of this case are neither complex nor contested. The plaintiff-appellant is Jennifer Smith, formerly known as Jennifer Gonsalves, who was, at all relevant times, a resident of New Bedford, Massachusetts and an employee of the U.S. Department of the Interior. The defendants-appellees are Solomon & Solomon, P.C., a law firm that specializes in debt collection, and Julie B. Solomon, an attorney who serves as a director at the firm.

In May 2010, the New Bedford District Court entered a default judgment against Smith in a suit filed by Solomon & Solomon to recover a consumer debt. In March 2011, Solomon & Solomon then brought a second suit in the Attleboro District Court, seeking to collect on the 2010 default judgment by attaching Smith's wages from the Department of the Interior, via trustee process. North Attleboro is one of the locations in which the Department of the Interior maintains a usual place of business.

In February 2012, Smith filed the present action to recover damages, alleging that the defendants-appellees violated the FDCPA venue provision, 15 U.S.C. § 1692i(a), when they brought the 2011 Attleboro suit in a district other than the one in which she resides or signed the underlying contract, *see id.* § 1692k (FDCPA civil liability provision); *Fox v. Citicorp Credit Services, Inc.*, 15 F.3d 1507, 1511 (9th Cir.1994) ("The parties agree that a violation of the venue provision may support civil liability."); *Pickens v. Collection Services of Athens, Inc.*, 165 F.Supp.2d 1376, 1379 (M.D.Ga.), *aff'd*, 273 F.3d 1121 (11th Cir.2001) (Table) ("Violation of the venue provision is sufficient to establish liability."). The defendants-appellees moved to dismiss, *see* Fed.R.Civ.P. 12(b)(6), and requested fees and costs, arguing that Smith's claim was baseless in that it ignored Massachusetts trustee process law. Although the district court granted the motion to dismiss, it denied the request for fees. *Smith v. Solomon & Solomon, P.C.*, 887 F.Supp.2d 334 (D.Mass.2012). This appeal followed; our review is de novo. *See Pruell v. Caritas Christi,* 645 F.3d 81, 83 (1st Cir.2011).

In Massachusetts, a plaintiff cannot attach a debtor's wages or salary "except on a claim that has first been reduced to judgment or otherwise authorized by law." Mass. R. Civ. P. 4.2(a). The defendants-appellees reduced their claim to judgment p.75 through the initial New Bedford District Court action, and Smith concedes that venue was proper in that suit. Thus, this case, unlike *Harrington v. CACV of Colo., LLC,* 508 F.Supp.2d 128, 131, 133-34 (D.Mass.2007), concerns the question of what venue is proper in a post-judgment enforcement proceeding, not an initial collections action.

The FDCPA venue provision requires "[a]ny debt collector who brings any legal action on a debt against any consumer" to do so "only in the judicial district or similar legal entity — (A) in which such consumer signed the contract sued upon; or (B) in which such consumer resides at the commencement of the action." 15 U.S.C. § 1692i(a). The parties agree that the defendants-appellees qualify as debt collectors, that the 2011 trustee process suit was a "legal action on a debt" within the meaning of the FDCPA, that it was not filed in a judicial district in which Smith "signed the contract sued upon" or in which she resided, and that the FDCPA venue provision applies only to legal actions brought "against any consumer." *Id.* What they vigorously dispute is whether a post-judgment enforcement proceeding — here, under Massachusetts trustee process law — qualifies as a legal action "against any consumer." *Id.* The text of the FDCPA provides no definition of that phrase and thus no guidance on the issue. *See id.*

As far as we are aware, only one circuit court has reviewed the exact question before us. In *Pickens,* 273 F.3d 1121, the Eleventh Circuit affirmed a district court's conclusion that a garnishment action under Georgia law is not against the consumer within the meaning of the FDCPA, 165 F.Supp.2d at 1380-81. The district court relied on the fact that the Georgia statutory scheme described a garnishment proceeding as an action between the judgment creditor and the garnishee and required venue to be based on the garnishee's place of business, *id.* at 1380, and on the fact that the judgment debtor had already had a chance to defend against the original debt action, *id.* at 1381.[1]

Smith points to *Fox,* in which the Ninth Circuit concluded generally that "[t]he plain meaning of the term 'legal action'" in the FDCPA venue provision "encompasses all judicial proceedings, including those in enforcement of a previously-adjudicated right." 15 F.3d at 1515; *see also Flores v. Quick Collect, Inc.,* No. 06-1564-AA, 2007 WL 2769003, at *3 (D.Or. Sept. 18, 2007) (following *Fox*). However, *Fox* did not address the "against any consumer" language in the FDCPA, nor was the court apparently asked to decide whether the garnishment process under the applicable state law fell within that definition. Our task today is to consider those issues.

Trustee process in Massachusetts is governed by Chapter 246 of the Massachusetts General Laws and Massachusetts Rule of Civil Procedure 4.2. We agree with the district court that the state statute and rule define trustee process as "a legal action directed against the third-party trustee, not the consumer." *Smith,* 887

F.Supp.2d at 338. We see no need to rehash the district court's thorough and persuasive opinion and will therefore keep our explanation brief.

Once the defendants-appellees obtained the default judgment against Smith, the
p.76 Massachusetts trustee process scheme required them to file their subsequent suit to collect on the judgment in a county in which the *trustee* (here, the Department of the Interior) resides or has a usual place of business. *See* Mass. Gen. Laws ch. 246, § 4 (mandating that "[n]o person shall be held to answer as a trustee in an action in a district court ... in any county other than that where he dwells or has a usual place of business"). Smith, the defendant debtor, could then move for a change of venue, *see id.* § 4A, but the fact that a trustee process action in Massachusetts can only be initiated in the venue in which the trustee is located indicates that the action is directed against the trustee, not the debtor.

The specific procedures for seeking trustee process laid out in Rule 4.2 provide further support for that proposition. The summons must be directed to the trustee, who is the party required to answer. *See* Mass. R. Civ. P. 4.2(b). The defendant debtor can appear to be heard on the motion for approval of attachment but does not thereby submit herself to the court's jurisdiction. *See* Mass. R. Civ. P. 4.2(c).[2] There is no doubt that the debtor has an interest in the proceeding; she must be given notice of the hearing and an opportunity to contest the attachment. *See id.* Fundamentally, however, a Massachusetts trustee process action is geared toward compelling the *trustee* to act, not the debtor. *See Smith,* 887 F.Supp.2d at 340.[3]

We find no conflict between that state statutory scheme and the FDCPA. The Congressional concern underlying the FDCPA venue provision was that a debt collector would file in an inconvenient forum, obtain a default judgment, and thereby deny the consumer an opportunity to defend herself. *See* S.Rep. No. 95-382, at 5 (1977), *reprinted in* 1977 U.S.C.C.A.N. 1695, 1699. That concern is not present in the case of a post-judgment enforcement proceeding under Massachusetts trustee process law. The original suit to collect on the debt occurred in a forum that was convenient for Smith, and she had an opportunity to defend against it. She was not, in the words of Congress, "denied [her] day in court." *Id.*

The Federal Trade Commission (FTC) seems to agree that the FDCPA venue provision does not control in a post-judgment enforcement proceeding like the one at issue here. The FTC's commentary to the FDCPA provides that, "[i]f a judgment is obtained in a forum that satisfies the requirements of [15 U.S.C. § 1692i], it may be enforced in another jurisdiction, because the consumer previously has had the opportunity to defend the original action in a convenient forum." *Statements of General Policy or Interpretation Staff Commentary On the Fair Debt Collection Practices Act,* 53 Fed.Reg. 50,097, 50,109 (Dec. 13, 1988). The commentary is not entitled to *Chevron* deference, *see id.* at 50,101; *Gulley v. Markoff & Krasny,* 664 F.3d 1073, 1074-75 (7th Cir.2011); *Brown v. Card Serv. Ctr.,* 464 F.3d 450, 455 (3d Cir.2006), but it lends further support to our conclusion today.

Smith relies heavily on the Ninth Circuit's contrary decision in *Fox,* 15 F.3d p.77
1507, and on *Adkins v. Weltman, Weinberg & Reis Co., L.P.A.,* No. 2:11-cv-00619, 2012 WL 604249 (S.D.Ohio Feb. 24, 2012). We find those cases unpersuasive. *Fox* did not consider the "against any consumer" language in the FDCPA venue provision at all, and *Adkins* considered it in the context of an entirely different state statutory scheme. *See Smith,* 887 F.Supp.2d at 339.[4] Furthermore, if we were to interpret the FDCPA

venue provision as *Fox* and *Adkins* do, it would be impossible for a debt collector to enforce a prior judgment through trustee process in Massachusetts unless the judgment debtor happened to reside or to have signed the underlying contract in the same county in which the trustee had a usual place of business. *See Smith,* 887 F.Supp.2d at 340. We do not read the FDCPA as mandating such a strange result.

We turn, finally, to the defendants-appellees' request for fees. They did not appeal the district court's denial of fees below but have requested fees on appeal, claiming that Smith's appeal was frivolous. "An application for an award of fees on appeal should be filed as a separate motion within 30 days of the entry of final judgment in this court." *Spooner v. EEN, Inc.,* 644 F.3d 62, 71 n. 6 (1st Cir.2011); *see also* 1st Cir. R. 39.1. Should the defendants-appellees wish to pursue their fee application further, they will need to follow the proper procedure.

The judgment of the district court is *affirmed.*

[*] Hon. David H. Souter, Associate Justice (Ret.) of the Supreme Court of the United States, sitting by designation.

[1] At least two district courts, in addition to the one below and the one in *Pickens,* have also weighed in on the issue. *Compare Schuback v. Law Offices of Phillip S. Van Embden, P.C.,* No. 1:12-CV-320, 2013 WL 432641, at *2-6 (M.D.Pa. Feb. 1, 2013) (holding that a writ of execution under New Jersey law is not an action against the consumer), *with Adkins v. Weltman, Weinberg & Reis Co., L.P.A.,* No. 2:11-cv-00619, 2012 WL 604249, at *4-7 (S.D.Ohio Feb. 24, 2012) (holding that a garnishment proceeding is an action against the consumer).

[2] An order approving trustee process can also be entered ex parte, without prior notice to the debtor. *See* Mass. R. Civ. P. 4.2(g). The debtor has a right to appear and challenge an ex parte order, but again "without thereby submitting his person to the jurisdiction of the court." Mass. R. Civ. P. 4.2(h).

[3] We agree with the district court that the fact that the complaint in this case named Smith as the defendant was merely a "procedural convention." *Smith,* 887 F.Supp.2d at 338.

[4] Although the *Adkins* court did not explicitly rely on the text of the relevant Ohio garnishment statute in reaching its conclusion, *see* 2012 WL 604249, at *6-7, the statute defined garnishment proceedings as being against the judgment debtor, not the garnishee, and thus differed significantly from the Massachusetts trustee process scheme, *see Smith,* 887 F.Supp.2d at 339 (citing Ohio Rev.Code Ann. § 2716.03).

SECOND CIRCUIT DECISIONS

Fair Debt Collection Practices Act

999 F.3d 151 (2021)

Cristian D. CORTEZ, Plaintiff-Appellee,
v.
FORSTER & GARBUS, LLP, Defendant-Appellant.

No. 20-1134 August Term 2020.

United States Court of Appeals, Second Circuit.

Argued: January 28, 2021.
Decided: June 4, 2021.

Cortez v. Forster & Garbus, LLP, 999 F. 3d 151 (2nd Cir. 2021)

In *Avila v. Riexinger & Associates, LLC,* 817 F.3d 72, 76 (2d Cir. 2016), we held that the Fair Debt Collection Practices Act, 15 U.S.C. § 1692e, requires "debt collectors, when they notify consumers of their account balance, to disclose that the balance may increase due to interest and fees." This appeal requires us to clarify whether *Avila*'s disclosure requirement applies to collection notices that extend offers to settle outstanding debt. We hold that it does not. Accordingly, the judgment of the United States District Court for the Eastern District of New York is REVERSED.

For Plaintiff-appellee: David M. Barshay, Craig B. Sanders, on the brief, Barshay Sanders PLLC, Garden City, New York, for Cristian D. Cortez.

For Defendant-Appellant: Robert L. Arleo, New York, New York, for Forster & Garbus, LLP.

Before: LIVINGSTON, Chief Judge, CABRANES, and LYNCH, Circuit Judges.

p.152 DEBRA ANN LIVINGSTON, Chief Judge:

The Fair Debt Collection Practices Act ("FDCPA") prohibits debt collectors from using "any false, deceptive, or misleading representation or means in connection with the collection of any debt." 15 U.S.C. § 1692e. In *Avila v. Riexinger & Associates, LLC,* 817 F.3d 72 (2d Cir. 2016), we held this provision to require "debt collectors, when they notify consumers of their account balance, to disclose that the balance may increase due to interest and fees." *Id.* at 76. This appeal requires us to clarify whether this disclosure requirement applies to collection notices that extend offers to settle outstanding debt. We hold that it does not. Consequently, we REVERSE and REMAND with directions to enter summary judgment in favor of Defendant Forster & Garbus, LLP.

BACKGROUND

Plaintiff Cristian D. Cortez incurred credit card debt to Discover Bank. Discover Bank placed Cortez's debt with Forster & Garbus for collection. In 2011, Forster & Garbus filed a collection action in New York state court and obtained a default judgment. Over the years, Forster & Garbus mailed Cortez a number of collection notices.

p.153 In one such notice dated February 2, 2017, Forster & Garbus indicated that Cortez's debt balance at that time was $13,457.65 and stated in relevant part:

> This office has been authorized to advise you that a settlement of the above account can be arranged. You are being offered a substantial discount off the current balance due. You may choose one of the three payment options as follows:
>
> A. One payment of $5,383.06, which we shall expect by February 24, 2017.
>
> B. Two payments of $3,364.42 each, totaling $6,728.84, which we shall expect by February 24, 2017, and March 24, 2017.
>
> C. Three payments of $2,691.53 each, totaling $8,074.59, which we shall expect by February 24, 2017, March 24, 2017, and April 24, 2017.
>
> Please note that we are not obligated to repeat this offer.
>
> Please return the bottom portion of this letter with your selection checked to confirm your settlement choice. If you are unable to take advantage of the above settlement opportunities, please contact this office so that we may arrange a payment plan on the account.

Joint App'x at 19. Cortez sued Forster & Garbus, claiming that this notice, by failing to disclose that interest was continuing to accrue on his balance, violated the FDCPA as interpreted by *Avila.*

Forster & Garbus moved for summary judgment, which the United States District Court for the Eastern District of New York (Block, *J.*) denied in a memorandum and order dated June 12, 2019. *See Cortez v. Foster & Garbus, LLP,* 382 F. Supp. 3d 259 (E.D.N.Y. 2019). The district court observed that the February 2 notice did not state whether interest and fees were accruing on Cortez's account even though *Avila* mandated that "debt collectors, when they notify consumers of their account balance," must "disclose that the balance may increase due to interest and fees." *Id.* at 261 (quoting *Avila,* 817 F.3d at 76). Forster & Garbus argued that the notice did not violate Section 1692e because under *Avila,* "a debt collector will not be subject to liability" under the FDCPA if it makes a settlement offer "clearly stat[ing] that the holder of the debt will accept payment of the amount set forth in full satisfaction of the debt if payment is made by a specified date," 817 F.3d at 77; the district court read *Avila* to require that such a settlement offer must nevertheless be accompanied by a disclosure of whether interest would continue to accrue if the debtor "do[es] not make the payment by the specified date." *Cortez,* 382 F. Supp. 3d at 261. In any event, the district court found it "debatable" whether the February 2 notice clearly stated that the specified amounts in the notice would fully satisfy Cortez's debt if made by the specified date. *Id.* at 262. The district court further decided that "because there are no genuine issues of material fact and [Forster & Garbus] has had adequate opportunity to develop and present its case," it would enter "summary judgment on the issue of liability in favor of [Cortez]." *Id.* (internal quotation marks omitted).

Forster & Garbus unsuccessfully moved for reconsideration, *Cortez v. Forster & Garbus, LLP,* No. 17-cv-06501, 2020 WL 1083680, at *1 (E.D.N.Y. Mar. 6, 2020), judgment in favor of Cortez entered March 6, 2020, and Forster & Garbus timely appealed the district court's grant of summary judgment for Cortez.

DISCUSSION

"We review a grant of summary judgment *de novo*, examining the evidence in the light most favorable to, and drawing p.154 all inferences in favor of, the non-movant." *Huebner v. Midland Credit Mgmt., Inc.*, 897 F.3d 42, 50 (2d Cir. 2018) (quoting *Blackman v. N.Y.C. Transit Auth.*, 491 F.3d 95, 98 (2d Cir. 2007) (per curiam)). Summary judgment is appropriate only when "there is no genuine dispute as to any material fact and the movant is entitled to judgment as a matter of law." Fed. R. Civ. P. 56(a).

I

The FDCPA provides that "[a] debt collector may not use any false, deceptive, or misleading representation or means in connection with the collection of any debt," 15 U.S.C. § 1692e, and, among other things, prohibits debt collectors from making any "false representation of the character, amount, or legal status of any debt," *id.* § 1692e(2)(A). To determine whether a debt collection notice violates these provisions, we employ the least sophisticated consumer standard, according to which a notice is deceptive or misleading if it is "open to more than one reasonable interpretation, at least one of which is inaccurate." *Clomon v. Jackson*, 988 F.2d 1314, 1319 (2d Cir. 1993).[1]

In *Avila*, we held that a collection notice that states a debtor's current balance but does not disclose whether interest and fees are accruing is "misleading within the meaning of Section 1692e" because "[a] reasonable consumer could read the notice and be misled into believing that she could pay her debt in full by paying the amount listed on the notice" when, in fact, "if interest is accruing daily, or if there are undisclosed late fees, a consumer who pays the 'current balance' stated on the notice will not know whether the debt has been paid in full." 817 F.3d at 76. Consequently, we held "that the FDCPA requires debt collectors, when they notify consumers of their account balance, to disclose that the balance may increase due to interest and fees." *Id.*

> However, we proceeded to explain that a debt collector will not be subject to liability under Section 1692e for failing to disclose that the consumer's balance may increase due to interest and fees if the collection notice either [1] accurately informs the consumer that the amount of the debt stated in the letter will increase over time, or [2] clearly states that the holder of the debt will accept payment in the amount set forth in full satisfaction of the debt if payment is made by a specified date.

Id. at 77. Together, these two disclosure options, or safe harbors, fully address the concern we articulated in *Avila* that a debtor might remit the listed balance without realizing that she has not fully paid off her debt. The first disclosure option contemplates debt collectors informing debtors that paying the specified amount *will not* satisfy the debt. *See, e.g., Kolbasyuk v. Capital Mgmt. Servs., LP*, 918 F.3d 236, 242 (2d Cir. 2019). The second disclosure option contemplates collectors informing debtors that paying the specified amount *will* satisfy the debt. When apprised of either of these two disclosures, no debtor reasonably could be unaware of the effect payment of the balance specified in the notice would have on her outstanding debt.

p.155 II

We reaffirm *Avila*'s holding that a debt collector "will not be subject to liability under Section 1692e for failing to disclose" in a collection notice whether an account is accruing interest and fees so long as the notice "clearly states that the holder of the debt will accept payment of the amount set forth in full satisfaction of the debt if payment is made by a specified date." 817 F.3d at 77. Such collection notices do not present the risk that a debtor might pay the listed balance only to find herself still owing more. Payment of an amount that the collector indicates will fully satisfy a debt excludes the possibility of further debt to pay.

Our decision in *Taylor v. Financial Recovery Services, Inc.*, 886 F.3d 212 (2d Cir. 2018), is instructive. There, debtors whose balances were static sued their debt collector, Financial Recovery Services ("FRS"), under the FDCPA for failing to disclose that interest and fees were *not* accruing on their accounts. They argued that under *Avila*, "a debt collector commits a per se violation of Section 1692e whenever it fails to disclose whether interest or fees are accruing on a debt." *Id.* at 214. We disagreed. While in *Avila* the collection notice's implication that payment of the outstanding balance would fully satisfy the debt was "prejudicially misleading," in *Taylor* "prompt payment of the amounts stated in [plaintiffs'] notices *would* have satisfied their debts." *Id.* (emphasis in original). For this reason, we held that FRS's notices to plaintiffs, which stated their respective balances without disclosing that interest and fees were not accruing on their accounts, did not violate the FDCPA. *Id.*; *see also Chuway v. Nat'l Action Fin. Servs., Inc.*, 362 F.3d 944, 949 (7th Cir. 2004) (Posner, *J.*) ("If the debt collector is trying to collect only the amount due on the date the letter is sent, then he complies with the Act by stating the 'balance' due . . . and asking the recipient to remit the balance listed — and stopping there[.]"). This reasoning extends to a collection notice proposing to accept a specified amount in full satisfaction of a debt. As with debtors faced with a collection notice for a static debt, who are not prejudicially misled by the collector's failure to disclose that interest is *not* accruing, debtors faced with a settlement offer are not misled by the failure to disclose that interest *is* accruing because in both situations, payment of the amount indicated in a collection notice would extinguish the debt.

Nevertheless, here the district court held that debt collectors extending offers of full satisfaction must also "advise consumers that their debt [is] still accruing interest and/or fees." *Cortez*, 382 F. Supp. 3d at 261. In doing so, the court was drawn to our suggestion in *Avila* that

> a debt collector who is willing to accept a specified amount in full satisfaction of the debt if payment is made by a specific date could considerably simplify the consumer's understanding by so stating, while advising that the amount due would increase by the accrual of additional interest or fees if payment is not received by that date.

Id. (quoting *Avila*, 817 F.3d at 77).

However, *Avila* held only that a debt collector must "*either*" disclose that interest and fees continue to accrue "*or*" offer to extinguish the debt in exchange for a specified payment. 817 F.3d at 77 (emphasis added). *Avila*'s use of a precatory word to suggest that a debt collector "could" simultaneously avail itself of both safe harbors is consistent with the conclusion, explained above, that either disclosure option alone dispels the risk of a collection notice misleading a debtor about the effect paying p.156 the specified amount would have on the outstanding debt.

The district court was concerned that a settlement offer from a debt collector could mislead the debtor if the offer set forth a payment deadline but failed to disclose whether interest or fees would accrue if payment were tendered *after* the deadline. The least sophisticated consumer, it reasoned, could interpret such an offer "as implying *either* that interest and/or fees would accrue after that date *or* that the balance will stay the same after that date." *Cortez*, 382 F. Supp. 3d at 262 (emphasis in original). We disagree that, to the extent such a settlement offer is ambiguous along the lines suggested by the district court, a collection notice containing it would be rendered misleading under Section 1692e. For one thing, as we have already explained, *Avila* expressly held that a debt collector clearly extending an offer of full satisfaction if payment is made by a specified date is not "subject to liability under Section 1692e for failing to disclose that the consumer's balance may increase due to interest and fees[.]" 817 F.3d at 77. But more generally, Section 1692e does not require that a collection notice anticipate every potential collateral consequence that could arise in connection with the payment or nonpayment of a debt. *See, e.g., Altman v. J.C. Christensen & Assocs., Inc.*, 786 F.3d 191, 194 (2d Cir. 2015) (settlement offer that did not factor potential tax liability into stated discount was not misleading); *Taylor*, 886 F.3d at 215 ("[C]ollection notice that fails to disclose that interest and fees are not currently accruing on a debt is not misleading[.]"). Instead, the FDCPA merely requires that a collection notice, *by its terms*, not be susceptible of a reasonable but inaccurate interpretation. *See Clomon*, 988 F.2d at 1319. Therefore, a settlement offer need not enumerate the consequences of failing to meet its deadline or rejecting it outright so long as it clearly and accurately informs a debtor that payment of a specified sum by a specified date will satisfy the debt.

III

With these principles in mind, we hold that Forster & Garbus's February 2 notice to Cortez did not violate Section 1692e because it extended a settlement offer that, if accepted through payment of the specified amount(s) by the specified date(s), would have cleared Cortez's account. The district court found it "debatable" that the notice "'clearly state[d] that [the defendant would] accept payment of the amount set forth in full satisfaction of the debt if payment is made by a specific date'" because the notice "[did] not state explicitly that the debt will be discharged *fully* upon receipt of payment." *Cortez*, 382 F. Supp. 3d at 262 (alterations and emphasis in original) (quoting *Avila*, 817 F.3d at 77). However, the notice extended three "settlement choice[s]," each affording a "substantial discount off the current balance due," Joint App'x at 19, unmistakably communicating that acceptance of one of the options would extinguish Cortez's debt. We therefore conclude that, even when viewed from the perspective of the least sophisticated consumer, the February 2 notice could only reasonably be read one way: as extending an offer to clear the outstanding debt upon payment of the specified amount(s) by the specified date(s). Since this sole reasonable interpretation was accurate, the notice did not violate the FDCPA.

CONCLUSION

For these reasons, we REVERSE and REMAND with directions to enter judgment p.157 in favor of Defendant Forster & Garbus, LLP.

[1] "This objective standard is designed to protect all consumers, 'the gullible as well as the shrewd,' while at the same time protecting debt collectors from liability for 'bizarre or idiosyncratic interpretations of collection notices.'" *Maguire v. Citicorp Retail Servs., Inc.,* 147 F.3d 232, 236 (2d Cir. 1998) (quoting *Clomon,* 988 F.2d at 1318, 1320); *see also Clomon,* 988 F.2d at 1319 ("[C]ourts have consistently applied the least-sophisticated-consumer standard in a manner that protects debt collectors against liability for unreasonable misinterpretations of collection notices.").

973 F.3d 154 (2020)

William J. WAGNER, Plaintiff-Appellant,
v.
CHIARI & ILECKI, LLP, Defendant-Appellee.

Docket No. 19-758 August Term, 2019.

United States Court of Appeals, Second Circuit.

Argued: February 5, 2020.
Decided: September 4, 2020.

Wagner v. Chiari & Ilecki, LLP, 973 F. 3d 154 (2nd Cir. 2020)

Appeal from the grant of summary judgment of the United States District Court for the Western District of New York (Frank P. Geraci, *C.J.*) to Defendant-Appellee Chiari & Ilecki, LLP ("C&I"). Plaintiff-Appellant William J. Wagner alleges that C&I violated various provisions of the Fair Debt Collection Practices Act, 15 U.S.C. § 1692, *et seq.,* by sending him a debt collection notice, information subpoena, subpoena duces tecum, and restraining notices in connection with C&I's efforts to collect on a state court judgment for an unpaid debt, though Wagner was not the debtor. We conclude that the district court erred in granting summary judgment to C&I as to the bona fide error defense under Section 1692k(c), vacate the order and judgment, and remand for further proceedings. We otherwise affirm the judgment of the district court.

Affirmed in part, vacated in part, and remanded.

BRIAN LEWIS BROMBERG, New York, NY, for Plaintiff-Appellant William J. Wagner.

KENNETH R. HILLER, Amherst, NY, for Plaintiff-Appellant William J. Wagner.

KATHERINE GRACE HOWARD, Connors LLP (Terrence M. Connors, on the brief), Buffalo, NY, for Defendant-Appellee Chiari & Ilecki, LLP.

Before: POOLER, LYNCH, and PARK, Circuit Judges.

p.156 POOLER, Circuit Judge.

Plaintiff-Appellant William J. Wagner alleges that Defendant-Appellee Chiari & Ilecki, LLP ("C&I") violated the Fair Debt Collection Practices Act ("FDCPA"), 15 U.S.C. § 1692, *et seq.,* by erroneously sending multiple debt collection communications to him, rather than to the actual debtor, William J. Wagner, Jr. ("Debtor"). p.157 The United States District Court for the Western District of New York (Frank P. Geraci, *C.J.*) granted C&I's motion for summary judgment. On appeal, Wagner argues that C&I committed violations of various provisions of the FDCPA that were not protected by the statutory exception from liability for bona fide errors, 15 U.S.C. § 1692k(c), by sending him a debt collection notice, information subpoena, subpoena duces tecum, and restraining notices in order to collect on a judgment against the Debtor. We affirm the district court's grant of summary judgment to C&I on Wagner's Section 1692e(5) and 1692f claims and vacate and remand in part on the bona fide error issue for further proceedings consistent with this opinion.

BACKGROUND

Wagner challenges C&I's use of several devices available under New York law to enforce a monetary judgment of the New York courts. We provide an overview of the relevant features of the collection devices at issue before we summarize the factual background and procedural history of the case.

I. Enforcement of Judgments Under New York Law

Article 52 of the New York Civil Practice Law and Rules "governs the enforcement and collection of money judgments in New York State courts." *Cruz v. TD Bank, N.A.*, 711 F.3d 261, 264 (2d Cir. 2013). A "money judgment" is defined as "a judgment, or any part thereof, for a sum of money or directing the payment of a sum of money," N.Y. C.P.L.R. § 105(q), and "may be enforced against any debt, which is past due or which is yet to become due, certainly or upon demand of the judgment debtor." *Id.* § 5201(a). When a creditor successfully obtains a money judgment against a judgment debtor, New York law allows the creditor, through an attorney, to use several statutory devices with force of law to collect on the judgment.

First, "the attorney for the judgment creditor as officer of the court" can issue a "restraining notice," which bars a "judgment debtor" from making "any sale, assignment, transfer or interference with any property in which he or she has an interest ... until the judgment or order is satisfied or vacated." N.Y. C.P.L.R. § 5222(b). While restraining notices can be served on a person other than a judgment debtor, such a restraining notice "is effective only if, at the time of service" (1) "he or she owes a debt to the judgment debtor," (2) the person "is in the possession or custody of property in which he or she knows or has reason to believe the judgment debtor or obligor has an interest," or (3) "the judgment creditor or support collection unit has stated in the notice that a specified debt is owed by the person served to the judgment debtor or obligor or that the judgment debtor or obligor has an interest in specified property in the possession or custody of the person served." *Id.*

Under New York Civil Practice Law and Rules Section 5223, "[a]t any time before a judgment is satisfied ... the judgment creditor may compel disclosure of all matter relevant to the satisfaction of the judgment, by serving upon any person a subpoena." Section 5224 authorizes several types of subpoenas to be served in connection with enforcement of money judgments, including (1) a "subpoena requiring attendance for the taking of a deposition," (2) a "subpoena duces tecum requiring the production of books and papers for examination at a time and place named therein," and (3) an "information subpoena," which requires that the recipient respond to a set of written questions. *Id.* § 5224(a). Each p.158 subpoena must, inter alia, specify the parties to, amount, and date of the judgment, and "state that false swearing or failure to comply with the subpoena is punishable as a contempt of court." *Id.* § 5223.

Information subpoenas have a "limited postjudgment discovery purpose," *N.Y. Cmty. Bank v. Bank of Am., N.A.*, 93 N.Y.S.3d 7, 10, 169 A.D.3d 35 (1st Dep't 2019), and can be served on "an individual or entity other than the judgment debtor... only if the judgment creditor or the judgment creditor's attorney has a reasonable belief that the party receiving the subpoena has in their possession information about the debtor that will assist the creditor in collecting his or her judgment." N.Y. C.P.L.R § 5224(a)(3)(i). The judgment creditor or his or her attorney must certify that "to the best of that person's knowledge, information and belief, formed after an inquiry reasonable under the circumstances, that the individual or entity receiving the [information] subpoena has relevant information about the debtor." *Id.*

While New York law thus "permits [a] creditor a broad range of inquiry through either the judgment debtor or any third person with knowledge of the debtor's property," *Gryphon Domestic VI, LLC v. GBR Info. Servs., Inc.*, 29 A.D.3d 392, 815 N.Y.S.2d 65, 66 (1st Dep't 2006), the discovery pursued must be "relevant to the judgment debtor's income and property." Siegel, Practice Commentaries, McKinney's Consol. Laws of N.Y., Book 7B, CPLR C5223:2.

Further, "[r]efusal or willful neglect of any person to obey" an information subpoena, subpoena duces tecum, or restraining notice issued in connection with the enforcement of the judgment of a New York court is "punishable as a contempt of court." *Id.* § 5251. Lawyers may use these enforcement tools in combination by, for example, adding a restraining notice to a subpoena. *See* Commentary, N.Y. C.P.L.R. § 5222 (McKinney) ("Some lawyers engaged in enforcement work will serve the restraining notice of CPLR 5222 together with a subpoena under CPLR 5224, the former imposing a restraint with the latter pursuing an inquiry into the judgment debtor's assets.").

Thus, a creditor generally can enforce repayment of debts by bringing an action in New York courts against the debtor. Once judgment is entered in their favor, the New York Civil Practice Law and Rules authorizes a creditor's attorney to facilitate collection of the judgment by, inter alia, (1) restraining the movement of the debtor's assets through service of a restraining notice, (2) issuing an information subpoena for written responses to questions, or (3) initiating limited supplementary proceedings by a subpoena duces tecum requiring the production of materials for a debtor's examination at a particular time and place. The creditor's attorney need not seek leave or make a motion for a court to exercise these statutory enforcement tools. Rather, an attorney may exercise these tools directly as an officer of the court, though "[t]he court may at any time, on its own initiative or the motion of any interested person, and upon such notice as it may require, make an order denying, limiting, conditioning, regulating, extending or modifying the use of any enforcement procedure." N.Y. C.P.L.R. § 5240.

II. Factual Background

In February 2005, Debtor submitted an application to M.J. Peterson LLC, a real estate company, to rent an apartment on Englewood Avenue in Buffalo, New York. The rental application stated that the applicant's name was "William J. Wagner, Jr.," and listed a Social Security number for the applicant ending in the digits "06." App'x at 163. The application stated the p.159 Debtor had lived with his parents at his then-current address on 356 Hartford Road in Amherst, New York, since 1960, and listed an emergency contact living at 1571 Eggert Road in Amherst, New York.

M.J. Peterson and the Debtor executed a lease agreement. Beginning on September 1, 2005, however, the Debtor failed to pay rent. In response, M.J. Peterson hired Goldstein, Bulan & Chiari LLP—a predecessor of C&I—to collect the unpaid rent. C&I submitted a "skip-trace" to the U.S. Postal Service Office in Kenmore, New York, requesting that the Post Office provide the new address for the Debtor. The skip-trace informed C&I that the Debtor's new address was 378 Windermere Boulevard, Amherst, New York.

C&I sued the Debtor for unpaid rent on behalf of M.J. Peterson in the City Court of the City of Buffalo, and on May 10, 2006, the court entered a default judgment of $1,437.15 against the Debtor. C&I listed the Debtor's address as 378 Windermere throughout the litigation, including for service of process, issuance of a summons, and in a collection letter and information subpoena following the default judgment. The Debtor did not comply with the information subpoena, and on August 8, 2007, the Buffalo City Court issued an order to show cause why it should not punish the Debtor with contempt. When the process server attempted to serve the show cause order at 378 Windermere, however, a resident explained that the Debtor no longer lived there.

C&I attempted unsuccessfully to locate the Debtor and communicate with him at various addresses for the next several years. C&I ran several credit reports, each of which returned three addresses associated with the Debtor: 356 Hartford Road, Buffalo, New York, which the Debtor previously listed as his parents' address in his rental application; 1571 Eggert Road, Buffalo, New York, which the Debtor previously listed as the address of his emergency contact in his rental application; and 378 Windermere Boulevard in Amherst, New York. Service at 378 Windermere already had been unsuccessful, and the U.S. Postal Service informed C&I that the Debtor did not receive mail at 356 Hartford Road. In April 2011, C&I attempted service of an information subpoena and restraining notice at 1571 Eggert, but these were returned as undeliverable. C&I also sent a collection letter, information subpoena, and restraining notice by certified mail to a William J. Wagner, Jr. at another address, 102 Reiman Street in Buffalo, New York, but they were returned as unclaimed. In June 2011, C&I sent a subpoena duces tecum with a restraining notice for service at this address. When the process server attempted service, however, the occupant explained that the William J. Wagner, Jr. who had lived there left in May 2010.

In February 2015, C&I attorney Melissa Overbeck took over the case. She began by reviewing C&I's file for the case.[1] Overbeck also ran a credit report and an employment search for the Debtor, as well as searches on LexisNexis, a public records database, and Real-Info, a real-estate information database, inter alia.[2]

Overbeck's Real-Info search returned a result for a property located at the address 5419 Roberts Road, Hamburg, New York. p.160 The report stated that William and Julie Wagner owned the Roberts Road property. C&I did not retain the results of this Real-Info search, however, and Overbeck testified that she could not recall if the name associated with the Roberts Road address in the Real-Info report used the suffix 'Jr.' Nevertheless, C&I recorded its debt collection activity on an events log, which includes the entry: "Real-Info: Dbtr owns 5419 Roberts Rd. w/wife." App'x at 511. After Wagner initiated this lawsuit, C&I ran a new Real-Info search. This report listed "William Wagner" as the owner of 5419 Roberts Road,

App'x at 303. Based on this Real-Info report, C&I does not dispute that the original Real-Info report referred to the owner of 5419 Roberts Road as 'William Wagner,' not 'William J. Wagner, Jr.'

Overbeck also did not retain the record of the results of the LexisNexis search. The events log states of this LexisNexis search, "Lx-nothing current," App'x at 511, and Overbeck testified that this meant the LexisNexis search provided no current information for the Debtor. C&I ran another LexisNexis search for the Debtor's name on December 15, 2015, after Wagner filed his complaint. The results of this Lexis-Nexis search included seven name variations for the Debtor, including "William J. Wagner," App'x at 294, and nine addresses associated with the Debtor's name, including 5419 Roberts Road, as well as the Eggert Road, Hartford Road, Windermere Boulevard, and Reiman Street addresses. This report identified four household members associated with 5419 Roberts Road: "Wagner, Andrew R," "Wagner, Julia Leona," "Wagner, William G," and "Wagner, William J." App'x at 295. Overbeck's declaration explains that the LexisNexis report indicated that 5419 Roberts Road "was one of the top possible addresses" for the Debtor. App'x at 426.

Citing the December 2015 LexisNexis report and Overbeck's declaration, C&I argued before the district court that the LexisNexis report supported 5419 Roberts Road as a potential address for the Debtor. *See* App'x at 375 (Def.'s Rule 56.1 Statement ¶ 4). Overbeck testified that she concluded that the Debtor lived at 5419 Roberts Road because she "saw that William J. Wagner, Junior had an address listed of 5419 Roberts Road" on LexisNexis and "to verify that, [she] looked on the Real Info website and confirmed that William J. Wagner, Junior did own 5419 Roberts Road with his wife, the wife being listed as a spouse on the Lexis report." App'x at 322. Overbeck's declaration explains further that she "was confident that the debtor was currently residing at 5419 Roberts Road," App'x at 426, because of the mutually corroborating reports and because C&I already had ruled out several of the potential addresses contained in the reports.

Plaintiff-Appellant William J. Wagner, not the Debtor, owned the home at 5419 Roberts Road. Wagner was born in 1950, and the last two numbers of his Social Security number are "18." He has resided at 5419 Roberts Road in Hamburg, New York, since he purchased the property with his wife, Julia Wagner, in 1984. On April 23, 2015, Wagner and Julia Wagner transferred title to 5419 Roberts Road to Wagner. Neither Wagner, his sons Andrew R. Wagner and William G. Wagner, nor anyone else in their family uses the suffix 'Jr.' Though Wagner and the Debtor have almost identical names, they are not members of the same family, have never lived at the same address, and do not know each other.

On February 9, 2015, C&I sent a debt collection notice pursuant to New York Civil Practice Law and Rules § 5222 to p.161 5419 Roberts Road.[3] The notice's cover letter was addressed to "William J. Wagner Jr.," stated that it pertained to the "Claim of M.J. Peterson, LLC," and was written under the letterhead "Chiari & Ilecki, LLP Attorneys and Counselors at Law." App'x at 550. The letter stated,

> Please find the enclosed Notice pursuant to CPLR 5222. This communication is from a debt collector. The debt collector is attempting to collect a debt, and any information obtained will be used for the purpose.

> The current Judgment balance as of February 9, 2015 is $2,570.17. Note—because of interest or other charges that may vary from day to day, the amount due on the day you pay may be greater. If you pay the amount shown above, an adjustment may be necessary after we receive the payment, in which event we will inform you.

App'x at 550. Wagner knew that he had not conducted business with M.J. Peterson and understood that C&I was not attempting to collect a debt from him. Wagner called C&I on February 12, 2015—the same day he received the collection notice —and spoke with Karen Sandford, a legal assistant. Wagner informed Sandford that though he lived at 5419 Roberts Road, he was not the debtor, and he explained that his name did not use the suffix 'Jr.' and that the last two digits of his Social Security number were "16."[4] Sandford told Wagner that she would inform an attorney. That same day, Sandford e-mailed Overbeck, stating, "A William Wagner called office who lives at the Roberts Rd address, claims not him. Gave me last 2 numbers of his SS# and didn't match with what we have." App'x at 514.

On February 11, 2015, C&I sent an information subpoena and restraining notice by certified mail addressed to "William J. Wagner, Jr." to Wagner's home. On February 15 and March 19, 2015, Wagner received notifications from the U.S. Postal Service that it was holding certified mail sent to "William J. Wagner, Jr." and "W. Wagner Jr.," respectively, at his address. App'x at 378-79, 857-58. Wagner understood that these communications were sent by C&I and intended for the Debtor and did not retrieve the letter from the post office.

Wagner called C&I on March 19, 2015, and spoke to Kristian Brown, a legal assistant. Wagner explained to Brown that he was not the Debtor, and he was "very upset" that he had continued to receive letters from C&I. App'x at 511. Wagner informed Brown that he was born in 1950, and Brown informed Wagner that an attorney at C&I had been e-mailed about Wagner's communications with C&I. Brown also stated that Wagner could send them a copy of his driver's license or Social Security number "if he'd like." App'x at 511. Though Wagner believed that C&I's initial communications were sent to him erroneously, based on his conversation with Brown and C&I's continued communications after the debt collection notice, he believed that C&I was "harassing" him, and attempting to collect a debt from him that he did not owe. App'x at 30. C&I contends that it never intended to collect a p.162 debt from Wagner, however, only from the Debtor.

The information subpoena was returned unclaimed on May 11, 2015. Shortly thereafter, C&I sent a subpoena duces tecum to a process server for service at 5419 Roberts Road. The subpoena duces tecum was addressed to "William J. Wagner, Jr.," and informed the recipient that the amount due had grown to $2,603.83. App'x at 551. The subpoena ordered the Debtor to testify at a debtor's examination in Buffalo on July 7, 2015, and to produce written materials relevant to the debt. The subpoena also included a restraining notice, stating that "pursuant to subdivision (b) of 5222 of the Civil Practice Law and Rules, ... you are hereby forbidden to make or suffer any sale, assignment or transfer of, or any interference with, any such property or pay over or otherwise dispose of any such debt, except as therein provided." App'x at 551. The subpoena warned that "disobedience of this restraining notice or ... failure to comply with this subpoena may subject you to fine and imprisonment for contempt of court." App'x at 552. The letter conveying the subpoena duces tecum to the process server stated that the person to be served (the Debtor) was born in 1958, and explained that the process server should "be sure to serve the correct William J. Wagner" because C&I "believe[d] there is a William J. Wagner, Sr. and William J. Wagner, Jr. living at the same address." App'x at 501.

On June 5, 2015, before service of the subpoena duces tecum, Overbeck ran a search for the Debtor on LexisNexis. Overbeck's notes in the events log state that the LexisNexis search indicated that it "looks like WW, Sr. and WW, Jr. live at the same address." App'x at 519. The events log noted that Overbeck had advised the process server to "be sure to serve [the] correct dbtr." App'x at 519.

On June 17, 2015, the process server served the subpoena duces tecum on Wagner at Wagner's home on Roberts Road. The process server's affidavit of personal service stated that the process server "knew the person [served] to be the person described as" the defendant, William J. Wagner, Jr. App'x at 503. Nevertheless, the affidavit also stated that "Defendant stated he was William Wagner, not the one we wanted. I asked him how old he was, he is 65 years old. He could have been what the dob listed: 1958." App'x at 503.

Wagner averred that he believed that the subpoena required his attendance at the debtor's examination. called C&I the same day and informed Sandford that he was served papers intended for the Debtor. Wagner reiterated that he was not the Debtor, explaining that no person using the suffix 'Jr.' lived at his address, and no one in his family used the suffix either. Sandford explained to Wagner that, based on a previous conversation with the legal assistant, Kristian Brown, Wagner was to send C&I his driver's license, but C&I never received it.

The events log states that on June 29, 2015, Overbeck pulled the physical case file and confirmed the Debtor's Social Security number. The events log further recounts that Overbeck also reviewed a credit report, LexisNexis search, and DMV records, and "[c]onfirmed there is a William Wagner" with a Social Security number ending in the numbers '18,' born in 1950, that lived at Roberts Road, and that this Wagner was not the debtor. App'x at 512. Overbeck testified that these notations did not mean that the Debtor did not reside at 5419 Roberts Road; rather, she testified, "all that tells me is that there was a William Wagner living at the Roberts Road address with that date of birth and social security number. I had no idea if our debtor was residing there as well." p.163 App'x at 334. She also testified that the LexisNexis and Real-Info reports told her "that our debtor with the social security number that I looked up is linked to 5419 Roberts Road." App'x at 776.

C&I has no written policies concerning debt collection activity where (1) employees of C&I believe that a debtor may live at a particular residence, but are not certain; (2) C&I has information about the location of a person with a name similar to a debtor's; or (3) a non-debtor with a name similar to a debtor informs C&I that they are not the debtor C&I sought to contact. C&I attorney William Ilecki averred that when "more than one potential address for the debtor is identified," C&I "compares reports and the information in [C&I's] file and utilizes experience, common sense, and reasoned judgment to attempt to determine which address is most likely the correct one." App'x at 417. Ilecki's declaration explains that C&I does "not proceed until [C&I's attorneys] feel confident that [they] have the right address for the debtor. In the event that an individual calls [C&I] claiming that (1) the firm has directed collection efforts towards his residence, (2) he has a name similar to that of the debtor, and (3) the debtor does not reside with him, ... [t]he legal assistant who takes the call requests that the alleged non-debtor provide verifiable proof of his identity (*e.g.*, date of birth or Social Security number) and may request the individual's driver's license and Social Security card in order to confirm that he is not the debtor." App'x at 417-18. A C&I attorney then "checks the events log for developments in the case before undertaking any additional collection efforts. If the attorney concludes that the caller has provided verifiable proof that he is not the debtor and that the debtor does not reside at his address, [C&I] immediately stops collection efforts directed to the debtor at that address." App'x at 418.

In the event that the "caller refuses to provide verifiable proof of his identity, the attorney performs additional skip tracing, including carefully reviewing the information contained in [C&I's] file and also running additional searches (such as on Lexis or Westlaw), to confirm the debtor's address." App'x at 418-19. If C&I continues to believe that "the debtor resides at the address in question, [C&I] may continue to undertake collection efforts against the debtor at that address. In that case, [C&I] takes steps to ensure that communications are directed at only the debtor and not anyone else at that address." App'x at 419.

Wagner contends that C&I did not follow these unwritten policies in his case, to the extent that C&I had unwritten policies at all. He testified that C&I's debt collection efforts caused him sleeplessness, nervousness, an upset stomach, and hypertension. Wagner explained, "I've been a person who has always paid any bills that I've owed. And to be basically accused of being a debtor and have to produce my financial records for people I don't even know, yes, that affects me greatly." App'x at 97.

On June 29, 2015, Overbeck informed Wagner's attorney that C&I would agree to a "general adjournment" of the subpoena duces tecum "pending the resolution of any alleged identity issues." App'x at 505.

III. Procedural Background

On July 15, 2015, Wagner brought suit in the United States District Court for the Western District of New York, claiming that C&I's debt collection communications violated various provisions of the FDCPA, including 15 U.S.C. §§ 1692d, 1692e, 1692e(2), 1692e(5), 1692e(10), 1692f, and p.164 1692f(1).[5] Following discovery, Wagner moved for summary judgment on his claims under all provisions other than 15 U.S.C. § 1692f(1), and C&I cross-moved for summary judgment on all of Wagner's claims.

The district court granted C&I's motion. It held that C&I had not violated 15 U.S.C. §§ 1692e(5) or 1692f(1), reasoning that C&I had legal authority to pursue the collection of the debt in the precise amount owed, but was alleged merely to have attempted to collect the debt from the wrong person. The court further held that C&I's conduct was not "unfair or unconscionable" for purposes of 15 U.S.C. § 1692f, reasoning that Wagner had not actually attended the debtor's examination, and C&I adjourned the debtor's examination upon Wagner's attorney's request.

The district court held that C&I had violated 15 U.S.C. §§ 1692e, 1692e(2)(A), and 1692e(10), by serving Wagner with the subpoena duces tecum after Wagner had twice informed them that he was not the Debtor. It determined that the restraining notice was not actionable on its own, however, reasoning that under the least sophisticated consumer standard applicable in actions under the FDCPA, a non-debtor would not have been deceived by the first debt collection communication sent to him or her in error. Finally, concluding that the FDCPA's bona fide error defense, 15 U.S.C. § 1692k(c), applied to shield C&I from liability for its violations of 15 U.S.C. §§ 1692e, 1692e(2)(A), and 1692e(10), the district court granted C&I's motion and entered judgment for C&I.[6] This appeal followed.

DISCUSSION

"We review de novo the award of summary judgment, construing the evidence in the light most favorable to the nonmoving party and drawing all reasonable inferences and resolving all ambiguities in its favor." *Jaffer v. Hirji,* 887 F.3d 111, 114 (2d Cir. 2018) (internal quotation marks and alterations omitted). Summary judgment is appropriate if "there is no genuine dispute as to any material fact and the movant is entitled to judgment as a matter of law." Fed. R. Civ. P. 56(a). "Material facts are those which might affect the outcome of the suit under the governing law, and a dispute is genuine if the evidence is such that a reasonable jury could return a verdict for the nonmoving party." *Coppola v. Bear Stearns & Co.,* 499 F.3d 144, 148 (2d Cir. 2007) (internal quotation marks omitted).

I. The Fair Debt Collection Practices Act

The statutory purposes of the FDCPA are to "eliminate abusive debt collection p.165 practices by debt collectors, to insure that those debt collectors who refrain from using abusive debt collection practices are not competitively disadvantaged, and to promote consistent State action to protect consumers against debt collection abuses." 15 U.S.C. § 1692(e). "The legislative history of the passage of the FDCPA explains that the need for the FDCPA arose" because of a number of different "collection abuses," such as the use of "'obscene or profane language, threats of violence, telephone calls at unreasonable hours, [and] misrepresentation of a consumer's legal rights.'" *Kropelnicki v. Siegel,* 290 F.3d 118, 127 (2d Cir. 2002) (quoting S. Rep. No. 95-382, at 2 (1977), *reprinted in* 1977 U.S.C.C.A.N. 1695, 1696). The legislative history of the FDCPA is clear that the statute also was intended to "eliminate the recurring problem of debt collectors dunning the wrong person." S. Rep. No. 95-382, at 4, reprinted in 1977 U.S.C.C.A.N. at 1699. The report of the House of Representatives explained:

> This bill also protects people who do not owe money at all. In the collector's zeal, collection efforts are often aimed at the wrong person either because of mistaken identity or mistaken facts. This bill will make collectors behave responsibly towards people with whom they deal.... Certainly a person who has a common name and is being hounded by a debt collector because of the debts of another person deserves the protection this legislation will offer. In far too many cases debt collectors do not even bother to double check common names before beginning collection efforts.

H.R. Rep. 95-131 at 8 (1977).

Two principles guide our inquiry into whether a communication from a debt collector to a consumer violates the FDCPA. First, "the FDCPA must be construed liberally to effectuate its stated purpose." *Taylor v. Fin. Recovery Servs., Inc.,* 886 F.3d 212, 214 (2d Cir. 2018); *see also* 15 U.S.C. § 1692(e). Second, "[i]n evaluating potential violations of the FDCPA, the court must use an objective standard based on whether the least sophisticated consumer would be deceived by the collection practice," looking to "the impression likely to be left upon the unsophisticated consumer." *Maguire v. Citicorp Retail Servs., Inc.,* 147 F.3d 232, 236 (2d Cir. 1998) (internal quotation marks and alterations omitted).

"[W]e review claims of FDCPA violations under the so-called least-sophisticated-consumer standard in order to: (1) ensure the protection of all consumers, even the naive and the trusting, against deceptive debt collection practices, and (2) protect debt collectors against liability for bizarre or idiosyncratic interpretations of collection notices." *Kropelnicki,* 290 F.3d at 127 (internal quotation marks and alterations omitted). "Pursuant to this standard, a collection notice can be misleading if it is open to more than one reasonable interpretation, at least one of which is inaccurate." *Taylor,* 886 F.3d at 214 (internal quotation marks omitted). "[E]ven if a debt collector accurately conveys the required information, a consumer may state a claim if she successfully alleges that the least sophisticated consumer would inaccurately interpret the message." *Carlin v. Davidson Fink LLP,* 852 F.3d 207, 216 (2d Cir. 2017). We have explained that "in crafting a norm that protects the naive and the credulous the courts have carefully preserved the concept of reasonableness, and some courts have held that even the least sophisticated consumer can be presumed to possess a rudimentary amount of information about the world and a willingness to read a collection notice with some care." *Altman v. J.C. Christensen & Assocs., Inc.,* 786 F.3d 191, 193-94 (2d Cir. p.166 2015) (internal quotation marks and alterations omitted).

II. Whether C&I's Conduct Violated Sections 1692e and 1692f

A single violation of Section 1692e or 1692f is sufficient to hold a debt collector liable under the FDCPA. *See* 15 U.S.C. § 1692k (authorizing the grant of actual and statutory damages against "any debt collector who fails to comply with *any* provision of this subchapter" (emphasis added)). While the same conduct can violate Section 1692e or 1692f, "[e]ach section primarily targets a different type of misconduct, even as both sections share the goal of protecting consumers from abuse by debt collectors. Section 1692e mainly targets practices that take advantage of a debtor's naivete or lack of legal acumen. Section 1692f, meanwhile, is aimed at practices that give the debt collector an unfair advantage over the debtor or are inherently abusive." *Arias v. Gutman, Mintz, Baker & Sonnenfeldt LLP,* 875 F.3d 128, 135-36 (2d Cir. 2017).

The district court held that C&I violated only 15 U.S.C. §§ 1692e, 1692e(2)(A), and 1692e(10), not 1692e(5), 1692f, or 1692f(1). Wagner argues that this was error.[7]

We first consider whether the district court correctly concluded that C&I was entitled to summary judgment on Wagner's Section 1692e(5) claim. Section 1692e of the FDCPA makes it unlawful for a debt collector to "use any false, deceptive, or misleading representation or means in connection with the collection of any debt." 15 U.S.C. § 1692e. It also provides a "non-exhaustive" list of "particular practices that debt collectors are forbidden to employ," *Kropelnicki,* 290 F.3d at 127, including making "threat[s] to take any action that cannot legally be taken or that is not intended to be taken," § 1692e(5).

On appeal, Wagner argues that the district court erred in granting summary judgment to C&I on his Section 1692e(5) claim, because (1) under N.Y. C.P.L.R. § 5222(b), C&I lacked the right to serve a restraining notice on Wagner without first having "reason to believe" that Wagner was the Debtor; and (2) New York case law holding that a subpoena duces tecum cannot "be used as a fishing expedition for the purpose of discovery or to ascertain the existence of evidence," *Decrosta v. State Police Laboratory,* 182 A.D.2d 930, 581 N.Y.S.2d 938, 939 (3d Dep't 1992), prohibited C&I from serving Wagner with the subpoena duces tecum.

Neither of Wagner's arguments is persuasive. As to Wagner's first argument, New York law provides that a restraining notice served on a non-debtor "is effective only if, at the time of service, he or she owes a debt to the judgment debtor or obligor or he or she is in the possession or custody of property in which he or she knows or has reason to believe the judgment debtor or obligor has an interest." N.Y. C.P.L.R. § 5222(b). Relying on this language, Wagner argues that "before a lawyer may serve a judgment debtor or garnishee, the lawyer must 'know[ ] or have reason to believe' that the person served is the judgment debtor or owes money to the judgment debtor." Appellant's Br. at 39-40. But Wagner misconstrues Section 5222(b), which plainly refers p.167 to the debtor's "reason to believe," not that of a debt collector or its lawyer.[8] Wagner's second argument fails because the case on which he relies, *Decrosta v. State Police Laboratory,* which considered a subpoena duces tecum sought under entirely different statutory provisions by a criminal defendant to procure laboratory records to defend against pending criminal charges, is inapposite. *See* 581 N.Y.S.2d at 939.

We thus conclude that the district court did not err in granting summary judgment to C&I on Wagner's Section 1692e(5) claim. In sending the debt collection communications, C&I sought to collect on a valid judgment of the City Court of the City of Buffalo entered against the Debtor. The record at least establishes that C&I did not intend to send the debt collection communications to a non-debtor: in fact, Overbeck explicitly instructed the process server to serve the subpoena duces tecum on Wagner, Jr., not Wagner, Sr. Stripped of Wagner's non-meritorious theories as to why the debt collection communications were unlawful, it is only established here that C&I unintentionally sent otherwise valid and lawful debt collection communications to a non-debtor. *Cf. Currier v. First Resolution Inv. Corp.,* 762 F.3d 529, 535 (6th Cir. 2014) (allegation that debt collector filed and maintained a lien that was invalid under state law was sufficient to state a claim under Section 1692e(5)). This is insufficient to constitute a violation of Section 1692e(5), and we therefore affirm the grant of summary judgment to C&I on this claim.

We also agree with the district court that C&I did not violate Section 1692f.[9] Under the FDCPA, a debt collector "may not use unfair or unconscionable means to collect or attempt to collect any debt." 15 U.S.C. § 1692f; *see also Todd v. Collecto, Inc.,* 731 F.3d 734, 739 (7th Cir. 2013) (collecting cases). "Although the FDCPA leaves the term 'unfair or unconscionable means' undefined, we have held that the term refers to practices that are 'shockingly unjust or unfair, or affronting the sense of justice, decency, or reasonableness.'" *Arias*, 875 F.3d at 135 (quoting *Gallego v. Northland Grp. Inc.*, 814 F.3d 123, 128 (2d Cir. 2016)).

Arias held that "a debt collector engages in unfair or unconscionable litigation conduct in violation of section 1692f when ... it in bad faith unduly prolongs legal proceedings or requires a consumer to appear at an unnecessary hearing." *Id.* at 138. Wagner was never forced to attend a debtor's examination or to respond to the information subpoena, however, and C&I ultimately agreed to hold the subpoena duces tecum—which incorporated the restraining notice—in abeyance. While a debt collector's bad faith or abusive exercise of New York's statutory devices to collect on a judgment of a New York court from a non-debtor might constitute an "unfair or unconscionable" means of debt collection, the record does not establish such p.168 conduct here. Accordingly, we agree with the district court that C&I's conduct did not constitute "unfair or unconscionable means" of debt collection for purposes of Section 1692f, and C&I was entitled to summary judgment on this claim.

III. Whether the Bona Fide Error Exception Applies

The FDCPA offers debt collectors an affirmative statutory defense for a violation of the FDCPA resulting from a bona fide error. The statute provides,

> A debt collector may not be held liable in any action brought under this subchapter if the debt collector shows by a preponderance of evidence that the violation was not intentional and resulted from a bona fide error notwithstanding the maintenance of procedures reasonably adapted to avoid any such error.

15 U.S.C. § 1692k(c). Thus, under the statute, a "debt collector asserting the bona fide error defense must show by a preponderance of the evidence that its violation of the Act: (1) was not intentional; (2) was a bona fide error; and (3) occurred despite the maintenance of procedures reasonably adapted to avoid any such error." *Edwards v. Niagara Credit Sols., Inc.*, 584 F.3d 1350, 1352-53 (11th Cir. 2009). While the bona fide error defense does not extend to intentional violations caused by mistakes of law, it does shield from liability unintentional "violations resulting from qualifying factual errors." *Jerman v. Carlisle, McNellie, Rini, Kramer & Ulrich LPA*, 559 U.S. 573, 594, 130 S.Ct. 1605, 176 L.Ed.2d 519 (2010).

On appeal, Wagner argues that the district court erred in granting summary judgment to C&I because a reasonable jury could conclude that C&I failed to establish one or more of the three prongs of the bona fide error defense. We address each prong in turn.

The district court concluded that no reasonable jury could find that the preponderance of the evidence established that C&I intentionally sent the subpoena duces tecum to a non-debtor, citing Overbeck's instruction to the process server to serve Wagner Jr., not Wagner Sr., and Overbeck's search on LexisNexis shortly before the subpoena was served to confirm the Debtor's connection to 5419 Roberts Road. We agree.

We nevertheless hold that C&I was not entitled to summary judgment on Wagner's claims because a reasonable jury could find that C&I's error was not bona fide and that C&I did not maintain procedures reasonably adapted to avoid its error.

Wagner twice informed C&I that he was not the Debtor before he was served with the subpoena duces tecum and restraining notice. C&I knew that the digits of Wagner's Social Security number that Wagner provided did not match that of the Debtor. Overbeck also knew from reviewing the events log that the Debtor's birthyear was 1958, and that Wagner told C&I that his birthyear was 1950. The December 2015 LexisNexis report—which C&I has proffered as a replacement for the search Overbeck ran before contacting Wagner—provided corroboration for Wagner's calls, listing a "Wagner, William J.," associated with 5419 Roberts Road and born in 1950, as a potential relative of the Debtor. This birthyear would have made Wagner too old to be the Debtor, and too young to be his father. And, the LexisNexis report identified a "Wagner, William G." associated with 5419 Roberts Road, who was born in 1977. In short, the LexisNexis report could be understood to state that two related William Wagners lived at 5419 Roberts Road, but neither was the Debtor.

C&I relies on the Real-Info and Lexis-Nexis reports to justify its pursuit of the p.169 Debtor at Wagner's address. Yet, C&I concedes that both reports identified 'William J. Wagner,' not 'William J. Wagner, Jr.' as the owner or resident of 5419 Roberts Road. While the former name could be an abbreviated form of the latter, the December 2015 LexisNexis report lists the dates for which Wagner was associated with the 5419 Roberts Road address as May 1985 to April 2015. This is inconsistent with the Debtor's residence in a rental in Buffalo in 2005; the same LexisNexis report, which stated that the Debtor lived at 356 Hartford Road—the Debtor's parents' address—from October 1986 to October 2015; and the Debtor's rental application, which stated that he had lived with his parents in Amherst, New York since 1960. In short, C&I was in possession of more than enough evidence that Plaintiff was neither the Debtor nor the Debtor's father to permit a reasonable jury to conclude that C&I's mistake, even if honestly made, was not made in good faith.

A reasonable jury could also conclude that C&I did not maintain procedures reasonably adapted to avoid its error. C&I concedes that it had no written policies for situations in which employees of C&I believe that a debtor may live at a particular residence, but are not certain; C&I has information about the location of a person with a name similar to a debtor's; or a non-debtor with a name similar to a debtor informs C&I that they are not the debtor C&I sought to contact. Though C&I maintains that it has unwritten policies addressing these circumstances, Ilecki averred that when "more than one potential address for the debtor is identified," C&I "compares reports and the information in [C&I's] file and utilizes experience, common sense, and reasoned judgment to attempt to determine which address is most likely the correct one," and C&I does "not proceed until [C&I's attorneys] feel confident that [they] have the right address for the debtor." App'x at 417. In light of the evidence available to C&I that Wagner was not the Debtor, a reasonable jury could conclude that a "feel[ing]" of "confidence" based on "experience, common sense, and reasoned judgment," App'x at 417, does not constitute a specific policy reasonably adapted to avoid the error at issue—"the kind of internal controls a debt collector might adopt to ensure its employees do not" dun the wrong person, *Jerman,* 559 U.S. at 587, 130 S.Ct. 1605. Further, in light of C&I's continued debt collection efforts despite possessing evidence that could reasonably be understood to refute a connection between Wagner and the Debtor, and Wagner's repeated calls expressing that he was not the Debtor, a reasonable jury could conclude that C&I either did not have or did not follow what Ilecki claimed were its unwritten policies.

Ilecki identifies several specific policies that C&I contends were sufficient for purposes of the bona fide error defense, including that (1) if a purported non-debtor refuses to provide verifiable identifying information, C&I reviews C&I's file and runs "additional searches (such as on Lexis or Westlaw), to confirm the debtor's address," and (2) if C&I concludes that the debtor nevertheless lives at the purported non-debtor's residence, it "takes steps to ensure that communications are directed at only the debtor and not anyone else at that address." App'x at 418-19. But a reasonable jury could conclude that C&I's "additional searches" were insufficient to avoid their error because C&I merely replicated the LexisNexis search C&I had relied on before Wagner informed C&I of his identity. And, a reasonable jury could conclude that Overbeck's instruction to the process server to "be sure to serve the correct William J. Wagner," App'x at 501, was insufficient, given that C&I had identifying p.170
information for Wagner such as his year of birth that could have allowed the process server to avoid dunning Wagner.

We therefore conclude that a reasonable jury could find that C&I did not make a bona fide error within the meaning of the FDCPA, and accordingly hold that the district court erred in granting summary judgment to C&I.

CONCLUSION

For the foregoing reasons, we affirm in part and vacate in part, and remand the judgment of the district court for further proceedings consistent with this opinion.

[1] On appeal, Wagner disputes that Overbeck reviewed the physical file. Wagner has waived this argument, however, because he did not dispute before the district court that Overbeck reviewed the information in C&I's case file. *See* App'x at 374 at ¶ 2, 853 at ¶ 2.

[2] The February 2015 credit report identified the same three addresses as the previous credit reports—on Hartford Road, Eggert Road, and Windermere Boulevard—and did not identify 5419 Roberts Road as a potential address.

[3] N.Y. C.P.L.R. § 5222(d) mandates that a debt collector, prior to sending a restraining notice to a debtor, send a "Notice to Judgment Debtor or Obligor" that explains that "property belonging to [the Debtor] may have been taken or held in order to satisfy a judgment" entered against them, among other statutorily required items.

[4] Wagner's statement of facts pursuant to Local Rule 56.1 states that the last four numbers of Wagner's social security number are "3918." App'x at 23. The reference to "16" appears to be an error. App'x 26.

[5] Section 1692e prohibits a debt collector from using a "false, deceptive, or misleading representation or means in connection with the collection of any debt," including in relevant part "[t]he false representation of ... the character, amount, or legal status of any debt," "[t]he threat to take any action that cannot legally be taken or that is not intended to be taken," and "[t]he use of any false representation or

deceptive means to collect or attempt to collect any debt or to obtain information concerning a consumer." *Id.* §§ 1692e(2), e(5), e(10). Section 1692f prohibits the use of "unfair or unconscionable means to collect or attempt to collect any debt," including "[t]he collection of any amount ... unless such amount is expressly authorized by the agreement creating the debt or permitted by law," *id.* § 1692f(1).

[6] Wagner's complaint alleged that C&I's conduct violated 15 U.S.C. § 1692d, which prohibits debt collection conduct "the natural consequence of which is to harass, oppress, or abuse any person in connection with the collection of a debt." The district court granted summary judgment to C&I on this claim after concluding that Wagner abandoned it. Wagner does not challenge this conclusion on appeal.

[7] On appeal, Wagner contends that the district court erred in holding that the February 9, 2015 debt collection notice was not actionable under Section 1692e on the basis that it was the first debt collection communication C&I erroneously directed to Wagner. We need not address this portion of the district court's reasoning, however, because whether the court correctly held that C&I violated Sections 1692e, e(2)(A), and e(10) is not at issue on appeal.

[8] Wagner makes a similar error in challenging the district court's ruling as to the restraining notice, relying on N.Y. C.P.L.R. § 5224(a)(3)(i), under which an information subpoena can be served "only if the judgment creditor or the judgment creditor's attorney has a reasonable belief that the party receiving the subpoena has in their possession information about the debtor that will assist the creditor in collecting his or her judgment." This provision governs information subpoenas, not restraining notices.

[9] Wagner makes no argument as to why the district court's grant of summary judgment to C&I on his Section 1692f(1) claim was error, and thus we do not consider this issue. *See Norton v. Sam's Club,* 145 F.3d 114, 117 (2d Cir. 1998) ("Issues not sufficiently argued in the briefs are considered waived and normally will not be addressed on appeal.").

955 F.3d 299 (2020)

Jean M. PETTAWAY, Individually and on Behalf of All Others Similarly Situated, Plaintiff-Appellant,
v.
NATIONAL RECOVERY SOLUTIONS, LLC, US Asset Management Inc., Defendants-Appellees,
John and Jane Does 1-50, Defendants.[*]

Docket No. 19-1453 August Term, 2019.

United States Court of Appeals, Second Circuit.

Argued: January 17, 2020.
Decided: April 9, 2020.

Pettaway v. Nat. Recovery Solutions, LLC, 955 F. 3d 299 (2nd Cir. 2020)

Appeal from the United States District Court for the Southern District of New York No. 1:19-cv-1328 — George B. Daniels, *Judge.*.

Plaintiff-Appellant Jean M. Pettaway challenges the district court's dismissal pursuant to Federal Rule of Civil Procedure 12(b)(6) of her FDCPA claim. Although we agree with Pettaway that her amended complaint was timely filed, notwithstanding the deficiency notice issued by the court clerk, we nevertheless conclude that when a plaintiff properly amends her complaint and a defendant has filed a motion to dismiss that is still pending, the district court has the option of either denying the pending motion as moot or evaluating the motion in light of the facts alleged in the amended complaint. Here, the district court did the latter and properly dismissed Pettaway's amended complaint on the merits because it fails to state a plausible claim for relief.

AFFIRMED.

Philip D. Stern (Andrew T. Thomasson, Francis R. Greene, on the brief), Stern Thomasson LLP, Springfield, NJ, for Plaintiff-Appellant.

Brian D. Gwitt, Andrea K. DiLuglio (on the brief), Woods Oviatt Gilman LLP, Buffalo, NY, for Defendants-Appellees.

Before: HALL, SULLIVAN, and BIANCO, Circuit Judges.

p.301 PER CURIAM:

Plaintiff-Appellant Jean M. Pettaway appeals from a judgment of the United States District Court for the Southern District of New York (Daniels, *J.*) entered on May 20, 2019 granting Defendants-Appellees' motion to dismiss pursuant to Federal Rule of Civil Procedure 12(b)(6) and denying Plaintiff-Appellant's motion for leave to file an amended complaint. Although we agree with Pettaway that her amended complaint was timely filed, and therefore leave to file an amended complaint was not required, we nevertheless conclude that the district court properly dismissed

Pettaway's amended complaint on the merits because it fails to state a plausible claim for relief.

I.

Pettaway co-signed a student loan, which subsequently fell into default and p.302 was charged-off. Defendant-Appellee US Asset Management Inc. ("US Asset") purchased the debt and placed it with Defendant-Appellee National Recovery Solutions, LLC ("NRS") for collection. NRS thereafter sent a form collection letter (the "Letter") to Pettaway on behalf of US Asset in an attempt to collect the debt; the Letter stated in pertinent part:

> As of the date of this letter, you owe $26,610.58. Because of interest, late charges, and other charges that may vary from day to day, the amount due on the day you pay may be greater. Hence, if you pay the amount shown above, an adjustment may be necessary after we receive your check, in which event we will inform you before depositing the check for collection.

App. at 18, 33 (emphasis in original). The letter also contained a "time sensitive" offer whereby NRS would accept $21,288.46 as a full settlement of the debt if the payment was received by a certain date. *Id.*

Pettaway filed a class action complaint against NRS, US Asset, and John and Jane Doe defendants in February 2019, alleging that they "used false, deceptive, and misleading practices, and other illegal practices, in connection with their attempts to collect an alleged debt from Plaintiff and other similarly situated customers," App. at 6, thereby violating the Fair Debt Collection Practices Act ("FDCPA"), 15 U.S.C. § 1692, *et seq.* Pettaway's initial complaint alleged that the Letter is "materially false, deceptive, and misleading," App. at 11, because it suggests that late charges and other charges will cause a customer's debt to increase even where, as here, such charges are not legally or contractually available.

NRS and US Asset timely filed a motion to dismiss the complaint under Rule 12(b)(6) and moved for attorneys' fees. In response, and pursuant to Federal Rule of Civil Procedure 15(a)(1)(B), Pettaway filed an amended complaint 21 days after Defendants-Appellees served their motion, adding allegations relating to the Letter's settlement offer and an allegation that Defendants-Appellees had not charged, and did not intend to charge, interest on the debt. The day after Pettaway filed her amended complaint, the clerk docketed a notice informing the parties that the amended complaint was deficient, and that Pettaway would be required to re-file. Since the 21-day window following a Rule 12 motion during which a plaintiff may file an amended complaint once as a matter of right was then closed, the notice stated that either the opposing party's consent or the district court's leave would be required to re-file.

Defendants-Appellees did not consent to a re-filing, so Pettaway filed a letter motion requesting leave to re-file the amended complaint. By order dated May 20, 2019, the district court granted Defendants-Appellees' motion to dismiss, denied their request for attorneys' fees and costs, and denied Pettaway's motion for leave to file the amended complaint. This appeal followed.

II.

On appeal, Pettaway first argues that her amended complaint was timely and properly filed on the 21st day following service of Defendants-Appellees' Rule 12 motion. Because the amended complaint followed the district court's Electronic Case Filing Rules & Instructions, she argues, it was served and filed in compliance with the Southern District of New York's local rules and was therefore "filed" within the meaning of Federal Rule of Civil Procedure 5 notwithstanding contrary online p.303 directions.[1] *See* S.D.N.Y. Local Civil Rule 5.2 ("A paper served and filed by electronic means in accordance with such instructions [published on the court's website] is, for purposes of Fed. R. Civ. P. 5, served and filed in compliance with the Local Civil Rules of the Southern [District] of New York."). Pettaway contends that the district court clerk was therefore incorrect to label her amended complaint as deficient and to require either the court's permission or the opposing party's consent to re-file and that the district court erred in concluding that the amended complaint was not correctly filed within the 21-day period.

We agree. Federal Rule of Civil Procedure 5(d)(4) prohibits a clerk from refusing "to file a paper solely because it is not in the form prescribed by these rules or by a local rule or practice." Pursuant to this directive, we have held that an error in a notice of appeal would not cause a party to lose his right to appeal, and the notice would be deemed timely filed notwithstanding the court's rejection of it for non-compliance with its rules on filing. *Contino v. United States,* 535 F.3d 124, 127 (2d Cir. 2008) (also citing Federal Rule of Civil Procedure 83(a)(2) for the proposition that "[a] local rule imposing a requirement of form must not be enforced in a way that causes a party to lose any right because of a nonwillful failure to comply"). Pettaway's amended complaint, filed as a matter of right and seemingly in compliance with the express instructions of the district court, should have been accepted by that court.

Pettaway next contends that because her amended complaint was properly and timely filed, it mooted the pending motion to dismiss. It is true that "an amended pleading ordinarily supersedes the original and renders it of no legal effect." *In re Crysen/Montenay Energy Co.,* 226 F.3d 160, 162 (2d Cir. 2000). This rule does not, however, dictate that a pending motion to dismiss is automatically rendered moot when a complaint is amended. District courts in this Circuit have repeatedly explained that, when faced with an amended complaint, they may either deny a pending motion to dismiss as moot or consider the merits of the motion, analyzing the facts as alleged in the amended pleading. *See, e.g., Conforti v. Sunbelt Rentals, Inc.,* 201 F. Supp. 3d 278, 291 (E.D.N.Y. 2016) ("Where a plaintiff seeks to amend his complaint while a motion to dismiss is pending, a court 'has a variety of ways in which it may deal with the pending motion to dismiss, from denying the motion as moot to considering the merits of the motion in light of the amended complaint.'" (quoting *Hamzik v. Office for People with Developmental Disabilities,* 859 F. Supp. 2d 265, 273-74 (N.D.N.Y. 2012))); *see also id.* (citing cases from the District of Connecticut and the Eastern District of New York for the same proposition). This is a sound approach that promotes judicial economy by obviating the need for multiple rounds of briefing addressing complaints that are legally insufficient. We now adopt this rule and hold that when a plaintiff properly amends her p.304 complaint after a defendant has filed a motion to dismiss that is still pending, the district court has the option of either denying the pending motion as moot or evaluating the motion in light of the facts alleged in the amended complaint.

The district court essentially followed the second approach described above. Although the district court explained that it would "consider Plaintiff's original complaint in evaluating [the] motion to dismiss and will separately assess the validity of Plaintiff's application to amend her complaint," App. at 37, it went on to say that Pettaway's amended complaint did not moot Defendants-Appellees' pending motion to dismiss because the new allegations did not save her claim. In effect, the district court's denial of Pettaway's application to amend her complaint was premised on its view that the amended complaint would not withstand a motion to dismiss. *See Dougherty v. Town of N. Hempstead Bd. of Zoning Appeals*, 282 F.3d 83, 88 (2d Cir. 2002) ("An amendment to a pleading will be futile if a proposed claim could not withstand a motion to dismiss pursuant to Rule 12(b)(6)."). Even though the district court conducted the bulk of its analysis of the motion to dismiss addressing the allegations in the original complaint, it also considered the motion in light of the allegations in the amended complaint. Because we agree that its methodology was satisfactory, we find no error in the district court's analysis.

III.

Pettaway contends that the "Amended Complaint alleged facts proving a cause of action." Appellant Br. at 10. We disagree. On independent review, we hold that the district court properly granted Defendants-Appellees' motion to dismiss. "We review *de novo* a grant of a motion to dismiss pursuant to Rule 12(b)(6), accepting the complaint's factual allegations as true and drawing all reasonable inferences in the plaintiff's favor." *Brown Media Corp. v. K&L Gates, LLP*, 854 F.3d 150, 156-57 (2d Cir. 2017) (internal quotation marks and citation omitted). "To survive a motion to dismiss, a complaint must contain sufficient factual matter, accepted as true, to state a claim to relief that is plausible on its face." *Ashcroft v. Iqbal*, 556 U.S. 662, 678, 129 S.Ct. 1937, 173 L.Ed.2d 868 (2009) (internal quotation marks and citation omitted).

In determining whether a communication violates the FDCPA, courts analyze the communication using a "least sophisticated consumer" standard. *Greco v. Trauner, Cohen & Thomas, L.L.P.*, 412 F.3d 360, 363 (2d Cir. 2005). Under this standard, "a collection notice can be misleading if it is open to more than one reasonable interpretation, at least one of which is inaccurate." *Taylor v. Fin. Recovery Servs.*, 886 F.3d 212, 214 (2d Cir. 2018) (internal quotation marks and citation omitted). The standard, however, will not render debt collectors liable for "bizarre or idiosyncratic interpretations of debt collection letters," *Greco*, 412 F.3d at 363 (internal quotation marks and citation omitted), or "unreasonable misinterpretations of collection notices," *Clomon v. Jackson*, 988 F.2d 1314, 1319 (2d Cir. 1993).

The district court held that Pettaway's original complaint failed to state a claim under the FDCPA because, *inter alia*, the Letter's language "clearly states that interest, late charges, and other charges '*may* vary from day to day,' not that they *will*." App. at 41 (citation omitted). The district court reasoned that the Letter is not inaccurate or misleading to the least sophisticated customer so long as one of these three components may accrue. Pettaway contends that her amended complaint p.305 changed the analysis because, unlike the initial complaint which alleged that only interest could accrue, the amended complaint alleged that neither interest, late charges, nor other charges could be added to her debt. But Pettaway overstates the allegations set out in the amended complaint. While her amended complaint does allege that the addition of late charges and other charges are impossible, it does not allege that interest could not accrue. Rather, the amended complaint simply asserts that Defendants-Appellees did not previously charge interest and did not intend to do so in the future. Even if there is no current intention to charge interest, the mere existence of that future possibility is completely consistent with the word "may" in the Letter's language. Nor do we read the Letter's acknowledgment that interest may accrue as threatening language prohibited by 15 U.S.C. § 1692e(5). The amended complaint therefore does not support the conclusion that the Letter was materially misleading, inaccurate, unfair, or unconscionable—thereby violating the FDCPA—simply by indicating that the balance *may* increase.[2]

Nor do the allegations related to the Letter's settlement language salvage the amended complaint. Pettaway argues that the Letter "falsely, deceptively, and misleadingly leads the least sophisticated consumer to think that if the payment of the reduced amount is not paid by the deadline, there will be no further chance to settle the Debt for less than the full amount." Appellant Br. at 6 (quoting Amend. Compl. ¶ 52). We do not think this is a fair reading of the Letter, even under the least sophisticated consumer standard. The Letter explains the process by which a consumer can negotiate her own settlement online, and that alone seriously undermines Pettaway's claim that a recipient would read the Letter and reasonably think that the proffered settlement terms were the only ones that would ever be available. Pettaway's "[t]hreadbare recitals of the elements of a cause of action, supported by mere conclusory statements" are insufficient to save her claim from dismissal. *Iqbal,* 556 U.S. at 678, 129 S.Ct. 1937.

***

For the foregoing reasons, we AFFIRM the judgment of the district court.

[*] The Clerk of Court is respectfully requested to amend the caption as stated above.

[1] Pettaway's attorneys selected the "All Defendants" radio button when delineating who the amended complaint was against, as it was brought against all defendants. S.D.N.Y.'s instructions read "Do not select 'all plaintiffs' or 'all defendants' unless it is appropriate." Electronic Case Filing Rules & Instructions, United States District Court Southern District of New York (Feb. 1, 2019). However, the clerk of court informed Pettaway's attorneys that the online directions during the filing process direct the filer not to use the "All Defendants" button and to select instead each individual defendant; the clerk further indicated that the use of the "All Defendants" button would result in the filing being deemed "deficient."

[2] In her reply brief, Pettaway also suggested that, even if the Letter's language regarding the possibility of accruing interest is not itself misleading, a plausible claim still exists because of the impossibility of late charges and other charges being

imposed. *See* Reply Br. at 19 (citing *Boucher v. Fin. Sys. of Green Bay,* 880 F.3d 362, 370 (7th Cir. 2018)). We need not address this argument because it was raised on appeal for the first time in Pettaway's reply brief and is therefore waved. *See Conn. Bar Ass'n v. United States,* 620 F.3d 81, 91 n. 13 (2d Cir. 2010) ("Issues raised for the first time in a reply brief are generally deemed waived." (citing *Norton v. Sam's Club,* 145 F.3d 114, 117 (2d Cir. 1998))).

954 F.3d 576 (2020)

Michael BRYAN, on behalf of himself and all others similarly situated, Plaintiff-Appellant,
v.
CREDIT CONTROL, LLC, p.577 **Defendant-Appellee.**[*]

Docket No. 19-244-cv August Term 2019.

United States Court of Appeals, Second Circuit.

Argued: November 20, 2019.
Decided: April 3, 2020.

Bryan v. Credit Control, LLC, 954 F. 3d 576 (2nd Cir. 2020)

Plaintiff-Appellant Michael Bryan, individually and on behalf of a class, appeals from an order of the United States District Court for the Eastern District of New York (Sandra J. Feuerstein, *J.*) granting judgment on the pleadings in favor of Defendant-Appellee Credit Control LLC ("Credit Control") in this action brought under the Fair Debt Collection Practices Act, 15 U.S.C. § 1692 *et seq.* Bryan alleged that Credit Control, in an effort to collect the outstanding debt on Bryan's Kohl's Department Stores, Inc. private label credit card account, sent him a letter that did not list the "creditor to whom the debt is owed," in violation of 15 U.S.C. § 1692g; he also alleged that Credit Control's letter constituted a false or misleading representation, in violation of 15 U.S.C. § 1692e. We conclude that the district court erred in finding that Credit Control disclosed the "name of the creditor to whom the debt is owed" by listing Kohl's, the servicer of the account, as the "client." Because the district court relied on this erroneous finding in further holding that the letter did not constitute a false or misleading representation, we do not reach the question of whether the letter violated Section 1692e. Accordingly, the judgment of the district court is REVERSED as to the Section 1692g claim and VACATED as to the Section 1692e claim. The case is REMANDED to the district court for further proceedings consistent with this Opinion.

TIFFANY N. HARDY (Daniel A. Edelman, on the brief) Edelman, Combs, Latturner & Goodwin, LLC, Chicago, IL, for Appellant.

PATRICK A. WATTS, Watts Law Group, LLC, St. Louis, MO (Donald S. Maurice, Jr., Thomas R. Dominczyk, Maurice Wutscher, LLP, Flemington, NJ, on the brief), for Appellee.

Before: WALKER, LYNCH, and SULLIVAN, Circuit Judges.

p.579 RICHARD J. SULLIVAN, Circuit Judge:

Section 1692g of the Fair Debt Collection Practices Act ("FDCPA"), 15 U.S.C. § 1692 *et seq.*, mandates that a debt collector disclose to a consumer "the creditor to whom the debt is owed," *id.* § 1692g(a)(1). This appeal requires us to consider whether a debt collector violates Section 1692g when, in a collection letter concerning private label credit card debt, it discloses the name of the retailer that services the credit card but not the financial institution that owns the debt.

Plaintiff-Appellant Michael Bryan, individually and on behalf of a class, brought suit alleging that Defendant-Appellee Credit Control, LLC ("Credit Control"), a debt collector, violated Section 1692g when it sent him a collection letter related to his Kohl's Department Stores, Inc. private label credit card debt. The letter listed Kohl's Department Stores, Inc., which services the credit card, as Credit Control's "client," but made no mention of Capital One, which owns the debt. Bryan also alleged that, because the letter failed to mention Capital One, it constituted a false or misleading communication in connection with a debt, in violation of 15 U.S.C. § 1692e. The district court (Sandra J. Feuerstein, *J.*) granted Credit Control's motion for judgment on the pleadings pursuant to Rule 12(c) of the Federal Rules of Civil Procedure.

On appeal, Bryan argues that the district court erred in holding that Credit Control did not violate Section 1692g — and therefore did not violate Section 1692e — because Kohl's was the "creditor to whom the debt is owed." We agree.

BACKGROUND[1]

The Kohl's private label credit card allows consumers to purchase goods at Kohl's online and brick-and-mortar stores. Until 2011, Kohl's issued its private label credit cards in partnership with Chase Bank; since then, it has issued the cards in partnership with Capital One. Various public documents make clear that Capital One, not Kohl's, owns the debt on these cards. Kohl's SEC Form 10-K states that "[t]he proprietary Kohl's credit card accounts are owned by an unrelated third-party, but [Kohl's] share[s] in the net risk-adjusted revenue of the portfolio." App'x 37. The Kohl's Cardmember Agreement ("Cardmember Agreement"), which is posted online, expressly states that Capital One is the "creditor and issuer" of the accounts. *Id.* at 117. The Private Label Credit Card Program Agreement between Kohl's and Capital One ("Program Agreement") further states that Capital One "offer[s] Private Label Credit Cards to qualified customers," p.580 *id.* at 63, "extend[s] credit on newly originated and existing Accounts," *id.* at 68, "own[s] ... all [a]ccounts," *id.* at 69, and has the exclusive right to "effect collection" of amounts owed, *id.* The Cardmember Agreement states that Kohl's services the accounts, and the Program Agreement specifies that Kohl's is responsible for, among other things, processing credit applications, establishing and monitoring accounts, handling collection and recovery efforts, and preparing and mailing billing statements.

After Bryan defaulted on his Kohl's private label credit card account debt, Credit Control, a debt collector as defined by the FDCPA, *see* 15 U.S.C. § 1692a(6), sent Bryan a debt collection letter. *See* App'x 46. The letter listed "Kohl's Department Stores Inc." as "Our Client" and "Chase Bank Usa N.A." as the "Original Credit Grantor." It further listed the "Client Account #" and the "Balance Due," but did not disclose that Capital One owned the debt.

Bryan filed this action on February 8, 2018, alleging that Credit Control violated the FDCPA because that letter did not list Capital One as "the creditor to whom the debt is owed." 15 U.S.C. § 1692g(a)(2). He further alleged that, because Credit Control did not disclose Capital One, the letter was misleading, in violation of 15 U.S.C. § 1692e. Credit Control filed its answer on March 23, 2018, and moved for judgment on the pleadings on July 18, 2018. In response, Bryan sought leave to amend his complaint to add an allegation that Kohl's was not the current creditor, and attached a proposed amended complaint and a number of exhibits, including the Cardmember Agreement and the Program Agreement.

The district court referred the motions to Magistrate Judge Locke, who considered the substance of the amended complaint and recommended judgment on the pleadings in favor of Defendant. Magistrate Judge Locke opined that Kohl's is the "creditor to whom the debt is owed," and the failure to disclose the owner of the debt was not misleading because it would not have materially affected a consumer's decision-making process. He thus recommended that the motion to amend the complaint be denied as futile. The district court considered Bryan's objections, but ultimately adopted the report and recommendation in its entirety. It therefore granted Credit Control's motion for judgment on the pleadings, denied Bryan's motion to amend the complaint, and dismissed the case.

STANDARD OF REVIEW

We review the district court's decision to grant judgment on the pleadings *de novo*. *See Hayden v. Paterson,* 594 F.3d 150, 160 (2d Cir. 2010). We must "accept all factual allegations in the complaint as true and draw all reasonable inferences in plaintiff['s] favor," and affirm the district court's decision only if plaintiff's complaint fails "to state a claim to relief that is plausible on its face." *Id.* (internal quotation marks omitted).

DISCUSSION

Bryan argues that the district court erred in holding that (1) by identifying Kohl's as the "client," Credit Control identified the "name of the creditor to whom the debt is owed," and (2) because the letter identified the "creditor to whom the debt is owed," it made no material misstatement in violation of Section 1692e. Because we conclude that the district court erred in finding that Credit Control identified the "name of the creditor to whom the debt is owed," we do not reach the question of whether there was a material misstatement in violation of Section 1692e.

p.581 I. Section 1692g

The FDCPA requires that a debt collector attempting to collect a debt must, within five days after its initial communication, send the consumer a written notice containing, among other things, "the name of the creditor to whom the debt is owed," unless it provided that information in the initial communication. 15 U.S.C. § 1692g(a)(2). "A debt collector violates the [FDCPA] if it fails to convey the information required by the [FDCPA]." *DeSantis v. Comput. Credit, Inc.,* 269 F.3d 159, 161 (2d Cir. 2001). "Even if a debt collector conveys the required information, the collector nonetheless violates [Section 1692g] if it conveys that information in a confusing or contradictory fashion so as to cloud the required message with uncertainty." *Id.* A collection letter is misleading if the "least sophisticated consumer — one not having the astuteness of a Philadelphia lawyer or even the sophistication of the average, everyday, common consumer," *Taylor v. Fin. Recovery Servs., Inc.,* 886 F.3d 212, 214 (2d Cir. 2018) (internal quotation marks omitted) — is left "uncertain as to the meaning of the message," *DeSantis,* 269 F.3d at 161 (internal quotation marks and citation omitted).

In arguing that Credit Control violated Section 1692g, Bryan insists that "the creditor to whom the debt is owed" is synonymous with the "owner" of the debt, and that Credit Control was therefore required to list Capital One — not Kohl's — as the creditor to whom Bryan's credit card debt was owed. The FDCPA provides that a "creditor" is "any person who offers or extends credit creating a debt or to whom a debt is owed," except if that person "receives an assignment or transfer of a debt in default solely for the purpose of facilitating collection of such debt for another." 15 U.S.C. § 1692a(4). Relying on the Program Agreement, the district court found that Kohl's qualified as a creditor because "Kohl's is the entity offering credit accounts to its customers ... and, in turn, facilitating the incurrence of monetary obligations through transactions by consumers exclusively at its stores." *Bryan v. Credit Control, LLC,* No. 18-CV-0865 (SJF)(SIL), 2018 WL 6520730, at *4 (E.D.N.Y. Dec. 11, 2018), *report and recommendation adopted,* 2019 WL 166100 (E.D.N.Y. Jan. 9, 2019).

But the mere fact that Kohl's participated in the credit card program with Capital One and played an active role in the servicing of accounts does not necessarily convert Kohl's into a creditor, and certainly not into the creditor to whom the debt is owed. Indeed, the Cardmember Agreement clarifies that Capital One is "the creditor and issuer of the Account," and that Kohl's is merely an "agent" responsible for "servicing [the] Account ... on [Capital One's] behalf." App'x 117 ¶ 1. Put simply, the terms of both Kohl's agreement with Capital One and Capital One's agreement with the cardholder make clear that Kohl's was not a creditor under the FDCPA at all. The collection letter appears to reflect as much, since it identified Chase as the "original credit grantor" and merely identified Kohl's as Credit Control's "client" — a term that says nothing about the department store's status as a creditor. By 2017, Capital One had replaced Chase as the "credit grantor," making Capital One, not Chase and certainly not Kohl's, the creditor to whom the debt was owed. Thus, since the collection letter did not identify Capital One at all, it did not comply with Section 1692g. Accordingly, the district court erred when it granted judgment on the pleadings in favor of Credit Control. Because Bryan has plausibly pleaded a cause of action pursuant to Section 1692g, we reverse the judgment of p.582 the district court and remand for further proceedings consistent with this opinion.

II. Section 1692e

In his amended complaint, Bryan also alleged that Credit Control's collection letter constituted a "false, deceptive, or misleading representation ... in connection with the collection of any debt," in violation of 15 U.S.C. § 1692e. As with Section 1692g, "[w]hether a communication is 'false, deceptive, or misleading' under [Section] 1692e 'is determined from the perspective of the objective least sophisticated consumer.'" *Cohen v. Rosicki, Rosicki & Assocs., P.C.,* 897 F.3d 75, 85 (2d Cir. 2018) (quoting *Easterling v. Collecto, Inc.,* 692 F.3d 229, 233 (2d Cir. 2012)). However, "not every technically false representation by a debt collector amounts to a violation of the FDCPA." *Id.* (internal quotation marks omitted). Instead, we have held that, as a natural "corollary" to the least sophisticated consumer test, only material errors violate Section 1692e. *Id.* That is, "a false statement is only actionable under the FDCPA if it has the potential to affect the decision-making process of the least sophisticated [consumer]." *Id.* (internal quotation marks omitted).

Although it is far from clear that Credit Control's failure to identify Capital One constituted a materially misleading statement under Section 1692e — indeed it might be argued that if Credit Control had identified Capital One and not Kohl's, such an action "likely would have *caused* confusion," *id.* at 86 — the fact remains that the district court dismissed Bryan's Section 1692e claim on the grounds that Kohl's was the creditor to whom the debt was owed. Since that finding was incorrect, and since the district court did not address the issue of materiality under Section 1692e, we vacate the district court's judgment and remand to the district court for further proceedings.

CONCLUSION

For the foregoing reasons, the judgment of the district court is REVERSED as to the Section 1692g claim and VACATED as to the Section 1692e claim. The case is REMANDED to the district court for further proceedings consistent with this Opinion.

[*] The Clerk of Court is respectfully requested to amend the caption as stated above.

[1] The following facts are taken from the amended complaint, the documents attached thereto, and SEC public filings, of which we are taking judicial notice, which both the magistrate judge and district court relied on without objection from the parties. *See Bryan v. Credit Control, LLC,* No. 18-CV-865 (SJF)(SIL), 2019 WL 166100, at *1 n.1 (E.D.N.Y. Jan. 9, 2019).

918 F.3d 236 (2019)

Yuri KOLBASYUK, on Behalf of Himself and All Others Similarly Situated, Plaintiff-Appellant,
v.
CAPITAL MANAGEMENT SERVICES, LP, Defendant-Appellee.

No. 18-1260-cv August Term 2018.

United States Court of Appeals, Second Circuit.

Argued: December 13, 2018.
Decided: March 12, 2019.

Kolbasyuk v. Capital Management Services, LP, 918 F. 3d 236 (2nd Cir. 2019)

Plaintiff-Appellant Yuri Kolbasyuk received a debt collection letter from Defendant-Appellee Capital Management Services, LP ("CMS"). Kolbasyuk sued CMS under the Fair Debt Collection Practices Act, 15 U.S.C. § 1692 et seq., but the United States District Court for the Eastern District of New York (Cogan, J.) rejected his claims. We hold that a debt collection letter that informs the consumer of the total, present quantity of his or her debt satisfies 15 U.S.C. § 1692g notwithstanding its failure to inform the consumer of the debt's constituent components or the precise rates by which it might later increase. We further hold that such a letter does not violate 15 U.S.C. § 1692e for failure to inform the consumer that his or her balance might increase due to interest or fees when the letter contains the "safe harbor" language previously ratified in *Avila v. Riexinger & Associates, LLC*, 817 F.3d 72 (2d Cir. 2016). Accordingly, the judgment of the district court is AFFIRMED.

For Plaintiff-Appellant: Levi Huebner, Levi Huebner & Associates, PC, Brooklyn, New York, for Yuri Kolbasyuk.

For Defendant-Appellee: Kirsten H. Smith (Bryan C. Shartle, on the brief), Sessions, Fishman, Nathan & Israel LLC, Metairie, Louisiana, for Capital Management Services, LP.

Before: SACK, LIVINGSTON, and CHIN, Circuit Judges.

p.238 DEBRA ANN LIVINGSTON, Circuit Judge:

The Fair Debt Collection Practices Act, 15 U.S.C. § 1692 *et seq.* ("FDCPA"), regulates certain communications from debt collectors to consumers with outstanding debts. Plaintiff-Appellant Yuri Kolbasyuk sought to invoke the FDCPA's protections when he received a debt collection letter from Defendant-Appellee Capital Management Services, LP ("CMS"). The United States District Court for the Eastern District of New York (Cogan, *J.*) dismissed Kolbasyuk's claims under 15 U.S.C. §§ 1692e ("Section 1692e") and 1692g ("Section 1692g"). We hold that CMS's letter complied with both provisions and therefore AFFIRM the district court's dismissal of Kolbasyuk's claims.

BACKGROUND

I. Factual Background[1]

Kolbasyuk owed a debt to Barclays Bank Delaware ("Barclays"). Barclays hired CMS to collect it. In an effort to accomplish that task, CMS sent Kolbasyuk a dunning letter dated July 21, 2017. The letter stated the present amount of Kolbasyuk's debt (about six thousand dollars) as well as the identity of the original and current creditor (Barclays). The letter contained CMS's address and contact information, including a website at which Kolbasyuk could submit his payment. The letter noted that it was a "communication ... from a debt collector." Joint App'x 22. It also contained the following language:

> As of the date of this letter, you owe $ 5918.69. Because of interest, late charges, and other charges that may vary from day to day, the amount due on the day you pay may be greater. Hence, if you pay the amount shown above, an adjustment may be necessary after we receive your check, in which event we will inform you before depositing the check for collection. For more information, p.239 write the undersigned or call 1-877-335-6949.

Id.

II. Procedural History

After receiving CMS's letter, Kolbasyuk filed a putative class action in the United States District Court for the Eastern District of New York. He alleged that the letter violated Sections 1692e and 1692g of the FDCPA. According to Kolbasyuk's complaint, the letter violated those provisions because it failed to inform him, *inter alia,* "what portion of the amount listed is principal," "what 'other charges' might apply," "if there is 'interest,'" "when such interest will be applied," and "what the interest rate is." Joint App'x 17. Kolbasyuk also claimed that the letter conveyed the mistaken impression "that the debt could be satisfied by remitting the listed amount as of the date of the letter, at any time after receipt of the letter." *Id.* at 18.

On April 14, 2018, the district court dismissed Kolbasyuk's complaint, holding that CMS's letter violated neither of the two provisions that Kolbasyuk cited. In so doing, the district court noted that the letter "stated the amount plaintiff owed as of its date" and "stated that the amount owed may increase due to interest and fees." *Kolbasyuk v. Capital Mgmt. Servs., LP,* No. 17-CV-07499 (BMC), 2018 WL 1785489, at *2 (E.D.N.Y. Apr. 14, 2018). Kolbasyuk timely appealed.

DISCUSSION

The district court dismissed Kolbasyuk's complaint under Federal Rule of Civil Procedure 12(b)(6). This Court reviews such dismissals *de novo. Forest Park Pictures v. Universal Television Network, Inc.,* 683 F.3d 424, 429 (2d Cir. 2012). To avoid dismissal under Rule 12(b)(6), the plaintiff's complaint must "state a claim to relief that is plausible on its face." *Bell Atl. Corp. v. Twombly,* 550 U.S. 544, 570, 127 S.Ct. 1955, 167 L.Ed.2d 929 (2007). The plaintiff must "plead[ ] factual content that allows the court to draw the reasonable inference that the defendant is liable for the misconduct alleged." *Ashcroft v. Iqbal,* 556 U.S. 662, 678, 129 S.Ct. 1937, 173 L.Ed.2d 868 (2009). In evaluating a motion to dismiss under Rule 12(b)(6), we assume as true all factual allegations asserted in the plaintiff's complaint. *Id.*

In the Second Circuit, "the question of whether a communication complies with the FDCPA is determined from the perspective of the 'least sophisticated consumer.'" *Jacobson v. Healthcare Fin. Servs., Inc.,* 516 F.3d 85, 90 (2d Cir. 2008). While the least sophisticated consumer may lack "the astuteness of a 'Philadelphia lawyer' or even the sophistication of the average, everyday, common consumer," *Russell v. Equifax A.R.S.,* 74 F.3d 30, 34 (2d Cir. 1996), he can nonetheless "be presumed to possess a rudimentary amount of information about the world and a willingness to read a collection notice with some care," *Clomon v. Jackson,* 988 F.2d 1314, 1319 (2d Cir. 1993). Under this standard, a collection notice may violate the FDCPA when it is sufficiently ambiguous to give rise to a reasonable, but inaccurate, interpretation. *See Clomon,* 988 F.2d at 1319.

I. Section 1692g

Kolbasyuk argues that CMS's letter violated Section 1692g. That section provides, in pertinent part:

> Within five days after the initial communication with a consumer in connection with the collection of any debt, a debt collector shall ... send the consumer a written notice containing—
>
> (1) the amount of the debt[.]

15 U.S.C. § 1692g(a). CMS's letter stated: "As of the date of this letter, you owe p.240 $ 5918.69." Joint App'x 22. Nevertheless, Kolbasyuk argues that CMS's letter did not include the required "amount of the debt" because it failed to inform him, *inter alia,* "what portion of the amount listed is principal," "what 'other charges' might apply," "if there is 'interest,'" "when such interest will be applied," and "what the interest rate is." Joint App'x 17. Absent these detailed disclosures, Kolbasyuk contends, an "otherwise accurate statement" of his debt violates Section 1692g. *Id.* at 16.

The text of Section 1692g clearly forecloses Kolbasyuk's argument. That provision required CMS to inform Kolbasyuk of the "amount of the debt" in question. 15 U.S.C. § 1692g(a). The word "amount" signifies a total, present quantity. *See Amount,* OXFORD ENGLISH DICTIONARY (2d ed. 1989) (defining "amount" as "the sum total to which anything mounts up or reaches ... in quantity"). The word "debt," as defined in the FDCPA, signifies an obligation to pay money. *See* 15 U.S.C. § 1692a(5) (defining "debt" as "any obligation or alleged obligation of a consumer to pay money arising out of a transaction"). The "amount of the debt," then, signifies the total, present quantity of money that the consumer is obligated to pay. And that is exactly the figure that CMS provided: the total, present quantity of money that Kolbasyuk was obligated to pay Barclays as of the date of CMS's letter.[2] Nothing in Section 1692g required CMS to inform Kolbasyuk of the constituent components of that debt or the precise rates by which it might later increase.[3]

Rather than relying on the text of Section 1692g, Kolbasyuk places great weight on our recent opinion in *Carlin v. Davidson Fink LLP,* 852 F.3d 207 (2d Cir. 2017).

But *Carlin* does not control this case. The debt collection letter at issue in *Carlin* included a "Payoff Statement" that allowed Carlin to retire his debt by paying the "Total Amount Due" stated in the letter through some future date. *Id.* at 211. That "Total Amount Due," however, was merely an estimate. Davidson Fink's letter noted that "the Total Amount Due may include estimated fees, costs, additional payments, and/or escrow disbursements that will become due prior to the 'Statement Void After' date, but which are not yet due as of the date this Payoff Statement is issued," and that Carlin would receive a refund in p.241 the amount of any overpayment. *Id.* The letter violated Section 1692g because Davidson Fink had only provided Carlin with an estimated, future amount that Carlin *might* owe, rather than the total, present amount that Carlin *did* owe. *Carlin* thus presented an altogether different question than CMS's letter to Kolbasyuk, which clearly states the total, present quantity of Kolbasyuk's debt as of the letter's date.

Kolbasyuk repeatedly quotes our statement in *Carlin* that a debt collection letter "is incomplete where, as here, it omits information allowing the least sophisticated consumer to determine the minimum amount she owes at the time of the notice, what she will need to pay to resolve the debt at any given moment in the future, and an explanation of any fees and interest that will cause the balance to increase." *Id.* at 216. For the reasons stated above, however, Kolbasyuk has taken that language out of context. *Carlin* establishes that an estimated, forward-looking "Payoff Statement" may need to inform the consumer of "what she will need to pay to resolve the debt at any given moment in the future" or provide "an explanation of any fees and interest that will cause the balance to increase." *Id.* But where, as here, the debt collector has *already* informed the consumer of the "minimum amount she owes at the time of the notice," *id., Carlin* simply lacks relevance.[4] We therefore create no inconsistency with our precedent in holding that a debt collection letter that informs the consumer of the total, present quantity of his or her debt satisfies Section 1692g, notwithstanding its failure to inform the consumer of the debt's constituent components or the precise rates by which it might later increase.

II. Section 1692e

Kolbasyuk also claims that CMS's letter violated Section 1692e. That section provides that "[a] debt collector may not use any false, deceptive, or misleading representation or means in connection with the collection of any debt." *Id.* Section 1692e provides a non-exhaustive list of sixteen potential violations of its terms, but Kolbasyuk invokes none of them here. Instead, he contends that CMS violated Section 1692e because "[t]he least sophisticated consumer could reasonably believe that the debt could be satisfied by remitting the listed amount as of the date of the letter, at any time after receipt of the letter." Joint App'x 18. With that argument, Kolbasyuk apparently seeks to capitalize on *Avila v. Riexinger & Associates, LLC,* 817 F.3d 72 (2d Cir. 2016), in which we held that a debt collector's failure to disclose that a consumer's balance might increase due to interest and fees violated Section 1692e, *id.* at 76. We stated in *Avila* that "[a] reasonable consumer could read the notice and be misled into believing that she could pay her debt in full by paying the amount listed on the notice." *Id.*

But Kolbasyuk overlooks a major difference between his case and Avila's. Here, CMS *did* disclose—quite explicitly—that Kolbasyuk's balance might increase. Specifically, CMS's letter stated the following:

> As of the date of this letter, you owe $ 5918.69. Because of interest, late charges, and other charges that may vary from day to day, *the amount due* p.242 *on the day you pay may be greater.* Hence, if you pay the amount shown above, an adjustment may be necessary after we receive your check, in which event we will inform you before depositing the check for collection. For more information, write the undersigned or call 1-877-335-6949.

Joint App'x 22 (emphasis added). CMS's unambiguous disclosure of the potential that Kolbasyuk's debt might increase vitiates Kolbasyuk's attempted analogy to *Avila.* Not even the least sophisticated consumer could conclude that his debt "could be satisfied by remitting the listed amount... at any time after receipt of the letter," Joint App'x 18, in the face of an explicit warning to the contrary.

Moreover, the above-quoted language from CMS's letter (excepting the numerical substitutions) identically tracks the "safe harbor" language adopted by the Seventh Circuit in *Miller v. McCalla, Raymer, Padrick, Cobb, Nichols, & Clark, L.L.C.,* 214 F.3d 872 (7th Cir. 2000). In *Avila,* we imported the *Miller* "safe harbor" language into Second Circuit law, holding that a debt collector who uses it "will not be subject to liability under Section 1692e for failing to disclose that the consumer's balance may increase due to interest and fees." *Avila,* 817 F.3d at 77; *see also id.* ("Using the language set forth in *Miller* will qualify for safe-harbor treatment...."). To be sure, this "safe harbor" language might not immunize debt collectors from *all* liability for "false, deceptive, or misleading representation[s] or means in connection with the collection of any debt," 15 U.S.C. § 1692e. But we nonetheless reaffirm today what we said previously in *Avila*: use of the *Miller* "safe harbor" language immunizes a debt collector from a Section 1692e claim predicated upon an alleged "fail[ure] to disclose that the consumer's balance may increase due to interest and fees." *Avila,* 817 F.3d at 77.[5]

Finally, to the extent that Kolbasyuk attempts to state a claim under Section 1692e based on CMS's failure to provide him with a precise breakdown of his debt or to inform him of the precise interest he might incur going forward, we reject that claim too. CMS has provided Kolbasyuk with the total, present quantity of his debt and informed him that this amount might increase due to additional fees and interest. A failure to provide the additional detailed disclosures that Kolbasyuk seeks does not transform CMS's otherwise-straightforward letter into a "false, deceptive, or misleading" one.

Kolbasyuk presents no other theory under which CMS might have violated Section 1692e. Nor can we imagine one. Absent additional facts not present on this record, nothing about CMS's letter could be fairly characterized as "false, deceptive, or misleading." Accordingly, the district court did not err in concluding that Kolbasyuk's complaint fails to state a claim that CMS "use[d] any false, deceptive, or misleading representation or means in connection p.243 with the collection" of the debt at issue here. 15 U.S.C. § 1692e.

CONCLUSION

We have considered Kolbasyuk's remaining arguments and conclude that they are waived or without merit. For the foregoing reasons, we AFFIRM the district court's judgment.

[1] The factual background presented below is derived from the allegations in Kolbasyuk's complaint, which we must accept as true in considering CMS's motion to dismiss. *See Ashcroft v. Iqbal,* 556 U.S. 662, 678, 129 S.Ct. 1937, 173 L.Ed.2d 868 (2009).

[2] On appeal, Kolbasyuk contests for the first time in this litigation not only the *sufficiency* of the figure that CMS provided, but also its *accuracy*. It is "a well-established general rule that an appellate court will not consider an issue raised for the first time on appeal." *Askins v. Doe No. 1,* 727 F.3d 248, 252 (2d Cir. 2013) (internal quotation marks omitted). Kolbasyuk seeks to avoid waiver by claiming that his initial complaint adequately alleged that CMS misstated the total quantity he owes. But it did not. Nothing in Kolbasyuk's complaint contested the accuracy of CMS's $ 5918.69 figure. Assertions like "[t]he Letter failed to inform Plaintiff whether the amount listed already includes 'interest,'" Joint App'x at 17, are not the same as an assertion that CMS's statement of Kolbasyuk's debt was *inaccurate*. Kolbasyuk has therefore failed to plausibly plead a violation of Section 1692g on the ground that CMS inaccurately stated the total amount of his debt. *See Iqbal,* 556 U.S. at 678, 129 S.Ct. 1937.

[3] Nor are we the first court to so conclude. *See, e.g., Barnes v. Advanced Call Ctr. Techs., LLC,* 493 F.3d 838, 840 (7th Cir. 2007) (stating that the "amount of the debt" means the "exact dollar amount owed" as of the date of the letter); *Wilson v. Trott Law, P.C.,* 118 F.Supp.3d 953, 963 (E.D. Mich. 2015) ("[T]here is no language in the FDCPA that requires a debt collector to provide a complete breakdown of the debt owed."); *Meier v. Law Offices of Weltman, Weinberg, & Reis Co., L.P.A.,* 2011 WL 2039113, at *7 (W.D. Pa. May 5, 2011) (finding "no merit to ... [the] argument that Defendant violated the FDCPA by failing to itemize the amounts due and how they increased over time").

[4] Indeed, applying *Carlin*'s language broadly to all debt collection letters would likely prove untenable as a practical matter. As the Seventh Circuit has recognized, it might well "be impossible" for a debt collector "to determine what the amount of the debt might be at some future date if for example the interest rate in the loan agreement was variable." *Miller v. McCalla, Raymer, Padrick, Cobb, Nichols, & Clark, L.L.C.,* 214 F.3d 872, 875 (7th Cir. 2000) (Posner, *J.*).

[5] Kolbasyuk argues, again for the first time on appeal, that the opinions in *Miller* and *Avila* exceed the boundaries of Article III of the Constitution by reaching issues not presented by the case or controversy before the court in each case. Even if this argument had any merit, we deem it waived due to Kolbasyuk's clear failure to raise it below. *See Askins,* 727 F.3d at 252. Moreover, even if Kolbasyuk were correct that *Avila* does not bind us, *this* case or controversy *does* present the relevant "safe harbor" language for our consideration because CMS used that language verbatim in

its notice. And under the circumstances of *this* case, we agree with the reasoning in *Miller* that "[n]o reasonable person could conclude that the statement" in CMS's letter "does not inform the debtor" that his balance might continue to increase. *Miller*, 214 F.3d at 876.

913 F.3d 297 (2019)

FEDERAL TRADE COMMISSION, Plaintiff-Appellee,
v.
William MOSES, Individually and as an Officer of One or More of the Corporate Defendants, Federal Check Processing Inc., a New York Corporation, Mark Briandi, Individually and as an Officer of One or More of the Corporate Defendants. Defendants-Appellants,
Federal Recoveries, LLC, et al., Defendants.

Docket No. 16-3811-cv 16-3805-cv August Term, 2018.

United States Court of Appeals, Second Circuit.

Argued: October 3, 2018.
Decided: January 11, 2019.

FTC v. Moses, 913 F. 3d 297 (2nd Cir. 2019)

The Federal Trade Commission brought this action in the United States District Court for the Western District of New York alleging that the defendants' debt collection practices had violated several provisions of the Federal Trade Commission Act and the Federal Fair Debt Collection Practices Act. The court (William M. Skretny, *Judge*) adopted a report and recommendation of Magistrate Judge Michael J. Roemer recommending that summary judgment be granted in favor of the FTC.

The defendant-appellant William Moses submitted no brief prior to the deadline for submission set by this Court. We therefore dismiss his appeal pursuant to Local Rule 31.2(d). The defendant-appellant Mark Briandi asserts that there are genuine issues of material fact as to whether he had knowledge of the businesses' practices at the heart of this action. He also contends that the disgorgement order against him is grossly excessive. The evidence before the court on summary judgment established as a matter of law that Briandi had control over the companies' affairs, was aware of their illegal practices, and, therefore, was liable for them. We conclude that the disgorgement assessed jointly and severally against all defendants, including Briandi and Moses, was in an appropriate amount because it was a reasonable approximation of the total amounts received by the defendant companies from consumers as a result of their unlawful acts. The judgment of the district court is therefore:

AFFIRMED.

HERBERT L. GREENMAN, Lipsitz Green Scime Cambria, LLP, Buffalo, NY, for Defendant-Appellant Mark Briandi.

MICHELE ARINGTON, (David C. Shonka, Joel Marcus, Katherine M. Worthman, Colin A. Hector, on the brief), Federal Trade Commission, Washington, D.C., for Plaintiff-Appellee.

Before: CABRANES, SACK, and PARKER, Circuit Judges.

p.301 SACK, Circuit Judge:

The Federal Trade Commission (the "FTC" or the "government") brought this action against thirteen corporate entities (the "Corporate Defendants") and defendants-appellants Mark Briandi ("Briandi") and William Moses ("Moses") alleging that the defendants' combined debt collection violated the Federal Trade Commission Act ("FTCA"), 15 U.S.C. § 45(a), and the Fair Debt Collection Practices Act ("FDCPA"), 15 U.S.C. § 1692 *et seq.* The p.302 United States District Court for the Western District of New York (William M. Skretny, *Judge*) adopted the report and recommendation of Magistrate Judge Michael J. Roemer, recommending the grant of summary judgment to the FTC on the grounds that the evidence before the court had established as a matter of law that the Corporate Defendants violated the FTCA and FDCPA, and that Briandi and Moses were personally liable for the amount of money that the defendants had received because of the violations.

Briandi and Moses appealed. Moses did not file a brief, and, there being no valid excuse proffered therefor, we dismiss his appeal pursuant to our Local Rule 31.2(d).[1]

Briandi does not contest the district court's conclusion that the Corporate Defendants violated the FTCA and FDCPA. He argues instead that the court erred by concluding that he is personally liable for the violations. He also contends that the district court erred by setting the measure of equitable monetary relief as the total proceeds of the debt collection enterprise. For the reasons set forth below, we agree with the district court on both issues, and, therefore, affirm its judgment.

BACKGROUND

General Factual Background[2]

In 2009, Briandi and Moses founded, and thereafter co-owned and co-directed, the first of the Corporate Defendants, Federal Recoveries, LLC. Over the next few years, Briandi or Moses incorporated twelve other Corporate Defendants, which were part of a single debt collection enterprise. The Corporate Defendants' business consisted largely of collecting payday loan debts,[3] which they bought from consumer-debt creditors and compiled into debt portfolios. These portfolios contained debtors' names, addresses, and general information about the debts allegedly owed.

At the Corporate Defendants' behest, nearly all of their approximately twenty-five employee-debt collectors would routinely contact debtors by telephone and falsely identify themselves as "processors," "officers," or "investigators" from a "fraud unit" or "fraud division," then accuse debtors of check fraud or a related crime and threaten them with criminal prosecution if they did not pay their debts. On some occasions, collectors called friends, family members, employers, or co-workers of debtors, telling them that the debtors owed a debt, had committed a crime in failing to pay it, and faced possible legal repercussions. When debtors or other interested parties sought further information about the debt, collectors typically refused to provide it.

After receiving a litany of consumer complaints about these activities, the Office p.303 of the New York State Attorney General began investigating the Corporate Defendants' businesses. On February 3, 2013, in an attempt to terminate the investigation, Briandi and Moses executed, on behalf of themselves and the relevant Corporate Defendants, a written "Assurance of Discontinuance" (the "AOD") with the State Attorney General. While not admitting fault, Briandi and Moses conceded in the AOD that the Corporate Defendants were subject to specified federal and state laws, including the FDCPA. Additionally, they agreed to dissolve some of the Corporate Defendants. And they stated that they would advise the New York State Attorney General's Office if any of the Corporate Defendants changed their principal place of business; if the individual defendants incorporated a new corporation or business entity; or if any of the Corporate Defendants did business under a new name. On May 8, 2013, Briandi and Moses also executed an affidavit in which they represented that they had implemented procedures — including the hiring of a "compliance officer" — to ensure that the Corporate Defendants met the requirements of the FDCPA.

Shortly after the AOD became effective, though, and without informing the Attorney General's Office, Briandi and Moses incorporated new Corporate Defendants, some in other states. And the Corporate Defendants continued to engage in the forsworn practices.

Briandi's Corporate Responsibilities

Briandi was a co-founder, co-owner, co-director, and general manager of all but perhaps one of the Corporate Defendants. He maintained a personal office within the Corporate Defendants' East Amherst, New York, office and a desk in the "collection call" area from which dunning calls were made by the companies' employees. Briandi had signature authority with respect to the companies' bank accounts, and in the more than four years between February 10, 2010, and February 26, 2014, received approximately $1.3 million in compensation from the Corporate Defendants.

Briandi's principal responsibilities for the companies included signing their checks; managing the banking side of their businesses; handling personnel matters, such as hiring and firing employees; maintaining the companies' phone systems and websites; receiving consumer payments; and — along with Moses, who was in charge of collections — operating the entity, bearing the mellifluous name "Flowing Streams," which purchased consumer debts. Prior to 2013, Briandi would himself also occasionally make collection calls on behalf of the Corporate Defendants.

After the instant litigation began, Briandi asserted in a deposition taken by FTC counsel on April 15, 2015, that, beginning in March of 2013, he had a diminished involvement with the Corporate Defendants. He testified that this resulted from his decision to become a pastor, which led to his spending much of his work days praying in his office and taking online bible classes. Although Briandi acknowledged that he continued to review corporate bank accounts from time to time, speak to managers, and occasionally take "hostile" consumer calls, Briandi Dep., April 15, 2015, at 65-66, 72; he denied having continued to visit his desk on the collection floor more than "once" or "twice" a day, *id.* at 134, 137, 143.

Procedural History

On February 24, 2014, the FTC filed a complaint against Briandi, Moses, and the Corporate Defendants in the United States District Court for the Western District of New York. It alleged two violations of Section 5(a) of the FTCA, 15 U.S.C. § 45(a) ("Unfair or Deceptive Acts or Practices"), and four violations of the p.304 FDCPA, 15 U.S.C § 1692 ("Debt Collection Practices"). The FTC accused the defendants of violating the statutes, despite having executed the AOD, by operating companies in which collectors continued to mask their identities, falsely accuse consumers of various crimes, and refuse to reveal to debtors the circumstances and nature of alleged debts. The FTC also sought and received from the district court an *ex parte* temporary restraining order prohibiting the defendants from using false representations or deceptive means to continue collecting debts, freezing all of the defendants' assets, and appointing a receiver to oversee the Corporate Defendants.

On June 17, 2014, Briandi and Moses asked the district court for one year in which to conduct discovery. A magistrate judge granted their request but noted that "no extensions of this order will be entertained." Dkt. No. 67.

Meanwhile, the FTC subpoenaed and received copies of a variety of scripts used by the Corporate Defendants' employees to make demand telephone calls, recordings of telephone calls between various collectors and consumers, and many consumer complaints and declarations detailing and challenging the companies' practices. The FTC also submitted interrogatories to the defendants and took oral depositions of Briandi and Moses. For their parts, though, Briandi, Moses, and the Corporate Defendants engaged in no discovery. And Briandi failed to answer interrogatories propounded by the FTC until after the discovery deadline had passed, and then only as part of his attempt to oppose the FTC's motion for summary judgment.

The FTC moved for summary judgment on August 27, 2015. The motion included a request for $10,852,396 in monetary relief, for which, the FTC asserted, all of the defendants, include Briandi and Moses, should be jointly and severally liable. That figure was based on "the gross total of consumer funds deposited by merchant processors" found "in the [d]efendants' settlement accounts." Second Suppl. Decl. of FTC Investigator Michael B. Goldstein ¶ 26 (July 24, 2015).

Briandi did not dispute the allegations that the Corporate Defendants engaged in wrongdoing. He denied, however, that he could be held individually liable for the Corporate Defendants' actions. He based that argument largely on his contention that he did not control the Corporate Defendants, did not participate in their activities, and lacked any knowledge of their alleged wrongdoing. Briandi also asserted that the government's requested relief vastly exceeded the Corporate Defendants' unlawful gains.

The District Court's Decision

On April 13, 2016, Michael J. Roemer, the magistrate judge to whom the matter had by then been referred by the district court "for all pre-trial matters, including preparation of a report and recommendation on dispositive motions," issued a report and recommendation concluding that the FTC's motion for summary judgment should be granted. *FTC v. Fed. Check Processing, Inc.*, No. 14-CV-122-WMS-MJR, 2016 WL 5956073, at *1, 2016 U.S. Dist. LEXIS 50589 (W.D.N.Y. Apr. 13, 2016), *adopted*, No. 14-CV-122S, 2016 WL 5940485, 2016 U.S. Dist. LEXIS 141998 (W.D.N.Y. Oct. 13, 2016). First, the magistrate judge concluded that the FTC had proved that Briandi both had "the authority to control the [C]orporate [D]efendants and knew of their wrongdoing." *Id.* at *14, 2016 U.S. Dist. LEXIS 50589 at *41-42. According to the magistrate judge, even if Briandi somehow lacked detailed knowledge of the Corporate Defendants' illicit collection practices, he could not plead ignorance p.305 after expressly agreeing to the 2013 AOD. *Id.* at *13, 2016 U.S. Dist. LEXIS 50589 at *40. The existence of the AOD executed by Briandi established that he had notice of the Corporate Defendants' illicit collection activities and was required to ensure that they followed the FTCA and the FDCPA. *Id.* at *13, 2016 U.S. Dist. LEXIS 50589 at *40.

Second, the magistrate judge concluded that the FTC's disgorgement request "reasonably approximate[d] the [C]orporate [D]efendants' unjust gains." *Id.* at *16, 2016 U.S. Dist. LEXIS 50589 at *48. As the magistrate judge observed, this amount was based on bank account data compiled by the FTC showing that "between May 2010 and March 2014 the [C]orporate [D]efendants collected $10,852,396 from consumers." *Id.* at *16, 2016 U.S. Dist. LEXIS 50589 at *48. The FTC had also demonstrated that "the defendants' misrepresentations were widely disseminated," and that their operation was "permeated with fraud." *Id.* at *16, 2016 U.S. Dist. LEXIS 50589 at *48. Finally, the magistrate judge noted that the defendant had failed to produce any evidence that would serve to dispute the recommended penalty. *Id.* at *16, 2016 U.S. Dist. LEXIS 50589 at *48.

On October 12, 2016, the district court adopted Magistrate Judge Roemer's report and recommendation in its entirety and entered judgment in the government's favor. *Fed. Trade Comm'n v. Fed. Check Processing, Inc.*, No. 14-CV-122S, 2016 WL 5940485, at *1, 2016 U.S. Dist. LEXIS 141998 (W.D.N.Y. Oct. 13, 2016).

DISCUSSION

Briandi makes three principal arguments on appeal. First, he contends that he should have been given time to conduct discovery. Second, he argues, based on the information contained in his deposition, that there were material facts at issue as to whether he could be held individually liable for the actions of the Corporate Defendants. He contends that these factual issues rendered summary judgment for the FTC improper. Finally, he asserts that the disgorgement amount adopted by the district court was grossly excessive. For the reasons that follow, we disagree with each of these contentions.

I. Standard of Review

A district court's decision on a party's request for "more time to conduct discovery ... is subject to reversal only if [the district court] abused its discretion." *Paddington Partners v. Bouchard*, 34 F.3d 1132, 1137 (2d Cir. 1994).

We review the "district court's decision to grant summary judgment *de novo*, resolving all ambiguities and drawing all permissible factual inferences in favor of the party against whom summary judgment is sought." *Burg v. Gosselin,* 591 F.3d 95, 97 (2d Cir. 2010) (internal quotation mark omitted). Summary judgment is appropriate only when "the movant shows that there is no genuine dispute as to any material fact and the movant is entitled to judgment as a matter of law." Fed. R. Civ. P. 56(a). However, "a party may not rely on mere speculation or conjecture as to the true nature of the facts to overcome a motion for summary judgment." *Fletcher v. Atex, Inc.,* 68 F.3d 1451, 1456 (2d Cir. 1995) (internal quotation marks omitted). "[C]onclusory allegations or denials" therefore "are not evidence and cannot by themselves create a genuine issue of material fact where none would otherwise exist." *Id.* (internal quotation marks omitted).

II. Additional Discovery

Briandi contends that the district court wrongly denied an extension to the p.306 one-year discovery period already provided. But Briandi has waived this argument. Federal Rule of Civil Procedure 56(d) provides that a party opposing summary judgment based on incomplete discovery must file an affidavit explaining why such discovery is necessary. *See id.* ("If a nonmovant shows by affidavit or declaration that, for specified reasons, it cannot present facts essential to justify its opposition, the court may ... allow time to obtain affidavits or declarations or to take discovery.") Briandi submitted no such affidavit to the magistrate judge or the district court; nor does he contend otherwise.

Also, it was Briandi and Moses who asked for the approximately one-year discovery period, and then chose, for unstated reasons, not to conduct any discovery at all during that period. Briandi now asserts that he did not understand the "circumstances of [his] position." Briandi Br. 22. However, he identifies no standard upon which to judge whether or not that is the case. Nor does he explain how the "circumstances of his position" were unclear or confusing, or provide any authority for the proposition that, if they were, he was therefore entitled to an extension on the lengthy period the court provided for discovery.

III. Briandi's Personal Liability

Briandi argues that the district court erred in granting summary judgment against him because genuine disputes of material fact exist regarding his control of the debt collection agencies, and therefore his personal liability for their actions. We disagree. In light of the undisputed evidence regarding the Corporate Defendants' operations and Briandi's relationship with them, we conclude that he had both sufficient authority over the Corporate Defendants, and knowledge of their practices, to be held individually liable for their misconduct as a matter of law.

A. Standard for Individual Liability Under the FTCA and FDCPA

Section 5(a)(1) of the FTCA, 15 U.S.C. § 45(a)(1), prohibits "[u]nfair or deceptive acts or practices in or affecting commerce." The FTC must show three elements to prove a deceptive act or practice in violation of § 5(a)(1): "[1] a representation, omission, or practice, that [2] is likely to mislead consumers acting reasonably under the circumstances, and [3], the representation, omission, or practice is material." *FTC v. Verity Int'l, Ltd.,* 443 F.3d 48, 63 (2d Cir. 2006) (brackets in the original; internal quotation marks omitted). "The deception need not be made with intent to deceive; it is enough that the representations or practices were likely to mislead consumers acting reasonably." *Id.*

An individual may be held liable under the FTCA for a corporation's deceptive acts or practices "if, with knowledge of the deceptive nature of the scheme, he either 'participate[s] directly in the practices or acts or ha[s] authority to control them.'" *FTC v. LeadClick Media, LLC,* 838 F.3d 158, 169 (2d Cir. 2016) (quoting *FTC v. Amy Travel Serv., Inc.,* 875 F.2d 564, 573 (7th Cir. 1989)).[4] To prevail on the issue, the FTC must therefore establish that

> p.307 the corporate practices were misrepresentations or omissions of a kind usually relied on by reasonably prudent persons and that consumer injury resulted. Once corporate liability is established, the FTC must show that the individual defendants participated directly in the practices or acts or had authority to control them. Authority to control the company can be evidenced by active involvement in business affairs and the making of corporate policy, including assuming the duties of a corporate officer.

Amy Travel, 875 F.2d at 573 (citations omitted). "The FTC is [also] required to establish the defendants had or should have had knowledge or awareness of the misrepresentations." *Id.* at 574 (citation omitted).

The FTC need not establish in this context that the defendant had actual and explicit knowledge of the particular deception at issue. We agree with our sister circuits that "knowledge 'may be established by showing that the individual [defendant] had actual knowledge of the deceptive conduct, [*or*] was recklessly indifferent to its deceptiveness, or had an awareness of a high probability of deceptiveness and intentionally avoided learning of the truth.'" *FTC v. Primary Grp., Inc.,* 713 F. App'x 805, 807 (11th Cir. 2017) (*per curiam*) (quoting *FTC v. Ross,* 743 F.3d 886, 892 (4th Cir. 2014)); *accord FTC v. World Media Brokers,* 415 F.3d 758, 764 (7th Cir. 2005).[5] And we agree with the Eleventh Circuit that "this standard correctly describes the breadth of individual liability under the FTC[A]." *Primary Grp.,* 713 F. App'x at 807. Imposing a more rigid knowledge requirement "would be inconsistent with the policies behind the FTCA and place too great a burden on the FTC." *Amy Travel,* 875 F.2d at 574.

Finally on this score, we conclude that the same standard applies when the FTC brings an action to enforce the FDCPA. "[V]iolations of the FDCPA are deemed to be unfair or deceptive acts or practices under the [FTCA]." *Jerman v. Carlisle, McNellie, Rini, Kramer & Ulrich LPA,* 559 U.S. 573, 577, 130 S.Ct. 1605, 176 L.Ed.2d 519 (2010); *see also* 15 U.S.C. § 1692l(a) ("[A] violation of [the FDCPA] shall be deemed an unfair or deceptive act or practice in violation of" the FTCA and is subject to enforcement "in the same manner as if the violation had been a violation of a[n] [FTC] trade regulation rule.") The FTC, then, is enforcing the FDCPA pursuant to its authority under the FTCA. And because the FTC can enforce compliance with the FDCPA only by employing the FTCA, and "in the same manner as a violation" of the FTCA, 15 U.S.C. § 1692l(a), it follows, we conclude, that the FTCA individual liability standard applies.

B. Briandi's Authority to Control the Corporate Defendants

Briandi was a founder of all but perhaps one of the Corporate Defendants, held a 50 percent ownership stake in them, had signatory authority over their bank accounts, and served as their co-director and general manager. In these various roles, Briandi had the authority to control the Corporate Defendants' deceptive actions. For example, in his deposition, Briandi admitted to having the power to hire and reprimand employees including those responsible for the Corporate Defendants' violations of the FTCA and FDCPA.

Briandi retained this authority after signing the AOD. From March 2013 until the time of the FTC's complaint, he remained p.308 a co-owner, co-director, and general manager of the Corporate Defendants, fielded hostile calls from consumers, continued to review the Corporate Defendants' financial activities, and, once or twice a day, would visit the collection floor, where he would speak to other managers about the corporations' business.

Briandi's deposition testimony that he contends was to the contrary was directed to the question of whether he *exercised* authority to control the Corporate Defendants' conduct, not whether he *possessed* authority to control it, which is the dispositive issue. Viewed in light of all the evidence properly before the district court on the motion for summary judgment, then, Briandi's denial of involvement in, rather than the authority to control the actions of, the Corporate Defendants did not create a dispute of material fact requiring the district court to deny the motion.

C. Briandi's Knowledge of the Corporate Defendants' Activities

The defendants were ordered to disgorge $10,852,396, an amount equal to all profits "resulting from [d]efendants' unlawful acts or practices," *Fed. Check Processing, Inc.,* 2016 WL 5940485, at *4, 2016 U.S. Dist. LEXIS 50589 (adopting magistrate judge's April 13, 2016 report and recommendation). This amount was calculated by the magistrate judge based on the Corporate Defendants' bank account data between May 2010 and March 2014. The FTC therefore was required to establish that Briandi had knowledge of the Corporate Defendants' wrongdoing during that entire period — both prior to and after his execution of the 2013 AOD — to hold him individually liable for the unlawful receipts of the Corporate Defendants during the same period. We conclude that the FTC did so.

We agree with the magistrate judge's report and recommendation that after the AOD was executed by Briandi in 2013, Briandi was at least aware "of a high probability of fraud and intentionally avoided learning the truth." *Fed. Check Processing, Inc.,* 2016 WL 5956073, at *13, 2016 U.S. Dist. LEXIS 50589. The AOD explicitly accused the Corporate Defendants of violating the FTC and FDCPA.

After executing the document, Briandi nonetheless continued to oversee the Corporate Defendants' collection activities. As the magistrate judge pointed out, the FTC found "numerous consumer complaints in Briandi's personal office." *Id.* at *13, 2016 U.S. Dist. LEXIS 50589, at *40. Briandi was thus aware of consumer complaints against the Corporate Defendants made to the New York Attorney General, the Better Business Bureau, and the FTC, complaints that numbered well into the hundreds.

To be sure, Briandi testified, as noted above, that beginning in March 2013, he neglected his managerial duties in favor of prayer and other spiritual pursuits. But he alleged that he began to neglect these managerial duties only after personally executing the AOD, in which he agreed to take measures to address the Corporate Defendants' deceptive conduct; and he did so after executing an affidavit in which he represented that he had implemented procedures — including the hiring of a "compliance officer" — to ensure that the Corporate Defendants met the requirements of the FDCPA. Therefore, when, according to Briandi, he retreated into spiritual pursuits at the expense of his managerial duties, he was not only on notice that the Corporate Defendants had been violating the FDCPA; he had taken on a personal duty to correct the Corporate Defendants' misbehavior. Briandi's withdrawal under these circumstances is at least evidence of p.309 reckless indifference to the Corporate Defendants' deceptive conduct after the 2013 AOD. *See Primary Grp.*, 713 F. App'x at 807.

We also agree with the district court that Briandi had knowledge of the Corporate Defendants' unlawful conduct *prior to* the 2013 AOD. *Fed. Check Processing, Inc.*, 2016 WL 5940485, at *1, 2016 U.S. Dist. LEXIS 141998 ("At *all times material to the Complaint* ... Defendant Mark Briandi ... had actual or constructive knowledge of the violative acts and practices" (emphasis added)). "[T]he degree of participation in business affairs" is a relevant factor in determining whether Briandi had knowledge of the Corporate Defendants' wrongful actions. *Amy Travel*, 875 F.2d at 574. Here, that factor is dispositive. Briandi served as the Corporate Defendants' co-director and general manager. In performing that role, Briandi was intimately involved with the unlawful activities at issue: the collection calls. The evidence before the magistrate judge and district court established that Briandi maintained a personal desk in the call center itself, which, he conceded, he visited at least daily. Adrian Fronczak, a former employee of the Corporate Defendants, testified in a deposition that Briandi sat at the desk "probably half the day." Fronczak Dep. 44. Fronczak also testified that Briandi and Moses would take over calls if asked to do so by one of the debt collectors. *Id.* at 44-45.

Far from demonstrating that the testimony was false, Briandi essentially corroborated it in his own deposition. There he admitted that he would take over from employees calls with hostile debtors, but said that he did so less frequently after he signed the AOD and became more engaged in his religious practices. According to his testimony, then, he was even *more* involved with the debt collection calls prior to the 2013 AOD. Indeed, Briandi made some of the more offensive collection calls himself; they were mentioned in nine consumer complaints filed before the AOD was executed. The magistrate judge and district court thus had ample evidence upon which to conclude that Briandi had knowledge of the Corporate Defendants' violations both before and after he executed the AOD.

IV. FTC Disgorgement

Finally, Briandi argues that the FTC's request that he be ordered to disgorge $10,852,396, which was adopted by the magistrate judge and confirmed by the district court, was grossly excessive. Briandi asserts that the FTC's calculation was predicated on "approximately 45 calls where it claimed that fraudulent claims were made," which is "a far cry from the court's finding that the entire operation was 'permeated with fraud.'" Briandi Br. 30-31 (quoting *Fed. Check Processing, Inc.,* 2016 WL 5956073, at *12, 2016 U.S. Dist. LEXIS 50589). Therefore, Briandi contends, "there was no basis to find that [he] should be [held] responsible for the entire amount of all the debt collected over [the] approximately four year period." Briandi Br. 34.

Section 13(b) of the FTCA provides that "in proper cases the [FTC] may seek, and after proper proof, the court may issue, a permanent injunction." 15 U.S.C. § 53(b). Although we have acknowledged that "the provision's express text refers only to injunctive relief," we have also held that the "unqualified grant of statutory authority to issue an injunction under [S]ection 13(b) carries with it the full range of equitable remedies, including the power to grant consumer redress and compel disgorgement of profits." *FTC v. Bronson Partners,* LLC, 654 F.3d 359, 365 p.310 (2d Cir. 2011) (internal quotation marks omitted).

We have adopted a "two-step burden-shifting framework for calculating equitable monetary relief. That framework requires a court to look first to the FTC to 'show that its calculations reasonably approximated the amount of the defendant[s'] unjust gains' and then shift the burden 'to the defendants to show that those figures were inaccurate.'" *Id.* at 364 (quoting *Verity Int'l,* 443 F.3d at 67).

To obtain equitable monetary relief, the FTC must also demonstrate that consumers relied on the misrepresentations at issue. Because "requir[ing] proof of each individual consumer's reliance on a defendant's misrepresentations would be an onerous task with the potential to frustrate the purpose of the FTC's statutory mandate," we concluded in *FTC v. Blue-Hippo Funding, LLC,* 762 F.3d 238, 244 (2d Cir. 2014), that "the FTC is entitled to a presumption of consumer reliance upon showing that (1) the defendant made material misrepresentations or omissions that were of a kind usually relied upon by reasonable prudent persons; (2) the misrepresentations or omissions were widely disseminated; and (3) consumers actually purchased the defendants' products." *Id.* (alteration in original; internal quotation marks omitted).

Here, in support of its motion for summary judgment, the FTC submitted more than five hundred consumer complaints regarding the defendants' debt collection practices, aggressive collection telephone scripts located in fifteen of the twenty-six Corporate Defendants' collection cubicles, and audio recordings of twenty-one of the twenty-five employee debt-collectors falsely telling consumers that the employees were law enforcement personnel or "processors." There is thus ample proof that the misrepresentations at issue were widely disseminated.

Briandi argues that those consumer complaints are inadmissible at the summary judgment stage. But he explicitly waived that challenge in the district court. As the magistrate judge correctly noted:

> The defendants do not argue that the FTC's evidence (*e.g.,* telephone calls, scripts, consumer complaints) is inadmissible, and their failure to do so may be construed as a waiver of any such argument. *DeCintio v. Westchester Cnty. Med. Ctr.,* 821 F.2d 111, 114 (2d Cir. 1987).

Fed. Check Processing, Inc., 2016 WL 5956073, at *2 n.6, 2016 U.S. Dist. LEXIS 50589.

Moreover, the case that Briandi relies on for the proposition that it is inappropriate to admit consumer complaints in support of a motion for summary judgment, *FTC v. Washington Data Resources,* No. 8:09-cv-2309, 2011 WL 2669661, 2011 U.S. Dist. LEXIS 72886 (M.D. Fla. July 7, 2011), was a district court decision without precedential effect that rejected the use of consumer complaints as a substitute for trial testimony, rather than in summary judgment proceedings.

Finally, even excluding consideration of these complaints, it is clear from the voluminous audio recordings and collection scripts submitted to the magistrate judge by the FTC that the magistrate judge did not err in concluding — nor did the district court in adopting the conclusion — that the defendants' operation was "permeated with fraud." *Fed. Check Processing, Inc.,* 2016 WL 5956073, at *12, 2016 U.S. Dist. LEXIS 50589.

The FTC has thus shown that it was entitled to a presumption of reliance. And when the FTC establishes such a presumption, it can "use[ ] the defendants' p.311 gross receipts as a baseline for calculating damages" at the first step of the burden-shifting framework. *BlueHippo Funding, LLC,* 762 F.3d at 245. That is exactly what the FTC did here. If the defendant wanted to attempt to refute the FTC's calculation, he had the burden to do so before the magistrate judge or the district court. *See Verity Int'l,* 443 F.3d at 67 (noting that burden-shifting framework requires "the FTC to first show that its calculations reasonably approximated the amount of the defendant's unjust gains, after which the burden shifts to the defendants to show that those figures were inaccurate" (internal quotation marks omitted)). The defendant chose not to submit any proof that the debt corporations earned "all or some of their revenue through lawful means." *Fed. Check Processing, Inc.,* 2016 WL 5956073, at *16, 2016 U.S. Dist. LEXIS 50589; *see also id.* at *16, 2016 U.S. Dist. LEXIS 50589, at *49 ("Had [the defendants challenged the accuracy of the FTC's figures] a hearing may have been required to determine the amount of disgorgement.") Accordingly, we conclude that it was appropriate for the district court to award the disgorgement in the amount sought by the FTC.

CONCLUSION

We have considered the appellants' remaining arguments on appeal and conclude that they are without merit. For the foregoing reasons, we DISMISS Moses's appeal, and AFFIRM the remainder of the judgment of the district court.

[1] Local Rule 31.2(d) provides: "Failure to File. The court may dismiss an appeal or take other appropriate action for failure to timely file a brief or to meet a deadline under this rule."

[2] The following statement of facts is taken primarily from the FTC's "Statement of Material Facts as to Which There is no Genuine Issue to be Tried," which is largely undisputed, and, where relevant, evidence Briandi proffered in attempting to establish the existence of a genuine dispute of material fact.

[3] "While there is no set definition of a payday loan, it is usually a short-term, high cost loan, generally for $500 or less, that is typically due on [the borrower's] next

payday." U.S. Consumer Financial Protection Bureau, "What is a payday loan?," available at https://www.consumerfinance.gov/ask-cfpb/what-is-a-payday-loan-en-1567/ (last visited December 16, 2018); *see also Fed. Trade Comm'n v. Fed. Check Processing, Inc.,* No. 14-CV-122-WMS-MJR, 2016 WL 5956073, at *2 n.5, 2016 U.S. Dist. LEXIS 50589 (W.D.N.Y. Apr. 13, 2016) (similar).

[4] The First, Fourth, Seventh, Ninth, Tenth, and Eleventh Circuits have also adopted this standard. *See FTC v. Direct Mktg. Concepts, Inc.,* 624 F.3d 1, 12 (1st Cir. 2010); *FTC v. Ross,* 743 F.3d 886, 892 (4th Cir. 2014); *FTC v. Amy Travel Serv., Inc.,* 875 F.2d 564, 573-74 (7th Cir. 1989); *FTC v. Grant Connect, LLC,* 763 F.3d 1094, 1101 (9th Cir. 2014); *FTC v. Freecom Commc'ns, Inc.,* 401 F.3d 1192, 1204, 1207 (10th Cir. 2005); *FTC v. IAB Mktg. Assocs., LP,* 746 F.3d 1228, 1233 (11th Cir. 2014).

[5] Under Eleventh Circuit Local Rule 36-2, "[u]npublished opinions are not considered binding precedent, but they may be cited as persuasive authority," as we do here.

897 F.3d 75 (2018)

Aaron COHEN, on behalf of himself and all others similarly situated, Plaintiff-Appellant,
v.
ROSICKI, ROSICKI & ASSOCIATES, P.C., Ditech Financial LLC, Defendants-Appellees.

Docket No. 17-950-cv August Term, 2017.

United States Court of Appeals, Second Circuit.

Argued: October 2, 2017.
Decided: July 23, 2018.

Cohen v. Rosicki, Rosicki & Associates, PC, 897 F. 3d 75 (2nd Cir. 2018)

Plaintiff-Appellant Aaron Cohen appeals from a judgment entered in favor of Defendants-Appellees Ditech Financial LLC and Rosicki, Rosicki & Associates, P.C., by the United States District Court for the Eastern District of New York (Leonard D. Wexler, *Judge*). Cohen alleges that the defendants violated the Fair Debt Collection Practices Act, 15 U.S.C. § 1692 *et seq.*, in connection with their attempt to initiate foreclosure proceedings on his home. The district court granted the defendants' motions to dismiss. We conclude that Cohen has failed to state a claim under the Fair Debt Collection Practices Act. Accordingly, the judgment of the district court is AFFIRMED.

DANIEL A. EDELMAN, Edelman, Combs, Latturner & Goodwin, LLC, Chicago, Illinois (Tiffany N. Hardy, Edelman, Combs, Latturner & Goodwin, LLC, Chicago, Illinois; Shimshon Wexler, The Law Office of p.78 Shimshon Wexler, PC, Decatur, Georgia, on the brief), for Plaintiff-Appellant.

HENRY MASCIA (Cheryl F. Korman, on the brief), Rivkin Radler LLP, Uniondale, New York, for Defendant-Appellee Rosicki, Rosicki & Associates, P.C.

MARTIN C. BRYCE, JR. (Adam P. Hartley, Alexander Kommatas, on the brief), Ballard Spahr LLP, New York, New York, for Defendant-Appellee Ditech Financial, LLC.

Mary McLeod, General Counsel, John R. Coleman, Deputy General Counsel, Steven Bressler, Assistant General Counsel, Nandan M. Joshi, Joseph Frisone, Counsel, Consumer Financial Protection Bureau, Washington, D.C., for Amicus Curiae Consumer Financial Protection Bureau, in support of Plaintiff-Appellant.

Before: SACK, RAGGI, and CARNEY, Circuit Judges.

p.77 SACK, Circuit Judge:

The plaintiff, Aaron Cohen, brings this putative class action against Ditech Financial LLC ("Ditech"), Cohen's mortgageloan servicer, and Rosicki, Rosicki & Associates, P.C. ("Rosicki"), the servicer's law firm, alleging violations of the Fair

Debt Collection Practices Act ("FDCPA"), 15 U.S.C. § 1692 *et seq.*, in connection with their attempt to initiate foreclosure proceedings on his home. The district court (the late Leonard D. Wexler, *Judge*) granted the defendants' motions to dismiss. We conclude that the district court erred in dismissing Cohen's FDCPA claims on the ground that the enforcement of a security interest through foreclosure proceedings is not debt collection for purposes of the FDCPA. We nevertheless affirm because Cohen has failed to plausibly allege that the defendants violated the FDCPA.

BACKGROUND

Factual Background[1]

On or about August 11, 2005, Cohen obtained a mortgage loan of $359,650 from Sterling Empire Funding Associates, Ltd. ("Sterling") to finance the purchase of his personal residence in Pomona, Rockland County, New York. Cohen has been in default on this mortgage since 2009. On June 1, 2010, Cohen's mortgage and note was assigned to Countrywide/Bank of America, which on June 10, 2013, transferred its rights in the mortgage and note to Green Tree Servicing LLC ("Green Tree"). Green Tree, through its attorney Rosicki, filed a foreclosure action summons and complaint with respect to the mortgaged property against Cohen in New York Supreme Court Rockland County on March 11, 2015. After the foreclosure action was filed, Green Tree changed its name to Ditech.[2] The defendants mailed copies of the summons and foreclosure complaint to Cohen.

The complaint in the foreclosure action asserts that Green Tree is the "holder of the subject note and mortgage, or has been delegated the authority to institute a mortgage foreclosure action by the owner and holder of the subject mortgage and note." App'x at 37. The summons states that Green Tree is "the creditor to whom
p.79 the debt is owed" and provides that "[u]pon your written request within 30 days after receipt of this notice, Rosicki, Rosicki & Associates P.C. will provide you with the name and address of the original creditor if different from the current creditor." App'x at 34.

New York law requires foreclosure plaintiffs to file two additional documents at the onset of a foreclosure proceeding. First, such a plaintiff must attach to the complaint a "Certificate of Merit" signed by the plaintiff's attorney that "certif[ies] that the attorney has reviewed the facts of the case and that . . . to the best of such attorney's knowledge, information and belief there is a reasonable basis for the commencement of such action and that the plaintiff is currently the creditor entitled to enforce rights under such documents." N.Y. C.P.L.R. § 3012-b(a). Second, "[a]t the time that proof of service of the summons and complaint is filed with the county clerk, plaintiff shall file with the county clerk a specialized request for judicial intervention (RJI), on a form prescribed by the Chief Administrator of the Courts." N.Y. Comp. Codes R. & Regs. tit. 22, § 202.12a(b)(1). The RJI must contain, *inter alia,* "the name of the mortgage servicer," and "shall request that a settlement conference be scheduled." *Id.*

Here, Green Tree filed in Supreme Court the Certificate of Merit (the "Certificate") on March 11, 2015, the same date that the foreclosure complaint was filed there. The Certificate was signed by Green Tree's attorney and certified that

Green Tree "is the creditor entitled to enforce rights" under the mortgage note and related documents. App'x at 93-94. Green Tree subsequently filed the RJI with the court on March 26, 2015. App'x at 99-101. The RJI identifies the nature of the action as a mortgage foreclosure proceeding and seeks a "Residential Mortgage Foreclosure Settlement Conference." App'x at 99-100. Cohen received copies of the Certificate and RJI from the defendants.

Cohen subsequently submitted a "qualified written request" to Ditech requesting information relating to the servicing of the loan.[3] On September 23, 2015, Ditech sent Cohen a letter in response, which states that "[t]he servicing of the above account was transferred from Bank of America, N.A. to Ditech effective June 1, 2013" and that the account is owned by "Fannie Mae."[4] App'x at 110. The letter further explains, "Please be aware Ditech did not originate nor owns [sic] the account; it merely services it for a third party and can provide information from the servicing transfer date forward." *Id.* Finally, the letter advises Cohen that "the owner does not service the account. All correspondence and inquiries concerning the account should be addressed to the account servicer, Ditech . . . . The servicer has authority to act on the owner's behalf with regard to the administration of the account and respond to any questions about the account." *Id.*

Procedural History

On December 1, 2015, Cohen filed this putative class action against Ditech and its foreclosure counsel, Rosicki, seeking to recover statutory damages under the FDCPA. *See* 15 U.S.C. § 1692k(a) (providing p.80 that a court may award up to $1,000 in statutory damages for violation of the FDCPA). Cohen alleges that the defendants violated two different provisions of the FDCPA by identifying Green Tree, and not the Federal National Mortgage Association ("Fannie Mae"), as the creditor in the foreclosure complaint, Certificate, and RJI. Specifically, Cohen alleges that the defendants violated 15 U.S.C. § 1692e, which prohibits false, deceptive, or misleading representations made in connection with collecting a debt, and 15 U.S.C. § 1692g(a), which requires debt collectors to provide debtors with the name of the "creditor to whom the debt is owed" within five days of an "initial communication with a consumer in connection with the collection of any debt."

The defendants moved to dismiss Cohen's complaint under Federal Rule of Civil Procedure 12(b)(6). On March 24, 2017, the district court dismissed Cohen's complaint, concluding that Cohen had failed to state a claim upon which relief can be granted because the "enforcement of a security interest through foreclosure proceedings that do not seek monetary judgments against debtors" does not qualify as debt collection within the scope of the FDCPA. *Cohen v. Ditech Fin. LLC*, No. 15-CV-6828 (LDW), 2017 WL 1134723, at *3, 2017 U.S. Dist. LEXIS 43443 (E.D.N.Y. Mar. 24, 2017). The district court reasoned that because "Green Tree elected to commence an action to foreclose on the mortgage and the 'communications' at issue were made in the context of enforcing its security interest . . . there was no attempt to enforce a debt actionable under the FDCPA." *Id.* Cohen then timely filed this appeal.

DISCUSSION

I. Standard of Review

"We review *de novo* a district court's grant of a defendant's motion to dismiss." *City of Pontiac Gen. Emps' Ret. Sys. v. MBIA, Inc.*, 637 F.3d 169, 173 (2d Cir. 2011). To survive a motion to dismiss, a complaint "must contain sufficient factual matter, accepted as true, to state a claim to relief that is plausible on its face." *Ashcroft v. Iqbal,* 556 U.S. 662, 678, 129 S.Ct. 1937, 173 L.Ed.2d 868 (2009) (internal quotation marks omitted). "A complaint is also deemed to include any written instrument attached to it as an exhibit, materials incorporated in it by reference, and documents that, although not incorporated by reference, are integral to the complaint." *L-7 Designs, Inc. v. Old Navy, LLC,* 647 F.3d 419, 422 (2d Cir. 2011) (brackets and internal quotation marks omitted).

II. Standing

Ditech argues that Cohen lacks standing under Article III of the Constitution to bring this action. Because standing is a "threshold matter" in determining whether the district court had jurisdiction to hear and decide this case, *Anderson Grp., LLC v. City of Saratoga Springs,* 805 F.3d 34, 44 (2d Cir. 2015) (internal quotation marks omitted), we address standing at the outset of our analysis.

To satisfy the "irreducible constitutional minimum" of Article III standing, a plaintiff must demonstrate (1) "injury in fact," (2) a "causal connection" between that injury and the complained-of conduct, and (3) a likelihood "that the injury will be redressed by a favorable decision." *Lujan v. Defs. of Wildlife,* 504 U.S. 555, 560-61, 112 S.Ct. 2130, 119 L.Ed.2d 351 (1992) (internal quotation marks omitted).

According to Ditech, Cohen lacks standing because he has alleged only a "bare [statutory] procedural violation, divorced from any concrete harm," which is p.81 insufficient to satisfy the injury-in-fact requirement under *Spokeo, Inc. v. Robins,* ___ U.S. ___, 136 S.Ct. 1540, 1549, 194 L.Ed.2d 635 (2016). Ditech Br. at 51. However, *Spokeo* does not "categorically . . . preclude[] violations of statutorily mandated procedures from qualifying as concrete injuries supporting standing." *Strubel v. Comenity Bank,* 842 F.3d 181, 189 (2d Cir. 2016) (citing *Spokeo,* 136 S.Ct. at 1550). It teaches, instead, that in order "to determine whether a procedural violation manifests injury in fact, a court properly considers whether Congress conferred the procedural right in order to protect an individual's concrete interests." *Id.* "[I]n the absence of a connection between a procedural violation and a concrete interest, a bare violation of the former does not manifest injury in fact." *Id.* However, "where Congress confers a procedural right in order to protect a concrete interest, a violation of the procedure may demonstrate a sufficient 'risk of real harm' to the underlying interest to establish concrete injury without 'need [to] allege any *additional* harm beyond the one Congress has identified.'" *Id.* (emphasis and brackets in original) (quoting *Spokeo,* 136 S.Ct. at 1549).

Here, Cohen alleges that the defendants violated 15 U.S.C. §§ 1692e and 1692g. We have held in the wake of *Spokeo,* albeit in non-binding summary orders,[5] that §§ 1692e and 1692g protect an individual's concrete interests, so that an alleged violation of these provisions satisfies the injury-in-fact requirement of Article III. *See Zirogiannis v. Seterus, Inc.*, 707 F. App'x 724, 727 (2d Cir. Sept. 12, 2017) (summary order) ("[W]e have no trouble concluding that § 1692g of the FDCPA protects an individual's concrete interests" (internal quotation marks and brackets omitted)); *Papetti v. Does 1-25*, 691 F. App'x 24, 26 (2d Cir. May 26, 2017) (summary order) (concluding that plaintiff's allegations of violations of §§ 1692e and 1692g by themselves entailed the concrete injury necessary for standing). We reach the same conclusion here.

Congress enacted the FDCPA "to protect against the abusive debt collection practices likely to disrupt a debtor's life." *Simmons v. Roundup Funding, LLC*, 622 F.3d 93, 96 (2d Cir. 2010) (internal quotation marks omitted). Sections 1692e and 1692g further this purpose: the former secures a consumer's right to be free from "false, deceptive, or misleading" practices by debt collectors, 15 U.S.C. § 1692e, and the latter requires a debt collector who solicits payment from a consumer to provide the consumer with "a detailed validation notice" so that he may confirm that he indeed owes the debt and its amount before paying it, *Russell v. Equifax A.R.S.*, 74 F.3d 30, 34 (2d Cir. 1996). Congress thus sought to protect consumers' concrete economic interests in enacting these provisions.

Both of Cohen's FDCPA claims are based on the defendants' allegedly incorrect identification of Green Tree as the creditor in the foreclosure complaint, Certificate, and RJI. Taken as true, this misrepresentation might have deprived Cohen of information relevant to the debt prompting the foreclosure proceeding, posing a "risk of real harm" insofar as it could hinder the exercise of his right to defend p.82 or otherwise litigate that action.[6] *See Strubel*, 842 F.3d at 190 (explaining that "consumer who is not given notice of his obligations is likely . . . unwittingly to lose the very . . . rights that the law affords him" (emphasis omitted)). We conclude that Cohen has alleged an injury-in-fact and therefore has standing. Accordingly, we proceed to the merits of this appeal.

III. The FDCPA and Mortgage Foreclosure Proceedings

We next address the district court's conclusion that actions taken within a foreclosure action do not categorically constitute debt collection within the scope of the FDCPA. We disagree and join those of our sister circuits that have concluded that a foreclosure action is an "attempt to collect a debt" as defined by the FDCPA. *See Kaymark v. Bank of Am., N.A.*, 783 F.3d 168, 174-79 (3d Cir. 2015); *Glazer v. Chase Home Fin. LLC*, 704 F.3d 453, 460-65 (6th Cir. 2013); *Wilson v. Draper & Goldberg, P.L.L.C.*, 443 F.3d 373, 376-78 (4th Cir. 2006); *see also Reese v. Ellis, Painter, Ratterree & Adams, LLP*, 678 F.3d 1211, 1216-18 (11th Cir. 2012) (concluding that letters threatening foreclosure are not exempt from the FDCPA because "communication related to debt collection does not become unrelated to debt collection simply because it also relates to the enforcement of a security interest"); *Kaltenbach v. Richards*, 464 F.3d 524, 527-29 (5th Cir. 2006) (same).[7]

We begin with the "language employed by Congress and the assumption that the ordinary meaning of that language accurately expresses the legislative purpose." *Gross v. FBL Fin. Servs., Inc.*, 557 U.S. 167, 175-76, 129 S.Ct. 2343, 174 L.Ed.2d 119 (2009) (internal quotation marks omitted). The FDCPA defines "debt" as "any obligation or alleged obligation of a consumer to pay money arising out of a transaction in which the money, property, insurance, or services which are the subject of the transaction are primarily for personal, family, or household purposes."[8] 15 U.S.C. § 1692a(5). This provision's p.83 "focus on the underlying transaction indicates that whether an obligation is a 'debt' depends not on whether the obligation is secured, but rather upon the purpose for which it was incurred." *Glazer,* 704 F.3d at 461. Cohen's payment obligations under the mortgage note fall within the plain language of § 1692a(5): Cohen is a consumer who must pay money to the mortgagee, and his obligation to do so arose from a transaction involving property that is for Cohen's personal, family, or household purposes (the mortgage note financed the purchase of his personal residence). *See Reese,* 678 F.3d at 1216-17; *Wilson,* 443 F.3d at 376. Cohen's obligation to pay off the mortgage note is therefore a "debt" for purposes of the FDCPA.

The defendants argue that the foreclosure action and the foreclosure filings at issue here — the complaint, summons, Certificate, and RJI — do not constitute an attempt to "collect" that debt. We disagree. To be liable under the relevant substantive provisions of the FDCPA, §§ 1692e and 1692g, a debt collector's targeted conduct must have been taken "in connection with the collection of any debt," 15 U.S.C. §§ 1692e, 1692g(a), *i.e.,* "any obligation or alleged obligation of a consumer to pay money," *id.* § 1692a(5). Thus, FDCPA liability is defined not in terms of whether the relief sought is money or property, but in terms of whether the debt collector's communication with the consumer is *in connection with* that consumer's obligation to pay money. In other words, the FDCPA does not make a distinction between an obligation itself grounded in money or property, and an obligation the breach of which can give rise to an award of money damages at law or of a property interest at equity.

Here, the purpose of the defendants' foreclosure proceeding was to obtain payment of the underlying mortgage note. Indeed, "*every* mortgage foreclosure, judicial or otherwise, is undertaken for the very purpose of obtaining payment on the underlying debt, either by persuasion (*i.e.,* forcing a settlement) or compulsion (*i.e.,* obtaining a judgment of foreclosure, selling the house at auction, and applying the proceedings from the sale to pay down the outstanding debt)." *Glazer,* 704 F.3d at 461 (emphasis in original). Moreover, mortgage foreclosure is contemplated in another portion of the statute. *See* 15 U.S.C. § 1692i(a)(1) (establishing venue requirements for a debt collector "in the case of an action [brought by the debt collector] to enforce an interest in real property securing the consumer's obligation"). We therefore conclude that mortgage foreclosure meets the FDCPA's broad definition of "debt collection."

The defendants counter that the foreclosure proceeding was not an attempt to collect a debt because the purpose of the proceeding was to enforce a security interest and obtain possession of property, rather than to obtain payment on a debt. However, New York law gives mortgagors redemption rights, N.Y. Real Prop. Acts § 1352, and allows mortgagees to obtain deficiency judgments if the proceeds from the foreclosure sale are less than the out-standing debt, *id.* § 1371. These provisions indicate that the purpose of foreclosure is to obtain payment on the underlying loan, rather than mere possession of the subject property. Indeed, "[s]uch remedies would not exist if foreclosure were not undertaken for the purpose of obtaining payment." *Glazer,* 704 F.3d at 461.

Moreover, contrary to the defendants' assertions, a foreclosure proceeding does not fall outside the scope of the FDCPA solely because it is an *in rem* legal proceeding. As an initial matter, we have determined in previous cases that debt collectors can be subject to FDCPA liability p.84 based on actions taken in legal proceedings. *See, e.g., Romea v. Heiberger & Assocs.,* 163 F.3d 111, 116 (2d Cir. 1998) (holding that a rent demand notice, required by New York law as a condition precedent to a summary eviction proceeding, was a "communication" to collect a debt within the meaning of the FDCPA); *cf. Heintz v. Jenkins,* 514 U.S. 291, 292, 115 S.Ct. 1489, 131 L.Ed.2d 395 (1995) (concluding that "a lawyer who 'regularly,' *through litigation,* tries to collect consumer debts" is a "debt collector" under the Act (emphasis in original)). Second, to accept the defendants' argument and exclude *in rem* proceedings from the scope of the FDCPA "would create an enormous loophole in the [FDCPA] immunizing any debt from coverage if that debt happened to be secured by a real property interest and foreclosure proceedings were used to collect the debt." *Wilson,* 443 F.3d at 376; *see also Kaymark,* 783 F.3d at 179; *Reese,* 678 F.3d at 1217-18. We therefore find it irrelevant that a mortgage foreclosure action is an *in rem* action in equity rather than an *in personam* action at law.

We conclude that mortgage foreclosure, at least under the circumstances presented here, constitutes debt collection under the FDCPA.

IV. Failure to State a Claim Under 15 U.S.C. § 1692e

We nonetheless affirm the dismissal of Cohen's § 1692e claim for failure to state a claim. Section 1692e prohibits debt collectors from making "any false, deceptive, or misleading representation or means in connection with the collection of any debt." Cohen's principal allegation is that the defendants violated § 1692e by falsely identifying Green Tree as the creditor with respect to Cohen's mortgage in the foreclosure complaint, the Certificate, and RJI. The defendants contend that Cohen failed to plausibly allege a violation of § 1692e for two reasons. First, the defendants argue that the Certificate and RJI accurately identified Green Tree as the creditor, so the defendants did not make any false or misleading statements in connection with the collection of a debt. In the alternative, the defendants contend that even if the identification of Green Tree as the creditor is false or misleading, it is not a *material* misrepresentation and therefore not actionable under the FDCPA.

The defendants' first argument requires us to consider whether the defendants' statement in the foreclosure documents that Green Tree is the "creditor" to whom Cohen's debt is owed was false or misleading. The FDCPA excludes from its definition of creditor "any person to the extent that he receives an assignment or transfer of a debt in default solely for the purpose of facilitating collection of such debt for another." 15 U.S.C. § 1692a(4). Here, Green Tree received the assignment of Cohen's loan on June 1, 2013, which was after Cohen defaulted, in order to facilitate the collection of Cohen's mortgage payments, suggesting that Green Tree falls within § 1692a(4)'s exclusion and therefore is not a creditor as defined by the FDCPA.

Green Tree nevertheless qualifies as a "creditor" under New York law and has standing to foreclose on Cohen's mortgage. New York law defines "creditor" as a "person having any claim, whether matured or unmatured, liquidated or unliquidated, absolute, fixed or contingent." N.Y. Debt. & Cred. Law § 270. A servicer entitled to receive mortgage payments and to pursue foreclosure — even on behalf of a third party — is a person having such a claim. *See N.Y. U.C.C.* § 3-301 ("The holder of an instrument whether or not he is the owner may . . . enforce payment in his own name."); *Aurora Loan Servs., LLC v. Taylor,* 25 N.Y.3d 355, 360-61, 12 N.Y.S.3d p.85
612, 34 N.E.3d 363 (2015) (concluding that mortgage servicer in possession of note at time foreclosure action commenced "was vested with standing to foreclose"). Accordingly, to determine whether the defendants' identification of Green Tree as the creditor was false or misleading, we would need to resolve this tension between the different definitions of "creditor" under the FDCPA and New York law.

We do not resolve this issue here because even if the defendants' creditor statement was inaccurate, it would not be material and Cohen's § 1692e claim therefore fails. Whether a communication is "false, deceptive, or misleading" under § 1692e "is determined from the perspective of the objective least sophisticated consumer." *Easterling v. Collecto, Inc.,* 692 F.3d 229, 233 (2d Cir. 2012) (internal quotation marks omitted). Under this standard, "collection notices can be deceptive if they are open to more than one reasonable interpretation, at least one of which is inaccurate." *Id.* (internal quotation marks omitted). However, we have explained that "not every technically false representation by a debt collector amounts to a violation of the FDCPA," *Gabriele v. Am. Home Mortg. Serv., Inc.,* 503 F. App'x 89, 94 (2d Cir. 2012) (summary order), and "FDCPA protection does not extend to every bizarre or idiosyncratic interpretation of a collection notice," *Easterling,* 692 F.3d at 233-34 (internal quotation marks omitted).

Several of our sister circuits have held that the least sophisticated consumer standard encompasses a materiality requirement; that is, statements must be materially false or misleading to be actionable under the FDCPA. *See Jensen v. Pressler & Pressler,* 791 F.3d 413, 421 (3d Cir. 2015); *Elyazidi v. SunTrust Bank,* 780 F.3d 227, 234 (4th Cir. 2015); *Donohue v. Quick Collect, Inc.,* 592 F.3d 1027, 1033-34 (9th Cir. 2010); *Miller v. Javitch, Block & Rathbone,* 561 F.3d 588, 596 (6th Cir. 2009); *Hahn v. Triumph P'ships LLC,* 557 F.3d 755, 757-58 (7th Cir. 2009). These courts have determined that a statement is material "if it is capable of influencing the decision of the least sophisticated [consumer]." *Jensen,* 791 F.3d at 421; *see also Hahn,* 557 F.3d at 758 ("A statement cannot mislead unless it is material, so a false but non-material statement is not actionable.").

We cited this line of cases with approval in a summary order without explicitly deciding that § 1692e incorporates a materiality requirement. *See Gabriele,* 503 F. App'x at 94. We reach that conclusion here, adopting the persuasive reasoning of these courts of appeals. As the Seventh Circuit observed, "[m]ateriality is an ordinary element of any federal claim based on a false or misleading statement," and there is no "reason why materiality should not equally be required in an action based on § 1692e." *Hahn,* 557 F.3d at 757. The FDCPA was designed to give consumers reliable information so that they can make informed decisions about how to address debts, and "by definition immaterial information neither contributes to that objective (if the statement is correct) nor undermines it (if the statement is incorrect)." *Id.* at 757-58.

The materiality requirement is thus a corollary to the well-established proposition that "[i]f a statement would not mislead the unsophisticated consumer, it does not violate the [FDCPA] — even if it is false in some technical sense." *Id.* at 758 (first brackets in original) (internal quotation marks omitted). In other words, "a false statement is only actionable under the FDCPA if it has the potential to affect the decision-making process of the least sophisticated [consumer]." *Jensen,* 791 F.3d at 421. This materiality requirement furthers the dual purposes of the least sophisticated consumer p.86 standard: the need to protect unsuspecting consumers from unscrupulous debt collectors and the need to ensure that debt collectors are not held liable "for unreasonable misinterpretations of collection notices." *Clomon v. Jackson,* 988 F.2d 1314, 1319 (2d Cir. 1993).

Applying this standard to the alleged misrepresentation here — the defendants' identification of Green Tree as the "creditor" — we conclude that it was immaterial and therefore not actionable under § 1692e. The materiality inquiry focuses on whether the false statement would "frustrate a consumer's ability to intelligently choose his or her response." *Donohue,* 592 F.3d at 1034. As we have explained, "[o]ur case law demonstrates that communications and practices that could mislead a putative-debtor as to the nature and legal status of the underlying debt, or that could impede a consumer's ability to respond to or dispute collection, violate the FDCPA." *Gabriele,* 503 F. App'x at 94. By contrast, "mere technical falsehoods that mislead no one" are immaterial and consequently not actionable under § 1692e. *Donohue,* 592 F.3d at 1034.

Here, there is no indication that the identification of Green Tree as the creditor misrepresented the nature or legal status of the debt or undermined Cohen's ability to respond to the debt collection. Although Ditech's response to the qualified written request stated that Fannie Mae owned Cohen's mortgage account, Green Tree was responsible for servicing the account. As the account servicer, Green Tree had the right to collect mortgage payments and to pursue foreclosure under New York law. Moreover, it is undisputed that the entity to whom Cohen's payments on his debt were owed in the first instance was Green Tree and that Green Tree was also the primary point of contact for any questions Cohen may have had about his mortgage. *See* App'x at 110 (instructions to Cohen in Ditech's response to Cohen's qualified written request that "[a]ll correspondence and inquiries concerning the account should be addressed to the account servicer, Ditech"). On the facts reflected in the complaint and attached documents, the false identification of Green Tree as the creditor would not have caused even a highly unsophisticated consumer to suffer a disadvantage in charting a course of action in response to the collection effort. Indeed, stating *accurately* that Fannie Mae was the creditor to whom the debt is owed likely would have *caused* confusion inasmuch as Cohen might then have been led to believe — wrongly, of course — that he should make his monthly mortgage payments to Fannie Mae.

We also think it significant that the challenged statements identifying Green Tree as the creditor were made in filings in a foreclosure action in state court. The "state foreclosure process is highly regulated and court controlled," and the "state court's authority to discipline will usually be sufficient to protect putative-debtors like [Cohen] from legitimately abusive or harassing litigation conduct." *Gabriele,* 503 F. App'x at 96 n.1. Moreover, as we have noted, Green Tree met the state law definition of "creditor." The identification of Green Tree as the creditor in the foreclosure filings was therefore accurate within the context of New York foreclosure law. Under these circumstances, we think that the identification of Green Tree as the "creditor" should be viewed as false only insofar as it results from the different definitions of "creditor" in the FDCPA and New York law.

Accordingly, although it may have technically been legally inaccurate to say that Green Tree was the "creditor" of Cohen's mortgage, considering the definition of the term in § 1692a(4), this statement was not p.87 false or misleading in any material way. The defendants' identification of Green Tree as the creditor was not deceptive as to the nature or legal status of Cohen's debt, nor would it have prevented the least sophisticated consumer from responding to or disputing the action.

We reach this conclusion based on the specific facts and circumstances of this case, *i.e.* a mortgage servicer that qualifies as a creditor under state law and that acts on behalf of a mortgage owner. We do not suggest that misrepresentations concerning the identity of the creditor are categorically immaterial. The identity of the creditor in debt collection communications can be a "serious matter." *Bourff v. Rubin Lublin, LLC,* 674 F.3d 1238, 1241 (11th Cir. 2012). The "entity to which a debtor owes money potentially affects the debtor in the most basic ways, such as what the debtor should write after 'pay to the order of on the payment check to ensure that the debt is satisfied." *Eun Joo Lee v. Forster & Garbus LLP,* 926 F.Supp.2d 482, 488 (E.D.N.Y. 2013). A misrepresentation concerning the creditor's identity in debt collection notices can cause a debtor "confusion and delay in trying to contact the proper party concerning payment on her loan and resolution of the problem." *Wallace v. Wash. Mut. Bank, F.A.,* 683 F.3d 323, 327 (6th Cir. 2012); *see also Tourgeman v. Collins Fin. Servs., Inc.,* 755 F.3d 1109, 1121-22 (9th Cir. 2014) (similar). Here, however, the facts and circumstances of the foreclosure proceeding and the foreclosure filings at issue in this lawsuit admit no plausible claim that the challenged misrepresentation of Green Tree rather than Fannie Mae as the creditor undermined Cohen's — or any other similarly situated mortgagor's — ability to respond to the debt.

V. Failure to State a Claim Under 15 U.S.C. § 1692g

We also affirm the district court's dismissal of Cohen's § 1692g claim for failure to state a claim upon which relief can be granted. Cohen claims that the defendants violated § 1692g(a)(2), which requires a debt collector, in its initial communication with the debtor, to identify the creditor to whom the debt is owed. Cohen contends that the Certificate and RJI[9] were initial communications as defined by § 1692g(a) and that because the defendants failed to identify the correct creditor in these documents, they are liable for damages under the FDCPA. The defendants counter that Cohen failed to state a § 1692g claim because the Certificate and RJI are exempt from the FDCPA's definition of initial communications. The defendants rely on § 1692g(d), which provides that "[a] communication in the form of a formal pleading in a civil action shall not be treated as an initial communication for purposes of subsection (a)." This "broad exclusion" applies not only to "the formal documents that make up a standard pleading," but also to "any communication forming any part" thereof, including "exhibits attached to a complaint." *Carlin v. Davidson Fink LLP*, 852 F.3d 207, 213 (2d Cir. 2017).

We conclude that the Certificate falls within § 1692g(d)'s pleading exclusion, and is therefore not an initial communication, because the defendants were legally obligated to file this document with the foreclosure complaint. *See* N.Y. C.P.L.R. p.88 § 3012-b(a) ("In any residential foreclosure action involving a home loan . . . the complaint shall be accompanied by a certificate. . . certifying that the attorney has reviewed the facts of the case and that . . . the plaintiff is currently the creditor entitled to enforce rights under such documents."). In *Carlin v. Davidson Fink LLP*, 852 F.3d 207, 213 (2d Cir. 2017), we held that documents attached to a foreclosure complaint — even a superfluous attachment — are covered by § 1692g(d)'s pleading exclusion. Therefore, under *Carlin*, legally required filings accompanying a complaint are also exempt. The fact that the Certificate is not denominated a "pleading" under the Federal Rules of Civil Procedure or the New York Civil Practice Law and Rules warrants no different conclusion. As *Carlin* instructs, Congress adopted a "broad exclusion that, on its face, applies to any communication *forming any part* of a pleading." *Id.* (emphasis added).

We also conclude that the RJI is not an initial communication as defined by the FDCPA. The RJI is dated fifteen days later than the foreclosure complaint, summons, and Certificate and it was not filed and served with the foreclosure complaint, summons, and Certificate. New York law nevertheless requires a foreclosure plaintiff to file the RJI at the time that proof of service of the summons and foreclosure complaint is filed. *See* 22 N.Y. Comp. Codes R. & Regs. tit. 22, § 202.12a. New York law thus requires the RJI as part of the initial assertion of a complaint seeking a foreclosure order, so the RJI can be viewed as "forming [a] part of a pleading." *Carlin*, 852 F.3d at 213. We conclude that *Carlin*'s reasoning applies not only to documents attached to an initial pleading but also to those documents that state law mandates a plaintiff to file shortly thereafter, and in relation to that pleading, to complete the initiation of the case.

Cohen's § 1692g claim therefore fails because the documents Cohen has identified as defective initial communications — the Certificate and RJI — are not initial communications as defined by the FDCPA.

CONCLUSION

We have considered the parties' remaining arguments on appeal and find them to be without merit. For the foregoing reasons, we AFFIRM the judgment of the district court.

[1] Because Cohen's complaint was dismissed under Federal Rule of Civil Procedure 12(b)(6), we accept the facts alleged in the complaint as true for purposes of our review. *Hutchison v. Deutsche Bank Sec., Inc.*, 647 F.3d 479, 481 (2d Cir. 2011). We also consider on review "any written instrument attached to the complaint, statements or documents incorporated into the complaint by reference"; here, those

include documents filed by Rosicki in its state mortgage foreclosure suit against Cohen. *Id.*

[2] We use "Ditech" and "Green Tree" to refer to the same entity.

[3] Under the Real Estate Settlement Procedures Act, a borrower who has a federally related mortgage loan may submit a written request to the servicer of the loan requesting information relating to the servicing of the loan. Such a request for information is termed a "qualified written request" and may impose on the loan servicer a duty to respond to the borrower's inquiry. 12 U.S.C. § 2605(e)(1)(B).

[4] The record does not appear to reflect the date on which Cohen's loan was sold to Fannie Mae or by whom.

[5] Although this Court's rulings by summary order do not have precedential effect, *see* 2d Cir. Local R. 32.1.1(a), "denying summary orders precedential effect does not mean that the court considers itself free to rule differently in similar cases," *Jackler v. Byrne,* 658 F.3d 225, 244 (2d Cir. 2011) (brackets omitted) (internal quotation marks omitted). In *Jackler* itself, though, we declined to follow the summary order in connection with which we made this observation.

[6] Ditech argues that Cohen "has failed to demonstrate any injury that could have possibly resulted from Ditech's failure to identify Fannie Mae as the creditor" and that this misinformation is too "trivial" to cause harm. Ditech Br. at 53 (quoting *Strubel,* 842 F.3d at 190). This argument goes to the materiality of the allegedly false information in the defendants' communications. As discussed *infra* in Part IV, materiality is a requirement for a successful § 1692e cause of action. We do not consider this merits issue as part of our standing analysis. *See, e.g., Whitmore v. Arkansas,* 495 U.S. 149, 155, 110 S.Ct. 1717, 109 L.Ed.2d 135 (1990) ("Our threshold inquiry into standing in no way depends on the merits of the [petitioner's] contention that particular conduct is illegal . . . ." (alteration in original) (internal quotation marks omitted)).

[7] The Ninth Circuit has concluded that "enforcement of security interests is not always debt collection" within the scope of the FDCPA. *Vien-Phuong Thi Ho v. ReconTrust Co., NA,* 858 F.3d 568, 573 (9th Cir. 2016). In *Ho,* the court decided that a trustee in a non-judicial foreclosure scheme that does not allow for deficiency judgments was not engaged in "debt collection" under the FDCPA. *Id.* at 571-74. In *McNair v. Maxwell & Morgan PC,* 893 F.3d 680 (9th Cir. 2018), however, the court subsequently observed that "*Ho* does not . . . preclude FDCPA liability for an entity that seeks to collect a debt through a *judicial* foreclosure scheme that allows for deficiency judgments" and concluded that actions taken by a law firm within a judicial foreclosure proceeding constitute debt collection under the FDCPA. *Id.* at 683 (emphasis in original). The instant case is like *McNair,* rather than *Ho,* because it involves a judicial foreclosure and as discussed below, the applicable state law (New York) permits mortgagees to seek deficiency judgments. Thus, we have no occasion to decide here if we would follow *Ho* in the circumstances presented there.

[8] "The term 'consumer' means any natural person obligated or allegedly obligated to pay any debt." 15 U.S.C. § 1692a(3).

[9] Cohen's complaint alleges that the foreclosure complaint itself is a "communication[]" as defined by the FDCPA, App'x at 11, but he does not raise this argument on appeal so we consider it abandoned, *see LoSacco v. City of Middletown,* 71

F.3d 88, 92 (2d Cir. 1995). In any event, the foreclosure complaint falls squarely within § 1692g(d)'s exclusion for "formal pleadings." *See Carlin v. Davidson Fink LLP*, 852 F.3d 207, 213 (2d Cir. 2017).

897 F.3d 433 (2018)

Yvette VANGORDEN, Plaintiff-Appellant,
v.
SECOND ROUND, LIMITED PARTNERSHIP, Defendant-Appellee.

No. 17-2186-cv August Term 2017.

United States Court of Appeals, Second Circuit.

Argued: March 6, 2018.
Decided: July 27, 2018.

Vangorden v. Second Round, Ltd. Partnership, 897 F. 3d 433 (2nd Cir. 2018)

On Appeal from the United States District Court for the Eastern District of New York.

On appeal from a judgment of the United States District Court for the Eastern District of New York (Feuerstein, J.), plaintiff challenges the dismissal of her Fair Debt Collection Practices Act complaint, which charges defendant with false representations and unfair practices in seeking payment on an already settled debt. See 15 U.S.C. §§ 1692e(2), (10), 1692f(1). Plaintiff argues that the district court erred in concluding that she could not state a claim because defendant had advised her of her right to dispute the debt, see id. § 1692g, which she did not do.

VACATED AND REMANDED.

DAVID N. McDEVITT, Thompson Consumer Law Group, PLLC, Mesa, Arizona, for Plaintiff-Appellant.

SHANNON MILLER (Thomas Robert Dominczyk, Donald S. Maurice, Jr., Maurice Wutscher, LLP, Flemington, New Jersey, on the brief), Maurice Wutscher, LLP, Wayne, Pennsylvania, for Defendant-Appellee.

Before: Cabranes and Raggi, Circuit Judges, Vilardo, District Judge.[*]

p.435 Reena Raggi, Circuit Judge:

Plaintiff consumer Yvette Vangorden sued defendant debt collector Second Round, Limited Partnership ("Second Round"), for violating the Fair Debt Collection Practices Act ("FDCPA"), 15 U.S.C. § 1692 *et seq.*, by sending her a letter representing that she still owed money on a debt that she had settled five years earlier, and requesting payment of that debt. She now appeals from the June 21, 2017 judgment of the United States District Court for the Eastern District of New York (Sandra J. Feuerstein, *Judge*), dismissing her complaint for failure to state a claim. *See Vangorden v. Second Round, Ltd. P'ship,* No. 16-CV-6227(SJF)(AKT), 2017 WL 4350438, at *4 (E.D.N.Y. June 20, 2017). Because we conclude that Vangorden has alleged plausible FDCPA claims, we vacate the judgment of dismissal and remand this case to the district court for further proceedings consistent with this opinion.

BACKGROUND

We draw the stated facts from Vangorden's complaint and the letters attached thereto. *See* Fed. R. Civ. P. 10(c); *Carlin v. Davidson Fink LLP,* 852 F.3d 207, 212 (2d Cir. 2017) (acknowledging that, on motion to dismiss, court may consider documents attached to complaint).

I. Settlement of the Underlying Debt

In 2011, New York resident Yvette Vangorden owed a personal credit card debt of $1,631.61 (the "Debt") to Synchrony Bank. Synchrony Bank offered to settle the Debt for $571.20, informing Vangorden, in an October 27, 2011 letter to her attorney, that upon receipt of that proposed settlement p.436 amount, it would consider the account paid and would report to credit bureaus that "the 'account [was] paid in full for less than the full balance.'" Compl. Ex. A.[1] On November 14, 2011, plaintiff paid Synchrony Bank $571.20, thus satisfying the terms of settlement set by her creditor.

II. Second Round Pursues Payment of the Debt

Almost five years later, on May 25, 2016, Second Round, which "purchases debts allegedly in default with the intent of collecting the debts for profit," *id.* at ¶ 19, purchased Vangorden's settled Debt from Synchrony Bank.

One month later, on June 22, 2016, Second Round sent Vangorden a letter (the "June Letter"),[2] which listed a "current outstanding balance" on the Debt of $1,365.39 and requested payment in that amount by use of a "detachable remittance voucher" or "online payment application." *Id.* at Ex. B. The letter also included a toll-free contact telephone number and the following notice:

> Unless you notify this office within 30 days after receiving this notice that you dispute the validity of this debt or any portion thereof, this office will assume this debt is valid. If you notify this office in writing within 30 days from receiving this notice that you dispute the validity of this debt or any portion thereof, this office will obtain verification of the debt or obtain a copy of a judgment and mail you a copy of such judgment or verification.

Id. The quoted text tracks the statutory notice that debt collectors must provide consumers regarding their right to dispute the validity of a debt. *See* 15 U.S.C. § 1692g(a). Finally, the June Letter warned Vangorden that Second Round "may report information about [her] account to credit bureaus," and that such information "may already appear on [her] credit report." Compl. Ex. B.

Vangorden did not notify Second Round that she disputed the Debt.

III. Procedural History

On November 9, 2016, Vangorden filed this lawsuit, charging Second Round with violating the FDCPA by falsely representing the character, amount, and legal status of the Debt, *see* 15 U.S.C. § 1692e(2); using false representations in connection with the collection of a debt, *see id.* § 1692e(10); and attempting to collect a debt amount not expressly authorized by agreement or law, *see id.* § 1692f(1). In her complaint, Vangorden asserts that "the least sophisticated consumer would be confused as to whether she owed any money on the Debt" and, "[r]ather than seek legal help, . . . may feel intimidated and simply pay the amount demanded." Compl. ¶¶ 37-38. She seeks statutory and actual damages, as well as attorneys' fees, costs, and interest. *See* 15 U.S.C. § 1692k.

On June 20, 2017, the district court granted Second Round's motion to dismiss the complaint under Fed. R. Civ. P. 12(b)(6). The district court determined that, even if the June Letter misrepresented the settled Debt as outstanding, Vangorden could not state a plausible FDCPA violation because the same letter notified Vangorden of her right to dispute the Debt, which she failed to do. *See Vangorden* p.437 *v. Second Round, Ltd. P'ship*, 2017 WL 4350438, at *4.

Vangorden timely appealed.

DISCUSSION

I. Standard of Review

This court "review[s] *de novo* a district court's grant of a motion to dismiss." *Deutsche Bank Nat'l Tr. Co. v. Quicken Loans Inc.*, 810 F.3d 861, 865 (2d Cir. 2015). To survive a motion to dismiss, a complaint must allege facts sufficient to "state a claim to relief that is plausible on its face." *Ashcroft v. Iqbal,* 556 U.S. 662, 678, 129 S.Ct. 1937, 173 L.Ed.2d 868 (2009) (internal quotation marks omitted). In deciding whether a complaint satisfies this standard, we "accept[] all factual allegations in the complaint as true, and draw[] all reasonable inferences in the plaintiff's favor." *Shomo v. City of New York,* 579 F.3d 176, 183 (2d Cir. 2009) (internal quotation marks omitted).

II. Sections 1692e and 1692f Claims

In deciding whether Vangorden states a plausible FDCPA claim, we begin with the text of the three statutory sections on which she relies. *See Federal Hous. Fin. Agency v. UBS Ams. Inc.,* 712 F.3d 136, 141 (2d Cir. 2013) ("In construing a statute, we begin with the plain language, giving all undefined terms their ordinary meaning."). First, § 1692e(2)(A) prohibits "[t]he false representation of the character, amount, or legal status of any debt." Second, § 1692e(10) prohibits "[t]he use of any false representation . . . to collect or attempt to collect any debt." Finally, § 1692f(1) prohibits "[t]he collection of any amount [on a debt] . . . unless such amount is expressly authorized by the agreement creating the debt or permitted by law."

Precedent instructs us to construe FDCPA text liberally to effectuate the overriding statutory purpose, which is "to 'eliminate abusive debt collection practices by debt collectors, to insure that those debt collectors who refrain from using abusive debt collection practices are not competitively disadvantaged, and to promote consistent State action to protect consumers against debt collection abuses.'" *Avila v. Riexinger & Assocs., LLC,* 817 F.3d 72, 75 (2d Cir. 2016) (quoting 15 U.S.C. § 1692(e)). Thus, this court has held that the FDCPA sections here at issue are not mutually exclusive because, although they "share the goal of protecting consumers from abuse by debt collectors," they each target "different type[s] of misconduct." *Arias v. Gutman, Mintz, Baker & Sonnenfeldt LLP,* 875 F.3d 128, 135 (2d Cir. 2017). While § 1692e "mainly targets practices that take advantage of a debtor's naivete or lack of legal acumen," § 1692f aims at "practices that give the debt collector an unfair advantage over the debtor or are inherently abusive." *Id.* at 136. Toward these ends, § 1692e and § 1692f each proscribe a "non-exhaustive" list of specific unfair practices, with this court recognizing that the same conduct may support claims brought under multiple subsections. *Id.* at 135-36.

The conduct here at issue is Second Round's transmittal to Vangorden of its June Letter representing that she had an outstanding Debt obligation of $1,365.39 and its request for payment of that Debt. Vangorden alleges that the letter misrepresented her indebtedness because she had settled the Debt some five years earlier by paying the creditor its requested settlement amount of $571.20. On review of a motion to dismiss, we must assume the truth of these facts. When we make that assumption here, we conclude that Vangorden plausibly pleaded that the June Letter falsely represented "the character, amount, or legal status" of her Debt in violation of § 1692e(2). The FDCPA is "a p.438 strict liability statute" and, thus, there is no need for a plaintiff to plead or prove that a debt collector's misrepresentation of a debt obligation was intentional. *See Arias v. Gutman, Mintz, Baker & Sonnenfeldt LLP,* 875 F.3d at 134. In sum, because Vangorden pleaded facts plausibly asserting Second Round's misrepresentation of her Debt obligation, her § 1692e(2) claim should not have been dismissed under Fed. R. Civ. P. 12(b)(6). *See generally Easterling v. Collecto, Inc.,* 692 F.3d 229, 234-35 (2d Cir. 2012) (concluding that collection letter's statement that debt was "'ineligible for bankruptcy discharge'" was false because plaintiff "at all times fully retained her right to seek bankruptcy discharge"); *cf. DiMatteo v. Sweeney, Gallo, Reich & Bolz, L.L.P.,* 619 F. App'x 7, 9 (2d Cir. 2015) (summary order) (concluding that "assertion that rent was unpaid was not false" for purposes of § 1692e claim because governing law was unclear as to whether landlord could lawfully refuse payment from co-tenant).

Further, because the June Letter, after allegedly misstating Vangorden's Debt obligation, requested payment of the Debt, we conclude that Vangorden has plausibly alleged that Second Round both used a "false representation" in a debt collection effort in violation of § 1692e(10), and attempted to collect a debt amount not "expressly authorized by the agreement creating the debt or permitted by law" in violation of § 1692f(1). *See Arias v. Gutman, Mintz, Baker & Sonnenfeldt LLP,* 875 F.3d at 135 (identifying "collection of an invalid debt" as one of § 1692f's "list of unfair practices"). As to the latter, this court has recognized that § 1692f's numbered subsections are "examples" of conduct manifesting the "unfair or unconscionable" means of debt collection identified in the section's first sentence. *Gallego v. Northland Grp. Inc.,* 814 F.3d 123, 125 (2d Cir. 2016). Thus, by pleading that defendant attempted to collect an amount not authorized by agreement or permitted by law, the plaintiff has stated a plausible claim under § 1692f(1) without need for further allegations of unfairness or unconscionability. *See generally Campbell v. MBI Assocs.,* 98 F.Supp.3d 568, 582 (E.D.N.Y. 2015) (observing that "[b]y its terms, § 1692f(1) prohibits the collection of *any* amount which is not expressly authorized by the agreement creating the debt or permitted by law," and holding that § 1692f(1) claim does not require demonstration of violation of "general proscription" on use of "unfair or unconscionable" collection means set forth in first sentence of section (emphasis in original)).

Our conclusion that Vangorden's pleadings state plausible FDCPA claims within the statutory text is consistent with rulings by our sister circuits. *See McLaughlin v. Phelan Hallinan & Schmieg, LLP,* 756 F.3d 240, 246 (3d Cir. 2014) (holding that where facts construed most favorably to plaintiff indicated that debt obligation was less than amount stated in defendant's letter, plaintiff stated plausible claim for misrepresentation of debt amount in violation of § 1692e(2), (10)); *Stratton v. Portfolio Recovery Assocs., LLC,* 770 F.3d 443, 451 (6th Cir. 2014) (holding that where defendant lacked right to collect interest on debt, statement to contrary was false representation of character and amount of debt); *Russell v. Absolute Collection Servs., Inc.,* 763 F.3d 385, 395 (4th Cir. 2014) (affirming judgment for plaintiff where statement that debt had not been satisfied was false on face and, thus, misrepresented character, amount, and legal status of debt).

On this appeal, Second Round does not contest Vangorden's allegation that the June Letter misrepresented her Debt obligation. Nor does it dispute that such a misrepresentation, coupled with a request p.439 for payment, can fall within the plain language of the three cited statutory provisions. Rather, Second Round argues that, here, its inclusion in the June Letter of the debt dispute notice mandated by § 1692g both (1) takes any technical falsity as to the amount or character of the Debt outside the sphere of actionable misrepresentation contemplated by § 1692e and § 1692f; and (2) precludes even the least sophisticated consumer from being misled as to the Debt at issue. We proceed to explain why these arguments do not persuade.

III. Second Round's Section 1692g Notice Does Not Preclude Vangorden from Stating Plausible Claims under Sections 1692e and 1692f

As already noted *supra* at 436, the FDCPA requires debt collectors to advise consumers of their right to dispute an asserted debt in writing "within thirty days after receipt of the notice." 15 U.S.C. § 1692g(a)(3). The consumer must further be advised that if it does not do so, "the debt will be assumed to be valid by the debt collector." *Id.* But if the consumer does dispute the debt, the debt collector "will obtain verification of the debt or a copy of a judgment against the consumer and a copy of such verification or judgment will be mailed to the consumer by the debt collector." *Id.* § 1692g(a)(4). Moreover, the debt collector is statutorily obliged to "cease collection of the debt" until it "obtains verification of the debt or a copy of a judgment, or the name and address of the original creditor," and mails that information to the consumer. *Id.* § 1692g(b).

Second Round argues that it is evident from this statutory scheme — which affords consumers the right to dispute debts, precludes efforts to collect disputed debts until verified, and affords a presumption of validity to undisputed debts — that the FDCPA does not obligate debt collectors to verify debts *prior to* sending initial communications to consumers. It therefore follows that there can be no FDCPA liability for an initial debt misrepresentation that is accompanied by a § 1692g notice of the right to dispute.

Like the Third and Fourth Circuits, we reject this argument because nothing in the text of the FDCPA suggests that a debtor's ability to state a § 1692e or § 1692f claim "is dependent upon the debtor first disputing the validity of the debt in accordance with § 1692g." *Russell v. Absolute Collection Servs., Inc.*, 763 F.3d at 392 [4th Cir.]; *see McLaughlin v. Phelan Hallinan & Schmieg, LLP*, 756 F.3d at 247-48 [3d Cir.] (holding that "statute's text provides no indication that Congress intended to require debtors to dispute their debts under § 1692g before filing suit under § 1692e"). The language of § 1692g is conditional, identifying a debt collector's obligations "*[i]f*" the consumer disputes a debt. 15 U.S.C. § 1692g(b) (emphasis added). The Third Circuit has observed that such language suggests that "disputing a debt" pursuant to § 1692g is an "option[]" available to consumers, not a condition precedent to the consumer bringing a § 1692e or § 1692f action. *McLaughlin v. Phelan Hallinan & Schmieg, LLP*, 756 F.3d at 247. If, instead, Congress had "intended for a debt collector's liability under the FDCPA to hinge upon a debtor's" first disputing the debt pursuant to § 1692g, one might expect "it would have so indicated with conspicuous language to that effect." *Russell v. Absolute Collection Servs., Inc.*, 763 F.3d at 392. This conclusion comports with the remedial nature of the statute and its solicitude for the least sophisticated consumer. *See McLaughlin v. Phelan Hallinan & Schmieg, LLP*, 756 F.3d at 248 ("Imposing a § 1692g dispute prerequisite in the absence of any statutory p.440 language requiring it would undermine the FDCPA's protection of unsophisticated debtors, who would have no reason to suspect that they would be prevented from filing suit concerning deceptive communications as a consequence of failing to invoke the optional statutory validation procedure."); *see generally Russell v. Equifax A.R.S.*, 74 F.3d 30, 34 (2d Cir. 1996) (holding that FDCPA claims should be reviewed by considering "how the least sophisticated consumer" — not "average, everyday, common consumer — understands the notice").

In urging otherwise, Second Round points to the FDCPA's "specific presumption that a debt is valid, subject to a properly conveyed dispute of its validation." Appellee Br. 14. In fact, what the relevant text does is impose a notice obligation on the debt collector to inform the consumer that, if the consumer does not dispute the debt, it "will be assumed to be valid by the debt collector." 15 U.S.C. § 1692g(a)(3). We do not think such a notice requirement can reasonably be construed to require extension of the presumption to other sections of the FDCPA — such as § 1692e and § 1692f — that make no mention of it.[3] *Cf. Loughrin v. United States*, ___ U.S. ___, 134 S.Ct. 2384, 2390, 189 L.Ed.2d 411 (2014) (observing that "when Congress includes particular language in one section of statute but omits it in another . . . this Court presumes that Congress intended a difference in meaning" (internal quotation marks and alterations omitted)).

In any event, Second Round's argument is undermined by language in the FDCPA stating that a consumer's "failure . . . to dispute the validity of a debt under [§ 1692g] may not be construed by any court as an admission of liability by the consumer." 15 U.S.C. § 1692g(c). Given this explicit protection of consumers who do not dispute their debts, "it would be anomalous to conclude that the debtor forfeits his or her ability to bring a lawsuit under the FDCPA simply because the debtor failed to invoke § 1692g's discretionary validation procedures." *Russell v. Absolute Collection Servs., Inc.*, 763 F.3d at 393. Indeed, to conclude otherwise would have the perverse effect of "immunizing" a debt collector's false statements after 30 days if a consumer does not dispute the debt within that time frame. *McLaughlin v. Phelan Hallinan & Schmieg, LLP,* 756 F.3d at 248; *see generally* 15 U.S.C. § 1692k(d) (establishing one-year statute of limitations for § 1692e and § 1692f claims).

Second Round nevertheless maintains that Vangorden's receipt of a § 1692g notice must be held to foreclose her § 1692e and § 1692f claims if § 1692g is not to be rendered "superfluous." Appellee Br. 7; *see Carlin v. Davidson Fink LLP,* 852 F.3d at 213 (recognizing "that courts should avoid statutory interpretations that render provisions superfluous" (internal quotation marks omitted)). The concern is misplaced. As the Third Circuit has observed, consumers who can challenge misrepresented debt obligations under other provisions of the FDCPA still have an incentive to dispute debts pursuant to § 1692g because that provision "enable[s] debtors to cheaply and quickly resolve disputes with debt collectors," as well as to "facilitate[] the exchange of information, [which] may ultimately help debtors bolster their FDCPA claims." *McLaughlin v. Phelan Hallinan & Schmieg, LLP,* 756 F.3d at 248.

Bleich v. Revenue Maximization Grp., Inc., 233 F.Supp.2d 496 (E.D.N.Y. 2002), relied on by both Second Round and the district court, although not controlling, took a different view. It concluded that p.441 consumers who ignored § 1692g validation procedure could not pursue FDCPA claims because "[t]o allow such lawsuits would discourage use of the detailed statutory procedure." *Id.* at 500-01. The district court reasoned that Congress "likely" included § 1692g's validation procedures in the FDCPA to "avoid . . . litigation." *Id.* at 500 ("The specific procedure for debt validation must have been intended to avoid FDCPA litigation based solely on the debt's validity as communicated to the collection agency by the creditor."). That is not, however, what Congress said when it enacted the FDCPA. Instead, Congress observed that § 1692g's validation procedures would "eliminate the recurring problem of debt collectors . . . attempting to collect debts which the consumer has already paid." S. Rep. No. 95-382, at 4 (1977), *as reprinted in* 1977 U.S.C.C.A.N. 1695, 1699. In sum, contrary to *Bleich,* the relevant legislative history focused on minimizing certain conduct by debt collectors, not enforcement actions by consumers.[4]

Our rejection of Second Round's argument is further reinforced by § 1692k(c), which states that a "debt collector may not be held liable . . . if the debt collector shows by a preponderance of evidence that [a] violation was not intentional and resulted from a bona fide error notwithstanding the maintenance of procedures reasonably adapted to avoid any such error." 15 U.S.C. § 1692k(c). In short, the FDCPA's text does not make consumer exhaustion of § 1692g dispute procedures a condition precedent to a consumer § 1692e or § 1692f claim; rather, the statutory language affords debt collectors an affirmative defense to such claims if they can show that their actions were bona fide and not intentional.[5] Thus, we need not quarrel with Second Round's assertion that the FDCPA "'anticipates that not all debts can or will be verified'" and that, "'in the real world, creditors and debt collectors make mistakes, and sometimes initiate collection activities against persons who do not owe a debt.'" Appellee Br. 15 (quoting *Jang v. A.M. Miller & Assocs.,* 122 F.3d 480, 483 (7th Cir. 1997)). We conclude only that the protection the FDCPA affords debt collectors in those circumstances is the affirmative defense stated in § 1692k(c), not an immunity from suit inferred from the dispute notice provision of § 1692g.[6]

p.442 Accordingly, we conclude that neither Second Round's compliance with § 1692g in allegedly misstating a Debt obligation to Vangorden, nor Vangorden's failure to avail herself of § 1692g verification procedures, precluded her as a matter of law from stating plausible FDCPA claims under § 1692e and § 1692f.

IV. Vangorden's Claims Do Not Fail the Least Sophisticated Consumer Standard

Second Round argues that even if a consumer who fails to act on § 1692g notices could state plausible § 1692e and § 1692f claims, Vangorden has not done so here because even the "least sophisticated consumer" could not be misled by the June Letter. The pleadings do not support that conclusion.

"[A] collection notice can be misleading if it is open to more than one reasonable interpretation, at least one of which is inaccurate." *Avila v. Riexinger & Assocs., LLC,* 817 F.3d at 75 (internal quotation marks omitted); *see Russell v. Equifax A.R.S.*, 74 F.3d at 35. Here, the June Letter's only interpretation is misleading; it told Vangorden that she had an out-standing debt obligation. In fact, that obligation had been settled some five years earlier. This court has held that even a partial misstatement of a consumer's debt obligation can be misleading under the FDCPA. *See Avila v. Riexinger & Assocs., LLC,* 817 F.3d at 76 (observing that accurate statement of balance due, "without notice that the amount is already increasing due to accruing interest or other charges, can mislead the least sophisticated consumer into believing that payment of the amount stated will clear her account"). The conclusion applies with even more force where a collection notice does more than misstate the extent of a consumer's debt obligation; it misstates the very existence of such an obligation.

Nor is such a misrepresentation rendered less false or misleading by the fact that the debt had existed at one time, but had been settled by the consumer. As Vangorden persuasively argues, upon receipt of a debt collection letter misstating a debt obligation and requesting payment, a consumer — and, particularly, a least sophisticated consumer — might question whether she had indeed satisfied the debt and make payment anew "out of fear and confusion." Appellant Br. 8; *see Russell v. Absolute Collection Servs., Inc.*, 763 F.3d at 395 (observing that "hypothetical least sophisticated consumer" would interpret statement that account was outstanding "to mean that the debt remains legally due and owing[,] . . . [despite plaintiff having] fully paid her debt"; thus, because statement that debt "'has not been satisfied' is false on its face and misrepresents the character, amount, and legal status of the debt," plaintiff states valid FDCPA claim (some internal quotation marks and alterations omitted)).

Section 1692g notice that the consumer could dispute the debt, thereby triggering verification obligations for the debt collector, warrants no different conclusion because, at the same time that Second Round gave Vangorden such notice, it also told her that it "may report information about your account to credit bureaus," and that such "information *may already appear* on your credit report." Compl. Ex. B (emphasis added). A least sophisticated consumer who was so advised might understand her right to dispute the misstated debt but, p.443 nevertheless, pay the debt out of fear that there was already an adverse effect on her credit that would continue as long as the obligation remained outstanding. A § 1692g notice hardly mitigates a debt misrepresentation when it sends this sort of "contradictory message" to the consumer. *Russell v. Equifax A.R.S.*, 74 F.3d at 34 (holding that least sophisticated consumer could be misled by communication that provided § 1692g debt dispute notice, but also advised consumer that if he did not dispute claim but, rather, paid it within 10 days, agency would not post collection to his credit file).

In urging otherwise, Second Round argues that its own intent bears on how a least sophisticated consumer would understand the June Letter. Second Round fails to demonstrate how Vangorden would have understood that its attempt to collect the Debt here was in good faith. *Cf. Hart v. FCI Lender Servs., Inc.*, 797 F.3d 219, 226 (2d Cir. 2015) (observing that court was "hard put" to understand how consumer would understand debt collector's professed purpose for sending letter at issue). No matter. As we have already explained, *supra* at 441-42, Second Round's intent is relevant not on a motion to dismiss, but only as an affirmative defense.

Thus, notwithstanding the June Letter's inclusion of § 1692g notice, we conclude that the letter could mislead a least sophisticated consumer about the misstated Debt obligation. We, therefore, adhere to our conclusion that Vangorden has pleaded plausible § 1692e and § 1692f claims, which should not have been dismissed.

CONCLUSION

To summarize, we conclude as follows:

1. Where, as here, a debt collector misreports a debt obligation to a consumer that she no longer owes, and requests payment on that debt, the consumer plausibly alleges violations of 15 U.S.C. § 1692e and § 1692f, notwithstanding the fact that the debt collector advised the consumer of her right to dispute the debt as required by *id.* § 1692g, and that the consumer did not exercise that right.
2. Inclusion of 15 U.S.C. § 1692g notice here does not prevent plaintiff from plausibly pleading that, on a least sophisticated consumer standard, defendant's debt communication was misleading and unfair under *id.* § 1692e and § 1692f.
3. Because the FDCPA is a strict liability statute, a consumer is not required to plead *mens rea* to state plausible FDCPA claims. Rather, a debt collector's intent is relevant as an element of the affirmative defense afforded by 15 U.S.C. § 1692k(c).

Accordingly, we VACATE the judgment of the district court dismissing plaintiff's FDCPA complaint, and we REMAND the case to the district court for further proceedings consistent with this opinion.

[*] Judge Lawrence J. Vilardo, of the United States District Court for the Western District of New York, sitting by designation.

[1] The letter is from GE Capital Retail Bank, a predecessor of Synchrony Bank.

[2] Although addressed to both Vangorden and a law firm, the June Letter was sent directly to Vangorden. It was the first, and only, communication between Vangorden and Second Round.

[3] We emphasize that § 1692g notice is a statutory requirement, *see* 15 U.S.C. § 1692g(a), not, as Second Round appears to suggest, a safe harbor.

[4] Other district court cases relied on by Second Round are equally unpersuasive insofar as they rely on *Bleich*'s reasoning or assume an FDCPA *mens rea* requirement that we have since rejected. *See Arias v. Gutman, Mintz, Baker & Sonnenfeldt LLP*, 875 F.3d at 134.

[5] Thus, Second Round cannot fault Vangorden for "mak[ing] no allegation that Second Round had knowledge, or was otherwise aware," that her Debt "had allegedly been settled with Synchrony," Appellee Br. 25, because the FDCPA does not require a consumer to plead *mens rea* to state a claim; rather, it allows the debt collector to avoid liability upon its proof that the violation was not intentional or that its actions were taken in good faith, *see Randolph v. IMBS, Inc.*, 368 F.3d 726, 728 (7th Cir. 2004) (acknowledging that "debt collector's false statement is presumptively wrongful" under FDCPA "even if the speaker is ignorant of the truth; but a debt collector that exercises care to avoid making false statements has a defense under § 1692k(c)"). Insofar as the parties' briefs dispute *mens rea,* that issue is properly pursued on remand. Our task on review of a Rule 12(b)(6) motion "is to test, in a streamlined fashion, the formal sufficiency of the plaintiff's statement of a claim for relief without resolving a contest regarding its substantive merits." *Halebian v. Berv,* 644 F.3d 122, 130 (2d Cir. 2011) (internal quotation marks omitted).

[6] In any event, *Jang* does not help Second Round because it is inapposite on its facts. Plaintiffs there alleged that defendants mailed dunning letters containing § 1692g notices knowing "that they would never provide verification" for disputed debts because they would simply return those accounts to creditors. *Jang v. A.M. Miller & Assocs.*, 122 F.3d at 482. The *Jang* court dismissed plaintiff's false statement claim, reasoning that the collection agencies had "technically complied" with the FDCPA because § 1692g does not require verification; instead, a debt collector can simply cease collection of a disputed debt. *Id.* at 481. By contrast, Vangorden's claims are based on alleged misrepresentations as to her debt obligations.

897 F.3d 42 (2018)

Levi HUEBNER, on behalf of himself and all other similarly situated consumers, Plaintiff-Appellant,
Poltorak PC, Elie C. Poltorak, Interested Party-Appellants,
v.
MIDLAND CREDIT MANAGEMENT, INC., Midland Funding, LLC., Defendants-Appellees.

Nos. 16-2363-cv, 16-2367-cv August Term 2017.

United States Court of Appeals, Second Circuit.

Argued: November 9, 2017.
Decided: July 19, 2018.

Huebner v. Midland Credit Management, Inc., 897 F. 3d 42 (2nd Cir. 2018)

Levi Huebner, Elie C. Poltorak, and Poltorak PC appeal a final judgment of the United States District Court for the Eastern District of New York (Cogan, *J.*). Huebner sued Midland Credit Management, Inc. and Midland Funding LLC. (collectively "Midland"), alleging that they violated the Fair Debt Collection Practices Act ("FDCPA"), 15 U.S.C. § 1692, *et seq.* Huebner alleged that when he called Midland to dispute his debt, Midland's representative harassed him by asking about the nature of his dispute. Huebner also alleged that, after his call, Midland did not report the debt as disputed to credit reporting agencies. The district court concluded that Huebner failed to produce any evidence raising a material issue as to either claim. Additionally, the court sanctioned: (1) Poltorak personally for misleading the court during the initial status conference; (2) Huebner for disregarding a protective order; and (3) both Huebner and Poltorak PC for needlessly multiplying the proceedings. Huebner, Poltorak, and Poltorak PC argue on appeal that the court erred in granting summary judgment for Midland and abused its discretion in sanctioning them. We disagree. Accordingly, the judgment of the district court is AFFIRMED.

FOR PLAINTIFF-APPELLANT: LAWRENCE KATZ, Valley Stream, NY, for Levi Huebner.

FOR INTERESTED PARTY-APPELLANTS: Elie C. Poltorak, Poltorak PC, Brooklyn, NY, pro se.

FOR DEFENDANTS-APPELLEES: ANDREW M. SCHWARTZ, Marshall Dennehey, Warner, Coleman & Goggin, P.C., Philadelphia, PA (Matthew B. Johnson, New York, NY, on the brief), for Midland Credit Management, Inc., Midland Funding LLC.

FOR AMICUS CURIAE: Brian Melendez, Dykema Gossett PLLC, Minneapolis, MN, for ACA International.

Before: LEVAL, LIVINGSTON, and CHIN, Circuit Judges.

p.45 DEBRA ANN LIVINGSTON, Circuit Judge:

Plaintiff-Appellant Levi Huebner ("Huebner") is an attorney who has litigated several cases under the Fair Debt Collection Practices Act ("FDCPA"), 15 U.S.C. §

1692, *et seq.*, which, among other things, prohibits debt collectors from using "false, deceptive, or misleading representation[s]. . . in connection with the collection of any debt," *id.* § 1692e. In October 2013, Huebner called Defendant-Appellee Midland Credit Management, Inc. ("Midland") to dispute a $131 debt that it had tried to collect from him.[1] Huebner surreptitiously p.46 recorded the call. Asked why he disputed the debt, Huebner would say only that the debt was "nonexistent." J.A. 371. After repeatedly declining to clarify what he meant, Huebner said he would call Midland back after reviewing his "files." *Id.* at 372. He filed this lawsuit instead.

Huebner's first amended complaint alleged that the Midland representative told him he could dispute his debt only in writing and then only if he gave cause for his dispute. Huebner's then-attorney, Interested Party-Appellant Elie C. Poltorak ("Poltorak"), repeated this allegation in a January 28, 2015 letter to the district court. During an initial status conference, Poltorak further assured the district court that Huebner's recording would show that Midland had told him that he could not dispute his debt orally. But upon listening to the recording of Huebner's call, Judge Cogan of the United States District Court for the Eastern District of New York learned that this allegation was false. The court sanctioned Poltorak $500 for failure to participate in the initial status conference in good faith.

To keep his case alive, Huebner amended his complaint twice more. His third amended complaint ultimately alleged that Midland had made multiple false or misleading representations in violation of 15 U.S.C. § 1692e. Concluding that Huebner had not raised a material issue of fact as to any of his claims, the court granted summary judgment for Midland. It also ordered Huebner and Poltorak's law firm, Interested Party-Appellant Poltorak PC, to pay some of Midland's legal fees because, the court determined, Huebner had tried to trick Midland into violating the FDCPA during his initial call; his claim was meritless and prosecuted in bad faith; and both he and Poltorak PC had needlessly multiplied the proceedings with, among other things, a baseless motion for recusal and a pretrial motion filed in flagrant disregard of the terms of the parties' joint protective order.

Huebner, Poltorak, and Poltorak PC now appeal the district court's grant of summary judgment and three separate sanctions orders issued over the course of this litigation. For the reasons stated below, we conclude that the district court did not err in granting summary judgment, nor did it abuse its discretion in sanctioning Huebner, Poltorak, and Poltorak PC. The judgment below is therefore AFFIRMED.

BACKGROUND

I. Factual Background[2]

In August 2013, Midland sent a collection letter to Huebner seeking to collect $131.21 from him. Verizon had originally billed Huebner for this sum in connection with work done on Huebner's phone line, but Huebner had refused to pay, advising Verizon that he should not have been charged for the work. Verizon told him that it would remove the charge from his invoice. On October 17, 2013, Huebner called Midland regarding the debt and secretly recorded the phone call. Huebner asked how he could dispute the debt. He was transferred to an employee named Emma Elliott ("Elliott"). The merits of this case turn largely on their conversation.

p.47 Huebner began by asking, "[W]hat do I have to do if I want to dispute the debt[?]" J.A. 369. "Just advise me what your dispute is[,] and I can see if I can assist you with that," responded Elliott. *Id.* Rather than answer, Huebner pivoted to a different question, "[H]ow do I get it off my credit report?" *Id.* Elliot replied, "Well, we need to . . . work with what your dispute is in order to remove it, sir. So why are you disputing?" *Id.* Huebner repeated his question: "I just can't get it off my credit report[?]" *Id.* "No," replied Elliott. "We just can't delete an account because the consumer wants it deleted. We need to know why [you] want it deleted and what [the] dispute is. I can assist you with your dispute here, sir." *Id.* at 369-70. Huebner tried a third time: "I can't get it off my credit card — my account without paying it?" *Id.* at 370. "That's not what I said, sir," Elliott corrected him. "I need to know what your dispute is before I can just delete it for you. . . . Why is it that you want to dispute it?" *Id.*

At last, Huebner answered her (in a manner of speaking): "Because it is a non-existent debt." *Id.* Elliott asked what he meant by "nonexistent" and even suggested answers Huebner might give her: "Did you already pay it with Verizon? Did you never have Verizon?" *Id.* Huebner claimed not to understand what she meant and declined to elaborate, eventually telling Elliott he would call her back after he reviewed his "files" to see if he could "find anything." *Id.* at 372. Elliott asked whether Huebner still wanted to dispute the debt. Huebner responded, "I told you I dispute it." *Id.* at 373. "But," Elliott said again, "[y]ou are just saying you are disputing. I need to know what you are disputing." *Id.*

Restating that the debt was "nonexistent" once more, Huebner then countered, "If you're telling me[] you are not going to take my dispute, that's fine. I'm just going to try to see if I can get more information." *Id.* at 373-74. No, insisted Elliott, "I am trying to help you with your dispute, sir, but you are not really helping me help you." *Id.* at 374. Shortly after, Huebner ended the call, saying that he might call back with "more information." *Id.* He never did.

According to Midland's internal procedures for managing debt disputes, when a consumer calls Midland to challenge a debt, Midland may mark the debt as "disputed" and report it as such to the credit reporting agencies while Midland attempts to confirm its validity. But sometimes resolving a difficult dispute is just not worth it, in which case, Midland will code the disputed account with the number "289." This denotes that Midland has deleted the account, that Midland will cease all collection, and that the credit reporting agencies will be informed of this.

The day Huebner called, Midland marked Huebner's account with "289" and sent advisories to the major credit reporting agencies requesting that Huebner's debt be deleted from his credit reports. Midland wrote Huebner a letter informing him that it had deleted his debt, would no longer collect it, and that Midland had informed the credit reporting agencies that they should delete the debt as well.[3]

II. Procedural History

A year later, Huebner sued Midland in the United States District Court for the
p.48 Eastern District of New York (Cogan, *J.*), alleging that Midland violated the FDCPA. According to Huebner's first amended complaint, Elliott told him "that he

could not orally dispute" his debt but must do so in writing and "that he must have a reason to dispute a debt." J.A. 51. Huebner sought to represent all consumers who had undergone similar treatment in a class action.

A

During the court's initial status conference, Poltorak, Huebner's counsel, told the court that Huebner's case was based exclusively on the recorded conversation and on the allegation that Elliott had told Huebner that he must dispute his debt in writing. Judge Cogan listened to the recording and discovered that Elliott had said nothing of the sort. Concluding that Huebner and Poltorak had misrepresented Huebner's call, which had "all the earmarks of a setup," the court ordered Huebner and Poltorak to show cause why the "action should not be dismissed, with fees [and] costs awarded under 15 U.S.C. § 1692k(a)(3), and sanctions issued pursuant to Rule 11." *Huebner v. Midland Credit Mgmt., Inc.*, 85 F.Supp.3d 672, 675 (E.D.N.Y. 2015).

Huebner and Poltorak moved to disqualify Judge Cogan. As evidence of the judge's purported bias, Huebner and Poltorak pointed primarily to the judge's ownership of a few shares in an exchange-traded fund, which held some shares of Midland's parent company Encore Capital Group, Inc. As to sanctions, Poltorak claimed that he "ha[d] no recollection" of making the no-verbal-disputes-allowed misrepresentation during the Initial Status Conference. J.A. 192 n.3. Huebner and Poltorak further insisted that dismissal was not proper because they had a new theory for relief: that Huebner never received a letter from Midland informing him that it had stopped collection on his debt.

In a May 1, 2015 decision and order, the district court denied the recusal motion. *Huebner v. Midland Credit Mgmt., Inc.*, No. 14 CIV. 6046 (BMC), 2015 WL 1966280 (E.D.N.Y. May 1, 2015). The judge's purported financial interest, $9 total, did not create a conflict because "ownership in a mutual or common investment fund that holds securities," like the exchange-traded fund at issue, does not create a conflict of interest "unless the judge participates in the management of the fund," according to Canon 3C(3)(c)(i) of the Code of Conduct for United States Judges and the Judicial Conference's Committee on Codes of Conduct Advisory Opinion No. 106 (2014). *Id.* at *2-*3.

Next, the court sanctioned Poltorak $500 under Fed. R. Civ. P. 16(f)(1)(B) for failure to participate in the initial status conference in good faith. Poltorak had initially "raised one claim and one claim only — that the recorded conversation between plaintiff and defendant's agent would show that defendant advised plaintiff that he could only dispute his debt in writing, not orally." *Id.* at *6. But after the status conference, Poltorak raised "new allegations that [were] not recently discovered, [were] relevant, and would have materially changed the posture of this case had they been disclosed at the proper time," thus frustrating the aim of the conference procedure to help cases proceed expeditiously. *Id.* The court nonetheless did not dismiss the action but instead scheduled a conference to plan discovery on Huebner's new theory. *Id.* at *7.

B

Three months and two amended complaints later, the district court approved the parties' joint protective order, which p.49 set out procedures for preserving documents' confidentiality. Any letter or memorandum that cited a protected document was to be filed under seal. A party who wanted to challenge a document's designation as "confidential" was to attempt to resolve the dispute with the other party first. If the parties could not resolve it between themselves, the challenging party could then ask the court to resolve it after ten days.

On November 4, 2015, Huebner's counsel wrote the court to outline contested areas of discovery. This letter, which cited Midland's confidential information, was filed on the court's open docket. The court ordered the letter sealed and warned the parties that it would sanction them if they failed to resolve outstanding discovery disputes. Huebner's counsel later requested, without first consulting with defense counsel, that the court revoke the confidential designations of certain documents. On November 13, 2015, the court imposed a $350 sanction on Huebner under Fed. R. Civ. P. 16(f)(1)(C) for filing a frivolous motion by failing to follow the protective order's procedures for challenging documents' confidential designations.

C

The district court granted Midland's motion for summary judgment after almost a year of discovery. *See Huebner v. Midland Credit Mgmt., Inc.,* No. 14 CIV. 6046 (BMC), 2016 WL 3172789 (E.D.N.Y. June 6, 2016). Although Huebner's third amended complaint had outlined four distinct claims for relief, his claims had essentially boiled down to just two theories by summary judgment. First, he argued that Elliott's questions about the nature of his dispute led him to believe that he could not dispute his debt without cause, in violation of 15 U.S.C. §§ 1692e(8) and 1692e(10). Second, Huebner alleged that Midland reported his debt to credit reporting agencies without mentioning that the debt was disputed, in violation of 15 U.S.C. §§ 1692e(5), 1692e(8), and 1692e(10), and also sent him a letter falsely claiming that Midland notified the credit reporting agencies that the debt was disputed, thereby violating 15 U.S.C. § 1692e(2)(A).

The district court rejected both arguments. The district court explained that the FDCPA does not make it illegal to ask a consumer questions about the nature of his dispute when the consumer calls to lodge one. Requesting that sort of information can help both the collector and the consumer resolve the dispute faster. To be sure, it might be unlawful to badger a consumer with harassing or browbeating questions "to deter him from disputing his debt." *Huebner,* 2016 WL 3172789 at *5. But here, it was Huebner, not Elliott, who was "bobbing and weaving, evading the questions and harassing the collection agent, who was just trying to do her job, find out what the problem was, and perhaps even resolve the dispute." *Id.* The court then concluded that no material issue of fact had been raised as to whether Midland informed the credit reporting agencies that the debt was deleted, and the record showed that deleted debts are a subset of disputed debts.[4] The court entered final judgment on June 6, 2016.

D

On June 13, 2016, Midland moved for the district court to sanction Huebner and Poltorak PC under 15 U.S.C. § 1692k(a)(3), 28 U.S.C. § 1927, and the court's inherent authority for pursuing this litigation in bad faith. Specifically, Midland p.50 sought to recover "all reasonable costs and fees it expended in defending" Huebner's suit. J.A. 1082. On November 10, 2016, the court granted Midland's motion in part. *See Huebner v. Midland Credit Mgmt., Inc.,* No. 14 CIV. 6046 (BMC), 2016 WL 6652722 (E.D.N.Y. Nov. 10, 2016). The court first noted that Poltorak PC's conduct was sanctionable under 28 U.S.C. § 1927 "because it pursued a claim that had no legal basis, and it acted in bad faith." *Id.* at *4. What is more, Poltorak PC had "unnecessarily multiplied the proceedings" with its "baseless motion for recusal," "frivolous motion to remove certain confidentiality designations," and frequent pre-motion conference letters that exceeded the court's page limit, all in disregard of Midland's warnings that it would seek fees and costs if the litigation continued. *Id.* at *4.

The court also ordered Huebner to pay fees under 15 U.S.C. § 1692k(a)(3) and the court's inherent authority to sanction. *Id.* at *5. Not only did Huebner — a lawyer so experienced with the FDCPA that he "whispered virtually every question into his attorney's ear" during a deposition, *id.* at *5 n.3 — change his legal theory several times, he also "attempt[ed] to entrap [Elliott] into committing an FDCPA violation" for the purpose of pursuing this lawsuit, *id.* at *5. Indeed, Huebner suggested in his opposition to sanctions that he had called Midland not to dispute his debt, but rather to "test[]" its FDCPA compliance. *Id.* at *5.

But Midland also deserved some blame, the court determined, because it "did not take its discovery obligations as seriously as it should have," having delayed document production several times. *Id.* at *6. "Under these circumstances, a substantial sanctions award would only further distort what should have been a minor litigation." *Id.* The court therefore ordered Huebner and Poltorak PC, jointly and severally, to pay only "the attorneys' fees and costs incurred in connection with [Midland's] motion for sanctions and some portion of [its] attorneys' fees and costs incurred in connection with opposing [Huebner's] class certification motion." *Id.* On December 23, 2016, after reviewing Midland's bill of fees, the court further reduced the award to only the fees that Midland incurred in connection with its motion for sanctions. This number was ultimately calculated as $9,850, less than a tenth of the full attorney's fees and costs that Midland incurred over the course of the litigation.

DISCUSSION

On appeal, Huebner — as well as Poltorak, and Poltorak PC, who have joined this case as interested parties — challenge the district court's June 6, 2016 final judgment and its three sanctions orders. For the reasons that follow, we AFFIRM the judgment of the district court and its sanctions orders.

I

We first address the district court's grant of summary judgment to Midland. "We review a grant of summary judgment *de novo,* examining the evidence in the light most favorable to, and drawing all inferences in favor of, the non-movant." *Blackman v. New York City Transit Auth.*, 491 F.3d 95, 98 (2d Cir. 2007) (per curiam) (quoting *Sheppard v. Beerman,* 317 F.3d 351, 354 (2d Cir. 2003)). "Summary judgment is appropriate only if it can be established 'that there is no genuine issue as to any material fact and that the moving party is entitled to judgment as a matter of law.'" *Sheppard,* 317 F.3d at 354-55 (quoting Fed. R. Civ. P. 56(c)). Huebner argues on appeal that the district court erred in granting summary judgment on each of his two principal theories p.51 under the FDCPA: (1) that Elliott's questions about the nature of his credit dispute amounted to a "misleading" communication about his debt; and (2) that Midland failed to report to the credit reporting agencies that he had "disputed" the debt. For the following reasons, we disagree.

A

Section 1692e of the FDCPA prohibits all "false, deceptive, or misleading representation[s] or means in connection with the collection of any debt." Apart from this blanket ban, § 1692e(8) more specifically renders it unlawful for a debt collector knowingly to communicate (or threaten to communicate) false credit information, while § 1692e(10) bars "deceptive means . . . to obtain information concerning a consumer." When interpreting § 1692e, we test whether a communication is "deceptive" by asking how the "least sophisticated consumer" would interpret it. *Eades v. Kennedy, PC Law Offices,* 799 F.3d 161, 173 (2d Cir. 2015) (quoting *Easterling v. Collecto, Inc.,* 692 F.3d 229, 233 (2d Cir. 2012)). This "is an objective standard, designed to protect all consumers, 'the gullible as well as the shrewd.'" *Ellis v. Solomon & Solomon, P.C.,* 591 F.3d 130, 135 (2d Cir. 2010) (quoting *Jacobson v. Healthcare Fin. Servs., Inc.,* 516 F.3d 85, 90 (2d Cir. 2008)).

Huebner's first theory of liability is that Midland violated § 1692e when Elliott, responding to Huebner's call, supposedly "overwhelm[ed]" him with "hassl[ing]" questions as to why he wished to dispute his debt. Br. for Pl.-Appellant at 38. This sort of questioning, he contends, misleads consumers into believing that they cannot dispute their debts without explaining the nature of their dispute, deters them from disputing their debts in violation of § 1692e(8), and allows collectors "to improperly extract information concerning the consumer," in violation of § 1692e(10). *Id.* In short, according to Huebner, as soon as he said the words "I want to dispute the debt," Elliott was obligated to record the dispute and end the conversation; she thus violated the FDCPA when she asked any follow-up questions inquiring into the nature of Huebner's dispute. We disagree.

Like the district court, we assume without deciding that at some point, a debt collector's questions about the nature of a consumer's dispute could become sufficiently inquisitorial to violate the FDCPA. But no reasonable jury could conclude that Elliott's questions were misleading or abusive in any way. *See, e.g., Ellis,* 591 F.3d at 135 ("While protecting those consumers most susceptible to abusive debt collection practices, this Court has been careful not to conflate lack of sophistication with unreasonableness."). The "least sophisticated consumer" would have interpreted Elliott not as threatening Huebner, or even conveying false information about his debt, but rather as endeavoring to learn more about Huebner's dispute so that Midland could resolve it. After all, Huebner had asked Elliott how he could "get [the debt] off [his] credit report." J.A. 369. Had she simply accepted his dispute and hung up the phone at that point, the debt would have stayed on his report pending a determination of the validity of the debt, rather than been deleted. And despite Huebner's purported misunderstanding of Elliott's basic questions throughout the call, Elliott remained patient, going so far as to feed him possible answers to her questions. *See Ellis,* 591 F.3d at 135 (explaining that, although a "hypothetical least sophisticated consumer" lacks "the sophistication of the average, everyday, common consumer," he is "neither irrational nor a dolt" (internal quotation marks omitted) (quoting *Russell v. Equifax A.R.S.*, 74 F.3d 30, p.52 34 (2d Cir. 1996))). Finally, even if Huebner had been at all confused about the status of his credit dispute when he ended the call, Midland sent him a letter that day telling him that his debt had been deleted.[5]

We thus agree with the district court that Huebner failed to raise a material issue on the theory that Midland violated § 1692e when Elliott politely asked Huebner what he meant when he said that his debt with Verizon was "nonexistent." *See id.* ("[T]he FDCPA does not aid plaintiffs whose claims are based on 'bizarre or idiosyncratic interpretations of collection notices.'" (quoting *Jacobson,* 516 F.3d at 90)); *Jacobson,* 516 F.3d at 90 (noting that our "least sophisticated consumer" objective test "protects debt collectors from unreasonable constructions of their communications"). The district court properly concluded that there were no genuine questions of fact as to whether Elliott misled Huebner with her questions, and was right to grant summary judgment to Midland on this issue.

B

Huebner next argues that Midland violated § 1692e(8), which requires debt collectors "to communicate that a disputed debt is disputed," by failing to so inform the credit reporting agencies. Nothing in the record, however, supports this meritless allegation either. Midland marked Huebner's debt with the code "289" the day he called, meaning that it deleted the account. Midland also sent several messages to the credit reporting agencies telling them to delete the debt, as well as a letter to Huebner informing him of this. Huebner has not pointed to any record evidence that creates a material question of fact on these issues.[6] As a result, we hold that summary judgment was also properly granted as to Huebner's second claim for relief.[7]

II

We next review the district court's sanctions orders. As discussed above, the district court sanctioned:

(1) Poltorak under Federal Rule of Civil Procedure 16(f)(1)(B) for failing to participate in the initial status conference in good faith;

(2) Huebner under Rule 16(f)(1)(C) for breaching the district court's protective order;

(3) Poltorak PC under 28 U.S.C. § 1927 for unreasonably multiplying the district court's proceedings; and

p.53 (4) Huebner under 15 U.S.C. § 1692k(a)(3) and the district court's inherent authority for pursuing a frivolous legal claim in bad faith.

We review the imposition of sanctions for abuse of discretion. *See Virginia Properties, LLC v. T-Mobile Ne. LLC,* 865 F.3d 110, 113 (2d Cir. 2017). "An abuse of discretion occurs when a district court bases its ruling on an erroneous view of the law or on a clearly erroneous assessment of the evidence, or renders a decision that cannot be located within the range of permissible decisions." *Star Mark Mgmt., Inc. v. Koon Chun Hing Kee Soy & Sauce Factory, Ltd.,* 682 F.3d 170, 175 (2d Cir. 2012) (quoting *Kiobel v. Millson,* 592 F.3d 78, 81 (2d Cir. 2010) (quotation marks and alterations omitted)). When a lower court sanctions a litigant for bad faith, the court must outline its factual findings with "a high degree of specificity." *Virginia Properties,* 865 F.3d at 113 (quoting *Weinberger v. Kendrick,* 698 F.2d 61, 80 (2d Cir. 1982)). But more often than not, "the district court is better situated than the court of appeals to marshal the pertinent facts and apply the fact-dependent legal standard that informs its determination as to whether sanctions are warranted." *Id.* (quoting *Revson v. Cinque & Cinque, P.C.,* 221 F.3d 71, 78 (2d Cir. 2000)).

A

Poltorak first argues that the district court abused its discretion when it sanctioned him $500 under Rule 16(f)(1)(B). Rule 16(f)(1)(B) allows a district court to sanction a party for failing to participate "in good faith" in a pretrial conference. Rule 16(f)'s "explicit reference to sanctions" reflects the Rule's intention to "encourage forceful judicial management." Fed R. Civ. P. 16(f) advisory committee's note to 1983 amendment. It vests a district court with "discretion to impose whichever sanction it feels is appropriate under the circumstances." *Id.* This sanctioning power accords with a district court's broader "'inherent power' and responsibility to manage [its] docket[] 'so as to achieve the orderly and expeditious disposition of cases.'" *In re World Trade Ctr. Disaster Site Litig.,* 722 F.3d 483, 487 (2d Cir. 2013) (per curiam) (quoting *Link v. Wabash R.R. Co.,* 370 U.S. 626, 630-31, 82 S.Ct. 1386, 8 L.Ed.2d 734 (1962)). "In deciding whether a sanction is merited, the court need not find that the party acted in bad faith. The fact that a pretrial order was violated is sufficient to allow some sanction." *See* 6A Charles Alan Wright *et al., Federal Practice and Procedure* § 1531 (3d ed. 2010).

Here, Poltorak had informed the court that the case turned on Elliott's telling Huebner that she would only accept disputes made in writing. Elliott, of course, said no such thing. Ordered to show cause why he should not be sanctioned, Poltorak denied having made the misrepresentation, even though Huebner's first amended complaint and Poltorak's statements in a January 28, 2015 pre-conference letter made the very same allegation. Then Poltorak changed the subject, moving to recuse Judge Cogan and alleging for the first time that Midland failed to tell credit reporting agencies that the debt was disputed. Because Poltorak's bait-and-switch routine delayed the litigation, the court sanctioned him $500. *See* Fed. R. Civ. P. 16(a) (explaining that pretrial conferences are meant to "expedit[e] disposition of the action," "discourag[e] wasteful pretrial activities," and "facilitate[] settlement"); *see also*

6A Charles Alan Wright *et al., Federal Practice and Procedure* § 1531 (3d ed. 2010) (describing orders to pay fees or costs under Rule 16(f) as "[l]ess drastic sanctions").

p.54 On appeal, Poltorak and Huebner suggest that any references to a "writing" were inadvertent and that, importantly, they never changed positions as to their legal theory. Huebner points out that both his first amended complaint and his third amended complaint allege that Elliott refused to accept his dispute unless he explained it. The third amended complaint, he asserts, is altogether in line with the first, but is just more specific in explaining that Elliott refused to acknowledge his dispute by asking him questions about it. We disagree.

As the district court observed, Poltorak's January 28, 2015 letter "raised one claim and one claim only — that the recorded conversation between plaintiff and defendant's agent would show that defendant advised plaintiff that he could only dispute his debt in writing, not orally." *Huebner,* 2015 WL 1966280, at *6. Poltorak's representation hardly appears inadvertent, since it can also be found in the first amended complaint. *See* J.A. 51 (alleging that Elliott "stated to the Plaintiff that he could not orally dispute the debt"). It does not hint at the theory that simply asking any follow-up questions posed a problem. Nor, for that matter, does the first amended complaint allege that Midland failed to report his debt as disputed to the credit reporting agencies: Huebner and Poltorak made this argument only after the court learned that their no-verbal-disputes claim was false. We therefore do not believe it was clearly erroneous for the district court to conclude that Poltorak "intentionally misl[ed] the [c]ourt and defendant as to his theory of the case," *Huebner,* 2015 WL 1966280, at *7, and we discern no abuse of discretion in the district court's decision to sanction Poltorak under Rule 16(f)(1)(B).

B

We next address Huebner's contention that the district court erred in sanctioning him on November 13, 2015 under Rule 16(f)(1)(C) for breaching the protective order. *See* Fed. R. Civ. P. 16(f)(1)(C) (authorizing courts to sanction parties who fail to "obey a . . . pretrial order"). Under the district court's August 2015 protective order, the parties were forbidden from quoting from confidential material in documents filed on the open docket. A party who wanted to challenge a document's designation as "confidential" was supposed to try to resolve the dispute with the other party first. If the parties could not resolve the dispute in ten days, the challenging party could ask the court to step in. In November 2015, Huebner filed a letter with the court that sought to challenge a document's confidential designations without first consulting Midland. Concluding that Huebner's letter was frivolous because he had ignored the protective order's procedures, the court sanctioned him $350.

Huebner's argument is not entirely clear, but he seems to believe that because the district court did not give him an opportunity to withdraw the offending submission, he was denied fair "notice of the particular sanctions sought." *Reilly v. Natwest Markets Grp. Inc.,* 181 F.3d 253, 270 (2d Cir. 1999). But attorneys "have no absolute right 'to be warned that they disobey court orders at their peril.'" *Id.* (quoting *Daval Steel Prods. v. M/V Fakredine,* 951 F.2d 1357, 1366 (2d Cir. 1991)); *see also Fonar Corp. v. Magnetic Resonance Plus, Inc.,* 128 F.3d 99, 102 (2d Cir. 1997) ("As a general rule, a court is not obliged to give a formal warning that sanctions might be imposed for violation of the court's orders."). What is more, this was Huebner's second violation of the protective order in eight days: on November 4, he had filed a letter on the court's open docket quoting from confidential documents. p.55 That same day, the court sealed Huebner's letter and warned the parties that failure to resolve discovery disputes could lead to sanctions. The district court's November 13 imposition of sanctions consequently "was, or should have been, entirely foreseeable to" Huebner. *Reilly*, 181 F.3d at 270; *see also Koehl v. Bernstein*, 740 F.3d 860, 863 (2d Cir. 2014) (affirming a sanctions order in part because the district court had given the litigant fair warning). We therefore discern no abuse of discretion in the district court's decision.

C

We next address the district court's decision to sanction Poltorak PC under 28 U.S.C. § 1927.[8] Section 1927 allows a court to require an attorney "who so multiplies the proceedings in any case unreasonably and vexatiously . . . to satisfy personally the excess costs, expenses, and attorneys' fees reasonably incurred because of such conduct." This statute "imposes an obligation on attorneys throughout the entire litigation to avoid dilatory tactics," and provides courts with a cudgel to use, in their discretion, "to deter unnecessary delays in litigation." *United States v. Int'l Bhd. of Teamsters, Chauffeurs, Warehousemen & Helpers of Am., AFLCIO,* 948 F.2d 1338, 1345 (2d Cir. 1991) (quoting H.R. Conf. Rep. No. 1234, 96th Cong., 2d Sess. 8). "To impose sanctions under [§ 1927], a court must find clear evidence that (1) the offending party's claims were entirely without color, and (2) the claims were brought in bad faith — that is, motivated by improper purposes such as harassment or delay." *Kim v. Kimm,* 884 F.3d 98, 106 (2d Cir. 2018) (internal quotation marks omitted) (quoting *Eisemann v. Greene,* 204 F.3d 393, 396 (2d Cir. 2000)). A court may infer bad faith when a party undertakes frivolous actions that are "completely without merit." *In re 60 E. 80th St. Equities, Inc.,* 218 F.3d 109, 116 (2d Cir. 2000) (quoting *Int'l Bhd. of Teamsters,* 948 F.2d at 1345).

Here, the district court cited numerous frivolous and vexatious actions by Poltorak PC attorneys over the course of this litigation. Poltorak himself, for example, had misrepresented to the court that Elliott told Huebner that he could only dispute his debt in writing. After the district court pointed this out, Poltorak moved to recuse Judge Cogan, citing the judge's ownership stake in a common investment fund, even though Canon 3C of the Judicial Code of Conduct and Advisory Opinion 106 expressly state that this sort of financial interest does not create a conflict. Poltorak PC also later changed its theory of the case, arguing first that Elliott, by trying to clarify Huebner's bewildering answers to her, questions, had somehow misled him, and second that Midland failed to report Huebner's debt properly to the credit reporting agencies. At summary judgment, the district court correctly concluded that the first claim "had no basis in the FDCPA," *Huebner,* 2016 WL 6652722, at *4, and that the second was plainly untrue. It also noted that Poltorak PC time and time again filed letters exceeding the court's page limit and ignored procedures set out in the court's protective order. *See generally Chambers v. NASCO, Inc.,* 501 U.S. 32, 52-53, 111 S.Ct. 2123, 115 L.Ed.2d 27 (1991) (upholding "the assessment of attorney's fees as a sanction for . . . disobedience of the court's orders and the attempt to defraud the court itself"). The district court thus had good reason to conclude that Poltorak PC "unreasonably and vexatiously" multiplied the proceedings in p.56 this case under 28 U.S.C. § 1927. *Kim,* 884 F.3d at 106.

Poltorak PC and Huebner raise two principal challenges to the district court's § 1927 fee award, neither of which we find convincing. First, they both argue that their principal claim for relief — that asking any questions about the nature of a consumer's dispute is a "misleading" statement under the FDCPA — was not frivolous because it turns on a question of law that was previously "undecided in this Circuit." *Simmons v. Roundup Funding, LLC,* 622 F.3d 93, 97 (2d Cir. 2010). But a legal theory may be frivolous even if we have never said so before. *See, e.g., Gollomp v. Spitzer,* 568 F.3d 355, 372 (2d Cir. 2009) (upholding a district court's conclusion that a plaintiff's argument was frivolous when the plaintiff failed to cite any "on point" cases in support of his legal theory). And the district court found that "any reasonable reading of [Huebner]'s recorded call" with Midland would show that he was specifically "trying to trick [Midland] into *not* complying with the FDCPA." *Huebner,* 2016 WL 3172789, at *3 (emphasis in original). We see nothing clearly erroneous about this finding, and thus nothing clearly erroneous about the district court's conclusion that Poltorak PC knew or should have known that Huebner's suit was devoid of merit. *See, e.g., Enmon,* 675 F.3d at 143 ("[A] claim is entirely without color when it lacks any legal or factual basis." (internal quotation marks omitted) (quoting *Schlaifer Nance & Co. v. Estate of Warhol,* 194 F.3d 323, 337 (2d Cir. 1999))). But even if this claim were not frivolous, it would not have been an abuse of discretion to award fees in light of Poltorak PC's "oppressive tactics" at the initial status conference and "willful violations of court orders." *Dow Chem. Pac. Ltd. v. Rascator Mar. S.A.,* 782 F.2d 329, 345 (2d Cir. 1986).

Second, because the district court did not fully grant Midland's motion for sanctions, which requested that the court award its total fees and costs, Huebner argues that this motion was meritless. And so, he contends, it was an abuse of discretion to impose a fee award that reimbursed Midland for preparing this motion. *Cf. Hensley v. Eckerhart,* 461 U.S. 424, 436, 103 S.Ct. 1933, 76 L.Ed.2d 40 (1983) (holding that courts should not award fees under 42 U.S.C. § 1988 to plaintiffs' lawyers who achieve "only partial or limited success"). But Midland's motion was not meritless. The court agreed with Midland that Poltorak PC should be sanctioned for their bad faith conduct; it just declined to give Midland as large a sanction as it requested. *See Enmon,* 675 F.3d at 148 (upholding a sanctions award for the cost of litigating a sanctions motion because the motion was "well founded," even though the district court "denied [it] in part"). We therefore conclude that the district court did not abuse its discretion in sanctioning Poltorak PC under 28 U.S.C. § 1927.

D

Finally, we examine the district court's decision to sanction Huebner under 15 U.S.C. § 1692k(a)(3) and its inherent authority. Section 1692k(a)(3) allows a district court to sanction a litigant for bringing an FDCPA suit "in bad faith and for the purpose of harassment." A court may also sanction a litigant pursuant to its inherent authority "if there is clear evidence that the [litigant's] conduct" was "(1) entirely without color and (2) motivated by improper purposes." *Wolters Kluwer Fin. Servs., Inc. v. Scivantage,* 664 F.3d 110, 114 (2d Cir. 2009); *see also Chambers,* 501 U.S. at 46, 111 S.Ct. 2123 (holding that such sanctions "vindicat[e] judicial authority without resort to the more drastic sanctions available for contempt of court" p.57 (quoting *Hutto v. Finney,* 437 U.S. 678, 689 n.14, 98 S.Ct. 2565, 57 L.Ed.2d 522 (1978)).

Here, the court sanctioned Huebner under § 1692k(a)(3) and its inherent authority for the same reasons as Poltorak PC, noting that, as an attorney experienced in FDCPA litigation, Huebner played a substantial role in crafting his case's litigation strategy. Huebner has not denied, for example, that at one point he fed his attorney all the questions he asked at a deposition. Huebner also suggested in his opposition to sanctions that he had called Elliott to "test" Midland's FDCPA compliance. The district court interpreted this as an admission that Huebner had been purposefully evasive during the call in an effort to provoke an FDCPA violation, and we see no clear error in this determination. The district court thus did not abuse its discretion in determining that Huebner's decision to initiate this lawsuit "was meritless and brought for improper purposes," and that a fee award was therefore appropriate. *Kerin v. U.S. Postal Serv.,* 218 F.3d 185, 195 (2d Cir. 2000). Huebner's arguments to the contrary are virtually identical to Poltorak PC's out-lined above, and we reject them for the same reasons.

In sum, we conclude that the district court set forth sufficiently detailed factual findings establishing that Huebner, Poltorak, and Poltorak PC brought a frivolous case and filed several frivolous motions in bad faith. The district court was therefore well within its discretion to sanction them.

CONCLUSION

We have considered Huebner, Poltorak, and Poltorak PC's remaining arguments and find them to be without merit. Accordingly, we AFFIRM the judgment of the district court.

[1] The record indicates that Defendant-Appellee Midland Funding LLC purchased the debt and placed it with Midland Credit Management, Inc. for servicing. Huebner purported to contest this fact below but, as the district court correctly noted, he raised no material issue as to the point. In any event, it is immaterial which of the two affiliated defendants technically owned the debt. For simplicity's sake, we will refer to both defendants collectively as "Midland."

[2] Because we are reviewing this case in part on appeal from a grant of summary judgment to Midland, the facts outlined below as to Huebner's substantive claims are either undisputed or viewed in the light most favorable to Huebner. *See, e.g., Raspardo v. Carlone,* 770 F.3d 97, 111 (2d Cir. 2014).

[3] Huebner alleges that Midland never sent him this letter and did not, in fact, inform the credit agencies that they should delete the debt. We agree with the district court that Huebner has failed to create a genuine dispute of material fact concerning this matter. *See* note 5, *infra.*

[4] The court separately held that, even if Huebner had not lost on the merits, it would have declined to certify Huebner's proposed class. *Huebner*, 2016 WL 3172789, at *7-10.

[5] As mentioned earlier, Huebner alleged below that Midland never sent him this letter, but on the evidence in the record, a reasonable jury could only find that Midland sent the letter.

[6] For the first time in his reply brief, Huebner argues that there is a legally significant difference between informing a credit reporting agency that a debt is "disputed" and instructing the agency to delete the debt. Whatever the merits of Huebner's argument, we need not address it. *See McCarthy v. S.E.C.*, 406 F.3d 179, 186 (2d Cir. 2005) (declining to consider "arguments not raised in an appellant's opening brief, but only in his reply brief").

[7] We need not consider Huebner's challenge to the district court's denial of class certification because we hold as a matter of law that Huebner did not suffer a legally cognizable injury. *See Gen. Tel. Co. of Sw. v. Falcon*, 457 U.S. 147, 156, 102 S.Ct. 2364, 72 L.Ed.2d 740 (1982) ("[A] class representative must be part of the class and possess the same interest and suffer the same injury as the class members." (internal quotation marks omitted) (quoting *East Texas Motor Freight System, Inc. v. Rodriguez*, 431 U.S. 395, 403, 97 S.Ct. 1891, 52 L.Ed.2d 453 (1977))).

[8] A court may sanction a law firm under § 1927 for the acts of its attorneys. *See Enmon v. Prospect Capital Corp.*, 675 F.3d 138, 147-48 (2d Cir. 2012).

THIRD CIRCUIT DECISIONS

Fair Debt Collection Practices Act

93 F.4th 136 (2024)

Paulette BARCLIFT, on behalf of herself and others similarly situated, Appellant
v.
KEYSTONE CREDIT SERVICES, LLC.

No. 22-1925.

United States Court of Appeals, Third Circuit.

Argued on March 30, 2023.
Opinion filed: February 16, 2024.

Barclift v. Keystone Credit Services, LLC, 93 F. 4th 136 (3rd Cir. 2024)

p.139 On Appeal from the United States District Court for the Eastern District of Pennsylvania, (D.C. Civil No. 5-21-cv-04335), District Judge: Honorable Joseph F. Leeson, Jr.

Jesse S. Johnson [ARGUED], Greenwald Davidson Radbil PLLC, 5550 Glades Road, Suite 500, Boca Raton, FL 33431, Eric J. Landes, Landes Law, LLC, 419 Oaktree Court, Sanatoga, PA 19464, Counsel for Appellant.

Lee J. Janiczek [ARGUED], Lewis Brisbois Bisgaard & Smith LLP, 550 E Swedesford Road, Suite 270, Wayne, PA 19087, Counsel for Appellee.

Before: MATEY, FREEMAN, and FUENTES, Circuit Judges.

OPINION OF THE COURT

FREEMAN, Circuit Judge.

To facilitate its efforts to collect a debt, Keystone Credit Services, LLC ("Keystone") sent Paulette Barclift's personal information to a mailing vendor, RevSpring, which then mailed Keystone's collection notice to Barclift. Barclift did not authorize p.140 Keystone's communications to RevSpring. So she sued Keystone for an unauthorized communication with a third party in violation of the Fair Debt Collection Practices Act ("FDCPA"), 15 U.S.C. § 1692 *et seq.*, and she sought to represent a class of similarly situated plaintiffs. The District Court found that Barclift did not allege an injury sufficient to establish standing for purposes of Article III of the United States Constitution and dismissed her suit with prejudice. We agree that Barclift lacks standing, but we will modify the District Court's order so that the dismissal will be without prejudice.

I

Keystone is a collection agency based in Lancaster, Pennsylvania.[1] It contracts with RevSpring to print and mail debt collection notices. RevSpring is a nationwide operation with multiple locations and hundreds of employees.

In October 2020, Barclift received a notice in the mail from Keystone regarding her outstanding debt for medical services. The notice was printed and mailed by RevSpring to Barclift's home in Pennsylvania. Keystone provided RevSpring with Barclift's name, address, debt balance, and other information about the debt to populate the mailing. Barclift did not give Keystone prior consent to share that information.

In October 2021, Barclift filed a class action complaint against Keystone on behalf of herself and other Pennsylvania residents who had received collection notices from Keystone through third-party mailing vendors. She claimed that Keystone violated the provision of the FDCPA that bars debt collectors from communicating with third parties in connection with a debt absent prior consent from the debtor (or absent exceptions that do not apply here). 15 U.S.C. § 1692c(b). She alleged that the disclosures had caused her embarrassment and stress, invaded her privacy, and inflicted reputational harm.

Keystone moved to dismiss the complaint for failure to state a claim. The District Court did not reach that argument because it concluded that it lacked jurisdiction, so it dismissed the action without prejudice on that basis and denied Keystone's motion as moot. In its opinion, the court assumed that Barclift had alleged a procedural violation of the FDCPA based on Keystone's communication with RevSpring, but it held that Barclift had not alleged a concrete injury sufficient to establish standing.

Barclift subsequently amended her complaint by adding allegations about RevSpring's operations and data collection processes. Specifically, she made several allegations "upon information and belief," including that RevSpring maintains electronic copies of the consumer data it receives from debt collectors for multiple years, during which time its employees can access sensitive information. She also alleged that RevSpring had mistakenly disseminated the personal information of more than 1,000 patients in the University of Pennsylvania Health System in 2014.

Keystone again moved to dismiss the complaint for failure to state a claim, and the District Court again concluded that Barclift lacked standing. It held that the mere possibility of public disclosure of private facts was not enough to establish a concrete injury and that her fear of future disclosure was too speculative. This time, it dismissed the action with prejudice, reasoning that any additional amendments would be futile because Barclift had not p.141 cured her claim's deficiencies when given the opportunity to do so.

Barclift timely appealed.

II

We have jurisdiction over the District Court's order pursuant to 28 U.S.C. § 1291. We exercise *de novo* review of a dismissal for a lack of standing, "accepting the facts alleged in the complaint as true and construing the complaint in the light most favorable to the non-moving party." *Potter v. Cozen & O'Connor,* 46 F.4th 148, 153 (3d Cir. 2022).

III

Article III of the Constitution grants federal courts "judicial Power" to resolve "Cases" and "Controversies." U.S. Const. art. III, §§ 1-2. The doctrine of standing ensures that courts do not overstep their role by "limit[ing] the category of litigants empowered to maintain a lawsuit in federal court to seek redress for a legal wrong." *Spokeo, Inc. v. Robins,* 578 U.S. 330, 338, 136 S.Ct. 1540, 194 L.Ed.2d 635 (2016). Plaintiffs seeking to vindicate their rights in federal court must therefore satisfy Article III's standing requirements. *See Lujan v. Defs. of Wildlife,* 504 U.S. 555, 561, 112 S.Ct. 2130, 119 L.Ed.2d 351 (1992); *Finkelman v. Nat'l Football League,* 877 F.3d 504, 511 (3d Cir. 2017). Standing consists of three main components: (1) an injury in fact that is concrete and particularized, (2) a causal connection between the injury and the challenged conduct, and (3) a likelihood that the injury will be redressed by a favorable judicial decision. *In re Horizon Healthcare Servs. Inc. Data Breach Litig.,* 846 F.3d 625, 633 (3d Cir. 2017) (quoting *Lujan,* 504 U.S. at 560, 112 S.Ct. 2130). Only the first component is at issue in this appeal: whether Keystone's alleged violation of the FDCPA resulted in a concrete and particularized injury to Barclift.

A

Congress enacted the FDCPA in 1977 to "eliminate abusive debt collection practices by debt collectors" that had contributed to "personal bankruptcies, to marital instability, to the loss of jobs, and to invasions of individual privacy." 15 U.S.C. §§ 1692(a), (e). To that end, section 1692c(b) prohibits debt collectors from "communicat[ing], in connection with the collection of any debt, with any person other than the consumer, his attorney, a consumer reporting agency if otherwise permitted by law, the creditor, the attorney of the creditor, or the attorney of the debt collector" "without the prior consent of the consumer." 15 U.S.C. § 1692c(b). And it creates a civil cause of action for any individual who sustains damages due to a debt collector's violation of the Act. 15 U.S.C. § 1692k.

For decades following the enactment of the FDCPA, consumers rarely sued over the use of third-party mailing vendors for debt collection practices. But in 2021, the United States Court of Appeals for the Eleventh Circuit held that consumers have standing under the FDCPA to bring so-called "mailing vendor theory" lawsuits. *Hunstein v. Preferred Collection & Mgmt. Servs., Inc.,* 994 F.3d 1341, 1344 (11th Cir. 2021) ("*Hunstein I*"), *vacated,* 48 F.4th 1236 (11th Cir. 2022) (en banc). In *Hunstein I,* the plaintiff alleged that a collection agency had sent his personal information to a mailing vendor to facilitate debt collection efforts. *Id.* at 1345. On the issue of Article III standing, the Eleventh Circuit considered *Spokeo, Inc. v. Robins,* in which the Supreme Court held that "a plaintiff [does not] automatically satisf[y] the injury-in-fact requirement whenever a statute grants a person a statutory right p.142 and purports to authorize [a suit] to vindicate [it]" because "Article III standing requires a concrete injury even in the context of a statutory violation." 578 U.S. at 341, 136 S.Ct. 1540. Applying *Spokeo*'s guidance, the Eleventh Circuit held that the injury Hunstein alleged was intangible but was nonetheless sufficiently concrete for Article III standing. *Hunstein I,* 994 F.3d at 1344, 1346. The court also concluded that Hunstein's allegations constituted a violation of section 1692c(b). *Id.* at 1344. That since-vacated decision led to a proliferation of similar suits across the country. *See, e.g., In re FDCPA Mailing Vendor Cases,* 551 F. Supp. 3d 57, 63 (E.D.N.Y. 2021) ("Each case addressed herein invokes a recently-developed 'mailing-vendor' theory.... These cases emanate from [*Hunstein I*]."); *Jackin v. Enhanced Recovery Co.,* 606 F. Supp. 3d 1031, 1034-35 (E.D. Wash. 2022).

Just two months after *Hunstein I,* the Supreme Court decided *TransUnion LLC v. Ramirez,* 594 U.S. 413, 141 S.Ct. 2190, 210 L.Ed.2d 568 (2021), which built upon *Spokeo* and provided additional guidance to courts seeking to determine whether an intangible harm suffices as a concrete injury. Because *TransUnion* is key to our decision today, we examine it in some detail here.

TransUnion was a class action suit seeking relief for individuals allegedly harmed by a violation of the Fair Credit Reporting Act ("FCRA"). A credit reporting agency mistakenly added an alert to numerous consumers' files indicating that they were a "potential match" with individuals on a national security threat list. *Id.* at 420, 141 S.Ct. 2190. For most of the affected consumers, the credit agency simply maintained alerts on internal records without disseminating them. *Id.* at 421, 141 S.Ct. 2190. But for others, the agency distributed reports containing the erroneous security alert to creditors. *Id.*

Invoking *Spokeo,* the Court explained that intangible harms can give rise to concrete injuries when they bear "a close relationship to harms traditionally recognized as providing a basis for lawsuits in American courts," such as "reputational harms, disclosure of private information, and intrusion upon seclusion." *Id.* at 425, 141 S.Ct. 2190. But even though this inquiry requires the identification of "a close historical or common-law analogue for the[] asserted injury," the Court clarified that there need not be "an exact duplicate." *Id.* at 424, 141 S.Ct. 2190. And while Congress may elevate certain harms to actionable legal status through legislation, the Court stressed that Congress's mere creation of a statutory cause of action does not "automatically satisf[y] the injury-in-fact requirement." *Id.* at 426, 141 S.Ct. 2190 (quoting *Spokeo,* 578 U.S. at 341, 136 S.Ct. 1540).

The *TransUnion* plaintiffs had sued, in relevant part, under a FCRA provision that requires agencies to "follow reasonable procedures to assure maximum possible accuracy of the [consumer's] information." 15 U.S.C. § 1681e(b). The plaintiffs contended that the erroneous security alerts bore a "close relationship" to the traditional harm associated with the tort of defamation. *TransUnion,* 594 U.S. at 432, 141 S.Ct. 2190. The credit agency countered by arguing that defamation required literal falsity, whereas the alerts (which only denoted "*potential* match[es]" with the threats list) were at most misleading. *Id.* at 433, 141 S.Ct. 2190.

The Supreme Court sided with the plaintiffs, explaining that—in the context of a national security threats list—"the harm from a misleading statement ... b[ore] a *sufficiently close relationship* to the harm from a false and defamatory p.143 statement." *Id.* (emphasis added). But because publication is "essential to liability" in a defamation claim, only the plaintiffs whose erroneous security alerts were actually disseminated to creditors suffered concrete injuries for standing purposes. *Id.* at 434, 141 S.Ct. 2190 (quoting Restatement (Second) of Torts § 577 cmt. a (1938)). By contrast, the remaining plaintiffs, whose alerts were never sent to third parties, lacked standing to sue. *Id.* ("The mere presence of an inaccuracy in an internal credit file, if it is not disclosed to a third party, causes no concrete harm."), 437, 141 S.Ct. 2190 ("[T]he [other] plaintiffs did not demonstrate that the risk of future harm materialized.... Nor did those plaintiffs present evidence that [they] were independently harmed by their exposure to the risk itself[.]").

In a footnote, the Court noted that the plaintiffs had forfeited an argument that the credit agency had "'published' the class members' information internally ... to employees within TransUnion and to the vendors that printed and sent the mailings that the class members received." *Id.* at 434 n.6, 141 S.Ct. 2190. In any event, the Court deemed the argument "unavailing" because "[m]any American courts did not traditionally recognize intra-company disclosures ... for purposes of the tort of defamation" and did not "necessarily recognize[] disclosures to printing vendors as actionable publications." *Id.* And even the courts that traditionally did so required a showing that the defendant "actually 'brought an idea to the perception of another'" or that the information "was actually read and not merely processed." *Id.* (quoting Restatement (Second) of Torts § 559 cmt. a); *see id.* (explaining that a theory that "circumvents a fundamental requirement of an ordinary defamation claim ... does not bear a sufficiently 'close relationship' to the traditional defamation tort to qualify for Article III standing").

Courts have interpreted *TransUnion*'s methodology in different ways, as exemplified by the subsequent developments in the *Hunstein* matter. The Eleventh Circuit reheard *Hunstein* twice (first before the original panel ("*Hunstein II*"), and then *en banc*) before concluding that Hunstein's alleged harm in his mailing vendor case was not a concrete injury. *Hunstein v. Preferred Collection & Mgmt. Servs., Inc.*, 48 F.4th 1236, 1240 (11th Cir. 2022) (en banc) ("*Hunstein III*"). The *en banc* court focused on elements. It reasoned that an alleged intangible harm is not closely related to a traditional harm if it is "missing an element 'essential to liability' under the comparator tort." *Id.* at 1242. It then compared Hunstein's alleged injury to the traditional tort of public disclosure of private facts. It recounted that Hunstein did not suggest in his complaint that the debt collector's communication "reached, or was sure to reach, the public. Quite the opposite—the complaint describe[d] a disclosure that reached a single intermediary, which then passed the information back to Hunstein without sharing it more broadly." *Id.* at 1248. So the court held that Hunstein's allegations lacked publicity—an element "essential to liability." *Id.* at 1244.

The *Hunstein III* dissent, however, took issue with the majority's "element-for-element" approach. *Id.* at 1261 (Newsom, J., dissenting). The four dissenting judges viewed that approach as a "dressed-up version of the very 'exact duplicate' standard that the Supreme Court ... flatly disavowed." *Id.* They reasoned that, because *TransUnion* held that misleading information was "close enough" to false and defamatory information, Hunstein's "allegation of *near* publicity[,] ... (*i.e.*, dissemination to an as-yet-unknown number of employees)" was "close enough" to an allegation of publicity. *Id.* at 1262.

p.144 As an alternative to comparing elements, the *Hunstein III* dissent embraced a "*kind* of harm" test, which would require a plaintiff suing on a statutory cause of action to "show that his alleged injury is similar in *kind* to the harm addressed by a common-law cause of action, but not that it is identical in *degree*." *Id.* at 1264. On that basis, the dissenting judges would have concluded that Hunstein's allegations (taken as true and paired with all reasonable and favorable inferences) were sufficient to show an injury in fact because Hunstein's injury was "close enough" to the *kind* of harm posed by publicity under the common-law tort of public disclosure of private facts, even if Hunstein's harm did not rise to the same *degree* of publicity-related harm. *Id.* at 1268-69.

A few months after *Hunstein III,* the Tenth Circuit considered the FDCPA mailing vendor theory in *Shields v. Professional Bureau of Collections of Maryland, Inc.,* 55 F.4th 823 (10th Cir. 2022). The Tenth Circuit implicitly adopted the kind-of-harm framework urged by the *Hunstein III* dissent, but held that the plaintiff lacked standing. *Shields,* 55 F.4th at 829. It stated that under *TransUnion,* "Shields did not have to plead and prove the [common law] tort's elements to prevail. But to proceed, she had to at least allege a similar harm." *Id.* The court concluded that Shields's assertion "that one private entity (and, presumably, some of its employees) knew of her debt" was "not the same kind of harm as *public* disclosure of private facts." *Id.*

After we heard oral argument in Barclift's appeal, the Seventh Circuit took a turn at deciding a FDCPA mailing vendor case. *Nabozny v. Optio Sols. LLC,* 84 F.4th 731 (7th Cir. 2023). It first used the element-based approach from *Hunstein III* and held that the plaintiff's "attempt to analogize her case to [the tort of public disclosure of private facts] [fell] apart on the threshold element of publicity." *Id.* at 735 (citing *Hunstein III,* 48 F.4th at 1245-49). Because the plaintiff did not allege publicity as that term is understood in traditional tort law, the court concluded that she had not suffered an injury "analogous to the harm at the core of the public-disclosure tort." *Id.* at 736; *id.* at 735 ("'Publicity' ... means that the matter is made public, by communicating it to the public at large, or to so many persons that the matter must be regarded as substantially certain to become one of public knowledge." (quoting Restatement (Second) of Torts § 652D cmt. a)). The Seventh Circuit then addressed the kind-or-degree question, stating that the difference between public and private communication "is not just a matter of numbers," but when a private communication is sent "with no expectation of further disclosure, it is not one that is 'sure to reach[] the public.'" *Id.* at 736 (alteration in original) (quoting Restatement (Second) of Torts § 652D cmt. a). Finally, it explained that "the harm at the core of the public-disclosure tort" is "the humiliation that accompanies the disclosure of sensitive or scandalizing private information to public scrutiny." *Id.* So "[w]ithout a public-exposure component," the plaintiff's alleged harm was not analogous. *Id.*

In sum, judges on our sister circuits have interpreted *TransUnion* in two different ways. Some espouse an element-based approach, wherein a plaintiff's alleged harm must not lack any element of the comparator tort that was essential to liability at common law. *E.g., Hunstein III,* 48 F.4th at 1244-45; *see* Element, *Black's Law Dictionary* (11th ed. 2019) (defining "element" as "[a] constituent part of a claim that must be proved for the claim to succeed"). Others compare the kind of harm a plaintiff alleges with the p.145 kind of harm caused by the comparator tort. *E.g., Shields,* 55 F.4th at 829. We view the second method as more faithful to *TransUnion.*

To determine the "concreteness" of intangible injuries, *TransUnion* instructs us to ask "whether the asserted harm has a 'close relationship' to a harm traditionally recognized as providing a basis for a lawsuit in American courts—such as physical harm, monetary harm, or various intangible harms including (as relevant here) reputational harm." 594 U.S. at 417, 141 S.Ct. 2190. *TransUnion* speaks only of harms, not elements. Indeed, the word "element" does not appear once in the body of the *TransUnion* opinion. We believe that if the Court wanted us to compare elements, it would have simply said so.[2] So when asking whether a plaintiff's intangible injury is "concrete," we will examine the kind of harm at issue.

B

Applying our interpretation of *TransUnion* to Barclift's allegations, we conclude that she cannot establish standing for her claim. She cannot demonstrate that the injury resulting from Keystone's communication of her personal information to a third-party mailing vendor bears a close relationship to a harm traditionally recognized by American courts. *See TransUnion,* 594 U.S. at 417, 141 S.Ct. 2190.

At common law, actionable invasions of privacy are typically categorized into four separate torts: intrusion upon seclusion, appropriation of name or likeness, unreasonable publicity given to another's private life, and false light. *See* Restatement (Second) of Torts § 652A; *see also Nabozny,* 84 F.4th at 735. The traditional harm that Barclift analogizes to lies at the heart of the unreasonable publicity given to another's private life, which is also known as the public disclosure of private information.[3] A defendant is liable under this tort when he "gives publicity to a matter concerning the private life of another... if the matter publicized is of a kind that (a) would be highly offensive to a reasonable person, and (b) is not of legitimate concern to the public." Restatement (Second) of Torts § 652D. The harm caused by this tort is "the humiliation that accompanies the disclosure of sensitive or p.146 scandalizing private information to public scrutiny." *Nabozny,* 84 F.4th at 736; *see also Jenkins v. Dell Publ'g Co.,* 251 F.2d 447, 450 (3d Cir. 1958) (explaining that privacy torts provide legal relief for "the embarrassment, humiliation[,] or other injury which may result from public disclosure concerning his personality or experiences"). The harm stems from both the offensive character of the information and its disclosure to the public.

Here, Barclift alleged that Keystone transmitted her information to RevSpring for one purpose: "to fashion, print, and mail debt collection letters." Appx. 39. She also alleged that she was "embarrassed and distressed" by the disclosure to RevSpring. Appx. 46. But she did not allege that anyone outside of Keystone or RevSpring accessed her personal information. In short, she alleged that Keystone transmitted her personal information to "a single ministerial intermediary," *Nabozny,* 84 F.4th at 736, causing her embarrassment.

While Barclift does not need to "exact[ly] duplicate" a traditionally recognized harm, *TransUnion,* 594 U.S. at 433, 141 S.Ct. 2190, she must still analogize to a harm "of the same character of previously existing 'legally cognizable injuries,'" *Kamal v. J. Crew Grp., Inc.,* 918 F.3d 102, 114 (3d Cir. 2019) (quoting *Susinno v. Work Out World Inc.,* 862 F.3d 346, 352 (3d Cir. 2017)). Like our sister circuits, we conclude that the harm from disclosures that remain functionally internal are not closely related to those stemming from public ones. *See Shields,* 55 F.4th at 829 ("Shields's alleged harm was that one private entity (and, presumably, some of its employees) knew of her debt. That is not the same kind of harm as *public* disclosure of private facts, which is concerned with highly offensive information being widely known."). When the communication of personal information only occurs between a debt collector and an intermediary tasked with contacting the consumer, the consumer has not suffered the kind of privacy harm traditionally associated with public disclosure.[4]

Our conclusion comports with the Supreme Court's observations (in dicta) from *TransUnion* about the internal publication of consumer data. While *TransUnion* compared FCRA violations to the traditional harms of defamation, the same logic applies here. The Court found unavailing plaintiffs' unpreserved argument that their information had been "published... internally ... to employees within [the credit reporting agency] and to the vendors that printed and sent the mailings that the class members received." *TransUnion,* 594 U.S. at 434 n.6, 141 S.Ct. 2190 (quotation marks omitted). The Court stated that American courts generally have not recognized "disclosures to printing vendors as actionable publications," and that harms associated with "internal publication... do[] not bear a sufficiently 'close relationship'" to defamation harms for standing purposes. *Id.* While this rationale is not binding, we believe it would p.147 apply to the mailing vendor theory claims here.[5] If there are no grounds to believe that the information will result in humiliation, then there is no comparable harm under *TransUnion.*[6]

Finally, Barclift cannot show that she has suffered a concrete injury due to anticipated harm. As a general matter, "[a]llegations of 'possible future injury' are not sufficient to satisfy Article III" in a p.148 suit for damages. *Reilly v. Ceridian Corp.,* 664 F.3d 38, 42 (3d Cir. 2011) (quoting *Whitmore v. Arkansas,* 495 U.S. 149, 158, 110 S.Ct. 1717, 109 L.Ed.2d 135 (1990)); *see TransUnion,* 594 U.S. at 437, 141 S.Ct. 2190 ("*Spokeo* did not hold that the mere risk of future harm, without more, suffices to demonstrate Article III standing in a suit for damages."). For a material risk of future harm to be concrete, a plaintiff must show that she was "independently harmed by [her] exposure to the risk itself." *TransUnion,* 594 U.S. at 437, 141 S.Ct. 2190. In *TransUnion,* it was not enough that "[the credit report company] could have divulged [the plaintiffs'] misleading credit information to a third party at any moment." *Id.* at 438, 141 S.Ct. 2190. Similarly, the mere assertion that RevSpring's employees *could* access and broadcast Barclift's personal information to the public is far too speculative to support standing. And even though RevSpring suffered a prior data breach in 2014, Barclift has not alleged facts supporting an inference of "a sufficient likelihood that [RevSpring] would ... intentionally or accidentally release [her] information to third parties." *Id.* Without an actual, materialized injury, "we cannot simply presume a material risk of concrete harm" absent a "serious likelihood of disclosure." *Id.* (quoting *Ramirez v. TransUnion,* 951 F.3d 1008, 1040 (9th Cir. 2020) (McKeown, J., concurring in part and dissenting in part)).[7]

In sum, the type of injury Barclift alleged "is not remotely analogous to the harm caused by the tortious public dissemination of sensitive facts about another's private life." *Nabozny,* 84 F.4th at 737-38 (emphasis omitted). Information transmission that neither travels beyond a private intermediary nor creates a sufficient likelihood of external dissemination cannot compare to a traditionally recognized harm that depends on the humiliating effects of public disclosure. Therefore, we conclude that Barclift lacks a concrete injury and cannot establish Article III standing.

C

Although the District Court correctly held that Barclift lacked a concrete injury, it erred in dismissing her complaint with prejudice. "Because the absence of standing leaves the court without subject matter jurisdiction to reach a decision on the merits, dismissals 'with prejudice' for lack of standing are generally improper." *Cottrell v. Alcon Lab'ys,* 874 F.3d 154, 164 n.7 (3d Cir. 2017). That general rule applies here, so we will modify the District Court's order to dismiss the complaint without prejudice and affirm that order as modified.

***

For the foregoing reasons, we will modify the District Court's order to dismiss the complaint without prejudice and affirm the order as modified.

MATEY, Circuit Judge, concurring in part, dissenting in part, and dissenting in the judgment.

"Standing" is a term found in every first-year law school outline, but absent from the text of the Constitution, Founding-era discussions, English and Roman history, and the reported decisions of our federal courts throughout most of the twentieth century. Ever shifting, the judicially p.149 created standard of modern standing confuses courts, commentators, and plaintiffs like Paulette Barclift who are told their claim is insufficiently "concrete" to decide. Barclift says Keystone Credit Services shared private information about her physical and financial health with "an untold number of individuals" at a mailing facility close to her home. App. 62. Can she file a lawsuit for her alleged harms? Congress said yes, inserting a private right of action in the Fair Debt Collection Practices Act (FDCPA). And the Supreme Court has explained that the "disclosure of private information" has been "traditionally recognized as providing a basis for lawsuits in American courts." *TransUnion LLC v. Ramirez,* 594 U.S. 413, 425, 141 S.Ct. 2190, 210 L.Ed.2d 568 (2021). I conclude that Barclift's "intangible harms" are sufficiently "concrete" for standing because they bear "a close relationship to harms traditionally recognized as providing a basis for lawsuits in American courts." *Id.*

But Barclift loses because the majority treats *TransUnion*'s footnote six as talismanic, turning dictum into precedent and, along the way, adopting the jot-for-jot reading of caselaw that the majority's opinion purports to reject. Respectfully, I cannot pour that much meaning into a note, particularly where the result only adds to the incoherence of modern standing. So I dissent in part and in the judgment because, while standing "needs a rewrite," as the requirement stands, Paulette Barclift is due her day in court. *Id.* at 461, 141 S.Ct. 2190 (Kagan, J., dissenting).[1]

I.

The majority surveys circuit caselaw, catalogues the divergent approaches, and selects a test that compares the harm a plaintiff asserts to a harm that traditionally provided a basis to sue in American courts to determine whether an intangible injury is concrete. I agree that conclusion is the best reading of *TransUnion,* even if a natural reading of the FDCPA and Article III make that difficult detour unnecessary.[2] I write separately to explain how the wandering began.

A. Article III provides that "[t]he judicial Power shall extend to *all* Cases, in Law and Equity, arising under ... the Laws of the United States, ..." U.S. Const. art. III, § 2 (emphasis added). Text that places no limits on either the judicial power to hear cases or on the legislative power to create causes of action under the laws of the United States. It seems to allow all suits arising under federal law.

Barclift's suit arises under the FDCPA, which prohibits a "debt collector" from "communicat[ing], in connection with the collection of any debt, with any person other than the consumer, his attorney, a consumer reporting agency if otherwise p.150 permitted by law, the creditor, the attorney of the creditor, or the attorney of the debt collector." 15 U.S.C. § 1692c(b). The FDCPA includes a private right of action against debt collectors. *See id.* § 1692k(d) ("An action to enforce any liability created by [the FDCPA] may be brought in any appropriate United States district court...."). If the text of Article III is the gate, Barclift's complaint says enough to walk through the doors of the federal courts. History confirms this unfussy understanding that Barclift's suit under the FDCPA constitutes a "case" under Article III.[3] Given the many thoughtful discussions on this subject, *see supra* note 1, a summary of standing will suffice.

1. Pre-Founding and early American jurists never used the term "standing" or required an injury in fact or special damage when a private party sued to enforce a private right.[4] "Historically, common-law courts possessed broad power to adjudicate suits involving the alleged violation of private rights, even when plaintiffs alleged only the violation of those rights and nothing more." *Spokeo, Inc. v. Robins,* 578 U.S. 330, 344, 136 S.Ct. 1540, 194 L.Ed.2d 635 (2016) (Thomas, J., concurring); *see also Muransky v. Godiva Chocolatier, Inc.,* 979 F.3d 917, 971 (11th Cir. 2020) (en banc) (Jordan, J., dissenting) ("English courts at common law heard suits involving private rights, regardless of whether the plaintiff suffered actual damage, ..."). Instead, "the English practice was to allow strangers to have standing in the many cases involving the ancient prerogative writs.... There were other English precedents for the citizen suit. In the seventeenth and eighteenth centuries, mandamus was available in England, even at the behest of strangers." Cass R. Sunstein, *What's Standing After* Lujan? *Of Citizen Suits, "Injuries," and Article III,* 91 Mich. L. Rev. 163, 171-72 (1992). Factual injury on top of legal injury was not a component of a completely pled complaint. *See, e.g.,* 3 William Blackstone, Commentaries *120 (explaining suits for assault could be brought even when "no actual suffering is proved" and for battery whether "accompanied with pain ... [or] attended with none").

p.151 The Framers wrote Article III against this backdrop. Federal question jurisdiction appeared at the Constitutional Convention in the Virginia Plan, broadly authorizing federal courts to hear "questions which may involve the national peace and harmony." James Madison, Resolutions Proposed by Mr. Randolph in Convention (May 29, 1787), *in* 1 The Records of the Federal Convention of 1787, at 22 (Max Farrand ed., 1911). The Committee of Detail removed the reference to "national peace and harmony" but preserved jurisdiction over "cases arising under laws passed by the Legislature of the United States." James Madison, Mr. Randolph's Delivery of the Report of the Committee of Detail (Aug. 6, 1787), *in* 2 The Records of the Federal Convention of 1787, *supra,* at 186. Few additional changes followed. And when the Committee of Style reported to the Convention in September 1787, the proposed federal judicial power extended "to all cases, both in law and equity, arising under this constitution, the laws of the United States, and treaties made, or which shall be made, under their authority." Report of Committee of Style, *in* 2 The Records of the Federal Convention of 1787, *supra,* at 600.

That troubled George Mason, who voiced concern that there would be no "limitation whatsoever, with respect to the nature or jurisdiction of [the federal] Courts." George Mason, Speech to the Virginia Convention (June 19, 1788), *in* 10 The Documentary History of the Ratification of the Constitution: Ratification of the Constitution by the States: Virginia, No. 3, at 1401 (John P. Kaminski & Gaspare J. Saladino eds., 1993). Responding, James Madison agreed that "it is so necessary and expedient that the Judicial power [of the national government] should correspond with the Legislative" and saw no problems posed by a broad judicial power. James Madison, Speech to the Virginia Convention (June 20, 1788), *in* The Documentary History of the Ratification of the Constitution: Ratification of the Constitution by the States: Virginia, No. 3, *supra,* at 1413. Neither Madison's nor Mason's writings, nor other Founding-era records, mention standing, the now-canonical injury-in-fact requirement, or anything else that would restrict Congress's power to create judicially enforceable rights.

Giants of the early American judiciary agreed, understanding Article III to confer broad power.[5] "It was also understood that p.152 Congress could create private rights by statute and that a plaintiff could sue based on a violation of that statutory right without regard to actual damages." *Muransky,* 979 F.3d at 971 (Jordan, J., dissenting) (citing Thomas M. Cooley, A Treatise on the Law of Torts or the Wrongs Which Arise Independent of Contract 271 (2d ed. 1888)); *see also Webb v. Portland Mfg. Co.,* 29 F. Cas. 506, 509 (C.C.D. Me. 1838) (Story, J.) ("[E]very violation imports damage; and if no other be proved, the plaintiff is entitled to a verdict for nominal damages."). Take the 1790 Copyright Act, which allowed patent holders to sue for damages those infringing on the patent, even in the absence of monetary loss. *See* Act of May 31, 1790, ch. 15, § 2, 1 Stat. 124, 124-25.

The factual injury requirement appeared only when a private individual sued to enforce a public right.[6] "Repeated attempts of private litigants to obtain a special stake in public rights have been consistently denied." *Scripps-Howard Radio v. F.C.C.,* 316 U.S. 4, 20, 62 S.Ct. 875, 86 L.Ed. 1229 (1942) (Douglas, J., dissenting) (collecting cases). If an individual sued over a public nuisance, for example, the person had to allege the violation caused them "some extraordinary damage, beyond the rest of the [community]." 3 Blackstone, Commentaries *220; *see also* Ann Woolhandler & Caleb Nelson, *Does History Defeat Standing Doctrine?,* 102 Mich. L. Rev. 689, 703 (2004) ("To be sure, when a public nuisance was threatening special injury to a private plaintiff and the plaintiff was able to win an injunction against the nuisance, the same remedy that protected the plaintiff against private harm also benefited the public as a whole. As a conceptual matter, however, this benefit to the public was 'incidental[]'; the private plaintiff was not thought of as representing the public, but rather as protecting his own private interest." (alteration in original) (quoting *Sparhawk v. Union Passenger Ry. Co.,* 54 Pa. 401, 422 (1867))).

That is the original understanding of Article III, and "courts for centuries held that injury in law to a private right was enough to create a case or controversy." *TransUnion,* 594 U.S. at 449, 141 S.Ct. 2190 (Thomas, J., dissenting). For most of American history, if Barclift sued as a private individual to enforce a private right created by Congress, her case would be p.153 heard without any obligation to make a threshold showing of factual injury.[7]

2. So what happened? The emergence of new federal agencies started to shift the landscape, although the public-private rights distinction continued without interruption. The idea, born from the minds of jurists like Brandeis and Frankfurter,[8] was "to insulate the nascent regulatory state from legal challenge. A strict requirement of *legal* injury fit well with efforts to limit challenges by regulated entities, which would generally be able to show factual costs from government action but often lacked either protected legal interests or established rights to sue." Ernest A. Young, *Standing, Equity, and Injury in Fact,* 97 Notre Dame L. Rev. 1885, 1890-91 (2022).[9] The Court formally introduced the concept of "injury in fact" in *Association of Data Processing Organizations v. Camp,* when it held that, in the context of the Administrative Procedure Act (APA), the plaintiff needed only to allege an "injury in fact, economic or otherwise" to sue under the APA. 397 U.S. 150, 152, 90 S.Ct. 827, 25 L.Ed.2d 184 (1970).[10] The Court added that "[t]he question of standing is different" from a test that looks to the plaintiff's legal interest, which "goes to the merits." *Id.* at 153, 90 S.Ct. 827. Rather, standing "concerns, apart from the 'case' or 'controversy' test, the question whether the interest sought to be protected by the complainant is arguably within the zone of interests to be protected or regulated by the statute or constitutional guarantee in question. Thus the [APA] grants standing to a person 'aggrieved by agency action within the meaning of a relevant statute.'" *Id.* (quoting 5 U.S.C. § 702). "Instead of a careful examination of the governing law to see if Congress had created a legal interest, the standing inquiry would be a simple one barely related to the underlying law. Henceforth the issue would turn on facts, not on law." Sunstein, *supra,* at 185. "Under the New Deal view, the common law was a regulatory system that should be evaluated pragmatically, in terms of whether it served human liberty and welfare. When it failed to do so, the system had to be supplemented or replaced." *Id.* at 187.

p.154 Standing's political valence shifted to an indirect limit on congressional power (ignoring, among other options, a fresh examination on the meaning of Article I, Section 8, Clause 3 of the Constitution). In 1983, then-Judge Scalia published an article explaining his view that "[t]he requirement of standing has been made part of American constitutional law through (for want of a better vehicle) the provision of Art. III, Sec. 2." Antonin Scalia, *The Doctrine of Standing as an Essential Element of the Separation of Powers,* 17 Suffolk U. L. Rev. 881, 882 (1983). He went on: "[t]here is no case or controversy, the reasoning has gone, when there are no adverse parties with personal interest in the matter. Surely not a linguistically inevitable conclusion, but nonetheless an accurate description of the sort of business courts had traditionally entertained, and hence of the distinctive business to which they were presumably to be limited under the Constitution." *Id.* (footnote omitted). He described the notion that Congress may create legal rights as "a peculiar characteristic of standing." *Id.* at 885. But he was bothered by Congress's control over the creation of legal rights given the increasing power of the regulatory state. With little discussion of constitutional text or history, Judge Scalia concluded that "the judicial doctrine of standing is a crucial and inseparable element of [the principle of separation of powers], whose disregard will inevitably produce ... an overjudicialization of the process of self-governance." *Id.* at 881.

In 1992, Justice Scalia penned the modern-day test for standing in *Lujan v. Defenders of Wildlife,* establishing the atextual tripart test for determining whether a party has standing to bring suit. *See* 504 U.S. 555, 560-61, 112 S.Ct. 2130, 119 L.Ed.2d 351 (1992). The broad, sweeping language of *Lujan* did not apply only in the public rights category, though the result, by happenstance, remained consistent with the historical public-private rights distinction.[11] Ever since, the Court has continued to march down *Lujan*'s path, while neglecting to engage with the public-private rights distinction.

3. Bringing us to *TransUnion.* That decision marked the first time the Supreme Court required a private individual to make some threshold showing of concrete harm, even though he was seeking to vindicate a private right. *See* 594 U.S. at 453-54, 141 S.Ct. 2190 (Thomas, J., dissenting) ("Never before has this Court declared that legal injury is *inherently* insufficient to support standing."); *see also Muransky,* 979 F.3d at 978-79 (Jordan, J., dissenting) (finding no "contemporary Supreme Court case in which a plaintiff had a private statutory right but was denied standing"). And the yardstick chosen to measure concreteness —the close-relationship test— swapped the text and history of Article III for unspecified and undetermined markers in American "history and tradition." *TransUnion,* 594 U.S. at 424, 141 S.Ct. 2190 (majority opinion). A plaintiff's allegations need not "exact[ly] duplicate" the elements of a common law cause of action, only resemble the "harm[s] *associated with*" p.155 those causes of action. *Id.* at 432-33, 141 S.Ct. 2190.

This illustrates a judicial test "displac[ing]... controlling, nonjudicial, primary texts." *OI Eur. Grp. B.V. v. Bolivarian Republic of Venez.,* 73 F.4th 157, 175 n.22 (3d Cir. 2023) (citation omitted); *see also* Peter Bozzo, Note, *The Jurisprudence of "As Though": Democratic Dialogue and the Signed Supreme Court Opinion,* 26 Yale J.L. & Human. 269, 289 (2014) (Judicial "tests often take on a life of their own, displacing the [source of law] from which they are drawn."). Leaving us to work with only a "metaphor for the law" instead of the law itself. Mitchel de S.-O.-l'E. Lasser, *"Lit. Theory" Put to the Test: A Comparative Literary Analysis of American Judicial Tests and French Judicial Discourse,* 111 Harv. L. Rev. 689, 768 (1998)).

But work with the shadow we must, for "unless we wish anarchy to prevail within the federal judicial system," precedent must be followed "by the lower federal courts no matter how misguided the judges of those courts may think it to be." *Hutto v. Davis,* 454 U.S. 370, 375, 102 S.Ct. 703, 70 L.Ed.2d 556 (1982) (per curiam). So I move to the best reading of *TransUnion.*

II.

TransUnion's close-relationship test starts from the premise that "Article III confines the federal judicial power to the resolution of 'Cases' and 'Controversies.'" *TransUnion,* 594 U.S. at 423, 141 S.Ct. 2190. "For there to be a case or controversy under Article III, the plaintiff must have a 'personal stake' in the case—in other words, standing." *Id.* (quoting *Raines v. Byrd,* 521 U.S. 811, 819, 117 S.Ct. 2312, 138 L.Ed.2d 849 (1997)). And to establish standing, "a plaintiff must show (i) that he suffered an injury in fact that is concrete, particularized, and actual or imminent; (ii) that the injury was likely caused by the defendant; and (iii) that the injury would likely be redressed by judicial relief." *Id.* (citing *Lujan,* 504 U.S. at 560-61, 112 S.Ct. 2130).

"If 'the plaintiff does not claim to have suffered an injury that the defendant caused and the court can remedy, there is no case or controversy for the federal court to resolve.'" *Id.* (citation omitted)). Barclift's case homes in on the injury-in-fact requirement—that the plaintiff's injury be "real, and not abstract." *Id.* at 424, 141 S.Ct. 2190 (quoting *Spokeo,* 578 U.S. at 340, 136 S.Ct. 1540). We can reduce that requirement to three questions.

First, when assessing whether a harm is sufficiently concrete for standing, "the Court has explained that 'history and tradition offer a meaningful guide to the types of cases that Article III empowers federal courts to consider.'" *Id.* (quoting *Sprint Commc'ns Co., L.P. v. APCC Servs., Inc.,* 554 U.S. 269, 274, 128 S.Ct. 2531, 171 L.Ed.2d 424 (2008)). "And with respect to the concrete-harm requirement in particular," *Spokeo* and *TransUnion* instruct courts to "assess whether the alleged injury to the plaintiff has a 'close relationship' to a harm 'traditionally' recognized as providing a basis for a lawsuit in American courts." *Id.*; *see also Spokeo,* 578 U.S. at 341, 136 S.Ct. 1540 ("[I]t is instructive to consider whether an alleged intangible harm has a close relationship to a harm that has traditionally been regarded as providing a basis for a lawsuit in English or American courts." (citing *Vt. Agency of Nat. Res. v. U.S. ex rel. Stevens,* 529 U.S. 765, 775-77, 120 S.Ct. 1858, 146 L.Ed.2d 836 (2000))). Under the close-relationship test, plaintiffs must identify "a close historical or common-law analogue for their asserted injury," but an "exact duplicate in American history and tradition" p.156 is not required. *TransUnion,* 594 U.S. at 424, 141 S.Ct. 2190.[12]

Second, while "traditional tangible harms, such as physical harms and monetary damages," "readily qualify as concrete injuries under Article III," certain "intangible harms can also be concrete." *Id.* at 425, 141 S.Ct. 2190. "Chief among them are injuries with a close relationship to harms traditionally recognized as providing a basis for lawsuits in American courts." *Id.* Qualifying intangible harms "include, for example, reputational harms, disclosure of private information, and intrusion upon seclusion." *Id.*

Third, along with common-law analogues, courts must consider "Congress's decision to impose a statutory prohibition or obligation on a defendant, and to grant a plaintiff a cause of action to sue over the defendant's violation of that statutory prohibition or obligation." *Id.* Indeed, Congress may enact a statute that "elevate[s]" certain "concrete, *de facto* injuries" "to the status of legally cognizable injuries" even though they "were previously inadequate in law." *Id.* at 426, 141 S.Ct. 2190 (quoting *Spokeo,* 578 U.S. at 341, 136 S.Ct. 1540). But while "Congress may 'elevate' harms that 'exist' in the real world before Congress recognized them to actionable legal status, it may not simply enact an injury into existence, using its lawmaking power to transform something that is not remotely harmful into something that is." *Id.* (citation omitted).

Putting it all together, we must evaluate whether Barclift's asserted harm bears a close relationship to a harm traditionally recognized as providing a basis for suit in American courts; and, if Barclift has a sufficiently concrete harm, evaluate whether Congress has elevated that harm to a legally cognizable injury. To that task I turn.

A. History

Barclift's "asserted harm has a 'close relationship' to a harm traditionally recognized as providing a basis for a lawsuit in American courts." *Id.* at 433, 141 S.Ct. 2190. That inquiry requires "a close historical p.157 or common-law analogue for [her] asserted injury," not "an exact duplicate." *Id.* at 424, 141 S.Ct. 2190.

1. Start with Barclift's alleged harm: the "disclosure of private information of a personal, sensitive nature" to a third party without her consent. App. 62. It stems from a "Notice of Account Placement" Barclift received stating that her "account with Main Line Fertility Center, Inc. ha[d] been assigned to" Keystone. App. 67. The letter listed Barclift's Keystone account number, the date of her purported delinquency, and the balance due. A bold notice advised "this communication is from a debt collection company. This is an attempt to collect a debt; any information obtained will be used for that purpose." App. 67.

Though the letter arrived on Keystone's letterhead, a third-party vendor, RevSpring, had prepared and mailed it. That must mean Keystone "provided information regarding [Barclift] and the Debt" to RevSpring and its hundreds of employees, including her "name and address, the amount of the Debt, the name of the current creditor, and other private details regarding the Debt." App. 56. Barclift says she "did not consent to [Keystone] communicating with RevSpring in connection with the collection of the Debt," nor did she authorize Keystone to engage in similar communications with other third-party vendors. App. 56. And she claims the unauthorized "disclosure of her personal financial details, as well as the sensitive details of her personal medical services, to an untold number of individuals affiliated with RevSpring" made her feel embarrassed, anxious, and stressed. App. 62. Take those allegations as true, and Barclift argues the unauthorized disclosure tracks two common-law privacy torts: public disclosure of private facts and breach of confidence. She is right.

The tort of public disclosure prohibits "unauthorized *disclosures* of information." *In re Horizon Healthcare Servs. Inc. Data Breach Litig.*, 846 F.3d 625, 638 (3d Cir. 2017), *quoted in Kamal v. J. Crew Grp., Inc.*, 918 F.3d 102, 114 (3d Cir. 2019). And "breach of confidence involves 'the unconsented, unprivileged disclosure to a third party of nonpublic information that the defendant has learned within a confidential relationship.'" *Kamal,* 918 F.3d at 114 (quoting Alan B. Vickery, Note, *Breach of Confidence: An Emerging Tort,* 82 Colum. L. Rev. 1426, 1455 (1982)).[13] As this Court p.158 held five years ago, "the harm underlying both of these actions transpires when a third party gains unauthorized access to a plaintiff's personal information." *Id.* Meaning the "unlawful disclosure of legally protected information" is itself a "*de facto* injury." *In re Nickelodeon Consumer Priv. Litig.*, 827 F.3d 262, 274 (3d Cir. 2016); *see also St. Pierre v. Retrieval-Masters Creditors Bureau, Inc.*, 898 F.3d 351, 357-58 (3d Cir. 2018) (same); *DiNaples v. MRS BPO, LLC,* 934 F.3d 275, 279-80 (3d Cir. 2019) (same).

The Supreme Court reached the same conclusion in *TransUnion.* It specifically listed the "disclosure of private information" as an example of a "harm[] traditionally recognized as providing a basis for lawsuits in American courts." 594 U.S. at 425, 141 S.Ct. 2190.[14] Because Barclift claims Keystone concretely harmed her by unlawfully disclosing her private information, she has done enough.

2. The majority sets a higher bar, requiring more fit between Barclift's asserted harm and the common-law analogues. In the majority's view, Barclift loses because her Amended Complaint lacks allegations of publicity, removing the kind of p.159 harm traditionally associated with public disclosure. But Barclift alleges that she suffered embarrassment, anxiety, and stress over the disclosure of her information to RevSpring—harms that are "of the same character" as privacy harms traditionally associated with public disclosure. *Susinno v. Work Out World Inc.*, 862 F.3d 346, 352 (3d Cir. 2017) (concluding that, although plaintiff's allegations "traditionally would provide no cause of action," Congress "sought to protect the same interests implicated in the traditional common law cause of action" when it enacted the statute at issue and thus plaintiff had standing under the statute). Nothing in *TransUnion* endorses, let alone requires, the majority's contrary result.

a. *TransUnion*'s close-relationship test directs courts to focus on harms (not causes of action) and look for comparisons in kind (not degree). *See Hunstein v. Preferred Collection & Mgmt. Servs., Inc.*, 48 F.4th 1236, 1264 (11th Cir. 2022) (en banc) (Newsom, J., dissenting) (discussing the "'kind-degree' framework"). And when comparing harms, *TransUnion* expressly disavows an "exact duplicate" requirement.[15]

TransUnion's reasoning follows this distinction to hold that the mere transmission of misleading information—with no further harms or consequences—constitutes a concrete injury. *See* 594 U.S. at 433, 141 S.Ct. 2190. TransUnion flagged thousands of individuals with a "potential match" to names on the U.S. Department of the Treasury Office of Foreign Assets Control (OFAC) list of "'specially designated nationals' who threaten America's national security." *Id.* at 419-20, 141 S.Ct. 2190. The OFAC list names "terrorists, drug traffickers, [and] other serious criminals." *Id.* at 419, 141 S.Ct. 2190. TransUnion's misleading labels imposed different kinds of harm. For Sergio Ramirez (the class representative), the label had real world consequences: he tried to buy a car, but the dealership refused to do business with him "because his name was on a 'terrorist list.'" *Id.* at 420, 141 S.Ct. 2190. For 1,853 class members (including Ramirez), "TransUnion provided third parties with credit reports containing" the misleading terrorist label. *Id.* at 432, 141 S.Ct. 2190. We do not know if other class members suffered harms beyond their credit reports; all the opinion tells us is that these class members had misleading information sent to third parties. *See id.* And for the Court, the mere transmission of that misleading information (with nothing further) constituted "a harm with a 'close relationship' to the harm associated with the tort of defamation." *Id.*

The Court could have required a more stringent connection to defamation. For one thing, the label was true: the class members' names were "potential" matches with those of terrorists. *See id.* at 420, 141 p.160 S.Ct. 2190. TransUnion argued that this undercut the defamation analogy. *See id.* at 433, 141 S.Ct. 2190. But the Court rejected TransUnion's push for "an exact duplicate," finding instead that "the harm from a misleading statement ... bears a sufficiently close relationship to the harm from a false and defamatory statement." *Id.*

The Court could have required more specificity. The hornbook definition of defamation requires some sort of "special harm." *See* Restatement (Second) of Torts § 558 (1977) (requiring either "the existence of special harm" or a statement actionable "irrespective of special harm" (i.e., defamation *per se*)). If the plaintiff lacks "special harm," he may only recover by showing that the statement constituted "defamation *per se.*" *Franklin Prescriptions, Inc. v. N.Y. Times Co.,* 424 F.3d 336, 343 (3d Cir. 2005) (citation omitted). And defamation *per se* historically applies to "words imputing (1) criminal offense, (2) loathsome disease, (3) business misconduct, or (4) serious sexual misconduct." *Synygy, Inc. v. Scott-Levin, Inc.,* 51 F. Supp. 2d 570, 580 (E.D. Pa. 1999), *aff'd sub nom. Synygy, Inc. v. Scott-Levin,* 229 F.3d 1139 (3d Cir. 2000) (citation omitted). The misleading terrorist label seems analogous to "words imputing ... criminal offense," *id.,* but the Court did not wade into, let alone rest on, that level of granularity. It instead drew an analogy to the general "reputational harm *associated with* the tort of defamation," and found that the mere transmission of a misleading (though literally true) statement implicated this kind of harm. *TransUnion,* 594 U.S. at 432, 141 S.Ct. 2190 (emphasis added).

Summed up, *TransUnion*'s text and reasoning support performing a general, kind-of-harm comparison that rejects exact duplication. I concur in the majority's adoption of this approach. But its application veers into an unnecessary jot-for-jot exactness to some common-law cause of action.[16]

b. Footnote six in *TransUnion* does not require a different outcome. I start by unpacking what the Court wrote. Recall that TransUnion sent the OFAC list to third-party vendors who printed and mailed the information to the class members. The class argued that "TransUnion 'published' the class members' information internally—for example, to employees within TransUnion and to the vendors that printed and sent the mailings that the class members received." *Id.* at 434 n.6, 141 S.Ct. 2190. The Court reasoned that communication requires "evidence that the defendant actually 'brought an idea to the perception of another,' and thus generally require[s] evidence that the document was actually read and not merely processed." *Id.* (quoting Restatement (First) of Torts § 559, cmt. a (1938)) (citing *Ostrowe v. Lee,* p.161 256 N.Y. 36, 38-39, 175 N.E. 505 (1931) (Cardozo, J.)). The Court then concluded that "the plaintiffs' internal publication theory circumvents a fundamental requirement of an ordinary defamation claim— publication—and does not bear a sufficiently 'close relationship' to the traditional defamation tort to qualify for Article III standing." *Id.*

Barclift still has standing despite *TransUnion*'s footnote six. To begin, the Court explained these class members failed to produce evidence at trial "that the [misleading credit reports were] actually read and not merely processed." *Id.* That makes sense: it is possible in our automated world that nobody even saw the data flowing from TransUnion's servers to the computers in the vendors' back offices. But the inverse does not follow—that, even if the challenged disclosures *were* read by a processor, they could not be actionable. I cannot read the lack of evidence to also mean that no evidence could suffice because *all* disclosures to intermediaries are beyond the ordinary meaning of publication. Not only would that defy logic, it would undermine *Ostrowe v. Lee,* the case cited by the Court to illustrate the meaning of publication. The plaintiff there sued a defendant for libel, alleging "that the defendant composed a letter accusing the plaintiff of the crime of larceny; that he dictated this letter to his stenographer; that the stenographer, in obedience to his orders, read the notes and transcribed them; and that the letter so transcribed was received by the plaintiff through the mails." 256 N.Y. at 38, 175 N.E. 505.

The defendant responded that no publication occurred because "[a] defamatory writing is not published if it is read by no one but the defamed." *Id.* But the New York Court of Appeals, per Chief Judge Cardozo, held that the "complaint [was] good upon its face" because someone else had read the defamatory writing: the stenographer. *Id.* at 38, 41, 175 N.E. 505. Indeed, publication occurs "as soon as read by any one else." *Id.* at 38, 175 N.E. 505. Cardozo takes care to show his homework, and the result is worth reprinting in full:

> The reader may be a telegraph operator (*Williamson v. Frere,* [(1874)] L. R. 9 C. P. 393), or the compositor in a printing house (*Baldwin v. Elphinston,* [(1775)] 2 W. Bl. 1037), or the copyist who reproduces a long hand draft (*Puterbaugh v. Gold Medal F. M. Co.,* [(1904)] 7 Ont. L. R. 582, 586). The legal consequence is not altered where the symbols reproduced or interpreted are the notes of a stenographer. Publication there still is as a result of the dictation, at least where the notes have been examined or transcribed (*Pullman v. Hill & Co.,* [1891] 1 Q. B. 524; *Boxsius v. Goblet Freres,* [1894] 1 Q. B. 842; *Gambrill v. Schooley,* 93 Md. 48, 48 A. 730 [(1901)]; *Ferdon v. Dickens,* 161 Ala. 181, 49 So. 888 [(1909)]; *Berry v. City of New York Ins. Co.,* 210 Ala. 369, 371, 98 So. 290 [(1923)]; *Nelson v. Whitten,* 272 F.[] 135 [(E.D.N.Y. 1921)]; *Puterbaugh v. Gold Medal F. M. Co., supra*; Gatley, Libel & Slander, p. 91; *cf. Kennedy v. Butler, Inc.,* 245 N. Y. 204, 156 N.E. 666 [(1927)]). Enough that a writing defamatory in content has been read and understood at the behest of the defamer (1 Street, Foundations of Legal Liability, p. 297).

Id. (fourth and fifth alterations in original). It is a strong line of cases traversing the continent, crossing the pond, and dating back dozens of decades directly undercutting the notion that no harm ever follows communication to intermediaries.[17] Under p.162 Barclift's Amended Complaint, RevSpring is the modern stenographer. Whether RevSpring "read and understood" the information Keystone sent is a question for p.163 discovery and another day. For today, it is enough that Barclift alleges Keystone "communicated with RevSpring"—as well as "an untold number of individuals affiliated with RevSpring"—and "provided [them] information regarding [Barclift] and the Debt ... —including [her] name and address, the amount of the Debt, the name of the current creditor, and other private details regarding the Debt." App. 56, 62. Accepting those factual allegations as true and extending all reasonable inferences in her favor, Barclift has done enough to show that she has standing. *See St. Pierre,* 898 F.3d at 354 n.1.

B. Judgment of Congress

The judgment of Congress confirms the concreteness of Barclift's asserted injury. *See TransUnion,* 594 U.S. at 425-26, 141 S.Ct. 2190. Courts consult "Congress's views" to determine whether Congress has "elevate[d] to the status of legally cognizable" a concrete injury that was "previously inadequate in law." *Id.* at 425, 141 S.Ct. 2190 (quoting *Spokeo,* 578 U.S. at 341, 136 S.Ct. 1540). Of course, "courts must presume that a legislature says in a statute what it means and means in a statute what it says there." *Conn. Nat'l Bank v. Germain,* 503 U.S. 249, 253-54, 112 S.Ct. 1146, 117 L.Ed.2d 391 (1992).

Congress has expressed its judgment in two provisions. First, Congress made it unlawful for a debt collector to communicate about "the collection of any debt" with "any person," unless the collector first obtains "the prior consent of the consumer." 15 U.S.C. § 1692c(b). And second, in a provision titled "Congressional findings and declarations of purpose," Congress listed the "invasion[] of individual privacy" as one of the harms to which the FDCPA was directed. *Id.* § 1692(a). Understood against the backdrop of common law privacy protections, the "legislative aim," *OI Eur. Grp. B.V.*, 73 F.4th at 170 (citing 1 Blackstone, Commentaries *87), of these provisions is clear: to elevate a real-world harm (the unauthorized disclosure of private information) to "actionable legal status," *TransUnion,* 594 U.S. at 426, 141 S.Ct. 2190 (citation omitted).

Maybe "Congress could have created... a [more] cumbersome scheme" to protect debtor privacy. *Krakauer v. Dish Network, L.L.C.*, 925 F.3d 643, 654 (4th Cir. 2019). One that requires the debtor to prove that her private information became public in the common-law sense of the word. Or maybe one that excepts third-party vendors from the general bar on communications (like the exceptions for attorney communications). Instead, Congress "opted for a more straightforward and manageable way of protecting personal privacy, and the Constitution in no way bars it from doing so." *Id.* That congressional judgment deserves the respect of the courts.

***

TransUnion warned that "the concrete-harm requirement can be difficult to apply in some cases." 594 U.S. at 429, 141 S.Ct. 2190. Few would argue otherwise. But under the path *TransUnion* paved, Barclift's asserted harm (the unauthorized disclosure of private information) bears a close relationship to the harm underlying claims for public disclosure of private facts and breach of confidence. The majority starts down the right road but loses footing on a footnote. I think *TransUnion* is made of sturdier stuff and would not wander further from the limited requirements of Article III. Barclift has shown standing sufficient for a federal court to hear her claim, and so I respectfully concur in part, dissent in part, and dissent in the judgment.

[1] We recount the facts as alleged in Barclift's complaint.

[2] It has done so in other contexts. *See, e.g., United States v. Dixon,* 509 U.S. 688, 696-97, 113 S.Ct. 2849, 125 L.Ed.2d 556 (1993) (referring to the *Blockburger* test for double jeopardy as a "same-elements test" (citing *Blockburger v. United States,* 284 U.S. 299, 304, 52 S.Ct. 180, 76 L.Ed. 306 (1932))); *cf. Descamps v. United States,* 570 U.S. 254, 260-61, 133 S.Ct. 2276, 186 L.Ed.2d 438 (2013) (describing the "categorical approach" to determining whether a state crime qualifies for a federal sentencing enhancement, which requires courts to ask whether the state crime "has the same elements as the 'generic' [federal] crime").

[3] The dissent accepts Barclift's argument that "breach of confidence" is also a common-law analogue for her alleged harm. Dissenting Op. at 157-58 & n.13. But we hesitate to conclude that the harm associated with a breach of confidence bears a "close relationship to a harm traditionally recognized as providing a basis for a

lawsuit in American courts." *TransUnion,* 594 U.S. at 440, 141 S.Ct. 2190. As Vickery (cited by Barclift and the dissent) writes, breach of confidence law in the United States is not a "traditional theor[y] of liability" —rather, it was "emerging" and "still rudimentary" in the 1980s. Alan B. Vickery, *Breach of Confidence: An Emerging Tort,* 82 Colum. L. Rev. 1426, 1426, 1451 (1982). Although it was mentioned in some texts much earlier, it "died out in its infancy," likely due to the "birth and explosive growth" of traditional privacy torts such as the public disclosure of private facts. *Id.* at 1454-55; *see Young v. U.S. Dep't of Just.,* 882 F.2d 633, 640 (2d Cir. 1989) (describing breach of confidence as "a relative newcomer to the tort family").

[4] We acknowledge that there is overlap between the nature of the traditional harm (humiliation stemming from the public disclosure of offensive information) and an element of the traditional tort (publicity). This is because a disclosure that remains nonpublic is unlikely to result in the type of humiliation associated with the traditional injury. Despite this overlap, and in accordance with the Supreme Court's directive in *TransUnion,* we focus our inquiry solely on the harm. And even though that inquiry necessarily considers whether a disclosure is "public" (for lack of a better term), our approach is not an exercise in element-matching.

[5] Indeed, numerous early twentieth century courts held that communications to an associate in the ordinary course of business did not support an action at common law. For example, in *Chalkley v. Atlantic Coast Line Railroad Co.,* 150 Va. 301, 143 S.E. 631 (1928), the Supreme Court of Virginia observed that

> in many cases the modern and more liberal rule is applied, *i.e.,* that where the communication of the libelous matter to the plaintiff is in the customary and usual course of the business of the defendant, in the discharge of an ordinary business duty, and is merely dictated to a stenographer, or copyist, who is charged with the duty of transcribing it, this is not such a publication of the alleged libel as will support an action.

143 S.E. at 638. *See also Globe Furniture Co. v. Wright,* 265 F. 873, 874-76 (D.C. Cir. 1920) (collecting cases); *Beck v. Oden,* 64 Ga.App. 407, 13 S.E.2d 468, 471 (1941) ("The more liberal rule, and the one which seemingly has the support of the weight of modern authority, is that, where the communication is made to a servant or business associate in the ordinary or natural course of business, there is no actionable libel."); *Rodgers v. Wise,* 193 S.C. 5, 7 S.E.2d 517, 519 (1940) ("This case seems to me to set out the sounder and more logical view [that] where a letter is dictated by a business man to his stenographer," the "cause of action ... fail[s] as a matter of law to allege a publication of the slanderous and libelous statements[.]"); *Cartwright-Caps Co. v. Fischel & Kaufman,* 113 Miss. 359, 74 So. 278, 279-80 (1917) ("It is inconceivable how the business of the country ... can be carried on, if a business man or corporation must be subject to litigation for every letter containing some statement too strong, where it is only sent to the person to whom directed, and only heard by a stenographer to whom the letter is dictated."); *Owen v. Ogilvie Publ'g Co.,* 32 A.D. 465, 53 N.Y.S. 1033, 1034 (1898) ("The writing and the copying were but parts of one act; i.e. the production of the letter. Under such conditions we think the dictation, copying, and mailing are to be treated as only one act of the corporation; and ... there was no publication of the letter[.]"); *Central of Ga. Ry. Co. v. Jones,* 18 Ga.App. 414, 89 S.E. 429, 429 (1916) (following *Owen*); *Nichols v. Eaton,* 110 Iowa 509, 81 N.W. 792,

793 (1900) ("One may make a publication to his servant or agent, without liability, which, if made to a stranger, would be actionable.").

The dissent posits that the *TransUnion* Court cited *Ostrowe v. Lee* in footnote 6 "to illustrate the meaning of publication." Dissenting Op. at 161. In *Ostrowe,* the New York Court of Appeals held that dictating a letter to a stenographer qualified as "publication" for defamation purposes because the contents of the letter had been read by someone other than the defamed person. 256 N.Y. 36, 175 N.E. 505, 505 (1931). In the dissent's view, "RevSpring is the modern stenographer," Dissenting Op. at 162, and Barclift's allegations are enough to suggest that her information was "read and not merely processed." *TransUnion,* 594 U.S. at 434 n.6, 141 S.Ct. 2190.

We agree that Barclift's allegations plausibly support an inference that Keystone caused someone at RevSpring to read (and not merely process) information about Barclift's alleged debt. But, in light of the authority mentioned above, we are not convinced that this inference or the Supreme Court's citation to *Ostrowe* means that Barclift's harm bears a close relationship to one that was actionable at common law.

[6] Our view also aligns with Congress's intent in enacting the FDCPA. As Congress explained, the Act's "purpose is to protect consumers from a host of unfair, harassing, and deceptive debt collection practices without imposing unnecessary restrictions on ethical debt collectors." S. Rep. No. 95-382, at 1 (1977). With limited exceptions, the Act prevents debt collectors from "contact[ing] third persons such as a consumer's friends, neighbors, relatives, or employer" because "[s]uch contacts are not *legitimate collection practices* and result in serious invasions of privacy." S. Rep. No. 95-382, at 4 (emphasis added). Using a mailing vendor to contact a consumer in a legitimate attempt to collect a debt is not a practice the statute was meant to prohibit.

[7] Of course, if RevSpring were to mistakenly release someone's personal information in the future, that person could have a cause of action. *Cf. Clemens v. ExecuPharm Inc.,* 48 F.4th 146, 155 (3d Cir. 2022) (holding, in the data breach context, that an alleged harm was sufficiently concrete because, among other things, there was actual "exposure of personally identifying information" on the dark web).

[1] *See also, e.g., TransUnion,* 594 U.S. at 442, 141 S.Ct. 2190 (Thomas, J., dissenting); *Sierra v. City of Hallandale Beach,* 996 F.3d 1110, 1115 (11th Cir. 2021) (Newsom, J., concurring); *Muransky v. Godiva Chocolatier, Inc.,* 979 F.3d 917, 971 (11th Cir. 2020) (en banc) (Jordan, J., dissenting); *Springer v. Cleveland Clinic Emp. Health Plan Total Care,* 900 F.3d 284, 290 (6th Cir. 2018) (Thapar, J., concurring); Erwin Chemerinsky, *What's Standing After* TransUnion LLC v. Ramirez, 96 N.Y.U. L. Rev. Online 269, 286-91 (2021); Daniel J. Solove & Danielle Keats Citron, *Standing and Privacy Harms: A Critique of* TransUnion v. Ramirez, 101 B.U. L. Rev. Online 62, 66-68 (2021); *cf.* Ernest A. Young, *Standing, Equity, and Injury in Fact,* 97 Notre Dame L. Rev. 1885 (2022).

[2] *See Fogle v. Sokol,* 957 F.3d 148, 165 (3d Cir. 2020) (Even where a doctrine "exceeds both [its] historic scope and the statutory text, we cannot use the original meaning of a statute as a 'makeweight' against precedent, nor hand-pick binding decisions to follow." (citation omitted)).

[3] As originally understood, a "controversy" was thought to include fewer matters within its realm than did a "case." *See Chisholm v. Georgia,* 2 U.S. (2 Dall.) 419, 431-32, 1 L.Ed. 440 (1793) (Iredell, J.) ("The [Judiciary Act of 1789] more particularly mentions *civil* controversies, a qualification of the general word in the Constitution, which I do not doubt every reasonable man will think well warranted, for it cannot be presumed that the general word 'controversies' was intended to include any proceedings that relate to criminal cases, which in all instances that respect the same Government, only, are uniformly considered of a local nature, and to be decided by its particular laws. The word 'controversy' indeed, would not naturally justify any such construction, but nevertheless it was perhaps a proper instance of caution in *Congress* to guard against the possibility of it."); *see also In re Pac. Ry. Comm'n,* 32 F. 241, 255 (C.C.N.D. Cal. 1887) (Field, J.) ("The judicial article of the constitution mentions cases and controversies. The term 'controversies,' if distinguishable at all from 'cases,' is so in that it is less comprehensive than the latter, and includes only suits of a civil nature." (quoting *Chisholm,* 2 U.S. (2 Dall.) at 431-32)).

[4] To the contrary, "[t]he word *standing* is rather recent in the basic judicial vocabulary and does not appear to have been commonly used until the middle of [the twentieth] century." Joseph Vining, Legal Identity: The Coming of Age of Public Law 55 (1978). Earlier judicial systems, well known to lawyers of the Founding era, used the phrase *stare in iudicium* ("to stand in court") to describe a person's "membership or position in a community" able to sue and be sued "separate from and largely independent of issues related to the merits of the lawsuit." Neil H. Cogan, *"Standing" Before the Constitution: Membership in the Community,* 7 L. & Hist. Rev. 1, 1-2 (1989) (tracing the meaning of standing through Roman to European sources familiar to American lawyers of the late 1700s).

[5] *See, e.g.,* 3 Joseph Story, Commentaries on the Constitution of the United States § 1640, at 507 (1833) ("A case, then, in the sense of this clause of the constitution, arises, when some subject, touching the constitution, laws, or treaties of the United States, is submitted to the courts by a party, who asserts his rights in the form prescribed by law. In other words, a case is a suit in law or equity, instituted according to the regular course of judicial proceedings; and, when it involves any question arising under the constitution, laws, or treaties of the United States, it is within the judicial power confided to the Union." (footnote omitted)); *Osborn v. Bank of U.S.,* 22 U.S. (9 Wheat.) 738, 819, 6 L.Ed. 204 (1824) (Marshall, J.) ("[Article III, Section 2] enables the judicial department to receive jurisdiction to the full extent of the constitution, laws, and treaties of the United States, when any question respecting them shall assume such a form that the judicial power is capable of acting on it. That power is capable of acting only when the subject is submitted to it by a party who asserts his rights in the form prescribed by law. It then becomes a case, and the constitution declares, that the judicial power shall extend to all cases arising under the constitution, laws, and treaties of the United States.").

The text of Article III supports this view. "Cases" extends "to all the cases described, without making in its terms any exception whatever, and without any regard to the condition of the party. If there be any exception, it is to be implied against the express words of the article." *Cohens v. Virginia,* 19 U.S. (6 Wheat.) 264, 378, 5 L.Ed. 257 (1821) (Marshall, J.). "Controvers[y]," by contrast, "depends entirely on the character of the parties," and if the parties asserting the controversy match those listed in Article III— "to which the United States shall be a Party," "between two or more States," "between a State and Citizens of another State," "between Citizens of different States," "between Citizens of the same State claiming Lands under Grants of different States," and "between a State, or the Citizens thereof, and foreign States, Citizens or Subjects," U.S. Const. art. III, § 2—"it is entirely unimportant what may be the subject of the controversy. Be it what it may, these parties have a constitutional right to come into the Courts of the Union." *Cohens,* 19 U.S. (6 Wheat.) at 378.

[6] *See TransUnion,* 594 U.S. at 447, 141 S.Ct. 2190 (Thomas, J., dissenting) ("But where an individual sued based on the violation of a duty owed broadly to the whole community, such as overgrazing of public lands, courts required 'not only *injuria* [legal injury] but also *damnum* [damage].'" (alterations in original) (citation omitted)); *see also* Caleb Nelson, *Adjudication in the Political Branches,* 107 Colum. L. Rev. 559, 562 (2007) ("Throughout our history, standing doctrine has raised no bar to private litigants with individualized legal interests. At least in the absence of public authorization, however, American courts have generally refused to entertain private lawsuits about matters in which the whole body politic was concerned and in which every individual had the same legal stake. From the early Republic on, such matters were controlled instead by the political branches.").

[7] *See* Adrian Vermeule, Common Good Constitutionalism 177 (2022) ("Until roughly the 1970s, the 'injury in fact' test in its current signification was no part of our law.").

[8] *See Coleman v. Miller,* 307 U.S. 433, 460, 59 S.Ct. 972, 83 L.Ed. 1385 (1939) (Frankfurter, J., concurring) (advancing the claim that the "[j]udicial power could come into play only in matters that were the traditional concern of the courts at Westminster and only if they arose in ways that to the expert feel of lawyers constituted 'Cases' or 'Controversies'").

[9] Like most scholarly explanations, this "insulation thesis" has its challengers. But there seems to be a consensus that expanded executive administration brought the discussion of standing to center stage. *See* Daniel E. Ho & Erica L. Ross, *Did Liberal Justices Invent the Standing Doctrine? An Empirical Study of the Evolution of Standing, 1921-2006,* 62 Stan. L. Rev. 591, 604-07 (2010). As Judge Fletcher reasoned, "private entities increasingly came to be controlled by statutory and regulatory duties" while "government increasingly came to be controlled by statutory and constitutional commands." William A. Fletcher, *The Structure of Standing,* 98 Yale L.J. 221, 225 (1988). When "individuals sought to control the greatly augmented power of the government through the judicial process, many kinds of plaintiffs and would-be plaintiffs sought the articulation and enforcement of new and existing rights in the federal courts." *Id.*

[10] On the same day, the Court applied its new injury-in-fact requirement to another APA challenge. *See Barlow v. Collins,* 397 U.S. 159, 163-64, 90 S.Ct. 832, 25 L.Ed.2d 192 (1970); *see also* Sunstein, *supra,* at 185-86 (tracing "injury in fact" to Kenneth Culp Davis's analysis of the APA (citing 3 Kenneth C. Davis, Administrative Law Treatise § 22.02, at 211-13 (1958))).

[11] The standing issue was teed up for the Court by the parties' briefs and the district and appellate court decisions that preceded it. But even those arguments were colored with uncertainty about the meaning or scope of standing. Prior to the

Supreme Court's review, the Eighth Circuit observed that "[t]he doctrines that stem from Article III, such as standing, mootness, ripeness, and political question, relate 'to an idea, which is more than an intuition but less than a rigorous and explicit theory, about the constitutional and prudential limits to the powers of an unelected, unrepresentative judiciary in our kind of government.'" *Defs. of Wildlife v. Hodel,* 851 F.2d 1035, 1038 (8th Cir. 1988) (quoting *Vander Jagt v. O'Neill,* 699 F.2d 1166, 1178-79 (D.C. Cir. 1982) (Bork, J., concurring)).

[12] Which history and tradition to consult is another challenge. *TransUnion* directs a search for "harms traditionally recognized as providing a basis for lawsuits in American courts," 594 U.S. at 425, 141 S.Ct. 2190, but cites tort law as restated in the twentieth century as "longstanding American law," *id.* at 432, 141 S.Ct. 2190 (citing Restatement (First) of Torts § 559 (1938)). But a twentieth-century translation does not necessarily nor accurately state current law, let alone tell us anything about law as traditionally understood. *Cf. Kansas v. Nebraska,* 574 U.S. 445, 476, 135 S.Ct. 1042, 191 L.Ed.2d 1 (2015) (Scalia, J., concurring in part and dissenting in part) ("[I]t cannot safely be assumed, without further inquiry, that a Restatement provision describes rather than revises current law.").

TransUnion also cites *Spokeo,* which cites *Vermont Agency* as an example of looking to traditionally recognized harms. *See TransUnion,* 594 U.S. at 425, 141 S.Ct. 2190 (citing *Spokeo,* 578 U.S. at 340-41, 136 S.Ct. 1540). *Vermont Agency* looks to "the long tradition of *qui tam* actions in England and the American Colonies," dating back to "around the end of the 13th century." 529 U.S. at 774-75, 120 S.Ct. 1858. So if looking to tradition means looking to England and the colonies, individuals alleging violations of private rights would not need to show harm. *See TransUnion,* 594 U.S. at 448, 141 S.Ct. 2190 (Thomas, J., dissenting) ("The principle that the violation of an individual right gives rise to an actionable harm was widespread at the founding, in early American history, and in many modern cases."); *Muransky,* 979 F.3d at 971 (Jordan, J., dissenting) ("English courts at common law heard suits involving private rights, regardless of whether the plaintiff suffered actual damage...."). But notice that *TransUnion* narrowed *Spokeo*'s class of permissible analogues from claims heard in "English or American courts," *Spokeo,* 578 U.S. at 341, 136 S.Ct. 1540, to claims heard only in "American courts," *TransUnion,* 594 U.S. at 424, 141 S.Ct. 2190.

[13] Keystone did not address Barclift's arguments about breach of confidence. And the majority "hesitate[s] to conclude" that the harm associated with breach of confidence bears a close relationship to a harm traditionally recognized as providing a basis for suit in American courts because "it 'died out in its infancy,' likely due to the 'birth and explosive growth' of traditional privacy torts such as the public disclosure of private facts." Majority Op. at 145 n.3 (quoting Vickery, *supra,* at 1454-55). But that only acknowledges breach of confidence existed in earlier American and English jurisprudence, even if it fell out of vogue for a time. And its reemergence in the 1980s demonstrates its continued distinction from other torts.

Barclift is correct that breach of confidence is a proper common-law analogue for her alleged harm. Considered by English courts as early as 1849 and American courts as early as 1894, breach of confidence has deep roots, at least as deep as those of public disclosure of private facts, a tort the majority and the Supreme Court accept as a traditionally recognized basis for suit in American courts. *See Prince Albert v. Strange* (1849) 41 Eng. Rep. 1171, 1178; 1 Mac. & G. 25, 44; *Corliss v. E.W. Walker*

Co., 64 F. 280, 281 (C.C.D. Mass. 1894); *see also* Samuel D. Warren & Louis D. Brandeis, *The Right to Privacy,* 4 Harv. L. Rev. 193, 207 (1890) ("It should be stated that, in some instances where protection has been afforded against wrongful publication, the jurisdiction has been asserted, not on the ground of property, or at least not wholly on that ground, but upon the ground of an alleged breach of an implied contract or of a trust or *confidence.*" (emphasis added)); *Pavesich v. New Eng. Life Ins. Co.,* 122 Ga. 190, 50 S.E. 68, 75 (1905) ("It must be conceded that the numerous cases decided before 1890 in which equity has interfered to restrain the publication of letters, writings, papers, etc., have all been based either upon the recognition of a right of property, or upon the fact that the publication would be a breach of contract, *confidence,* or trust. It is well settled that, if any contract or property right or trust relation has been violated, damages are recoverable. There are many cases which sustain such a doctrine." (emphasis added)). Its failure to gain popularity over alternative privacy torts in the early twentieth century is not fatal to this conclusion. The mere fact that, for a time, plaintiffs chose to utilize alternative causes of action does not render the underutilized cause of action unable to sustain a suit at common law.

Barclift's alleged harm bears a close relationship to the harm arising from breach of confidence. The confidential relationship is legally significant to the tort only because it imposes a duty on the defendant to maintain the plaintiff's private information. *See* Vickery, *supra,* at 1456-57. Here that duty is imposed by the FDCPA. *See* 15 U.S.C. § 1692c(b).

[14] A proposition the Court supported by citing *Davis v. Federal Election Commission,* which held that a candidate had standing to challenge a campaign finance law requiring him to disclose personal contributions beyond a certain amount. *See* 554 U.S. 724, 733, 128 S.Ct. 2759, 171 L.Ed.2d 737 (2008). At common law, the tort of public disclosure requires "the matter publicized" to be "of a kind that (a) would be highly offensive to a reasonable person, and (b) is not of legitimate concern to the public." Restatement (Second) of Torts § 652D (1977). But neither of these elements mattered to the Court in *Davis,* nor did the Court mention them in *TransUnion. See Clemens v. ExecuPharm Inc.,* 48 F.4th 146, 155 n.5 (3d Cir. 2022) ("[W]hether a plaintiff has successfully made out claims under a particular cause of action is a separate question."). The "disclosure of private information" alone constituted the classic example of a concrete intangible harm. *TransUnion,* 594 U.S. at 425, 141 S.Ct. 2190.

A conclusion with support dating back to at least 1905. *See Pavesich,* 50 S.E. at 80-81 ("So thoroughly satisfied are we that the law recognizes, within proper limits, as a legal right, the right of privacy, and that the publication of one's picture without his consent by another as an advertisement, for the mere purpose of increasing the profits and gains of the advertiser, is an invasion of this right, that we venture to predict that the day will come that the American bar will marvel that a contrary view was ever entertained by judges of eminence and ability."); *see also Cox Broad. Corp. v. Cohn,* 420 U.S. 469, 488-89, 95 S.Ct. 1029, 43 L.Ed.2d 328 (1975) (acknowledging that "the century has experienced a strong tide running in favor of the so-called right of privacy," explaining that "a 'right of privacy' has been recognized at common law" in much of the country, and discussing "[t]he version of the privacy tort ... termed ... 'the tort of public disclosure'" (quoting *Time, Inc. v. Hill,* 385 U.S. 374, 383 n.7, 87 S.Ct. 534, 17 L.Ed.2d 456 (1967))).

[15] *See* 594 U.S. at 433, 141 S.Ct. 2190 ("[W]e do not require an exact duplicate."); *id.* at 424, 141 S.Ct. 2190 ("*Spokeo* does not require an exact duplicate in American history and tradition."); *see also id.* ("[C]ourts should assess whether the alleged injury to the plaintiff has a 'close relationship' to a harm 'traditionally' recognized as providing a basis for a lawsuit in American courts."); *id.* at 425, 141 S.Ct. 2190 (requiring "injuries with a close relationship to harms traditionally recognized as providing a basis for lawsuits in American courts"); *id.* at 432, 141 S.Ct. 2190 (assessing plaintiffs' contention that their "injury bears a 'close relationship' to a harm traditionally recognized as providing a basis for a lawsuit in American courts"); *id.* (finding certain class members "suffered a harm with a 'close relationship' to the harm associated with the tort of defamation"); *id.* at 433, 141 S.Ct. 2190 (stating courts should "look[] to whether a plaintiff's asserted harm has a 'close relationship' to a harm traditionally recognized as providing a basis for a lawsuit in American courts").

[16] In an attempt to fit its analysis under the kind-of-harm approach, the majority distinguishes between the harms arising from public dissemination and private dissemination. But as the Supreme Court recognized, the degree of dissemination only affects the "*extent* of the protection accorded a privacy right." *Dep't of Just. v. Reps. Comm. for Freedom of Press,* 489 U.S. 749, 763, 109 S.Ct. 1468, 103 L.Ed.2d 774 (1989) (emphasis added). Meaning Barclift might be unable to recover on a claim for public disclosure at common law. But she has still suffered *some* intrusion on her right to privacy through the unauthorized disclosure. While that harm may be a mere "trifle of injury," that is all we require for her to stand in court. *Danvers Motor Co., Inc. v. Ford Motor Co.,* 432 F.3d 286, 294 (3d Cir. 2005) (citation omitted). Recall that Barclift need not establish the elements of a common-law analogue to have standing to assert her FDCPA claim. *See TransUnion,* 594 U.S. at 433, 141 S.Ct. 2190 ("[W]e do not require an exact duplicate."). She only needs to assert a harm with a "'close relationship' to a harm traditionally recognized as providing a basis for a lawsuit in American courts." *Id.* She has done so.

[17] The majority "agree[s] that Barclift's allegations plausibly support an inference that Keystone caused someone at RevSpring to read (and not merely process) information about Barflict's alleged debt," but is "not convinced that this inference or the Supreme Court's citation to *Ostrowe* means that Barclift's harm bears a close relationship to one that was actionable at common law." Majority Op. at 147 n.5. A conclusion the majority supports with cites to cases showing that "communications to an associate in the ordinary course of business did not support an action at common law." Majority Op. at 147 n.5. But those cases deal with *privileged* communications. *See, e.g., Chalkley v. Atl. Coast Line R. Co.,* 150 Va. 301, 334, 143 S.E. 631 (1928) ("Here, however, the communication was privileged and the typist had a duty to discharge in the ordinary course of business in connection with the transcription of the communication."); *Globe Furniture Co. v. Wright,* 265 F. 873, 876 (D.C. Cir. 1920) ("But we prefer to put our decision upon the ground that the occasion was conditionally privileged, that the letter was within the privilege, that there was no malice, and therefore that the letter is not actionable."); *Rodgers v. Wise,* 193 S.C. 5, 7 S.E.2d 517, 517-19 (1940) (finding satisfactory the conclusions of the lower court, which held that the letter was "privileged and that the writing and mailing of it [was] not a publication"); *Cartwright-Caps Co. v. Fischel & Kaufman,* 113

Miss. 359, 74 So. 278, 279 (1917) (concluding that "the letters were privileged, and that there was not, in a legal sense, a publication of the letters in question"); *Owen v. Ogilvie Publ'g Co.,* 32 A.D. 465, 466-67, 53 N.Y.S. 1033 (N.Y. App. Div. 1898) (explaining that "[i]t may be that the dictation to the stenographer and her reading of the letter would constitute a publication of the same by the person dictating it, if the relation existing between the manager and the copyist was that of master and servant, and the letter be held not to be privileged. Such, however, was not the relation of these persons. They were both employed by a common master, and were engaged in the performance of duties which their respective employments required. Under such circumstances we do not think that the stenographer is to be regarded as a third person in the sense that either the dictation or the subsequent reading can be regarded as a publication by the corporation"); *Cent. of Ga. Ry. Co. v. Jones,* 18 Ga.App. 414, 89 S.E. 429, 429 (1916) (reversing judgment and following rule in *Owen*); *Nichols v. Eaton,* 110 Iowa 509, 81 N.W. 792, 793 (1900) ("One may make a publication to his servant or agent, without liability, which, if made to a stranger, would be actionable," if "[t]he occasion was undoubtedly privileged").

The presence of a privilege separates the claims in *Ostrowe,* the cases it cites, and the decisions that reach the same conclusions as Cardozo. *See also, e.g., Rickbeil v. Grafton Deaconess Hosp.,* 74 N.D. 525, 542, 23 N.W.2d 247 (1946); *State v. McIntire,* 115 N.C. 769, 20 S.E. 721, 722 (1894). Conclusions that constitute no outlier or minority approach. *See, e.g.,* Martin L. Newell, The Law of Slander and Libel in Civil and Criminal Cases § 195, 242-43 (4th ed. 1924) (describing the rule later adopted by *Ostrowe* as the "leading" American approach); Restatement (First) of Torts § 577, cmt. h (1938) (adopting *Ostrowe*'s publication holding). Rather, *Ostrowe*'s rule that disclosing private information to intermediaries constitutes publication is the starting point, subject to attacks to the *prima facie* case such as privilege. *See Rickbeil,* 74 N.D. at 542, 23 N.W.2d 247 ("A defamatory writing, which on its face is libelous per se, is presumed to be unprivileged and therefore when the plaintiff proved the publication of this libel he made out a cause of action showing an unprivileged publication."); *Kennedy,* 245 N.Y. at 207, 156 N.E. 666 ("Whether such a publication were privileged —a privileged communication—is another matter. Privilege presupposes publicity. The plea of privilege is unnecessary if there has been no publication."). *Ostrowe* and the majority's cases both show that the disclosure of private information to an intermediary was actionable at common law. Whether a plaintiff may successfully recover is a different— and premature—question in our standing inquiry.

In any event, that courts allowed both approaches —in different jurisdictions at different times—does not mean that disclosures to intermediaries were not actionable at common law. *TransUnion* did not insist on harms traditionally recognized in *every* American court. Nor harms that would withstand every defense against them.

84 F.4th 132 (2023)

Jamie HUBER, individually and on behalf of all others similarly situated,
v.
SIMON'S AGENCY, INC., Appellant.

No. 22-2483.

United States Court of Appeals, Third Circuit.

Argued April 25, 2023.
Opinion filed: October 12, 2023.

Huber v. Simon's Agency, Inc., 84 F. 4th 132 (3rd Cir. 2023)

p.140 On Appeal from the United States District Court for the Eastern District of Pennsylvania, (D.C. No. 2-19-cv-01424), District Judge: Honorable Anita B. Brody.

Yitzchak Zelman [ARGUED], Ari H. Marcus, Marcus & Zelman, 701 Cookman Avenue, Suite 300, Asbury Park, NJ 07712, Counsel for Appellee

David B. Shaver [ARGUED], Surdyk Dowd & Turner, 8163 Old Yankee Street, Suite C, Dayton, OH 45458, Counsel for Appellant

Before: KRAUSE, BIBAS, and RENDELL, Circuit Judges.

OPINION OF THE COURT

KRAUSE, Circuit Judge.

Since it entered the scene in 1989, the informational injury doctrine of Article III standing has generated its share of confusion, and with each new case, its contours have come into sharper focus. In this case, Appellee Jamie Huber and the class of consumers she seeks to represent brought suit under the Fair Debt Collection Practices Act ("FDCPA"), 15 U.S.C. §§ 1692-1692p, after receiving confusing collection letters from Appellant Simon's Agency, Inc. (SAI). The District Court agreed the letters were "misleading and deceptive" in p.141 violation of the Act, certified the class, and granted summary judgment in its favor. App. 41. It also rejected SAI's jurisdictional challenge to the plaintiffs' standing under Article III, holding that while confusion from the letter, without more, would not suffice, Huber had standing under the informational injury doctrine because she suffered a concrete financial consequence as a result of her confusion, and the other class members had standing under "the same theory" because they "inevitably" could be expected to suffer the same harm. App. 48.

We agree with the District Court that Huber has standing, but not under the informational injury doctrine. After the District Court rendered its ruling, we decided *Kelly v. RealPage Inc.*, which clarified that a plaintiff who seeks to establish standing based on an "informational injury" must identify "omitted information to which she has entitlement[.]" 47 F.4th 202, 213 (3d Cir. 2022). Huber did not do so and, therefore, did not suffer an informational injury.

But she does have standing on a different basis—that the financial harm she suffered in reliance on the letter bears a "close relationship" to the harm associated with the tort of fraudulent misrepresentation. *Spokeo, Inc. v. Robins,* 578 U.S. 330, 341, 136 S.Ct. 1540, 194 L.Ed.2d 635 (2016). If the other proposed class members can also make that showing, they, too, will have standing, but confusion alone does not constitute concrete injury, and the present record does not reflect whether any of the class members suffered any consequences beyond confusion.

For these reasons, we will affirm the District Court's determination that SAI's letter violated the FDCPA, 15 U.S.C. § 1692e, and that Huber herself has standing, but we will remand for the District Court to consider the extent to which unnamed class members may have standing to "recover individual damages," *TransUnion LLC v. Ramirez,* 594 U.S. 413, 141 S. Ct. 2190, 2208, 210 L.Ed.2d 568 (2021), and the implications of that determination for class certification under Federal Rule of Civil Procedure 23(b)(3).

I. Factual and Procedural Background

A. Huber's Dealings with SAI

In 2018, Huber visited doctors in the Crozer Health Network (Crozer) on four separate occasions. As a result, she incurred the following debts to Crozer: $178 on February 9, $78 on February 22, $83.50 on March 27, and $178 on May 22. Crozer contracted with SAI—a debt collection agency that specializes in medical billing—to collect outstanding bills from Huber and other patients. Whenever Crozer placed a debt with SAI, SAI sent a form collection letter to the debtor. That letter set out an "Account Summary" that provided the debtor with two figures: in one box, the specific debt SAI sought to collect, entitled "Amount," and in another box, a second figure, entitled "Various Other Acc[oun]ts Total Balance." App. 7. By way of example, the fourth such letter Huber received between May and September of 2018—one for each of her debts to Crozer—appeared as follows:

p.142

Thus, the "Account Summary" informed Huber that she owed an "Amount" of $178, while her "Various Other Accounts Total Balance" was listed at $517.50. *Id.*

According to her deposition testimony, Huber was confused after reading the letter as to how much she owed in total: Was it $695.50 (the sum of the "Amount" and "Various Other Accounts Total Balance") or $517.50 (just the "Various Other Accounts Total Balance")? Uncertain which amount was due, she paid neither. Instead, she sent the letter to a financial advisor she had retained to help her "take care of [her] financial situation." App. 111.

B. The Proceedings Below

Huber filed this putative class action against SAI in 2019 alleging, among other things, that the fourth collection letter constituted a "false, deceptive, or misleading" means of collecting a debt in violation of 15 U.S.C. § 1692e. Huber also alleged that SAI's letter failed to disclose the "amount of the debt" as required by 15 U.S.C. § 1692g(a)(1). But the District Court remarked that the letter straightforwardly stated that the "Amount" of Huber's fourth debt was $178, so there was no actionable failure to disclose. Accordingly, the Court granted summary judgment in favor of SAI on Huber's § 1692g(a)(1) claim, and Huber does not challenge that ruling on appeal.

Following discovery, both parties moved for summary judgment on Huber's § 1692e claim, and Huber prevailed. Applying our Court's objective "least sophisticated debtor standard," App. 17, the District Court observed such a debtor could reasonably read SAI's collection letter in two ways: the recipient's total debt could be either the sum of the "Amount" and the "Various Other Accounts Total Balance," or the latter already representing that sum. Because the former reading is inaccurate— the "Various Other Accounts Total Balance" in fact represents the total debt— the District Court ruled that SAI's form letter was indeed deceptive and therefore violated § 1692e as a matter of law.

Claiming that hundreds of other debtors were also subject to this violation, Huber moved to certify a class under Federal Rule of Civil Procedure 23(b)(3). Her proposed class consisted of "all consumers in Clifton Heights, PA (1) who received a [form] Collection letter from the Defendant (2) containing a reference to 'Various Other Accounts[,'] (3) on an obligation owed or allegedly owed to Crozer, (4) during the time period of April 4, 2018 to May 30, 2018." App. 28. The District Court granted that motion, holding the proposed class satisfied the numerosity, commonality, typicality, and adequacy requirements of Rule 23(a), and the predominance and superiority requirements of Rule 23(b)(3).

p.143 SAI, now facing class-wide liability, moved for reconsideration on the ground that Huber and the unnamed members of her class had not suffered a concrete injury for purposes of Article III standing. The District Court disagreed. Correctly observing that this Court "ha[d] not [yet] issued a precedential opinion on injury-in-fact stemming from the misleading communications of debt collectors," App. 45, the District Court thoughtfully sought to determine what constitutes such an injury in the FDCPA context. It did so under the auspices of the "informational injury doctrine."

Because we had treated improper disclosures of private information as concrete, if intangible, informational injuries in prior FDCPA cases, the District Court inferred that the dissemination of misleading information likewise should be viewed as a species of informational harm—at least where that that misleading information "influences a plaintiff's credit or management of their debt." App. 46. For this intangible harm to be concrete, it recognized, "confusion itself is not enough," App. 47; rather, the plaintiff must have engaged in "consequential action or inaction following receipt of [the] misleading or deceptive collection letter," App. 47. Such action could "lead[] a plaintiff to pay extra money, affect[] a plaintiff's credit, or otherwise alter[] a plaintiff's response to a debt." App. 46 (quoting *Markakos v. Medicredit, Inc.*, 997 F.3d 778, 780 (7th Cir. 2021)).

On that basis, the District Court concluded that Huber had standing because "[s]he was not merely confused or anxious," but also suffered two types of "financial consequences" as a result of her confusion: (1) "seeking assistance from a professional to figure out how to interpret the letter and how to handle her debt"; and (2) being "unable to pay down her debts or otherwise take appropriate action (other than turning to a third party at her own additional cost) because of the misinformation in SAI's letter." App. 47-48. As for the other class members, the District Court extrapolated that they all had standing under "the same theory of harm" because they received the same confusing letter from SAI, and "being provided with misleading or deceptive information about a debt" would "inevitably" prevent each member's "appropriate action to manage their debt." App. 48. The District Court therefore denied SAI's motion for reconsideration.

Ten days later, the parties stipulated to the statutory damages Huber and the class would receive under the FDCPA if the District Court's rulings were upheld on appeal. Huber would receive $1,000 in statutory damages; the unnamed class members would collectively receive $5,000 in statutory damages to be "distributed on a pro rata basis"; and Huber would also receive a $5,000 service award "for her work in representing the class over the past three years."[1] *Id.* at 52-53. The District Court entered the stipulation as a final appealable order, and SAI timely appealed.

II. Jurisdiction and Standard of Review

The District Court had putative jurisdiction under 28 U.S.C. § 1331 and 15 p.144 U.S.C. § 1692k(d). We have jurisdiction under 28 U.S.C. § 1291, which includes our "jurisdiction to determine our own jurisdiction." *United States v. Kwasnik,* 55 F.4th 212, 215 (3d Cir. 2022).

Our review of an order granting summary judgment "is plenary, meaning we review anew the District Court's summary judgment decision[], applying the same standard it must apply." *Ellis v. Westinghouse Elec. Co., LLC,* 11 F.4th 221, 229 (3d Cir. 2021). Summary judgment is appropriate when "there is no genuine dispute as to any material fact and the movant is entitled to judgment as a matter of law." Fed. R. Civ. P. 56(a).

Our review of class certification orders, on the other hand, is for abuse of discretion, "which occurs if the district court's decision rests upon a clearly erroneous finding of fact, an errant conclusion of law or an improper application of law to fact." *Marcus v. BMW of N. Am., LLC,* 687 F.3d 583, 590 (3d Cir. 2012) (quotation omitted). In assessing whether a district court applied the correct legal standard during class certification, we exercise *de novo* review. *Id.*

Finally, we review denials of motions for reconsideration for abuse of discretion. *United States ex rel. Ascolese v. Shoemaker Constr. Co.,* 55 F.4th 188, 193 (3d Cir. 2022). When a district court's "denial is based on legal issues, we review that determination *de novo.* However, factual findings are reviewed for clear error." *Gibson v. State Farm Mut. Auto. Ins. Co.,* 994 F.3d 182, 186 (3d Cir. 2021) (citation omitted).

III. Discussion

We begin as "we must begin every case: with the question of jurisdiction." *Gayle v. Warden Monmouth Cnty. Corr. Inst.,* 838 F.3d 297, 303 (3d Cir. 2016). Because a plaintiff's standing implicates this Court's Article III jurisdiction, we will address that as a "threshold matter," *St. Pierre v. Retrieval-Masters Creditors Bureau, Inc.,* 898 F.3d 351, 356 (3d Cir. 2018), before turning to the merits of Huber's FDCPA claim and SAI's challenges to her class action.

A. Huber's Article III Standing

While we agree with the District Court's determination that Huber herself has Article III standing, we reach that conclusion on different grounds. Below, we address (1) the requirements of standing and the informational injury doctrine; (2) why that doctrine is inapplicable to Huber's case; and (3) why Huber nonetheless has standing under traditional standing principles.

1. The "Informational Injury" Doctrine

To establish standing under Article III, a plaintiff must show that she suffered: "(1) an injury-in-fact; (2) that is fairly traceable to the defendant's challenged conduct; and (3) that is likely to be redressed by a favorable judicial decision." *Id.* (citing *Lujan v. Defs. of Wildlife,* 504 U.S. 555, 590, 112 S.Ct. 2130, 119 L.Ed.2d 351 (1992)). The injury-in-fact requirement "preserves the vitality of the adversarial process," *Lujan,* 504 U.S. at 581, 112 S.Ct. 2130 (Kennedy, J., concurring in part and concurring in the judgment), by ensuring the plaintiff has "a 'personal stake' in the case," *TransUnion,* 141 S. Ct. at 2203 (quoting *Raines v. Byrd,* 521 U.S. 811, 819, 117 S.Ct. 2312, 138 L.Ed.2d 849 (1997)). Accordingly, her injury must be "concrete," *i.e.,* "real, and not abstract." *Spokeo,* 578 U.S. at 340, 136 S.Ct. 1540 (quotations omitted).

In response to the proliferation of information as both an engine of economic activity and fixture of daily life, the Supreme Court acknowledged in two seminal
p.145 opinions that even the nondisclosure of information can sometimes constitute a "concrete" injury. *See Pub. Citizen v. DOJ,* 491 U.S. 440, 448-49, 109 S.Ct. 2558, 105 L.Ed.2d 377 (1989) (reasoning that the DOJ's denial of information on judicial candidates under consideration by the ABA prevented plaintiffs from "participat[ing] more effectively in the judicial selection process"); *FEC v. Akins,* 524 U.S. 11, 13-14, 21, 118 S.Ct. 1777, 141 L.Ed.2d 10 (1998) (concluding that the FEC's "political committee" determination effectively exempting the AIPAC from disclosing its membership, contributions, and expenditures imperiled plaintiffs' ability to "evaluate candidates for public office").

In the decades that followed, we had occasion to apply that informational injury doctrine, but we did not expound on its requirements. Last year, however, in *Kelly v. RealPage, Inc.,* we specified the criteria a plaintiff must meet to establish an informational injury: "she [must be] denied information to which she [is] legally entitled [by statute], and ... the denial [must] cause[] some adverse consequences related to the purpose of the statute." 47 F.4th at 212. Recognizing that the Supreme Court had developed the informational injury doctrine to address the distinctly modern needs of the Information Age, we deemed that doctrine an exception to the usual concreteness requirement that a plaintiff identify a close historical or common-law analogue to her cause of action. *See id.* at 212 n.8 (declining "to import a historical analogue requirement into the standing analysis for informational injury claims").

But exceptions must be limited, lest they swallow the rule. And, as we explained in *Kelly,* there is no more fundamental limitation on the informational injury doctrine than the need for a plaintiff to show "the denial of information ... to which she has entitlement." *Id.* at 212-13. The Supreme Court made that clear in *TransUnion LLC v. Ramirez,* when a credit reporting agency had mailed plaintiffs credit files omitting certain required information but sent them that information in separate mailings. 141 S. Ct. at 2213. Those plaintiffs had not suffered an informational injury because, the Court explained, they "did not allege that they failed to receive any required information." *Id.* at 2214. In contrast, the plaintiffs in *Kelly* established standing where they had requested a file disclosure from a credit reporting agency pursuant to the Fair Credit Reporting Act, the file produced by the agency omitted information the statute required, and the plaintiffs suffered the kinds of consequences that the disclosure requirements were designed to prevent. *See* 47 F.4th at 214-15.

In short, entitlement to the information allegedly withheld is the *sine qua non* of the informational injury doctrine.

2. Huber's Injury Does Not Qualify As "Informational Harm"

Kelly makes clear why the doctrine is inapplicable to Huber: she has not alleged "the omission of information to which [she] claim[s] entitlement[.]"[2] 47 F.4th at 214. The very reason the District Court granted summary judgment on Huber's § 1692g(a)(1) claim was that Huber had received all the information to which she was entitled. That is, § 1692g(a)(1) required SAI to disclose "the amount of the debt" for the specific service at issue in the letter, and the box labeled "Amount" p.146 did so by telling Huber that she owed $178 for her fourth visit to Crozer. App. 6, 16. That conclusion not only had obvious consequences for Huber's § 1692g(a)(1) claim, but also has consequences for her surviving § 1692e claim because it forecloses the informational injury doctrine of Article III standing.[3]

Because she cannot identify a failure to disclose, Huber urges us instead to extend the informational injury doctrine to the failure to disclose *clearly and effectively*. In support of that capacious theory, she cites decisions interpreting the scope of debt collectors' obligations under the FDCPA. But Huber's argument "confuses standing with the merits," *Frank v. Autovest, LLC,* 961 F.3d 1185, 1189 (D.C. Cir. 2020), as those statutory decisions do not answer the constitutional question of when a harm qualifies as an informational injury for purposes of Article III. And constitutional decisions undermine Huber's proposed expansion of the doctrine. In *TransUnion,* for example, the Supreme Court admonished that an informational injury consists in the "fail[ure] to receive [legally] required information," not merely "receiv[ing] it *in the wrong format.*" 141 S. Ct. at 2214; *see also Trichell v. Midland Credit Mgmt., Inc.,* 964 F.3d 990, 1004 (11th Cir. 2020) (reasoning the informational injury doctrine was inapt when plaintiffs were not "denied desired information, but [instead] ... received unwanted communications that were misleading").

Simply put, unclear disclosures do not equate to outright omissions. Opening the courthouse doors whenever required disclosures could arguably be clearer would vitiate the concrete injury requirement in almost any case involving information. Neither we nor the Supreme Court has suggested that the informational injury doctrine stretches so far, and we reject that proposition today. Because Huber has not alleged that SAI omitted information to which she was entitled, she did not suffer an informational injury.

3. Huber Has Standing Under Traditional Standing Principles

The informational injury doctrine, however, is just one path to standing, and an exceptional one at that. So having ruled it out in Huber's case, we must also consider the more traditional path prescribed by the Supreme Court in *TransUnion:* whether an alleged injury "has a 'close relationship' to a harm 'traditionally' recognized as providing a basis for a lawsuit in American courts." 141 S. Ct. at 2204 (quoting *Spokeo,* 578 U.S. at 341, 136 S.Ct. 1540).

In that case, the Court considered the standing of a purported class of consumers claiming that TransUnion "failed to 'follow reasonable procedures to assure maximum possible accuracy' of the plaintiffs' credit files" in its possession, in violation of the Fair Credit Reporting Act, by including alerts in the consumers' files that erroneously labeled them as potential terrorists on a government watchlist. *Id.* at 2208 (quoting 15 U.S.C. § 1681e(b)). Because "[e]very class member must have Article III standing in order to recover individual damages," *id.*, the Court considered separately those class members whose credit files had been transmitted to third parties and those whose credit files were maintained by TransUnion but had not been disseminated. *Id.* at 2208-09.

Class members in the first category had standing, the Court concluded, because they "suffered a harm with a 'close relationship' p.147 to the harm associated with the tort of defamation." *Id.* Specifically, the Court explained that "the harm from a misleading statement of this kind [*i.e.*, actually disseminated] bears a sufficiently close relationship to the harm from a false and defamatory statement" to satisfy Article III's concrete injury requirement. *Id.* at 2209. In contrast, those whose credit files contained the same misleading statement but were not disseminated lacked standing because the "retention of information lawfully obtained, without further disclosure, traditionally has not provided the basis for a lawsuit in American courts." *Id.* (quotation omitted). Although Congress intended "to assure maximum possible accuracy" of both categories of credit files, 15 U.S.C. § 1681e(b), the mere presence of "misleading information in the internal credit files" did not qualify as a "concrete harm" sufficient to support standing, *TransUnion,* 141 S. Ct. at 2210.

That distinction brought needed clarity to the proper treatment of Article III standing. Before *TransUnion,* courts sometimes conflated the concepts of "statutory" or "prudential" standing with Article III standing by failing to distinguish between "(i) a plaintiff's statutory cause of action to sue a defendant over the defendant's violation of federal law," *i.e.,* the merits of a plaintiff's claim, with "(ii) a plaintiff's suffering concrete harm because of [a] defendant's violation of federal law," *i.e.,* a particular plaintiff's standing to bring that claim. *Id.* at 2205. *TransUnion* put that confusion to rest, explaining that Congress may create an "injury in law," but for an individual plaintiff to proceed in federal court, Article III requires that she show her own "injury in fact." *See id.* at 2205-06. As the Court explained, allowing "*unharmed* plaintiffs to sue defendants who violate federal law not only would violate Article III but also would infringe on the Executive Branch's Article II authority" to decide "how to prioritize and how aggressively to pursue legal actions against defendants who violate the law." *Id.* at 2207.

But why not allow any plaintiff seeking to serve as private attorney general to enforce the statutory right alongside the Executive Branch? Because, the Court explained, in contrast to federal agencies empowered to enforce statutory rights, "[p]rivate plaintiffs are not accountable to the people and are not charged with pursuing the public interest in enforcing a defendant's general compliance with regulatory law." *Id.* Thus, a private party may sue to enforce a statute only when (1) Congress has authorized a private right of action, *and* (2) the prospective plaintiff has established her own individual standing under Article III, *i.e.*, a "physical, monetary, or cognizable intangible harm traditionally recognized as providing a basis for a lawsuit in American courts." *Id.* at 2206.

When it comes to the FDCPA, Congress authorized general enforcement by the Federal Trade Commission (FTC), which may seek civil penalties for the dissemination of a "false, deceptive, or misleading representation ... in connection with the collection of any debt." 15 U.S.C. §§ 1692e, 1692l(a); *see also id.* § 57b. And Congress also provided a private right of action for individual plaintiffs. *Id.* § 1692k. But as *TransUnion* makes clear, "under Article III, an injury in law is not an injury in fact. Only those plaintiffs who have been *concretely harmed* by [the] defendant's statutory violation may sue that private defendant over that violation in federal court." 141 S. Ct. at 2205.

Helpfully, in clarifying the need for an injury-in-fact to establish standing, the Court also clarified the nature of that injury. To establish standing, a plaintiff p.148 must show that she suffered an injury for which there exists a sufficiently "close historical or common-law analogue." *Id.* at 2204. While it is not necessary to find "an exact duplicate in American history and tradition," *id.*, or to show facts that would "give rise to a cause of action under common law," *In re Horizon Healthcare Servs. Inc. Data Breach Litig.*, 846 F.3d 625, 639 (3d Cir. 2017), the *de jure* injury must "'protect essentially the same interests' as 'traditional causes of action,'" *Long v. Se. Pa. Transp. Auth.*, 903 F.3d 312, 324 (3d Cir. 2018) (quoting *Susinno v. Work Out World Inc.*, 862 F.3d 346, 351 (3d Cir. 2017)).

Here, Huber asserts that the receipt of deceptive collection letters meets that test because "the common law has long reflected an interest in avoiding the harms inherent to receiving misleading information." Ans. Br. 34-35 (quoting *Cunningham v. Credit Bureau of Lancaster Cnty., Inc.*, No. 17-cv-5102, 2018 WL 6062351, at *6 (E.D. Pa. Nov. 20, 2018)). We take this as an oblique reference to the tort of fraudulent misrepresentation and agree it is an apt analogue. Like fraudulent misrepresentation, a § 1692e violation involves deception, and the statutory prohibition on the use of "any false, deceptive, or misleading representation or means in connection with the collection of any debt," 15 U.S.C. § 1692e, "protect[s] essentially the same interests" as that "traditional cause[] of action," *Long*, 903 F.3d at 324 (quotation omitted).

But to establish standing, *TransUnion* requires more than a statute's analogue in a common-law action; it requires that "*the harm* [the prospective plaintiff suffered as a result of the statutory violation] bears a sufficiently close relationship to *the harm* from [that common-law action]." 141 S. Ct. at 2209 (emphasis added). It was not sufficient in *TransUnion* that Congress sought to protect the "maximum possible accuracy" of all consumer credit files maintained by credit companies; class members who were labeled potential terrorists but whose credit files had not been disseminated to third parties had not suffered any "concrete injury" because "[t]he mere presence of an inaccuracy in an internal credit file, if it is not disclosed to a third party, causes no concrete harm," *id.* at 2210. Those whose files were disseminated, on the other hand, had standing because "the harm [they suffered] from a misleading statement of [that] kind bears a sufficiently close relationship to the harm from a false and defamatory statement." *Id.* at 2209. Likewise, in the FDCPA context, it is not sufficient for a debtor's standing that Congress sought to protect all debtors from the receipt of false or misleading information from debt collectors; each plaintiff asserting a § 1692e violation must establish that "the harm [she suffered] from a misleading statement of this kind bears a sufficiently close relationship to the harm from [fraudulent misrepresentation]." *Id.*

Notably, however, the "harm traditionally recognized as providing a basis for [fraudulent misrepresentation] in American courts," *id.* at 2206, is not the mere receipt of a misleading statement, or even confusion, without any further consequence. It is the "physical, monetary, or cognizable intangible harm," *id.,* such as a reputational or emotional harm, *id.* at 2208; *Clemens v. ExecuPharm Inc.,* 48 F.4th 146, 155-56 (3d Cir. 2022), that may follow from a plaintiff's "*reliance* upon the misrepresentation," Restatement (Second) of Torts § 525 (Am. L. Inst. 1977) (emphasis added); *see also* John C.P. Goldberg et al., *The Place of Reliance in Fraud,* 48 Ariz. L. Rev. 1001, 1012 (2006) ("[U]nless and until a deception occurs—unless and until there is reliance by the victim—the tort of fraud has not been committed."). p.149 The "mere risk" that a plaintiff who receives a misleading letter from a debt collector will suffer such a cognizable injury is "too speculative to support Article III standing." *TransUnion,* 141 S. Ct. at 2211-12.

We therefore agree with the District Court that confusion, without, more, is not a concrete injury.[4] Instead, to analogize to the tort of fraudulent misrepresentation, a § 1692e claimant must suffer some cognizable harm that flows from that confusion. Namely, she must identify what the District Court aptly described as a "consequential action or inaction following receipt of a misleading or deceptive collection letter[.]" App. 47.[5] Only then will her injury be of the "same character" as the harm from fraudulent misrepresentation, *Thorne v. Pep Boys Manny Moe & Jack Inc.,* 980 F.3d 879, 890 (3d Cir. 2020) (quotation omitted), for only then will the "interests" protected by her statutory cause of action align with those of her common-law analogue, *Long,* 903 F.3d at 324 (quotation omitted).

Huber has established that detrimental action for the reasons the District Court adeptly summarized. She did not merely suffer from confusion, but from two resulting "financial consequences": one in consulting with her financial advisor, which the District Court found was "at her own additional cost," and the other in her failure to "pay down her debts or otherwise take appropriate action" beyond that consultation.[6] App. 47-48. Those detrimental consequences are sufficiently similar to the kind of harm protected by the tort of fraudulent misrepresentation to establish Huber's standing.[7]

***

p.150 In sum, because we had not yet clarified the informational injury doctrine in *Kelly,* the District Court mistakenly believed Huber had standing as a result of an informational injury. Nevertheless, "[w]e may affirm on any basis supported by the record, even if it departs from the District Court's rationale." *TD Bank N.A. v. Hill,* 928 F.3d 259, 270 (3d Cir. 2019). And here, tracking the common-law analogy to fraudulent misrepresentation, Huber has identified both an allegedly deceptive communication and specific harmful action and inaction she took as a result of that communication. She therefore suffered a concrete injury for Article III purposes, and having "assure[d] ourselves of [Huber's] standing," *DiNaples v. MRS BPO, LLC,* 934 F.3d 275, 279 (3d Cir. 2019), we can turn to the merits of her claim.

B. Fair Debt Collection Practices Act

To prevail on an FDCPA claim, a plaintiff must establish that: "(1) she is a consumer, (2) the defendant is a debt collector, (3) the defendant's challenged practice involves an attempt to collect a 'debt' as the [FDCPA] defines it, and (4) the defendant has violated a provision of the FDCPA in attempting to collect the debt." *St. Pierre,* 898 F.3d at 358 (quoting *Douglass v. Convergent Outsourcing,* 765 F.3d 299, 303 (3d Cir. 2014)). The first three elements are uncontested here, so the only question for us is whether the District Court correctly determined that SAI's form letter transgresses the FDCPA— specifically, the prohibition on the "use [of] any false, deceptive, or misleading representation or means in connection with the collection of any debt." 15 U.S.C. § 1692e.

Like the District Court, we make that assessment applying the "least sophisticated debtor" standard. *Moyer v. Patenaude & Felix, A.P.C.,* 991 F.3d 466, 470 (3d Cir. 2021) (quoting *Jensen v. Pressler & Pressler,* 791 F.3d 413, 418 (3d Cir. 2015)); *see also Riccio v. Sentry Credit, Inc.,* 954 F.3d 582, 594 (3d Cir. 2020) (en banc). Under that test, we consider "whether a debt collector's statement in a communication to a debtor would *deceive* or *mislead* the least sophisticated debtor." *Jensen,* 791 F.3d at 420. Because the standard is objective, "the specific plaintiff need not prove that *she* was actually confused or misled, only that the objective least sophisticated debtor would be." *Id.* at 419.

Although the least sophisticated debtor test "protects naïve consumers, it also prevents liability for bizarre or idiosyncratic interpretations of collection notices by preserving a quotient of reasonableness and presuming a basic level of understanding and willingness to read with care." *Wilson v. Quadramed Corp.,* 225 F.3d 350, 354-55 (3d Cir. 2000) (quotation omitted). Accordingly, we have held that a collection letter is deceptive when "it can be reasonably read to have two or more different meanings, one of which is inaccurate." *Moyer,* 991 F.3d at 470 (quoting *Wilson,* 225 F.3d at 354).

Here, the District Court correctly observed that the "Account Summary" in SAI's form letter could be reasonably interpreted in two ways because, without further explanation, it sets out both an "Amount" and "Various Other Accounts Total Balance." App. 7, 17. Thus, a least sophisticated debtor could read the latter as "Various Other Accounts *Total Balance,*" meaning the sum total of her out-standing debt, including the "Amount." Alternatively, a least sophisticated debtor could read it as "*Various Other Accounts* Total Balance," meaning she owes that figure in addition to the "Amount." So as SAI itself acknowledges, "[i]n a vacuum, the Letter could reasonably be read to p.151 have the two meanings ascribed by the District Court," Opening Br. 30, and "one of [them] is inaccurate," *Moyer,* 991 F.3d at 470 (quotation omitted). That is the very definition of a "deceptive" communication, in violation of § 1692e.

SAI resists that conclusion by arguing that a debtor in Huber's situation would have deduced the meaning of "Various Other Accounts Total Balance" by comparing the fourth letter she received with the three prior collection letters SAI sent her. *See* Opening Br. 31 ("Each correspondence was about a separate account and the 'Total Balance' identified increased each time by the amount owed for that specific amount.").

That argument highlights the open question whether the least sophisticated debtor standard is "purely objective" or instead "look[s] to what an objective debtor in [the plaintiff's] situation . . . would have thought or done," *Jensen*, 791 F.3d at 422 n.4, but it is not a question to answer today. SAI sent those letters to Huber on May 24, June 14, and July 12, 2018—months before it mailed her its fourth collection letter on September 6, 2018, App. 281-84—and in the intervals between the collection letters, a least sophisticated debtor "may have lost the [prior letters] and forgotten the amount of the debt completely," *Fields v. Wilber L. Firm, P.C.*, 383 F.3d 562, 566 (7th Cir. 2004); *see also Lukawski v. Client Servs., Inc.*, No. 3:12-cv-02082, 2013 WL 4647482, at *3 (M.D. Pa. Aug. 29, 2013) ("[A] least sophisticated consumer, gullible, trusting, and naïve . . . cannot be expected to recall . . . a collection letter received six weeks prior to a current communication."). So even if we look beyond the four corners of SAI's letter, we would not expect a least sophisticated debtor in Huber's position to recall the precise figures in the prior letters, much less understand clearly what amount was due.

In short, whether we examine the fourth collection letter from the perspective of a purely objective least sophisticated debtor or a least sophisticated debtor in Huber's position, SAI's letter is "deceptive" for purposes of § 1692e. We therefore affirm the District Court's grant of summary judgment in Huber's favor on that claim.

C. Class Considerations

Finally, SAI contends that even if Huber could bring an individual claim under the FDCPA, the District Court erred in permitting her suit to proceed on behalf of a class whose members may or may not have individual standing. We consider SAI's challenges, first, to the justiciability of the class action for the unnamed class members' lack of standing and, second, to Huber's ability to satisfy the requirements of Federal Rule of Civil Procedure 23.

1. Justiciability

According to SAI, Huber failed to establish that the unnamed class members individually have standing because she did not "present any evidence that [they] acted to their detriment after receiving a letter from SAI in the same form as the [challenged] Letter." Opening Br. 14. And absent that showing of individual standing, SAI asserts, Huber's suit is nonjusticiable under Article III. We consider both arguments below.

i. The Standing of the Unnamed Class Members

The District Court generalized from Huber's own injury, holding that all unnamed class members also had standing because their receipt of SAI's letter would "inevitably" cause them similar financial harm to Huber. App. 48. Our dissenting colleague appears to go further and to believe that p.152 no individualized determination of standing is necessary for the class members (or Huber, for that matter) because Congress, in creating a private right of action under the FDCPA, ensured their injuries were "concrete[ ]." Dissent at 162-63. We cannot agree with either analysis.

We part ways with the District Court because Huber did not present evidence that any class member other than herself suffered a "consequential action or inaction" as a result of receiving SAI's letter. App. 47. The District Court correctly observed that Congress "may not simply enact an injury into existence," so regardless of whether the defendant violated the law, the plaintiff must establish that she herself suffered a concrete harm. App. 44 (quoting *TransUnion,* 141 S. Ct. at 2205). But neither theory of standing can float the entire class. Just as Huber did not suffer an informational injury, neither did these class members, so the informational injury doctrine cannot support their standing. *Kelly,* 47 F.4th at 214. And while the District Court found that Huber had experienced specific "financial consequences" as a result of SAI's letter, App. 47—rendering her injury analogous to the harm associated with fraudulent misrepresentation and thus concrete for purposes of Article III—it could not make such findings as to any other class member because Huber offered no such evidence.

Some class members may not have been confused at all; some may have been confused but nonetheless paid the correct sum; and some may have cleared up their confusion with a glance at their prior notices. It is also true that some, like Huber, may have suffered sufficiently concrete harm, financial or otherwise, to satisfy Article III. But standing cannot be based on speculative injury. *See Clapper v. Amnesty Int'l USA,* 568 U.S. 398, 409, 133 S.Ct. 1138, 185 L.Ed.2d 264 (2013); *Thorne,* 980 F.3d at 893 (explaining that standing will not be found when the "alleged harm, even if concrete, is hypothetical or conjectural"). So while the District Court correctly recognized that mere "receipt of a misleading or deceptive collection letter," without some "consequential action or inaction following [that] receipt," would be insufficient to establish informational harm, App. 47, it was too quick to assume that financial harm was an "inevitable consequence[ ]" for each and every class member, App. 49.

We part ways with our dissenting colleague to the extent she rejects the need for individualized inquiry and asserts that, because SAI's letter violated the FDCPA, any and all recipients of the letter automatically have standing to bring suit. But that position misapprehends the fundamental distinction between "statutory standing" and Article III standing. According to the dissent, a plaintiff has standing to bring a claim based on a cause of action created by Congress whenever Congress has "impose[d] a statutory prohibition and grant[ed] a plaintiff a cause of action to sue over a 'defendant's violation of that statutory prohibition or obligation,'" Dissent at 158 (quoting *TransUnion,* 141 S. Ct. at 2204). Harm is "concrete[ ]" simply because "Congress has provided a remedy." *Id.* at 165. And a plaintiff's standing depends on "harm to the interest that [Congress sought] to be protected, not actual harm to the plaintiff." *Id.* at 162-63; *see also id.* at 163-64 (stating that "what actually happened to Ms. Huber[ ] . . . and what happened to every plaintiff in the class," is "irrelevant" because there is no requirement that we consider "the actual impact or consequences of the violation on a particular plaintiff"). From these premises, the dissent concludes that here, because Congress wanted "debtors to be protected p.153 from misleading information from collection agencies," the receipt of misleading information—in and of itself—effects a concrete injury, without any need for individualized inquiry. *Id.* at 164-65.

The Supreme Court has repudiated each of those premises. In *Spokeo,* the Court expressly "rejected the proposition that 'a plaintiff automatically satisfies the injury-in-fact requirement whenever a statute grants a person a statutory right and purports to authorize that person to sue to vindicate that right.'" *TransUnion,* 141 S. Ct. at 2205 (quoting *Spokeo,* 578 U.S. at 341, 136 S.Ct. 1540). In *TransUnion,* it explained that Congress's creation of a statutory remedy does not make harm "concrete"; what matters is whether the particular plaintiff has suffered "any physical, monetary, or cognizable intangible harm traditionally recognized" in common law. *Id.* at 2206; *see id.* (concrete injury is required "[e]ven if Congress affords . . . a cause of action (with statutory damages available) to sue over [a] defendant's legal violation"). It also made clear that actual or imminent injury to the plaintiff herself is the *sine qua non* of standing—requiring that a plaintiff "seek[s] to remedy . . . harm to herself" and not "merely . . . to ensure a defendant's 'compliance with regulatory law.'" *Id.* (quoting *Spokeo,* 578 U.S. at 345, 136 S.Ct. 1540 (Thomas, J., concurring)).

The dissent is therefore mistaken that Congress can create not just the right, but Article III standing to enforce it, simply by legislating an "interest to be protected. . . in not receiving false or misleading information," Dissent at 164, or that Congress's desire to protect that interest—in the absence of any detrimental consequence to the prospective plaintiff—imbues that plaintiff with standing in "the same way as common law sought to protect people from fraudulent misrepresentations," *id.* at 165. It is precisely because Congress "may not . . . us[e] its lawmaking power to transform something that is not remotely harmful into something that is," *TransUnion,* 141 S. Ct. at 2205, that any plaintiff alleging intangible harm must show an actual or imminent injury "with a close relationship to harms traditionally recognized as providing a basis for lawsuits in American courts,"[8] *id.* at 2204.

In *TransUnion,* the cognizable harm from wrongly identifying the class members as potential terrorists was akin to the harm from defamation. *Id.* at 2208-09. In *Horizon,* the cognizable harm from the unauthorized release of the plaintiffs' sensitive information was akin to the harm from invasion of privacy, *Horizon,* 846 F.3d at 639-40, as was the disclosure of the plaintiff's financial information in *St. Pierre,* 898 F.3d at 357-58, and the intrusion of an unauthorized robocall in *Susinno,* 862 F.3d at 351-52 & n.3.[9] Here, however, p.154 the only harm that we can say with certainty was suffered by the unnamed class members is the receipt of misleading information.

Even assuming *arguendo* that the receipt of that information actually confused each and every class member, confusion, without more, is not "harm traditionally recognized as providing a basis for [fraudulent misrepresentation] in American courts." *TransUnion,* 141 S. Ct. at 2206; *see Island Insteel Sys., Inc. v. Waters,* 296 F.3d 200, 212-13 (3d Cir. 2002); Restatement (Second) of Torts §§ 525, 549. Nor has

Huber identified any other tort that would make the mere receipt of misleading information akin to an "intangible harm traditionally recognized" in common law. *TransUnion,* 141 S. Ct. at 2206. The need for individualized inquiry to determine the standing of the unnamed class members thus stems not from our requirement that plaintiffs prove reliance as "an element of a cause of action for fraudulent misrepresentation," Dissent at 159, but from Article III's requirement of a concrete injury to establish standing, *see TransUnion,* 141 S. Ct. at 2204.

ii. Consequences for Justiciability

That uncertainty, however, does not render the class action itself non-justiciable. To the contrary, we have held that "the 'cases or controversies' requirement is satisfied so long as a class representative has standing, whether in the context of a settlement or litigation class." *Neale v. Volvo Cars of N. Am., LLC,* 794 F.3d 353, 362 (3d Cir. 2015); *see also Mielo v. Steak'n Shake Operations, Inc.,* 897 F.3d 467, 478 (3d Cir. 2018) (same). And the Supreme Court has remarked that "federal courts lack jurisdiction if no *named* plaintiff has standing." *Frank v. Gaos,* ___ U.S. ___, 139 S. Ct. 1041, 1046, 203 L.Ed.2d 404 (2019) (emphasis added).

SAI urges us to depart from *Neale* and *Mielo* based on *TransUnion*'s purported requirement that each unnamed class member have standing for a class action to present a justiciable case or controversy. But SAI misapprehends *TransUnion,* which held only that individual standing was required for a class member to obtain damages. As the Supreme Court explained: "Every class member must have Article III standing in order *to recover individual damages.* 'Article III does not give federal courts the power *to order relief* to any uninjured plaintiff, class action or not.'" 141 S. Ct. at 2208 (emphasis added) (quoting *Tyson Foods, Inc. v. Bouaphakeo,* 577 U.S. 442, 466, 136 S.Ct. 1036, 194 L.Ed.2d 124 (2016) (Roberts, C.J., concurring)). The Court also underscored the limited scope of its holding in a footnote, clarifying: "We do not here address the distinct question whether every class member must demonstrate standing *before* a court certifies a class." *Id.* at 2208 p.155 n.4 (citing *Cordoba v. DIRECTV, LLC,* 942 F.3d 1259, 1277 (11th Cir. 2019)).

TransUnion suggests that the need for unnamed class members to demonstrate Article III standing depends on the stage of litigation. At the remedial phase, each class member must establish standing to recover individual damages. *See id.* at 2208. By contrast, at certification, the standing of individual class members may inform whether a proposed class satisfies the requirements of Federal Rule of Civil Procedure 23, *see infra*; *see also Neale,* 794 F.3d at 368, but it is not necessary for each member to prove his or her standing for the class action to be justiciable, *TransUnion,* 141 S. Ct. at 2208 n.4.

We therefore abide by *Neale*'s precept that "so long as a named class representative has standing, a class action presents a valid 'case or controversy' under Article III." 794 F.3d at 369. In doing so, we respect *stare decisis* by "assum[ing] that the law is stable unless there is clear precedent to the contrary. And that means that we do not assume that the Supreme Court has altered the law unless it says so." *Horizon,* 846 F.3d at 638. Our cases since *TransUnion* have similarly hewed to *Neale* and *Mielo,* albeit without explicitly grappling with the Supreme Court's remarks on standing in class actions. *See Boley v. Universal Health Servs., Inc.,* 36 F.4th 124, 133 (3d

Cir. 2022); *Duncan v. Governor of V.I.*, 48 F.4th 195, 203 (3d Cir. 2022); *Clemens*, 48 F.4th at 153 n.4.

Because Huber has Article III standing, her proposed class action presents a justiciable case or controversy even though some unnamed class members may lack standing.

2. Certification

On the other hand, the possibility that some unnamed class members lack standing may prevent certification under Federal Rule of Civil Procedure 23. While *TransUnion* left open "whether every class member must demonstrate standing *before* a court certifies a class," 141 S. Ct. at 2208 n.4 (citing *Cordoba*, 942 F.3d at 1277), our precedent supplies an answer to that query: We do not "requir[e] Article III standing of absent class members" prior to certification, but the potential inclusion of some members without standing in a class can result in "legitimate Rule 23 challenges." *Neale*, 794 F.3d at 367-68.

SAI raises three certification challenges here, contending Huber's failure to establish unnamed class members' standing means her proposed class cannot satisfy the commonality, typicality, and predominance requirements of Federal Rule of Civil Procedure 23. We address each objection in turn.

The commonality prerequisite to certification derives from Federal Rule of Civil Procedure 23(a)(2)'s insistence that there be "questions of law or fact common to the class." Fed. R. Civ. P. 23(a)(2). According to SAI, Huber's class does not satisfy commonality because Huber has not shown that "she and the class members suffered the same injury." Reply Br. 19 (citing *Wal-Mart Stores, Inc. v. Dukes*, 564 U.S. 338, 349-50, 131 S.Ct. 2541, 180 L.Ed.2d 374 (2011)). Here, SAI conflates the common injury the Supreme Court demanded in *Dukes* for purposes of Federal Rule of Civil Procedure 23(a)(2) with the injury-in-fact component of standing. As *Dukes* explained, class members suffer a common injury for Rule 23(a)(2) when their claims "depend upon a common contention. . . capable of classwide resolution." 564 U.S. at 350, 131 S.Ct. 2541. Huber's suit raises a common contention as to every class member—namely, that the form collection letter they all received violates 15 U.S.C. § 1692e. *Cf. Dukes*, 564 p.156 U.S. at 350, 131 S.Ct. 2541 (observing a class would satisfy commonality by asserting, for example, "discriminatory bias on the part of the same supervisor"). The class thus asserts a "common contention" and so shares common questions of law or fact for Rule 23(a)(2) purposes. *Id.*

Next, SAI suggests the class founders on the requirement that Huber's "claims or defenses . . . [be] typical of the claims or defenses of the class." Fed. R. Civ. P. 23(a)(3). Huber's claim is atypical, according to SAI, because Huber has not submitted evidence of the specific detrimental consequences unnamed class members experienced after receiving the form collection letter. Yet the typicality requirement merely serves to ensure that class representatives do not have "unique interests that might motivate them to litigate against or settle with the defendants in a way that prejudices the absentees," *Duncan*, 48 F.4th at 207 (quotation omitted), and here the merits of Huber's FDCPA claim are identical to those of the unnamed class members',[10] *see Boley*, 36 F.4th at 134 ("[A] violative practice can support a class action embracing a variety of injuries so long as those injuries can all be linked to the practice."). As a result, Huber's interests are "sufficiently aligned with those of the class" to satisfy typicality. *Id.*

In a last challenge to certification, SAI contends that the individualized questions regarding unnamed class members' standing will overwhelm common questions, such that Huber cannot meet the predominance requirement of Federal Rule of Civil Procedure 23(b)(3) (stating "questions of law or fact common to class members [must] predominate over any questions affecting only individual members").

The predominance inquiry "asks whether the common, aggregation-enabling, issues in the case are more prevalent or important than the non-common, aggregation-defeating, individual issues." *Ferreras v. Am. Airlines, Inc.,* 946 F.3d 178, 185 (3d Cir. 2019) (quoting *Tyson,* 577 U.S. at 453, 136 S.Ct. 1036). To answer that question, "court[s] must look first to the elements of the plaintiffs' underlying claims . . . through the prism of Rule 23" to assess whether the class members can prove their claims with "evidence that is common to the class rather than individual to its members." *Reinig v. RBS Citizens, N.A.,* 912 F.3d 115, 127-28 (3d Cir. 2018) (quotations omitted). But "the presence of individual questions does not *per se* rule out a finding of predominance." *In re Prudential Ins. Co. Am. Sales Prac. Litig. Agent Actions,* 148 F.3d 283, 315 (3d Cir. 1998). Rather, as the Supreme Court has counseled:

> When "one or more of the central issues in the action are common to the class and can be said to predominate, the action may be considered proper under Rule 23(b)(3) even though other important matters will have to be tried separately, such as damages or some affirmative defenses peculiar to some individual class members."

Tyson, 577 U.S. at 453, 136 S.Ct. 1036 (quoting 7AA Charles A. Wright et al., *Federal Practice and Procedure* § 1778 (3d ed. 2005)).

No doubt, predominance concerns can arise when unnamed class members must submit individualized evidence to satisfy standing and recover damages. We have previously recognized as much, *see* p.157 *Neale,* 794 F.3d at 368 (explaining that differences between injuries suffered by class members can "affect . . . predominance analyses"), as did the Supreme Court in tacitly endorsing the Eleventh Circuit's decision in *Cordoba, see TransUnion,* 141 S. Ct. at 2208 n.4 (citing *Cordoba,* 942 F.3d at 1277). Although the named plaintiff in *Cordoba* had Article III standing, 942 F.3d at 1271, the evidence in the record was inconclusive as to the proportion of unnamed class members who could make a similar showing, *id.* at 1275. To recover damages, the Eleventh Circuit explained, unnamed class members would have to submit individualized evidence of their standing. *Id.* at 1274. Depending on the number of class members able to satisfy that burden and the difficulty of identifying those class members, "individualized determinations might overwhelm issues common the class," *id.* at 1275, so the district court needed "to address whether common issues predominate under Rule 23(b)(3) when this [standing] issue is baked into the analysis," *id.* at 1277. Accordingly, the Eleventh Circuit vacated the class certification order and remanded.

Like the Eleventh Circuit in *Cordoba,* we conclude that remand is necessary here owing to the lack of evidence in the record indicating how many members of Huber's class are likely to have standing and how burdensome that showing will be for both the District Court and the parties. Because the District Court decided that Huber and the unnamed members of her class suffered informational injuries, the Court had no occasion to consider how individualized evidence of unnamed class members' standing would affect the balance of common versus individual issues for purposes of predominance, or what proportion of the class could be expected to establish standing. Thus, the District Court must assess the implications of those individualized showings for the predominance requirement of Federal Rule of Civil Procedure 23(b)(3).[11] *See Neale,* 794 F.3d at 368.

On remand, Huber should submit evidence enabling the District Court to estimate "how many class members (or what proportion of them)" have standing.[12] *Cordoba,* 942 F.3d at 1275. Additionally, the Court should evaluate the feasibility of receiving individualized evidence on class members' standing. If the Court surmises that few class members will be able to show they undertook the kind of detrimental action or inaction required for standing or that "it will be extraordinarily difficult to identify those who did," *id.* at 1275, then Huber's proposed class is not "sufficiently cohesive to warrant adjudication by representation," *Reinig,* 912 F.3d at 127 (quoting *In re Hydrogen Peroxide Antitrust Litig.,* 552 F.3d 305, 311 (3d Cir. 2008)). By contrast, if many class members appear likely to satisfy standing "or if there is a p.158 plausible straightforward method to sort them out at the back end of the case, then the class might appropriately proceed as it is currently defined." *Cordoba,* 942 F.3d at 1275.

We have no doubt that our esteemed colleague on the District Court—given her deep familiarity with this case and vast experience on the bench—is well-equipped to make those determinations. We will therefore vacate the class certification order and remand for the District Court to decide whether Huber's proposed class satisfies Federal Rule of Civil Procedure 23(b)(3) notwithstanding the individualized evidence class members must submit to demonstrate standing and recover damages. In addition, because the District Court's damages award was predicated on its class certification decision, *see* App. 51-52, we will also vacate that order to enable the District Court to reassess damages, if needed to avoid any anomalous windfall. The District Court can then exercise its wide discretion, depending on its determinations as to certification and the number of class members expected to have standing and to recover damages, to ensure appropriate amounts of both statutory damages and attorney's fees. *See* 15 U.S.C. § 1692k(a)(2)-(3).

IV. Conclusion

For the foregoing reasons, we will affirm the District Court's rulings that Huber has Article III standing and that SAI's form collection letter violated 15 U.S.C. § 1692e. However, we will vacate the District Court's orders certifying Huber's proposed class and awarding damages and will remand for proceedings consistent with this opinion.

RENDELL, Circuit Judge, concurring in part and dissenting in part.

Jamie Huber received misleading notices from a collection agency that, under our case law, were deceptive as a matter of law. The same goes for members of the class certified by the District Court. I agree with the Majority that Huber has standing. But unlike the Majority, I adopt the analysis that comports with our precedent and would affirm outright without any need for a remand to examine the propriety of the class certification. So, I part ways with the Majority and respectfully dissent as to the proper analysis and ultimate disposition.

The Majority's reasoning disregards both controlling Supreme Court precedent in *Spokeo, Inc. v. Robins,* 578 U.S. 330, 136 S.Ct. 1540, 194 L.Ed.2d 635 (2016), and *TransUnion LLC v. Ramirez,* 549 U.S. 413, 141 S. Ct. 2190, 210 L.Ed.2d 568 (2021), and our precedent, namely our opinions in *Susinno v. Work Out World Inc.,* 862 F.3d 346 (3d Cir. 2017) (Hardiman, J.), and *In re Horizon Healthcare Servs. Inc. Data Breach Litig.,* 846 F.3d 625 (3d Cir. 2017) (Jordan, J.). The Majority purports to follow *Spokeo* and *TransUnion,* but it fails to emphasize that the issue before us involves the unique question of concreteness for purposes of determining the standing of a plaintiff bringing a claim based on a cause of action created by Congress. Moreover, the Majority conflates standing in such cases with the injury required in other Article III standing cases, focusing on the extent of harm or injury. *Spokeo* and *TransUnion* do not ever refer to an inquiry along these lines. This is a distinct type of standing, as we afford "due respect" to Congress's decision to impose a statutory prohibition and grant a plaintiff a cause of action to sue over a "defendant's violation of that statutory prohibition or obligation." *TransUnion,* 141 S. Ct. at 2204 (citing *Spokeo,* 578 U.S. at 341, 136 S.Ct. 1540). This "respect" means that we allow Congress to provide a p.159 remedy to plaintiffs in certain situations where they might not have satisfied the traditional notions of harm required at common law. Congress "has the power to define injuries that were previously inadequate in law." *Horizon,* 846 F.3d at 638 (internal quotation marks omitted) (quoting *Spokeo,* 578 U.S. at 341, 136 S.Ct. 1540). Otherwise, why create a special test for "concreteness" in these cases?

The analysis in this situation is quite specific and straightforward. We ask whether the claim vindicates a right traditionally recognized at common law (*i.e.,* is there a common law analog?) taking into account Congress's view regarding the need to vindicate that right.[1] We must also make sure that the situation actually implicates the interest to be protected so that a plaintiff is not simply complaining of a "bare procedural violation" of a statute unconnected to any impact on her. *Spokeo,* 578 U.S. at 342, 136 S.Ct. 1540. Checking these boxes leads to a plaintiff's satisfying the "concreteness" test for standing to pursue a congressionally created claim based on an alleged intangible harm. "Case closed"—or, actually, opened—because Huber's claim meets this test, as I discuss more fully below.

We performed this analysis correctly in *Horizon* and in *Susinno.*

In *Horizon,* plaintiffs' laptops containing highly sensitive and private personal information were stolen. 846 F.3d at 630. The complaint alleged that their insurance company, Horizon, failed to maintain the confidentiality of the plaintiffs' information, giving rise to a cause of action under the Fair Credit Reporting Act (FCRA). *Id.* at 629. It did not allege that the false information was actually used to the plaintiffs' detriment. *Id.* The district court had dismissed the case, concluding that "standing requires some form of additional 'specific harm' beyond 'mere violations of statutory and common law rights.'" *Id.* at 634. We reversed based on our own precedent in *In re Google Inc. Cookie Placement Consumer Priv. Litig.,* 806 F.3d 125 (3d Cir. 2015), and *In re Nickelodeon Consumer Priv. Litig.,* 827 F.3d 262 (3d Cir. 2016), citing the principle that "Congress has long provided plaintiffs with the right to seek redress for unauthorized disclosures of information that, in Congress's judgment, ought to remain private." *Horizon,* 846 F.3d at 636 (quotation marks omitted) (quoting *Nickelodeon,* 827 F.3d at 274). We noted that *Spokeo* did not compel a different outcome and commented on *Spokeo*'s recognition of Congress's role:

> We reaffirm that conclusion today. *Spokeo* itself does not state that it is redefining the injury-in-fact requirement. Instead, it reemphasizes that Congress "has the power to define injuries that were previously inadequate in law." In the absence of any indication to the contrary, we understand that the *Spokeo* Court meant to reiterate traditional notions of standing, rather than erect any new barriers that might prevent Congress from identifying new causes of action though they may be based on intangible harms.

Id. at 638 (internal citations omitted) (quoting *Spokeo,* 578 U.S. at 341, 136 S.Ct. 1540). And in *Susinno,* we summarized *Horizon*'s rule as follows:

> p.160 When one sues under a statute alleging "the very injury [the statute] is intended to prevent," and the injury "has a close relationship to a harm . . . traditionally. . . providing a basis for a lawsuit in English or American courts," a concrete injury has been pleaded.

862 F.3d at 351 (quoting *Horizon,* 846 F.3d at 639-40) (alteration in original). We then proceeded to conclude that the plaintiff in *Susinno* had pled a concrete, albeit intangible, injury by complaining of one prerecorded call and voice message to her cellular telephone that violated the Telephone Consumer Protection Act (TCPA):

> Where a plaintiff's intangible injury has been made legally cognizable through the democratic process, and the injury closely relates to a cause of action traditionally recognized in English and American courts, standing to sue exists.

Id. at 352.

After we decided *Horizon* and *Susinno,* the Supreme Court revisited, and reiterated, the appropriate test in *TransUnion.* There, the plaintiffs complained of "misleading" alerts in their credit reports that indicated each of the plaintiffs was a "potential match to names on the OFAC list [of suspected terrorists]." *TransUnion,* 141 S. Ct. at 2202. This was based on the credit reporting agencies' matching first and last names against the list. The Supreme Court once again laid out the test for "concreteness" of an intangible harm, explaining that the harm experienced by "the 1,853 class members whose reports [containing potentially misleading information] were disseminated to third parties suffered a concrete injury in fact under Article III" because "the harm from a misleading statement . . . bears a *sufficiently close relationship* to the harm from a false and defamatory statement." *Id.* at 2209 (emphasis added). End of analysis. As the Majority points out, the other class of plaintiffs in *TransUnion,* whose reports were not disseminated, did not suffer a concrete injury because there was "no historical or common law analog where the mere existence of inaccurate information, absent dissemination, amounts to concrete injury." *TransUnion,* 141 S. Ct. at 2209 (quoting *Owner-Operator Indep. Drivers, Inc. v. U.S. Dep't of Transp.,* 879 F.3d 339, 344-45 (D.C. Cir. 2018)) (quotation marks omitted). The Majority states that the distinction between the plaintiffs whose misleading reports were sent and plaintiffs whose misleading reports were not "brought needed clarity to the proper treatment of Article III standing." Maj. Op., Section III.A.3, *supra.* It then expands on the need for a "personal stake." I agree. Here, if the misleading notice had never been sent to *Huber,* she would have no claim. Or, if, as the Majority's quotation from *TransUnion* notes, Huber had no personal stake because she was only pursuing a mere procedural violation with no connection to her she would lack standing.[2] But no one has contended that Huber lacks a personal stake or is pursuing a mere procedural violation.[3]

p.161 The Majority quotes *TransUnion* regarding the need to find a "sufficiently close relationship" between a statutory harm and a common law harm, but it fails to heed the Supreme Court's essential conclusion: once a close relationship is found with a common law analog, the plaintiff has standing because the injury is concrete as a matter of law. Rather than reasoning along these lines and asking, "does the harm from a misleading communication from a collection agency have a sufficiently close relationship to the harm from a fraudulent misrepresentation?" (the answer is, yes), the Majority focuses on "consequences" flowing from the receipt of a misleading communication and asserts that there is no match, or "close relationship," because to state a claim for fraudulent misrepresentation the plaintiff must have detrimentally relied on the communication, *i.e.,* there must be some "further consequence." Maj. Op. Section III.A.3., *supra.* To analogize to the tort of fraudulent misrepresentation, the Majority concludes, a § 1692e claimant must suffer some cognizable harm that flows from the confusion that attends her receipt of the misleading communication.

But in *TransUnion,* the Court noted that "[i]n looking to whether a plaintiff's asserted harm has a 'close relationship' to a harm traditionally recognized as providing a basis for a lawsuit in American courts, we do not require an exact duplicate." *Id.* Bearing that principle in mind, the Court concluded that saying someone was a "potential terrorist" was "sufficiently close" to saying that he is an actual terrorist so as to be analogized to defamation. *Id.* In truth, the statement was more misleading than defamatory. If the Supreme Court had wanted the relationship to defamation to be something more than "sufficiently close," the analogy may not have worked because truth might have been a defense. Indeed, based on the matching of the names, the "potential match" was true (*i.e.,* the name "Susan Smith" appeared on the OFAC list). Moreover, a match may have been true for some plaintiffs (*i.e.,* if the "Susan Smith" identified by the credit report was, in fact, the same "Susan Smith" identified on the OFAC list). So, the element of falsity normally associated with defamation was tenuous at best. That did not concern the Court: an exact match to the common law cause of action is not required.

The Majority here appears to heed our, and the Supreme Court's, directives by analogizing Huber's situation to the common law tort of fraudulent misrepresentation:

> Huber asserts that the receipt of deceptive collection letters meets that test, because the common law has long reflected an interest in avoiding the harms inherent to receiving misleading information. We take this as an oblique reference to the tort of fraudulent misrepresentation and agree it is an apt analogue. Like fraudulent misrepresentation, a § 1692e violation involves deception[,] and the statutory prohibition on the use of any false, deceptive, or misleading representation or means in connection with the collection of

> any p.162 debt protects essentially the same interests as that traditional cause of action.

Maj. Op., Section III.A.3, *supra* (cleaned up and bracketed alteration added). The Majority should have ended its reasoning there and concluded with a statement similar to the one that the Supreme Court made in *TransUnion*: "In short, a plaintiff who received a misleading statement regarding the amount of the debt she owes suffered a concrete injury in fact under Article III." Instead, the Majority considers two unnecessary issues: first, whether there has been some "consequential action or inaction following receipt of [the] misleading or deceptive collection letter," Maj. Op., Section III.A.3, *i.e.,* did the plaintiffs detrimentally rely on the misleading information? And second, what was the extent of the harm caused by the detrimental reliance?

As to the first inquiry, action in reliance on the misrepresentation is an element of a cause of action for fraudulent misrepresentation. But in discussing the common law analog in *Horizon,* we specifically rejected any notion that a plaintiff's allegations need to state a cause of action:

> We are not suggesting that Horizon's actions would give rise to a cause of action under common law. No common law tort proscribes the release of truthful information that is not harmful to one's reputation or otherwise offensive.

Horizon, 846 F.3d at 639. Although the Majority quotes this language from *Horizon,* it proceeds to disregard it by focusing its attention on the proposition that "until a deception occurs—unless and until there is reliance by the victim—the tort of fraud has not been committed." Maj. Op., Section III.A.3, *supra.* In *Horizon,* the personal information that was on the stolen computers was not false, so there really was no cause of action at common law for the employers' failure to safeguard the plaintiffs' personal information. But we reasoned that the 'intangible harm' that the FCRA seeks to remedy had a sufficiently close relationship to a harm—invasion of privacy—that has traditionally been regarded as providing a basis for a lawsuit in English and American courts. It was a stretch to say that the insurer, by being negligent in keeping the information sufficiently secure, had invaded its members' privacy. No matter; the harm was close enough based on the interest to be protected. And in *Susinno,* we reiterated that the focus should be on the interest to be protected:

> [A] close relationship does not require that the newly proscribed conduct would "give rise to a cause of action under common law." But it does require that newly established causes of action protect *essentially the same interests that traditional causes of action sought to protect.*

Susinno, 862 F.3d at 351 (internal citation omitted) (emphasis added). To be clear, the historical analysis in *Susinno* centered on the link between the common law analog and the statutory cause of action itself—not any specific theory of liability under the statute. The plaintiff's allegation of receiving a single unwanted robocall amounted to an unadorned, garden-variety TCPA claim. We still concluded that the mere violation of the TCPA provision at issue worked a sufficiently concrete injury for Article III standing. So, our precedent leaves no room to ask for more than that in this case.

In *TransUnion,* the Court analogized the asserted harm to the harm of defamation looking only at the dissemination of misleading information, and it respected Congress's decision to protect an individual's interest in not having misleading information disseminated by credit reporting agencies. While the Majority says p.163 there must be "reputational or emotional harm," Maj. Op., Section III.A.3., the Court in *TransUnion* did not concern itself with whether the information was false, or whether anyone receiving the report actually read it or denied credit to the plaintiffs, or whether there was harm to plaintiffs' reputations—all relevant considerations in a defamation case. Rather, the Court was concerned with the interest at stake, not with mirroring the cause of action.

By adding a requirement of consequences resulting from reliance, the Majority drastically limits the remedy Congress provided, undermining Congressional policy and the separation of powers. As we noted in *Sussino,* this is a matter for the democratic process. Furthermore, not only is the imposition of this reliance element contrary to precedent, but the error of imposing this element is compounded by the Majority's holding that the predominance inquiry of the class action certification analysis cannot be conducted unless and until the District Court inquires into whether each class member did or did not detrimentally rely on the defendant's misleading collection letter, and the extent of harm. This is not only analytically incorrect, but it also dooms all class actions under § 1692e of the FCRA.[4] This undermines the statutory scheme.

Once the relationship to common law is found, there is no place for further inquiry, let alone any inquiry into the extent of the harm. This is the Majority's second error. The Majority insists upon "further consequences" that follow from the detrimental reliance and opines that "confusion, without more, is not a concrete injury." Maj. Op., Section III.A.3, *supra.* However, as I have explained, as long as an analog is identified, plaintiffs have "suffered a concrete injury in fact under Article III," whether or not plaintiff is subjectively confused. *TransUnion,* 141 S. Ct. at 2209. Confusion is a red herring.[5] When we speak of harm in this context, we speak of the harm envisioned by Congress, *i.e.,* "a harm . . . traditionally . . . providing a basis for a lawsuit in English or American courts." *Susinno,* 862 F.3d at 351 (quoting *Horizon,* 846 F.3d at 639-40). It is the p.164 harm to the interest that is to be protected, not actual harm to the plaintiff. Otherwise, why would the Supreme Court and we not have considered actual harm in the precedents we rely on? The Majority's focus on finding a tangible harm, and determining the extent of this harm and injury—a sort of "analog plus" analysis—is misplaced.

The Majority seems to reject the notion that an intangible harm can be concrete but that is what *TransUnion* is all about. *TransUnion,* 141 S. Ct. at 2204 ("Various intangible harms can also be concrete."). The intangible harms at the core of all of the statutory causes of action we have been describing confer standing without proof of tangible injury. *See id.* (gathering examples). So, the Majority's "analog plus" analysis, which insists upon proof of tangible harm is at odds with the precedents that are our guide.

Instead, we should look at the interest that Congress sought to protect and ask whether there is similarity between that interest and the interest that common law sought to protect.

So, too, here, the interest to be protected is the interest in not receiving false or misleading information, and the harm of a misleading communication from a collection agency to a debtor regarding the amount that is owed has a *close relationship* to the harm caused by a fraudulent misrepresentation at common law.[6] As I noted above, the Majority says so itself.

So, in *TransUnion,* the Court did not ask how harmful it was to the plaintiff that a third party would read that he is a potential match to the OFAC list, or what negative consequences actually flowed from it. Instead, it concluded that plaintiffs whose reports were disseminated had "demonstrated concrete reputational harm" even though the plaintiffs made no showing of any tangible harm to their reputation. And in *Susinno,* we found an analog because the plaintiff's right of freedom from invasion of privacy was protected at common law. *Susinno,* 862 F.3d at 351-52. That was enough. We did not look to see whether the defendant's phone call really intruded upon the plaintiff's privacy or how great the intrusion was. The call may have been merely annoying, but that did not concern us. In fact, we specifically rejected the notion that repeated calls "with such persistence and frequency as to amount to . . . hounding," would be necessary. *Susinno,* 862 F.3d at 351 (citation omitted). We focused on the right Congress chose—"it sought to protect the same interests implicated in the traditional common law cause of action"—and found that it was traditionally worthy of protection. *Id.* at 352. And, contrary to the Majority's desire for additional negative consequences or more harm than what a p.165 robocall involves, we did not hesitate to find the right worthy of protection notwithstanding that the plaintiff had received *only one robocall.* Congress recognized the harm was worthy of protection, and "*Spokeo* addressed, and approved, such a choice by Congress." *Id.*

In no case relevant to the inquiry at hand has the Supreme Court or our court considered the actual harm or extent of injury. Yet, the Majority wishes to engage with what actually happened to Ms. Huber, what she did, and what happened to every plaintiff in the class. But this is irrelevant to our analysis. Standing in this type of case should be decided as a preliminary matter, and nowhere in the jurisprudence is there any indication that we should consider evidence regarding the actual impact or consequences of the violation on a particular plaintiff.[7]

To ask how harmful it was to the plaintiff to receive this misinformation is to add to the straightforward and objective analog test that applies here. The question the Court asked in *TransUnion* was whether the "harm from a misleading statement of this kind bears a sufficiently close relationship to the harm from a false and defamatory statement." *TransUnion,* 141 S. Ct. at 2209. The answer was "yes." And here, substitute "fraudulent misrepresentation" for "a false and defamatory statement" in the last phrase: does the harm from a misleading statement from a debt collector to a debtor about the amount owed bear a sufficiently close relationship to the harm from a fraudulent misrepresentation? The answer is "yes."[8]

Our precedent has established a specific test for concreteness where Congress has provided a remedy. Using that test, we should conclude that the match to the harm at issue in the tort of fraudulent misrepresentation is more than "sufficiently close," and the relevant interest at stake is for debtors to be protected from misleading information from collection agencies, much the same way as common law sought to protect people from fraudulent misrepresentations. The Majority reached this very conclusion. Standing to pursue the statutory remedy requires nothing more; our precedent says that is enough. To require more in the name of "standing" is unwarranted where Congress has chosen to provide a remedy that meets the p.166 test that the Supreme Court established in *Spokeo* and *TransUnion* and we have followed in *Horizon* and *Sussino.*

The Majority's approach does mischief to the approach that the Supreme Court and our Court have endorsed. Therefore, I must respectfully part ways with the Majority.

[1] The parties recognized that these damages awards "represent[ed] the maximum amount of statutory damages available" under the FDCPA. App. 52. That is because, "in the case of a class action," the FDCPA permits "each named plaintiff" to recover "damages as the court may allow, but not exceeding $1,000" and "such amount as the court may allow for all other class members, without regard to a minimum individual recovery, not to exceed the lesser of $500,000 or 1 per centum of the net worth of the debt collector." 15 U.S.C. § 1692k(a)(2). Prevailing plaintiffs are also entitled to costs and attorney's fees, so long as they are "reasonable ... as determined by the court." *Id.* § 1692k(a)(3).

[2] We therefore need not address whether Huber demonstrated "'adverse effects' that flow from [an] omission, and ... the requisite nexus to [a] 'concrete interest' Congress intended to protect." *Kelly,* 47 F.4th at 214.

[3] As Huber does not contend that SAI's letter provided inaccurate information, whether a false disclosure amounts to an omission for purposes of the informational injury doctrine is not at issue here. *Cf. Davidson v. Kimberly-Clark Corp.,* 889 F.3d 956, 971 (9th Cir. 2018).

[4] Our sister circuits are in agreement. *See Perez v. McCreary, Veselka, Bragg & Allen, P.C.,* 45 F.4th 816, 825 (5th Cir. 2022); *Ward v. Nat'l Patient Acct. Servs. Sols., Inc.,* 9 F.4th 357, 363 (6th Cir. 2021); *Brunett v. Convergent Outsourcing, Inc.,* 982 F.3d 1067, 1068 (7th Cir. 2020); *Bassett v. Credit Bureau Servs., Inc.,* 60 F.4th 1132, 1137 (8th Cir. 2023); *Adams v. Skagit Bonded Collectors, LLC,* 836 F. App'x 544, 547 (9th Cir. 2020); *Shields v. Pro. Bureau of Collections of Md., Inc.,* 55 F.4th 823, 830 (10th Cir. 2022); *Trichell,* 964 F. 3d at 1004.

[5] *Cf. Shields,* 55 F.4th at 830 ("Shields never pleaded reliance. In other words, she did not allege the same kind of harm as required by the tort of fraud." (citation omitted)); *Pierre v. Midland Credit Mgmt., Inc.,* 29 F.4th 934, 939 (7th Cir. 2022) ("[C]ritically, [the plaintiff] didn't ... act to her detriment in response to anything in or omitted from the letter.").

[6] Judge Bibas would not read the record and statements at oral argument as enough to show detrimental reliance. He does not read the record as showing that Huber paid an incremental cost to have her financial advisor help her with this letter. Thus, he would find no standing. But because both of his colleagues find standing here, he joins the rest of the opinion of the Court. *Cf. Hanover 3201 Realty, LLC v. Vill. Supermarkets, Inc.,* 806 F.3d 162, 196 (3d Cir. 2015) (Ambro, J., dissenting in part and concurring in part).

[7] Given the District Court's findings, even SAI's counsel conceded Huber had demonstrated detrimental reliance sufficient for individual standing:

Q: ... [T]here are other ways you might characterize what happened—like ... she sent these documents to her credit advisor and she did testify that she paid for his services.

A: I'm not sure if she did or not. I think that was presumed or implied in the record that she had hired Mr. Ramsey, that she had paid him something at some point.

Q: Why isn't that enough? Let's put the concrete financial loss to the side but, just for reliance, why aren't those actions or omissions sufficient to show reliance?

A: They might be, right? In Ms. Huber, we have evidence of that ...

Q: Just to be clear, do you concede for her individual case that there is reliance?

A: Based on her testimony, she has said that she relied to her detriment.

Oral Arg. at 21:04-22:29.

[8] Although we made the broader statement in *Horizon* that Congress "has the power to define injuries . . . that were previously inadequate in law," 846 F.3d at 638, the dissent places more weight on that statement than it can bear, Dissent at 159. First, we still assured ourselves in *Horizon* that the injury at issue "ha[d] a close relationship" to "invasion of privacy," which "has traditionally been regarded as providing a basis for a lawsuit in English or American courts." *Horizon,* 846 F.3d at 639-40 (quoting *Spokeo,* 578 U.S. at 341, 136 S.Ct. 1540). Second, the Supreme Court later clarified in *TransUnion* that a congressionally defined injury lacking a common-law analogue would not suffice for Article III purposes. *TransUnion,* 141 S. Ct. at 2206.

[9] The dissent attaches significance to the fact that we recognized a concrete injury in *Horizon* without requiring that the plaintiffs' stolen data be "actually used to the plaintiffs' detriment." Dissent at 159. But again, this appears to reflect doctrinal confusion—this time between the requirement that an injury be "concrete and particularized" and the requirement that it be "actual or imminent." *Lujan,* 504 U.S. at 560, 112 S.Ct. 2130 (quotation omitted). The question of whether the data was already used to plaintiffs' detriment in *Horizon* went to imminence, not concreteness, *see* 846 F.3d at 634, 639 n.19 (discussing plaintiffs' alternative argument that, even if they had not yet suffered a concrete injury, the data breach put them at "imminent . . . risk of harm" for identify fraud), and later cases have made the distinction even clearer; *compare Reilly v. Ceridian Corp.,* 664 F.3d 38, 46 (3d Cir. 2011) (declining to find that plaintiffs had standing because, while a data breach may have exposed their personal data to misuse by third parties, "[s]uch misuse is only speculative—not imminent"), *with Clemens v. ExecuPharm Inc.,* 48 F.4th 146, 156-57 (3d Cir. 2022) (finding injury "imminent" in the data breach context when a "known," "sophisticated ransomware group" had already demanded ransom and published the named plaintiff's data on the "Dark Web").

[10] Nor is she "subject to a defense that is both inapplicable to many members of the class and likely to become a major focus of the litigation." *Duncan,* 48 F.4th at 207 (quoting *In re Schering Plough Corp. ERISA Litig.,* 589 F.3d 585, 599 (3d Cir. 2009)).

[11] Although SAI does not contest Huber's ability to satisfy numerosity under Federal Rule of Civil Procedure 23(a)(1), a plaintiff cannot satisfy that requirement

by "resorting to mere speculation." *Mielo,* 897 F.3d at 484. Thus, on remand, the District Court should also consider the implications of unnamed class members' potential lack of standing for the numerosity requirement.

[12] At the certification stage, Huber need not prove the exact number of class members who have standing. Instead, as often is the case in assessments of the Rule 23 criteria, Huber can resort to any number of mechanisms to offer a sufficiently reliable estimate of the proportion of class members who will be able to demonstrate standing. *Cf. Reinig,* 912 F.3d at 128 (recognizing "representative evidence [can] satisfy the commonality/predominance requirements of Rule 23"); *Marcus,* 687 F.3d at 596 (explaining a "plaintiff [need not] offer direct evidence of the exact number and identities of the class members").

[1] This is an abbreviated version of what the Supreme Court outlined in both *Spokeo* and *TransUnion. See Spokeo,* 578 U.S. at 340-41, 136 S.Ct. 1540; *TransUnion,* 141 S. Ct. at 2204-05. In *Horizon,* Judge Jordan provided a thorough explanation of *Spokeo*'s reasoning, *see* 846 F.3d at 636-39, which Judge Hardiman relied upon in *Susinno, see* 862 F.3d at 350-51. A few years later, *TransUnion* expanded further, but it did so consistent with *Spokeo.*

[2] Indeed, to make this point, the Supreme Court considered a hypothetical Hawaii resident complaining of a factory's environmental pollution of a Maine resident's land—in such a situation, the Hawaii resident would have no standing to sue the factory. *TransUnion,* 141 S. Ct. at 2205-06.

[3] The Majority returns later in its opinion to *TransUnion*'s distinction between the "sent" report and "non-sent" report plaintiffs as if it supports its argument regarding the need for harmful consequences, but it really has no bearing on that issue. Maj. Op., Section III. A.3, *supra.* Indeed, the quotations it uses from *TransUnion* that purportedly support its position regarding the need for consequences (*i.e.,* its assertion that the "mere receipt" of a misleading communication is not enough and its statement that the mere risk that a plaintiff who receives a misleading letter from a debt collector will suffer such a cognizable injury is "too speculative to support Article III standing") are from *TransUnion*'s rejection of the argument that the non-sent report plaintiffs should have standing because there is a risk that the reports might be sent. That is the "speculation" it is discussing. As Justice Kagan recently advised, "when you see that my description of precedent differs from the majority's go take a look at the decision. . . . I'll take my chances on readers' good judgment." *Andy Warhol Found, for Visual Arts, Inc. v. Goldsmith,* 598 U.S. 508, 560, n.2, 143 S.Ct. 1258, 1293, n.2, 215 L.Ed.2d 473 (2023) (Kagan, J., dissenting).

[4] Moreover, I am not sure as a practical matter what such an inquiry will "look like." The Majority states only that, on remand, Huber should submit evidence that would allow the District Court to estimate how many class members have standing, yet it also suggests that the District Court could potentially find that receiving individualized evidence on class members' standing is not feasible. Maj. Op. Section III.C.2, *supra.* Beyond that guidance, what is the District Court to do on remand? Are the class members to be asked if they detrimentally relied on the misleading notice? What does "detrimentally relied on" mean? Are the negative consequences here really "detrimental reliance" or just obvious consequences? What would a class member

need to have done to satisfy this requirement? What if they lost sleep? Or suffered from anxiety? Why does it matter? The harm that Congress sought to prevent was the harm experienced by the receipt of misleading information by debtors. If the information is misleading as a matter of law—as this was—presumably the debtor was deceived. That is the same harm that an action for fraudulent misrepresentation was aimed at, at common law. That is all we need to know for purposes of standing. Why do we need to know what the debtor did after receiving the misleading letter? What if they did nothing because they did not know what to do? It matters not.

[5] The District Court also seemed confused by the issue of confusion, but it ultimately reasoned more along the lines of the inevitable nature of harm here: "In matters of debt collection, informational harm leads to financial harm." *Huber v. Simon's Agency, Inc.*, Civ. A. No. 2:19-01424, 2022 WL 1801497, at *4 (E.D. Pa. June 2, 2022). This is the judgment that Congress made, and we need not inquire further.

[6] Our analysis in *Susinno* also confirms that statutory causes of action can have multiple analogs and that a plaintiff has standing as long as the court can identify one that fits—whether or not the plaintiff does so. Thus, even though we thought intrusion upon seclusion was the *best* analog, we agreed with the Ninth Circuit "that TCPA claims closely relate to [other] traditional claims for 'invasions of privacy . . . and nuisance [which] have long been heard by American courts.'" *Susinno,* 862 F.3d at 351 (quoting *Van Patten v. Vertical Fitness Grp., LLC,* 847 F.3d 1037, 1043 (9th Cir. 2017)) (second alteration in original). Likewise, colleagues on our sister courts have suggested that torts other than fraudulent misrepresentation bear a close relationship to the interest protected by § 1692e: intrusion upon seclusion, abuse of process, emotional distress from negligent transmission of misleading information, *see Trichell v. Midland Credit Mgmt., Inc.,* 964 F.3d 990, 1008-09 (11th Cir. 2020) (Martin, J., concurring in part and dissenting in part), or intentionally or recklessly caused emotional distress, *see Pierre v. Midland Credit Mgmt., Inc.,* 29 F.4th 934, 946-48 (7th Cir. 2022) (Hamilton, J., dissenting).

[7] In explaining the requirement of standing and why courts must ensure that plaintiffs have a personal stake in the litigation, the Majority asks rhetorically: "Why not allow any plaintiff seeking to serve as a private attorney general to enforce the statutory right alongside the Executive Branch?" No doubt this question would help hone the analysis in some cases, but not in this one. There is no dispute that Huber received a misleading collection letter and that she suffered a harm. She is not, thus, acting as a "private attorney general," she is acting on her own behalf to obtain relief for the harm she has suffered. There is no risk in this case that Huber or any member of the putative class are acting as private attorneys general and the reference to this concept does little to advance our understanding of standing in this context.

[8] And even if the impact on the plaintiff were the focus, the Majority overlooks the context of the FDCPA. The entire premise underlying congressional action in this area is the fragile state of debtors preyed upon by collection agencies. In passing the FDCPA, the Senate noted that the "suffering and anguish which [unscrupulous debt collectors] regularly inflict is substantial." S. Rep. No. 95-382, at 2 (1977). While we have concluded that this was not an informational injury as such, can there be any doubt that a misleading statement of the amount owed leading to an inability to pay the amount due is any less harmful than a failure to indicate an amount at all? And just as in the context of the TCPA, we have deferred to Congress's judgment

that one robocall is actionable because of the interests at stake, here, too, we need to respect Congress's view that debtors need protection from misleading information of this nature.

49 F.4th 323 (2022)

Michael LUTZ, individually and on behalf of all others similarly situated, Appellant,
v.
PORTFOLIO RECOVERY ASSOCIATES, LLC.

No. 21-1656.

United States Court of Appeals, Third Circuit.

Argued: May 4, 2022.
(Filed: September 19, 2022).

Lutz v. Portfolio Recovery Associates, LLC, 49 F. 4th 323 (3rd Cir. 2022)

On Appeal from the United States District Court for the Western District of Pennsylvania, (D.C. No. 2:20-cv-00676), District Judge: Honorable Christy C. Wiegand.

Kevin J. Abramowicz [ARGUED], Kevin W. Tucker, East End Trial Group, 6901 Lynn Way, Suite 215, Pittsburgh, PA 15208, Counsel for Michael Lutz.

Tammy L. Adkins [ARGUED], Amy Gilbert, David L. Hartsell, McGuireWoods, 77 West Wacker Drive, Suite 4100, Chicago, IL 60601, Jarrod D. Shaw, McGuireWoods, 260 Forbes Avenue, Suite 1800, Pittsburgh, PA 15222, Counsel for Portfolio Recovery Associates, LLC.

Stefanie Hamilton, Carlton M. Smith, Commonwealth of Pennsylvania, Department of Banking and Securities, 17 North Second Street, Suite 1300, Harrisburg, PA 17101, Counsel for Amicus Curiae.

Before: GREENAWAY, JR., KRAUSE, and PHIPPS, Circuit Judges.

p.325 OPINION OF THE COURT

PHIPPS, Circuit Judge.

In this case, a consumer, who seeks to represent a putative class, sues a debt collection firm for attempting to collect an outstanding credit-card debt, which had accrued interest at an annual rate of 22.90%. After the consumer had not paid the balance for several months, the bank canceled the card, ceased charging interest, closed the account, and sold it to the debt-collection firm. The firm did not charge interest on the account balance after purchasing it, but the firm did attempt to collect the outstanding balance inclusive of the previously accrued interest.

In his amended complaint, the consumer claimed that the debt collection firm violated the Fair Debt Collection Practices Act p.326 by making false statements about the amount of the debt, *see* 15 U.S.C. § 1692e, and by collecting a debt not permitted by law, *see id.* § 1692f. Both of those claims rest on the premise that a

Pennsylvania statute prohibits the debt collection firm from collecting the interest that had previously accrued at an annual rate greater than 6%. *See* 7 P.S. § 6203.A; *see also* 41 P.S. § 201(a).

The debt collection firm moved to dismiss those claims and the others brought by the consumer, all for failure to state a claim upon which relief can be granted. *See* Fed. R. Civ. P. 12(b)(6). The District Court granted that motion and did not afford the consumer another opportunity to amend the complaint.

Through a timely appeal, the consumer argues that the District Court erred in dismissing the FDCPA claims and that the District Court should have permitted him an opportunity to amend his complaint again. But the consumer does not plausibly allege that Pennsylvania law prohibited the debt collection firm from collecting interest that had previously accrued at greater than 6% annually. Thus, as elaborated below, on *de novo* review of the motion to dismiss[1] and abuse-of-discretion review of the denial of the motion to amend the pleadings,[2] we will affirm the judgment of the District Court.

I. FACTUAL BACKGROUND (AS ALLEGED IN THE COMPLAINT)

In July 2014, Michael Lutz received a credit card from Capital One Bank (USA), N.A. The card provided him with a revolving line of credit with which he could make purchases and obtain cash advances. For several months, Lutz made purchases and obtained cash advances with the card for personal, family, and household purposes. Lutz had an obligation to repay Capital One for those purchases and cash advances. By the terms of the credit card agreement, he could do so over time through minimum installment payments. That agreement also permitted Capital One to charge interest at an annual rate up to 22.90% on any unpaid monthly balance.

Lutz failed to make the required monthly installment payments, and Capital One charged interest on the outstanding monthly balance. By July 2015, his account balance was $2,343.76, inclusive of at least $341.67 in interest that had accrued at an annual rate of 22.90%. At that time, Capital One charged off the account: it canceled the card, ceased charging interest, closed the account, and regarded the outstanding balance as a loss.

Capital One sold the charged-off account to Portfolio Recovery Associates, LLC ('PRA'). PRA is not a bank and cannot issue credit cards, but it does hold a license from the Pennsylvania Department of Banking and Securities to make motor vehicle loans and to charge interest at 18% to 21% on those loans. Despite that license, PRA's sole business involves purchasing defaulted consumer debt at a discount and then attempting to collect the full amount due.

As part of its collection efforts, PRA sued Lutz in a Magisterial District Court in Allegheny County, Pennsylvania in August p.327 2019 for the outstanding account balance. PRA obtained a default judgment against Lutz. But Lutz timely appealed to the Allegheny County Court of Common Pleas, and before a hearing in that case occurred, PRA discontinued the lawsuit.

II. PROCEDURAL HISTORY

In his original complaint, Lutz sued PRA in the District Court for the Western District of Pennsylvania for violating two provisions of the Fair Debt Collection Practices Act, 15 U.S.C. §§ 1692e, 1692f. *See* 28 U.S.C. § 1331 (conferring federal jurisdiction over "all civil actions arising under" the laws of the United States). Lutz based his FDCPA claims on an alleged underlying violation of Pennsylvania's Consumer Credit Code. *See* 12 Pa. Cons. Stat. § 6309. Instead of answering the complaint, PRA moved to dismiss it for failure to state a claim upon which relief could be granted. *See* Fed. R. Civ. P. 12(b)(6). Rather than opposing PRA's motion, Lutz amended his complaint. *See* Fed R. Civ. P. 15(a)(1) (allowing a party to amend a pleading once as a matter of course within 21 days after service of a Rule 12(b)(6) motion to dismiss).

The amended complaint did more than just attempt to cure the purported pleading deficiencies. It added additional FDCPA claims also under §§ 1692e and 1692f, which were premised on PRA's alleged violations of Pennsylvania's Consumer Discount Company Act, commonly abbreviated as the 'CDCA.'

PRA moved to dismiss Lutz's amended complaint, again for failure to state a claim for relief. This time, Lutz opposed PRA's motion to dismiss, but as part of his opposition, Lutz requested an opportunity to amend his complaint if the District Court dismissed any or all of his claims.

The District Court granted PRA's motion and dismissed with prejudice Lutz's original claims as well as the claims added in the amended complaint. As part of that order, the District Court denied Lutz's request for leave to amend.

Lutz sought reconsideration of that order. In briefing that issue, Lutz identified another alleged underlying violation of the CDCA by PRA that he had not previously raised. The District Court rejected that attempt to present a new argument and denied his motion.

Through a timely appeal, Lutz invokes this Court's appellate jurisdiction. *See* 28 U.S.C. § 1291; Fed. R. App. P. 4(a). To supplement the briefing provided by the parties, the Pennsylvania Department of Banking and Securities responded to an invitation for an amicus filing on the issues raised in the appeal.[3]

III. DISCUSSION

Under the plausibility pleading standard, this Circuit uses a three-step process to evaluate a motion to dismiss a complaint for failure to state a claim for relief. *See Connelly v. Lane Constr. Corp.*, 809 F.3d 780, 787 (3d Cir. 2016); *see also Burtch v. Milberg Factors, Inc.*, 662 F.3d 212, 220-21 (3d Cir. 2011); *Santiago v. Warminster Twp.*, 629 F.3d 121, 130 (3d Cir. 2010). The first step in that process requires an articulation of the elements of the claim. *See Connelly*, 809 F.3d at 787 (quoting *Ashcroft v. Iqbal*, 556 U.S. 662, 675, 129 S.Ct. 1937, 173 L.Ed.2d 868 (2009)); *see also Santiago*, 629 F.3d at 130 (quoting *Iqbal*, 556 U.S. at 675, 129 S.Ct. 1937). The second step involves reviewing the complaint and disregarding any "'formulaic recitation of the elements of a ... claim' or other legal conclusion," *Connelly*, p.328 809 F.3d at 789 (alteration in original) (quoting *Iqbal*, 556 U.S. at 681, 129 S.Ct. 1937); *see also Burtch*, 662 F.3d at 224;

Santiago, 629 F.3d at 131, as well as allegations that are "so threadbare or speculative that they fail to cross the line between the conclusory and the factual," *Connelly,* 809 F.3d at 790 (citation omitted); *see also Fowler v. UPMC Shadyside,* 578 F.3d 203, 210-11 (3d Cir. 2009). The third step evaluates the plausibility of the remaining allegations. That involves assuming their veracity, construing them in the light most favorable to the plaintiff, and drawing all reasonable inferences in the plaintiff's favor. *See Connelly,* 809 F.3d at 787, 790; *see also Iqbal,* 556 U.S. at 679, 129 S.Ct. 1937; *Fowler,* 578 F.3d at 210-11.

If, after completing this process, the complaint alleges "enough fact[s] to raise a reasonable expectation that discovery will reveal evidence of" the necessary elements of a claim, then it plausibly pleads a claim. *Bell Atl. Corp. v. Twombly,* 550 U.S. 544, 556, 127 S.Ct. 1955, 167 L.Ed.2d 929 (2007). But if "a complaint pleads facts that are merely consistent with a defendant's liability, it stops short of the line between possibility and plausibility of entitlement to relief." *Iqbal,* 556 U.S. at 678, 129 S.Ct. 1937 (citation and internal quotation marks omitted). In the latter scenario, a district court should generally "permit a curative amendment, unless an amendment would be inequitable or futile." *Phillips v. County of Allegheny,* 515 F.3d 224, 236 (3d Cir. 2008).

Following those three steps here on *de novo* review, the District Court's judgment dismissing Lutz's FDCPA claims should be affirmed.

A. The Elements of an FDCPA Claim (Only One of Which Is Disputed)

In this Circuit, a claim under the FDCPA has four elements. *See Douglass v. Convergent Outsourcing,* 765 F.3d 299, 303 (3d Cir. 2014). The first three involve statutorily defined terms: the plaintiff must be a "consumer," 15 U.S.C. § 1692a(3); the defendant must be a "debt collector," *id.* § 1692a(6); and the challenged practice must relate to the collection of a "debt," *id.* § 1692a(5). *See Douglass,* 765 F.3d at 303; *see also Zimmerman v. HBO Affiliate Grp.,* 834 F.2d 1163, 1167 (3d Cir. 1987) ("A threshold requirement for application of the FDCPA is that the prohibited practices are used in an attempt to collect a 'debt[.]'"). The fourth element, the one contested here, requires the defendant to have violated "the FDCPA in attempting to collect the debt." *Douglass,* 765 F.3d at 303.

For that fourth element, Lutz asserts that PRA violated two provisions of the FDCPA in attempting to collect his account balance: § 1692e and § 1692f. Section 1692e imposes civil liability for the use of false, deceptive, or misleading representations, subject to a bona fide error exception. *See* 15 U.S.C. § 1692e; *see also id.* § 1692k(c). That extends to false representations relating to "the character, amount, or legal status of any debt." 15 U.S.C. § 1692e(2)(A). Section 1692f outlaws unfair or unconscionable means of collecting debts. *See id.* § 1692f. That includes a prohibition on debt collectors from collecting:

> any amount (including any interest, fee, charge, or expense incidental to the principal obligation) unless such amount is expressly authorized by the agreement creating the debt or permitted by law.

Id. § 1692f(1).

Both of Lutz's FDCPA claims hinge on the premise that PRA violated p.329 Pennsylvania law by attempting to collect interest that had previously accrued at greater than 6% annually. For context, the Commonwealth has a long history, dating back to colonial times, of outlawing annual interest rates above 6%.[4] Even now, Pennsylvania generally prohibits annual interest above 6% on loans or the use of money of $50,000 or less. *See* 41 P.S. § 201(a). But, during the Great Depression, the Pennsylvania Department of Banking and Securities, despite acknowledging the problem of usury, recommended that credit be extended more readily to consumers.[5] In response, the Pennsylvania legislature enacted the Consumer Discount Company Act, which permits entities licensed by the Pennsylvania Department of Banking and Securities to charge interest at a higher annual rate, up to 24%, for loans under a certain amount, currently $25,000. *See* 7 P.S. §§ 6203.A, 6213.E, 6217.1.A; *see also Cash Am. Net of Nev., LLC v. Dep't of Banking,* 607 Pa. 432, 8 A.3d 282, 285-86 (2010). But the CDCA imposed restrictions on unlicensed entities "in the business of negotiating or making loans or advances of money on credit, in the amount or value of twenty-five-thousand dollars ($25,000) or less." 7 P.S. § 6203.A.[6] Those unlicensed entities may not "charge, *collect,* contract for[,] or receive interest" at an annual interest rate above 6%. *Id.* (emphasis added); *see also* 41 P.S. § 201(a).

Lutz's theory of PRA's liability under the FDCPA depends on PRA being subject to those restrictions in the CDCA. On the premise that PRA is an unlicensed entity subject to the CDCA, Lutz contends that it was illegal for PRA to attempt to *collect* interest that previously accrued on Lutz's account at greater than 6% — even though Capital One, as a bank not subject to the CDCA, *see* 7 P.S. § 6217, could legally charge that rate. With that alleged violation of the CDCA as a foundation, Lutz claims that PRA violated the FDCPA by making false statements about the amount of the debt, *see* 15 U.S.C. § 1692e, and by collecting a debt not permitted by law, *see id.* § 1692f.

In moving to dismiss Lutz's FDCPA claims, PRA denied that it was subject to the CDCA's restrictions on unlicensed entities on two grounds. First, PRA disputed p.330 the applicability of the CDCA's restrictions because it is not "in the business of negotiating or making loans or advances." 7 P.S. § 6203.A. Second, PRA argued that even if it were in the business of negotiating or making loans or advances, it could still collect interest at an annual rate above 6% because it held a license from the Department of Banking and Securities, albeit one for motor vehicle loans under the Consumer Credit Code, 12 Pa. Cons. Stat. § 6201, *et seq.,* not one issued under the CDCA. *See* 7 P.S. § 6217 (exempting from the CDCA's licensing requirements any company "licensed by the Secretary of Banking of the Commonwealth of Pennsylvania under the provisions of any other statute"). The District Court granted PRA's motion, rejecting the first argument, but relying on the second. On appeal, Lutz argues that both rationales are deficient, and PRA urges affirmation of the District Court's order on both grounds.

As briefed, the first argument — whether PRA is 'in the business of negotiating or making loans or advances' — narrows a bit. No one contends that PRA is in the business of *making* loans or advances. With that focus, the keystone of Lutz's case becomes his assertion that PRA is in the business of *negotiating* loans or advances and thus subject to the CDCA. If PRA is not in that business, then the CDCA does not apply here, and PRA would prevail regardless of the scope of its license under the Consumer Credit Code.

B. Certain Allegations in the Amended Complaint Must Be Disregarded.

The second step of the plausibility analysis involves disregarding allegations in the complaint that are legal conclusions, speculative, or threadbare. *See Connelly,* 809 F.3d at 789; *see also Santiago,* 629 F.3d at 131; *Fowler,* 578 F.3d at 210-11. In evaluating whether PRA is in the business of negotiating loans or advances, only allegations bearing on that topic need to be scrutinized.

Even still, several allegations must be disregarded. For example, the statement that "PRA's collection of the interest and fees on [Lutz's account] was subject to the CDCA" is a legal conclusion. Am. Compl. ¶ 61 (JA31). *See Connelly,* 809 F.3d at 789-90. Seven other paragraphs include similar legal conclusions about the CDCA's applicability to PRA.[7] *See Connelly,* 809 F.3d at 789-90. Also, three statements merely paraphrase the CDCA's requirements.[8] p.331 *See id.* at 790 (disregarding allegations that "paraphrase[d] in one way or another the pertinent statutory language or elements of the claims in question"). None of those allegations may be considered in assessing whether PRA is in the business of negotiating loans or advances.

C. The Amended Complaint Lacks Plausible Allegations that PRA Is in the Business of Negotiating Loans or Advances.

The third stage of the plausibility analysis evaluates whether the non-disregarded allegations in the complaint plausibly state a claim for relief. When, as here, a motion to dismiss challenges less than all elements of a claim, only the sufficiency of the allegations pertaining to the disputed elements require evaluation. The critical dispute here concerns whether PRA is in the business of negotiating loans or advances, and that depends on the meaning of the term 'negotiate.'

1. As used in the CDCA, the term 'negotiate' is best understood to mean 'to bargain.'

In enacting the CDCA in 1937, the Pennsylvania legislature did not define or incorporate a preexisting definition for the term 'negotiate.' *See* 7 P.S. § 6202 (defining terms used in the CDCA). Under Pennsylvania law, an undefined statutory term takes on its "common and approved usage." 1 Pa. Cons. Stat. § 1903; *Orson, Inc. v. Miramax Film Corp.,* 79 F.3d 1358, 1374 (3d Cir. 1996) (stating that, under Pennsylvania law, any undefined word "must be construed according to the rules of grammar and according to the common and approved usage"); *see also Perrin v. United States,* 444 U.S. 37, 42, 100 S.Ct. 311, 62 L.Ed.2d 199 (1979) ("A fundamental canon of statutory construction is that, unless otherwise defined, words will be interpreted as taking their ordinary, contemporary, common meaning."). And following the principle that a statutory term has a fixed meaning over time,[9] dictionaries from the time of a statute's enactment illuminate an undefined term's common and approved meaning. *See Phila. Eagles Football Club, Inc. v. City of Philadelphia,* 573 Pa. 189, 823 A.2d 108, 127 n.31 (2003); *see also Wis. Cent. Ltd. v. United States,* ___ U.S. ___, 138 S. Ct. 2067, 2070-71, 201 L.Ed.2d 490 (2018); *Delaware Cnty. v. Fed. Hous. Fin. Agency,* 747 F.3d 215, 221 (3d Cir. 2014).

Dictionaries contemporaneous with the CDCA's enactment identify two p.332 common and approved meanings of 'negotiate.' It could mean "to bargain,"[10] and it also could mean "to transfer," especially with respect to a negotiable instrument.[11] When, as here, a term has multiple common and approved meanings, context may inform the term's meaning. *See United States v. TRW Rifle 7.62X51mm Caliber, One Model 14 Serial 593006*, 447 F.3d 686, 690 (9th Cir. 2006) ("As with most words, the dictionary gives multiple definitions. But we do not ascertain ordinary meaning in the abstract. Rather, we must decide which of these definitions, if any, is consistent with the context of the statute."); *see also* Scalia & Garner, at 70 (noting that "[m]any words have more than one ordinary meaning" and that "[o]ne should assume the contextually appropriate ordinary meaning unless there is reason to think otherwise").

One tool for evaluating context, the *noscitur a sociis* canon, instructs that neighboring words inform the meaning of a term.[12] Looking at nearby words in § 6203.A, the transitive verb 'negotiate,' used as a gerund in a gerund phrase, is linked with another transitive verb 'make,' also a gerund in the same gerund phrase, and each has two direct objects: loans and advances.[13] *See* 7 P.S. § 6203.A. The direct objects show little preference for either meaning of 'negotiate' because loans and advances can be bargained for and transferred. But the other verb, 'make,' applies to the initiation and formation of loans and advances. *See Make*, Black's Law Dictionary (3d ed. 1933) (defining 'make' as "[t]o cause to exist"). And the pairing of 'negotiating' with 'making' in § 6203.A suggests that 'negotiate' should also relate to the p.333 initiation of loans or advances. Since bargaining occurs at the loan initiation phase and transferring does not, 'negotiate' is better understood to mean 'bargain.' That conclusion is not automatic, however, because the terms 'negotiating' and 'making' are separated by an 'or,' and that may mean that they are alternatives rather than complements of each other.[14] But the term 'or' may also be used to identify two separate but related actions.[15]

Additional context resolves that uncertainty. In the subsequent subsection, the CDCA again uses the term 'negotiate' to define the scope of the CDCA's coverage. *See* 7 P.S. § 6203.B. That subsection extends the CDCA to "[a]ny person who shall hold himself out as willing or able to arrange for or *negotiate* such loans ... or who solicits prospective borrowers of such loans." *Id.* (emphasis added). The related phrases in that subsection — 'arrange for' and 'solicits' — concern loan initiation and formation, and not the transferability of the debt. *See* Webster's New International Dictionary 152 (2d ed. 1934) (defining 'arrange'); *Solicit*, Black's Law Dictionary (3d ed. 1933). Thus, for purposes of that subsection, 'negotiate' is best understood to mean 'to bargain,' not 'to transfer.' Although not absolute,[16] the consistent-usage canon holds that a term should have the same meaning each time it is used throughout a statute.[17] And for 'negotiate' to have a consistent meaning in the CDCA, it must mean 'to bargain.'

In sum, as applied here, *noscitur a sociis* and the consistent usage canon counteract the other's limitations, and together they yield the conclusion that the term 'negotiate' as used in § 6203A means 'to bargain.'

2. The remnant allegations in the complaint do not plausibly allege that PRA is in the business of negotiating loans or advances.

Lutz does not specifically allege that PRA is in the business of negotiating — or bargaining for — loans or advances. The amended complaint contains two sets of allegations related to PRA's business practices. One paragraph describes PRA's business practice without a specific reference to negotiating loans: "PRA's sole business is purchasing defaulted consumer debt with the purpose of collecting debt for profit." Am. Compl. ¶ 9 (JA24). A later paragraph adds a layer of detail, but still makes no specific reference to PRA negotiating loans: "PRA is in the business of purchasing loans or advances of money or credit, as PRA purchases debt for the purpose of collecting debt for profit." *Id.* ¶ 63 (JA31). In addition, eight paragraphs in the amended complaint address Lutz's specific interactions with PRA — and none of those remotely suggest that PRA is in the business of negotiating p.334 loans. Those paragraphs allege that "PRA filed a lawsuit against Lutz," *id.* ¶ 38 (JA28), and that PRA "purchased [Lutz's] Account from Capital One Bank," *id.* ¶ 39 (JA28). They also state that "PRA sought to collect and receive interest and fees charged on the Account's purchases and cash advance balances," *id.* ¶ 40 (JA28), and that "[t]he interest and fees ... [had been] charged at a rate that aggregated in excess of 22.90% per year," *id.* ¶ 41 (JA28). They further indicate that "PRA obtained a default judgment against Lutz," *id.* ¶ 42 (JA28), that Lutz appealed that judgment, *id.* ¶ 43 (JA28), and that PRA discontinued the action before a hearing could be held in the appeal, *id.* ¶¶ 44-45 (JA28). In short, nowhere does Lutz allege that PRA is in the business of negotiating loans or advances.

Despite the absence of such allegations, Lutz's pleading receives the benefit of reasonable inferences at the motion-to-dismiss stage. *See Connelly,* 809 F.3d at 790; *see also Iqbal,* 556 U.S. at 678, 129 S.Ct. 1937. Lutz's allegations indicate that PRA *purchases* debt, such as Lutz's credit card account that Capital One charged off. But even with that allegation as a starting point, it is not reasonable to infer that an entity that purchases charged-off debt would also be in the business of negotiating or bargaining for the initial terms of loans or advances. If anything, the amended complaint cuts against such an inference: it alleges that Capital One, not PRA, set the annual interest rate for Lutz's use of the credit card for loans and advances at 22.90%. Thus, with the understanding that negotiate means 'to bargain' and not 'to transfer,' Lutz's allegations do not support an inference that PRA is in the business of negotiating loans or advances.

Without such a favorable inference, Lutz cannot establish that PRA is subject to the CDCA and its limitations on collecting interest. And because his FDCPA claims depend on an underlying violation of the CDCA, they collapse.[18]

D. The District Court Did Not Abuse Its Discretion in Denying Lutz Leave to Amend His Complaint Again.

Lutz also argues that the District Court erred by dismissing his claims with prejudice and denying him leave to amend his complaint for a second time. He contends that through further amendment he could allege that PRA's license to charge interest on motor vehicle loans at an annual rate of up to 21% did not permit it to collect interest that Capital One charged. But amendments along those lines could be curative only if the CDCA applies to PRA. And as explained above, the allegations do not establish that PRA is in the business of negotiating loans or advances, and therefore the amended complaint fails to place PRA within the CDCA's regulatory p.335 grasp. Because the proposed amendments do not cure those deficient allegations, the amendments would be futile, and the District Court did not abuse its discretion in dismissing Lutz's claims with prejudice and denying Lutz leave to amend. *See Mullin v. Balicki,* 875 F.3d 140, 150 (3d Cir. 2017).

IV. CONCLUSION

For the foregoing reasons, we will affirm the District Court's judgment.

KRAUSE, Circuit Judge, concurring.

I join my colleagues' excellent opinion in full but write separately to address two additional issues that were raised by the parties and that have benefited from the Secretary of Banking's thoughtful and illuminating analysis as amicus.

First is the type of license that permits an entity under Pennsylvania's Consumer Discount Company Act ("CDCA") to charge in excess of 6% on loans under $25,000, notwithstanding the statute's general prohibition. *See* 7 P.S. §§ 6203, 6217. As the District Court interpreted the statute, it authorizes the charging of excess interest not just by entities licensed under the CDCA, but by any entity to which the Secretary of Banking has issued a license to do business under any statute. Because Portfolio Recovery Associates ("PRA") fell into that category, the District Court viewed its collection of excess interest as permissible, ruling out a Fair Debt Collections Practices Act ("FDCPA") claim predicated on a CDCA violation. According to Lutz and the Secretary of Banking, however, the District Court misinterpreted the statute, and for the reasons explained below, I believe they are correct.

Second, I consider whether—if Lutz cannot base his FDCPA claim on a CDCA violation—he can base it instead on PRA's alleged violation of Pennsylvania's Loan Interest and Protection Law ("LIPL"), 41 P.S. § 101, *et seq.* I join my colleagues in holding that he cannot because the LIPL does not regulate the "collection" of interest, and PRA is in the collection business. *See supra* n.18. But there is a second, independent reason that the LIPL is inapplicable, which I also address below.

I. PRA's Consumer Credit Code License Does Not Confer the Authority to Charge Interest as a CDCA Licensee.

We begin with PRA's contention that we need not wade into the intricacies of what it means to "negotiate" loans or advances under the CDCA because, regardless, the fact that PRA holds a Consumer Credit Code license means that it is exempted from the CDCA's prohibition on collecting interest at a rate of more than 6%.[1] As the theory goes, the CDCA bars any entity "engage[d] ... in the business of negotiating or making loans or advances of money on credit" from charging over 6% interest on direct loans under $25,000 "if not licensed under this act." 7 P.S. § 6203. But the CDCA does not apply to certain kinds of entities, including entities that are "licensed by the Secretary of Banking ... under the provisions of any other statute." 7 P.S. § 6217. *Ergo,* says PRA, it is exempted p.336 from the CDCA's general prohibition and can charge excess interest.

The problem for PRA, however, is that the plain language of the statute compels a different reading, which the Secretary, as amicus, corroborates, *i.e.,* that § 6217 merely permits an entity licensed by the Secretary under another statute to engage in the activities for which it is licensed without, in addition, obtaining a CDCA license—even when those activities would also fall within the CDCA's ambit.

We start with a textual analysis. As noted, the parties differ as to what it means that the CDCA does not "apply" to corporations licensed under a different statute. But we must "[a]ssum[e] that every word in a statute has meaning" and "avoid interpreting part of a statute so as to render another part superfluous." *Allen ex. rel. Martin v. LaSalle Bank, N.A.,* 629 F.3d 364, 367 (3d Cir. 2011). Here, § 6203 of the CDCA provides that only CDCA licensees may collect over 6% interest on direct loans under $25,000. 7 P.S. § 6203. So if we were to conclude, as PRA would have us do, that § 6217 allows *any* licensee of the Secretary under any statute to collect over 6% interest, it would render § 6203 superfluous.

The broader context of § 6217 further supports Lutz's and amicus's interpretation. The first sentence announces that the CDCA "shall not affect any existing laws... authorizing a charge for the loan of money in excess of interest at the legal rate." 7 P.S. § 6217. As the Secretary of Banking points out, that is exactly what the provision at issue in this case does: It ensures that the CDCA does not interfere with the privileges conferred by other kinds of licenses issued by the Department even when they authorize activity that would otherwise require a CDCA license. In other words, § 6217 provides that entities authorized under other laws to charge and collect interest on direct loans at a rate greater than that permitted by the CDCA (such as banks operating under the Banking Code or pawnbrokers licensed under the Pawnbrokers License Act, 63 P.S. § 281-1 *et seq.*) need not also obtain a CDCA license and comply with the CDCA's requirements. *See* Amicus Br. 3 ("As long as those licensees lawfully engage in the activities for which they are licensed, the CDCA will not apply to their conduct."). Similarly, entities authorized by other laws to charge fees not provided for by the CDCA, such as sales finance companies licensed under the CCC, are not prohibited by the CDCA from doing so. *Id.*

PRA's interpretation would also produce just the sort of absurdity that Pennsylvania's statutory rules of construction direct us to avoid. *See* 1 PA. CONS. STAT. § 1922(1)-(2). PRA, echoing the District Court, argues that its reading of § 6217 is consistent with the purpose of the CDCA, which it believes to be "concerned about *unregulated, unlicensed* entities—not entities licensed by the Secretary of Banking," because the Secretary "has oversight and other authority over [all of] its licensees, even those which are licensed under other statutes." Answering Br. 28, 32 (quoting Appx. 11-12). But the Secretary of Banking issues licenses to a wide variety of entities, including money transmitters, check cashers, debt management and debt settlement companies, pawnbrokers, mortgage brokers, lenders, servicers, loan correspondents or originators, and motor vehicle sales finance companies.[2] So under p.337 PRA's theory, the General Assembly would have authorized all these licensees—some of which engage in businesses far afield from lending—to charge, collect, contract for, and receive interest and other charges of over 6% per year on direct loans under $25,000. 7 P.S. § 6203. To put a fine point on it, it would mean that money transmitters and check cashers, among others, would be authorized to charge and collect interest in excess of the CDCA's 6% cap solely by virtue of the fact that they hold licenses to engage in their primary business. But "in ascertaining legislative intent, the Statutory Construction Act requires a presumption that the General Assembly did not intend a result that is absurd or unreasonable," *Cash Am. Net of Nev., LLC v. Dep't of Banking,* 607 Pa. 432, 8 A.3d 282, 289 (2010) (citing 1 PA. CONS. STAT. § 1922(1)), so the CDCA should not be construed in that nonsensical manner.

Comparing the licensing regime for pawnbrokers to the licensing regime set forth in the CDCA reinforces our conclusion. *See* 1 PA. CONS. STAT. § 1932(b) (instructing courts to construe statutes relating to the same things together). On April 6, 1937, just two days before the passage of the CDCA, Pennsylvania Governor George H. Earle signed the Pawnbrokers License Act into law. 63 P.S. § 281-1 (originally enacted as Act of April 6, 1937, P.L. 200, No. 51). It contained many provisions parallel to the original version of the CDCA, but included less stringent requirements for pawnbrokers. For example, both statutes required applicants to include a bond with their application for licensure: $2,000 for prospective Pawnbrokers License Act licensees and $5,000 for prospective CDCA licensees. These bond requirements remain in the same amounts to this day. *See* 63 P.S. § 281-5; 7 P.S. § 6205.

Similarly, the CDCA as enacted in 1937 required corporations to have a minimum capitalization of $25,000 in order to be eligible for a license; the Pawnbrokers License Act contained no minimum capitalization requirement. *See* Act of April 8, 1937, P.L. 262, No. 66, § 7; Act of April 6, 1937, P.L. 200, No. 51. Today, the minimum capitalization requirement for CDCA licensees is $75,000, and there is still no analogous requirement for licensed pawnbrokers. *See* 7 P.S. § 6207; 63 P.S. § 281-1 *et seq.*

The fact that the two statutes were passed contemporaneously demonstrates that the General Assembly made intentional choices as to which requirements would apply to consumer discount companies and which would apply to pawnbrokers. *See* 1 PA. CONS. STAT. § 1921(c)(7). If the General Assembly intended licensed pawnbrokers—who indisputably fall within the category of entities "licensed by the Secretary of Banking ... under the provisions of any other statute," 7 P.S. § 6217—to enjoy the same privileges conferred by a CDCA license, there would have been no reason for it to have constructed an entirely different licensing regime. But it did, signaling that being a licensee under another statute does not equate to being licensed under the CDCA. And it does not exempt such licensees, if they are covered by the CDCA, from the strictures of that statute.

Here, PRA's CCC license does not authorize it to charge over 6% interest on direct loans under $25,000, and for the reasons explained, the mere fact that it p.338 holds such a license does not exempt it from § 6203's general prohibition. The next question I would reach is whether PRA can avoid liability under that section by showing that it is not "in the business of negotiating or making loans or advances." 7 P.S. § 6203. Our majority opinion aptly addresses that issue with which I am in full agreement. *See supra* Section III.C. In sum, under neither of Lutz's theories of CDCA liability can his FDCPA claim rest on a violation of that statute.

II. PRA Also Did Not Violate the LIPL.

Nor has Lutz established a LIPL violation as a basis for his FDCPA claim. The LIPL caps at 6% "the maximum lawful rate of interest" for a loan of $50,000 or less, 41 P.S. § 201, with the proviso that if this rule is "inconsistent with the provision of any other act establishing, permitting or removing a maximum interest rate, or prohibiting the use of usury as a defense, the provision of such other act shall prevail," 41 P.S. § 604. The LIPL also exempts banks, which "may charge a maximum rate of interest as authorized by [the Banking Code] or other applicable Federal or State law," *id.,* so there is no question that Capital One, the originator of Lutz's credit card account, was in compliance with the LIPL when it charged interest at a rate of 22.9%. *See* 7 P.S. § 6217. The question remains, however, whether Capital One can validly assign its right to collect on that interest to a non-bank, like PRA, that itself *is* subject to the LIPL's interest cap.

Pennsylvania law answers in the affirmative. Section 2210 of Pennsylvania's Commercial Code provides that contract rights—including rights to collect debt and interest—are freely assignable, meaning that "the assignee stands in the same shoes as the assignor," *U.S. Steel Homes Credit Corp. v. S. Shore Dev. Corp.,* 277 Pa.Super. 308, 419 A.2d 785, 789 (1980), and although "[a]n assignment does not confer on the assignee any greater rights than those possessed by the assignor ... the assignee's rights are not inferior to those of the assignor," *id.* (citation omitted). But interpreting § 201 of the LIPL to abrogate an assignee's contractual right to collect debt with over 6% interest would render § 201 "inconsistent with" Pennsylvania's assignment statute. 41 P.S. § 604. So, under the LIPL's proviso, the assignment statute, 13 PA. CONS. STAT § 2210, "shall prevail." *Id.*

It is also telling that the LIPL, unlike some other Pennsylvania statutes, does not prohibit assignments. The CDCA, for example, explicitly provides that "a license may not be transferred or assigned," 7 P.S. § 6208, as does the CCC, which states that a debt arising from an installment sale contract for a motor vehicle is not enforceable if "the holder was not licensed under this chapter when the holder acquired the contract," 12 PA. CONS. STAT § 6236(a)(2). There is no such restriction in the LIPL, which, to the contrary, indicates in the proviso that the LIPL will yield to "other acts"—presumably including the law of assignments, codified at 13 PA. CONS. STAT § 2210—if they would be inconsistent with the 6% cap. *See* 41 P.S. § 604. So as applied here, this means that because PRA acquired the charged-off account from Capital One, PRA had the same rights as Capital One to collect the total amount of both the debt and interest that accrued.

We draw support for our conclusion from our decision in *Pollice v. National Tax Funding, L.P.,* 225 F.3d 379 (3d Cir. 2000), *abrogated on other grounds by Henson v. Santander Consumer USA Inc.,* ___ U.S. ___, 137 S. Ct. 1718, 198 L.Ed.2d 177 (2017). Although that case dealt with assignment of government entities' claims against homeowners who failed to pay p.339 their property and utility taxes, rather than consumer debt originated by a bank, its reasoning carries over to this context. In *Pollice,* we cited a Pennsylvania Commonwealth Court decision holding that a provision of the Municipal Claims and Tax Liens Law permitted a municipality to assign or transfer any claim, tax or municipal, to a party that is a stranger to the original transaction. *Id.* at 389 (citation omitted). Because the statute provided that "such assignee[s] shall have all the rights of the original holder thereof," 53 P.S. § 7147, we found that the purchaser of the claims—a company in the business of purchasing such delinquent claims from municipalities in several states—had the authority to collect interest and penalties to the same extent as the government entities under relevant state and local law, including the authority to exceed the LIPL's six percent cap on interest rates, *Pollice,* 225 F.3d at 389-90, 392.

Our reading of the LIPL also aligns with the Seventh Circuit's interpretation of Illinois's usury statute, 815 Ill. Comp. Stat. § 205/5. In *Olvera v. Blitt & Gaines, P.C.,* the court considered whether Illinois's usury statute prohibits an unlicensed debt buyer from charging the same interest rate as the original lender where the lender was authorized by license or by its status as a bank to charge a higher interest rate. 431 F.3d 285, 286 (7th Cir. 2005). By its terms, § 205/5 forbids anyone from charging a higher interest rate "than is expressly authorized by this Act or other laws of this State." *Id.* at 287 (quoting § 205/5). The Seventh Circuit noted that "other laws of this State" included the "law of assignments, whereby the assignee steps into the shoes of the assignor," and concluded that the usury statute did not prevent debt buyers from collecting interest at the higher rate. *Id.* at 288-89. Here, the same is true for the LIPL's proviso, which by its terms gives precedence to "other acts" like § 2210 that would "permit[] or remov[e] a maximum interest rate." 41 P.S. § 604.

Finally, a regulation issued by the Office of the Comptroller of the Currency after the events of this suit confirms the reasonableness of this interpretation and ensures that any confusion on this score is eliminated going forward. That regulation—12 C.F.R. § 7.4001(e)—provides: "[i]nterest on a loan that is permissible under 12 U.S.C. § 85 shall not be affected by the sale, assignment, or other transfer of the loan." Any contrary state law is preempted.[3] *See id.*; *Barnett Bank of Marion Cnty., N.A. v. Nelson,* 517 U.S. 25, 33, 116 S.Ct. 1103, 134 L.Ed.2d 237 (1996) (establishing preemption for state regulation of national banks). And under 12 U.S.C. § 85, national banks like Capital One may charge interest on a loan in accordance with the law of the state where the bank is located, so their assignees can as well.

In sum, without either a LIPL or a CDCA violation on which to base his FDCPA claim, Lutz cannot survive a motion to dismiss. For these reasons, I join the Majority in affirming the judgment of the District Court.

[1] *See Klotz v. Celentano Stadtmauer & Walentowicz LLP,* 991 F.3d 458, 462 (3d Cir. 2021) (applying *de novo* review to a motion to dismiss under Rule 12(b)(6)); *see also Delaware Cnty. v. Fed. Hous. Fin. Agency,* 747 F.3d 215, 220 (3d Cir. 2014) (applying *de novo* review to questions of statutory interpretation).

[2] *See Walker v. Coffey,* 905 F.3d 138, 143 (3d Cir. 2018) (applying abuse-of-discretion review to a denial of leave to amend); *cf. U.S. ex rel. Schumann v. Astrazeneca Pharms. L.P.,* 769 F.3d 837, 849 (3d Cir. 2014) (reviewing a determination of the futility of amendment *de novo*).

[3] The Court extends its gratitude to the Pennsylvania Department of Banking and Securities and to Deputy Chief Carlton Smith for responding to the Court's invitation for an amicus submission.

[4] *See, e.g.*, Act of 2d March, 1723 (2d vol. chap. 262, § 1) ("[N]o person shall, directly nor indirectly ... take for the loan or use of money, or any other commodities, above the value of six pounds for the forbearance of one hundred pounds, or the value thereof, for one year[.]"); Act of 28 May 1858 § 1, P.L. No. 557 ("[T]he lawful rate of interest for the loan or use of money, in all cases where no express contract shall have been made for a less rate, shall be six per cent. per annum."). *But see, e.g.*, Small Loans Act of June 17, 1915 § 1, P.L. No. 432 (capping the interest rate between 2-3% for loans of $300 or less made by licensed small loan companies).

[5] *See* Commonwealth of Pa. Dep't of Banking, Report on Small Loan Companies, at 5, 26 (Feb. 9, 1937), https://hdl.handle.net/2027/mdp.39015076020364 (last visited August 22, 2022) (recognizing that "[v]olumes have been written in condemnation and in defense of the taking of interest" and that "[t]he problem is as old as history of mankind," but nonetheless, "wisdom and common sense demand that every effort be made to support and enlarge the general purchasing power of the consumer to prevent underconsumption from retarding recovery").

[6] In an invited amicus filing, the Pennsylvania Department of Banking and Securities submits that this provision contains a scrivener's error added during the 1963 amendments which inadvertently changed "advances of money *or* credit" to "advances of money *on* credit." *Compare* Act of April 8, 1937, P.L. 262, No. 66, § 3 (emphasis added), *with* 7 P.S. § 6203.A (emphasis added). *See* Dep't of Banking & Securities Amicus Ltr. at 2 n.1 (Feb. 15, 2022) (ECF No. 47); *see also* Dep't of Banking Interpretive Ltr. at 4 (Nov. 19, 2001) (JA45). That issue of Pennsylvania law does not require resolution in this case.

[7] *See* Am. Compl. ¶ 69 (JA32) ("Since PRA does not have a CDCA license or any other license that specifically provides for charging or collecting interest and fees on direct loans or revolving lines of credit, PRA is limited to charging or collecting no more than six percent simple interest per year on direct loans or revolving lines of credit."), ¶ 71 (JA32) ("PRA did not have legal authority to collect or receive such interest and fees because PRA was not licensed under the CDCA and was not otherwise licensed to collect or receive such interest and fees in Pennsylvania."), ¶ 72 (JA32) ("By seeking to collect and receive interest and fees charged in excess of six percent simple interest per year on the Account's cash advances, PRA falsely represented its ability to collect the full amount of the Account."), ¶ 73 (JA32) ("Additionally, by seeking to collect and receive such interest and fees, PRA sought to collect and receive interest and fees it had no legal authority to collect or receive."), ¶ 92 (JA34) ("PRA's attempt to collect and receive such interest and fees was unlawful, as PRA could not lawfully collect or receive such interest and fees."), ¶ 93 (JA34) ("PRA's attempt to collect and receive such interest and fees misrepresented PRA's ability to collect or receive such interest and fees."), ¶ 94 (JA35) ("By seeking to collect interest and fees charged on cash advance balances of credit card accounts at rates in excess of six percent simple interest per year, PRA sought to collect amounts it could not lawfully collect from Lutz or the class members.").

[8] *See id.* ¶ 20 (JA25) ("The CDCA applies to debt buyers that purchase and attempt to collect loans or advances of money or credit in amounts of $25,000 or less."), ¶ 21 (JA25) ("Debt buyers must obtain a CDCA license to charge, collect, contract for, or receive interest and fees that 'aggregate in excess of the interest ... the [debt buyer] would otherwise be permitted by law to charge if not licensed under th[e CDCA].'" (alterations in original)), ¶ 24 (JA26) ("Debt buyers seeking to collect cash advances on credit card accounts must obtain a CDCA license if they seek to collect interest and fees in excess of six percent simple interest per year because this type of credit constitutes a loan or advance of money or credit under the CDCA."), ¶ 60 (JA31) ("The CDCA applies to entities in the business of issuing or purchasing loans or advances of money or credit in amounts of $25,000 or less when such entities attempt to charge, collect, contract for, or receive interest and fees 'in excess of the interest ... the [entity] would otherwise be permitted by law to charge if not licensed under th[e CDCA].'" (alterations in original)).

[9] *See United States v. Jabateh,* 974 F.3d 281, 296 (3d Cir. 2020) (second alteration in original) ("[U]nder the fixed-meaning canon '[w]ords must be given the meaning they had when the text was adopted." (quoting Antonin Scalia & Bryan Garner, Reading Law: The Interpretation of Legal Texts 78 (2012))).

[10] *Negotiate,* Black's Law Dictionary (3d ed. 1933) (defining 'negotiate' as "To transact business, to treat with another respecting a purchase and sale, to hold intercourse, to bargain or trade, to conduct communication or conferences. It is that which passes between parties or their agents in the course of or incident to the making of a contract; it is also conversation in arranging terms of contract" and "To discuss or arrange a sale or bargain; to arrange the preliminaries of a business transaction"); *see also* Webster's New International Dictionary 1638 (2d ed.1934) (defining 'negotiation' as "a treating with another with a view to coming to terms, as for a sale or purchase").

[11] *Negotiate,* Black's Law Dictionary (3d ed. 1933) ("An instrument is 'negotiated,' when it is transferred from one person to another in such manner as to constitute the transferee the holder thereof."); Bouvier's Law Dictionary 843 (Baldwin's Century Ed. 1934) (defining 'negotiate' as "to conclude a contract or to transfer or arrange" and "The power to negotiate a bill or note is the power to indorse and deliver it to another, so that the right of action thereon shall pass to the indorser or holder. A note transferred by delivery is negotiated. A national bank, under the power to negotiate evidences of debt, may exchange government bonds for registered bonds"); Webster's 1638 (defining 'negotiate' as "To transfer for a valuable consideration under rules of commercial law").

[12] *Freeman v. Quicken Loans, Inc.,* 566 U.S. 624, 634-35, 132 S.Ct. 2034, 182 L.Ed.2d 955 (2012) ("[T]he 'commonsense canon of *noscitur a sociis* ... counsels that a word is given more precise content by the neighboring words with which it is associated.'" (quoting *United States v. Williams,* 553 U.S. 285, 294, 128 S.Ct. 1830, 170 L.Ed.2d 650 (2008))); *see also United States v. Taylor,* ___ U.S. ___, 142 S. Ct. 2015, 2023, 213 L.Ed.2d 349 (2022); *United States v. Yung,* 37 F.4th 70, 80 (3d Cir. 2022); *Mountain Vill. v. Bd. of Supervisors of Longswamp Twp.,* 582 Pa. 605, 874 A.2d 1, 8-9 (2005) (quoting *Northway Vill. No. 3, Inc. v. Northway,* 430 Pa. 499, 244 A.2d 47, 50 (1968)).

[13] *See generally* Sister Miriam Joseph, The Trivium: The Liberal Arts of Logic, Grammar, and Rhetoric 55-57 (Marguerite McGlinn ed., First Paul Dry Books 2002) (1937) (explaining that a "transitive verb expresses action that begins in the subject ... and 'goes across' ... to the object" and that a gerund "is a verbal which, like the infinitive, may perform all the functions of a substantive").

[14] *See Or,* Black's Law Dictionary (3d ed. 1933).

[15] *See id.*

[16] *See United States v. Adair,* 38 F.4th 341, 353 (3d Cir. 2022).

[17] *See Pereira v. Sessions,* ___ U.S. ___, 138 S. Ct. 2105, 2115, 201 L.Ed.2d 433 (2018) ("[I]t is a normal rule of statutory construction that identical words used in different parts of the same act are intended to have the same meaning." (quoting *Taniguchi v. Kan Pac. Saipan, Ltd.,* 566 U.S. 560, 571, 132 S.Ct. 1997, 182 L.Ed.2d 903 (2012)); *see also United States v. Castleman,* 572 U.S. 157, 174, 134 S.Ct. 1405, 188 L.Ed.2d 426 (2014) (Scalia, J., concurring in part and concurring in the judgment) (invoking "the presumption of consistent usage — the rule of thumb that a term generally means the same thing each time it is used"); *Bayview Loan Servicing, LLC v. Lindsay,* 646 Pa. 381, 185 A.3d 307, 313 (2018) (same).

[18] For closure, PRA's collection of Lutz's account balance from Capital One, inclusive of the 22.90% annual interest rate, does not violate Pennsylvania's general usury statute, which prohibits annual interest at a rate over 6%. As a bank, Capital One was authorized to charge interest at a higher rate, and the general usury prohibition, unlike the CDCA, does not regulate collection — only the interest on a loan or use of money. *Compare* 7 P.S. § 6203.A (prohibiting unlicensed covered entities from "charg[ing], *collect[ing],* contract[ing] for or receiv[ing] interest") (emphasis added), *with* 41 P.S. § 201(a) (setting "the maximum lawful interest rate for the *loan* or *use of money*") (emphasis added). *See also Roethlein v. Portnoff Law Assocs., Ltd.,* 623 Pa. 1, 81 A.3d 816, 821-24 (2013) ("[T]he plain language of [the general usury statute] restricts its application to claims involving the loan or use of money."); *Pollice v. Nat'l Tax Funding, L.P.,* 225 F.3d 379, 394-97 (3d Cir. 2000) (concluding that the general usury statute's application is limited to "the loan or use of money").

[1] The Majority does not contend with the § 6217 issue, instead dispensing with Lutz's CDCA claim on the grounds that the CDCA does not apply to PRA because PRA does not "negotiate" loans within the meaning of the Act. As I see it, there would be no need to construe "negotiate" if PRA's Consumer Credit Code (CCC) license—which is issued by the Secretary of Banking and permits PRA to collect on motor vehicle loans, *see* 12 PA. CONS. STAT. § 6201, *et seq.,*—exempts it from the CDCA in any event. So, I would consider this issue at the outset. Regardless, however, we reach the same conclusion in the end.

[2] *See* 7 P.S. § 6102 (money transmitters); 63 P.S. § 2311 (check cashers); 63 P.S. § 2403 (debt management and debt settlement companies); 63 P.S. § 281-3 (pawnbrokers); 7 PA. CONS. STAT. § 6111 (mortgage brokers, lenders, servicers, loan correspondents or originators); 12 PA. CONS. STAT. § 6211 (motor vehicle sales finance companies). Notably, the Department of Banking merged with the Pennsylvania Securities Commission in 2012, so the Department is now responsible

for licensing "a broad range of entities and industries that were never contemplated by the General Assembly when the CDCA was enacted." Amicus Br. 4.

[3] Opponents of the regulation have argued that the OCC lacked authority to preempt state usury law in the manner that it did. *See Permissible Interest on Loans That Are Sold, Assigned, or Otherwise Transferred,* 85 Fed. Reg. 33,530 (June 2, 2020) (summarizing comments). We need not wade into this debate for our purposes.

991 F.3d 466 (2021)

Candace MOYER, Individually and on Behalf of All Others Similarly Situated, Appellant
v.
PATENAUDE & FELIX, A.P.C.

No. 20-1937.

United States Court of Appeals, Third Circuit.

Submitted Under Third Circuit L.A.R. 34.1(a): January 26, 2021.
Filed: March 16, 2021.

Moyer v. Patenaude & Felix, APC, 991 F. 3d 466 (3rd Cir. 2021)

On Appeal from the United States District Court for the Eastern District of Pennsylvania,>Edward M. Koch (D.C. Civil Action No. 5-18-cv-04711), District Judge: Honorable Joshua D. Wolson.

Ari H. Marcus, Yitzchak Zelman, Marcus & Zelman, 701 Cookman Avenue, Suite 300, Asbury Park, NJ 07712, Counsel for Plaintiff-Appellant Candace Moyer.

Edward M. Koch, Marc L. Penchansky, White & Williams, One Liberty Place, Suite 1800, 1650 Market Street, Philadelphia, PA 19103, Counsel for Defendant-Appellee Patenaude & Felix, A.P.C.

Before: RESTREPO, BIBAS, and PORTER, Circuit Judges.

p.468 OPINION OF THE COURT

PORTER, Circuit Judge.

Candace Moyer brought a putative class action against Patenaude & Felix, A.P.C. under the Fair Debt Collection Practices Act ("FDCPA") after Patenaude sent her a collection letter inviting her to "eliminate further collection action" by calling Patenaude. Moyer claimed that this invitation to call Patenaude (1) deceives debtors by making them think a phone call is a "legally effective" means of ceasing collection activity, and (2) makes debtors uncertain about their right to dispute a debt in writing. Moyer's claims fail, so we will affirm the District Court's grant of summary judgment in favor of Patenaude.

I

Moyer failed to pay her credit-card debt, so the card issuer hired Patenaude to collect it. Patenaude sent Moyer a one-page, p.469 single-sided collection letter that stated the following:

> Please be advised that the above-referenced debt has been assigned to this firm to initiate collection efforts regarding your delinquent outstanding balance to our client. If you wish to eliminate further collection action, please contact us at 800-832-7675 ext. 8500.
>
> Unless you notify this office within THIRTY (30) days of receiving this notice that you dispute the validity of this debt, or any portion thereof, this office will assume this debt is valid.
>
> If you notify this office in writing within THIRTY (30) days of receiving this notice that this debt, or any portion thereof, is disputed, this office will obtain verification of the debt, or a copy of a judgment against you, and mail you a copy of such verification or judgment. Further, if you make a written request upon this office within THIRTY (30) days of receiving this notice, this office will provide you with the name and address of the original creditor, if different from the current creditor.
>
> This is an attempt to collect a debt and any information obtained will be used for that purpose.

App. 29.

Moyer sued Patenaude for violating the FDCPA. According to Moyer, the letter's second sentence—"[i]f you wish to eliminate further collection action, please contact us at 800-832-7675 ext. 8500" (the "Contact Sentence")—would deceive a debtor. Moyer argues that the Contact Sentence would lead a debtor to believe that a phone call is a "legally effective way to stop such collection action" when, in reality, only written communication can legally stop collection activity. Appellant's Br. 13. In addition, Moyer claimed that the Contact Sentence would make a debtor uncertain about her right to dispute the debt in writing.

The District Court disagreed with Moyer and granted summary judgment in favor of Patenaude. This timely appeal followed.

II

The District Court had subject-matter jurisdiction under 28 U.S.C. § 1331. We have appellate jurisdiction under 28 U.S.C. § 1291. We review the District Court's grant of summary judgment de novo and apply the same standard employed by the District Court. *Pa. Dep't of Env't Prot. v. Trainer Custom Chem., LLC,* 906 F.3d 85, 91 n.7 (3d Cir. 2018). Summary judgment is appropriate only if, after drawing all reasonable inferences in favor of the non-moving party, there exists "no genuine dispute as to any material fact" and the movant "is entitled to judgment as a matter of law." *Shuker v. Smith & Nephew, PLC,* 885 F.3d 760, 770 (3d Cir. 2018) (internal quotation marks omitted) (quoting Fed. R. Civ. P. 56(a)).

Whether Patenaude's collection letter violates the FDCPA is a question of law. *Wilson v. Quadramed Corp.,* 225 F.3d 350, 353 n.2 (3d Cir. 2000).

III

"Congress enacted the FDCPA 'to eliminate abusive debt collection practices by debt collectors, to insure that those debt collectors who refrain from using abusive debt collection practices are not competitively disadvantaged, and to promote consistent State action to protect consumers against debt collection abuses.'" *Rotkiske v. Klemm*, ___ U.S. ___, 140 S. Ct. 355, 358, 205 L.Ed.2d 291 (2019) (quoting 15 U.S.C. § 1692(e)). "The FDCPA pursues these stated purposes by imposing affirmative requirements on debt collectors and p.470 prohibiting a range of debt-collection practices." *Id.* (citing 15 U.S.C. §§ 1692b-1692j). The law authorizes private civil actions against debt collectors. 15 U.S.C. § 1692k(a).

"To prevail on an FDCPA claim, a plaintiff must prove that (1) she is a consumer, (2) the defendant is a debt collector, (3) the defendant's challenged practice involves an attempt to collect a 'debt' as the Act defines it, and (4) the defendant has violated a provision of the FDCPA in attempting to collect the debt." *Jensen v. Pressler & Pressler*, 791 F.3d 413, 417 (3d Cir. 2015) (internal quotation marks omitted) (quoting *Douglass v. Convergent Outsourcing*, 765 F.3d 299, 303 (3d Cir. 2014)). The parties dispute only the fourth element —whether Patenaude's collection letter violated a provision of the FDCPA.

When deciding if a debt-collection action violates the FDCPA, we employ the "least sophisticated debtor" standard. *Id.* at 418. "The standard is an objective one, meaning that the specific plaintiff need not prove that *she* was actually confused or misled, only that the objective least sophisticated debtor would be." *Id.* at 419. This standard "protects naive consumers, [but] also 'prevents liability for bizarre or idiosyncratic interpretations of collection notices by preserving a quotient of reasonableness and presuming a basic level of understanding and willingness to read with care.'" *Wilson*, 225 F.3d at 354-55 (quoting *United States v. Nat'l Fin. Servs., Inc.*, 98 F.3d 131, 136 (4th Cir. 1996)). Moyer relies on two provisions of the FDCPA in her suit against Patenaude.

First, under 15 U.S.C. § 1692e, "[a] debt collector may not use any false, deceptive, or misleading representation or means in connection with the collection of any debt." Section 1692e specifies several types of forbidden false communications and includes a catch-all provision that forbids "[t]he use of any false representation or deceptive means to collect or attempt to collect any debt or to obtain information concerning a consumer." *Id.* § 1692e(10). "[A] collection letter 'is deceptive when it can be reasonably read to have two or more different meanings, one of which is inaccurate.'" *Wilson*, 225 F.3d at 354 (quoting *Russell v. Equifax A.R.S.*, 74 F.3d 30, 35 (2d Cir. 1996)).

Second, under 15 U.S.C. § 1692g, a debt collector must provide the consumer with a written notice containing the following:

(1) the amount of the debt;

(2) the name of the creditor to whom the debt is owed;

(3) a statement that unless the consumer, within thirty days after receipt of the notice, disputes the validity of the debt, or any portion thereof, the debt will be assumed to be valid by the debt collector;

(4) a statement that if the consumer notifies the debt collector in writing within the thirty-day period that the debt, or any portion thereof, is disputed, the debt collector will obtain verification of the debt or a copy of a judgment against the consumer and a copy of such verification or judgment will be mailed to the consumer by the debt collector; and

(5) a statement that, upon the consumer's written request within the thirty-day period, the debt collector will provide the consumer with the name and address of the original creditor, if different from the current creditor.

Id. § 1692g(a). "Paragraphs 3 through 5 of section 1692g(a) contain the validation notice [the "Validation Notice"]—the statements that inform the consumer how to obtain verification of the debt and that p.471 [s]he has thirty days in which to do so." *Wilson,* 225 F.3d at 353-54 (second alteration in original). As shown above, Patenaude provided the Validation Notice in the second and third paragraphs of its collection letter.

If a consumer follows § 1692g(a)(4) or (5) by writing to the debt collector to dispute the debt or to request the name of the original creditor, then § 1692g requires the debt collector to "cease collection of the debt ... until the debt collector obtains verification of the debt or a copy of a judgment, or the name and address of the original creditor, and [these materials are] mailed to the consumer by the debt collector." *Id.* § 1692g(b). "Any collection activities and communication during the 30-day period may not overshadow or be inconsistent with the disclosure of the consumer's right to dispute the debt or request the name and address of the original creditor." *Id.* A debt collector violates this provision if the contents of the letter cause the least sophisticated debtor to be "confused or mislead" as to her "rights to dispute or seek validation of the debt." *Wilson,* 225 F.3d at 353.

A

Moyer first contends that the letter is a deceptive means of debt collection in violation of § 1692e(10) because Patenaude indicated that a phone call was a "legally effective" means of stopping collection activity. Appellant's Br. 13. Section 1692g(b) requires a debt collector to "cease all collection efforts if the consumer provides written notice" that she disputes the debt. *Wilson,* 225 F.3d at 354. A phone call from a debtor would not legally require Patenaude to cease collection efforts. But, according to Moyer, Patenaude's invitation to "eliminate" collection action through a phone call would deceive a debtor into believing that the call would, by law, require collection efforts to cease.

Moyer's argument fails because Patenaude never claimed the phone call was a "legally effective" means of stopping collection efforts. Patenaude invited Moyer to call to "eliminate" collection action, but never asserted, explicitly or implicitly, that the phone call would, by law, force Patenaude to cease its collection efforts. Moyer reads into the invitation an implication that it does not create. For this reason, the district court decisions cited by Moyer are inapposite. They each involve a debt collector who *did* state that a phone call would legally require collection activity to cease. *See, e.g., Langley v. Weinstein & Riley, P.S.,* No. H-12-1562, 2013 WL 2951057, at *5, 7-8 (S.D. Tex. June 14, 2013) (holding that a debtor collector's letter was deceptive when the letter stated that "the law requires [the debt collector] to suspend its [collection] efforts" if the debtor placed a phone call with the debt collector).

B

Moyer next contends that Patenaude's insertion of the invitation to call in the Contact Sentence before the Validation Notice causes confusion regarding how to pursue her rights contained in the Validation Notice. According to Moyer, when an invitation to call appears directly before an acknowledgment that the debtor can write to exercise her rights under § 1692g, the debtor would be left uncertain about whether she should call or write to exercise her rights.

Moyer sees confusion where none exists. The Validation Notice instructs the debtor to write to exercise their § 1692g rights, leaving no suggestions that a phone call would suffice. Likewise, the Contact Sentence does not suggest that a debtor could exercise any § 1692g rights over the p.472 phone. And the order of the paragraphs does not create confusion about what each one conveys. *See Wilson,* 225 F.3d at 356 (holding that a paragraph demanding immediate payment of a debt that preceded a Validation Notice did not create "an actual or apparent contradiction" with the Validation Notice in violation of § 1692g).

***

For the foregoing reasons, we will affirm the judgment of the District Court.

991 F.3d 458 (2021)

Terry L. KLOTZ, on behalf of herself and those similarly situated, Appellant
v.
CELENTANO STADTMAUER AND WALENTOWICZ LLP.

No. 19-3703.

United States Court of Appeals, Third Circuit.

Argued: September 24, 2020.
Filed: March 16, 2021.

Klotz v. Celentano Stadtmauer and Walentowicz LLP, 991 F. 3d 458 (3rd Cir. 2021)

On Appeal from the United States District Court for the District of New Jersey, (D.C. Civil Action No. 2-19-cv-00248), District Judge: Honorable Susan D. Wigenton.

Scott C. Borison, [ARGUED], Borison Firm, 30 North Gould Street, Sheridan, WY 82801, Yongmoon Kim, Kim Law Firm, 411 Hackensack Avenue, Hackensack, NJ 07601, Counsel for Plaintiff-Appellant Terry L. Klotz.

Lawrence J. Bartel, [ARGUED], Andrew M. Schwartz, Gordon Rees Scully Mansukhani, Three Logan Square, 1717 Arch Street, Philadelphia, PA 19103, Counsel for Defendant-Appellee Celentano Stadtmauer and Walentowicz LLP.

Before: AMBRO, PORTER, and ROTH, Circuit Judges.

p.461 OPINION OF THE COURT

PORTER, Circuit Judge.

Terry Klotz's now-deceased husband received medical services from Hackensack University Medical Center (the "Hospital") and incurred a $1,580 debt. Klotz's husband did not pay the medical debt before he died, and he left no estate. The Hospital retained Celentano, Stadtmauer and Walentowicz, LLP ("CSW") to collect the debt, and it mailed two collection letters to Klotz.

p.462 Klotz claims she is not liable for the debt and asks us to hold that the Equal Credit Opportunity Act ("ECOA"), 15 U.S.C. § 1691 *et seq.*, preempts New Jersey's common-law doctrine of necessaries (where a spouse is jointly liable for necessary expenses incurred by the other spouse). Preemption of this doctrine would allow her to pursue a case against CSW for an alleged violation of the Fair Debt Collection Practices Act ("FDCPA"), 15 U.S.C. § 1692 *et seq*. We hold that the ECOA does not preempt New Jersey's doctrine of necessaries. Klotz also argues that CSW failed to follow the procedural requirements of the doctrine of necessaries and that she should be allowed to amend her complaint. We reject these additional arguments and will affirm the District Court's judgment.

I

Klotz believed that she was not liable for the debt, so she sued CSW for violating 15 U.S.C. §§ 1692e and 1692f of the FDCPA because CSW's collection letters sought payment of a debt that she did not owe. CSW moved to dismiss the complaint under Federal Rule of Civil Procedure 12(b)(6), arguing that Klotz owed the debt under New Jersey's common-law doctrine of necessaries because her deceased husband incurred the debt for medical treatment. The District Court agreed with CSW and dismissed the complaint with prejudice. Klotz moved under Federal Rule of Civil Procedure 59(e) for reconsideration of the District Court's order and for leave to file an amended complaint with additional allegations. The District Court denied the motion, reasoning that amendment would be futile. Klotz timely appealed.

II

The District Court had subject-matter jurisdiction under 28 U.S.C. § 1331 and 15 U.S.C. § 1692k(d). We have appellate jurisdiction under 28 U.S.C. § 1291.

We review de novo a district court's grant of a motion to dismiss for failure to state a claim under Rule 12(b)(6). *Foglia v. Renal Ventures Mgmt., LLC,* 754 F.3d 153, 154 n.1 (3d Cir. 2014). To survive a Rule 12(b)(6) motion, a complaint must set forth enough factual allegations to "state a claim to relief that is plausible on its face." *Bell Atl. Corp. v. Twombly,* 550 U.S. 544, 570, 127 S.Ct. 1955, 167 L.Ed.2d 929 (2007). A claim is facially plausible "when the plaintiff pleads factual content that allows the court to draw the reasonable inference that the defendant is liable for the misconduct alleged." *Ashcroft v. Iqbal,* 556 U.S. 662, 678, 129 S.Ct. 1937, 173 L.Ed.2d 868 (2009). When reviewing a Rule 12(b)(6) motion, we accept as true all factual allegations in the complaint and view those facts in the light most favorable to the non-moving party. *Foglia,* 754 F.3d at 154 n.1.

We review a district court's denial of a Rule 59(e) motion to amend the complaint for abuse of discretion, but we review the district court's underlying legal determinations de novo and factual determinations for clear error. *Burtch v. Milberg Factors, Inc.,* 662 F.3d 212, 220 (3d Cir. 2011). When a plaintiff moves to amend her complaint under Rule 59(e), we apply the same factors as when a party files a motion to amend a pleading under Federal Rule of Civil Procedure 15(a). *See Adams v. Gould Inc.,* 739 F.2d 858, 864 (3d Cir. 1984). Those factors include whether the amendment would be futile. *Burtch,* 662 F.3d at 231. A proposed amendment to a complaint is futile if the amended complaint would fail to state a claim for relief under Rule 12(b)(6). *See Alvin v. Suzuki,* 227 F.3d 107, 121 (3d Cir. 2000).

p.463 III

The FDCPA prohibits debt collectors from using false, misleading, and unfair debt-collection practices by seeking to collect on a debt that is not authorized by law. *See* 15 U.S.C. §§ 1692e, 1692f. As noted, Klotz believes that she does not owe her husband's medical debt. She argues that CSW's debt-collection letters misrepresent "the character, amount, or legal status of [the] debt" in violation of the FDCPA. 15 U.S.C. § 1692e(2)(A).

In response, CSW argues that Klotz had a legal obligation to pay the debt under New Jersey's common-law doctrine of necessaries. In *Jersey Shore Medical Center-Fitkin Hospital v. Estate of Baum,* the Supreme Court of New Jersey held that "both spouses are liable for necessary expenses incurred by either spouse in the course of the marriage." 84 N.J. 137, 417 A.2d 1003, 1005 (1980). Additionally, a non-debtor is liable for the debts of her spouse only if "the assets of the spouse who incurred the debt are insufficient." *Id.* at 1010. CSW's arguments prevailed in the District Court.

Klotz argues the following on appeal: (1) federal law preempts the doctrine of necessaries, and thus CSW's collection effort violated the FDCPA; (2) CSW failed to follow the doctrine's procedural requirement that CSW seek repayment from her husband before seeking repayment from her; and (3) she should be permitted to amend her complaint. All three arguments fail.

A

First, Klotz argues that the ECOA preempts the doctrine of necessaries. Federal law[1] can preempt state law in three ways: (1) express preemption; (2) field preemption; or (3) conflict preemption. *Farina v. Nokia Inc.,* 625 F.3d 97, 115 (3d Cir. 2010). Conflict preemption, the only type of preemption relevant here, "exists where compliance with both state and federal law is impossible, or where the state law stands as an obstacle to the accomplishment and execution of the full purposes and objectives of Congress." *Oneok, Inc. v. Learjet, Inc.,* 575 U.S. 373, 377, 135 S.Ct. 1591, 191 L.Ed.2d 511 (2015) (internal quotation marks omitted) (quoting *California v. ARC Am. Corp.,* 490 U.S. 93, 100-01, 109 S.Ct. 1661, 104 L.Ed.2d 86 (1989)).

Two principles guide a conflict-preemption analysis. First, "all preemption arguments[] must be grounded in the text and structure of the [federal] statute at issue." *Kansas v. Garcia,* ___ U.S. ___, 140 S. Ct. 791, 804, 206 L.Ed.2d 146 (2020) (internal quotation marks omitted) (quoting *CSX Transp., Inc. v. Easterwood,* 507 U.S. 658, 664, 113 S.Ct. 1732, 123 L.Ed.2d 387 (1993)). Second, "there is a strong presumption against preemption in areas of the law that States have traditionally occupied." *Sikkelee v. Precision Airmotive Corp.,* 822 F.3d 680, 687 (3d Cir. 2016) (citing *Medtronic, Inc. v. Lohr,* 518 U.S. 470, 485, 116 S.Ct. 2240, 135 L.Ed.2d 700 (1996)).

The ECOA prohibits "any creditor" from "discriminat[ing] against any applicant, with respect to any aspect of a credit transaction[] on the basis of ... marital status." 15 U.S.C. § 1691(a)(1). As relevant here, one regulation implementing the ECOA provides that "a creditor shall not require the signature of an applicant's spouse ... on any credit instrument if the p.464 applicant qualifies under the creditor's standards of creditworthiness for the amount and terms of the credit requested." 12 C.F.R. § 202.7(d)(1) (2021).

Klotz argues that the doctrine of necessaries conflicts with the spousal-signature prohibition found at 12 C.F.R. § 202.7(d)(1).[2] By imposing liability for her deceased husband's debt, Klotz argues, the doctrine effectively treats her as a spousal co-signer on the debt in violation of the spousal-signature prohibition. This conflict means the spousal-signature prohibition preempts the doctrine.

Putting aside questions such as whether CSW is a "creditor" and Klotz an "applicant" under the spousal-signature prohibition, we hold that the ECOA does not preempt the doctrine of necessaries because the debt is "incidental credit" exempt from the prohibition. The Federal Reserve Board may exempt certain categories of transactions from the scope of the ECOA "after making an express finding that the application of ... any provision... would not contribute substantially to effecting the purposes of [the ECOA]." 15 U.S.C. § 1691b(b). The agency exercised this authority by exempting "incidental credit" from the § 202.7(d) spousal-signature prohibition. *See* 12 C.F.R. § 202.3(c)(2)(v) (2021); Equal Credit Opportunity, 68 Fed. Reg. 13,144, 13,145 (March 18, 2003) (to be codified at 12 C.F.R. pt. 202). "Incidental credit refers to extensions of consumer credit ... (i) [t]hat are not made pursuant to the terms of a credit card account; (ii) [t]hat are not subject to a finance charge ... and (iii) [t]hat are not payable by agreement in more than four installments." *Id.* § 202.3(c)(1).

Klotz's medical debt qualifies as incidental credit because it satisfies all three criteria. She does not dispute that the debt is not related to a credit card account, not subject to a finance charge, and not subject to installment payments. *See* Equal Credit Opportunity, 68 Fed. Reg. at 13,188 (listing medical debt from a hospital or doctor that "allows the client or customer to defer the payment of a bill" as an example of incidental credit); *Mays v. Buckeye Rural Elec. Coop., Inc.,* 277 F.3d 873, 877-79 (6th Cir. 2002) (holding that money owed to an electrical utility was incidental credit under 12 C.F.R. § 202.3(c) because the utility "ha[d] no credit card accounts, d[id] not permit installment payments for electrical service, and d[id] not impose finance charges"). Because the medical debt CSW sought to collect is incidental credit exempt from the spousal-signature prohibition, CSW's attempt to collect the debt cannot violate the prohibition.

Given that the spousal-signature prohibition does not apply, we hold the ECOA and its regulations do not conflict-preempt the doctrine of necessaries. To succeed on a conflict-preemption argument, Klotz must demonstrate that the doctrine of necessaries either (1) makes compliance with the ECOA impossible or (2) "stand[s] as an obstacle to the accomplishment and execution of the full purposes" of the ECOA. *Garcia,* 140 S. Ct. at 806 (internal quotation marks omitted). The identification of the purpose "cannot be based on a free-wheeling judicial inquiry into whether a state statute is in tension with federal objectives." *Id.* at 801 (internal quotation marks and citation omitted).

p.465 CSW's use of the doctrine of necessaries complies with the ECOA because the medical debt is incidental credit exempt from the spousal-signature prohibition. Further, Klotz's attempt to invoke the general objectives of the ECOA fails, as the statute was focused on ensuring the availability of credit rather than the allocation of liability between spouses. *See Moran Foods, Inc. v. Mid-Atlantic Mkt. Dev. Co., LLC,* 476 F.3d 436, 441 (7th Cir. 2007) ("[I]t is apparent that what the Act was intended to do was to forbid a creditor to deny credit to a [married] woman on the basis of a belief that she would not be a good credit risk."). Because CSW's use of the doctrine of necessaries complies with the ECOA and does not frustrate the purpose of the ECOA, we hold the ECOA has not preempted the doctrine. *Garcia,* 140 S. Ct. at 804.

B

Klotz next argues that CSW failed to comply with the requirements of the doctrine of necessaries. But she did not plead adequate facts to support her argument, and her husband does not have an estate that could pay the debt, so the argument fails.

Before resorting to the doctrine of necessaries, a creditor must "first seek satisfaction from the income and other property of the spouse who incurred the debt." *Jersey Shore,* 417 A.2d at 1005. This step ensures that the doctrine applies "only where the financial resources of the spouse who incurred the necessary expense are insufficient." *Id.* at 1010. Klotz's complaint does not allege that CSW flouted the doctrine's requirement that it first seek satisfaction from her deceased husband. Nor does the complaint allege that her husband's estate possessed funds to cover the debt. Public records—which we may consider when reviewing the grant of a Rule 12(b)(6) motion, *see Mayer v. Belichick,* 605 F.3d 223, 230 (3d Cir. 2010)— explain this omission: they show that Klotz's husband does not have an estate.

Klotz argues that CSW should have sought administration of her husband's estate under N.J. Rev. Stat. § 3B:10-2 (explaining who can seek administration of an estate). *Jersey Shore* forecloses this argument. There, the "defendant's late husband[] died at the hospital after a long illness which exhausted his medicaid benefits and left a balance due the hospital of $25,709.50." *Jersey Shore,* 417 A.2d at 1004. "[The husband's] estate was insolvent, and no one [had] sought letters of administration." *Id.* Yet the Supreme Court of New Jersey permitted the creditor hospital to assert a doctrine-of-necessaries argument against the surviving wife. *See id.* at 1006-07. Klotz fails to explain what other action CSW should have taken to satisfy the requirements of *Jersey Shore.*

C

Third, Klotz argues that the District Court abused its discretion by denying her motion for leave to file an amended complaint. The District Court denied Klotz's motion because the amendment would be futile. We agree.

A proposed amendment to a complaint is futile if the complaint, as amended, would fail to state a claim upon which relief could be granted. *See Suzuki,* 227 F.3d at 121. Klotz argues that her proposed amended complaint would not be futile because it would plead that CSW's letters sought to collect an amount beyond what the doctrine of necessaries permits. CSW's letters sought to collect a debt of $1,580. Klotz pleads that her husband was a Medicare beneficiary with a Medicare deductible of $1,316, thus implying that some amount of p.466 the debt in the collection letter was not covered by Medicare. She also pleads that the collection amount "included copayments, expenses, fees, costs and/or other charges incurred on additional dates beyond the 'Date of Service' specified in the [collection letters]." App. at 123.

Even if the debt included a small amount of ancillary charges beyond the Medicare deductible of Klotz's husband, these allegations do not change whether the debt resulted from the provision of a necessary service. Indeed, necessaries can be costs that "directly or *indirectly* are designed to preserve the assets of [a] marriage or to permit [a debtor spouse] to continue his normal life, including the ability to make income and support the family either through employment or providing services or emotional well-being in the household." *See DuBois v. DeLarm,* 243 N.J.Super. 175, 578 A.2d 1250, 1255 (1990) (emphasis added). None of Klotz's proposed allegations challenge whether the debt incurred falls outside the definition of a necessary under New Jersey law. Her "complaint pleads facts that are 'merely consistent with' [CSW]'s liability" but "stops short of the line between possibility and plausibility of entitlement to relief." *Iqbal,* 556 U.S. at 678, 129 S.Ct. 1937 (internal quotation marks omitted). The District Court did not abuse its discretion when it denied Klotz's request for leave to amend for futility.

***

The ECOA does not preempt New Jersey's doctrine of necessaries, so the doctrine permitted CSW to send its collection letters to Klotz without violating the FDCPA. Additionally, CSW followed the procedural requirements of the doctrine, and Klotz's filing an amended complaint would be futile. So we will affirm the District Court's judgment dismissing Klotz's complaint.

[1] Federal regulations can also have preemptive effect. *See Fellner v. Tri-Union Seafoods, L.L.C.,* 539 F.3d 237, 243 (3d Cir. 2008).

[2] We cite to the Federal Reserve Board's regulations but note for completeness that much of the rulemaking authority under the ECOA was transferred to the Consumer Financial Protection Bureau ("CFPB") in 2011. The CFPB restated the Federal Reserve's regulations at 12 C.F.R. pt. 1002, 76 Fed. Reg. 79,442 (Dec. 21, 2011); *see also Tyson v. Sterling Rental, Inc.*, 836 F.3d 571, 578 (6th Cir. 2016).

994 F.3d 117 (2021)

Randy HOPKINS, Individually and on behalf of those similarly situated, Appellant
v.
COLLECTO, INC., dba EOS CCA; US Asset Management, Inc.; John Does 1 To 10.

No. 20-1955.

United States Court of Appeals, Third Circuit.

Submitted under Third Circuit L.A.R. 34.1(a) January 19, 2021.
Filed April 12, 2021.

Hopkins v. Collecto, Inc., 994 F. 3d 117 (3rd Cir. 2021)

On Appeal from the United States District Court for the District of New Jersey, (D.C. No. 2:19-cv-18661), District Judge: The Honorable William J. Martini.

Yongmoon Kim Evan W. Lehrer Philip D. Stern THE KIM LAW FIRM LLC 411 Hackensack Avenue, Suite 701 Hackensack, NJ 07601 Counsel for Appellant.

Lawrence J. Bartel Andrew M. Schwartz GORDON REES SCULLY MANSUKHANI, LLP Three Logan Square 1717 Arch Street, Suite 610 Philadelphia PA 19103 Counsel for Appellees.

Derick K. Sohn, Jr CONSUMER FINANCIAL PROTECTION BUREAU 1700 G Street, N.W. Washington DC 20552 Counsel for Amicus Appellee.

Before: SMITH, Chief Judge, HARDIMAN and ROTH, Circuit Judges.

p.119 OPINION OF THE COURT

SMITH, Chief Judge.

Is there anything materially deceptive or misleading about a debt collection letter that accurately itemizes a debt as including "$0.00" in interest and fees when the debt cannot accrue interest and fees? To ask the question is essentially to answer it. Even our case law's hypothetical "least sophisticated consumer"—gullible though he may be—reads a debt collection letter without speculating about what could happen in the future based on true statements concerning the past. In other words, he is not a litigious claim-seeker who hunts, Lagotto-like, for truffles in dunning letters. The District Court properly dismissed the complaint, so we will affirm.

I. FACTUAL AND PROCEDURAL BACKGROUND

On behalf of US Asset Management, Inc. ("USAM"), Collecto, Inc. d/b/a EOS CCA ("Collecto") sent a letter to Randy Hopkins to collect on a debt that Hopkins initially owed to Verizon but which was later sold to USAM. The letter itemized Hopkins's debt in the following table:

FEES PRINCIPAL INTEREST COLL COSTS BALANCE $1,088.34 $00.0 $0.00 $1.088.34 TOTAL DUE: $1.088.34

p.120 Compl. ¶ 23. The letter concluded that Hopkins owed $1,088.34 on the debt and offered to "resolve this debt in full" if he paid a reduced amount of $761.84. *Id.* at Ex. A.

Hopkins filed a putative class action complaint in the District of New Jersey against USAM and Collecto (and John Does), alleging that Collecto's letter violated the Fair Debt Collection Practices Act, 15 U.S.C. § 1692 *et seq.* ("FDCPA"). Hopkins claimed that the debt could not or was not intended to accrue interest or collection fees. Hopkins alleged that by itemizing interest and collection fees for his "static debt" and by assigning a "$0.00" value to those columns, the letter's table falsely implied—in violation of § 1692e and § 1692f of the FDCPA—that interest and fees could accrue and thereby increase the amount of his debt over time. Compl. ¶¶ 24, 26, 29, 53; Appellant's Br. 12-13. According to Hopkins, consumers prioritize what debts to pay and, by suggesting that the debt might accrue interest and fees (when, in fact, it was static), the Collecto letter gave him the false impression that the debt needed to be prioritized.

Collecto and USAM moved to dismiss Hopkins's complaint for failure to state a claim.[1] The District Court dismissed Hopkins's complaint with prejudice, identifying as the "central issue" whether "Defendants' inclusion of language... stating that Plaintiff owed $0.00 in interest and $0.00 for fees or collection costs for a static debt violated the FDCPA." JA6.[2] Looking to a pair of decisions from the Second Circuit, *Dow v. Frontline Asset Strategies, LLC,* 783 F. App'x 75 (2d Cir. 2019), and *Taylor v. Financial Recovery Services, Inc.,* 886 F.3d 212 (2d Cir. 2018), the District Court held that Hopkins's complaint failed to plausibly allege that Collecto's debt itemization violated the FDCPA. It neither "leave[s] the least sophisticated consumer in doubt of the nature and legal status of the underlying debt" nor "impede[s] the consumer's ability to respond to or dispute collection." JA7. The District Court declined to require assurances by debt collectors that itemized amounts "will not change in the future," reasoning that doing so would lead to "complex and verbose debt collection letters" that would confuse consumers. *Id.*

II. DISCUSSION

We review the District Court's dismissal of Hopkins's complaint de novo.[3] We accept the truth of all factual allegations in the complaint and draw all reasonable inferences in favor of Hopkins, the non-movant. *See, e.g., Levins v. Healthcare Revenue Recovery Grp., LLC,* 902 F.3d 274, 278 n.1 (3d Cir. 2018).

According to Hopkins, the itemized table in Collecto's letter denoting "$0.00" in interest and collection fees falsely implied that interest and collection fees were materially likely to accrue. And because the debt was static,[4] Hopkins contends that p.121 the letter violated the FDCPA's prohibition on deceptive (§ 1692e) and unfair or unconscionable (§ 1692f) means of collecting consumer debts. For two reasons, we are unconvinced.

1. *Recent decisions from other Circuits are to the contrary.* Ours is not the first court to be confronted with a claim similar to Hopkins's. For example, in *Degroot v. Client Services, Inc.,* 977 F.3d 656 (7th Cir. 2020), the Seventh Circuit held that a debt collection letter spoke only about the past and thus was not misleading about the future when it listed a debt as including $0.00 in interest and fees. *Id.* at 660-61. "[M]ere[ly] raising ... an open question about future assessment of other charges," as the $0.00 itemization did, does not mislead the unsophisticated consumer. *See id.* at 661. Likewise, in *Salinas v. R.A. Rogers, Inc.,* 952 F.3d 680 (5th Cir. 2020), the Fifth Circuit analyzed a dunning letter "from the perspective of an unsophisticated or least sophisticated consumer" yet concluded that it did not violate the FDCPA. *Id.* at 683-84 & n.3. The letter listed $0.00 due in interest and fees, stating, "in the event there is interest or other charges accruing on your account, the amount due may be greater than the amount shown above after the date of this notice." *Id.* (cleaned up).

Hopkins points out that such cases were decided under an "unsophisticated debtor" standard and maintains that the Third Circuit's "least sophisticated debtor" standard is more forgiving. The *least* sophisticated debtor, he posits, is less savvy than the merely unsophisticated debtor, and is thus plausibly misled or deceived about the nature of his static debt when a collection letter lists it as including $0.00 in interest and fees.

But our court's framework is functionally equivalent to the unsophisticated debtor standard on which claims like Hopkins's have foundered. We have described the "least sophisticated debtor" standard as "almost universally employed by Courts of Appeals in interpreting [the FDCPA]," even though we recognize variance in how the standard is worded. *Jensen v. Pressler & Pressler,* 791 F.3d 413, 419 & n.3 (3d Cir. 2015) (noting that it is "sometimes referred to as the 'least sophisticated consumer' or 'unsophisticated debtor' standard"). Among the authorities cited in *Jensen* as comprising this near "universal" consensus were cases decided under the "unsophisticated debtor" or "unsophisticated consumer" standard, including from the First, Fifth, and Seventh Circuits. *See, e.g., Pollard v. Law Office of Mandy L. Spaulding,* 766 F.3d 98, 103 (1st Cir. 2014) ("[W]e hold that, for FDCPA purposes, a collection letter is to be viewed from the perspective of the hypothetical unsophisticated consumer."); *McMurray v. ProCollect, Inc.,* 687 F.3d 665, 669 (5th Cir. 2012) ("We must evaluate any potential deception in the letter under an unsophisticated or least sophisticated consumer standard." (cleaned up)); *Wahl v. Midland Credit Mgmt., Inc.,* 556 F.3d 643, 645-46 (7th Cir. 2009) ("In deciding whether collection letters violate the FDCPA, we have consistently viewed them through the eyes of the 'unsophisticated consumer.'" (citations omitted)). Our Circuit's word choice may invite an argument that our standard is less exacting than that of these Circuits. But we do, in fact, analyze FDCPA claims from a similar vantage. So we find the rationale of the Fifth Circuit in *Salinas* and Seventh Circuit in *Degroot* persuasive, and follow those decisions here because they were decided under a standard functionally identical to our own. We thus conclude p.122 that Collecto's letter to Hopkins did not violate the FDCPA by itemizing $0.00 in interest and fees on his static debt.

2. *We would affirm dismissal even if confined to least-sophisticated-debtor case law.* If, in applying the least sophisticated debtor standard, we were constrained to focus on a hypothetical debtor even less savvy than the "unsophisticated debtor," we would still affirm the District Court's dismissal of Hopkins's complaint. The least sophisticated

debtor of our case law, though gullible, does not subscribe to "bizarre or idiosyncratic interpretations of collection notices." *Wilson v. Quadramed Corp.*, 225 F.3d 350, 354-55 (3d Cir. 2000) (citation omitted). Such naïve consumers are still deemed to possess a "quotient of reasonableness" consistent with "a basic level of understanding and willingness to read with care." *Id.* (citation omitted).

To begin with, the Second Circuit has rejected claims like Hopkins's under a "least sophisticated consumer" standard similar to our own. *See, e.g., Taylor,* 886 F.3d at 214-15 (letters seeking to collect static debts that "stated their respective balances due without discussing interest or fees" were not misleading to "the least sophisticated consumer"); *Dow,* 783 F. App'x at 76-77 (dunning letter listing "interest and charges or fees accrued on the balance as separate line items, even though the amounts accrued explicitly reflect $0," would not mislead "the least sophisticated consumer" into believing "their debt is dynamic"). Based on the identity of standards, the District Court justifiably relied on the reasoning of Second Circuit decisions to dismiss Hopkins's complaint.

At all events, certain assumptions are fundamental to our court's conception of the least sophisticated debtor. For example, even the least sophisticated debtor understands that collection letters—as reflected by their fonts, formatting, content, and fields—often derive from templates and may contain information not relevant to his or her particular situation. *See, e.g., Campuzano-Burgos v. Midland Credit Mgmt., Inc.*, 550 F.3d 294, 300 (3d Cir. 2008) (noting how "frequent use of capital letters, exclamation points, and boldfaced type, as well as ... bar-codes [and] a toll-free telephone number" suggest a mass-mailed communication). Hopkins himself alleged that Collecto's letter wasn't bespoke, but a "mass-produced, computer-generated form letter[]." Compl. ¶ 32. It did not even address him by name. To see $0.00 in each of the form letter's interest and fees columns, and yet fail to understand that they are inapplicable vestiges of a template letter, is to be callow to an "unrealistic and fanciful" degree. *Campuzano-Burgos,* 550 F.3d at 299. And yet, as Hopkins tells it, this same person is also shrewdly speculative—extrapolating that he or she needs to pay off the debt post haste because interest and penalties are materially likely to accrue in the future. *But see Reyes v. Associated Credit Servs.*, No. 19-cv-1670, 2020 WL 3642441, at *2-3 (M.D. Pa. July 6, 2020) (least sophisticated consumer would not interpret line itemizations of "Interest: $0.00" and "Fees: $0.00" as debt collector's threat to charge them in future). Our FDCPA case law does not support attributing to the least sophisticated debtor simultaneous naïveté and heightened discernment.

Were we for some reason constrained to consider only the law of Circuits that employ the word "least" in their FDCPA standards, we would still affirm.[5]

p.123 III. CONCLUSION

Hopkins's complaint fails to state a claim, whether our court's "least sophisticated debtor" standard is functionally the same as the "unsophisticated debtor" standard applied by other Circuits or is instead an independent and less demanding framework. We will affirm the District Court's dismissal of Hopkins's complaint.

[1] USAM did not argue for dismissal based on its owning Hopkins's debt. As the Supreme Court held in *Henson v. Santander Consumer USA Inc.*, ___ U.S. ___, 137 S. Ct. 1718, 198 L.Ed.2d 177 (2017), an entity has to attempt to collect debts owed *to another* before it can qualify as a "debt collector" under the FDCPA. *Id.* at 1724-26.

[2] Citations preceded by "JA" are to the parties' Joint Appendix.

[3] The District Court had jurisdiction under 28 U.S.C. §§ 1331 and 1337 to adjudicate claims arising under the FDCPA. We have jurisdiction under 28 U.S.C. § 1291 to review the judgment of the District Court dismissing Hopkins's complaint.

[4] For purposes of this appeal, we assume the truth of Hopkins's allegation that the debt was static. We do not decide whether any applicable laws or contract provisions precluded application of interest and fees to his debt.

[5] The Consumer Financial Protection Bureau (CFPB) recently proposed detailed rules that seemingly condone itemizing interest and fees as Collecto did. *See* 84 Fed. Reg. 23274 (May 21, 2019); *see also* 85 Fed. Reg. 12672 (Mar. 3, 2020) (supplemental notice). Those proposed rules were issued in final form on January 19, 2021, and are slated to take effect on November 30, 2021. *See* 86 Fed. Reg. 5766 (Jan. 19, 2021). Under the pending rules, debt collectors must include in certain notices a table showing the interest, fees, payments, and credits that have been applied—even if *none* have actually been applied—to a consumer's debt since the itemization date. 84 Fed. Reg. at 23404 (proposed 12 C.F.R. § 1006.34(c)(2)(ix)); 86 Fed. Reg. at 5803-06. And "a debt collector may indicate that the value of a required field is '0,' 'none,' or may state that no interest, fees, payments, or credits have been assessed or applied to the debt." 86 Fed. Reg. at 5807, 5860; *see also* 84 Fed. Reg. at 23415 (proposed comment 34(c)(2)(ix)-1).

954 F.3d 582 (2020)

Maureen RICCIO, on behalf of herself and all others similarly situated, Appellant
v.
SENTRY CREDIT, INC.; John Does 1-25.

No. 18-1463.

United States Court of Appeals, Third Circuit.

Argued February 19, 2020.
Filed: March 30, 2020.

Riccio v. Sentry Credit, Inc., 954 F. 3d 582 (3rd Cir. 2020)

On Appeal from the United States District Court for the District of New Jersey District Court No. 3-17-cv-01773 District Judge: The Honorable Brian R. Martinotti

Joseph K. Jones [ARGUED], Benjamin J. Wolf, Jones Wolf & Kapasi, 375 Passaic Avenue, Suite 100, Fairfield, NJ 07004, Counsel for Appellant.

Jacob C. Cohn [ARGUED], Gordon Reese Scully Mansukhani, Three Logan Square, 1717 Arch Street, Suite 610, Philadelphia, PA 19103, Peter G. Siachos, Gordon Reese Scully Mansukhani, 18 Columbia Turnpike, Suite 220, Florham Park, NJ 07932, Counsel for Appellee.

Before: SMITH, Chief Judge, McKEE, AMBRO, CHAGARES, JORDAN, HARDIMAN, GREENAWAY, JR., SHWARTZ, KRAUSE, RESTREPO, BIBAS, PORTER, MATEY, and PHIPPS, Circuit Judges.

p.584 OPINION OF THE COURT

SMITH, Chief Judge.

This case presents a question of statutory interpretation: does 15 U.S.C. § 1692g(a)(3) allow debtors to orally dispute a debt's validity?

It also presents a question of stare decisis: should our en banc Court resolve a circuit conflict by overturning a three-decades-old panel decision which has been p.585 eroded by intervening Supreme Court authority?

Because we answer both questions affirmatively, we will overrule *Graziano v. Harrison*'s contrary interpretation of § 1692g(a)(3) and affirm.

I

A

The statutory interpretation question arises from language which appears in the Fair Debt Collection Practices Act, 15 U.S.C. §§ 1692-1692p (FDCPA). The FDCPA protects against abusive debt collection practices by imposing restrictions and obligations on third-party debt collectors. *See* §§ 1692b-1692j.

This case concerns one of those requirements: that debt collectors send debtors a letter notifying them of their right to dispute the debt. *See* § 1692g. Section 1692g(a) specifies five things the letter, often called a "validation notice," must include:

> (1) the amount of the debt;
>
> (2) the name of the creditor to whom the debt is owed;
>
> (3) a statement that unless the consumer, within thirty days after receipt of the notice, disputes the validity of the debt, or any portion thereof, the debt will be assumed to be valid by the debt collector;
>
> (4) a statement that if the consumer notifies the debt collector in writing within the thirty-day period that the debt, or any portion thereof, is disputed, the debt collector will obtain verification of the debt or a copy of a judgment against the consumer and a copy of such verification or judgment will be mailed to the consumer by the debt collector; and
>
> (5) a statement that, upon the consumer's written request within the thirty-day period, the debt collector will provide the consumer with the name and address of the original creditor, if different from the current creditor.

The question presented is whether the letter must require all disputes to be in writing, or whether § 1692g(a)(3) permits oral disputes.

Before answering that question, it is instructive to examine other protections the FDCPA provides when debts are disputed. For instance, § 1692g(b) demands that:

> If the consumer notifies the debt collector in writing within the thirty-day period described in subsection (a) that the debt, or any portion thereof, is disputed, or that the consumer requests the name and address of the original creditor, the debt collector shall cease collection of the debt, or any disputed portion thereof, until the debt collector obtains verification of the debt or a copy of a judgment, or the name and address of the original creditor, and a copy of such verification or judgment, or name and address of the original creditor, is mailed to the consumer by the debt collector.

In addition, debt collectors are prohibited from reporting disputed debts to credit agencies without noting the fact of a dispute. *See* § 1692e(8) (prohibiting collectors from "[c]ommunicating or threatening to communicate to any person credit information which is known or which should be known to be false, including the failure to communicate that a disputed debt is disputed"). Finally, collectors seeking payments on multiple debts owed by the same debtor cannot apply a payment to any disputed debts. *See* § 1692h ("If any consumer owes multiple debts and makes any single payment to any debt collector with respect to such debts, such debt collector p.586 may not apply such payment to any debt which is disputed by the consumer and, where applicable, shall apply such payment in accordance with the consumer's directions.").

B

We first considered the import of § 1692g(a)(3) in *Graziano v. Harrison. See* 950 F.2d 107 (3d Cir. 1991). There, a three-judge panel expressed "the view that, given the entire structure of section 1692g, subsection (a)(3) must be read to require that a dispute, to be effective, must be in writing":

> Adopting [a contrary] reading of the statute would thus create a situation in which, upon the debtor's non-written dispute, the debt collector would be without any statutory ground for assuming that the debt was valid, but nevertheless would not be required to verify the debt or to advise the debtor of the identity of the original creditor and would be permitted to continue debt collection efforts. We see no reason to attribute to Congress an intent to create so incoherent a system. We also note that there are strong reasons to prefer that a dispute of a debt collection be in writing: a writing creates a lasting record of the fact that the debt has been disputed, and thus avoids a source of potential conflicts.

Id. at 112; *accord Caprio v. Healthcare Revenue Recovery Grp., LLC,* 709 F.3d 142, 148 (3d Cir. 2013) ("In *Graziano v. Harrison,* we specifically concluded that 'subsection (a)(3), like subsections (a)(4) and (a)(5), contemplates that any dispute, to be effective, must be in writing.'" (citation omitted) (quoting *Graziano,* 950 F.2d at 112)).

C

In the matter now before us, Maureen Riccio fell behind on payments to M-Shell Consumer Oils. Sentry Credit bought the debt and sought to collect on it. So it sent Riccio a letter containing the following notification:

Compl. Ex. A.

p.587 Riccio sued,[1] alleging the letter violated § 1692g(a)(3) by providing a debtor with multiple options for contacting Sentry Credit rather than explicitly requiring any dispute be in writing. App. 53-54. Sentry Credit agreed that it had to require Riccio to dispute the debt in writing under *Graziano,* but the company viewed its letter as complying with that requirement. It therefore moved for judgment on the pleadings, and the District Court granted the motion. *See Riccio v. Sentry Credit, Inc.,* 2018 WL 638748, at *4-6 (D.N.J. Jan. 31, 2018).

Riccio timely appealed. The District Court exercised jurisdiction under 28 U.S.C. § 1331. We have jurisdiction under 28 U.S.C. § 1291 and review statutory interpretation questions de novo. *See United States v. Hodge,* 948 F.3d 160, 162 (3d Cir. 2020).

II

As noted, a panel of this Court previously concluded § 1692g(a)(3) requires that "any dispute, to be effective, must be in writing." *Graziano,* 950 F.2d at 112. Yet reading the statutory text with fresh eyes—and more importantly, with the past three decades of Supreme Court statutory-interpretation caselaw—we think § 1692g(a)(3) permits oral disputes.

A

We begin by looking at § 1692g(a)(3) itself. That provision refers only to "disputes," without specifying oral or written. Used generally, the word fairly encompasses both forms of communication. *See, e.g., Dispute,* Oxford English Dictionary (2d ed. 1989) ("To discuss, debate, or argue (a question); ... To argue against, contest, controvert; To call in question or contest the validity or accuracy of a statement, etc., or the existence of a thing.").

We must read § 1692g as a whole. Subsection (a)(3) merely calls for "the consumer" to "dispute[] the validity of the debt" in order to rebut the statutory presumption of validity. But (a)(4) requires "the consumer [to] notif[y] the debt collector *in writing*" before forcing the collector to mail documentation verifying the debt. (emphasis added). And (a)(5) similarly demands that the consumer make a "*written* request within the thirty-day period" to compel the collector to "provide the consumer with the name and address of the original creditor, if different from the current creditor." (emphasis added). Subsection (b) then echoes (a)(4) and (5), obliging collectors to "cease collection ... until ... obtain[ing] verification" if the debtor "notifie[d] the debt collector" of a dispute or requested the creditor's identity "*in writing*." (emphasis added). That intra-section variation strongly signals that § 1692g permits oral disputes. "We refrain from concluding here that the differing language in the [various] subsections has the same meaning in each." *Russello v. United States,* 464 U.S. 16, 23, 104 S.Ct. 296, 78 L.Ed.2d 17 (1983).

We must also consider the entirety of the FDCPA. Like § 1692g(a)(3)—but unlike (a)(4), (a)(5), and (b)—§§ 1692e(8) and 1692h also discuss "dispute[s]" without specifying a method of communication. That inter-section variation amplifies the variation within § 1692g and, in our view, refutes Riccio's suggestion that Congress inadvertently omitted a writing requirement from § 1692g(a)(3). "[W]here Congress includes particular language in one section of a statute but omits it in another section of the same Act, it is generally p.588 presumed that Congress acts intentionally and purposely in the disparate inclusion or exclusion." *Russello,* 464 U.S. at 23, 104 S.Ct. 296 (alteration in original) (quoting *United States v. Wong Kim Bo,* 472 F.2d 720, 722 (5th Cir. 1972)).

Finally, we consider one of the most venerable of our interpretive canons: the rule against surplusage. *See Gustafson v. Alloyd Co.,* 513 U.S. 561, 574, 115 S.Ct. 1061, 131 L.Ed.2d 1 (1995) ("[T]he Court will avoid a reading which renders some words altogether redundant."); *see also Marbury v. Madison,* 5 U.S. (1 Cranch) 137, 174, 2 L.Ed. 60 (1803) (using this canon to interpret U.S. Const. art. III, § 2, cl. 2). Collectively, the text of § 1692g(a)(3), (a)(4), and (b) signifies that if a debtor makes the effort to dispute the debt in writing, the collector must immediately stop collecting, verify the debt, and respond. Yet if the debtor merely disputes the debt orally, the collector can continue attempts to collect the debt. It will, though, eventually have to prove the debt's validity.

Injecting a writing requirement into (a)(3) effectively strikes that provision from the statute. It is a truism that if a debt isn't presumed valid, the debt collector must eventually verify it. Subsection (a)(3) merely restates that point: if the debtor disputes the debt, the collector must verify it at some point down the road. But (a)(4) and (b) demand that if the debtor disputes the debt in writing, the collector must prove its validity immediately. So if every dispute must be conveyed in writing, collectors must prove every debt immediately —no collector can ever count on its future ability to prove a debt. Put differently, inserting a writing requirement into (a)(3) means that every dispute triggers (a)(4) and (b). That simply can't be right. If every dispute triggers (a)(4) and (b), then (a)(3) has no independent effect.

***

The upshot: § 1692g(a)(3)'s plain meaning permits a debtor to dispute a debt orally. And when a "'statute's language is plain, the sole function of the courts'—at least where the disposition required by the text is not absurd—'is to enforce it according to its terms.'" *Hartford Underwriters Ins. Co. v. Union Planters Bank, N.A.*, 530 U.S. 1, 6, 120 S.Ct. 1942, 147 L.Ed.2d 1 (2000) (quoting *United States v. Ron Pair Enters.*, 489 U.S. 235, 241, 109 S.Ct. 1026, 103 L.Ed.2d 290 (1989)).

Riccio tries using this absurd-result exception to shoehorn a writing requirement into § 1692g(a)(3).[2] But that dog won't hunt. "An absurd interpretation is one that 'defies rationality or renders the statute nonsensical and superfluous.'" *Encompass Ins. Co. v. Stone Mansion Rest. Inc.*, 902 F.3d 147, 152 (3d Cir. 2018) (quoting *United States v. Moreno,* 727 F.3d 255, 259 (3d Cir. 2013)). As long as Congress could have any conceivable justification for a result—even if the result carries negative consequences—that result cannot be absurd. *See United States v. Fontaine,* 697 F.3d 221, 228 (3d Cir. 2012) ("[S]tandard interpretive doctrine ... defines an 'absurd result' as an outcome so p.589 contrary to perceived social values that Congress could not have 'intended' it." (quoting John F. Manning, *The Absurdity Doctrine,* 116 Harv. L. Rev. 2387, 2390 (2003))); *Hanif v. Attorney Gen.*, 694 F.3d 479, 487 (3d Cir. 2012); *see also In re Visteon Corp.*, 612 F.3d 210, 234 (3d Cir. 2010) ("Virtually all laws would be absurd if judged by whether they accomplish a perfect solution to an underlying legislative concern.").

Reading § 1692g(a)(3) to permit oral disputes falls far short of the high bar this Court has set. In fact, allowing oral disputes makes sense: it provides debtors multiple methods to dispute debts while assigning various rights depending on the method.[3] An oral dispute can still defeat the presumption of validity, still prevent collectors from reporting the debt without noting the dispute, and still preclude debt collectors holding multiple debts of the same debtor from applying a payment to the disputed debt. It just doesn't force the debt collector to immediately stop, verify, and respond in the way the FDCPA requires if a dispute is in writing. That's hardly absurd. If nothing else, it is easier to prove written disputes and therefore easier to enforce the additional protections that attach.[4]

Lest any doubt remains, *Lamie v. United States Trustee* should settle the matter. There, the Supreme Court refused to "read an absent word into [a] statute" despite "an apparent legislative drafting error" that rendered the statute "awkward, and even ungrammatical." 540 U.S. 526, 530-38, 124 S.Ct. 1023, 157 L.Ed.2d 1024 (2004). "With a plain, nonabsurd meaning in view, we need not proceed in this way," the Court said, noting their "longstanding" "unwillingness to soften the import of Congress' chosen words even if we believe the words lead to a harsh outcome." *Id.* at 538, 124 S.Ct. 1023.

So too here. Even if we thought Congress inadvertently omitted a writing requirement from § 1692g(a)(3), and even if we thought permitting oral disputes precipitated an incoherent system, we must still recognize the validity of oral disputes based on § 1692g's plain meaning. "If Congress enacted into law something different from what it intended, then it should amend the statute.... 'It is beyond our province to rescue Congress from its drafting errors, and to provide for what we might think ... is the preferred result.'" *Id.* at 542, 124 S.Ct. 1023 (second omission in original) (quoting *United States v. Granderson,* 511 U.S. 39, 68, 114 S.Ct. 1259, 127 L.Ed.2d 611 (1994) (Kennedy, J., concurring in the judgment)).

B

Other courts have reached the same conclusion. The Second, Fourth, and Ninth Circuits reject a writing requirement, openly splitting with *Graziano. See Clark v. Absolute Collection Serv., Inc.,* 741 F.3d 487, 490-91 (4th Cir. 2014) (per curiam); p.590 *Hooks v. Forman, Holt, Eliades & Ravin, LLC,* 717 F.3d 282, 285-86 (2d Cir. 2013); *Camacho v. Bridgeport Fin. Inc.,* 430 F.3d 1078, 1080-81 (9th Cir. 2005). And without noting the split, the First, Fifth, Sixth, and Seventh Circuits have taken the same position. *See Macy v. GC Servs. Ltd.,* 897 F.3d 747, 757-58 (6th Cir. 2018); *Evans v. Portfolio Recovery Assocs., LLC,* 889 F.3d 337, 347 n.6 (7th Cir. 2018); *Sayles v. Advanced Recovery Sys., Inc.,* 865 F.3d 246, 249-50 (5th Cir. 2017); *Brady v. Credit Recovery Co.,* 160 F.3d 64, 66-67 (1st Cir. 1998).

C

In sum, we no longer think § 1692g(a)(3) requires written disputes. Simply put, "Congress did not write the statute that way." *United States v. Naftalin,* 441 U.S. 768, 773, 99 S.Ct. 2077, 60 L.Ed.2d 624 (1979). Subsections (a)(4), (a)(5), and (b) command a written dispute; (a)(3) does not. "We would not presume to ascribe this difference to a simple mistake in draftsmanship." *Russello,* 464 U.S. at 23, 104 S.Ct. 296.

III

The foregoing details our reasoning, and our disagreement with *Graziano.* Yet we must consider whether stare decisis justifies our upholding that precedent. "*Stare decisis*—in English, the idea that today's Court should stand by yesterday's decisions—is 'a foundation stone of the rule of law.'" *Kimble v. Marvel Entm't, LLC,* 576 U.S. 446, 135 S. Ct. 2401, 2409, 192 L.Ed.2d 463 (2015) (quoting *Michigan v. Bay Mills Indian Cmty.,* 572 U.S. 782, 798, 134 S.Ct. 2024, 188 L.Ed.2d 1071 (2014)). To be sure, stare decisis "is not an inexorable command," but it is critical to "promote[] the evenhanded, predictable, and consistent development of legal principles, foster[] reliance on judicial decisions, and contribute[] to the actual and perceived integrity of the judicial process." *Payne v. Tennessee,* 501 U.S. 808, 827, 111 S.Ct. 2597, 115 L.Ed.2d 720 (1991). In fact, sometimes it "means sticking to some wrong decisions." *Kimble,* 135 S. Ct. at 2409. After all, "it is usually 'more important that the applicable rule of law be settled than that it be settled right.'" *Id.* (quoting *Burnet v. Coronado Oil*

& Gas Co., 285 U.S. 393, 406, 52 S.Ct. 443, 76 L.Ed. 815 (1932) (Brandeis, J., dissenting)). That's especially true in statutory interpretation cases like this one, because Congress can correct unintended interpretations. *See id.* at 2409-10.

Before overruling its own precedent, the Supreme Court looks for "'special justification[s]' [] over and above the belief 'that the precedent was wrongly decided.'" *Kimble*, 135 S. Ct. at 2409 (quoting *Halliburton Co. v. Erica P. John Fund, Inc.*, 573 U.S. 258, 266, 134 S.Ct. 2398, 189 L.Ed.2d 339 (2014)). Those include "the quality of [the prior case]'s reasoning, the workability of the rule it established, its consistency with other related decisions, developments since the decision was handed down, and reliance on the decision." *Janus v. AFSCME*, ___ U.S. ___, 138 S. Ct. 2448, 2478-79, 201 L.Ed.2d 924 (2018). Though we, as a lower court, "play a different role in the federal system," we join virtually every other Circuit in weighing those same considerations before overturning our own caselaw. *Critical Mass Energy Project v. NRC*, 975 F.2d 871, 876 (D.C. Cir. 1992) (en banc); *see also United States v. Sykes*, 598 F.3d 334, 338 (7th Cir. 2010), *aff'd*, 564 U.S. 1, 131 S.Ct. 2267, 180 L.Ed.2d 60 (2011), *overruled on other grounds by Johnson v. United States*, ___ U.S. ___, 135 S. Ct. 2551, 192 L.Ed.2d 569 (2015); *Shi Liang Lin v. U.S. Dep't of Justice*, 494 F.3d 296, 310 (2d Cir. 2007) (en banc); *United States v. Heredia*, 483 F.3d 913, 918-19 (9th Cir. 2007) (en p.591
banc); *Glazner v. Glazner*, 347 F.3d 1212, 1216 (11th Cir. 2003) (en banc); *Festo Corp. v. Shoketsu Kinzoku Kogyo Kabushiki Co.*, 234 F.3d 558, 575 (Fed. Cir. 2000) (en banc), *vacated on other grounds*, 535 U.S. 722, 122 S.Ct. 1831, 152 L.Ed.2d 944 (2002); *Stewart v. Dutra Constr. Co.*, 230 F.3d 461, 467 (1st Cir. 2000), *rev'd on other grounds*, 543 U.S. 481, 125 S.Ct. 1118, 160 L.Ed.2d 932 (2005); *Coats v. Penrod Drilling Corp.*, 61 F.3d 1113, 1137-38 (5th Cir. 1995) (en banc); *McKinney v. Pate*, 20 F.3d 1550, 1565 n.21 (11th Cir. 1994) (en banc).

We also consider three factors unique to courts of appeals. *First*, prior en banc decisions carry more stare decisis weight than prior panel decisions. *See United States v. Games-Perez*, 695 F.3d 1104, 1124 (10th Cir. 2012) (Gorsuch, J., dissental) ("[I]t is surely uncontroversial to suggest that the point of the *en banc* process, the very reason for its existence, is to correct grave errors in panel precedents when they become apparent, even if the panel precedents in question happen to be old or involve questions of statutory or regulatory interpretation."); *Igartua v. United States*, 654 F.3d 99, 100 (1st Cir. 2011) (statement of Lynch, C.J., and Boudin & Howard, JJ.) (declining "to reopen settled issues which have already been given en banc treatment"); *McKinney*, 20 F.3d at 1565 n.21 ("It must be recalled that this is the first time this court sitting en banc has addressed this issue; thus, the implications of *stare decisis* are less weighty than if we were overturning a precedent established by the court en banc."). *See generally* Letter from Justice Sandra Day O'Connor to Ret. Justice Byron R. White (June 23, 1998), *published in Review of the Report by the Commission on Structural Alternatives for the Federal Courts of Appeals Regarding the Ninth Circuit and the Ninth Circuit Reorganization Act: Hearing on S. 253 Before the Subcomm. on Admin. Oversight & the Courts of the S. Comm. on the Judiciary*, 106th Cong. 71 (1999) [hereinafter *Ninth Circuit Review*] ("It is important to the federal system as a whole that the Courts of Appeals utilize en banc review to correct panel errors within the circuit that are likely to otherwise come before the Supreme Court."); Letter from Justice Antonin Scalia to Ret. Justice Byron R. White (Aug. 21, 1998), *published in Ninth Circuit Review* 72 ("[T]he function of en banc hearings ... is not only to eliminate intra-circuit conflicts, but also to correct and deter panel opinions that are pretty clearly wrong.... The disproportionate segment of [the Supreme Court's] discretionary docket that is consistently devoted to reviewing [a court of appeals's] judgments, and to reversing them by lop-sided margins, suggests that this error-reduction function is not being performed effectively.").

Second, "[w]hile we generally 'decide cases before us based on our own examination of the issue, not on the views of other jurisdictions,' the[] more recent [contrary] decisions [from other circuits] suggest that we should 'consider whether the reasoning applied by our colleagues elsewhere is persuasive.'" *Bastardo-Vale v. Attorney Gen.,* 934 F.3d 255, 267 (3d Cir. 2019) (en banc) (quoting *In re Grossman's Inc.,* 607 F.3d 114, 121 (3d Cir. 2010) (en banc)); *see also United States v. Corner,* 598 F.3d 411, 414 (7th Cir. 2010) (en banc) ("Although ... it is rarely appropriate to overrule circuit precedent just to move from one side of a [circuit] conflict to another, reconsideration is more appropriate when [we] can eliminate the conflict by overruling a decision that lacks support elsewhere."); *cf. Wagner v. PennWest Farm Credit, ACA,* 109 F.3d 909, 912 (3d Cir. 1997) ("In light of such an array of [unanimous] precedent [from other courts of appeals], we would p.592 require a compelling basis to hold otherwise before effecting a circuit split."); *Butler Cty. Mem'l Hosp. v. Heckler,* 780 F.2d 352, 357 (3d Cir. 1985) ("[T]his Court should be reluctant to contradict the unanimous position of other circuits.").

Third, "on rare occasions a circuit precedent, though not directly overruled or superseded, nonetheless might crumble" if "case law postdating 'the original decision, although not directly controlling, nevertheless offers a sound reason for believing that the former panel, in light of fresh developments, would change its collective mind.'" *Stewart,* 230 F.3d at 467 (quoting *Williams v. Ashland Eng'g Co.,* 45 F.3d 588, 592 (1st Cir. 1995)).

All three factors support overturning *Graziano.* Given *Lamie* and other recent Supreme Court decisions, we believe the panel that decided *Graziano* would decide it differently today. And what's more, *Graziano* was only a panel decision; our en banc Court has never expressed a view on the issue presented. By expressing our view today, we put an end to a circuit split and restore national uniformity to the meaning of § 1692g.

Traditional stare decisis considerations point in the same direction. For starters, district courts applying *Graziano* have split over whether identical language violates its rule. *See Cadillo v. Stoneleigh Recovery Assocs., LLC,* No. 17-7472, 2019 WL 1091391, at *4 (D.N.J. Mar. 8, 2019) (collecting cases), *appeal docketed,* 19-2811 (3d Cir. Aug. 8, 2019).

Additionally, "the growth of judicial doctrine" has undermined *Graziano*'s reasoning. *Patterson v. McLean Credit Union,* 491 U.S. 164, 173, 109 S.Ct. 2363, 105 L.Ed.2d 132 (1989), *superseded on other grounds by statute,* Civil Rights Act of 1991, Pub. L. No. 102-166, 105 Stat. 1071, *as recognized in Jones v. R.R. Donnelley & Sons Co.,* 541 U.S. 369, 383, 124 S.Ct. 1836, 158 L.Ed.2d 645 (2004). Recall how *Graziano* framed its own conclusion: "subsection (a)(3) ... *contemplates* that any dispute, to be effective, must be in writing." 950 F.2d at 112 (emphasis added). That is a curious verb choice, since it suggests the panel thought § 1692g(a)(3) meant something other than what it says. *See, e.g., Contemplate,* Oxford English Dictionary (2d ed. 1989) ("To have in view, look for, expect, take into account as a contingency to be provided for. To have in view as a purpose; to intend, purpose.").

But that is not how we read statutes today. In the years before *Graziano,* the Supreme Court engaged in statutory interpretation with statements like, *"[a]bsent a clearly expressed legislative intention to the contrary,* th[e statutory] language must ordinarily be regarded as conclusive." *Consumer Prod. Safety Comm'n v. GTE Sylvania, Inc.,* 447 U.S. 102, 108, 100 S.Ct. 2051, 64 L.Ed.2d 766 (1980) (emphasis added). In the years since *Graziano,* the Court has instructed us "that [the] legislature says ... what it means and means ... what it says." *Henson v. Santander Consumer USA Inc.,* ___ U.S. ___, 137 S. Ct. 1718, 1725, 198 L.Ed.2d 177 (2017) (alteration and omissions in original) (quoting *Dodd v. United States,* 545 U.S. 353, 357, 125 S.Ct. 2478, 162 L.Ed.2d 343 (2005)). In other words, "[a]s Justice Kagan recently stated, 'we're all textualists now.'" Brett M. Kavanaugh, *Fixing Statutory Interpretation,* 129 Harv. L. Rev. 2118, 2118 (2016) (reviewing Robert A. Katzmann, *Judging Statutes* (2014)) (quoting Justice Elena Kagan, The Scalia Lecture: A Dialogue with Justice Kagan on the Reading of Statutes at 8:28 (Nov. 17, 2015), http://perma.cc/BCF-FEFR). We decline to breathe new life into *Graziano*'s atextual interpretation of § 1692g(a)(3), an interpretation that has already made us the "legal last-man-standing" among the p.593 courts of appeals. *Kimble,* 135 S. Ct. at 2411.

Moreover, any legitimate reliance interests seem minimal. Overturning *Graziano* merely requires debt collectors to prospectively tweak their collection notice template. If anything, since debt collectors may operate nationwide, overturning *Graziano* should make their job easier by allowing them to use the same form no matter where a debtor resides. By contrast, resuscitating *Graziano* would mean collectors must use one notice in Pennsylvania, New Jersey, Delaware, and the Virgin Islands, but another everywhere else. And overturning *Graziano* helps debtors too, since the case's atextual rule requires more than the statutory text mandates for them to dispute a debt's validity. *See supra* note 3 and accompanying text.

***

By today's standards, *Graziano*'s "reasoning was clearly wrong"; changes in the way we interpret statutes "have unmoored the case from its doctrinal anchors." *Morrow v. Balaski,* 719 F.3d 160, 180 (3d Cir. 2013) (Smith, J., concurring). Both traditional stare decisis principles and considerations unique to courts of appeals convince us that *Graziano* should be, and now is, overruled.

IV

Perhaps anticipating the result we announce today, Riccio asks us to curb our holding's retroactive application so that *Graziano* still governs her claim. Her only support for that argument is New Jersey precedent allowing state-court judges to limit a holding's retroactive application "when 'considerations of fairness and justice, related to reasonable surprise and prejudice to those affected' counsel [them] to do so." *Malinowski v. Jacobs,* 189 N.J. 345, 915 A.2d 513, 517 (2007) (quoting *N.J. Election Law Enf't Comm'n v. Citizens to Make Mayor-Council Gov't Work,* 107 N.J. 380, 526 A.2d 1069, 1073 (1987)).

Yet federal courts follow a different rule. Our holding today "is the controlling interpretation of federal law and must be given full retroactive effect in all cases still open on direct review and as to all events, regardless of whether such events predate or postdate our announcement of the rule." *Harper v. Va. Dep't of Taxation,* 509 U.S. 86, 97, 113 S.Ct. 2510, 125 L.Ed.2d 74 (1993). "[W]e can scarcely permit 'the substantive law [to] shift and spring' according to 'the particular equities of [individual parties'] claims' of actual reliance on an old rule and of harm from a retroactive application of the new rule." *Id.* (alterations in original) (quoting *James B. Beam Distilling Co. v. Georgia,* 501 U.S. 529, 543, 111 S.Ct. 2439, 115 L.Ed.2d 481 (1991) (opinion of Souter, J.)). We will, therefore, apply to this case our new rule that debt collectors need not require debtors to dispute the validity of their debt in writing.[5]

V

Our new rule dooms Riccio's claim. As we and several other Circuits have held, p.594 debt collection notices must intelligibly convey the § 1692g(a) requirements. *See Wilson v. Quadramed Corp.,* 225 F.3d 350, 354-55 (3d Cir. 2000) (collecting cases). Put another way, a hypothetical "least sophisticated debtor" should be able to read the notice and reasonably discern her rights. *Id.; cf. United States v. Nat'l Fin. Servs., Inc.,* 98 F.3d 131, 136 (4th Cir. 1996) (noting the least sophisticated debtor standard "also prevents liability for bizarre or idiosyncratic interpretations of collection notices by preserving a quotient of reasonableness and presuming a basic level of understanding and willingness to read with care").[6]

Sentry Credit's collection notice easily clears that bar. Its plainspoken language reproduces § 1692g(a)(3)-(5) nearly word-for-word, alerting the least sophisticated debtor of her rights as effectively as does the statute itself. A collection notice can never mislead the least sophisticated debtor by relying on the language Congress chose. And since that's all this notice did, Sentry Credit did not violate § 1692g.

VI

In short, we conclude that debt collection notices sent under § 1692g need not require that disputes be expressed in writing. In doing so, we overrule *Graziano*'s contrary holding. Because Sentry Credit's notice perfectly tracked § 1692g's text, we will affirm the judgment of the District Court.

[1] The FDCPA authorizes private actions and imposes strict liability for violations, with statutory damages up to $1000 and potential fee-shifting. *See* § 1692k.

[2] Riccio also uses *United States v. American Trucking Associations,* 310 U.S. 534, 543, 60 S.Ct. 1059, 84 L.Ed. 1345 (1940), to argue she need not show that permitting oral disputes would be absurd, just that it would be unreasonable. Simply put, that misrepresents the current state of the law. To depart from a statute's plain meaning today, the text must dictate a result so unreasonable that it amounts to an absurdity. *See Tenn. Valley Auth. v. Hill,* 437 U.S. 153, 187 n.33, 98 S.Ct. 2279, 57 L.Ed.2d 117 (1978); *see also MORI Assocs., Inc. v. United States,* 102 Fed. Cl. 503, 537-39 (2011) (detailing *American Trucking Associations*'s practical abrogation).

[3] On this point, it bears noting that purposively reading the FDCPA underscores our textual conclusion. At bottom, expanding the ways a debtor can dispute a debt's validity makes it easier for debtors to invoke its protections. So demanding written disputes not only flouts the FDCPA's text—it also hoodwinks the Act's purpose.

[4] Relatedly, at oral argument, Riccio's counsel argued that permitting oral disputes would spawn conundrums over the "magic words" that distinguish a formal dispute from informal grumbling. Oral Argument at 3:16, 4:57 (Feb. 19, 2020), https://www2.ca3.uscourts.gov/oralargument/audio/18-1463Ricciov.%20SentryCreditInc.mp3; *see also id.* at 6:05, 50:31. We think district courts are more than capable of that linedrawing. In fact, they already do it when reviewing a debtor's written communication.

[5] We do not suggest that debt collectors who sent *Graziano*-compliant letters before today will be on the hook for failing to foresee our change in the law. Just as collectors who act "in good faith in conformity with any [agency] advisory opinion" cannot be liable if that "opinion is amended, rescinded, or" judicially invalidated, § 1692k(e), collectors should not be penalized for good-faith compliance with then-governing caselaw. To that end, we note district courts can withhold damages for unintentional errors, § 1692k(b), award no damages for trivial violations, § 1692k(a)(1), and even award attorney's fees to the collector if the debtor's suit "was brought in bad faith and for the purpose of harassment," § 1692k(a)(3). *See generally Jerman v. Carlisle, McNellie, Rini, Kramer & Ulrich LPA,* 559 U.S. 573, 597-99, 130 S.Ct. 1605, 176 L.Ed.2d 519 (2010). We have confidence in district courts to exercise that discretion appropriately.

[6] Although Judge Matey reaches the same conclusion as the Court, it is his view that the atextual "least sophisticated debtor" test announced in *Graziano* warrants reexamination. *See Jensen v. Pressler & Pressler,* 791 F.3d 413, 418 (3d Cir. 2015) (noting that the "least sophisticated debtor" requirement "appears nowhere in the text of the statute"). In his view, in an appropriate case, we should revisit whether that standard comports with the ordinary meaning of the FDCPA.

934 F.3d 275 (2019)

Donna DINAPLES, on behalf of herself and all others similarly situated
v.
MRS BPO, LLC; John Does 1-25 MRS BPO, LLC, Appellant.

No. 18-2972.

United States Court of Appeals, Third Circuit.

Argued: June 27, 2019.
Filed August 12, 2019.

DiNaples v. MRS BPO, LLC, 934 F. 3d 275 (3rd Cir. 2019)

On Appeal from the United States District Court for the Western District of Pennsylvania, (D.C. No. 2-15-cv-01435), Chief District Judge: Honorable Mark R. Hornak.

Michael D. Alltmont [ARGUED], Bryan C. Shartle, Sessions Fishman Nathan & Israel, 3850 North Causeway Boulevard, Lakeway Two, Suite 200, Metairie, LA 70002, Andrew J. Blady, Sessions Fishman Nathan & Israel, 3682 Green Ridge Road, Furlong, PA 18925, Ross Enders, Law Offices of J. Scott Watson, 24 Regency Plaza, Glen Mills, PA 19342, Counsel for Appellant MRS BPO, LLC.

Ari H. Marcus, Yitzchak Zelman [ARGUED], Marcus & Zelman, 701 Cookman Avenue, Suite 300, Asbury Park, NJ 07712, Mark G. Moynihan, Suite 1-N, 112 Washington Place, Pittsburgh, PA 15219, Counsel for Appellee Donna DiNaples.

Before: SMITH, Chief Judge, and CHAGARES and GREENAWAY, JR., Circuit Judges.

p.277 OPINION OF THE COURT

CHAGARES, Circuit Judge.

Five years ago, in Douglass v. Convergent Outsourcing, 765 F.3d 299 (3d Cir. 2014), we held that a debt collector violated p.278 the Fair Debt Collection Practices Act ("FDCPA"), 15 U.S.C. §§ 1692-1692p, when it sent a collection letter in an envelope displaying the debtor's internal account number with the collection agency. We are now asked to decide whether the same is true when the envelope does not, on its face, show the account number but does display an unencrypted "quick response," or "QR," code that reveals the number when scanned. The District Court held that such conduct violates the FDCPA. We agree and will affirm.

I.

The facts underlying this appeal are undisputed. Donna DiNaples had a credit card through Chase Bank. Eventually, she fell behind on her payments, so Chase assigned her account to a debt collection agency called MRS BPO, LLC ("MRS"). MRS sent DiNaples a collection letter as a pressure-sealed envelope that had a QR code printed on its face. QR codes, including the one here, can be scanned by a reader downloadable as an application (better known as an "app") on a smartphone. And this QR code, when scanned with a QR-code reader, revealed the following sequence: "LU4.###1813.3683994."[1] The string "LU4.###1813" was the internal reference number associated with DiNaples's account at MRS.

DiNaples filed a class action lawsuit against MRS, alleging that the collection agency, by printing the QR code on the envelope, had violated the FDCPA, which prohibits debt collectors from "[u]sing any language or symbol, other than the debt collector's address, on any envelope when communicating with a consumer by use of the mails." 15 U.S.C. § 1692f(8). Each side eventually filed a motion for summary judgment.

The District Court granted DiNaples's motion on liability, concluding that MRS violated the FDCPA. The District Court explained that this conclusion was required by our decision in Douglass, in which we held that a debt collector violates § 1692f(8) by placing on an envelope the consumer's account number with the debt collector. 765 F.3d at 303, 306. For the District Court, there was no meaningful difference between displaying the account number itself and displaying a QR code — scannable "by any teenager with a smartphone app" — with the number embedded. Dinaples v. MRS BPO, LLC, No. 2:15-cv-01435-MAP, 2017 WL 5593471, at *2 (W.D. Pa. Nov. 21, 2017). The District Court further rejected MRS's contention that DiNaples had not "suffered a concrete injury," explaining that DiNaples was injured by "the disclosure of confidential information." Id. And the District Court rejected MRS's argument that it was protected by the FDCPA's "bona fide error defense." Id. at *3. The District Court also certified the proposed class.

The parties thereafter stipulated that, to the extent that there was liability, the damages would be $11,000. The District Court granted judgment for DiNaples and the class for that amount, and this timely appeal followed.

II.

We consider first a jurisdictional issue — DiNaples's standing to sue.[2] The District Court, while it did determine that DiNaples had suffered a concrete injury, p.279 never explicitly addressed standing, seemingly assuming it was a non-issue. We, though, must assure ourselves of DiNaples's standing. Anthony v. Council, 316 F.3d 412, 416 (3d Cir. 2003).

Article III of the Constitution limits the federal courts to adjudication of "Cases" and "Controversies." U.S. Const. art. III, § 2, cl. 1. "Courts enforce the case-or-controversy requirement" by requiring the plaintiff to have standing to sue. Toll Bros., Inc. v. Twp. of Readington, 555 F.3d 131, 137 (3d Cir. 2009). Standing has three elements: "[t]he plaintiff must have (1) suffered an injury in fact, (2) that is fairly traceable to the challenged conduct of the defendant, and (3) that is likely to be redressed by a favorable judicial decision." Spokeo, Inc. v. Robins, ___ U.S. ___, 136 S. Ct. 1540, 1547, 194 L.Ed.2d 635 (2016). An "injury in fact" is one that is "concrete and particularized." Id. at 1548 (quoting Lujan v. Defenders of Wildlife, 504 U.S. 555, 560, 112 S.Ct. 2130, 119 L.Ed.2d 351 (1992)). To be concrete, the injury "must actually exist." Id. It must be "real," not "abstract." Id.

The question here is whether DiNaples suffered a concrete injury when her debt collector sent her a letter in an envelope displaying a QR code that, when scanned, revealed her account number with the debt collection agency. We conclude that she did.

Because DiNaples's injury was intangible, we begin our analysis with the Supreme Court's decision in Spokeo. There, the Court reaffirmed that, while tangible injuries are typically easier to identify, "intangible injuries can nevertheless be concrete." 136 S. Ct. at 1549. The Court in Spokeo offered guidance for determining the concreteness of an intangible injury. The Court explained that "both history and the judgment of Congress play important roles." Id. As to history, courts should "consider whether an alleged intangible harm has a close relationship to a harm that has traditionally been regarded as providing a basis for a lawsuit in English or American courts." Id. Congress's "judgment is also instructive and important," because Congress "is well positioned to identify intangible harms that meet minimum Article III requirements." Id. Granted, just because a plaintiff asserts a congressionally created cause of action does not necessarily mean that the plaintiff has suffered a concrete injury. Id. A "bare procedural violation" will not meet the concreteness requirement. Id. But "the violation of a procedural right granted by statute can be sufficient in some circumstances to constitute injury in fact," and "a plaintiff in such a case need not allege any additional harm beyond the one Congress has identified." Id.

We have already applied the principles set forth in Spokeo to a similar situation. In St. Pierre v. Retrieval-Masters Creditors Bureau, 898 F.3d 351 (3d Cir. 2018), we held that a debtor suffered a concrete injury when a debt collector, in violation of the FDCPA, sent him a collection letter in an envelope displaying his account number with the debt collector. Id. at 355, 358. We explained that our earlier decision in Douglass — though not a decision directly addressing standing — resolved the matter. Id. at 357-58. In Douglass, we had held that displaying a consumer's account number on an envelope was not "benign," explaining that such conduct "implicates a core concern animating the FDCPA—the invasion of privacy." 765 F.3d at 303. That number, we emphasized in Douglass, was "a core piece of information" relating to the debtor's status as such, and, if "[d]isclosed to the public, it could be used to expose her financial predicament." Id. Thus, in St. Pierre, we concluded that the harm inflicted by exposing the debtor's p.280 account number was "a legally cognizable injury." 898 F.3d at 358. We explained that, because the harm involves the invasion of privacy, it "is closely related to harm that has traditionally been regarded as providing a basis for a lawsuit in English and American courts." Id. (citing Douglass, 765 F.3d at 303, and Spokeo, 136 S. Ct. at 1549). And therefore, per Spokeo, the plaintiff in St. Pierre had standing.

St. Pierre, to be sure, did not involve the precise situation we have here — an account number displayed not on the face of the envelope but embedded in a QR code. And in St. Pierre we explicitly declined to address that scenario. See id. at 357 n.6 ("[W]e need not reach the question whether exposure of the 'quick response' code on the envelope, without more, would be sufficient to confer standing under the FDCPA because exposure of one's account number itself suffices."). We similarly declined to consider our QR-code issue in Douglass. See 765 F.3d at 301 n.4

("Douglass no longer presses her argument that Convergent violated the FDCPA by including the QR Code on the envelope.... We therefore do not decide that issue.").

Nonetheless, we conclude that the reasoning of those two cases inevitably dictates that DiNaples has suffered a concrete injury. Disclosure of the debtor's account number through a QR code, which anyone could easily scan and read, still "implicates core privacy concerns." Id. at 304. The debt collector has "displayed core information relating to the debt collection" that is "susceptible to privacy intrusions." Id. at 305. Whether disclosed directly on the envelope or less directly through a QR code, the protected information has been made accessible to the public. And as we concluded in St. Pierre, such an invasion of privacy "is closely related to harm that has traditionally been regarded as providing a basis for a lawsuit in English and American courts." 898 F.3d at 357-58. It thus follows from our Douglass and St. Pierre decisions that DiNaples has suffered a sufficiently concrete harm.

MRS is incorrect to suggest that "to establish Article III standing, [DiNaples] would have to show that someone actually intercepted her mail, scanned the barcode, read the unlabeled string of numbers and determined the contents related to debt collection — or it was imminent someone might do so." MRS Br. 16 (emphases omitted). The teaching of Douglass and St. Pierre is that the disclosure of an account number is itself the harm — it "implicates core privacy concerns," Douglass, 765 F.3d at 304, and therefore is sufficiently concrete under Spokeo to establish an injury-in-fact, St. Pierre, 898 F.3d at 357-58. In other words, because the disclosure is the concrete harm here, DiNaples "need not allege any additional harm beyond the one Congress has identified." Spokeo, 136 S. Ct. at 1549. Her evidence that she received an envelope with a QR code containing private information was enough to establish a concrete injury.[3]

We hold that DiNaples has standing to sue.

III.

Satisfied that DiNaples has standing, we now consider whether the District Court correctly determined that she had a successful claim under the FDCPA. Our review p.281 is de novo. See Tundo v. Cty. of Passaic, 923 F.3d 283, 286 (3d Cir. 2019).

A.

The FDCPA, specifically 15 U.S.C. § 1692f(8), prohibits debt collectors from:

> [u]sing any language or symbol, other than the debt collector's address, on any envelope when communicating with a consumer by use of the mails or by telegram, except that a debt collector may use his business name if such name does not indicate that he is in the debt collection business.

There is no dispute that that provision plainly prohibits the QR code. Still, as other courts have observed, § 1692f(8) is rather expansive when read literally. It would seemingly prohibit including "a debtor's address and an envelope's pre-printed postage," as well as "any innocuous mark related to the post, such as 'overnight mail' and 'forwarding and address correction requested.'" Strand v. Diversified Collection

Serv., Inc., 380 F.3d 316, 318 (8th Cir. 2004); see also Goswami v. Am. Collections Enter., Inc., 377 F.3d 488, 493 (5th Cir. 2004). To avoid these "bizarre results," Strand, 380 F.3d at 318, many courts, as well as the Federal Trade Commission, have read a "benign language exception" into § 1692f(8), see Goswami, 377 F.3d at 493-94. Although we have never adopted such an exception, MRS asks us to do so here and conclude that the QR code falls within it.

But once again, we return to our decision in Douglass. To repeat, Douglass involved an envelope displaying the debtor's account number with the debt collector. 765 F.3d at 300-01. There, as here, the debt collector urged us to read a benign language exception into § 1692f(8), and like MRS, the debt collector in Douglass argued that the account number should fall within that exception. See id. at 301. We declined to decide whether § 1692f(8) contains such an exception because, regardless, the account number was not benign. Id. at 301, 303. That number, we explained, was "a core piece of information," the disclosure of which "implicate[d] a core concern animating the FDCPA—the invasion of privacy." Id. at 303. We thus rejected the debt collector's contention that the "account number is a meaningless string of numbers and letters, and its disclosure has not harmed and could not possibly harm Douglass." Id. at 305-06.

As with standing, the question is whether the analysis changes when the account number is not on the face of the envelope but is embedded in a QR code. The panel in Douglass explicitly left that question open. See id. at 301 n.4. But, keeping in mind that "the FDCPA must be broadly construed in order to give full effect to [its remedial] purposes," Caprio v. Healthcare Revenue Recovery Grp., LLC, 709 F.3d 142, 148 (3d Cir. 2013), we agree with the District Court that the reasoning of Douglass applies fully to an account number embedded in a QR code. As explained above with respect to standing, the harm here is still the same — the unauthorized disclosure of confidential information. And if such disclosure was not benign, disclosure via an easily readable QR code is not either. Protected information has still been compromised.

MRS argues that Douglass is distinguishable. There, the account information was on the face of the envelope, capable of being seen by all. Here, by contrast, the envelope facially displayed no connection to debt collection. It just revealed a QR code, which is facially neutral and appears on many commercial mailings. Any account information, according to MRS, is hidden from public sight and could only be seen by "unlawfully scanning" the envelope. MRS Br. 24 n.3. MRS suggests that "scanning p.282 the QR Code on an envelope addressed to another is akin to opening a letter addressed to another." MRS Br. 23.

We are not persuaded. While we do not decide here whether a benign language exception to § 1692f(8) exists, it would apply only to language truly benign relative to the purposes of the FDCPA. See Douglass, 765 F.3d at 303 ("[W]e cannot find language exempt from § 1692f(8) if its disclosure on an envelope would run counter to the very reasons Congress enacted the FDCPA."). If, as we held in Douglass, disclosure of a debtor's account number is an invasion of privacy, it follows that disclosure of a QR code embedded with that number is not benign. A QR code is still "susceptible to privacy intrusions," even if it does not facially display any "core information relating to the debt collection."[4] Id. at 305. There is no material difference between disclosing an account number directly on the envelope and doing so via QR code —the harm is the same, especially given the ubiquity of smartphones.[5] Whether it is illegal to scan someone's mail, as MRS argues, is beside the point. The debt collector has still exposed private information to the world in violation of the FDCPA.[6]

We therefore hold that a debt collector violates § 1692f(8) when it sends to a debtor an envelope displaying an unencrypted QR code that, when scanned, reveals the debtor's account number. We thus agree with the District Court that MRS, in doing so here, violated the FDCPA.

B.

MRS argues that, even if its conduct violated the FDCPA, it is subject to the bona fide error defense. We disagree.

The FDCPA's bona fide error defense is found in 15 U.S.C. § 1692k(c), which provides:

> [a] debt collector may not be held liable in any action brought under this subchapter if the debt collector shows by a preponderance of evidence that the violation was not intentional and resulted from a bona fide error notwithstanding the maintenance of procedures reasonably adapted to avoid any such error.

In Jerman v. Carlisle, McNellie, Rini, Kramer & Ulrich L.P.A., 559 U.S. 573, 130 S.Ct. 1605, 176 L.Ed.2d 519 (2010), the Supreme Court held "that the bona fide error defense in § 1692k(c) does not apply to a violation of the FDCPA resulting from a debt collector's incorrect interpretation of the requirements of that statute." Id. at 604-05, 130 S.Ct. 1605. Put differently, "FDCPA violations forgivable under § 1692k(c) must result from 'clerical or factual mistakes,' not mistakes of law." Daubert v. NRA Grp., LLC, 861 F.3d 382, 394 (3d Cir. 2017) (quoting Jerman, 559 U.S. at 587, 130 S.Ct. 1605).

MRS contends that it committed a mistake of fact. It argues that it "erred by using industry standards for processing p.283 return mail and appreciating that no person has ever used a QR Code to determine a letter concerned debt collection." MRS Br. 26. MRS insists that it "did not mistakenly interpret the FDCPA." MRS Br. 26. But that is precisely what it did. While MRS tries to characterize its error as one of fact, MRS ultimately just misunderstood its obligations under the FDCPA. Indeed, MRS all but admits that point when it argues that it "mistakenly believed that its conduct could not conceivably violate the FDCPA." MRS Br. 31. That is not a mistake of fact; it is a mistake of law. Had MRS's printing of the QR code been the result of a clerical mistake, accidentally included contrary to the agency's normal procedures, then it could conceivably avail itself of the bona fide error defense. See Jerman, 559 U.S. at 587, 130 S.Ct. 1605. But that is not MRS's argument; indeed, MRS explains that using QR codes is "the industry standard." MRS Br. 34. MRS may not have intended "to disclose that the contents of the envelope pertain to debt collection," MRS Br. 27, but the bona fide error defense does not protect every well-intentioned act, see Jerman, 559 U.S. at 584-85, 130 S.Ct. 1605. It applies only to clerical or factual mistakes. See Daubert, 861 F.3d at 394. The bona fide error defense is therefore inapplicable here.

IV.

For the foregoing reasons, we will affirm the judgment of the District Court.

[1] Pursuant to Federal Rule of Civil Procedure 5.2(a)(4), MRS and DiNaples omitted the first three digits of her account number from their summary-judgment filings.

[2] As long as DiNaples has standing, the District Court had jurisdiction under 28 U.S.C. § 1331. We have appellate jurisdiction under 28 U.S.C. § 1291.

[3] For this reason, MRS's attempt to distinguish St. Pierre as involving a motion to dismiss, and hence a lower evidentiary standard, falls flat. Though the motion here is for summary judgment, DiNaples has offered sufficient evidence of her concrete injury, namely the envelope's displaying a QR code embedded with her account number.

[4] We do not consider whether a debt collector violates § 1692f(8) by including on an envelope a QR code that does not contain a consumer's account number.

[5] For this reason, it also does not matter where on the envelope the QR code is printed, which MRS suggests makes a difference. The account number has still been disclosed, regardless of its location on the envelope.

[6] And contrary to MRS's contentions, there is a difference between scanning a letter and opening it. The former can be done surreptitiously without leaving any evidence of tampering. Not so when a letter is physically opened.

916 F.3d 260 (2019)

Mary BARBATO
v.
GREYSTONE ALLIANCE, LLC; Turning Point Capital Inc; Crown Asset Management LLC Crown Asset Management LLC, Appellant.

No. 18-1042.

United States Court of Appeals, Third Circuit.

Argued: September 6, 2018.
Opinion Filed: February 22, 2019.

Barbato v. Greystone Alliance, LLC, 916 F. 3d 260 (3rd Cir. 2019)

On Appeal from the United States District Court for the Middle District of Pennsylvania, (M.D. Pa. Civil Action No. 3-13-cv-02748), Honorable Malachy E. Mannion, U.S. District Judge.

Anthony J. Gingo, Michael J. Palumbo, Gingo Palumbo Law Group, 4700 Rockside Road, Suite 440, Independence, OH 44131, Matthew R. Rosenkoff, [ARGUED], Taylor English Duma, 1600 Parkwood Circle, Suite 200, Atlanta, GA 30339, Counsel for Defendant-Appellant Crown Asset Management LLC.

Daniel A. Edelman, [ARGUED], Edelman Combs Latturner & Goodwin, 20 South Clark Street, Suite 1500, Chicago, IL 60603, Brett M. Freeman, Carlo Sabatini, Sabatini Law Firm, 216 North Blakely Street, Dunmore, PA 18512, Counsel for Plaintiff-Appellee Mary Barbato.

Before: HARDIMAN, KRAUSE, and BIBAS, Circuit Judges.

p.261 OPINION OF THE COURT

KRAUSE, Circuit Judge.

The Fair Debt Collection Practices Act ("FDCPA") protects consumers from abusive, deceptive, or otherwise unfair debt collection practices. 15 U.S.C. § 1692(a). It applies to "debt collectors," defined alternatively as those engaged "in any business the principal purpose of which is the collection of any debts" and those "who regularly collect[]" debts "owed or due another." *Id.* § 1692a(6). This appeal concerns only the first definition and requires us to determine whether an entity that acquires debt for the "purpose of ... collection" but outsources the actual collection activity qualifies as a "debt collector." The District Court held that it does, and we agree: an entity that otherwise meets the "principal purpose" definition cannot avoid the dictates of the FDCPA merely by hiring a third party to do its collecting. We therefore will affirm.

p.262 I. Background

A. Factual Background

Appellant Crown Asset Management ("Crown") is a purchaser of charged-off receivables, that is, accounts on which a consumer has stopped paying the debt owed. When Crown purchases an account, it determines if the debtor has filed for bankruptcy or is deceased. If neither is the case, Crown does not collect on the account itself; rather, it refers the charged-off receivable to a third-party servicer for collection or it hires a debt collection law firm to file a collection lawsuit on its behalf. Although Crown does not contact consumers directly, it principally derives revenue from liquidating the consumer debt it has acquired.

In this case, Appellee Mary Barbato obtained a consumer credit card from GE Electric Capital Corporation and GE Money Bank (collectively "GE") in 2007. She made her last payment on the account in November 2010, leaving an outstanding balance. GE subsequently charged off that balance and, after a number of sales and assignments, Crown purchased Barbato's debt. Pursuant to its standing service agreement with collection agency Turning Point Capital, Inc. ("Turning Point"), Crown then referred that debt to Turning Point for collection.

Crown's service agreement with Turning Point explained that Crown was seeking "to procure certain collection services" from Turning Point, and Turning Point was agreeing to "undertake collection on each Account placed" with it by Crown. App. 376. In addition, the agreement said that Crown had the "sole and absolute discretion," App. 378, as to which accounts it would forward, that Crown's obligation to pay Turning Point was contingent upon Turning Point's success, and that Crown could establish settlement guidelines from which Turning Point would have to obtain permission in order to deviate.

Pursuant to this agreement, Turning Point sent Barbato a collection letter in February 2013, identifying itself as a "National Debt Collection Agency" and Crown as its client. Turning Point also called Barbato and left her two voicemail messages. For its part, Crown did not have any direct communication with Barbato regarding her account, nor did it review or approve the letter sent to her by Turning Point. When Barbato filed for bankruptcy, however, Crown recalled Barbato's account from Turning Point and subsequently closed it.

B. Procedural Background

Several months later, after Turning Point was absorbed by Greystone Alliance, LLC ("Greystone"), Barbato filed a state court complaint against Greystone, alleging that it had violated the FDCPA. And after Greystone removed the action to federal court, Barbato filed an amended complaint in which she added Turning Point and Crown as defendants and alleged that each was a "debt collector" as defined by the FDCPA.[1] Turning Point was served but never answered. Barbato eventually dismissed both Turning Point and Greystone from the action, leaving only Crown as a defendant.

Barbato and Crown subsequently filed cross-motions for summary judgment on, p.263 among other issues, the question whether Crown was a debt collector.

Barbato did not argue that Crown satisfied the "regularly collects" definition, i.e., that it "regularly collect[ed]" debts "owed or due another." 15 U.S.C. § 1692a(6). Rather, she argued that Crown was a "debt collector" because: (1) it purchased debts when they were in default, which, under then-controlling precedent, was a prerequisite to being considered a "debt collector" as opposed to a "creditor"[2]—statuses we had deemed mutually exclusive under § 1692a(6), *see F.T.C. v. Check Inv'rs, Inc.*, 502 F.3d 159, 171 (3d Cir. 2007)—and (2) it satisfied the statute's "principal purpose" definition because the principal purpose of its business was the collection of those defaulted debts, even if it hired third-party debt collectors to do the collecting. 15 U.S.C. § 1692a(6); App. 209-10 (citing *Pollice v. Nat'l Tax Funding, L.P.*, 225 F.3d 379, 403-04 (3d Cir. 2000)). Crown countered that, regardless of the default status of the debt, Barbato could not prove it fit the "principal purpose" definition because it took no collection action towards her and its principal purpose was not the collection of debt but, rather, its acquisition.

Siding with Barbato on these issues, the District Court held that Crown was "acting as [a] 'debt collector'" because: (1) it acquired debts like Barbato's when they were in default and (2) the summary judgment record supported that Crown's "principal purpose" was the "collection of 'any debts.'" *Barbato v. Greystone All., LLC*, No. 3:13-CV-2748, 2017 WL 1193731, at *10 (M.D. Pa. Mar. 30, 2017). As to the second ground, the Court found little difference between collecting on charged-off receivables and referring charged-off receivables to third-party independent servicers for collection. Instead, given that Crown purchased debt, that ninety to ninety-five percent of that debt came from consumers, and that Crown referred all of that debt out for collection, the District Court concluded that "Crown's principal purpose is to acquire accounts in 'default' for the purpose of collection." *Id.* The District Court nevertheless denied Barbato's motion for summary judgment, holding that she had not established that Crown was vicariously liable for Turning Point's conduct because (1) in the District Court's view, vicarious liability could be imputed to Crown in these circumstances only if the agent too was a "debt collector," and (2) the evidence in the record was insufficient to hold that Turning Point was a debt collector under the FDCPA. The Court granted the parties leave to file renewed motions for summary judgment to address Turning Point's status as a debt collector.

While these proceedings continued in the District Court, however, the Supreme Court issued a decision that prompted Crown to seek reconsideration of the District Court's ruling that it was a "debt collector." In *Henson v. Santander, Consumer USA Inc.*, in interpreting the "regularly collects" definition and deciding whether the entity there "regularly collect[ed]... debts owed or due another," 15 U.S.C. § 1692a(6), the Supreme Court held that it was irrelevant whether the debt acquired and sought to be collected was in default; instead, it held "[a]ll that matters is whether the target of the lawsuit regularly seeks to collect debts for its own account or does so for 'another,'" ___ U.S. ___, 137 S.Ct. 1718, 1721, 1724, 198 L.Ed.2d 177 (2017). Construing that language to apply to § 1692a(6) generally, Crown urged that it could no longer be considered a debt collector, even under the "principal purpose" definition, because it p.264 too was collecting debts on its own behalf and not for another. The District Court disagreed, holding that *Henson* pertained only to the "regularly collects" definition of "debt collector" and did not affect its holding that Crown was a debt collector under the "principal purpose" definition. *See Barbato v.*

Greystone All., LLC, No. CV 3:13-2748, 2017 WL 5496047, at *1, *9-*10 (M.D. Pa. Nov. 16, 2017).

Nevertheless, the District Court certified its decision for interlocutory appeal and presented a controlling question of law to this Court: "whether *Henson* requires a finding that Crown is not a debt collector in this case when it was a third-party buyer of the debt, and the debt was in default at the time it purchased it." App. 34. Crown then filed a petition for permission to file the interlocutory appeal and to appeal the District Court's denial of its motion for reconsideration, which we granted.

II. Jurisdiction and Applicable Standards

The District Court had jurisdiction under 28 U.S.C. § 1331, and we have jurisdiction over this interlocutory appeal under 28 U.S.C. § 1292(b). When reviewing an interlocutory appeal under 28 U.S.C. § 1292(b), we exercise plenary review over the question certified. *Florence v. Bd. of Chosen Freeholders of Cty. of Burlington,* 621 F.3d 296, 301 (3d Cir. 2010). The scope of our review, however, is not limited to the question set forth in the certification motion but, rather, includes any issue fairly included within the certified order. *See Yamaha Motor Corp., U.S.A. v. Calhoun,* 516 U.S. 199, 205, 116 S.Ct. 619, 133 L.Ed.2d 578 (1996) ("As the text of § 1292(b) indicates, appellate jurisdiction applies to the *order* certified to the court of appeals, and is not tied to the particular question formulated by the district court.").

"We review a denial of a motion for reconsideration for abuse of discretion, but we review the District Court's underlying legal determinations"—its denial of summary judgment to Crown in this case—"de novo and factual determinations for clear error." *Howard Hess Dental Labs. Inc. v. Dentsply Int'l, Inc.,* 602 F.3d 237, 246 (3d Cir. 2010). Summary judgment is appropriate only where there is no genuine issue as to any material fact. Fed. R. Civ. P. 56(c).

III. Discussion

On appeal, Crown contends that it does not qualify as a "debt collector" under the "principal purpose" definition for three reasons: First, the Supreme Court's decision in *Henson* undermined our prior precedent that would render it a debt collector. Second, its principal purpose is the acquisition—not the collection—of debt, and a faithful interpretation of the statute requires that we distinguish between the two. And third, the legislative history demonstrates that Congress intended to regulate the proverbial "repo man," not a "passive debt owner" like Crown. Appellant Br. 32. We begin with a brief overview of the FDCPA and, with that context for Crown's arguments, address—and reject—each in turn.

A. The FDCPA

Congress enacted the FDCPA in 1977 "to eliminate abusive debt collection practices by debt collectors" and "to insure that those debt collectors who refrain from using abusive debt collection practices are not competitively disadvantaged." 15 U.S.C. § 1692(e). It provides a private right of action against debt collectors who violate its provisions. 15 U.S.C. § 1692k; *see also Brown v. Card Serv. Ctr.*, 464 F.3d 450, 453 (3d Cir. 2006). "As remedial legislation, p.265 the FDCPA must be broadly construed in order to give full effect to these purposes." *Caprio v. Healthcare Revenue Recovery Grp., LLC,* 709 F.3d 142, 148 (3d Cir. 2013).

"To prevail on an FDCPA claim, a plaintiff must prove that (1) she is a consumer, (2) the defendant is a debt collector, (3) the defendant's challenged practice involves an attempt to collect a 'debt' as the [FDCPA] defines it, and (4) the defendant has violated a provision of the FDCPA in attempting to collect the debt." *St. Pierre v. Retrieval-Masters Creditors Bureau, Inc.,* 898 F.3d 351, 358 (3d Cir. 2018) (quoting *Douglass v. Convergent Outsourcing,* 765 F.3d 299, 303 (3d Cir. 2014)). The only element at issue in this case is the second—whether Crown qualifies as a "debt collector."

As noted, the statute defines "debt collector" as any person (1) "who uses any instrumentality of interstate commerce or the mails in any business the principal purpose of which is the collection of any debts" (the "principal purpose" definition), or (2) "who regularly collects or attempts to collect, directly or indirectly, debts owed or due or asserted to be owed or due another" (the "regularly collects" definition).[3] 15 U.S.C. § 1692a(6). The statute thus provides two separate paths to establishing an entity's status as a "debt collector." *See Henson,* 137 S.Ct. at 1721.

As we recently had occasion to remark, the debt collection industry has changed since Congress enacted the FDCPA in 1977, and the simple creditor-debt collector duo has been complicated by the advent and growth of debt buying. *See Tepper v. Amos Fin., LLC,* 898 F.3d 364, 366 (3d Cir. 2018). With the proliferation of debt buying have come questions about the boundaries of the statute's definitions.

In *Henson v. Santander,* the Supreme Court clarified the "regularly collects" definition. There, Santander Bank purchased loans once they were already in default and sought to collect on them. 137 S.Ct. at 1720. Focusing on the plain language of the statutory definition at issue, the Court held that a third-party buyer of debt that seeks to collect debt owed to it does not fit the second definition because it does not "regularly seek to collect debts 'owed ... another.'" *Id.* at 1721. It rejected the petitioners' arguments that either the origin of the debt or the default status of the debt had any bearing on that analysis. As to the debt's origin, it reasoned that the statutory language did not suggest that "whether the owner originated the debt or came by it only through a later purchase" was relevant. *Id.* The Court similarly saw no basis in the text for concluding that an entity that obtains debts after default automatically qualifies as a "debt collector" under the definition. *See id.* at 1724. "All that matters," the Court concluded, "is whether the target of the lawsuit regularly seeks to collect debts for its own account or does so for 'another.'" *Id.* at 1721. Relevant for our purposes, the Court explicitly declined to address whether such debt buyers could nevertheless qualify as debt collectors under the "principal purpose" definition. *Id.*

p.266 B. *Henson* and Third Circuit Precedent

Crown's primary argument on appeal is that *Henson* abrogated our prior precedent such that it no longer qualifies as a "debt collector" under the statute. Crown contends this is so for two reasons: first, because *Henson* renders it a creditor, not a debt collector, and the two statuses are mutually exclusive; and second, because *Henson* rejected the so-called "default" test on which we relied, thereby undermining "the very foundation" of our prior caselaw. Appellant Br. 30. Crown overstates the effect of *Henson.*

We need not dwell on Crown's first argument because our recent decision in *Tepper v. Amos* forecloses it. In *Tepper,* the defendant was a company whose "sole business [wa]s purchasing debts entered into by third parties and attempting to collect them." 898 F.3d at 369. The defendant claimed that because it met the statutory definition of creditor—it was trying to collect debts it owned and was thus an entity "to whom [the] debt is owed"—it could not also be a debt collector. *Id.* at 371 (quoting 15 U.S.C. § 1692a(4)). Like Crown, the defendant based this argument on Third Circuit precedent that characterized the two statuses as "mutually exclusive." *Id.* (citing *Check Inv'rs,* 502 F.3d at 173); *see also Pollice,* 225 F.3d at 403. Until *Henson,* as we explained, we relied on the "default" test to determine whether an entity was a creditor or a debt collector: either the entity obtained the debt before default and was a creditor or it acquired the debt afterwards and was a debt collector. *Tepper,* 898 F.3d at 366-67. Given the binary nature of default status, an entity could be only one or the other. But, we observed, *Henson* rejected the "default" test, *id.* at 367, and with it, the basis for treating the terms "debt collector" and "creditor" as mutually exclusive. Following the Supreme Court's direction to hew more closely to the statutory definitions, we concluded that "an entity that satisfies both [definitions] is within the Act's reach." *Id.* at 371. The same is true here.

As to Crown's second argument about *Henson*'s overall effect on our caselaw, it simply proves too much. While it is no doubt true that *Henson* abrogated the default test on which we relied to distinguish between creditors and debt collectors and that it clarified the scope of the "regularly collects" definition of debt collector, *Henson* did not address the other prong of § 1692a(6)—the wholly separate "principal purpose" definition. To the contrary, the Court conducted a close textual analysis of the "regularly collects" definition, deriving from that portion of the statute—which requires the entity to "collect" debt "owed or due another"—that "[a]ll that matters is whether the target of the lawsuit regularly seeks to collect debts for its own account or does so for 'another.'" 137 S.Ct. at 1721. That requirement, however, does not appear in the "principal purpose" definition, and the Supreme Court went out of its way in *Henson* to say that it was not opining on whether debt buyers could also qualify as debt collectors under that prong of § 1692a(6). *See id.*

But we have previously opined on this question—and in similar circumstances. In *Pollice v. National Tax Funding, L.P.,* a debt buyer, National Tax Funding L.P. ("NTF"), purchased delinquent municipal tax and utility claims from the government. 225 F.3d at 385. Like Crown, NTF had no direct contact with debtors; rather, it outsourced all of its collection activities to others. *Id.* at 386. We concluded that NTF was a debt collector both because it purchased debt in default—a fact *Henson* has since rendered irrelevant—*and also* because "there [was] no question that the 'principal purpose' of NTF's business is p.267 the 'collection of any debts,' namely, defaulted obligations which it purchases from municipalities." *Id.* at 404. The fact that someone else did the actual collecting did not deter us from concluding that NTF was a "debt collector" given that "NTF exist[ed] *solely* for the purpose of holding claims for delinquent taxes and municipal obligations." *Id.* at 404 n.27

(emphasis added). True, *Pollice* predated *Henson,* but for the reasons we explain below, we continue to find its logic persuasive.

C. Statutory Interpretation

To determine whether Crown is a "debt collector" under the "principal purpose" definition, we look first to the plain meaning of the statutory text. *See S.H. ex rel. Durrell v. Lower Merion Sch. Dist.*, 729 F.3d 248, 257 (3d Cir. 2013). The text states that "any person who uses any instrumentality of interstate commerce or the mails in any business the principal purpose of which is the collection of any debts" is a "debt collector." 15 U.S.C. § 1692a(6). Focusing on the word "collection," which it defines as "the act or process of collecting," Crown argues that the "principal purpose" definition applies only to those that engage in "overt acts of collection" by interacting with consumers —not entities like Crown that purchase debt and outsource the collection. Appellant Br. 25, 31, 33.

As much as Crown might wish that it were otherwise, nothing suggests that the definition is so limited. An entity qualifies under the definition if the "principal purpose" of its "business" is the "collection of any debts." "Principal" is defined as "most important, consequential, or influential," *Principal,* Webster's Third New International Dictionary 1802 (1976) ("Webster's Third"), and "purpose" is defined as "something that one sets before himself as an object to be attained : an end or aim" and "an object, effect, or result aimed at, intended, or attained," *id.* at 1847. Thus, an entity that has the "collection of any debts" as its "most important" "aim" is a debt collector under this definition. While it is true that "collection" can be defined as "the act or process of collecting," it can also be defined as "that which is collected." *Collection,* Random House Dictionary of the English Language 290 (1973). So defined, the focus shifts from the *act* of collecting to *what* is collected, namely, the acquired debts. As long as a business's *raison d'être* is obtaining payment on the debts that it acquires, it is a debt collector. Who actually obtains the payment or how they do so is of no moment.

The statutory context of the "principal purpose" definition casts further doubt on Crown's argument that Congress meant to limit it to only those entities that actively collect from consumers. *See Allen ex rel. Martin v. LaSalle Bank, N.A.*, 629 F.3d 364, 367 (3d Cir. 2011) ("If the plain language fails to express Congress' intent unequivocally ... we will examine the surrounding words and provisions in their context.") (citing *Tavarez v. Klingensmith,* 372 F.3d 188, 190 (3d Cir. 2004)). In contrast to the "regularly collects" definition, where Congress explicitly used the verb "to collect" in describing the actions of those it intended the definition to cover, in the "principal purpose" definition, Congress used the noun "collection" and did not specify who must do the collecting or to whom the debt must be owed.[4] 15 U.S.C. § 1692a(6); *see also Tepper,* 898 F.3d at 370. Thus, by its terms, the "principal purpose" definition sweeps more p.268 broadly than the "regularly collects" definition, and we must presume that the "legislature says ... what it means and means... what it says." *Henson,* 137 S.Ct. at 1725 (quoting *Dodd v. United States,* 545 U.S. 353, 357, 125 S.Ct. 2478, 162 L.Ed.2d 343 (2005)).

In a plain language argument of its own, Crown retorts that to find that it qualifies under the "principal purpose" definition even though it outsources its collection activities would be to read the word "indirectly" into the statute where it does not appear. This is especially problematic, Crown contends, because the "regularly collects" definition does specify that an entity can collect "directly or indirectly," while Congress omitted this qualifier from the "principal purpose" definition.

We are unpersuaded. Again, the fact that the "regularly collects" definition employs a verb and the "principal purpose" definition employs a noun is critical. In the "regularly collects" definition, the "directly or indirectly" qualification is necessary because one could reasonably interpret "collect" to refer to only direct efforts to collect—it is, after all, "a verb that requires action." Appellant Reply Br. 15 (citation omitted).

The "principal purpose" definition, however, needs no such qualification. "Collection" by its very definition may be indirect, and that is the type of collection in which Crown engages: it buys consumer debt and hires debt collectors to collect on it.[5] The existence of a middleman does not change the essential nature—the "principal purpose"—of Crown's business. As Barbato points out, Crown could buy debt for the charitable purpose of forgiving it, or it could buy debt for the purpose of reselling it to unrelated parties at a profit. In both of those cases, the entity's "principal purpose" would not be collection. But Crown does neither of those things. Indeed, the record reflects that Crown's only business is the purchasing of debts for the purpose of collecting on those debts, and, as Crown candidly acknowledged at oral argument, without the collection of those debts, Crown would cease to exist. In short, Crown falls squarely within § 1692a(6)'s "principal purpose" definition.

D. Crown's Purpose and Legislative History Argument

Finally, Crown argues that the legislative history of the FDCPA demonstrates that Congress did not intend for the statutory definition of "debt collector" to apply to a "passive debt owner" like itself but only to a repo man who was personally hounding debtors to hand over the money they owe. Appellant Br. 32. This argument is flawed in two respects.

First, it proves too much. There is no doubt that "[d]isruptive dinnertime calls, downright deceit, and more besides drew Congress's eye to the debt collection industry." *Henson,* 137 S.Ct. at 1720. But even if the purpose of the statute was to reach repo men, that purpose is furthered by recognizing Crown as a debt collector under § 1692a(6). Unlike a traditional creditor, such as a bank or a retail outlet p.269 that has its own incentive to cultivate good will among its customers and for which debt collection is one of perhaps many parts of its business, an independent debt collector like Crown has only one need for consumers: for them to pay their debts. As market-based incentives go, that makes it far more like a repo man than a creditor and gives it every incentive to hire the most effective repo man to boot.

Second, while the Supreme Court acknowledged in *Henson* that "[e]veryone agrees that the term embraces the repo man," *id.,* the language on which Congress settled sweeps more broadly to include "*any* business the principal purpose of which is the collection of any debts," 15 U.S.C. § 1692a(6) (emphasis added), without regard to whether that entity delegates its collecting activities. The statute is clear, and Crown's argument fails for this reason as well: "[R]ecourse to legislative history or underlying legislative intent is unnecessary when a statute's text is clear and does not lead to an absurd result." *In re Phila. Newspapers, LLC,* 599 F.3d 298, 317 (3d Cir. 2010) (quoting *Hay Grp., Inc. v. E.B.S. Acquisition Corp.,* 360 F.3d 404, 406 (3d Cir. 2004)).

E. Issues for Remand

Of course, our holding that Crown is a debt collector does not answer the ultimate question of liability, which turns here on principles of vicarious liability. As the District Court recognized, "when Congress creates a tort action, it legislates against a legal background of ordinary tort-related vicarious liability rules," *Barbato,* 2017 WL 1193731, at *12 (quoting *Meyer v. Holley,* 537 U.S. 280, 285, 123 S.Ct. 824, 154 L.Ed.2d 753 (2003)), and we have relied on traditional agency principles in holding parties vicariously liable under the FDCPA, *see Pollice,* 225 F.3d at 404-05, as have other Courts of Appeals in the context of analogous remedial statutes, *see, e.g., Jones v. Federated Fin. Reserve Corp.,* 144 F.3d 961, 965 (6th Cir. 1998) (applying agency principles to determine vicarious liability under the Fair Credit Reporting Act).

As Crown's ultimate liability for the acts of Turning Point was not the question certified in this interlocutory appeal nor the focus of the parties' briefing, we will leave that issue for the District Court's consideration in the first instance. By way of guidance on remand, however, we offer two brief observations. First, to the extent Crown argues that the District Court was obligated to find that Crown exerted actual control over Turning Point in order to be held vicariously liable, Crown misunderstands the tenets of agency law and our precedent. *See Meyer,* 537 U.S. at 285-86, 123 S.Ct. 824 (explaining that the principal-agent relationship requires that the principal either control "*or [have] the right to direct or control*" the agent) (emphasis added); *see also Janetos v. Fulton Friedman & Gullace, LLP,* 825 F.3d 317, 326 (7th Cir. 2016) (interpreting *Pollice* to mean that vicarious liability need not be based "on a showing of actual control over the specific activity alleged to violate the [FDCPA]").

Second, in inviting further development of the record on Turning Point's own status as a "debt collector," the District Court assumed that Crown could not be held vicariously liable for the acts of an agent under the FDCPA unless the agent qualified as a "debt collector" in its own right. *Barbato,* 2017 WL 1193731, at *13. But our case law imposes no such requirement; to the contrary, we have focused on whether the *principal* qualifies as a debt collector because "an entity which itself meets the definition of 'debt collector' may be held vicariously liable for unlawful collection activities carried out by another on its behalf." p.270 *Pollice,* 225 F.3d at 404. And as we explained in *Pollice,* and we reinforce today, this is "a fair result because an entity that is itself a 'debt collector'—and hence subject to the FDCPA—should bear the burden of monitoring the activities of those it enlists to collect debts on its behalf." *Id.* at 405.

IV. Conclusion

For the foregoing reasons, we will affirm the District Court's order denying reconsideration of its summary judgment decision and will remand for further proceedings consistent with this opinion.

[1] Although of limited relevance for this appeal, the specific conduct that Barbato alleged violated the FDCPA was (1) that Turning Point left her voicemail messages without disclosing that the calls were from a debt collector, as required under 15 U.S.C. § 1692e(11), and (2) that Turning Point's letter neglected to inform her how to properly exercise her validation rights, as required under 15 U.S.C. § 1692g. Barbato purported to bring this latter claim on behalf of a putative class of Pennsylvania residents.

[2] The statute defines "creditor" as "any person who offers or extends credit creating a debt or to whom a debt is owed." 15 U.S.C. § 1692a(4).

[3] The statute also provides two other definitions of "debt collector," neither of which is relevant here:. "any creditor who, in the process of collecting his own debts, uses any name other than his own which would indicate that a third person is collecting or attempting to collect such debts" and "any person who uses any instrumentality of interstate commerce or the mails in any business the principal purpose of which is the enforcement of security interests." 15 U.S.C. § 1692a(6). Excluded from the definition's reach are, among others, a creditor's officers and employees who collect debts for the creditor, an entity collecting a debt it originated, and an entity collecting a debt it obtained that was not in default at the time of purchase. *Id.* §§ 1692a(6)(A), (F).

[4] At both oral argument and in its supplemental briefing, Crown argued that the word "collection" is a verb. It is not. It is a noun. *See Collection,* Webster's Third at 444 (denoting with the abbreviation "*n*" that the word being defined is a noun).

[5] Although not addressed by the District Court or the focus of the parties' arguments on appeal, Barbato has suggested that Crown itself collects debt because it is the named plaintiff in many collection lawsuits. Because Crown's litigation efforts did not give rise to this appeal and we conclude that Crown otherwise satisfies the "principal purpose" definition, we need not address this argument. We note, however, that Crown's answer to it—that its litigation efforts are irrelevant because its counsel, not Crown itself, does the collecting by, for example, drafting the pleadings—is in tension with our precedent, *e.g., Pollice,* 225 F.3d at 404-05 (recognizing that a debt collector may be held vicariously liable for the conduct of its attorneys), and squarely refuted by our holding today.

882 F.3d 422 (2018)

Michelle TATIS, Individually and on behalf of all others similarly situated, Appellant
v.
ALLIED INTERSTATE, LLC; John Does 1-25

No. 16-4022.

United States Court of Appeals, Third Circuit.

Argued September 5, 2017.
Filed: February 12, 2018.

Tatis v. Allied Interstate, LLC, 882 F. 3d 422 (3rd Cir. 2018)

On Appeal from the United States District Court for the District of New Jersey, (D.C. No. 2-16-cv-00109), District Judge: Honorable John M. Vazquez.

p.425 Ari H. Marcus (Argued), Yitzchak Zelman, Marcus & Zelman, 1500 Allaire Avenue, Suite 101, Ocean, NJ 07712, Counsel for Appellant.

James C. Martin (Argued), Kellie A. Lavery, Reed Smith, 136 Main Street, Suite 250, Princeton, NJ 08540, Counsel for Appellee.

Before: CHAGARES, JORDAN, and HARDIMAN, Circuit Judges.

OPINION OF THE COURT

HARDIMAN, Circuit Judge.

This appeal arises under the Fair Debt Collection Practices Act (FDCPA or Act). The question presented is whether a collection letter sent to collect a time-barred debt that makes a "settlement offer" to accept payment "in settlement of" the debt could violate the Act's general prohibition against "any false, deceptive, or misleading representation or means in connection with the collection of any debt." 15 U.S.C. § 1692e. We hold that it could.

I

Over ten years ago, Appellant Michelle Tatis incurred a debt of $1,289.86 to Bally Total Fitness Holding Corp. Appellee Allied Interstate, LLC—a debt collector— sent Tatis a letter dated May 18, 2015 that read as follows: "[The creditor] is willing to accept payment in the amount of $128.99 in settlement of this debt. You can take advantage of this settlement offer if we receive payment of this amount or if you make another mutually acceptable payment arrangement within 40 days...." App. 37. At the time Allied sent its letter, the six-year New Jersey statute of limitations applicable to debt-collection actions had already run. *Tatis v. Allied Interstate, LLC,* 2016 WL 5660431, at *1, *3 (D.N.J. Sept. 29, 2016); *see also* N.J. STAT. ANN. § 2A:14-1.

Tatis filed a class action in the United States District Court for the District of New Jersey, alleging that Allied's letter violated the FDCPA. The complaint alleged that Tatis interpreted the word "settlement" in the letter to mean that she had a "legal obligation" to pay the debt, and the least-sophisticated debtor would hold a similar belief. Compl. ¶ 27, App. 32. She also claimed the letter was a "false, deceptive, or misleading representation or means in connection with" collecting the debt. Compl. ¶ 37, App. 34. Specifically, Tatis alleged that Allied "[f]alsely represent[ed] the legal status of the debt in violation of 15 U.S.C. § 1692e(2)(A)," made "false threats to take action that cannot legally be taken in violation of 15 U.S.C. § 1692e and 1692e(5)," and used "false representations and/or deceptive means to collect or attempt to collect [the] debt in violation of 15 U.S.C. § 1692e(10)." Compl. ¶ 38, App. 34.

Allied filed a motion to dismiss the complaint under Rule 12(b)(6) of the Federal Rules of Civil Procedure for failure to state a claim, and the District Court granted the motion.[1] *See Tatis*, 2016 WL p.426 5660431, at *10. In doing so, the Court looked primarily to our decision in *Huertas v. Galaxy Asset Management*, 641 F.3d 28, 32-33 (3d Cir. 2011) (per curiam), which it read to hold that an attempt to collect a timebarred debt does not violate the FDCPA unless it is accompanied by the threat of legal action. *See Tatis*, 2016 WL 5660431, at *5. And because Allied's use of the word "settlement" did not constitute threatened legal action, the Court found dismissal of the complaint appropriate. *Id.* at *8-9. The Court also found it significant that, under New Jersey law, partial repayment of the debt would not revive the statute of limitations. *Id.* at *9. Thus, the letter could not deceive or mislead a consumer into inadvertently reviving a timebarred legal claim. *Id.*[2]

Tatis filed this appeal.

II[3]

A

We review de novo the District Court's order dismissing Tatis's complaint under Rule 12(b)(6). *Wilson v. Quadramed Corp.*, 225 F.3d 350, 353 (3d Cir. 2000). "[W]e accept as true all allegations in the plaintiff's complaint as well as all reasonable inferences that can be drawn from them, and we construe them in a light most favorable to the non-movant." *Sheridan v. NGK Metals Corp.*, 609 F.3d 239, 262 n.27 (3d Cir. 2010). To survive dismissal, "a complaint must contain sufficient factual matter, accepted as true, to 'state a claim to relief that is plausible on its face.'" *Ashcroft v. Iqbal*, 556 U.S. 662, 678, 129 S.Ct. 1937, 173 L.Ed.2d 868 (2009) (quoting *Bell Atl. Corp. v. Twombly*, 550 U.S. 544, 570, 127 S.Ct. 1955, 167 L.Ed.2d 929 (2007)). Plausibility means "more than a sheer possibility that a defendant has acted unlawfully." *Id.* "A claim has facial plausibility when the plaintiff pleads factual content that allows the court to draw the reasonable inference that the defendant is liable for the misconduct alleged." *Id.* (citing *Twombly*, 550 U.S. at 556, 127 S.Ct. 1955).

B

Congress enacted the FDCPA to curb "abusive, deceptive, and unfair debt collection practices." 15 U.S.C. § 1692(a). Among other things, the Act seeks "to eliminate abusive debt collection practices by debt collectors [and] to insure that those debt collectors who refrain from using abusive debt collection practices are not competitively disadvantaged." *Id.* § 1692(e). To effectuate these purposes, Congress proscribed the use of "any false, deceptive, or misleading representation or means in connection with the collection of any debt" and provided a list of sixteen examples of such prohibited conduct. *Id.* § 1692e. These include making "false representation[s]" about "the character, amount, or legal status of any debt," *id.* § 1692e(2)(A), and "threat[ening] to take any action that cannot legally be taken or that is not intended to be taken," *id.* § 1692e(5). As we have noted, "[b]ecause the list of the sixteen subsections is non-exhaustive, a debt collection practice can be a 'false, deceptive, or misleading' practice in violation of section 1692e even if it does not fall within any of the subsections." p.427 *Lesher v. Law Offices of Mitchell N. Kay, PC,* 650 F.3d 993, 997 (3d Cir. 2011).

The FDCPA is remedial, so we "construe its language broadly, so as to effect its purpose." *Brown v. Card Serv. Ctr.,* 464 F.3d 450, 453 (3d Cir. 2006). In addition, we employ a "least sophisticated debtor" standard to evaluate whether a particular debt-collection practice violates the Act. *Jensen v. Pressler & Pressler,* 791 F.3d 413, 418 (3d Cir. 2015) (citing *Rosenau v. Unifund Corp.,* 539 F.3d 218, 221 (3d Cir. 2008)). This standard aims to "protect[] the gullible as well as the shrewd," *id.* (alteration in original) (quoting *Campuzano-Burgos v. Midland Credit Mgmt., Inc.,* 550 F.3d 294, 298 (3d Cir. 2008)), but it nevertheless "preserv[es] a quotient of reasonableness and presum[es] a basic level of understanding and willingness to read with care," *id.* (alterations in original) (quoting *Rosenau,* 539 F.3d at 221); *see also Lesher,* 650 F.3d at 997 (characterizing the least-sophisticated debtor standard as a "low standard"). The standard is objective, "meaning that the specific plaintiff need not prove that *she* was actually confused or misled, only that the objective least sophisticated debtor would be." *Jensen,* 791 F.3d at 419.

C

To prevail on her FDCPA claim, Tatis must demonstrate that "(1) she is a consumer, (2) the defendant is a debt collector, (3) the defendant's challenged practice involves an attempt to collect a 'debt' as the Act defines it, and (4) the defendant has violated a provision of the FDCPA in attempting to collect the debt." *Douglass v. Convergent Outsourcing,* 765 F.3d 299, 303 (3d Cir. 2014). Only the fourth element is disputed in this appeal.

In arguing whether Allied violated the FDCPA, the parties offer competing interpretations of our opinion in *Huertas.* Allied contends that *Huertas* imposed a "threat of litigation" requirement that must be present for an attempt to collect a time-barred debt to violate the FDCPA. By contrast, Tatis attempts to distinguish *Huertas,* arguing that an "offer to settle may mislead the least sophisticated [debtor] into believing that a time-barred debt is legally enforceable, even when litigation is not threatened." *Tatis,* 2016 WL 5660431, at *2.

In *Huertas,* the plaintiff received a letter seeking to collect a time-barred debt. 641 F.3d at 31. Suit was brought under 15 U.S.C. § 1692e(2)(A), alleging that the collection letter Huertas received falsely represented the legal status of his debt which, like Tatis's, was time-barred under New Jersey law. *Huertas v. Galaxy Asset Mgmt.,* 2010 WL 936450, at *4 (D.N.J. Mar. 9, 2010); *see also Huertas,* 641 F.3d at 32. We disagreed for several reasons.

First, we explained that Huertas's debt remained valid under New Jersey law even after the statute of limitations had run. *Huertas,* 641 F.3d at 32. But even though the debt was still owed, Huertas "ha[d] a complete legal defense against having to pay it." *Id.* Next, we explained that "when the expiration of the statute of limitations does not invalidate a debt, but merely renders it unenforceable, the FDCPA permits a debt collector to seek voluntary repayment of the time-barred debt so long as the debt collector does not initiate or threaten legal action in connection with its debt collection efforts." *See id.* at 32-33. In reaching this conclusion, we cited with approval the Eighth Circuit's decision in *Freyermuth v. Credit Bureau Services, Inc.,* 248 F.3d 767, 771 (8th Cir. 2001). Consistent with *Freyermuth,* "Huertas's FDCPA claim hinge[d] on whether [the p.428 collection] letter threatened litigation," as "analyzed from the perspective of the 'least sophisticated debtor.'" *Huertas,* 641 F.3d at 33 (quoting *Brown,* 464 F.3d at 453). We concluded that the letter—which informed Huertas that his debt had been reassigned and requested that he contact the agency to "resolve this issue"—contained no such impermissible threat. *Id.*

Thus, *Huertas* stands for the proposition that debt collectors do not violate 15 U.S.C. § 1692e(2)(A) when they seek voluntary repayment of stale debts, so long as they do not threaten or take legal action. But the FDCPA sweeps far more broadly than the specific provision found in § 1692e(2)(A). It prohibits "*any* false, deceptive, *or misleading representation*" associated with debt-collection practices. 15 U.S.C. § 1692e (emphasis added). Accordingly, this appeal requires us to decide whether collection letters may run afoul of the FDCPA by misleading or deceiving debtors into believing they have a legal obligation to repay time-barred debts even when the letters do not threaten legal action.

D

Since *Huertas,* three other United States Courts of Appeals have addressed the question presented in this appeal. All three have determined that, even absent threats of litigation, it is plausible that offers to "settle" time-barred debts could mislead the least-sophisticated debtor.

The first of the three decisions is *McMahon v. LVNV Funding, LLC,* 744 F.3d 1010 (7th Cir. 2014). In *McMahon,* the Seventh Circuit held that an offer to settle a time-barred debt may violate the FDCPA if it "uses language ... that would mislead an unsophisticated consumer into believing that the debt is legally enforceable." *Id.* at 1020. In particular, the court observed that "a settlement offer on a timebarred debt implies that the creditor could successfully sue on the debt." *Id.* at 1022; *see also id.* at 1021 ("If a consumer received an 'offer for settlement' and searched on Google to see what is meant by 'settlement,' she might find the Wikipedia entry for 'settlement offer,'" which includes a discussion of civil lawsuits). Accordingly, "[i]f unsophisticated consumers believe either that the settlement offer is their chance to avoid court proceedings where they would be defenseless, or if they believe that the debt is legally enforceable at all, they have been misled, and the debt collector has violated the FDCPA." *Id.* at 1022. The *McMahon* court also stated that the Act "cannot bear" any reading requiring a threat of litigation, noting that "[t]he plain language of the FDCPA prohibits not only threatening to take actions that the collector cannot take, but also the use of any false, deceptive, or misleading representation." *Id.* at 1020-21.

A year after *McMahon,* the Sixth Circuit in *Buchanan v. Northland Group, Inc.* held that a settlement offer could "plausibly mislead an unsophisticated consumer into thinking her lender could enforce the debt in court." 776 F.3d 393, 395 (6th Cir. 2015). The court supported this conclusion by looking to definitions of the terms "settle," "settlement," and "settlement agreement" in six formal and informal dictionaries. *Id.* at 399 (providing direct quotations from *Webster's Third New International Dictionary, The Oxford English Dictionary Online, The American Heritage Dictionary of the English Language, Wiktionary, Dictionary.com,* and *Black's Law Dictionary*). Though each source provided numerous definitions, they all included one that referred to the conclusion and/or the avoidance of a lawsuit. *Id.* And like *McMahon,* the *Buchanan* court observed that "the addition of the term 'misleading' confirms[that] the statute outlaws more than p.429 just falsehoods[,] ... [such that] even a true statement may be banned for creating a misleading impression." *Id.* at 396 (citation omitted). After *Buchanan,* the Fifth Circuit joined the chorus, endorsing the same view expressed by the Sixth and Seventh Circuits. *Daugherty v. Convergent Outsourcing, Inc.,* 836 F.3d 507, 513 (5th Cir. 2016).

Although we are not bound by these precedents of our sister courts, we are persuaded that their considered view is the best interpretation of the FDCPA. As the Seventh Circuit noted in *McMahon,* construing the Act to *require* a threat of legal action for any FDCPA violation interposes a mandate that is not found in its text. 744 F.3d at 1020-21. Section 1692e prohibits three discrete categories of conduct: false, misleading, or deceptive representations. So adding a "threat of litigation" requirement to all time-barred debt-collection efforts curtails the reach of the Act by excising conduct otherwise covered by the terms "deceptive" or "misleading." Common sense, our case law, and traditional tools of statutory interpretation foreclose such a construction.

For example, "in certain contexts[,] a completely accurate statement can be deceptive or misleading." *Campuzano-Burgos,* 550 F.3d at 301; *see also Buchanan,* 776 F.3d at 396 (noting that the term "misleading" bans "more than just falsehoods"). Moreover, a communication subject to the FDCPA is deceptive if "it can be reasonably read to have two or more different meanings, one of which is inaccurate." *Id.* at 298 (quoting *Rosenau,* 539 F.3d at 222). Thus, conduct by a debt collector can be unlawfully misleading or deceptive while still falling short of an explicit threat of litigation. Since our task is "to give effect, if possible, to every clause and word of a statute," *Duncan v. Walker,* 533 U.S. 167, 174, 121 S.Ct. 2120, 150 L.Ed.2d 251 (2001) (quoting *United States v. Menasche,* 348 U.S. 528, 538-39, 75 S.Ct. 513, 99 L.Ed. 615 (1955)), we decline Allied's invitation to construe the FDCPA in a manner that narrows the broad language Congress enacted. *See Brown,* 464 F.3d at 453 (noting that we "construe [the FDCPA's] language broadly, so as to effect its purpose"); *see also Disabled in Action v. Se. Pa. Transp. Auth.,* 539 F.3d 199, 210 (3d Cir. 2008) (noting the

Court "assume[s] ... that every word in a statute has meaning and avoid[s] interpreting one part of a statute in a manner that renders another part superfluous").

We also agree with our sister courts that, in the specific context of a debt-collection letter, the least-sophisticated debtor could be misled into thinking that "settlement of the debt" referred to the creditor's ability to enforce the debt in court rather than a mere invitation to settle the account. App. 37. *See Buchanan,* 776 F.3d at 395; *McMahon,* 744 F.3d at 1021. As the *Buchanan* court's survey of sources suggests, multiple dictionaries define "settle" to refer not only to "settling accounts," but also to the avoidance or resolution of litigation.[4] *See* 776 F.3d at p.430 399. Moreover, the chance that the letter could mislead the least-sophisticated debtor increases with the use of phrases such as "settlement offer," which *Black's Law Dictionary* defines as "[a]n offer by one party to settle a dispute amicably (usu[ally] by paying money) to avoid or end a lawsuit or other legal action." (10th ed. 2014).

These textual sources and the reasoning of the Fifth, Sixth, and Seventh Circuits indicate that Tatis has "state[d] a facially plausible claim for relief." *Caprio v. Healthcare Revenue Recovery Grp., LLC,* 709 F.3d 142, 147 (3d Cir. 2013). Because the words "settlement" and "settlement offer" could connote litigation, the least-sophisticated debtor could be misled into thinking Allied could legally enforce the debt. *Cf., e.g., Huertas,* 641 F.3d at 33 (analyzing a letter using the more general verb "to resolve"). We recognize that some debtors might properly interpret Allied's letter as referring solely to the settlement of an account. *See Buchanan,* 776 F.3d at 400-01 (Kethledge, J., dissenting) (noting that many debtors receive multiple collection letters without a suit ever being brought). But others may not. *See Wilson,* 225 F.3d at 354 (noting that the "least sophisticated debtor" standard is lower than the "reasonable debtor" standard). Both the context in which the letter is received and the available textual sources indicate that, far from being a "bizarre or idiosyncratic interpretation[]" not covered by the least-sophisticated debtor standard, interpreting the settlement offer as creating a legally-enforceable obligation is a mistake even a debtor "willing[] to read with care" might make. *Campuzano-Burgos,* 550 F.3d at 299 (quoting *Rosenau,* 539 F.3d at 221).

In sum, because we conclude that the least-sophisticated debtor could plausibly be misled by the specific language used in Allied's letter, we will vacate the District Court's order granting Allied's motion to dismiss and remand for further proceedings. In doing so, we reiterate what we said both in *Huertas* and elsewhere: standing alone, settlement offers and attempts to obtain voluntary repayments of stale debts do not necessarily constitute deceptive or misleading practices. *See Huertas,* 641 F.3d at 32-33; *see also Campuzano-Burgos,* 550 F.3d at 299 (noting that "[t]here is nothing improper about making a settlement offer"). Nor do we impose any specific mandates on the language debt collectors must use, such as requiring them to explicitly disclose that the statute of limitations has run. We do not, therefore, hold that the use of the word "settlement" is "misleading as a matter of federal law." *Buchanan,* 776 F.3d at 400 (Kethledge, J., dissenting). Rather, in keeping with the text and purpose of the FDCPA, we merely reiterate that any such letters, when read in their entirety, must not deceive or mislead the least-sophisticated debtor into believing that she has a legal obligation to pay the time-barred debt. *See, e.g., Caprio,* 709 F.3d at 149 (noting that "even the 'least sophisticated debtor' is expected to read any notice in its entirety"); *Huertas,* 641 F.3d at 33 (examining the specific language used in the letter from the perspective of the least-sophisticated debtor); *Campuzano-Burgos*, 550 F.3d at 300 (analyzing letters "as a whole").

III

For the reasons stated, we will vacate the District Court's order granting Allied's p.431 motion to dismiss and remand the case for further proceedings consistent with this opinion.

[1] Allied filed a motion for judgment on the pleadings, but the District Court construed it as a motion to dismiss for failure to state a claim because it was filed before the pleadings were closed. *Tatis*, 2016 WL 5660431, at *3.

[2] Tatis also alleged that Allied used "unfair or unconscionable means" when attempting to collect the debt. The District Court dismissed that count, *Tatis*, 2016 WL 5660431, at *9, and Tatis has not made an argument challenging that ruling on appeal, Tatis Br. 4-5. *See Linder & Assocs., Inc. v. Aetna Cas. & Sur. Co.*, 166 F.3d 547, 552 n.5 (3d Cir. 1999).

[3] The District Court had jurisdiction under 28 U.S.C. § 1331. We have jurisdiction under 28 U.S.C. § 1291.

[4] Our own survey confirms this point. *Settle*, CONCISE OXFORD DICTIONARY OF CURRENT ENGLISH (7th ed. 1982) ("[T]erminate (lawsuit) by mutual agreement."); *Settle*, AMERICAN HERITAGE DICTIONARY OF THE ENGLISH LANGUAGE (4th ed. 2000) ("To decide (a lawsuit) by mutual agreement of the involved parties without court action."; "To come to an agreement, especially to resolve a lawsuit out of court."); *Settle*, WEBSTER'S THIRD NEW INTERNATIONAL DICTIONARY OF THE ENGLISH LANGUAGE UNABRIDGED (3d ed. 1993) ("[T]o conclude (a lawsuit) by agreement between the parties usu. out of court."); *see also Settlement*, AMERICAN HERITAGE DICTIONARY OF THE ENGLISH LANGUAGE (4th ed. 2000) ("An arrangement, adjustment, or other understanding reached, as in financial or business proceedings: *a divorce settlement*."); *Settlement*, WEBSTER'S THIRD NEW INTERNATIONAL DICTIONARY OF THE ENGLISH LANGUAGE UNABRIDGED (3d ed. 1993) ("[P]ayment or adjustment of an account: satisfaction of a claim by agreement often with less than full payment.").

890 F.3d 422 (2018)

Kevin C. ROTKISKE, Appellant
v.
Paul KLEMM, Esq., DBA Nudelman, Klemm & Golub, P.C., DBA Nudelman, Nudelman & Ziering, P.C., Klemm & Associates; Nudelman, Klemm & Golub, P.C., DBA Nudelman, Nudelman & Ziering, P.C., DBA Klemm & Associates; Nudelman, Nudelman & Ziering, P.C., DBA Nudelman, Klemm & Golub, P.C., Klemm & Associates; Klemm & Associates, DBA Nudelman, Klemm & Golub, P.C., Nudelman, Nudelman & Ziering, P.C.; John Does 1-10.

No. 16-1668.

United States Court of Appeals, Third Circuit.

Argued January 18, 2017.
En Banc Rehearing Ordered September 7, 2017.
Reargued En Banc February 21, 2018.
Filed: May 15, 2018.

Rotkiske v. Klemm, 890 F. 3d 422 (3rd Cir. 2018)

On Appeal from the United States District Court for the Eastern District of Pennsylvania, (D.C. No. 2-15-cv-03638), District Judge: Honorable Gene E. K. Pratter.

Matthew B. Weisberg [Argued], Weisberg Law, 7 South Morton Avenue, Morton, PA 19070, Adina H. Rosenbaum, Esq. [Argued], Public Citizen Litigation Group, 1600 20th Street, N.W., Washington, DC 20009, Counsel for Plaintiff-Appellant.

Carl E. Zapffe [Argued], Fenton & McGarvey Law Firm, 2401 Stanley Gault Parkway, Louisville, KY 40223, Counsel for Defendants-Appellees.

Before: SMITH, Chief Judge, McKEE, AMBRO, CHAGARES, JORDAN, HARDIMAN, GREENAWAY, JR., VANASKIE, SHWARTZ, KRAUSE, RESTREPO, BIBAS, and FISHER[*], Circuit Judges.

p.423 OPINION OF THE COURT

HARDIMAN, Circuit Judge.

This appeal requires us to determine when the statute of limitations begins to run under the Fair Debt Collection Practices Act (FDCPA or Act), 91 Stat. 874, 15 p.424 U.S.C. § 1692 *et seq.* The Act states that "[a]n action to enforce any liability created by this subchapter may be brought in any appropriate United States district court. . . within one year from the date on which the violation occurs." 15 U.S.C. § 1692k(d). The United States Courts of Appeals for the Fourth and Ninth Circuits have held that the time begins to run not when the violation occurs, but when it is discovered. *See Lembach v. Bierman,* 528 Fed.Appx. 297 (4th Cir. 2013) (per curiam); *Mangum v. Action Collection Serv., Inc.,* 575 F.3d 935 (9th Cir. 2009). We respectfully disagree. In our view, the Act says what it means and means what it says: the statute of limitations runs from "the date on which the violation occurs." 15 U.S.C. § 1692k(d).

I

The relevant facts of this case are undisputed. Appellant Kevin Rotkiske accumulated credit card debt between 2003 and 2005, which his bank referred to Klemm & Associates (Klemm) for collection. Klemm sued for payment in March 2008 and attempted service at an address where Rotkiske no longer lived, but eventually withdrew its suit when it was unable to locate him. Klemm tried again in January 2009, refiling its suit and attempting service at the same address.[1] Unbeknownst to Rotkiske, somebody at that residence accepted service on his behalf, and Klemm obtained a default judgment for around $1,500. Rotkiske discovered the judgment when he applied for a mortgage in September 2014.

On June 29, 2015, Rotkiske sued Klemm and several associated individuals and entities asserting, *inter alia,* that the above-described collection efforts violated the FDCPA. Defendants moved to dismiss Rotkiske's FDCPA claim as untimely and the United States District Court for the Eastern District of Pennsylvania agreed. The District Court rejected Rotkiske's argument that the Act's statute of limitations incorporates a discovery rule which "delays the beginning of a limitations period until the plaintiff knew of or should have known of his injury." *Rotkiske v. Klemm,* No. 15-3638, 2016 WL 1021140, at *3 (E.D. Pa. Mar. 15, 2016). It found the "actual statutory language" sufficiently clear that the clock began to run on Defendants' "last opportunity to comply with the statute," not upon Rotkiske's discovery of the violation. *Id.* at *4. The Court also rejected Rotkiske's request for equitable tolling as duplicative of his discovery rule argument. *Id.* at *5.

Rotkiske timely appealed the judgment of the District Court and a panel of this Court heard oral argument on January 18, 2017. Prior to issuing an opinion and judgment, on September 7, 2017, the Court sua sponte ordered rehearing en banc, and argument was held on February 21, 2018.

II[2]

"Statutory interpretation, as we always say, begins with the text." *Ross v.* p.425 *Blake,* ___ U.S. ___, 136 S.Ct. 1850, 1856, 195 L.Ed.2d 117 (2016). The text at issue in this appeal reads:

> An action to enforce any liability created by this subchapter may be brought in any appropriate United States district court . . . within one year from the date *on which the violation occurs.*

15 U.S.C. § 1692k(d) (emphasis added). In declining Rotkiske's request to read the statute to imply a discovery rule, the District Court found that this language spoke clearly. We agree, and will affirm its judgment dismissing Rotkiske's untimely FDCPA claim.

Statutes of limitation provide "security and stability to human affairs" and are "vital to the welfare of society." *Gabelli v. S.E.C.,* 568 U.S. 442, 448-49, 133 S.Ct. 1216, 185 L.Ed.2d 297 (2013) (citations omitted). The standard rule is that a statute of limitations "commences when the plaintiff has 'a complete and present cause of action.'" *Bay Area Laundry & Dry Cleaning Pension Tr. Fund v. Ferbar Corp. of Cal.*, 522 U.S. 192, 201, 118 S.Ct. 542, 139 L.Ed.2d 553 (1997) (quoting *Rawlings v. Ray*, 312 U.S. 96, 98, 61 S.Ct. 473, 85 L.Ed. 605 (1941)). By fixing an end point for civil liability, Congress advances "the basic policies of all limitations provisions: repose, elimination of stale claims, and certainty about a plaintiff's opportunity for recovery and a defendant's potential liabilities." *Gabelli*, 568 U.S. at 447-48, 133 S.Ct. 1216 (quoting *Rotella v. Wood*, 528 U.S. 549, 555, 120 S.Ct. 1075, 145 L.Ed.2d 1047 (2000)).

We recently summarized the two basic models that "a legislature may choose" in fixing the start of a limitations period. *G.L. v. Ligonier Valley Sch. Dist. Auth.*, 802 F.3d 601, 613 (3d Cir. 2015). First, a statute can run from "the date the injury actually occurred, an approach known as the 'occurrence rule.'" *Id.* Alternatively, Congress may delay the start of the limitations period until "the date the aggrieved party knew or should have known of the injury, that is, the 'discovery rule.'" *Id.*

Sometimes Congress clearly picks one model or another. When a statute of limitations begins to run only when "the plaintiff acquired or should have acquired actual knowledge of the existence of such cause of action," the discovery rule plainly applies. *See, e.g.*, 29 U.S.C. § 1451(f)(2); *Bay Area Laundry*, 522 U.S. at 204, 118 S.Ct. 542 (interpreting 29 U.S.C. § 1451(f)(2) to impose a discovery rule); *Merck & Co. v. Reynolds*, 559 U.S. 633, 648, 130 S.Ct. 1784, 176 L.Ed.2d 582 (2010) (interpreting similar language in 28 U.S.C. § 1658(b)(1)). Likewise, when Congress specifies that the "date on which the violation occurs" starts the limitations period, the occurrence rule plainly applies. Accordingly, we hold that § 1692k(d)'s one-year limitations period begins to run when a would-be defendant violates the FDCPA, not when a potential plaintiff discovers or should have discovered the violation.

Congress does not, of course, always express statutes of limitations so directly. Instead of expressly enacting an occurrence or a discovery rule, Congress often articulates statutes of limitations in terms somewhere between those two poles. Some statutes of limitations begin when a "claim first accrue[s]." *See, e.g.*, *Gabelli*, 568 U.S. at 447-48, 133 S.Ct. 1216 (interpreting 28 p.426 U.S.C. § 2462). Others start when the "cause of action arises" or when "liability arises." *See, e.g.*, *McMahon v. United States*, 342 U.S. 25, 27, 72 S.Ct. 17, 96 L.Ed. 26 (1951) (interpreting Suits in Admiralty Act); *Bay Area Laundry*, 522 U.S. at 201, 118 S.Ct. 542 (interpreting 29 U.S.C. § 1451(f)(1)). And we have little doubt that an exhaustive search would yield still other variations—some subtle, some stark. This appeal does not implicate the less-determinate language of those statutes, however.

III

Despite the "occurrence" language of the FDCPA, Rotkiske insists that the discovery rule applies. His argument relies on the text of the FDCPA, the policies underlying the Act, decisions of two of our sister courts of appeals finding a discovery rule in the FDCPA, and decisions of this Court applying a discovery rule to other federal statutes. We consider each point in turn.

A

For starters, we reject summarily Rotkiske's assertion that the text of the FDCPA is silent on the discovery rule. *See* Rotkiske Supp. Br. 6. While it is true that the Act does not state *in haec verba* that "the discovery rule shall not apply," the Supreme Court made clear in *TRW Inc. v. Andrews,* 534 U.S. 19, 28, 122 S.Ct. 441, 151 L.Ed.2d 339 (2001), that Congress may "implicitly" provide as much. In that Fair Credit Reporting Act (FCRA) case, the Court held that Congress had "implicitly excluded a general discovery rule by explicitly including a more limited one." 534 U.S. at 28, 122 S.Ct. 441. The same natural reading applies to the FDCPA in this appeal: Congress's explicit choice of an occurrence rule implicitly excludes a discovery rule. A quotidian example illustrates why this is so. When a bill states that payment is timely if it is "received at the bank by 5:00," it goes without saying that a check arriving at 6:00 is late even if it was postmarked a week earlier. Short of the express command that *TRW* tells us is not required, it is hard to imagine how Congress could have more clearly foreclosed the discovery rule.

B

Rotkiske also highlights the remedial purpose of the FDCPA, which was enacted to combat the national problem of abusive debt-collection practices. Rotkiske Supp. Br. 10-11. Rotkiske emphasizes that those practices may involve fraud, deception, or self-concealing behavior such that the failure to apply the discovery rule would thwart the principal purpose of the Act. *Id.* at 11-13. He warns that "[a]bsent the discovery rule, vulnerable consumers will be left without redress if the harm caused by debt collectors' abusive or deceptive acts remains concealed for over a year." *Id.* at 16. We disagree for two reasons.

First, to the extent Rotkiske contends that the collection practices the FDCPA proscribes are inherently fraudulent, deceptive, or self-concealing, the statute belies his argument. Debtors are often vexed by overzealous or unscrupulous debt collectors precisely because of repetitive contacts by phone or mail. As the language of the FDCPA makes clear, many violations will be apparent to consumers the moment they occur. *See, e.g.,* 15 U.S.C. § 1692c(a)(1) (proscribing communication regarding debt collection "at any unusual time or place"); *id.* § 1692d (proscribing various forms of harassment in the service of debt collection, including "[t]he use of obscene or profane language" and "[t]he publication of a list of consumers who allegedly refuse to pay debts"); *id.* § 1692f(7) (proscribing "[c]ommunicating with a consumer regarding a debt by post p.427 card"). The Act's statute of limitations applies to all of its provisions, so we decline Rotkiske's invitation to interpret the Act as if it contemplated only concealed or fraudulent conduct.[3]

Second, to the extent that FDCPA claims *do* deal with "false, deceptive, or misleading representation[s]," *id.* § 1692e, nothing in the Act impairs the discretion district courts possess to avoid patent unfairness in such cases. As we shall explain, equitable tolling remains available in appropriate cases.

C

In addition to his textual and purposive arguments, Rotkiske asks us to follow the Ninth Circuit's decision in *Mangum v. Action Collection Service, Inc.*, and the Fourth Circuit's decision in *Lembach v. Bierman,* both of which implied a discovery rule in the Act's statute of limitations. We respectfully decline to do so.

Most fundamentally, neither opinion analyzed the "violation occurs" language of the FDCPA. In *Mangum,* the Ninth Circuit did not engage the text of the Act, relying instead on its expansive holding in *Norman-Bloodsaw v. Lawrence Berkeley Lab.*, 135 F.3d 1260, 1266 (9th Cir. 1998), that "the discovery rule applies to statutes of limitations in federal litigation." *Mangum,* 575 F.3d at 940. The Ninth Circuit did acknowledge that the Supreme Court had reversed its application of the *Norman-Bloodsaw* rule to the FCRA in *TRW*. *Id.* at 940-41. Nevertheless, after brushing aside *TRW*'s analysis as "food for thought. . . worth musing on," *id.* at 941, the majority of the panel in *Mangum* concluded that *TRW* neither overruled nor undermined that circuit's prior precedent regarding the general applicability of the discovery rule, *id.*[4]

Like the Ninth Circuit in *Mangum,* the Fourth Circuit in *Lembach* failed to engage the statutory text on its way to determining that a discovery rule would vindicate the policies underlying the FDCPA. *Lembach,* 528 Fed.Appx. at 302. The Court reasoned—without mentioning equitable tolling—that because plaintiffs "had no way of discovering the alleged violation," the defendant "should not be allowed to profit from the statute of limitations when its wrongful acts have been concealed." *Id.* For these reasons, we decline to join either the Ninth or the Fourth Circuits in holding that the statute means something other than what it plainly says.

D

In addition to the opinions of our sister courts in *Mangum* and *Lembach,* Rotkiske places substantial weight on our opinion in *Oshiver v. Levin, Fishbein, Sedran & Berman,* 38 F.3d 1380 (3d Cir. 1994). In dictum in that case, we applied the discovery rule to Title VII, even though the statutory language required charges to be filed within 180 days "after the alleged unlawful p.428 employment practice occurred." 42 U.S.C. § 2000e-5(e).

The problem with Rotkiske's reliance on *Oshiver* is that its dictum is in obvious tension with the Supreme Court's decision in *TRW*. Instead of focusing on the statutory text (which we relegated to a footnote, 38 F.3d at 1385 n.3), we described a "general rule" that "the statute of limitations begins to run . . . [on] the date on which the plaintiff *discovers*" an injury rather than "the date on which the wrong that injures the plaintiff occurs," *id.* at 1385 (emphasis in original). The Supreme Court's approach in *TRW* counsels in favor of reconsidering our earlier practice of presuming that federal statutes of limitations include an implied discovery rule. Indeed, to the extent that our decisions have relied on such a general presumption in applying a discovery rule to statutes that expressly begin to run when a violation "occurs," they cannot be reconciled with the Supreme Court's mandate that when "the text [of a statute] and reasonable inferences from it give a clear answer," that is "the end of the matter." *Brown v. Gardner,* 513 U.S. 115, 120, 115 S.Ct. 552, 130 L.Ed.2d 462 (1994) (citations omitted). *See Oshiver,* 38 F.3d at 1385 (presuming applicability of discovery rule); *Podobnik v. U.S. Postal Serv.*, 409 F.3d 584, 590 (3d Cir. 2005) (same, following *Oshiver*).

Rather than imply a discovery rule by rote "in the absence of a contrary directive from Congress," *see, e.g., Disabled in Action of Pa. v. S.E. Pa. Transp. Auth.*, 539 F.3d 199, 209 (3d Cir. 2008), we must parse each limitations period using ordinary principles of statutory analysis—beginning with the statutory text and then proceeding to consider its structure and context. *See, e.g., TRW*, 534 U.S. at 28-33, 122 S.Ct. 441. As part of that inquiry into context, it may sometimes prove appropriate to consider whether there are "historical[ ] or equitable reasons" to adopt either an occurrence or a discovery rule. *Gabelli*, 568 U.S at 454, 133 S.Ct. 1216. *See, e.g., TRW*, 534 U.S. at 27-28, 122 S.Ct. 441 (noting that latent disease and medical malpractice, but not the FCRA, are contexts that "cr[y] out for application of a discovery rule"); *Stephens v. Clash*, 796 F.3d 281, 285-88 (3d Cir. 2015) (noting the secretive nature of trade in child pornography and the likelihood that an occurrence rule would frustrate Congress's objective to provide a remedy to blameless minor victims). This is not such a case, however, because the text of § 1692k(d) plainly incorporates an occurrence rule.

IV

We conclude by emphasizing that our holding today does nothing to undermine the doctrine of equitable tolling. Indeed, we have already recognized the availability of equitable tolling for civil suits alleging an FDCPA violation. *See Glover v. F.D.I.C.*, 698 F.3d 139, 151 (3d Cir. 2012) (considering and rejecting an equitable tolling argument where no extraordinary barrier existed to plaintiff's suit). We do not reach the question in this case only because Rotkiske failed to raise it on appeal. Accordingly, our opinion should not be read to forclose the possibility that equitable tolling might apply to FDCPA violations that involve fraudulent, misleading, or self-concealing conduct. *See, e.g., Bailey v. Glover*, 88 U.S. (21 Wall.) 342, 348, 22 L.Ed. 636 (1874) ("[W]here the party injured by the fraud remains in ignorance of it without any fault or want of diligence or care on his part, the bar . . . does not begin to run until the fraud is discovered, though there be no special circumstances or efforts on the part of the p.429 party committing the fraud to conceal it. . . .").[5]

V

Civil actions alleging violations of the Fair Debt Collection Practices Act must be filed within one year from the date of the violation. Because Rotkiske's action was filed well after that period expired, his action was untimely. We will affirm the judgment of the District Court.

[*] Honorable D. Michael Fisher, United States Circuit Judge for the Third Circuit, assumed senior status on February 1, 2017.

[1] In a certification accompanying Defendants' motion to dismiss, Klemm's managing partner stated that by the time of the second suit he had moved to a new firm named Nudelman, Nudelman & Ziering. Because Rotkiske has sued (among

others) both Klemm and Nudelman, and the complaint's allegations do not distinguish between them, for the sake of simplicity we refer only to Klemm.

[2] The District Court had jurisdiction under 28 U.S.C. § 1331. We have jurisdiction under 28 U.S.C. § 1291. Our review of an order dismissing a complaint for failure to state a claim is plenary, *Evancho v. Fisher,* 423 F.3d 347, 350 (3d Cir. 2005), as is our review of questions of statutory interpretation, *United States v. Zavrel,* 384 F.3d 130, 132 (3d Cir. 2004). We will affirm an order dismissing a complaint only when the complaint fails to "contain sufficient factual matter, accepted as true, to 'state a claim to relief that is plausible on its face.'" *Ashcroft v. Iqbal,* 556 U.S. 662, 678, 129 S.Ct. 1937, 173 L.Ed.2d 868 (2009) (quoting *Bell Atl. Corp. v. Twombly,* 550 U.S. 544, 570, 127 S.Ct. 1955, 167 L.Ed.2d 929 (2007)).

[3] The fact that the conduct proscribed by the FDCPA will usually be obvious to its victims distinguishes this case from our decision in *Stephens v. Clash,* 796 F.3d 281 (3d Cir. 2015). There, we considered a child sexual abuse claim governed by a statute that required a filing "within six years after the right of action first accrues." 796 F.3d at 285 (quoting 18 U.S.C. § 2255(b) (2012)). We reasoned that since "child pornography is most often distributed in secret and without the victim's immediate knowledge," the statute's fundamental objective of providing redress to exploited children would most often "be thwarted without the discovery rule." *Id.* at 285-86.

[4] Judge O'Scannlain disagreed, relying on essentially the same reading of the statutory text that we adopt here. *Mangum,* 575 F.3d at 944 (O'Scannlain, J., specially concurring).

[5] If Rotkiske had preserved reliance on equitable tolling on appeal, then Judges McKee, Ambro, Vanaskie, and Shwartz would have remanded to allow the District Court to consider whether he would be entitled to rely on this doctrine because our precedent had not previously recognized that a defendant's self-concealing conduct may be a basis for equitable tolling.

898 F.3d 351 (2018)

Thomas E. ST. PIERRE, Appellant in No. 17-1731
v.
RETRIEVAL-MASTERS CREDITORS BUREAU, INC., Appellant in No. 17-1941.

Nos. 17-1731 & 17-1941.

United States Court of Appeals, Third Circuit.

Argued: January 23, 2018.
Opinion Filed: August 7, 2018.

St. Pierre v. Retrieval-Masters Creditors Bureau, 898 F. 3d 351 (3rd Cir. 2018)

On Appeal from the United States District Court for the District of New Jersey, (D.N.J. Civil Action No. 3-15-cv-02596), Honorable Freda L. Wolfson, U.S. District Judge.

Michael J. Quirk, Esq. [ARGUED], Berezofsky Law Group, 40 West Evergreen Avenue, Suite 104, Philadelphia, PA 19118-3324, Peter Colonna Romano, Esq., Berezofsky Law Group, Woodland Falls Corporate Center, 210 Lake Drive East, Suite 101, Cherry Hill, NJ 08002, Christopher Markos, Esq., Williams Cedar, 1515 Market Street, Suite 1300, Philadelphia, PA 19102, Attorneys for Plaintiff-Appellant Thomas E. St. Pierre.

Joel D. Bertocchi, Esq. [ARGUED], Carlos A. Ortiz, Esq., Louis J. Manetti, Jr., David M. Schultz, Esq., Hinshaw & Culbertson LLP, 151 North Franklin Street, Suite 2500, Chicago, IL 60606, Han Sheng Beh, Esq., Hinshaw & Culbertson, 800 Third Avenue, 13th Floor, New York, NY 10022, Attorneys for Defendant-Appellee Retrieval-Masters Creditors Bureau, Inc.

Before: GREENAWAY, JR., KRAUSE, Circuit Judges, and JONES, District Judge.[*]

p.354 OPINION OF THE COURT

KRAUSE, Circuit Judge.

In this appeal following the District Court's dismissal of Appellant Thomas E. St. Pierre's class action complaint, we consider a matter of first impression among the Courts of Appeals: whether unpaid highway tolls constitute the type of "debt" that could support a consumer claim under the Fair Debt Collection Practices Act. Because we conclude they do not, we will affirm.

I. Background[1]

A. Factual Background

St. Pierre is a New Jersey resident and the registered owner of a car that he sometimes drives on New Jersey highways. p.355 On those occasions, he is subject to New Jersey's statutory toll requirements, including that "[n]o vehicle shall be permitted to make use of any highway project or part thereof operated by the New Jersey Turnpike Authority [("Authority")]... except upon the payment of such tolls, if any, as may from time to time be prescribed by the Authority," N.J. Stat. Ann. § 27:23-25, and that the owner of the vehicle is liable for the payment of highway tolls even if "such vehicle was used or operated" by someone other than the owner, *id.* § 27:23-34.2(b).

Like many car owners in New Jersey, St. Pierre chose to sign up for New Jersey E-ZPass ("E-ZPass"), an electronic toll payment program that facilitates toll collection. E-ZPass accountholders agree to certain terms and conditions (the "E-ZPass Contract"), including that they maintain a positive balance in a prepaid E-ZPass account from which the toll fare is automatically deducted when they pass through an E-ZPass lane and that their "failure to pay charges posted to [their] [a]ccount, including tolls, may result in additional penalties as provided by law."[2] JA 66. When St. Pierre's E-ZPass account fell into arrears because he failed to maintain a positive balance, E-ZPass assigned it to Appellee Retrieval-Masters Credit Bureau, Inc. ("RMCB"), a private debt collection agency, which, in turn, sent St. Pierre a collection letter "for outstanding violations owed for toll evasions in the amount of $1,200.75."[3] JA 70. At issue in this case, however, is not the letter itself but the envelope in which the letter was sent. Visible through the glassine window of that envelope was not only St. Pierre's name and address, but also a "quick response" code[4] and St. Pierre's account number.

St. Pierre's amended class action complaint alleges that the disclosure of these p.356 two pieces of information on the envelope violated the Fair Debt Collection Practices Act ("FDCPA"), 15 U.S.C. §§ 1692a-1692p, which prohibits the use of any "unfair or unconscionable means to collect or attempt to collect any debt," *id.* § 1692f, including "any language or symbol, other than the debt collector's address, on any envelope when communicating with a consumer by use of the mails," *id.* § 1692f(8). That prohibition, however, applies only to the collection of a "debt," which the FDCPA defines as an "obligation ... of a consumer to pay money arising out of a transaction in which the money, property, insurance, or services which are the subject of the transaction are primarily for personal, family, or household purposes." *Id.* § 1692a(5). And there lies the crux of this appeal: Do unpaid highway tolls reflect a consumer's "obligation ... arising out of a transaction in which the ... services which are the subject of the transaction are primarily for personal, family, or household purposes," *id.,* or a legal obligation in the nature of a tax that falls outside the scope of the FDCPA?

The District Court concluded the latter. Although it held as a threshold matter that St. Pierre had alleged an injury sufficiently "concrete" to confer Article III standing and, by extension, federal jurisdiction, *St. Pierre v. Retrieval-Masters Creditors Bureau, Inc.,* No. 15-cv-2596, 2017 WL 1102635, at *6 (D.N.J. Mar. 24, 2017), it dismissed St. Pierre's complaint on the ground that unpaid highway tolls do not constitute "debt" and therefore failed to state a claim for a violation of the FDCPA, *id.* at *10.

St. Pierre filed this appeal challenging the District Court's characterization of the obligation to pay highway tolls, and RMCB cross-appealed, challenging the Court's ruling on standing.

II. Jurisdiction and Standard of Review

The District Court had jurisdiction pursuant to 28 U.S.C. § 1331, and we have jurisdiction pursuant to 28 U.S.C. § 1291. We review de novo both the District Court's decision to dismiss for failure to state a claim, *In re Lipitor Antitrust Litig.*, 868 F.3d 231, 249 (3d Cir. 2017), and its conclusion as to standing, *Edmonson v. Lincoln Nat'l Life Ins. Co.*, 725 F.3d 406, 414 (3d Cir. 2013).

III. Discussion

Because St. Pierre's standing to bring this case implicates the Court's jurisdiction, it must be resolved as a threshold matter. *Hartig Drug Co. v. Senju Pharm. Co.*, 836 F.3d 261, 269 (3d Cir. 2016). We therefore will address RMCB's cross-appeal before turning to the merits of St. Pierre's FDCPA claim.[5]

A. Standing

To establish standing, St. Pierre must allege facts demonstrating that he suffered (1) an injury-in-fact; (2) that is fairly traceable to the defendant's challenged conduct; and (3) that is likely to be redressed by a favorable judicial decision. *Lujan v. Defenders of Wildlife,* 504 U.S. 555, 590, 112 S.Ct. 2130, 119 L.Ed.2d 351 (1992). RMBC argues that St. Pierre failed to make that showing because he alleged only a *de minimis* procedural violation of p.357 the FDCPA and not an injury-in-fact. Although we previously held in *Douglass v. Convergent Outsourcing,* 765 F.3d 299 (3d Cir. 2014), that a debt collector's disclosure of a debtor's account number through a glassine window is not a *de minimis* violation, RMCB contends the Supreme Court's interim decision in *Spokeo, Inc. v. Robins,* ___ U.S. ___, 136 S.Ct. 1540, 194 L.Ed.2d 635 (2016), casts doubt on that holding and requires denial of St. Pierre's argument on standing grounds. It does not.

In *Spokeo,* the Supreme Court provided a lens through which to determine whether an intangible injury is sufficiently "concrete and particularized" and "actual or imminent" to qualify as an injury-in-fact. 136 S.Ct. at 1548. We first ask "whether an alleged intangible harm has a close relationship to a harm that has traditionally been regarded as providing a basis for a lawsuit in English or American Courts." *Id.* at 1549. If so, it is likely to satisfy the injury-in-fact element of standing; if not, we next ask whether Congress has expressed an intent to make an injury redressable by "elevat[ing] [it] to the status of [a] legally cognizable injur[y]" even if that injury was previously inadequate in law. *Id.* Here too, if Congress expressed such an intent, the injury is likely to satisfy Article III. Thus, while "a bare procedural violation, divorced from any concrete harm" will not suffice, "the violation of a procedural right granted by statute can be sufficient in some circumstances to constitute injury in fact. In other words, a plaintiff in such a case need not allege any *additional* harm beyond the one Congress has identified." *Id.*

As we recently observed in *In re Horizon Healthcare Servs. Inc. Data Breach Litig.*, 846 F.3d 625 (3d Cir. 2017), however, *Spokeo* merely "reiterate[d] traditional notions of standing" and "reemphasize[d] that Congress has the power to define injuries that were previously inadequate at law," rather than "erect[ing] any new barriers that might prevent Congress from identifying new causes of action though they may be based on intangible harms." *Id.* at 638 (internal quotation marks omitted). For that reason, we concluded in *Horizon* that "the improper disclosure of one's personal data in violation of [the Fair Credit Reporting Act] is a cognizable injury for Article III standing purposes," *id.* at 641, and that "the unauthorized dissemination of personal information ... causes an injury in and of itself — whether or not the disclosure of that information increased the risk of identity theft or some other future harm," *id.* at 639. We also cited approvingly to our prior precedent — *In re Google Inc. Cookie Placement Consumer Privacy Litigation*, 806 F.3d 125 (3d Cir. 2015), where we held that claims "that the defendants, in the course of serving advertisements to their *personal* web browsers, implanted tracking cookies on their *personal* computers" alleged "concrete, particularized, and actual" injuries, *id.* at 134-35, and *In re Nickelodeon Consumer Privacy Litigation*, 827 F.3d 262 (3d Cir. 2016), where we concluded that "the unlawful disclosure of legally protected information" constitutes "a clear *de facto* injury," *id.* at 272-74 — identifying those as other examples of intangible but concrete injuries that Congress had defined to protect consumers. *Horizon*, 846 F.3d at 636-39; *id.* at 642-43 (Shwartz, J., concurring).

Spokeo thus reinforces, rather than undermines, our holding in *Douglass*. And that holding squarely resolves the standing issue here. In *Douglass*, we observed that the exposure of a plaintiff's account number through a glassine window[6] "implicates
p.358 a core concern animating the FDCPA — the invasion of privacy" — and thus is closely related to harm that has traditionally been regarded as providing a basis for a lawsuit in English and American courts. *Douglass*, 765 F.3d at 303; *see Spokeo*, 136 S.Ct. at 1549. We also explained that even if § 1692f(8) contains a "benign language exception," the exposure of a debtor's account number through a glassine window "is not benign" because "we cannot find language exempt from § 1692f(8) if its disclosure on an envelope would run counter to the very reasons Congress enacted the FDCPA." *Douglass*, 765 F.3d at 303.

As *Douglass* controls here, the District Court properly concluded that a violation of § 1692f(8) is a legally cognizable injury that confers standing on St. Pierre.

B. Merits

Having satisfied ourselves of our jurisdiction, we turn to the substance of St. Pierre's claim under the FDCPA. The FDCPA, which is a remedial statute passed by Congress in 1977 and geared towards eliminating abusive practices by debt collectors, creates a private right of action against debt collectors who violate its provisions. 15 U.S.C. § 1692k; *see also Brown v. Card Serv. Ctr.*, 464 F.3d 450, 453 (3d Cir. 2006). "To prevail on an FDCPA claim, a plaintiff must prove that (1) she is a consumer, (2) the defendant is a debt collector, (3) the defendant's challenged practice involves an attempt to collect a 'debt' as the [FDCPA] defines it, and (4) the defendant has violated a provision of the FDCPA in attempting to collect the debt." *Douglass,* 765 F.3d at 303.

Here, the only disputed prong is the "threshold requirement" that the prohibited collection practices relate to a "debt," *Zimmerman v. HBO Affiliate Grp.,* 834 F.2d 1163, 1167 (3d Cir. 1987), which the FDCPA defines as "any obligation ... of a consumer to pay money arising out of a transaction in which the money, property, insurance, or services which are the subject of the transaction are primarily for personal, family, or household purposes," 15 U.S.C. § 1692a(5). As the terms "transaction" and "personal, family, or household purposes" are not further defined in the statute, the definition of "debt" has proven elusive.[7] In an effort to pin it down as to highway tolls, we review the few cases to date in which we have marked its bounds.

1. Relevant Precedent Concerning FDCPA "Debt"

We have addressed the definition of FDCPA "debt" in only four cases. In *Staub v. Harris,* 626 F.2d 275 (3d Cir. 1980), we held that a delinquent per capita tax levied by a Pennsylvania taxing district against the plaintiffs was not "debt" encompassed by the FDCPA. *Id.* at 278. Without deciding whether the term "'transaction' as used in the FDCPA always connotes the existence of an underlying contractual relationship," we concluded that, "at a minimum, the statute contemplates p.359 that the debt has arisen as a result of the rendition of a service or purchase of property or other item of value." *Id.* By contrast, "[t]he relationship between taxpayer and taxing authority," we held, "does not encompass that type of pro tanto exchange which the statutory definition envisages" because tax revenue is a "public burden[] imposed generally upon the inhabitants" used for "nonpersonal purposes [such] as prisons, roads, defense, courts and other governmental services," and "without reference to peculiar benefits to particular individuals[.]" *Id.* (quoting *Black's Law Dictionary* 1307 (5th ed. 1979)).

Next, in *Zimmerman v. HBO Affiliate Group,* 834 F.2d 1163 (3d Cir. 1987), we held that the obligation that arose out of allegedly abusive collection letters sent by defendant cable television companies attempting to collect a sum of money to settle potential tort claims against plaintiffs for the "illegal reception of HBO signals" was not "debt" under the FDCPA because the source of the obligation was an "asserted tort liability" rather than a consensual transaction. *Id.* at 1165-68. While we recognized that "the concept of a 'transaction' is broader than that of a contract... nothing in the statute or the legislative history leads us to believe that Congress intended to equate asserted tort liability with asserted consumer debt" or, for that matter, that the FDCPA was intended to protect against "abusive practices in collecting tort settlements from alleged tortfeasors through threats of legal action." *Id.* at 1168.

Over a decade later, in *Pollice v. National Tax Funding, L.P.,* 225 F.3d 379 (3d Cir. 2000), we addressed whether homeowners' obligations to pay their property taxes, as well as their water and sewer utilities, qualified as "debt" under the statute.[8] *Id.* at 401. As for the property taxes, we held that "*Staub* [wa]s controlling" because "[u]nlike a sales tax, for example, which arguably arises from the sale transaction, the property taxes ... arose not from the purchase of property but from the *fact of ownership*." *Id.* at 401-02. We rejected the plaintiff's attempt to distinguish *Staub* on the basis that "the tax obligations changed in character and became 'debts'" when they were assigned to a private entity that was in the business of purchasing such claims, explaining that even after that assignment, "there still had not been a 'transaction' involving the homeowners; their obligation to pay [the private entity] still arose from the levying of taxes." *Id.* at 402. We also concluded that the fact that the homeowners could pay their delinquent property taxes pursuant to a payment plan did not distinguish the nature of the property taxes from the per capita tax in *Staub*. *Id.* at 403. In that context, we explained, the payment plan itself was not the obligation but rather was "simply [] one aspect of defendants' course of conduct in attempting to collect the *original* ... obligations which were owed to the government entities[.]" *Id.* at 402-03.

We had a different view, however, of the homeowners' water and sewer utility obligations. Those obligations, we held, did p.360 constitute FDCPA "debt" because "[a]t the time [they] first arose, homeowners ('consumers' of water and sewer services) had an 'obligation ... to pay money' to the government entities which arose out of a 'transaction' (requesting water and sewer services) the subject of which was 'services... primarily for personal, family, or household purposes.'" *Id.* at 400. The consumer's affirmative "request," we explained, transformed the relationship between the government and homeowner into a "transaction,"[9] *id.*, and the flow of the water directly into the household for personal consumption by the consumer rendered that transaction "primarily for personal, family, or household purposes," *id.* (quoting 15 U.S.C. § 1692a(5)).

Finally, in *Piper v. Portnoff Law Associates, Ltd.*, 396 F.3d 227 (3d Cir. 2005), we again held that transactions involving utility services gave rise to "debt" because "whenever a homeowner voluntarily elects to avail himself of municipal water/sewer services, in whatever manner, and thereby incurs an obligation to pay for such services, there is the kind of *pro tanto* exchange contemplated by the FDCPA." *Id.* at 233 n.8. We also observed that "[t]he consensual nature of the transaction distinguishe[d] [Pennsylvania water and sewer service] from tax assessments which *Pollice* held to not be debts within the meaning of the FDCPA," emphasizing that the consumer's usage "was metered in the normal fashion and ... the amount of their obligation to pay was based on the amount of water they chose to use." *Id.*

From these cases, we distill a three-part test to evaluate whether an obligation constitutes "debt" under the FDCPA. First, we consider whether the underlying obligation "aris[es] out of a transaction," 15 U.S.C. § 1692a(5) — that is, a consensual exchange involving an affirmative "request," *Pollice,* 225 F.3d at 400, and "the rendition of a service or purchase of property or other item of value," *Staub,* 626 F.2d at 278, such as a contract — or whether, instead, it arises by virtue of a legal status — that is, an involuntary obligation attendant to the fact of having a specific legal status such as that of a property owner, *see Pollice,* 225 F.3d at 401, legal resident, *see Staub,* 626 F.2d at 278, or tortfeasor or other type of offender under criminal or civil law, *see Zimmerman,* 834 F.2d at 1168.[10]

p.361 Second, if we conclude that the obligation arises out of a transaction, we next identify what "money, property, insurance, or services ... [] are the subject of the transaction," 15 U.S.C. § 1692a(5), *i.e.,* what it is that is being rendered in exchange for the monetary payment. And third, we consider the characteristics of that "money, property, insurance, or services" to ascertain whether they are "primarily for personal, family, or household purposes." *Id.*

2. The Obligation to Pay Highway Tolls

Applying this framework to the obligation to pay highway tolls, we conclude it does not satisfy the definition of "debt" under the FDCPA.

Step One: Arising out of a Transaction. At the first step, we consider the two arguments raised by St. Pierre as to why the obligation to pay highway tolls arises out of a "transaction." His first, that the transaction out of which his obligation to pay highway tolls arises is the E-ZPass Contract, is a non-starter. We were clear in *Pollice* that the original source of the obligation — not the subsequent method of collection — determines whether an obligation constitutes "debt" under the FDCPA, 225 F.3d at 402, and, like the payment plan in *Pollice,* the contract with E-ZPass is merely "directed toward the collection of the original obligations, not any obligations which may have arisen from [the E-ZPass Contract]," *id.* at 403.

St. Pierre attempts to distinguish *Pollice* by arguing that the E-ZPass Contract imposes a $50 per violation fee even for "inadvertent violations" that are otherwise exempted by statute. Reply Br. 10-11. But this too is a false start. St. Pierre cites to no authority for that reading of the E-ZPass Contract, and the E-ZPass Contract expressly provides that drivers are required to pay penalties only "as required by law," JA 66, and thus appears coextensive with the statutory requirement that "an owner that proves an inadvertent toll violation has occurred shall be required only to pay the toll and shall not incur the administrative fee."[11] N.J. Admin. Code § 19:9-9.2(b).

St. Pierre makes more headway with his second argument in support of a "transaction," *i.e.,* that he did not have to drive on the toll roads and voluntarily chose to do so. Here, we find the analogy to the utilities in *Piper* compelling: Just as "a homeowner voluntarily elects to avail himself of municipal water/sewer services ... and thereby incurs an obligation to pay for such services ... based on the amount of water [the homeowner] chose to use," 396 p.362 F.3d at 233 n.8, so too does St. Pierre, by electing to drive on toll roads (or authorizing another driver to do so in his vehicle), "voluntarily elects to avail himself" of the Authority's highway services in exchange for a per-use fee — a classic *pro tanto* exchange, *id.*

We acknowledge this presents a closer case than *Piper* in two respects. For one, the obligation to pay highway tolls is non-consensual in the sense that it involves a statutory requirement. But that is not dispositive: In *Pollice,* we recognized that water and sewer obligations were "debt," notwithstanding the fact that "a City ordinance... provides for a twelve percent annual rate of interest on claims for unpaid sewer charges," 225 F.3d at 386, and we observed in dictum that a sales tax — which is, of course, a statutorily-imposed obligation — might constitute "debt" because, unlike property tax, sales tax "arguably arises from the sale transaction" for goods or services rather than "from the *fact of ownership,*" *id.* at 402. In neither discussion did we indicate that the mere codification of an obligation precluded the exchange from constituting a transaction.

For another, highway tolls are, in a sense, a "tax for the use of highways," *Safeway Trails, Inc. v. Furman,* 41 N.J. 467, 197 A.2d 366, 376 (1964), and there is some facial appeal to the argument that highway tolls, like the property taxes in *Pollice,* derive "from the *fact of ownership,*" 225 F.3d at 402, because liability is assessed on the registered owner of the vehicle that made use of the "highway," N.J. Stat. Ann. § 27:23-25, even if that vehicle was operated by a different driver, *id.* § 27:23-34.2(b). But in contrast to the property taxes in *Pollice,* or the per capita taxes in *Staub,* the liability imposed on vehicle owners is not merely from the fact of ownership or residency but from the voluntary election to drive the owned vehicle on toll roads. *See Pollice,* 225 F.3d at 401; *Staub,* 626 F.2d at 278. That is, St. Pierre would have no obligation to pay highway tolls had he chosen to use alternative routes or to keep his car parked rather than drive on the Authority's roads; the homeowners in *Pollice* and the residents in *Staub* had no such choice.

In sum, St. Pierre's obligation to pay highway tolls does arise out of a "transaction" within the meaning of the FDCPA, 15 U.S.C. § 1692a(5), but while that gives him some momentum, he cannot cross the finish line for an FDCPA claim unless "the subject of the transaction [is] primarily for personal, family, or household purposes," *id.* We thus turn to the next step of our inquiry.

Step Two: The Subject of the Transaction. Before we can determine whether the subject of a transaction is "primarily for personal, family, or household purposes," *id.,* we must identify the subject of the transaction itself: what is being rendered in exchange for payment? Here is where the proverbial rubber meets the road, for while St. Pierre contends that what he receives is access to New Jersey highways and bridges, what is "payable from tolls" under the New Jersey statute is the Authority's mandate to "facilitate vehicular traffic and remove the present handicaps and hazards on the congested highways in [New Jersey]," and "to acquire, construct, maintain, improve, manage, repair and operate transportation projects." N.J. Stat. Ann. § 27:23-1. As the New Jersey Supreme Court observed in *City of East Orange v. Palmer,* the Authority's mission is "the construction and operation of a highway, on a self-sustaining toll basis." 52 N.J. 329, 245 A.2d 327, 330 (1968).

The toll booths dispersed throughout the roads, in other words, are merely the collection point for tolls, and access to the p.363 roads or bridges is thus incident to the payment of tolls, not the service rendered in exchange for them. Instead, highway tolls "compensate the state for the cost, maintenance and repair of its highways," *Safeway Trails,* 197 A.2d at 375, and in exchange for those tolls all drivers benefit from "safer, faster, and more convenient travel in and through the State," *id.* at 370.

Step Three: The Primary Purpose of the Subject of the Transaction. Having identified the services rendered in exchange for highway tolls, it is clear that what St. Pierre receives in exchange for the payment of highway tolls is not the private benefit of a "personal, family, or household" service or good but the very public benefit of highway maintenance and repair. 15 U.S.C. § 1692a(5). This stands in stark contrast to the services rendered in *Pollice* and *Piper,* where, as the District Court recognized, "the homeowners consumed the water and sewer services, within the confines of their home, for their personal benefit," *St. Pierre,* 2017 WL 1102635, at *8, or, for that matter, any transaction in which the service rendered in exchange for the consumer's money is personal or individual to the consumer, *see, e.g., Franklin v. Parking Revenue Recovery Servs., Inc.,* 832 F.3d 741, 745 (7th Cir. 2016) (holding that the obligation to pay for an *individual* parking space in a government-owned parking lot constitutes FDCPA "debt"). Rather, the public nature of the construction, maintenance, or operations of highways steers the obligation away from a "debt" and towards the tax obligations in *Staub,* which, as we observed there, were not primarily personal because they were "used for more general purposes." 626 F.2d at 278.

Moreover, the fact that highway tolls resemble taxes — while not a sufficient basis on which to conclude they do not arise out of a "transaction" at the first stage of our inquiry — does at this step reinforce the conclusion that the services rendered are not primarily for personal purposes. Like taxes, highway tolls are imposed for public benefit and "without reference to peculiar benefits to particular individuals or property." *Staub,* 626 F.2d at 278 (quoting *Black's Law Dictionary* 1307 (5th ed. 1979)). While one component of the obligation to pay highway tolls is the distance traveled, it is also, like taxes, largely determined categorically by the type and class of vehicle being driven[12] and thus is not simply "metered in the normal fashion... based on the amount [used]." *Piper,* 396 F.3d at 233 n.8. And just as the amount paid in taxes does not entitle an individual taxpayer to "better" parks, schools, or government systems, the amount paid in tolls does not entitle the payor to better maintenance or construction of highways. Rather, to the extent the services rendered by the Authority benefit an individual like St. Pierre, they do so only "secondarily." *Staub,* 626 F.2d at 278 (internal quotation marks omitted).

Focusing on access to the roads, St. Pierre contends that the benefit is personal and protests that because "[t]he FDCPA defines covered consumer debt based on the alleged *debtor's* — not a creditor's — purposes," his obligation to pay highway tolls should be considered "debt" because his purpose was to attain access not available to the general public and to serve the personal purpose of getting where he was going. Appellant's Br. 20-21. That argument, however, mistakenly conflates two distinct inquiries: whether, subjectively, p.364 an individual chooses to enter into the transaction primarily for his own personal purposes, and whether, objectively, the subject of the transaction — that is, "the money, property, insurance, or services" being rendered, 15 U.S.C. § 1692a(5) — is primarily for personal purposes. While in some cases, the two will be aligned, as in the case of utilities, *e.g., Pollice,* 225 F.3d at 400, they are not where the subject of the transaction is the rendition of services that benefit the public generally. And here, even accepting that road access could be considered a good or service in exchange for toll payments — and not merely an opportunity for toll collection — the other, far more significant services rendered by the Authority in exchange for highway tolls are the public services that follow from its statutory mandate, funded through tolls, "to acquire, construct, maintain, improve, manage, repair and operate transportation projects." N.J. Stat. Ann. § 27:23-1. The subject of the transaction, in other words, would still not be "primarily" for personal purposes.

In sum, the FDCPA is not implicated where, as here, the bulk, if not all of the services rendered, are made "without reference to peculiar benefits to particular individuals or property." *Staub,* 626 F.2d at 278 (quoting *Black's Law Dictionary* 1307 (5th ed. 1979)). St. Pierre's toll liability thus does not constitute "an[] obligation... primarily for personal, family, or household purposes," and does not qualify as "debt" under the FDCPA. 15 U.S.C. § 1692a(5).

IV. Conclusion

For the foregoing reasons, we will affirm the judgment of the District Court.

[*] The Honorable John E. Jones III, United States District Judge for the Middle District of Pennsylvania, sitting by designation.

[1] As this appeal arises from the grant of a motion to dismiss, we accept as true the factual allegations in St. Pierre's amended class action complaint. *See Bridge v. Phx. Bond & Indem. Co.*, 553 U.S. 639, 642 n.1, 128 S.Ct. 2131, 170 L.Ed.2d 1012 (2008). St. Pierre's complaint was originally filed in New Jersey state court before the case was removed to the District Court in April 2015.

[2] The New Jersey Administrative Code defines E-ZPass as an "Electronic toll collection system" ("ETC System"), which is an electronic system "employed or utilized by the Authority to register and collect the toll required to be paid for a vehicle entering a toll plaza owned and/or operated by, or upon the behalf of, the Authority." N.J. Admin. Code § 19:9-9.1 (2010). Through E-ZPass, "drivers can establish an account, prepay tolls and attach a small electronic device, called a tag or a transponder, to their vehicles. Tolls are automatically calculated and deducted from the prepaid account as an E-ZPass customer passes through the toll lanes." *FAQ's, NJ E-ZPass,* https://www.ezpassnj.com/en/about/faqs.shtml (last visited July 12, 2018). The Administrative Code also authorizes the Authority to adopt a "form of contract" governing the responsibilities of ETC System subscribers, *see* N.J. Admin. Code § 19:9-9.2(h), which New Jersey E-ZPass has utilized by requiring its subscribers to agree to Terms and Conditions available by way of hyperlinks on its website. *Terms and Conditions, NJ E-ZPass,* https://www.ezpassnj.com/en/about/i_terms.pdf (last visited July 12, 2018).

[3] St. Pierre's FDCPA claim is based only on this letter, which was sent on June 16, 2014. RMCB also had sent St. Pierre a collection letter in an envelope disclosing the same information on November 11, 2013, attempting to recover $60.06 that "consisted of allegedly unpaid tolls and additional fees." Appellant's Br. 4. However, St. Pierre concedes that the FDCPA's one-year limitations period, 15 U.S.C. § 1692k(d), had expired as to that letter by the time he filed his complaint on March 2, 2015.

[4] Here, a "quick response" code is a code that, "when scanned by a device such as a smart phone, reveal[s] the same information as that displayed through the glassine window, as well as a monetary amount corresponding to [a debtor's] alleged debt." *Douglass v. Convergent Outsourcing,* 765 F.3d 299, 301 (3d Cir. 2014).

[5] St. Pierre also cross-appealed, asserting that RMCB lacks standing to challenge this Court's jurisdiction. We need not tarry over that argument, for "[e]ven if the parties have not raised the issue" of standing, this Court would "examine its authority *sua sponte* during its review of the case." *Samuel-Bassett v. KIA Motors Am., Inc.,* 357 F.3d 392, 395-96 (3d Cir. 2004); *see Hayes v. Wal-Mart Stores, Inc.,* 725 F.3d 349, 360 n.9 (3d Cir. 2013).

[6] Here, as in *Douglass,* we need not reach the question whether exposure of the "quick response" code on the envelope, without more, would be sufficient to confer

standing under the FDCPA because exposure of one's account number itself suffices. *See Douglass,* 765 F.3d at 301 n.4.

[7] *See, e.g., Rosenzweig v. Transworld Sys. Inc,* No. 16-227, 2017 WL 3025557, at *6 (D.N.J. July 14, 2017) (agreeing with the reasoning of the District Court here and concluding that highway tolls are not "debt" because "tolls are akin to taxes for using the particular route"); *Yazo v. Law Enf't Sys., Inc.,* No. 08-cv-3512, 2008 WL 4852965, at *3 (C.D. Cal. Nov. 7, 2008) (reasoning that because failure to pay highway tolls violates California law, the court "cannot conclude that the obligation to pay arose out of a consensual consumer transaction").

[8] As we explain in *Tepper v. Amos Fin., LLC,* No. 17-2851, 898 F.3d 364 (3d Cir. Aug. 7, 2018), issued contemporaneously with this opinion, another aspect of *Pollice* — that is, our conclusion that the assignee of an obligation is a "debt collector" under 15 U.S.C. § 1692a(6) if the obligation is in default at the time of the assignment, 225 F.3d at 403 — was recently abrogated by the Supreme Court in *Henson v. Santander Consumer USA Inc., LLC,* ___ U.S. ___, 137 S.Ct. 1718, 1721, 198 L.Ed.2d 177 (2017). *Henson,* however, did not address the meaning of "debt" under § 1692a(5) and that aspect of *Pollice* remains valid and instructive for our purposes here.

[9] In clarifying that the homeowners' water and sewer obligations constituted "debt" under the FDCPA "even though the government entities did not extend homeowners any right to defer payment of their obligations," *Pollice,* 225 F.3d at 401, we also expressly "disavowed" our dictum in *Zimmerman* where we had stated that "the type of transaction which may give rise to a 'debt' as defined in the FDCPA" is "one involving the offer or extension of credit to a consumer," *id.* (quoting *Zimmerman,* 834 F.2d at 1168) (emphasis omitted).

[10] The other Courts of Appeals that have considered the meaning of FDCPA "debt" have likewise excluded from coverage those obligations that arise out of a legal status rather than a consensual exchange of goods or services. *See, e.g., Boyd v. J.E. Robert Co.,* 765 F.3d 123, 126 n.4 (2d Cir. 2014) (holding the obligation to pay water and sewer charges in New York City did not constitute "debt" because, unlike the "character" of the water and sewer obligations in *Pollice,* "nothing in the record here suggests that plaintiffs must 'request' water and sewer services in order to be charged by the City. Rather, the charges are levied automatically *in connection with the property ownership*") (emphasis added); *Gulley v. Markoff & Krasny,* 664 F.3d 1073, 1074-75 (7th Cir. 2011) (holding the obligation to pay government-imposed fines is not "debt" under the FDCPA because a "fine is a penalty imposed for breaking the law — not the result of a consensual transaction"); *Hawthorne v. Mac Adjustment, Inc.,* 140 F.3d 1367, 1371-72 (11th Cir. 1998) (holding the obligation of a tortfeasor to pay damages is not "debt" under the FDCPA because it is not a "consensual or contractual arrangement" but rather amounts to a "damage obligation[] thrust upon one as a result of no more than her own negligence"); *Fleming v. Pickard,* 581 F.3d 922, 925 (9th Cir. 2009) (same); *Bass v. Stolper, Koritzinsky, Brewster & Neider, S.C.,* 111 F.3d 1322, 1326 (7th Cir. 1997) (same).

[11] As the District Court observed, we do not foreclose the "possib[ility] that certain obligations, unrelated to tolls and penalties, may arise out of the [E-ZPass Contract]," *St. Pierre,* 2017 WL 1102635, at *10 n.6, and thus amount to independent liabilities that qualify as "debt," *see, e.g., Brown v. Transurban USA, Inc.,* 144 F.Supp.3d 809, 842 (E.D. Va. 2015) (holding that E-ZPass "overcharges" that arose out of the

E-ZPass contract itself were "properly understood" as a consensual transaction). Here, while the District Court astutely observed that the E-ZPass monthly membership fee of $1 "could arguably be considered a 'debt' because it was created by the [E-ZPass Contract], and not by operation of law," *St. Pierre,* 2017 WL 1102635, at *10 n.6, St. Pierre does not allege that RMCB attempted to collect the $1 membership fee, and, even if he had, he would be hard pressed to explain how that distinct and *de minimis* obligation could convert the obligation to pay highway tolls into one that arises out of the E-ZPass Contract, *see Pollice,* 225 F.3d at 402-03.

[12] *See New Jersey Turnpike Authority Toll Calculator,* http://www.njta.com/toll-calculator (last visited July 12, 2018).

898 F.3d 364 (2018)

James TEPPER; Allison Tepper
v.
AMOS FINANCIAL, LLC, Appellant.

No. 17-2851.

United States Court of Appeals, Third Circuit.

Argued June 5, 2018.
Opinion filed: August 7, 2018.

Tepper v. Amos Financial, LLC, 898 F. 3d 364 (3rd Cir. 2018)

Appeal from the United States District Court for the Eastern District of Pennsylvania, (D.C. Civil Action No. 2-15-cv-05834), District Judge: Honorable J. Curtis Joyner.

Erik M. Helbing (Argued), Helbing Law, LLC, 1328 Second Avenue, Berwick, PA 18603, Counsel for Appellant.

Michael J. Palumbo, Anthony J. Gingo, Gingo Palumbo Law Group, 4700 Rockside Road, Suite 440, Independence, OH 44131, Matthew R. Rosenkoff, Taylor English Duma LLP, 1600 Parkwood Circle, Suite 200, Atlanta, GA 30339, Counsel for Amicus Appellant.

Gleb Epelbaum, John J. Jacko, III (Argued), Fellheimer & Eichen, 50 South 16th Street, Two Liberty Place, Suite 3401, Philadelphia, PA 19102, Counsel for Appellee.

Carlo Sabatini, Brett Freeman, Sabatini Law Firm, 216 North Blakely Street, Dunmore, PA 18512, Daniel A. Edelman, Francis Greene, Edelman, Combs, Latturner & Goodwin LLC, 20 S. Clark Street, Suite 1500, Chicago, IL 60603, Counsel for Amicus Appellee.

Before: AMBRO, JORDAN, and VANASKIE, Circuit Judges.

p.365 OPINION OF THE COURT

AMBRO, Circuit Judge.

Many would gladly pay Tuesday for a hamburger today. Of course, not all of those who fall into debt make payments timely, and debt collection has become a professional trade. The Fair Debt Collection Practices Act (the "FDCPA" or "Act"), 15 U.S.C. § 1692, *et seq.*, regulates their efforts. Under it, debt collectors are prohibited from engaging in deceptive, abusive, or otherwise unfair practices to collect debts. When these practices occur, the Act gives debtors a private right of action to seek recourse, with the possibility of receiving statutory damages.

The Act does not apply, however, to all entities who collect debts; only those whose principal purpose is the collection of any debts, and those who regularly collect debts owed another are subject to its proscriptions. Those entities whose principal business is to collect the defaulted debts they purchase seek to avoid the Act's reach. We believe such an entity is what it is — a debt collector. If so, the Act applies.

I. Background

A. "Debt Collectors" Under the Fair Debt Collection Practices Act

The FDCPA is a "remedial legislation" aimed, as already noted, "to eliminate abusive debt collection practices by debt collectors." p.366 *Kaymark v. Bank of Am., N.A.*, 783 F.3d 168, 174 (3d Cir. 2015) (quoting § 1692(e); *Caprio v. Healthcare Revenue Recovery Grp., LLC,* 709 F.3d 142, 148 (3d Cir. 2013)). Importantly, it applies only to "debt collectors," *Pollice v. Nat'l Tax Funding, L.P.*, 225 F.3d 379, 403 (3d Cir. 2000), defined as any person: (1) "who uses any instrumentality of interstate commerce or the mails in any business the principal purpose of which is the collection of any debts" (the "principal purpose" definition); or (2) "who regularly collects or attempts to collect, directly or indirectly, debts owed or due or asserted to be owed or due another" (the "regularly collects for another," or "regularly collects," definition).[1] § 1692a(6). Specifically excluded from the definition's reach are, in relevant part, a creditor's officers and employees collecting debts for the creditor, a company collecting debts only for its non-debt-collector sister company, an entity collecting a debt it originated, and one collecting a debt it obtained that was not in default at the time of purchase. § 1692a(6)(A), (B), (F).

"Creditors — as opposed to 'debt collectors' — generally are not subject to the [Act]." *Pollice,* 225 F.3d at 403. A "creditor" is any person: (1) "who offers or extends credit creating a debt[;] or" (2) "to whom a debt is owed." § 1692a(4). Excluded is "any person to the extent that he receives an assignment or transfer of a debt in default solely for the purpose of facilitating collection of such debt for another." *Id.* Notably, the Act, by its terms, contemplates that an entity may be both a debt collector and a creditor, stating that "debt collector" also includes "any creditor who, in the process of collecting his own debts, uses any name other than his own which would indicate that a third person is collecting or attempting to collect such debts." § 1692a(6).

The landscape of debt collection has changed since the FDCPA's enactment in 1977, and not all those who collect debt look like the classic "repo man." The Federal Trade Commission reported in 2009 that "[t]he most significant change in the debt collection business in recent years has been the advent and growth of debt buying." Federal Trade Commission, Collecting Consumer Debts: The Challenges of Change — A Workshop Report 13 (2009). No longer do creditors simply hire debt collectors to serve their named role; rather, with increased frequency creditors sell debt to purchasers, who may again resell the debt, hire outside debt collectors to undertake collection efforts, or attempt to collect on their own. *See* Federal Trade Commission, The Structure and Practices of the Debt Buying Industry 1 (2013). Since this shift, courts have had to find new ways to distinguish "debt collectors" from "creditors" to determine whether the FDCPA applies to a particular entity.

In *Pollice* we followed the "default" test to make that determination. Per that test, "an assignee of an obligation is not a 'debt collector' if the obligation is not in default at the time of the assignment; conversely, an assignee may be deemed a 'debt collector' if the obligation is already in default when it is assigned." 225 F.3d at 403. Applying the test to an entity alleged to be a "debt collector," we held that because "there [was] no dispute that the various claims assigned to [it] were in default prior to their assignment[,] ... [and] there [was] no question that the 'principal purpose' of [its] business [was] the 'collection p.367 of any debts,'" the entity was a debt collector. *Id.* at 404.

In *Federal Trade Commission v. Check Investors, Inc.*, 502 F.3d 159 (3d Cir. 2007), we applied *Pollice* to similarly situated entities whose principal business was the collection of debts. *Id.* at 172. The alleged debt collectors argued they were "creditors" because they collected debts owed to themselves as opposed to "debt collectors" who collect debts owed to another. *Id.* Because they owned the debt they collected, they claimed they were not subject to the Act. *Id.* We noted in a *dictum* that the entities "appear[ed] at first blush to satisfy the statutory definition of a creditor," yet, "as to a specific debt, one cannot be both a 'creditor' and a 'debt collector,' as defined in the [Act], because those terms are mutually exclusive." *Id.* at 173.

We again followed the "default" test to determine whether the entity was a creditor or instead a debt collector, but pointed out that "focusing on the status of the debt when it was acquired overlooks ... that the person engaging in the collection activity may actually be owed the debt and is, therefore, at least nominally a creditor." *Id.* We justified our use of the "default" test by reasoning that "Congress ... unambiguously directed our focus to the time the debt was acquired in determining whether one is acting as a creditor or debt collector under the [Act]." *Id.* We noted that the Act's legislative history explained the term "debt collector" as "intended to cover all third persons who regularly collect debts," *id.*, because independent debt collectors, unlike creditors, are not "restrained by the desire to protect their good will when collecting past due accounts." *Id.* (quoting S. Rep. No. 95-382, at 2, 1977 U.S.C.C.A.N. 1695, 1696). Instead, they likely will have "no future contact with the consumer and often are unconcerned with the consumer's opinion of them." *Id.*

The Supreme Court, in *Henson v. Santander Consumer USA Inc.*, ___ U.S. ___, 137 S.Ct. 1718, 198 L.Ed.2d 177 (2017), has recently repealed the "default" test we followed. Debtors claimed that Santander Bank, which had purchased their loans already in default and attempted to collect on them, met the second definition of "debt collector," *i.e.*, one who "regularly collects or attempts to collect ... debts owed or due ... another." *Id.* at 1721 (quoting § 1692a(6)). They asserted as well that the Bank met the "principal purpose" definition, but the Court did not review that claim because it was not litigated in the District Court. *Id.*

The Supreme Court began "with a careful examination of the statutory text," in particular the definition's limitation to debts "owed ... another." *Id.* It reasoned that "by its plain terms this language seems to focus our attention on third party collection agents working for a debt owner — not on a debt owner seeking to collect debts for itself." *Id.* This language does not suggest that "whether the owner originated the debt or came by it only through later purchase" determines if it is a debt collector. *Id.* "All that matters is whether the target of the lawsuit regularly seeks to collect debts for its own account or does so for 'another.'" *Id.* Hence the Bank, which collected debts for its own account, did not meet the "regularly collects for another" definition. *Id.* at 1721-22.

The debtors in *Henson* further argued that the "default" test ought to apply because the statute excludes from the definition of "debt collector" those who obtain debts before default, and therefore those who obtain debts after default must fit the definition. *Id.* at 1724 (citing § 1692a(6)(F)(iii)). The Court held that argument untenable because "it doesn't necessarily follow that the ['regularly collects'] definition [of 'debt collector'] must include p.368 anyone who regularly collects debts acquired after default;" to meet that definition, those debts must be "owed *another.*" *Id.* (emphasis in original).

The Court also addressed the suggestion that everyone who attempts to collect debt is either a "debt collector" or a "creditor" with respect to a particular debt, but cannot be both. *Id.* "[S]potting (without granting) th[at] premise," it stated that a company such as the Bank, which collects on debt it purchased for its own account, "would hardly seem to be barred from qualifying as a creditor under the statute's plain terms." *Id.* But excluded from the definition of "creditor" are those who acquire a debt after default when the debt is assigned or transferred "*solely* for the purpose of facilitating collection of such debt *for another.*" *Id.* (quoting § 1692a(4)) (emphases in original).

Only one of our sister circuits has applied *Henson* thus far in a precedential opinion.[2] In *Bank of New York Mellon Trust Co. N.A. v. Henderson,* 862 F.3d 29 (D.C. Cir. 2017), the D.C. Circuit ruled on whether the Bank of New York, which regularly purchased and collected on defaulted loans, was a "debt collector" or instead a "creditor" under the Act. *Id.* at 33-34. As there was "no evidence to indicate the Bank's 'principal' business is debt collection[,] []or [that] the debt the Bank is seeking to collect [is] 'due another,'" the Court (following *Henson*) held the Bank of New York was not a debt collector. *Id.* No sister circuit has yet opined on *Henson*'s applicability to the "principal purpose" definition of "debt collector," the task before us today.

B. Facts

Appellees James and Allison Tepper, husband and wife, entered into a home equity line of credit with NOVA Bank secured by a mortgage on their Pennsylvania home. *Tepper v. Amos Financial, LLC,* No. 15-cv-5834, 2017 WL 3446886, at *1 (E.D. Pa. Aug. 11, 2017). The Teppers received periodic statements regarding their loan, and made timely payments, until the Pennsylvania Department of Banking and Securities closed the Bank and the Federal Deposit Insurance Corporation was appointed as receiver. *Id.* at *2.

The Teppers were notified of the Bank's closure, the FDIC's role as receiver, and its intention to market and sell all of the Bank's assets, including their loan. *Id.* Though the Teppers stopped receiving periodic statements, they attempted to remit a periodic payment to the FDIC, but it neither cashed nor returned their check. *Id.* Rather than attempt to make further payments to the FDIC, the couple decided to wait until they received a periodic statement from the loan's new servicer. *Id.*

Some months later, the FDIC declared the loan to be in default and sold it, also assigning the mortgage securing the loan, to Appellant Amos Financial, LLC. *Id.* at *2-3. It is an Illinois limited liability company that first registered to conduct business p.369 in Pennsylvania in October 2015. Not a financial institution or lender, its sole business is purchasing debts entered into by third parties and attempting to collect them. *Id.* at *1. The FDIC notified the Teppers of both the loan's default and its transfer to Amos, who made several attempts to collect the amount due. *Id.* at *1, 3-4. Amos mailed the Teppers three letters demanding lump-sum payments and sent them a notice, containing a higher amount due, stating that it intended to foreclose on their home. *Id.* at *3-4. It then filed a foreclosure action in Pennsylvania court in March 2015. *Id.* at *4. At that time, Amos was not registered to do business in Pennsylvania. *Id.* at *1, 4.

James Tepper reached out to Amos to request loan statements and to resolve the loan's default and avoid foreclosure. *Id.* at *4-5. Nareg Korogluyan, an Amos officer, returned his call. *Id.* at *5. He refused to give Mr. Tepper any loan statements, said the Teppers' home belonged to Amos, and warned they could not stop its foreclosure. *Id.* at *5-6. An attorney, acting on behalf of Amos, then sent Mr. Tepper an email attempting to collect the debt, but at an even higher amount. *Id.* at *6.

C. Procedural History

The Teppers filed a complaint alleging Amos violated the FDCPA and Amos timely replied. In their pretrial filings, the Teppers argued that Amos was a "debt collector" as defined in § 1692a(6) of the Act because their loan was in default and Amos considered the loan to be in default when it was purchased. They alleged Amos violated the Act through its written and oral communications with the Teppers, in part because it was not registered to do business in Pennsylvania when it threatened and filed foreclosure.

Amos, in its pretrial filings, did not contest its status as a "debt collector" under the Act. Rather, it argued it was not required to register in Pennsylvania as a foreign business entity because its sole business was acquiring and collecting debt. During the one-day bench trial that followed, Korogluyan testified to the same and added that the higher loan amount was calculated using an increased interest rate.

The District Court requested post-trial memoranda from the parties. In their memorandum, the Teppers argued Amos violated the FDCPA because it increased their loan's interest rate without first terminating and accelerating the loan, which their credit agreement required. Amos, in its memorandum, again did not challenge its status as a debt collector, and repeated that it was not required to register in the Commonwealth because its sole business was collecting the debt it acquired.

After the trial and post-trial supplemental briefing, but before the District Court issued a decision, the Supreme Court decided *Henson*. In response, the District Court ordered additional briefing for the parties to address whether, in light of *Henson,* Amos qualifies as a debt collector.

Thereafter the Court decided: (1) Amos is a "debt collector" as defined in § 1692a(6); (2) the Teppers' loan is a "debt" as defined in § 1692a(5) of the Act; and (3) Amos violated the Act.[3] *Tepper,* p.370 2017 WL 3446886, at *7-10. Amos was not liable for failing to register as a foreign business in Pennsylvania, however, because it is a debt collector. *Id.* at *10. It appeals the District Court's decision, arguing that it is not a debt collector. Accordingly, we summarize only the Court's reasoning for that part of its decision.

Taking heed from *Henson,* the District Court looked first to the statute's text. *Id.* at *7. It explained there are two ways for a plaintiff to prove a defendant is a debt collector: either (1) its "principal purpose... is the collection of any debts," or (2) it "regularly collects or attempts to collect... debts owed or due ... another." *Id.* at *8 (quoting § 1692a). It explained that, following *Henson,* an entity that purchases debts and then seeks to collect them for its own account is ineligible for the second definition because it is limited to those who regularly collect debts due a third party. *Id.* By contrast, the first definition applies to "collection of any debts" so long as that activity is the entity's "principal purpose." *Id.* (citing § 1692a). The parties did not dispute that Amos's sole business activity is purchasing and then attempting to collect debts. *Id.* Hence the Court held Amos meets the first definition of debt collector. *Id.*

II. Jurisdiction and Standard of Review

The District Court had jurisdiction under 28 U.S.C. § 1331 and we have jurisdiction to review its decision under 28 U.S.C. § 1291. We review *de novo* the Court's conclusions of law and review for clear error its factual findings. *Battoni v. IBEW Local No. 102 Employee Pension Plan,* 594 F.3d 230, 233 (3d Cir. 2010).

III. Discussion

Henson did not decide, but nonetheless affects, who fits the "principal purpose" definition of "debt collector." Whereas, prior to the Supreme Court's decision, our precedent in *Pollice* and *Check Investors* instructed us to look at whether the debt was in default at the time it was purchased, after *Henson* the "default" test falls away for a "principal purpose" framework.

We take our cue from the Court to begin by carefully examining the statute's text. *Henson,* 137 S.Ct. at 1721. Both Amos and the Teppers contend the plain text of the statute supports their desired outcome — Amos arguing that it fits the definition of "creditor" and therefore it is not a "debt collector" because the terms are mutually exclusive, and the Teppers arguing it fits the "principal purpose" definition of "debt collector."

We do not overlook Amos's omission of the "principal purpose" definition from its argument. Its admitted sole business is collecting debts it has purchased. It uses the mails and wires for its business. It can be no plainer that Amos "uses any instrumentality of interstate commerce or the mails in any business the principal purpose of which is the collection of any debts." § 1692a(6). "Any debts" does not distinguish to whom the debt is owed. And it stands in contrast to "debts owed or due... another," which limits only the "regularly collects" definition. *See Henson,* 137 S.Ct. at 1723 ("[W]hen we're engaged in the business of interpreting statutes we presume differences in language ... convey differences in meaning."). Asking if Amos is a debt collector is thus akin to p.371 asking if Popeye is a sailor. He's no cowboy.

Amos claims that because it also meets the definition of creditor — it is the entity "to whom [the] debt is owed," § 1692a(4) — it is not a debt collector. In *Check Investors* we noted an entity may satisfy the statutory definition of "creditor" and yet be a "debt collector." 502 F.3d at 173. Our conclusion today does not require us to sort out what *Check Investors* intended by its statement that those terms are mutually exclusive. Suffice it to say that, following *Henson,* an entity that satisfies both is within the Act's reach.

Amos argues as its fallback position that if we do not find it is a creditor (to the exclusion of being a debt collector), we should hold that it is not a debt collector under the definition's exclusion for "officer[s] [and] employee[s] of a creditor [who], in the name of the creditor, [are] collecting debts for [the] creditor." § 1692a(6)(A). This exception clearly does not fit; for even if Amos is a nominal creditor, the Teppers sued Amos, a limited liability company, and not any of its officers or employees.

*****

In sum, Amos may be one tough gazookus when it attempts to collect the defaulted debts it has purchased, but when its conduct crosses the lines prescribed by the FDCPA, it opens itself up to the Act's penalties. The District Court held that Amos's debt-collection attempts with the Teppers crossed those lines, and it must face the statute's penalties for its bad behavior. We affirm the portion of the Court's opinion Amos has challenged on appeal — that it is a debt collector under the "principal purpose" definition. The Court decided correctly in light of *Henson*'s repeal of the "default" test. Whether an entity acquired the debts it collects after they became defaulted does not resolve whether that entity is a debt collector. Instead, we follow the plain text of the statute: an entity whose principal purpose of business is the collection of any debts is a debt collector regardless whether the entity owns the debts it collects.

Thus we affirm.

[1] Though not relevant here, the definition of "debt collector" also includes "any person who uses any instrumentality of interstate commerce or the mails in any business the principal purpose of which is the enforcement of security interests." § 1692a(6).

[2] The Fifth Circuit, in a non-precedential opinion, ruled that because *Henson* held "that debt purchasers who collect for their own accounts are not 'debt collectors' under the 'regularly collects' alternative," the plaintiff failed to state a claim to that effect. *Infante v. Law Office of Joseph Onwuteaka, P.C.,* No. 17-41071, 735 Fed.Appx. 839, 842, 2018 WL 2438153, at *2 (5th Cir. May 30, 2018). The Sixth Circuit ruled much the same, also in a non-precedential opinion. *Garner v. Select Portfolio Servicing, Inc.,* No. 17-1303, 2017 WL 8294293, at *3 (6th Cir. Oct. 27, 2017). In addition, the Eleventh Circuit has since applied its pre-*Henson* standard that "a non-originating debt holder [does not qualify as] a 'debt collector' ... solely because the debt was in default at the time it was acquired" (which, it noted, *Henson* confirmed). *Kurtzman v. Nationstar Mortgage LLC,* 709 F. App'x 655, 659 (11th Cir. 2017) (citation omitted) (first alteration in original).

[3] Specifically, the Court held: (1) Amos's foreclosure notice and email that failed to disclose sufficient details about the amount and character of the debt were incomplete and misleading in violation of §§ 1692e(2) and (10); (2) its calculation of

the loan amount at an increased interest rate without following the credit agreement's required procedures violated § 1692e; and (3) Korogluyan's statements that Amos owned the Teppers' home and they could not stop the foreclosure constituted false representations and deceptive means to collect on the loan in violation of § 1692e(10). *Tepper,* 2017 WL 3446886, at *10. The Court also ordered $1,000 in statutory damages to the Teppers and deemed them entitled to recoup costs and reasonable attorneys' fees. *Id.* at *11.

902 F.3d 274 (2018)

Elaine LEVINS; William Levins, on behalf of themselves and others similarly situated, Appellants

v.

HEALTHCARE REVENUE RECOVERY GROUP LLC, a/k/a ARS Account Resolution Services; John and Jane Does 1 through 25.

No. 17-3330.

United States Court of Appeals, Third Circuit.

Argued June 5, 2018.

Filed: August 22, 2018.

Levins v. Healthcare Revenue Recovery Group LLC, 902 F. 3d 274 (3rd Cir. 2018)

On Appeal from the United States District Court for the District of New Jersey, (D.C. No. 1-17-cv-00928), District Judge: Honorable Robert B. Kugler.

Daniel A. Frischberg, 525 Route 73 South, Evesham Commons, Marlton, NJ 08053, Philip D. Stern [ARGUED], Andrew T. Thomasson, Stern Thomasson, 150 Morris Avenue, 2nd Floor, Springfield, NJ 07081, Counsel for Appellants.

Sean X. Kelly, Christian M. Scheuerman [ARGUED], Marks O'Neill O'Brien Doherty & Kelly, 535 Route 38 East, Suite 501, Cherry Hill, NJ 08002, Counsel for Appellee.

Before: AMBRO, JORDAN, and VANASKIE, Circuit Judges.

p.277 OPINION

JORDAN, Circuit Judge.

In this appeal, we interpret three provisions of the Fair Debt Collection Practices Act ("FDCPA"), 15 U.S.C. §§ 1692-1692p. Elaine and William Levins allege that Healthcare Revenue Recovery Group LLC ("HRRG") violated §§ 1692e(14), 1692d(6), and 1692e(10) by leaving telephone voice messages that did not use its true name, did not meaningfully disclose its identity, and used false representations and deceptive means to collect or attempt to collect a debt or obtain information about a consumer. In particular, the Levinses complain that voicemail messages in which HRRG went by the name of "ARS" were insufficient to identify it as HRRG or even as "ARS ACCOUNT RESOLUTION SERVICES," which is an alternative business name used by HRRG. HRRG moved to dismiss the complaint, as amended, for failure to state a claim, and the District Court granted that motion.

We conclude that the Levinses have stated a plausible claim that HRRG violated § 1692e(14)'s "true name" provision, but they have not stated plausible claims under §§ 1692d(6) or 1692e(10). Accordingly, p.278 we will vacate in part and affirm in part the dismissal of their case.

I. BACKGROUND

A. Allegations In The Complaint[1]

The Levinses, who live in New Jersey, purportedly incurred a debt that was transferred to HRRG for collection. HRRG then began leaving pre-recorded voicemail messages on the Levinses' phone in an attempt to collect the debt. The following is a transcription of the message:

> ARS calling. Please return our call at 1-800-694-3048. ARS is a debt collector. This is an attempt to collect a debt. Any information obtained will be used for that purpose. Again, our number is 1-800-694-3048. Visit us at www.arspayment.com.

(App. at 22 ¶ 31.)

At the time the Levinses received that message over and over, they did not know the identity of the caller. They had never received any written communication from HRRG. Having recently gone through bankruptcy, they knew of a debt collector with the full name "ARS National Services, Inc." that was known as "ARS" for short. That company, however, turns out to be wholly unrelated to HRRG. While it has registered the name "ARS ACCOUNT RESOLUTION SERVICES" in New Jersey, HRRG has neither registered the stand-alone name "ARS" nor taken any other legal steps to do business under that specific name.

There are numerous businesses that use the name "ARS," including the debt collector the Levinses had heard of, which is a California corporation registered to transact business in New Jersey. According to the Levinses, "by reputation the name 'ARS' is, without more, associated in the nation's debt collection industry with ARS National Services Inc." (App. at 23 ¶ 41.) A Google search of "ARS" along with "debt" or "collector" will result in links to many debt collectors other than HRRG. Reference to www.arspayment.com, the website that HRRG mentioned in the pre-recorded messages it left for the Levinses, does not narrow the field. It only leads to a browser privacy warning that blocks access to the website. And, if one ignores the warning and accesses the site, the website begins tracking and storing information about the computer user.

B. Procedural History

Within a year of receiving the voicemail messages from HRRG, the Levinses filed their putative class-action complaint alleging that HRRG violated the FDCPA when attempting to collect debts from them and others similarly situated. They eventually filed an amended complaint in which they claimed that the pre-recorded messages violate 15 U.S.C. §§ 1692e(14), 1692d(6), and 1692e(10) because they "use the name of any business, company or organization other than the true name of the debt collector's business, company, or organization"; "fail to provide meaningful disclosure of HRRG's identity"; and "use false representations and deceptive means to collect or attempt to collect any debt and to obtain information concerning a consumer[.]" (App. at 19 ¶ 13.)

HRRG moved to dismiss the case, invoking Federal Rule of Civil Procedure 12(b)(6). Along with its motion, HRRG filed an attorney declaration with supporting documents. Among those was a certificate stating that it is registered to do p.279 business in New Jersey under the name "ARS ACCOUNT RESOLUTION SERVICES," and a collection letter that it purports to have sent to Elaine Levins in November 2015. The Levinses opposed HRRG's motion and submitted their own attorney declaration with documents listing hundreds of businesses registered in New Jersey under names that include "ARS." After reviewing the parties' submissions, the District Court granted the motion to dismiss.

The Levinses have timely appealed.

II. DISCUSSION[2]

In appealing the order dismissing their complaint for failure to state a claim, the Levinses make three arguments. First, they say that HRRG violated § 1692e(14) because it did not use its true name in the voicemail messages. Next, they argue that HRRG violated § 1692d(6) because the messages did not meaningfully disclose the caller's identity. And finally, they assert that HRRG violated § 1692e(10) because forcing consumers to call HRRG or navigate its website is a deceptive means to collect debts and obtain information about a consumer.

HRRG of course disputes all of those contentions. It says that it did not violate § 1692e(14) because "ARS" is an abbreviation of its registered alternative business name "ARS Account Resolution Services," which is a true name. It then contends that it did not violate § 1692d(6) because the messages said that the caller was a debt collector, pointed out that the purpose of the call was to collect a debt, and provided a phone number and website for the consumer to use, all of which was a sufficient disclosure of identity. And, last, it argues that it did not use deceptive collection practices in violation of § 1692e(10) because the messages informed consumers that any information obtained would be used to collect a debt.

Before turning to the parties' competing arguments, though, we must determine which materials can properly be considered in evaluating the District Court's decision to dismiss the claims under Rule 12(b)(6).

A. We Decline To Rely On The Collection Letter Attached To HRRG's Motion To Dismiss Because The Complaint Does Not Reference Or Rely On It.

We "generally consider only the allegations contained in the complaint, exhibits attached to the complaint[,] and matters of public record" when evaluating whether dismissal under Rule 12(b)(6) was proper. *Pension Benefit Guar. Corp. v. White Consol. Indus., Inc.*, 998 F.2d 1192, 1196 (3d Cir. 1993). But we can also consider "an undisputedly authentic document that a defendant attaches as an exhibit to a motion to dismiss if the plaintiff's claims are based on the document." *Id.* We may do so because "the primary problem raised by looking to documents outside the complaint p.280 — lack of notice to the plaintiff — is dissipated where the plaintiff has actual notice ... and has relied upon [those] documents in framing the complaint." *Schmidt v. Skolas,* 770 F.3d 241, 249 (3d Cir. 2014) (internal quotation marks, alteration, and citation omitted).

Here, HRRG asks us to consider the collection letter that it claims to have mailed to the Levinses in November 2015. The letter bears a company logo consisting of the letters "ARS," says in the letterhead that "Account Resolution Services" is "a division of HRRG, LLC," and, in the body of the letter, uses "ARS" as an abbreviated name. (App. at 38.) HRRG urges us to conclude that the Levinses received that collection letter before the phone messages and so would have understood ARS and HRRG to be one and the same. The Levinses respond that the letter is off limits at this stage of the litigation, and they are right. We will not consider it because the claims in the Levinses' complaint are not based on it. Rather, the claims are based on the pre-recorded phone messages that the Levinses allegedly received. Indeed, the Levinses specifically allege that they have never received any written communication from HRRG, and we must take that as true, *see Tatis v. Allied Interstate, LLC,* 882 F.3d 422, 426 (3d Cir. 2018) (construing allegations in the complaint in the light most favorable to the non-moving party).[3]

Of course, our decision not to consider the letter at this stage does not mean that it is irrelevant or forever precluded from consideration. Assuming it is properly tendered to the District Court, HRRG may rely on it later in a motion for summary judgment or at trial.

With that decided, we can now consider whether the Levinses have stated their FDCPA claims with sufficient plausibility to withstand the motion to dismiss.

B. The Levinses Have Stated A Plausible Claim Under § 1692e(14).

Congress enacted the FDCPA "to eliminate abusive debt collection practices by debt collectors[.]" 15 U.S.C. § 1692. Because it is a remedial statute, "we construe its language broadly, so as to effect its purpose." *Tatis,* 882 F.3d at 427 (internal quotation marks and citation omitted). In evaluating whether a particular debt-collection practice violates the Act, "we employ a 'least sophisticated debtor' standard[.]" *Id.* (citation omitted). "The standard is objective, meaning that the specific plaintiff need not prove that she was actually confused or misled, only that the objective least sophisticated debtor would be." *Id.* (internal quotation marks, emphasis, and citation omitted). "[That] standard aims to protect the gullible as well as the shrewd, but it nevertheless preserves a quotient of reasonableness[.]" *Id.* (internal quotation marks, alterations, and citations omitted).

To state a claim under the FDCPA, a plaintiff must allege that "(1) she is a consumer, (2) the defendant is a debt collector, (3) the defendant's challenged practice involves an attempt to collect a 'debt' as the Act defines it, and (4) the defendant has violated a provision of the FDCPA in attempting to collect the debt." *Id.* Here, the parties only dispute p.281 the fourth element, *i.e.,* whether the messages violated §§ 1692e(14), 1692d(6), or 1692e(10) of the Act.

We conclude that the Levinses have stated a plausible claim under § 1692e(14) because, as alleged in the complaint, "ARS" is neither HRRG's full business name, the name under which it usually transacts business, nor a commonly used acronym of its registered name "ARS ACCOUNT RESOLUTION SERVICES." Section

1692e prohibits a debt collector from "us[ing] any false, deceptive, or misleading representation or means in connection with the collection of any debt." 15 U.S.C. § 1692e. It contains a non-exhaustive list of prohibited conduct, one sort of which is "[t]he use of any business, company, or organization name other than the true name of the debt collector's business, company, or organization." *Id.* § 1692e(14).

The FDCPA is enforced by the Federal Trade Commission ("FTC"), which has offered guidance on how to interpret that statute. *Hawthorne v. Mac Adjustment, Inc.*, 140 F.3d 1367, 1372 n.2 (11th Cir. 1998). Although the FTC's guidance "does not have the force of law and is not entitled to deference in FDCPA cases[,]" we may adopt its interpretation when we find its logic persuasive. *Brown v. Card Serv. Ctr.*, 464 F.3d 450, 455 (3d Cir. 2006) (internal quotation marks, alterations, and citation omitted). The FTC has interpreted the "true name" requirement in § 1692e(14) to permit a debt collector to "use its full business name, the name under which it usually transacts business, or a commonly-used acronym[,]" as long as "it consistently uses the same name when dealing with a particular consumer." *Statements of General Policy or Interpretation Staff Commentary On the Fair Debt Collection Practices Act*, 53 Fed. Reg. 50097, 50107 (Dec. 13, 1988) [hereinafter *FTC Commentary*]. That is a sound interpretation of the statutory requirement, and we adopt it as our own.

Here, at this early stage in the case, when we must take the allegations in the complaint as true, the Levinses have plausibly alleged facts suggesting that "ARS" is not the "true name" of HRRG. While they do not deny that "ARS" is a name HRRG may use, they say that the acronym is commonly associated with other debt collection companies, including "ARS National Services, Inc.," and that it could refer to hundreds of other businesses registered to do business in New Jersey under names that include "ARS." (App. at 23 ¶¶ 37, 41; App. at 41.) *See also Sayles v. Advanced Recovery Sys., Inc.*, 865 F.3d 246, 248 (5th Cir. 2017) (abbreviating defendant "Advanced Recovery Systems, Inc." as "ARS"); *Koby v. ARS Nat'l Servs., Inc.*, 846 F.3d 1071, 1074 (9th Cir. 2017) (abbreviating defendant "ARS National Services, Inc." as "ARS"). Nothing in the information properly before us indicates that "ARS" is HRRG's full business name, the name under which it usually transacts business, or its commonly used acronym. To the extent HRRG argues to the contrary, it is doing so without proper record support. It will have an opportunity later to expand the record, but for now taking the allegations in the complaint as true, we conclude that the Levinses have stated a plausible claim for relief under § 1692e(14).[4]

p.282 C. The Levinses Have Not Stated A Plausible Claim Under § 1692d(6).

Section 1692d prohibits a debt collector from "engag[ing] in any conduct the natural consequence of which is to harass, oppress, or abuse any person in connection with the collection of a debt." 15 U.S.C. § 1692d. It too, like § 1692e, contains a non-exhaustive list of prohibited conduct, one type of which is "the placement of telephone calls without meaningful disclosure of the caller's identity." *Id.* § 1692d(6). Here, though the issue is close, we conclude that the District Court was correct to rule that the Levinses have not stated a claim under § 1692d(6). The voicemail messages provided enough information about the caller's identity for the least sophisticated debtor to know that the call was from a debt collector and was an attempt to collect a debt.

The statute does not define "meaningful disclosure[,]" but in *Hart v. Credit Control, LLC,* the United States Court of Appeals for the Eleventh Circuit interpreted "meaningful disclosure" as requiring a debt collector's voice message to provide two types of information: first, "the name of the debt collection company[,]" and second, "the nature of the debt collection company's business, which can be satisfied by disclosing that the call is on behalf of a debt collection company[.]" 871 F.3d 1255, 1260 (11th Cir. 2017). The court held that there was no violation of § 1692d(6) when the individual calling on behalf of the debt collector did not leave his or her personal name in a message because that individual provided a company name and stated that the call was from a debt collector. *Id.* at 1259-60; *see also id.* at 1256 ("This is Credit Control calling with a message. This call is from a debt collector. Please call us at 866-784-1160. Thank you."). District courts in our Circuit have similarly interpreted "meaningful disclosure" as requiring a debt collector "to reveal itself as a collection agency when leaving messages" because "[m]eaningful disclosure requires a debt collector to disclose enough information so as not to mislead the recipient as to the purpose of the call." *See Pisarz v. GC Servs. Ltd. P'ship,* No. 16-4552, 2017 WL 1102636, at *6 (D.N.J. Mar. 24, 2017) (internal quotation marks and citation omitted); *see also id.* (citing district court cases).

The Levinses claim that saying "ARS" was not enough meaningful disclosure of the caller's identity to be lawful under § 1692d(6). As with their claim under § 1692e(14), they again argue that, from the words of the messages, it is not clear that "ARS" would uniquely refer to HRRG because there are other companies in the debt collection industry that are associated with the name "ARS," and there are other businesses registered in New Jersey with business names or associated names that include "ARS." Although we agreed with that contention with respect to § 1692e(14)'s "true name" requirement, it p.283 has less force in the context of § 1692d(6) for two reasons.

First, although it is possible for a debt collector's phone message to violate both §§ 1692d(6) and 1692e(14),[5] a violation of one provision is not necessarily a violation of the other because "meaningful disclosure of the caller's identity" is not restricted to providing the name of the debt collector. As explained above, "meaningful disclosure of the caller's identity" has been interpreted to include information that discloses the call is from a debt collector so as not to mislead the least sophisticated debtor of the purpose of the call. Here, the voicemail messages would not mislead the least sophisticated debtor because the messages gave some identifying information about the caller, stated that the call was from a debt collector, and stated that the call was an attempt to collect a debt. Even though the Levinses have sufficiently alleged that "ARS" is, as already discussed, less than a "true name" as defined by § 1692e(14), they have not plausibly alleged that using the abbreviation "ARS," which is associated with a registered identity of HRRG, amounts to a lack of meaningful disclosure of the sort forbidden by § 1692d(6). Nothing in the messages rises to the level of "harass[ment], oppress[ion], or abuse ... in connection with the collection of a debt," which is the target of § 1692d.

Second, and closely related, if we were to say that use of anything less than a debt collector's "true name" was a violation of § 1692d(6), we would make § 1692d(6) superfluous in light of § 1692e(14). *See Everage v. Nat'l Recovery Agency,* No. 14-2463, 2015 WL 1071757, at *5 (E.D. Pa. Mar. 11, 2015) (declining to import § 1692e(14)'s "true name" requirement into § 1692d(6)). When Congress enacted the FDCPA, it used the term "true name" in § 1692e(14), whereas it used "meaningful disclosure of the caller's identity" in § 1692d(6). Fair Debt Collection Practices Act, Pub. L. No. 95-109, 91 Stat. 874, 877-78 (1977). The difference must have significance. If Congress had wanted § 1692d(6) also to require that a debt collection company use its "true name[,]" then it would have so specified. *See Loughrin v. United States,* 573 U.S. 351, 134 S.Ct. 2384, 2390, 189 L.Ed.2d 411 (2014) (noting "when Congress includes particular language in one section of a statute but omits it in another[,]... th[e Supreme] Court presumes that Congress intended a difference in meaning" (internal quotation marks, citation, and alteration omitted)). We will not rewrite the statute and import the "true name" requirement of § 1692e(14) into § 1692d(6).

For those reasons, the District Court properly dismissed the Levinses' claim under § 1692d(6).

D. The Levinses Have Not Stated A Plausible Claim Under § 1692e(10).

Finally, we also agree with the District Court's conclusion that the Levinses failed p.284 to state a claim under § 1692e(10) because the messages adequately warned that any information obtained would be used to collect a debt. Section 1692e(10) prohibits "[t]he use of any false representation or deceptive means to collect or attempt to collect any debt or to obtain information concerning a consumer." 15 U.S.C. § 1692e(10).

Violations of § 1692e(10) usually "include impersonating a public official, falsely representing that unpaid debts will be referred to an attorney, and misrepresenting the amount of the debt owed." *Harvey v. Great Seneca Fin. Corp.,* 453 F.3d 324, 331 (6th Cir. 2006) (internal citations omitted); *see also, e.g., Crossley v. Lieberman,* 868 F.2d 566, 571 (3d Cir. 1989) (holding attorney violated § 1692e(10) when he sent a collection letter that falsely represented that a mortgage foreclosure case was already in litigation, that threatened to take action within one week, and that failed to inform debtor of her right to cure). To state a claim under § 1692e, a false statement "must be material when viewed through the least sophisticated debtor's eyes[,]" which means "it has the potential to affect the decision-making process of the least sophisticated debtor[.]" *Jensen v. Pressler & Pressler,* 791 F.3d 413, 421 (3d Cir. 2015) (emphasis omitted).

Here, nothing in the messages rises to the level of being materially deceptive, misleading, or false. The plain language of each message reveals that the caller is a debt collector, that the call is part of an attempt to collect a debt, and that any information obtained will be used in that attempt. Given those clear disclosures, even the least sophisticated debtor is fairly on notice that calling the phone number provided in the message or visiting the website might result in the debt collector obtaining information that it could use in trying to collect the debt. The caller's purpose is transparent and the messages are far removed from the false representations that typically have been held to violate § 1692e(10). The District Court thus properly dismissed the claim brought under that FDCPA subsection.

III. CONCLUSION

For the foregoing reasons, we will vacate the District Court's dismissal of the § 1692e(14) claim and remand for further proceedings. We will affirm, however, the District Court's dismissal of the claims under §§ 1692d(6) and 1692e(10).

[1] For convenience, we refer to the amended complaint simply as "the complaint." We construe the allegations of that pleading in the light most favorable to the Levinses. *See infra* note 2.

[2] The District Court had jurisdiction under 28 U.S.C. § 1331. We have jurisdiction pursuant to 28 U.S.C. § 1291. "We exercise plenary review over a district court's dismissal for failure to state a claim under Rule 12(b)(6), applying the same standard as the district court." *Glover v. FDIC,* 698 F.3d 139, 144 (3d Cir. 2012). "We will affirm an order dismissing a complaint only when the complaint fails to contain sufficient factual matter, accepted as true, to state a claim to relief that is plausible on its face." *Rotkiske v. Klemm,* 890 F.3d 422, 424 n.2 (3d Cir. 2018) (en banc) (internal quotation marks omitted). "A claim has facial plausibility when the plaintiff pleads factual content that allows the court to draw the reasonable inference that the defendant is liable for the misconduct alleged." *Tatis v. Allied Interstate, LLC,* 882 F.3d 422, 426 (3d Cir. 2018). We construe the allegations in the complaint in the light most favorable to the non-moving parties, the plaintiffs. *Id.*

[3] The District Court's decision likewise did not reference that collection letter. We will, however, consider the certificate stating that HRRG is registered to do business in New Jersey under the name "ARS ACCOUNT RESOLUTION SERVICES," (App. at 35), because it is a matter of public record, *Pension Benefit Guar. Corp.,* 998 F.2d at 1196. The District Court referenced the certificate in its decision, and neither party disputes that choice on appeal. That is the limit of what we are considering outside of the complaint.

[4] The District Court reached the opposite conclusion by relying on *Pescatrice v. Elite Recovery Service, Inc.,* No. 06-61130, 2007 WL 1192441 (S.D. Fla. Apr. 23, 2007), and *Strand v. Diversified Collection Service, Inc.,* 380 F.3d 316 (8th Cir. 2004). Those cases, however, are distinguishable.

In *Pescatrice,* the court held that there was no violation of § 1692e(10) when a debt collector used an abbreviation of its company name in the return address of a mailing. 2007 WL 1192441, at *4; *see also* 15 U.S.C. § 1692e(10) (prohibiting "[t]he use of any false representation or deceptive means to collect or attempt to collect any debt or to obtain information concerning a consumer"); *infra* Section II.D. Similarly, in *Strand,* the court held that a collection agency's practice of using its initials and corporate logo on an envelope's exterior did not violate § 1692f(8). 380 F.3d at 319; *see also* 15 U.S.C. § 1692f(8) (prohibiting "[u]sing any language or symbol, other than the debt collector's address, on any envelope when communicating with a consumer by use of the mails or by telegram, except that a debt collector may use his business name if such name does not indicate that he is in the debt collection business"). Both of those cases were based on different provisions of the FDCPA, and we do not interpret them as deciding the "true name" question that is at issue here.

[5] The FTC regards a debt collector's use of "a false business name in a phone call" as violating both §§ 1692e(14) and 1692d(6). *See FTC Commentary,* 53 Fed. Reg. at 50105 ("A debt collector who uses a false business name in a phone call to conceal his identity violates [§ 1692e(14)], as well as [§ 1692d(6)]."); *id.* at 50107 ("When a debt collector uses a false business name in a phone call, he violates [§ 1692d(6)] as well as [§ 1692e(14)]."). We agree that such conduct would violate both §§ 1692e(14) and 1692d(6), but here the Levinses have not alleged that "ARS" is a "false business name" of HRRG. They have only alleged and argued that the name "ARS" could refer to any number of companies that use the name "ARS," which falls short of saying that "ARS" is a "false business name" of HRRG.

905 F.3d 159 (2018)

Robert A. SCHULTZ, Jr.; Donna Schultz, on behalf of themselves and those similarly situated, Appellants
v.
MIDLAND CREDIT MANAGEMENT, INC.; John Does 1-10.

Case No. 17-2244.

United States Court of Appeals, Third Circuit.

Argued January 23, 2018.
Opinion Filed: September 24, 2018.

Schultz v. Midland Credit Management, Inc., 905 F. 3d 159 (3rd Cir. 2018)

On Appeal from the United States District Court for the District of New Jersey (D.C. Civil No. 2-16-cv-04415) District Judge: Hon. Jose L. Linares.

Cary L. Flitter, Esq., Andrew M. Milz, Esq. [ARGUED], Flitter Milz, 450 North Narberth Avenue, Suite 101, Narberth, PA 19072, Yongmoon Kim, Esq., Kim Law Firm, 411 Hackensack Avenue, Suite 701, Hackensack, NJ 07601, Counsel for Plaintiffs-Appellants Robert A. Schultz, Jr. and Donna Schultz.

Han Sheng Beh, Esq., Ellen B. Silverman, Esq., Hinshaw & Culbertson, 800 Third Avenue, 13th Floor, New York, NY 10022, Joel D. Bertocchi, Esq., David M. Schultz, Esq. [ARGUED], Hinshaw & Culbertson, 151 North Franklin Street, Suite 2500, Chicago, IL 60606, Counsel for Defendant-Appellee Midland Credit Management, Inc.

Before: HARDIMAN, VANASKIE, and SHWARTZ, Circuit Judges.

p.160 OPINION OF THE COURT

VANASKIE, Circuit Judge.

The question before us in this matter is whether a statement in a debt collection letter to the effect that forgiveness of the debt may be reported to the Internal Revenue Service constitutes a violation of the Fair Debt Collection Practices Act ("FDCPA"), 15 U.S.C. § 1692 *et seq.* The District Court concluded that the statement found in dunning letters sent by Appellee Midland Credit Management Inc., ("Midland") to Appellants Robert A. Schultz, Jr., and his wife, Donna (the "Schultzes") could not constitute a violation of the FDCPA, and dismissed their putative class action complaint. We disagree, and hold that the statement in question may violate the FDCPA. Accordingly we will reverse the dismissal of this action and remand for further proceedings.

I.

On four dates in 2015 — July 21, August 24, September 2, and October 23 — Midland sent letters to Robert Schultz, Jr., attempting to collect three separate outstanding debts that had been outsourced to Midland for collection after Robert had defaulted on them. On August 24 and October 23, 2015, Midland sent Donna Schultz separate letters likewise attempting to collect a separate outstanding debt from her. None of the Schultzes debts exceeded $600. Each letter offered to settle the amount of indebtedness for less than the full amount owing.[1] Four of the p.161 letters noted that "[i]f you pay your full balance we will report your account as Paid in Full. If you pay less than your full balance, we will report your account as Paid in Full for less than the full balance." (App. 24, 30, 32, 36). All of the aforementioned letters contained the following language: "We are not obligated to renew this offer. We will report forgiveness of debt as required by IRS regulations. Reporting is not required every time a debt is canceled or settled, and might not be required in your case." (App. 17). Since the Department of the Treasury only requires an entity or organization to report a discharge of indebtedness of $600 or more to the IRS, and because each of the debts linked to the Schultzes was less than $600, the Schultzes claimed that the inclusion of the foregoing language was "false, deceptive and misleading" in violation of the FDCPA, (App. 18), which broadly prohibits the use of any false, deceptive, or misleading representation in connection with the collection of any debt. *See* 15 U.S.C. § 1692e.

On July 20, 2016, the Schultzes filed a putative class action complaint on behalf of themselves and others similarly situated asserting violations of the FDCPA. Midland moved pursuant to Fed. R. Civ. P. 12(b)(6) to dismiss on the ground that the Schultzes failed to plead a plausible violation of the FDCPA. The District Court granted Midland's motion on May 8, 2017, concluding that the Schultzes indeed failed to plausibly allege a violation of the FDCPA because the language set forth in the dunning letters was not "deceptive" or "otherwise violative of the FDCPA." (App. 8). In the District Court's view, the language:

> [did] not threaten the reader of the letter with a legal action that cannot be taken, nor [did] the letter include any false or deceptive statements designed to enhance its ability to collect the out-standing debt. Rather, Defendant's letter, when read in its entirety by the least sophisticated consumer, [could] only have one interpretation. That interpretation is simply that, in certain circumstances, debt settlement and/or discharge] may be reportable to the IRS, not all settlements and/or discharges are reportable, and that the subject statement may not be applicable to the reader.

(App. 8-9).[2] The Schultzes timely appealed the District Court's ruling to our Court.

II.

The District Court had subject matter jurisdiction under 28 U.S.C. § 1331. We have jurisdiction pursuant to 28 U.S.C. § 1291. We afford plenary review to a district court's order granting a motion to dismiss for failure to state a claim. *Black v. Montgomery Cty.*, 835 F.3d 358, 364 (3d Cir. 2016).

III.

Congress enacted the FDCPA in 1977 after noting the "abundant evidence of the use of abusive, deceptive, and unfair debt collection practices by many debt collectors." p.162 15 U.S.C. § 1692(a); *see also Brown v. Card Serv. Ctr.,* 464 F.3d 450, 453 (3d Cir. 2006). The Act's purpose is twofold: It seeks not only to eliminate abusive practices by debt collectors, but also "to insure that those debt collectors who refrain from using abusive debt collection practices are not competitively disadvantaged." *Brown,* 464 F.3d at 453 (quoting 15 U.S.C. § 1692(e)).

The portion of the FDCPA relevant here, § 1692e, states that "[a] debt collector may not use any false, deceptive, or misleading representation or means in connection with the collection of any debt." The section goes on to describe the following as violations of the FDCPA:

> The threat to take any action that cannot legally be taken or that is not intended to be taken.
>
> . . .
>
> The use of any false representation or deceptive means to collect or attempt to collect any debt or to obtain information concerning a consumer.

Id. §§ 1692e(5), (10). Whether a collection letter is "false, deceptive, or misleading" under § 1692e is determined from the perspective of the "least sophisticated debtor." *Brown,* 464 F.3d at 453. In *Brown,* we articulated the standard for deception under § 1692e as follows:

> The least sophisticated debtor standard requires more than simply examining whether particular language would deceive or mislead a reasonable debtor because a communication that would not deceive or mislead a reasonable debtor might still deceive or mislead the least sophisticated debtor. This lower standard comports with a basic purpose of the FDCPA: as previously stated, to protect all consumers, the gullible as well as the shrewd, the trusting as well as the suspicious, from abusive debt collection practices.

Id. at 454 (citations and internal quotation marks omitted). The plaintiff's burden is low under this objective standard. She need not prove that she was confused or misled, but only that the least sophisticated consumer would be. *Jensen v. Pressler & Pressler,* 791 F.3d 413, 419 (3d Cir. 2015).

On appeal, the Schultzes argue that by including the language, "[w]e will report forgiveness of debt as required by IRS regulations," Midland presented a false or misleading view of the law — one designed to scare or intimidate the Schultzes into paying the outstanding debts listed on the debt collection letters even though Midland knew that any discharge of the Schultzes' debt would not result in a report to the IRS. We agree.

Here, the reporting requirement under the Internal Revenue Code is wholly inapplicable to the Schultzes' debts because none of them totaled $600 or more, and IRS regulations clearly state that only discharges of debt of $600 or more "must" be included on a Form 1099-C and filed with the IRS. *See* 26 C.F.R. § 1.6050P-1(a).[3] By including the reporting language on collection letters addressing debts of less than $600, we believe that the least sophisticated debtor might be persuaded into thinking that the discharge of any portion of their debt, regardless of amount discharged, may be reportable.

Midland argues that, in order to conclude that a consumer would be misled by this statement, one would have to read the first sentence in isolation while paying no attention to the second qualifying statement — *i.e.,* that "[r]eporting is not required p.163 every time a debt is canceled or settled, and might not be required in your case." (App. 17). However, even with this qualifying statement, the least sophisticated debtor could be left with the impression that reporting *could* occur. Indeed, this is precisely what happened in the Schultzes' case — there was no possibility of IRS reporting in light of the fact that the debt was less than $600, but use of the conditional "might" suggested that reporting was a possibility.

Midland argues that if we were to adopt the Schultzes' interpretation of the language contained in the letters, we would essentially give credence to a "bizarre or idiosyncratic" interpretation of the letters, which does not preserve "a quotient of reasonableness and ... a basic level of understanding and willingness to read with care." *Wilson v. Quadramed Corp.,* 225 F.3d 350, 354-55 (3d Cir. 2000). For Midland, the use of the conditional "might" should signal to the least sophisticated debtor that only under certain circumstances will reporting occur. The problem with this argument, however, is that, for the Schultzes, under *no* set of circumstances will reporting ever occur. As we held in *Brown,* even if the language in a letter is true, it can still be deceptive where "it can be reasonably read to have two or more different meanings, one of which is inaccurate." 464 F.3d at 455 (citation omitted). And the facts here are not so different than those in *Brown,* such that our holding here should be different. In *Brown,* a debt collector suggested that if a debtor did not pay her outstanding debt within five days it could result in a lawsuit against her. *Id.* at 451-53. While the debt collector had the authority to bring such a suit, because five days passed and it failed to do so and rarely had done so in the past, the threat of legal action was considered deceptive in violation of the FDCPA. *Id.* at 455 (stating that "it would be deceptive under the FDCPA for [the debt collector] to assert that it *could* take an action that it had no intention of taking and has never or very rarely taken before" and that "where the debt collector 'has reason to know there are facts that make the action unlikely in the particular case, a statement that the action was possible would be misleading'" (citation omitted)).

The FDCPA sweeps broadly — it is not just outright lies that it condemns. As the Ninth Circuit held in *Gonzales v. Arrow Financial Services, LLC,* 660 F.3d 1055, 1063 (9th Cir. 2011), anytime a debt collector includes "language in a debt collection letter [that] can reasonably be interpreted to imply that the debt collector will take action it has no intention or ability to undertake, the debt collector that fails to clarify that ambiguity does so at its peril." Similar to *Brown,* although even more egregious, *Gonzales* dealt with a debt collector who had bought up years of debts owed to health clubs, all of which were more than seven years old, and thereby pursuant to the Fair Credit Reporting Act, ineligible for reporting to a credit reporting agency. *Id.* at 1059. In its collection notices, the following statement was made: "[I]f we are reporting the account, the appropriate credit bureaus will be notified that this account has been settled." *Id.* (emphasis omitted). Because there was no possible way that all of the debts could be legally reported, the Ninth Circuit deemed this statement misleading. *Id.* at 1063. The Court went on to say that "[w]here the law places affirmative limits on a debt collector's actions, the debt collector that 'goes perilously close to an area of proscribed conduct takes the risk' that it will be liable under the FDCPA for misleading consumers." *Id.* at 1063 (citation omitted). And, of particular note, the Court also stated "[c]onditional language, particularly in the absence of any language clarifying or explaining p.164 the conditions, does not insulate a debt collector from liability." *Id.*; *see also Campuzano-Burgos v. Midland Credit Mgmt., Inc.*, 550 F.3d 294, 301 (3d Cir. 2008) ("in certain contexts a completely accurate statement can be deceptive or misleading").[4]

The Seventh Circuit has held that "a dunning letter is false and misleading if it 'impl[ies] that certain outcomes might befall a delinquent debtor, when legally, those outcomes cannot come to pass.'" *Boucher v. Fin. Sys. of Green Bay, Inc.*, 880 F.3d 362, 367 (7th Cir. 2018) (quoting *Lox v. CDA Ltd.*, 689 F.3d 818, 825 (7th Cir. 2012)). Thus, it is not merely the inclusion of a lie but also incomplete or inapplicable language in a collection letter that may form the basis for a potential FDCPA violation.[5]

Finally, we would be remiss if we did not address two cases that Midland submitted in support of its position after oral argument: *Ceban v. Capital Management Services, L.P.*, No. 17-CV-4554 (ARR) (CLP), 2018 WL 451637, at *1 (E.D.N.Y. Jan. 17, 2018), and *Antista v. Financial Recovery Services*, No. 2:17-cv-3567 (WJM), 2018 WL 259771, at *1 (D.N.J. Jan. 2, 2018). In *Ceban*, the district court held that the statement "[t]his settlement may have tax consequences" was not false, deceptive, or misleading. "[T]he statement simply — and correctly — put plaintiff on notice that a settlement 'may' have tax consequences." *Ceban*, 2018 WL 451637, at *7. In *Antista*, the court held that we must presume that even the least sophisticated debtor can distinguish between "may" and "must" when it comes to any statement regarding the IRS reporting requirement. *Antista*, 2018 WL 259771, at *3.

Neither case is persuasive. First, *Ceban* dealt with a debt that was over $600. Therefore, the district court's analysis was written in reference to a completely different set of circumstances than those applicable to the Schultzes in this case. Second, even if we accept *Antista*'s statement that p.165 the least sophisticated debtor can distinguish between "may" and "must", the circumstances in our case demonstrate that the language at issue references an event that would never occur, distinguishing it from *Antista*. Here, it is reasonable to assume that a debtor would be influenced by potential IRS reporting and that, if that reporting cannot come to pass, it could signal a potential FDCPA violation regardless of the use of conditional language.

While we recognize that Midland, like many debt collection companies, uses form letters when contacting its debtors, we must reinforce that convenience does not excuse a potential violation of the FDCPA. We therefore are obligated to reverse the order of the District Court granting Midland's motion to dismiss, as a reasonable juror may find a violation of the FDCPA in this instance.

IV.

Based on the foregoing, we will reverse the May 8, 2017, Order of the District Court as we find that the Schultzes have pled sufficient factual allegations that state a plausible claim upon which a court may grant relief under the FDCPA. We will therefore remand for further proceedings consistent with this opinion.

[1] All but one of the letters offered a 10% discount on the indebtedness if prompt payment was made. For example, the July 21, 2015 letter to Robert offered to settle the amount then due — $389.59 — for $350.64 if that amount was paid by August 20, 2015. (App. at 24). The October 23, 2017 letter to Donna offered a 40% discount on the amount then due, $479.83. (*Id.* at 36).

[2] Midland had also filed a Motion to Compel Arbitration in this matter because it maintained that the claims raised in Mr. Schultz's original complaint, concerning the Synchrony Bank/Lowe's indebtedness of $389.59, were subject to an Arbitration Clause in the pertinent credit card agreement. (App. 63). The District Court, after granting Midland's dismissal motion, declined to address Defendant's Motion to Compel Arbitration, owing to mootness. (*Id.* at 9). Because we are remanding, this issue should be reviewed in the first instance by the District Court.

[3] Significantly, "multiple discharges of indebtedness of less than $600 are not required to be aggregated." 26 C.F.R. § 1.6050P-1(a)(2).

[4] Several district courts in our Circuit have found similar collection letter language to be sufficiently deceptive to survive a motion to dismiss. *See, e.g., Disla v. Northstar Location Servs., LLC,* No. 16-cv-4422, 2017 WL 2799691, at *1, *4 (D.N.J. June 27, 2017) (concluding that the statement "Barclays Bank Delaware is required to report the amount of the debt forgiven to the Internal Revenue Service" could be misleading because the "language does not accurately reflect 26 C.F.R. § 1.6050P-1 because it discusses no exceptions to the reporting requirement") (emphasis omitted); *Medina v. Allianceone Receivables Mgmt., Inc.,* No. 16-4664, 2017 WL 220328, at *2 (E.D. Pa. Jan. 19, 2017) (finding that the statement "Department Store National Bank will report forgiveness of debt as required by IRS regulations" to be deceptive because "[a] reasonable recipient of the letter could rightly interpret *as* to mean not *when* but *because*" and thereby understand the IRS reporting requirement to be mandatory even though exceptions may apply); *Good v. Nationwide Credit, Inc.,* 55 F. Supp. 3d 742, 744, 748 (E.D. Pa. 2014) (finding the statement that "GE CAPITAL RETAIL BANK is required to file a form 1099C with the Internal Revenue Service for any cancelled debt of $600 or more" to be deceptive because exceptions may apply).

[5] Midland argues that including tax consequence language in a letter can be helpful to the consumer, as it gives the debtor more information to make an informed choice about what to do with a debt. Yet, as Midland also concedes, the Second Circuit has already held that "a debt collector need not warn of possible tax consequences when making a settlement offer for less than the full amount owed to comply with FDCPA." *Altman v. J.C. Christensen & Assocs., Inc.,* 786 F.3d 191, 192 (2d Cir. 2015). Furthermore, the suggestion that forgiveness of the debt may be reported to the IRS could compel the unsophisticated debtor to pay the full amount of the indebtedness to avoid having to deal with the potential tax ramifications when debt forgiveness is reported to the IRS.

FOURTH CIRCUIT DECISIONS

Fair Debt Collection Practices Act

23 F.4th 370 (2022)

Ashly ALEXANDER; Cedric Bishop, On behalf of themselves individually and similarly situated persons, Plaintiffs-Appellants,
v.
CARRINGTON MORTGAGE SERVICES, LLC, Defendant-Appellee.

No. 20-2359.

United States Court of Appeals, Fourth Circuit.

Argued: December 8, 2021.
Decided: January 19, 2022.

Alexander v. Carrington Mortgage Services, LLC, 23 F. 4th 370 (4th Cir. 2022)

Appeal from the United States District Court for the District of Maryland, at Baltimore. Richard D. Bennett, Senior District Judge. (1:20-cv-02369-RDB).

ARGUED: Hassan A. Zavareei, TYCKO & ZAVAREEI LLP, Washington, D.C., for Appellants. Fredrick S. Levin, BUCKLEY LLP, Santa Monica, California, for Appellee. ON BRIEF: Phillip R. Robinson, CONSUMER LAW CENTER, LLC, Silver Spring, Maryland; Dia Rasinariu, TYCKO & ZAVAREEI LLP, Washington, D.C.; Patricia M. Kipnis, BAILEY GLASSER LLP, Cherry Hill, New Jersey, for Appellants. Sarah B. Meehan, BUCKLEY LLP, Washington, D.C., for Appellee.

Before WILKINSON, KING, and DIAZ, Circuit Judges.

Affirmed in part, reversed in part, vacated in part, and remanded by published opinion. Judge WILKINSON wrote the opinion, in which Judge KING and Judge DIAZ joined.

p.372 WILKINSON, Circuit Judge.

Plaintiffs Ashly Alexander and Cedric Bishop brought this case as a class action against Carrington Mortgage Services, LLC. They alleged that Carrington violated the Maryland Consumer Debt Collection Act and the Maryland Consumer Protection Act by charging $5 convenience fees to borrowers who paid monthly mortgage bills online or by phone. Because Carrington, a collector, charged an amount that was not permitted by law, plaintiffs can proceed with some (but not all) of their claims. For the following reasons, we affirm in part, reverse in part, vacate in part, and remand for further proceedings consistent with this opinion.

I.

A.

The Maryland Consumer Debt Collection Act (MCDCA) and the Maryland Consumer Protection Act (MCPA) are remedial consumer protection statutes aimed at "protect[ing] the public from unfair or deceptive trade practices by creditors engaged in debt collection activities." *Andrews & Lawrence Pro. Servs. v. Mills,* 467 Md. 126, 223 A.3d 947, 950 (2020). The MCDCA prohibits debt collectors from engaging in an extensive list of practices, while the MCPA both functions as a "statutory enforcement umbrella" and contains its own prohibitions. *Id.*

Two provisions of the MCDCA are relevant in this case. First, "[i]n collecting or attempting to collect an alleged debt," a "collector" may not "engage in any conduct that violates §§ 804 through 812 of the federal Fair Debt Collection Practices Act." Md. Code Ann., Com. Law § 14-202(11). Maryland thus incorporates the substantive provisions of the Fair Debt Collection Practices Act (FDCPA). One of those provisions, at issue here, is the p.373 FDCPA's proscription on "[t]he collection of any amount (including any interest, fee, charge, or expense incidental to the principal obligation) unless such amount is expressly authorized by the agreement creating the debt or permitted by law." FDCPA § 808, 15 U.S.C § 1692f(1). Section 14-202(11) contains no scienter requirement. Second, a "collector" may not "claim, attempt, or threaten to enforce a right with knowledge that the right does not exist." Md. Code Ann., Com. Law § 14-202(8). The MCDCA defines "collector" to mean "a person collecting or attempting to collect an alleged debt arising out of a consumer transaction," and a "consumer transaction" is "any transaction involving a person seeking or acquiring real or personal property, services, money, or credit for personal, family, or household purposes." *Id.* § 14-201(b), (c).

The MCPA provides that "[a] person may not engage in any unfair, abusive, or deceptive trade practice ... in the sale, lease, rental, loan, or bailment of any consumer goods, consumer realty, or consumer services" or "in the collection of consumer debts." *Id.* § 13-303(1), (5). "Unfair, abusive, or deceptive trade practices" are defined to include "any false, falsely disparaging, or misleading oral or written statement ... or other representation of any kind which has the capacity, tendency, or effect of deceiving or misleading consumers," as well as "any failure to state a material fact if the failure deceives or tends to deceive." *Id.* § 13-301(1), (3). An MCDCA violation "is also a per se violation" of the MCPA. *Mills,* 223 A.3d at 950; *see also* Md. Code Ann., Com. Law § 13-301(14)(iii) ("Unfair, abusive, or deceptive trade practices include any violation of a provision of ... the [MCDCA].").

If a collector violates the MCDCA, it is "liable for any damages proximately caused by the violation." Md. Code Ann., Com. Law § 14-203. And under the MCPA, any person who is awarded damages "may also seek, and the court may award, reasonable attorney's fees." *Id.* § 13-408(b).

B.

In 2005, Ashly Alexander took out a residential mortgage loan to purchase her property in Baltimore, Maryland. The Note evidencing her loan required her to "make all payments under this Note in the form of cash, check or money order" at a P.O. Box in Dallas, Texas "or at a different place if required by the Note Holder." J.A. 116. In 2017, Carrington was retained to service and collect on Alexander's loan.

In 2010, Cedric Bishop took out a residential mortgage loan to refinance his property in Gaithersburg, Maryland. Bishop's Note stated that "[p]ayment shall be made" at an address in Irvine, California "or at such other place as Lender may designate in writing by notice to Borrower." J.A. 137. In 2018, Carrington was retained to service and collect on Bishop's loan.

Carrington gave Alexander and Bishop, in addition to the free pay-by-mail option specified in the initial mortgage documents, the choice to make payments online or by phone if they paid a $5 convenience fee. Borrowers opting to pay their bills online pressed an "I agree" button after reviewing Carrington's terms and conditions (thereby entering into a clickwrap agreement) and then selected "Continue" after manually inputting their payment amount and seeing the convenience fee displayed. Both Alexander and Bishop paid their mortgages online, and they each incurred the $5 fee at least nine times in 2018 or 2019.

Alexander filed a class-action complaint in Maryland court challenging Carrington's convenience fees; Carrington promptly p.374 removed the action to federal court under 28 U.S.C. § 1332(d). Alexander then filed an amended complaint which added Bishop as a plaintiff. Count I of that complaint, at issue here, alleged two violations of the MCDCA: engaging in conduct that violates the FDCPA, Md. Code Ann., Com. Law § 14-202(11), and attempting to enforce a right with knowledge that the right does not exist, *id.* § 14-202(8). It also alleged two violations of the MCPA: a standalone unfair-and-deceptive-trade-practices claim and a derivative claim based on the MCDCA violations.[1]

Carrington moved to dismiss plaintiffs' complaint, and the district court granted Carrington's motion. The district court first held that in charging the convenience fees, Carrington was not a "collector" for either MCDCA claim. As to the § 14-202(11) claim, the district court further held that Carrington was not a "debt collector" under the FDCPA, that plaintiffs' choice to use the online-payment option was "permitted by law," and that Carrington's convenience fees were not "incidental" to plaintiffs' mortgage debt. *See* 15 U.S.C. § 1692f(1). As to the § 14-202(8) claim, the district court held that Carrington had the "right" to collect the convenience fees, since none of the mortgage documents expressly prohibited the fees and plaintiffs voluntarily chose to make payments online.

Because the district court found that plaintiffs' MCDCA claims failed, it also dismissed their derivative MCPA claim. On the standalone MCPA claim, the district court found no unfair practice or misrepresentation upon which plaintiffs relied. As a result, it dismissed all of plaintiffs' claims with prejudice.

We review de novo the district court's dismissal of plaintiffs' claims. *Weidman v. Exxon Mobil Corp.*, 776 F.3d 214, 219 (4th Cir. 2015).

II.

The MCDCA and the MCPA are, as noted, remedial consumer protection statutes. As such, they "must be liberally construed, in order to effectuate [their] broad remedial purpose." *Mills,* 223 A.3d at 968 (quoting *Lockett v. Blue Ocean Bristol, LLC,* 446 Md. 397, 132 A. 3d 257, 272 (2016)); *see also Washington Home Remodelers, Inc. v. State,* 426 Md. 613, 45 A.3d 208, 219 (2012) (The MCPA "constitutes remedial legislation that is intended to be construed liberally in order to promote its purpose of providing a modicum of protection for the State's consumers."). In fact, Maryland's high court has expressly warned against construing these statutes in a "narrow or grudging" manner so as to "exemplify and perpetuate the very evils to be remedied." *Mills,* 223 A.3d at 968 (quoting *Pak v. Hoang,* 378 Md. 315, 835 A.2d 1185, 1191 (2003)). Relatedly, "exemptions from remedial legislation must be narrowly construed." *Id.* (quoting *Lockett,* 132 A.3d at 272). So we must not "read[] additional exemptions into a remedial statute"; we instead defer to the legislature's judgments. *Id.*

Keeping these principles in mind, we turn to plaintiffs' central claim under the MCDCA: that, by charging its convenience fees, Carrington engaged in conduct violating the FDCPA. We hold that Carrington is a "collector" who charged an "amount" that was not "expressly authorized by the agreement creating the debt or permitted by law" in violation of the FDCPA. *See* 15 U.S.C. § 1692f(1). As a result, we reverse p.375 the district court's dismissal of plaintiffs' § 14-202(11) claim.

A.

We first find that Carrington is a "collector" under the MCDCA. The MCDCA broadly defines a "collector" as "a person collecting or attempting to collect an alleged debt arising out of a consumer transaction." Md. Code Ann., Com. Law § 14-201(b). Here there is no dispute that Carrington is a person, as the MCDCA defines "person" to include "an individual, corporation, business trust, statutory trust, estate, trust, partnership, association, two or more persons having a joint or common interest, or any other legal or commercial entity." *Id.* § 14-201(d). Nor is there any dispute that plaintiffs' debt arose out of a consumer transaction, which the statute defines as "any transaction involving a person seeking or acquiring real or personal property, services, money, or credit for personal, family, or household purposes." *Id.* § 14-201(c). And it is plain that, by collecting borrowers' monthly mortgage payments, Carrington is collecting a debt. Each piece of the statutory puzzle thus fits together: Carrington counts as a "collector" under the MCDCA.

To avoid this result, Carrington offers three arguments. Yet each would have us add safe-harbor exceptions which are nowhere to be found within the MCDCA. First, Carrington would have us distinguish between loan servicing and debt collection, exempting the former from the MCDCA's reach. Passively accepting monthly payments, Carrington says, is a world away from actively enforcing the payment obligations of defaulting borrowers. Maybe so, but the statute draws no such distinction. Because "[r]eading additional exemptions into a remedial statute limits the possibility of remedies beyond what the Legislature intended," *Mills,* 223 A.3d at 968, we decline Carrington's invitation to do just that.

Next, Carrington argues that plaintiffs must challenge a "method of collection" and not simply the validity of the fees. Until recently, that argument may have held some water. But in *Chavis v. Blibaum & Assocs., P.A.,* 476 Md. 534, 559-60, 264 A.3d 1254 (Md. Aug. 27, 2021), the Court of Appeals of Maryland rejected it altogether. Interpreting § 14-202(8), Maryland's high court found that "nothing in the MCDCA generally, or in § 14-202 specifically," limited § 14-202(8)'s applicability to methods of debt collection. *Id.* The same reasoning applies to § 14-202(11), which likewise says nothing about methods. So while "it is not inaccurate to say that § 14-202 deals with methods of debt collection, it is more accurate to describe the statute as regulating the conduct of a person while engaged in debt collection." *Id.* To put it simply, Carrington is collecting a debt; the means it chooses does not make it any less of a collector. We therefore refuse to place Carrington's extra-statutory hurdle in plaintiffs' path.

Carrington has one final arrow in its quiver. It argues that even if it is a "collector" under the MCDCA, plaintiffs must also show that Carrington is a "debt collector" under the FDCPA to establish a § 14-202(11) violation. We disagree. While the FDCPA's definition of "debt collector" includes a requirement that the debt be in default, the MCDCA's definition has no similar limitation. *Compare* 15 U.S.C. § 1692a(6)(F)(iii) *with* Md. Code Ann., Com. Law § 14-201(b).

The MCDCA's broader definition controls here, as it is not displaced by the federal definition. Indeed, the Maryland legislature was intentional on this front: it incorporated only the FDCPA's "substantive p.376 provisions" (sections 804 through 812). *Chavis,* 476 Md. at 565 n.14, 264 A.3d 1254; *see* Md. Code Ann., Com. Law § 14-202(11). It did not incorporate section 803, which includes the FDCPA's narrower definition of "debt collector." *See* FDCPA § 803, 15 U.S.C. § 1692a(6). Nor did it incorporate, for example, the FDCPA's remedial structure as to affirmative defenses, the statute of limitations, or civil remedies. *See* FDCPA § 813, 15 U.S.C. § 1692k. The end result, as Maryland district courts have recognized, is that "the MCDCA applies more broadly than the FDCPA." *Aghazu v. Severn Savings Bank,* 2017 WL 1020828, at *8 n.21 (D. Md. Mar. 16, 2017); *see also Awah v. Cap. One Bank,* 2015 WL 302880, at *4 n.8 (D. Md. Jan. 22, 2015) ("The MCDCA contains a broader definition of 'collector' than the definition of 'debt collector' under the FDCPA."). And the FDCPA itself specifies that state laws affording greater protection to consumers are not inconsistent with its own safeguards. *See* 15 U.S.C. § 1692n.

This makes good sense. Just as federal law need not totally preempt state law, so also state law need not totally incorporate federal law. *See, e.g.,* Kevin M. Clermont, *Degrees of Deference: Applying vs. Adopting Another Sovereign's Law,* 103 Cornell L. Rev. 243, 270 (2018); Ronald J. Greene, *Hybrid State Law in the Federal Courts,* 83 Harv. L. Rev. 289, 290-91 (1969). Instead, state legislatures can incorporate federal law to the extent that they see fit; incorporation is no all-or-nothing enterprise. So while some states only incorporate federal definitions (as to, say, the tax code), Clermont, *supra,* at 308, other states are well within their rights to incorporate federal substance while retaining definitions of their own. This is precisely what Maryland has done, and so Carrington need not be a debt collector under federal standards for plaintiffs' state claim to proceed.

B.

We next hold that Carrington's convenience fees qualify as an "amount" under the FDCPA. The FDCPA prohibits "[t]he collection of *any amount* (including any interest, fee, charge or expense incidental to the principal obligation) unless such amount is expressly authorized by the agreement creating the debt or permitted by law." 15 U.S.C. § 1692f(1) (emphasis added). Carrington claims that the FDCPA only prohibits fees that are "incidental" to the mortgage debt. But this misreads the statute.

Examine the statutory language, which forbids the collection of "any" amount and gives a non-exhaustive list of examples "includ[ed]" within this ban. This linguistic construction ought to be read broadly. As the Supreme Court has indicated, "[r]ead naturally, the word 'any' has an expansive meaning, that is, 'one or some indiscriminately of whatever kind.'" *Ali v. Fed. Bureau of Prisons,* 552 U.S. 214, 219,

128 S.Ct. 831, 169 L.Ed.2d 680 (2008) (quoting *United States v. Gonzales,* 520 U.S. 1, 5, 117 S.Ct. 1032, 137 L.Ed.2d 132 (1997)). And "including" is "not [a term] of all-embracing definition, but connotes simply an illustrative application of the general principle." *Fed. Land Bank of St. Paul v. Bismarck Lumber Co.,* 314 U.S. 95, 100, 62 S.Ct. 1, 86 L.Ed. 65 (1941); *see also United States v. Hawley,* 919 F.3d 252, 256 (4th Cir. 2019) (explaining that including "is an introductory term for an *incomplete* list of examples"); *Include, Black's Law Dictionary* (10th ed. 2014) ("The participle *including* typically indicates a partial list."). All told, "any amount" means what it says—*any* amount, whether or not that amount is incidental to the principal obligation.

p.377 To see why Carrington's approach is misguided, imagine a statute that prohibits gambling on "any sporting event (including any game, race, or match broadcast on television)." While such a statute gives helpful examples illustrating what "any sporting event" means, this is no exhaustive list. No one would think that the legislature intended for people to bet with impunity on college football games airing exclusively online—or on high-school sports not broadcast anywhere. Yet Carrington's approach would have us narrowly focus on one specified category (games broadcast on television) at the expense of the overarching prohibition (any sporting event).

The FDCPA's far-reaching language straightforwardly applies to the collection of "any amount." While convenience fees are not explicitly enumerated, Congress certainly did not want debt collectors to skirt statutory prohibitions through linguistic sophistry. So we have no trouble in concluding that convenience fees are an "amount" under the FDCPA.[2]

C.

We now turn to the final component of plaintiffs' § 14 202(11) claim and hold that Carrington's convenience fees were not "permitted by law." Once more, the FDCPA prohibits "[t]he collection of any amount ... unless such amount is expressly authorized by the agreement creating the debt or permitted by law." 15 U.S.C. § 1692f(1). While Carrington concedes that the agreements creating the debt do not expressly authorize the convenience fees, the parties vigorously dispute whether those fees are "permitted by law." Plaintiffs argue that "permitted by law" requires express sanction or approval; Carrington thinks that the phrase indicates only a lack of express prohibition. In our view, plaintiffs' interpretation aligns best with the statute: here, "permitted by law" requires affirmative sanction or approval, typically (though not always) from a statute.

By itself, "permit" is susceptible to differing interpretations. It can mean, for instance, either "to consent to formally" or "to allow or admit of." *Permit, Black's Law Dictionary* (10th ed. 2014). However, "*allow* and *permit* have an important connotative difference. *Allow* ... suggests merely the absence of opposition, or refraining from a proscription. In contrast, *permit* suggests affirmative sanction or approval." Garner's Dictionary of Legal Usage 46 (3d ed. 2011). Here, the legislature chose the word "permit." And it did not use that word by itself, but as part of the phrase "permitted by law." These choices suggest that some form of affirmative sanction (that is, some "law"), rather than mere lack of prohibition, is required.

Other circuits have likewise read "permitted by law" to require an affirmative sanction. *See Tuttle v. Equifax Check*, 190 F.3d 9, 13 (2d Cir. 1999) ("If state law neither *affirmatively permits* nor expressly prohibits service charges, a service charge can be imposed only if the customer expressly agrees to it in the contract." (emphasis added)); *Seeger v. AFNI, Inc.*, 548 F.3d 1107, 1112 (7th Cir. 2008) ("Neither a law *expressly permitting* a collection p.378 fee ... nor an agreement between the [parties] exists here." (emphasis added)). As early as 1988, so did the FTC, which had primary enforcement authority over the FDCPA at that time. *See* Staff Commentary on the Fair Debt Collection Practices Act, 53 Fed. Reg. 50,097, 50,108 (Dec. 13, 1988) ("A debt collector may attempt to collect a fee or charge in addition to the debt if ... the contract [creating the debt] is silent but the charge is otherwise *expressly permitted* by state law." (emphasis added)). After enforcement authority shifted to the CFPB in 2010, it subsequently issued guidance that also required express permission. *See* CFPB Compliance Bulletin 2017-01, 82 Fed. Reg. 35,936, 35,938 (Aug. 2, 2017) ("Supervision has found that one or more mortgage servicers ... violated the [FDCPA] when they charged fees for taking mortgage payments over the phone to borrowers whose mortgage instruments did not expressly authorize collecting such fees and who reside in states where applicable law does not *expressly permit* collecting such fees." (emphasis added)). While none of this authority is controlling, it buttresses our conclusion as to the statutory meaning.

So too does the linguistic context. Start with the statute's focus, in the first prong, on the original agreement. This protects consumers from later add-ons in the way of various fees, preventing them from being blindsided down the road. When choosing a mortgage lender, for example, consumers have different options. While bargaining power is certainly not equal between lender and borrower at the out-set, there is at least some element of notice as to the terms of the original agreement. Yet consumers have no say in choosing their debt collectors, and they may well be over a barrel at that later point in time. To allow debt collectors to subsequently modify the terms of the original agreement as they see fit, based solely on the mere absence of legal prohibition, would thus frustrate the FDCPA's goals.

Next look at how the provision works as a whole. Collecting "any amount" is prohibited "unless such amount is expressly authorized by the agreement creating the debt or permitted by law." 15 U.S.C. § 1692f(1). The incorporated FDCPA provision sets a "no collection" default, subject to two narrow exceptions. And these two exceptions mirror one another. Each lays out a particular source of authority (either the agreement creating the debt or law), and each requires that the source of authority affirmatively speaks to the amount's collection (either through express authorization or through permission). Our interpretation preserves this parallelism.

Carrington's contrary reading gives the phrase "permitted by law" a very loose meaning. So long as the law does not expressly prohibit it from doing so, Carrington claims, it can charge whatever fees it wishes. Yet this reading both shifts the default and also places the statute's two exceptions at war with one another. We reject an interpretation that carries such worrisome consequences. After all, we must interpret a statute "as a symmetrical and coherent regulatory scheme and fit, if possible, all parts into an harmonious whole." *FDA v. Brown & Williamson Tobacco Corp.*, 529 U.S. 120, 133, 120 S.Ct. 1291, 146 L.Ed.2d 121 (2000) (internal quotation marks and citations omitted); *see also* Antonin Scalia & Bryan A. Garner, *Reading Law: The*

Interpretation of Legal Texts 180-82 (2012) (The "harmonious-reading canon" counsels that "[t]he provisions of a text should be interpreted in a way that renders them compatible, not contradictory."). Carrington's reading suggests that a narrow exception sits right next to a broad license and thereby fails on p.379 this score. While it rightly acknowledges that express authorization in the original agreement is a carefully guarded and narrow gate to pass through, it wrongly suggests that permission by law is an unattended and broad entrance to the same venue. If a fan can get into the North London Derby either by presenting an expensive ticket at Gate A or by waltzing freely through Gate B, no one in their right mind would choose the first option. Why pay to watch Arsenal beat Tottenham when you can enjoy the spectacle for free?

In this particular case, Carrington's argument hits another snag. Carrington places great emphasis on plaintiffs' manifestation of assent in the online clickwrap agreements, arguing that common principles of contract render its convenience fees "permitted by law." But if general contract principles are enough to permit the charging of such fees, then the statute's prong permitting amounts "expressly authorized by the agreement creating the debt" becomes superfluous. There would be no need to say this if Carrington is right, for an "agreement creating the debt" is by definition a valid contract. Because we "disfavor interpretations of statutes that render language superfluous," *Conn. Nat. Bank v. Germain,* 503 U.S. 249, 253, 112 S.Ct. 1146, 117 L.Ed.2d 391 (1992), Carrington's argument runs into yet another barrier.

As one last throw of the dice, Carrington complains that we are punishing it for offering additional choices to consumers. It tries to make hay out of the fact that those consumers who pay online or over the phone receive the satisfaction of immediate payment and posting, and it contends that these options need not be provided for free. But here's the inconvenient truth: Carrington's alternative payment options are likely more cost-effective and less time-consuming for Carrington. While paying by check is free for consumers, it generally costs debt collectors between $1 and $4 to process those checks. Association for Financial Professionals, *Payments Cost Benchmarking Survey,* at 7 (2015). By contrast, processing payments made online or by phone typically costs debt collectors substantially less, about $0.50 per transaction. *See id.* at 8 (finding median cost to be between $0.37 and $0.75); *see also* J.A. 7-8 (alleging that Carrington's fees range "from 10 to 50 times ... its actual costs"). And because it is in Carrington's interest to get consumers to pay, it is also in Carrington's interest to offer convenient methods for doing so. Nothing we have said prevents Carrington from extending this payment option to consumers. If it does so, however, it must do so without the imposition of a statutorily prohibited convenience fee.

Because Carrington is a collector who charged an amount that was not expressly authorized by the agreement creating the debt or permitted by law, it violated the MCDCA. We thus reverse the district court's dismissal of plaintiffs' § 14-202(11) claim.

III.

A few words as to plaintiffs' remaining claims. First, because we hold that Carrington has violated the MCDCA by engaging in conduct violating the FDCPA, plaintiffs' derivative MCPA claim can also proceed, and the district court's dismissal of that claim must also be reversed.

Second, plaintiffs argue that because the fees are prohibited under § 14-202(11), Carrington asserts rights that "do[] not exist" under § 14-202(8). As explained above, Carrington is an MCDCA "collector" whose convenience fees are not "permitted by law." So the district court's dismissal, predicated as it was on its view of the MCDCA's definition of "collector" and p.380 plaintiffs' voluntary assent, was in error. We vacate this dismissal and remand plaintiffs' § 14-202(8) claim to allow the district court's further consideration of that claim consistent with this opinion.

Third and finally, plaintiffs' standalone MCPA claim alleging "unfair, abusive, or deceptive trade practices" cannot proceed. To plead a standalone claim under the MCPA, a consumer must allege "(1) an unfair or deceptive practice or misrepresentation that is (2) relied upon, and (3) causes them actual injury." *Stewart v. Bierman,* 859 F. Supp. 2d 754, 768 (D. Md. 2012) (citing *Lloyd v. General Motors Corp.,* 397 Md. 108, 916 A.2d 257, 277 (2007)). While plaintiffs perfunctorily allege that they "reasonably relied upon the direct and indirect material acts and actions of Carrington," J.A. 35, this looks more like a "threadbare recital[] of the elements of a cause of action" than a "plausible claim for relief." *Ashcroft v. Iqbal,* 556 U.S. 662, 678, 679, 129 S.Ct. 1937, 173 L.Ed.2d 868 (2009). We thus affirm the district court's dismissal of this claim.

IV.

We do not know if disallowing these fees is a wise policy choice. But it is the choice that Maryland has made, and our role is simply to respect it. For the foregoing reasons, we affirm in part, reverse in part, vacate in part, and remand for further proceedings consistent with this opinion.

AFFIRMED IN PART, REVERSED IN PART, VACATED IN PART, AND REMANDED

[1] Counts II and III of plaintiffs' amended complaint alleged violations of Maryland's law prohibiting usury and violations of a separate FDCPA provision. The district court dismissed those Counts, and they are not at issue in this appeal.

[2] As a result, we need not reach Carrington's argument that its fees are not "incidental" here. But in any event, its argument is unpersuasive. Carrington argues that "the convenience fee is not *dependent* upon the monthly payment of the mortgage, but upon the borrower's decision to make their mortgage payment online and thereby enjoy the convenience of immediate payment and posting." Appellee's Br. at 36. But we have a hard time seeing how the convenience fee is not incidental to the debt. Without the mortgage payment, there is of course no convenience fee.

963 F.3d 403 (2020)

Robert L. BENDER; Deborah A. Bender, Plaintiffs-Appellants,
v.
ELMORE & THROOP, P.C., Defendant-Appellee.
Consumer Financial Protection Bureau, Amicus Supporting Appellant.

No. 19-1325.

United States Court of Appeals, Fourth Circuit.

Submitted: May 22, 2020.
Decided: July 2, 2020.

Bender v. Elmore & Throop, PC, 963 F. 3d 403 (4th Cir. 2020)

Appeal from the United States District Court for the District of Maryland, at Baltimore. Catherine C. Blake, District Judge. (1:18-cv-00979-CCB)

E. David Hoskins, THE LAW OFFICE OF E. DAVID HOSKINS, LLC, Baltimore, Maryland, for Appellants. John S. Vander Woude, ECCLESTON & WOLF, P.C., Hanover, Maryland, for Appellee. Mary McLeod, General Counsel, John R. Coleman, Deputy General Counsel, Steven Y. Bressler, Assistant General Counsel, Kevin E. Friedl, CONSUMER FINANCIAL PROTECTION BUREAU, Washington, D.C., for Amicus Curiae.

Before AGEE, KEENAN, and RICHARDSON, Circuit Judges.

Vacated and remanded by published opinion. Judge KEENAN wrote the opinion, in which Judge AGEE and Judge RICHARDSON joined.

p.405 BARBARA MILANO KEENAN, Circuit Judge:

Robert and Deborah Bender (the Benders) appeal from the district court's dismissal of their complaint brought under the Fair Debt Collection Practices Act, 15 U.S.C. § 1692 *et seq.* (FDCPA, or the Act). The district court dismissed the Benders' complaint after concluding that it was barred by the FDCPA's one-year statute of limitations. In reaching this conclusion, the court acknowledged that the Benders had alleged violations of the Act occurring within one year of the date the suit was filed. Nevertheless, the court held that the entire complaint was time-barred because the more recent violations that the Benders alleged were of the "same type" as other violations that occurred outside the one-year limitations period.

We disagree with the district court's analysis and hold that each violation of the FDCPA gives rise to a separate claim governed by its own limitations period. We therefore vacate the district court's judgment and remand the case for further proceedings.

I.

The complaint in this case arose from a dispute between the Benders and their homeowners' association (HOA). Because the Benders' suit was dismissed under Federal Rule of Civil Procedure 12(b)(6), we accept as true the facts stated in their complaint and draw all reasonable inferences in the Benders' favor. *Ray v. Roane*, 948 F.3d 222, 226 (4th Cir. 2020).

On April 16, 2016, the Benders found a notice taped to the door of their home. The notice originated from the defendant, Elmore & Throop, P.C. (Elmore), a law firm retained by the Benders' HOA. The letter stated that the Benders had failed to pay $77.09 in HOA assessments, and included a demand that the Benders pay a total of more than $1,000 to satisfy both the HOA assessments and the costs and attorneys' fees attributable to the asserted delinquency. In response, the Benders delivered a letter to Elmore together with copies of cancelled checks showing that they had paid the assessments. Elmore acknowledged that the disputed payments had been received, but nonetheless asserted that the Benders owed the costs and attorneys' fees detailed in the initial letter.

Over the next several months, the Benders exchanged additional correspondence with Elmore. The Benders continued to deny ever having made any late payments, and Elmore persisted in maintaining that late fees, costs, interest, and attorneys' fees were owed. On May 18, 2016, following another demand for payment, the Benders personally delivered a letter to Elmore "requesting that [it] stop contacting us about this claim" and stating that the Benders would consider "any further attempt to collect a debt against us or record a lien on our property [as] harassment[.]"

In January 2017, Mr. Bender attended the annual HOA meeting and hand-delivered payment for a quarterly HOA assessment unrelated to this action. The President of the HOA directed Mr. Bender to leave the meeting, and Mr. Bender later received a notice that he had been banned from the HOA's premises for one year. In February 2017, the Benders received another letter (the February letter) from Elmore. The February letter acknowledged receipt of the HOA payment made by Mr. Bender at the meeting in January 2017, but noted as outstanding the accumulated fees and costs associated with the original disputed payment from 2016.

On March 10, 2017, the Benders responded to the February letter, writing that "in our correspondence to you on this p.406 matter, we had requested that you stop contacting us about that claim ... As both my wife and I dispute the debt referenced in your most recent letter, I am now requesting once again that you stop all communications with my wife and myself concerning this debt." The Benders received additional correspondence from Elmore on March 14, 2017, including an updated ledger of the Benders' account showing that a fee had been added for preparation of the February letter.

In January 2018, Mr. Bender sent a letter to the HOA, requesting to attend its upcoming annual meeting. In response, the Benders received a voicemail from an Elmore attorney seeking to discuss Mr. Bender's letter. When Mr. Bender returned the call, the attorney told Mr. Bender that he would not be allowed to attend the annual meeting, and that "this whole thing would not have happened if you would just pay your bills." When Mr. Bender responded by stating that his account was current, the attorney informed Mr. Bender that a lien had been placed on the Benders' property.

On February 6, 2018, the Benders received further correspondence from Elmore, including an updated ledger, which showed additional fees for sending "balance due" notices and "acknowledgement letters" to the Benders. Although this correspondence from Elmore purported to provide the Benders with "verification of your account as you requested," the Benders deny having made any such request for verification. The Benders filed the present action against Elmore on April 5, 2018.

In their complaint, the Benders alleged that Elmore violated various provisions of the FDCPA by engaging in unfair debt collection practices and by improperly communicating with the Benders after they had disputed the debt and had made a written request that Elmore cease further communications. Elmore responded by seeking dismissal of the complaint as untimely or, in the alternative, summary judgment.

The district court granted Elmore's motion under Rule 12(b)(6) and dismissed the complaint based on the statute of limitations. Relying on a series of cases from the District of Maryland, the court held that the FDCPA's limitations period runs from the date of the first violation, and that later violations of the same type do not trigger a new limitations period under the Act. Accordingly, although some of the challenged communications from Elmore occurred less than one year from the date that the Benders filed their complaint, the district court held that the entire complaint was time-barred. The Benders appealed.

II.

The Benders' sole contention on appeal is that the district court erred in concluding that all their claims were barred by the FDCPA's statute of limitations. We review de novo the district court's interpretation of the Act, as well as the court's ultimate decision to dismiss the Benders' complaint under Rule 12(b)(6). *King v. Rubenstein,* 825 F.3d 206, 214 (4th Cir. 2016); *Sayyed v. Wolpoff & Abramson,* 485 F.3d 226, 229 (4th Cir. 2007).

The Benders argue that the district court erred in dismissing all their claims as time-barred because two of the alleged violations occurred less than one year from the date they filed suit. These alleged violations were: (1) the January 2018 phone call, in which an Elmore attorney informed the Benders that a lien had been placed on their property, and that "this whole thing would not have happened if you would just pay your bills"; and (2) the unsolicited February 2018 letter listing the alleged p.407 debts still owed by the Benders. According to the Benders, under the language of 15 U.S.C. § 1692k(d), a new statute of limitations arose with each "violation" of the Act. Thus, although the Benders concede that several of the alleged violations fall outside the one-year limitations period, they contend that the district court erred in dismissing the entirety of their complaint, which was filed in April 2018 and contained allegations of FDCPA violations arising from the January and February 2018 communications.

In response, Elmore argues that the district court did not err in dismissing the entire complaint, because the *first* alleged violation of the FDCPA occurred outside the limitations period and all later communications by Elmore arose from its attempt to collect the same debt. In support of this argument, Elmore relies on the same rationale articulated by the district court, namely, that the statute of limitations for FDCPA claims runs from the date of the initial violation, and that later violations of the same kind do not reset the limitations period.[1] Thus, Elmore argues that the district court properly determined that a single limitations period applied to the Benders' complaint dating from the first allegedly unlawful communication. We disagree with Elmore's argument.

Under the FDCPA, claims must be brought "within one year from the date on which the violation occurs." 15 U.S.C. § 1692k(d). This language "unambiguously sets the date of *the violation* as the event that starts the one-year limitations period."[2] *Rotkiske v. Klemm,* ___ U.S. ___, 140 S. Ct. 355, 360, 205 L.Ed.2d 291 (2019) (emphasis added). Moreover, nothing in the FDCPA suggests that "similar" violations should be grouped together and treated as a single claim for purposes of the FDCPA's statute of limitations. To the contrary, we long have held that a "separate violation" of the FDCPA occurs "every time" an improper communication, threat, or misrepresentation is made. *United States v. Nat'l Fin. Servs., Inc.,* 98 F.3d 131, 141 (4th Cir. 1996). Accordingly, we conclude that Section 1692k(d) establishes a separate one-year limitations period for each violation of the FDCPA.

This interpretation avoids creating a safe harbor for unlawful debt collection activity. Under the district court's approach, so long as a debtor does not initiate suit within one year of the first violation, a debt collector would be permitted to violate the FDCPA with regard to that debt indefinitely and with impunity. No matter how frequent or abusive such collection efforts might become, the debtor would be left entirely without a remedy simply because the debtor did not timely pursue the first violation. As the statutory text makes clear, Congress did not intend such a result.

Finally, we observe that two of our sister circuits likewise have concluded in p.408 published decisions that the FDCPA's limitations period runs anew from the date of each violation. *See Demarais v. Gurstel Chargo, P.A.,* 869 F.3d 685, 694 (8th Cir. 2017); *Llewellyn v. Allstate Home Loans, Inc.,* 711 F.3d 1173, 1188 (10th Cir. 2013). As these courts have recognized, it simply "does not matter that the debt collector's violation restates earlier assertions—if the plaintiff sues within one year of the violation, [the suit] is not barred by § 1692k(d)." *Demarais,* 869 F.3d at 694; *see also Llewellyn,* 711 F.3d at 1188.

Accordingly, applying the plain language of the FDCPA in 15 U.S.C. § 1692k(d), we conclude that the district court erred in dismissing the Benders' complaint as time-barred. The Benders have alleged at least two potential violations of the FDCPA that are not barred by the one-year limitations period provided in the Act. We express no opinion on the merits of the Benders' claims, and likewise offer no opinion on the validity of the alternative bases for affirmance that Elmore asserts on appeal. The district court did not rule on these alternative arguments in its decision, and we decline to address them in the first instance.

III.

For these reasons, we vacate the district court's judgment and remand the case to the district court for further proceedings consistent with this opinion.

VACATED AND REMANDED[*]

[1] Elmore relies on two unpublished opinions issued by this Court supporting Elmore's view of the FDCPA's statute of limitations. *See Jackson v. Ocwen Loan Servicing, LLC,* 747 F. App'x 159, 160 (4th Cir. 2019); *Bey v. Shapiro Brown & Alt, LLP,* 584 F. App'x 135, 135 (4th Cir. 2014). However, because those opinions are unpublished, they do not have precedential effect and we do not address them here. *Booker v. S.C. Dep't of Corr.,* 855 F.3d 533, 543 (4th Cir. 2017) (citing *Hogan v. Carter,* 85 F.3d 1113, 1118 (4th Cir. 1996) (en banc)).

[2] In *Rotkiske,* the Supreme Court considered whether the limitations period under the FDCPA begins on the date of the violation or the date that the plaintiff discovers the violation. 140 S. Ct. at 360. The Court held that the plain language of the Act identifies the date of the violation as the starting point for computing the limitations period. *Id.*

[*] This opinion is published without oral argument pursuant to this Court's Standing Order 20-01, http://www.ca4.uscourts.gov/docs/pdfs/amendedstandingorder20-01.pdf (amended Apr. 7, 2020).

834 F.3d 522 (2016)

IN RE: Eric DUBOIS, Debtor.
Chaille Dubois, f/k/a Chaille Gaines, f/k/a Candace DuBois, f/k/a Candace Gaines, f/k/a Candi Gaines, f/k/a Candi DuBois; Kimberly Adkins, Plaintiffs-Appellants,
v.
Atlas Acquisitions LLC, Defendant-Appellee, and Timothy P. Branigan; Nancy Spencer Grisby, Trustees.

No. 15-1945.

United States Court of Appeals, Fourth Circuit.

Argued: May 10, 2016.
Decided: August 25, 2016.

In re Dubois, 834 F. 3d 522 (4th Cir. 2016)

p.524 Appeal from the United States Bankruptcy Court for the District of Maryland, at Greenbelt, Thomas J. Catliota, Bankruptcy Judge, (15-00110; 14-28589).

ARGUED: Morgan William Fisher, LAW OFFICES OF MORGAN FISHER LLC, Annapolis, Maryland, for Appellants. Donald S. Maurice, Jr., MAURICE WUTSCHER, LLP, Flemington, New Jersey, for Appellee. ON BRIEF: Courtney L. Weiner, LAW OFFICES OF MORGAN FISHER LLC, Washington, D.C., for Appellants. Alan C. Hochheiser, BUCKLEY KING, LPA, Cleveland, Ohio, for Appellee.

Before DIAZ, FLOYD, and THACKER, Circuit Judges.

p.525 Affirmed by published opinion. Judge FLOYD wrote the majority opinion, in which Judge THACKER joined. Judge DIAZ wrote a dissenting opinion.

FLOYD, Circuit Judge:

Appellants Kimberly Adkins and Chaille Dubois filed separate Chapter 13 bankruptcy petitions in the Bankruptcy Court for the District of Maryland. Appellee Atlas Acquisitions LLC (Atlas) filed proofs of claim in their bankruptcy cases based on debts that were barred by Maryland's statute of limitations.[1] The issue on appeal is whether Atlas violated the Fair Debt Collection Practices Act (FDCPA) by filing proofs of claim based on time-barred debts. We hold that Atlas's conduct does not violate the FDCPA, and affirm the bankruptcy court's dismissal of Appellants' FDCPA claims and related state law claim.

I.

The facts of Appellants' cases are similar. Adkins filed for Chapter 13 bankruptcy on August 29, 2014. Atlas filed two proofs of claim in her case. The first proof of claim indicated that Adkins owed Atlas $184.62 based on a loan that originated with payday lender Check N Go and that Atlas purchased from Elite Enterprise Services, LLC (Elite Enterprise) on September 15, 2014.[2] The proof of claim identified the last transaction date on the account as May 19, 2009. Atlas's second proof of claim was for $390.00 based on a loan that originated with payday lender Impact Cash USA and that Atlas purchased from Elite Enterprise on November 18, 2014. The proof of claim identified the last transaction date on that account as September 10, 2009. It is undisputed that both debts were beyond Maryland's three-year statute of limitations when Atlas purchased and attempted to assert the debts in Adkins's bankruptcy case. See Md. Code Ann., Cts. & Jud. Proc. § 5-101. Adkins neither listed the debts on her bankruptcy schedules nor sent a notice of bankruptcy to Atlas.

Dubois filed for Chapter 13 bankruptcy on December 6, 2014. Atlas filed a proof of claim for $135.00 based on a loan that originated with payday lender Iadvance and that Atlas purchased from Elite Enterprise on January 5, 2015. The proof of claim identified the last transaction date on the account as October 18, 2008. It is undisputed that this debt was also beyond Maryland's statute of limitations when Atlas purchased and attempted to assert the debt in Dubois's bankruptcy case. Dubois did not list the debt on her bankruptcy schedules nor did she send a notice of bankruptcy to Atlas.

Adkins and Dubois filed separate adversary complaints against Atlas. Both objected to Atlas's claims as being time-barred and further alleged that Atlas violated the FDCPA by filing proofs of claim on stale debts. Appellants sought disallowance of Atlas's claims as well as damages, attorney's fees, and costs under the FDCPA.[3]

p.526 Atlas conceded that its claims were based on time-barred debts and stipulated to their disallowance. However, Atlas moved to dismiss Appellants' FDCPA claims under Federal Rule of Civil Procedure 12(b)(6) for failure to state a claim upon which relief could be granted. See Fed. R. Bankr. P. 7012(b) (incorporating Rule 12(b)(6) into adversary proceedings). After hearing consolidated oral arguments, the bankruptcy court concluded that filing a proof of claim does not constitute debt collection activity within the meaning of the FDCPA and granted Atlas's motion to dismiss. Pursuant 28 U.S.C. § 158(d)(2), we permitted Appellants to appeal the bankruptcy court's decision directly to this Court. We review the bankruptcy court's dismissal of Appellants' claims under Rule 12(b)(6) de novo. See, e.g., In re Mwangi, 764 F.3d 1168, 1173 (9th Cir. 2014); In re McKenzie, 716 F.3d 404, 412 (6th Cir. 2013).

II.

Before addressing the substance of Appellants' claims, we provide a brief overview of the relevant statutes in this case: the Bankruptcy Code (the "Code") and the FDCPA.

A.

"The principal purpose of the Bankruptcy Code is to grant a 'fresh start' to the 'honest but unfortunate debtor.'" Marrama v. Citizens Bank, 549 U.S. 365, 367, 127 S.Ct. 1105, 166 L.Ed.2d 956 (2007) (quoting Grogan v. Garner, 498 U.S. 279, 286, 287, 111 S.Ct. 654, 112 L.Ed.2d 755 (1991)). Through bankruptcy, the debtor's assets are collected for equitable distribution among creditors and his remaining debts are discharged. See Covert v. LVNV Funding, LLC, 779 F.3d 242, 248 (4th Cir. 2015); In re Jahrling, 816 F.3d 921, 924 (7th Cir. 2016). A bankruptcy debtor must file with the bankruptcy court a list of creditors, a schedule of assets and liabilities, and a statement of the debtor's financial affairs. 11 U.S.C. § 521(a)(1). "[B]eing all-inclusive on the schedules is consistent with the Code's principle of honest and full disclosure." In re Vaughn, 536 B.R. 670, 676 (Bankr. D.S.C. 2015). Scheduling a debt notifies the creditor of the bankruptcy and of the creditor's opportunity to file a proof of claim asserting a right to payment against the debtor's estate. See id. at 679; 11 U.S.C. § 501(a).

The bankruptcy court may "allow" or "disallow" claims from sharing in the distribution of the bankruptcy estate. 11 U.S.C. § 502. In Chapter 13 proceedings, allowed claims are typically paid, either in whole or in part, out of the debtor's future earnings pursuant to a repayment plan proposed by the debtor and confirmed by the bankruptcy court. See id. § 1322(a)(1); 4-501 Collier on Bankruptcy ¶ 501.01 (Collier). Upon completion of all payments under the plan, the bankruptcy court "grant[s] the debtor a discharge of all debts provided for by the plan or disallowed." 11 U.S.C. § 1328(a). Thus, at the end of the process the debtor receives the "fresh start" contemplated by the Bankruptcy Code.

B.

Congress enacted the FDCPA to eliminate abusive debt collection practices and to ensure that debt collectors who refrain from such practices are not competitively disadvantaged. 15 U.S.C. § 1692(a), (e). The FDCPA regulates the conduct of "debt collectors," defined to include "any person who uses any instrumentality of interstate commerce or the mails in any business the principal purpose of which is the collection of any debts, or who regularly collects or attempts to collect, directly or indirectly, debts owed or due or asserted p.527 to be owed or due another." Id. § 1692a(6). Among other things, the FDCPA prohibits debt collectors from using "any false, deceptive, or misleading representation or means in connection with the collection of any debt," and from using "unfair or unconscionable means to collect or attempt to collect any debt." Id. §§ 1692e-1692f. The statute provides a non-exhaustive list of conduct that is deceptive or unfair (e.g., falsely implying that the debt collector is affiliated with the United States, id. § 1692e(1)). Debt collectors who violate the FDCPA are liable for actual damages, statutory damages of up to $1,000, and attorney's fees and costs. See id. § 1692k(a).

C.

Federal courts have consistently held that a debt collector violates the FDCPA by filing a lawsuit or threatening to file a lawsuit to collect a time-barred debt. See Crawford v. LVNV Funding, LLC, 758 F.3d 1254, 1259-60 (11th Cir. 2014) (collecting cases), cert. denied, ___ U.S. ___, 135 S.Ct. 1844, 191 L.Ed.2d 724 (2015). Appellants contend that filing a proof of claim on a time-barred debt in a bankruptcy proceeding similarly violates the FDCPA. Atlas counters that filing a proof of claim is not debt collection activity and is therefore not subject to the FDCPA. Alas further argues that, even if the FDCPA applies, filing a proof of claim on a time-barred debt does not violate its provisions. These arguments are addressed in turn.

III.

Atlas does not dispute that it is a debt collector but argues that filing a proof of claim does not constitute debt collection activity regulated by the FDCPA. See 15 U.S.C. § 1692e (prohibiting deceptive or misleading representations "in connection with the collection of any debt"); id. § 1692f (prohibiting unfair or unconscionable means "to collect or attempt to collect any debt"). Instead, Atlas contends that a proof of claim is merely a "request to participate in the bankruptcy process." Appellee's Br. 20.

Determining whether a communication constitutes an attempt to collect a debt is a "commonsense inquiry" that evaluates the "nature of the parties' relationship," the "[objective] purpose and context of the communication[ ]," and whether the communication includes a demand for payment. Gburek v. Litton Loan Servicing LP, 614 F.3d 380, 385 (7th Cir. 2010); see also Olson v. Midland Funding, LLC, 578 Fed. Appx. 248, 251 (4th Cir. 2014) (citing Gburek factors approvingly). Here, the "only relationship between [the parties] [is] that of a debtor and debt collector." Olson, 578 Fed.Appx. at 251. Moreover, the "animating purpose" in filing a proof of claim is to obtain payment by sharing in the distribution of the debtor's bankruptcy estate. See Grden v. Leikin Ingber & Winters PC, 643 F.3d 169, 173 (6th Cir. 2011); 4-501 Collier ¶ 501.01. This fits squarely within the Supreme Court's understanding of debt collection for purposes of the FDCPA. See Heintz v. Jenkins, 514 U.S. 291, 294, 115 S.Ct. 1489, 131 L.Ed.2d 395 (1995) (explaining that in ordinary English, an attempt to "collect a debt" is an attempt "to obtain payment or liquidation of it, either by personal solicitation or legal proceedings" (quoting Black's Law Dictionary 263 (6th ed. 1990))). Precedent and common sense dictate that filing a proof of claim is an attempt to collect a debt. The absence of an explicit demand for payment does not alter that conclusion, Gburek, 614 F.3d at 382, nor does the fact that the bankruptcy court may ultimately disallow the claim.

Atlas argues that treating a proof of claim as an attempt to collect a debt would conflict with the Bankruptcy Code's automatic stay provision. The automatic stay provides that filing a bankruptcy petition p.528 "operates as a stay" of "any act to collect, assess, or recover a claim against the debtor that arose before the commencement of the case." 11 U.S.C. § 362(a)(6). Atlas argues that if filing a proof of claim were an act to collect debt, then such filing would violate the automatic stay, "an absurd result." Appellee's Br. 21.

Atlas's quandary is easily resolved as the automatic stay simply bars actions to collect debt outside of the bankruptcy proceeding. See, e.g., Cent. States, Se. & Sw. Areas Pension Fund v. Basic Am. Indus., Inc., 252 F.3d 911, 918 (7th Cir. 2001) ("'[D]emanding' payment from a debtor in bankruptcy other than in the bankruptcy proceeding itself is normally a violation of the automatic stay"); Campbell v. Countrywide Home Loans, Inc., 545 F.3d 348, 354 (5th Cir. 2008) (explaining that the automatic stay "merely suspends an action to collect the claim outside the procedural mechanisms of the Bankruptcy Code"). The automatic stay helps channel debt collection activity into the bankruptcy process. It does not strip such activity of its debt collection nature for purposes of the FDCPA.

Finally, Atlas argues that filing a proof of claim is not an attempt to collect debt because the proof of claim is directed to the bankruptcy court and trustee rather than to the debtor. However, collection activity directed toward someone other than the debtor may still be actionable under the FDCPA. See, e.g., Sayyed v. Wolpoff & Abramson, 485 F.3d 226, 232-33 (4th Cir. 2007) (finding that FDCPA "plainly" applies to communications made by debt collector to debtor's counsel rather than debtor); Horkey v. J.V.D.B. & Assocs., Inc., 333 F.3d 769, 774 (7th Cir. 2003) (finding that debt collector's phone call to debtor's co-worker was "in connection with the collection of a debt" where purpose of the call was to induce debtor to settle her debt). Although a proof of claim is filed with the bankruptcy court, it is done with the purpose of obtaining payment from the debtor's estate. That the claim is paid by the debtor's estate rather than the debtor personally is irrelevant for purposes of the FDCPA. See 15 U.S.C. §§ 1692e, 1692f (prohibiting the use of deceptive or unfair means to collect "any debt," without specifying a payor).

Accordingly, we find that filing a proof of claim is debt collection activity regulated by the FDCPA.

IV.

We next consider whether filing a proof of claim based on a debt that is beyond the applicable statute of limitations violates the FDCPA. Deciding this issue requires closer examination of the claims process in bankruptcy.

The Federal Rules of Bankruptcy Procedure specify the form, content, and filing requirements for a valid proof of claim. See, e.g., Fed. R. Bankr. P. 3001. A properly filed proof of claim is prima facie evidence of the claim's validity, and the claim is "deemed allowed" unless "a party in interest" objects. 11 U.S.C. § 502. The bankruptcy trustee and debtor are parties in interest who may object.[4] Indeed, the trustee has a statutory duty to "examine p.529 proofs of claims and object to the allowance of any claim that is improper." Id. § 704(a)(5).

If objected to, the Code disallows claims based on time-barred debts. See id. § 502(b)(1) (stating that a claim shall be disallowed if it is "unenforceable against the debtor ... under any agreement or applicable law"); id. § 558 (stating that the bankruptcy estate has "the benefit of any defense available to the debtor ... including statutes of limitation"). As previously noted, debts that are "provided for by the plan or disallowed under section 502" may be discharged. Id. § 1328 (emphasis added).

Appellants contend that the FDCPA should be applied to prohibit debt collectors from filing proofs of claim on time-barred debts. Appellants argue that a time-barred debt is not a "claim" within the meaning of the Bankruptcy Code and that filing claims on time-barred debts is an abusive practice because such claims are seldom objected to and therefore receive payment from the bankruptcy estate to the detriment of the debtor and other creditors. Atlas, meanwhile, argues that a time-barred debt is a valid "claim" and that filing such a claim should not be prohibited because only debts that are treated in the bankruptcy system may be discharged.

A.

The Bankruptcy Code defines the term "claim" broadly to mean a "right to payment, whether or not such right is reduced to judgment, liquidated, unliquidated, fixed, contingent, matured, unmatured, disputed, undisputed, legal, equitable, secured, or unsecured." 11 U.S.C. § 101(5)(A). By using the "broadest possible definition," the Code "contemplates that all legal obligations of the debtor, no matter how remote or contingent, will be able to be dealt with in the bankruptcy case," thereby providing the debtor the "broadest possible relief." H.R. Rep. No. 95-595, p. 309 (1977); S. Rep. No. 95-989, p. 22 (1978).

"[W]hen the Bankruptcy Code uses the word claim ... it is usually referring to a right to payment recognized under state law." Travelers Cas. & Sur. Co. of Am. v. Pac. Gas & Elec. Co., 549 U.S. 443, 451, 127 S.Ct. 1199, 167 L.Ed.2d 178 (2007) (quotation omitted). Under Maryland law, the statute of limitations "does not operate to extinguish [a] debt, but to bar the remedy." Potterton v. Ryland Grp., Inc., 289 Md. 371, 424 A.2d 761, 764 (1981) (quotation omitted); see also Higginbotham v. Pub. Serv. Comm'n of Md., 412 Md. 112, 985 A.2d 1183, 1191 (2009) ("[W]e have regarded limitations as not denying the plaintiff's right of action, but only the exercise of the right." (quotation omitted)). Indeed, a stale debt may be revived if the debtor sufficiently acknowledges the debt's existence. Potterton, 424 A.2d at 764; see also FTC, Time-Barred Debts (July 2013), https://www.consumer.ftc.gov/articles/0117-time-barred-debts ("Although the [debt] collector may not sue you to collect [a time-barred] debt, you still owe it. The collector can continue to contact you to try to collect .... [and] [i]n some states, if you pay any amount on a time-barred debt or even promise to pay, the debt is 'revived.'") (saved as ECF opinion attachment). Thus, under Maryland law, a time-barred debt still constitutes a "right to payment" and therefore a "claim" that the holder may file under the Bankruptcy Code.[5]

p.530 Appellants note that a debt must be enforceable to constitute a claim, citing the Supreme Court's statement that "[t]he plain meaning of a 'right to payment' is nothing more nor less than an enforceable obligation." Pa. Dep't of Pub. Welfare v. Davenport, 495 U.S. 552, 559, 110 S.Ct. 2126, 109 L.Ed.2d 588 (1990). However, we do not read the Supreme Court's statement to mean that a debt must be enforceable in court to be a claim. Indeed, the Bankruptcy Code treats debts that are "contingent" or "unmatured" as claims notwithstanding that such debts are not presently enforceable in court. 11 U.S.C. § 101(5)(A). Furthermore, in Davenport, the Supreme Court found restitution orders to be claims even though "neither the Probation Department nor the victim can enforce restitution obligations in civil proceedings." 495 U.S. at 558, 110 S.Ct. 2126. Instead, such obligations are enforced by the "substantial threat of revocation of probation and incarceration." Id.

It is also notable that while the Bankruptcy Code provides that time-barred debts are to be disallowed, see, e.g., 11 U.S.C § 558, the Code nowhere suggests that such debts are not to be filed in the first place. Indeed, the Bankruptcy Rules were recently amended to facilitate the assessment of a claim's timeliness by requiring that claims such as the ones at issue in this appeal be filed with a statement setting forth the last transaction date, last payment date, and charge-off date on the account. Fed. R. Bankr. P. 3001, advisory committee notes to 2012 Amendments (discussing filing requirements for claims based on open-end or revolving consumer credit agreements). This Rule suggests the Code contemplates that untimely debts will be filed as claims but ultimately disallowed. Lastly, excluding time-barred debts from the scope of bankruptcy "claims," and thus excluding them from the bankruptcy process, would frustrate the Code's "intended effect to define the scope of the term 'claim' as broadly as possible," 2-101 Collier ¶ 101.05, and thereby provide the debtor the broadest possible relief. Accordingly, we conclude that when the statute of limitations does not extinguish debts, a time-barred debt falls within the Bankruptcy Code's broad definition of a claim.

B.

Next, we consider whether filing a proof of claim on a time-barred debt violates the FDCPA notwithstanding that the Bankruptcy Code permits such filing. As noted above, the FDCPA has been interpreted to prohibit filing a lawsuit on a time-barred debt. The rationale has been explained as follows:

> As with any defendant sued on a stale claim, the passage of time not only dulls the consumer's memory of the circumstances and validity of the debt, but heightens the probability that she will no longer have personal records detailing the status of the debt. Indeed, the unfairness of such conduct is particularly clear in the consumer context where courts have imposed a heightened standard of care — that sufficient to protect the least sophisticated consumer. Because few unsophisticated consumers would be aware that a statute of limitations could be used to defend against lawsuits based on stale debts, such consumers would unwittingly acquiesce to such lawsuits. And, even if the consumer realizes that she can use time as a defense, she will more than likely still give in rather than fight the lawsuit because p.531 she must still expend energy and resources and subject herself to the embarrassment of going into court to present the defense; this is particularly true in light of the costs of attorneys today.

Kimber v. Fed. Fin. Corp., 668 F.Supp. 1480, 1487 (M.D. Ala. 1987); see also Crawford, 758 F.3d at 1260; Phillips v. Asset Acceptance, LLC, 736 F.3d 1076, 1079 (7th Cir. 2013).[6]

We note at the outset a unique consideration in the bankruptcy context: if a bankruptcy proceeds as contemplated by the Code, a claim based on a time-barred debt will be objected to by the trustee, disallowed, and ultimately discharged, thereby stopping the creditor from engaging in any further collection activity.[7] If the debt is unscheduled and no proof of claim is filed, the debt continues to exist and the debt collector may lawfully pursue collection activity apart from filing a lawsuit. This is detrimental to the debtor and undermines the bankruptcy system's interest in "the collective treatment of all of a debtor's creditors at one time." 1 Norton Bankr. L. & Prac. 3d § 3:9. Clearly, then, when a time-barred debt is not scheduled the optimal scenario is for a claim to be filed and for the Bankruptcy Code to operate as written.

Appellants complain, however, that trustees often lack the time and resources to examine each proof of claim and object to those that are based on time-barred debts. See Appellants' Br. 17-18 (explaining that Maryland has only three Chapter 13 trustees to manage approximately 5,000 cases per year, with approximately 10 proofs of claim filed in each case). Debt collectors like Atlas purportedly take advantage of this by filing claims on stale debts in hopes that the claims will go unnoticed and receive some payment from the bankruptcy estate. When successful, these debt collectors reduce the amount of money available to legitimate creditors and may sometimes cause debtors to pay more into their Chapter 13 plans.

We appreciate the harm that can be wrought if time-barred claims go unnoticed. However the solution, in our view, is not to impose liability under the FDCPA that would categorically bar the filing of such claims, but to improve the Code's administration such that it operates as written.[8] This may be accomplished, for example, by allocating additional resources to trustees or through action of the United States Trustee, who appoints and supervises all Chapter 13 trustees. 28 U.S.C. § 586.

Another consideration that counsels against finding FDCPA liability is that, for p.532 most Chapter 13 debtors, the amount they pay into their bankruptcy plans is unaffected by the number of unsecured claims that are filed. Chapter 13 debtors typically do not enter into 100 percent repayment plans; thus, their unsecured creditors receive only partial payment of their claims, with the remainder being discharged. See 8-1328 Collier ¶ 1328.02 ("Congress clearly contemplated chapter 13 plans paying little or nothing on unsecured debts ...."). As additional claims are filed, unsecured creditors receive a smaller share of available funds but the total amount paid by the debtor remains unchanged. Thus, from the perspective of most Chapter 13 debtors, it may in fact be preferable for a time-barred claim to be filed even if it is not objected to, as the debtor will likely pay the same total amount to creditors and the debt can be discharged. See In re Gatewood, 533 B.R. 905, 909 (8th Cir. BAP 2015) (explaining that "debtors have less at stake in claims allowance than they would when facing enforcement of an adverse judgment in a collection action" because the allowance of additional claims would not affect the total amount the debtor would pay).[9]

Various other considerations also differentiate filing a proof of claim on a time-barred debt from filing a lawsuit to collect such debt. First, the Bankruptcy Rules require claims like the ones filed by Atlas to accurately state the last transaction and charge-off date on the account, making untimely claims easier to detect and relieving debtors from the burden of producing evidence to show that the claim is time-barred.[10] Second, a bankruptcy debtor is protected by a trustee and often by counsel who are responsible for objecting to improper claims even if, as Appellants argue, they currently do not always do so. Third, unlike a debtor who is unwillingly sued, a Chapter 13 debtor voluntarily initiates the bankruptcy case, diminishing concerns about the embarrassment the debtor may feel in objecting to a stale claim. In sum, the reasons why it is "unfair" and "misleading" to sue on a time-barred debt are considerably diminished in the bankruptcy context, where the debtor has additional protections and potentially benefits from having the debt treated in the bankruptcy process.

Lastly, Appellants concede that a debt collector would not violate the FDCPA by filing a proof of claim on a time-barred debt that the debtor had scheduled and did not designate as "disputed." Appellants explain that scheduling a debt as undisputed is an "invitation to participate" because it provides "'notice to a creditor that its debt will be paid ... in accordance with the filed proof of claim, claims objection process, and other bankruptcy provisions.'" Appellants' Br. 28 n.14 (quoting Vaughn, 536 B.R. at 678). However, such notice is sent whether a scheduled debt is disputed or not. Moreover, a time-barred debt that is disputed is less likely to be inadvertently allowed. Thus, we see no reason to attach FDCPA liability to a claim filed on a time-barred debt that is scheduled as disputed. Finally, the interests in discharge and collective treatment of claims discussed above convince us that FDCPA liability should p.533 not attach where a debtor fails to schedule a time-barred debt.

We conclude that filing a proof of claim in a Chapter 13 bankruptcy based on a debt that is time-barred does not violate the FDCPA when the statute of limitations does not extinguish the debt.[11]

V.

For the foregoing reasons, we affirm the district court's dismissal of Appellants' FDCPA and MCDCA claims.

AFFIRMED

DIAZ, Circuit Judge, dissenting:

I join Part III of the majority opinion, which concludes that filing a proof of claim is debt-collection activity regulated by the Fair Debt Collection Practices Act (FDCPA), 15 U.S.C. § 1692 et seq.

And while I agree that Atlas's time-barred claim is a "claim" under the Bankruptcy Code (as the majority concludes in Part IV.A), I cannot agree that Atlas's alleged conduct is consistent with the FDCPA (or the Maryland Consumer Debt Collection Act (MCDCA), Md. Code Ann., Com. Law § 14-201 et seq.).[1] Atlas buys the time-barred debt of people in bankruptcy and tries to collect by filing proofs of claim in their bankruptcy proceedings. As Atlas concedes, these claims should fail — the debt is unenforceable in court. But, absent objection, the Bankruptcy Code automatically allows all properly filed claims. 11 U.S.C. § 502. So Atlas plays the odds, representing itself as entitled to part of the debtors' estates. If someone notices the claims and objects, as happened here Atlas grins sheepishly — "You caught me!" — and admits that the claim is meritless. But if the claim slips through, Atlas uses the bankruptcy court to garner a payoff on unenforceable debts. In my view, this sharp practice is misleading and unfair to debtors and other creditors, and it gives rise to a cause of action under the FDCPA.

Moreover, I would hold that the Bankruptcy Code does not impliedly repeal the FDCPA or preempt the MCDCA. Accordingly, I would vacate the opinion of the district court and remand for further proceedings.

I.

The FDCPA aims to "protect[ ] consumers from abusive and deceptive practices by debt collectors, and ... non-abusive debt collectors from competitive disadvantage." United States v. Nat'l Fin. Servs., Inc., 98 F.3d 131, 135 (4th Cir.

1996). The statute prohibits a wide variety of collection tactics, including the use of "any false, deceptive, or misleading representation or means" of debt collection, 15 U.S.C. § 1692e, and "unfair or unconscionable means to collect or attempt to collect any debt," § 1692f.

Although the FDCPA enumerates specific examples of these broad prohibitions, it does so "[w]ithout limiting [their] general application." Id. For example, "[t]he false representation of ... the character, amount, or legal status of any debt" is a specific violation of the general ban on false, deceptive, or misleading representations. § 1692e(2)(A). But Congress chose not to limit the general prohibitions, to "enable the courts, where appropriate, to proscribe other improper conduct which is not specifically addressed." Stratton v. Portfolio Recovery Assocs., LLC, 770 F.3d 443, 450 (6th Cir. 2014) (quoting S. Rep. p.534 No. 95-382 at 4 (1977), as reprinted in 1977 U.S.C.C.A.N. 1695, 1698).

One such court-imposed proscription applies to lawsuits to collect time-barred debt. Crawford v. LVNV Funding, LLC, 758 F.3d 1254, 1259-60 & n.6 (11th Cir. 2014) (citing cases). Such lawsuits raise two major concerns in the consumer context. First, the "least sophisticated consumer" — from whose vantage point we view FDCPA communications, see Russell v. Absolute Collection Servs., Inc., 763 F.3d 385, 394 (4th Cir. 2014) — may be unaware of the existence of a statute-of-limitations defense and may therefore "unwittingly acquiesce to such lawsuits," Kimber v. Fed. Fin. Corp., 668 F.Supp. 1480, 1487 (M.D. Ala. 1987). Second, "the passage of time not only dulls the consumer's memory of the circumstances and validity of the debt, but heightens the probability that [the consumer] will no longer have personal records detailing the status of the debt." Phillips v. Asset Acceptance, LLC, 736 F.3d 1076, 1079 (7th Cir. 2013) (quoting Kimber, 668 F.Supp. at 1487).

These same considerations support recognizing FDCPA liability for filing time-barred claims on unscheduled debts in bankruptcy.[2] Crawford, 758 F.3d at 1260-61. But see Nelson v. Midland Credit Mgmt., Inc., No. 15-2984, 828 F.3d 749, 752, 2016 WL 3672073, at *2 (8th Cir. July 11, 2016) (published opinion) (refusing to "extend[ ] the FDCPA to time-barred proofs of claim" because the Bankruptcy Code's "protections against harassment and deception satisfy the relevant concerns of the FDCPA"). Here, where the proofs of claim provide enough information to determine the debt is time barred, the first consideration is of particular importance. An unsophisticated debtor reviewing a proof of claim may be unaware of the statute-of-limitations defense and — perhaps not appreciating the legal significance of even accurately listed last-transaction and charge-off dates — may nevertheless "acquiesce" to the claims.

While some courts have found the role of the bankruptcy trustee in weeding out time-barred claims critical in distinguishing the bankruptcy context from civil lawsuits, see, e.g., Nelson, 828 F.3d at 751-52, 2016 WL 3672073, at *2, I am not persuaded. At best, a debt collector who files such a claim wastes the trustee's time. At worst, the debt collector catches the trustee asleep at the switch and collects on an invalid claim to the detriment of other creditors and, in many cases, the debtor. In either case, the debt collector misleadingly represents to the debtor that it is entitled to collect through bankruptcy when it is not.

Moreover, there is reason to doubt the efficacy of the trustee as a vigilant steward of the debtor's estate. See, e.g., In re Edwards, 539 B.R. 360, 365 (Bankr.

N.D. Ill. 2015) ("Chapter 13 trustees in this district do not object to proofs of claim based on statute of limitations defenses. This is not surprising because objecting to claims based on affirmative defenses would require trustees to examine the details of virtually every unsecured proof of claim, which is simply impracticable."). Indeed, if trustees performed their duties flawlessly, Atlas would have little incentive to engage in its scheme.

Like filing a lawsuit on time-barred debt, Atlas's alleged debt-collection activity in this case is precisely the sort of unfair and misleading practice that Congress intended the courts to recognize as a violation. After the debtors entered bankruptcy, Atlas bought their debts, or rather, p.535 as the bill of sales said, "charged-off receivables." J.A. 58, 132, 143. All of these charged-off debts were more than five-years old, well outside Maryland's three-year statute of limitations. Nevertheless, Atlas filed proofs of claim to recover the unenforceable debts in the bankruptcy court. The relevance of the statute of limitations was not lost on Atlas, which included the following notice on two of the three proof-of-claim forms it filed: "This proof of claim is being filed pursuant to 11 USC Secs. 101(5), 501(a) and 502(b) as said claim may be outside of the statute of limitations." J.A. 55, 140. Section 502(b) explains that if a claim is objected to, the court will allow the claim "except to the extent that ... such claim is unenforceable against the debtor and the property of the debtor, under any agreement or applicable law." § 502(b)(1). In short, Atlas knew exactly what it was doing — exploiting a weakness in the bankruptcy system and preying on potential error to collect on debts where it should not. The practice subverts a core purpose of bankruptcy by diverting estate assets from the creditors entitled to receive them.

Atlas rather stunningly argues that it is doing a public service: "[B]ut for Atlas' filing of its proofs of claim, those debts would not be subject to discharge and at the conclusion of Appellants' chapter 13 cases, Atlas could restart collection activity with respect thereto so long as it does not otherwise violate the FDCPA." Appellee's Br. at 40. Really? While the statement is literally true, the (unintended) possibility that the time-barred debts will be disallowed and discharged hardly justifies Atlas's tactics. Moreover, that the debtors did not schedule the debts is some evidence that collection efforts have stopped. And it would not be surprising if they had; the time for enforcement has passed, and the combination of the statute of limitations and the FDCPA seriously limits what a debt collector can do to recover old debts. Ideally, debtors would remember all their old debts, realize they were time barred, schedule them as disputed, and see that they were disallowed. But the FDCPA asks what the least sophisticated consumer would do, not the ideal one. Atlas's conduct games the bankruptcy process; it does not ensure its integrity.

Accordingly, I would hold that Atlas's conduct constitutes a violation of the FDCPA. Such a holding would not impose a great burden on debt collectors. "[A] debt collector is not liable in an action brought under the [FDCPA] if [it] can show 'the violation was not intentional and resulted from a bona fide error notwithstanding the maintenance of procedures reasonably adapted to avoid any such error.'" Jerman v. Carlisle, McNellie, Rini, Kramer & Ulrich LPA, 559 U.S. 573, 576, 130 S.Ct. 1605, 176 L.Ed.2d 519 (2010) (quoting 15 U.S.C. § 1692k(c)). Atlas and other debt collectors can avoid FDCPA liability by putting in place a reasonable procedure to screen unscheduled, time-barred claims — if Atlas already has such a procedure, it can prove it in the district court.

II.

Because the majority determines that the FDCPA does not reach Atlas's conduct, it does not address the question whether — if the FDCPA on its own terms would apply to the filing of time-barred claims — the Bankruptcy Code nevertheless precludes such an action. To determine whether two federal statutes are compatible, we employ ordinary statutory interpretation principles. See POM Wonderful LLC v. Coca-Cola Co., ___ U.S. ___, 134 S.Ct. 2228, 2236, 189 L.Ed.2d 141 (2014). Because the circuits are split on this issue and the arguments have been made extensively on both sides, I explain briefly my p.536 position that the two statutes do not conflict in this instance.

The Second and Ninth Circuits have concluded that the Bankruptcy Code precludes certain FDCPA suits. Simmons v. Roundup Funding, LLC, 622 F.3d 93, 95-96 (2d Cir. 2010) (rejecting an FDCPA claim brought during the pendency of bankruptcy proceedings for the filing of an inflated proof of claim); Walls v. Wells Fargo Bank, N.A., 276 F.3d 502, 510-11 (9th Cir. 2002) (barring an FDCPA claim for post-bankruptcy debt collection in violation of the discharge order). Both rely on the comprehensive provisions and protections of the Bankruptcy Code to hold that it leaves no room for FDCPA claims. Simmons, 622 F.3d at 96; Walls, 276 F.3d at 510.

The Third, Seventh, and Eleventh Circuits have rejected the notion that FDCPA actions may not be brought in the context of bankruptcy. Johnson v. Midland Funding LLC, 823 F.3d 1334, 1341-42 (11th Cir.2016) (published opinion) (holding that the Bankruptcy Code does not impliedly repeal FDCPA actions for filing proofs of claim on time-barred debt); Simon v. FIA Card Servs., N.A., 732 F.3d 259, 274 (3d Cir. 2013) (permitting an FDCPA claim for the violation of the Bankruptcy Code's subpoena requirements); Randolph v. IMBS, Inc., 368 F.3d 726, 730-31 (7th Cir. 2004) (comparing the FDCPA and Bankruptcy Code and concluding they are compatible). In the view of these courts, the statutes do not expressly contradict one another, nor are they in "irreconcilable conflict" because "any debt collector can comply with both simultaneously." Randolph, 368 F.3d at 730; accord Johnson, 823 F.3d at 1340-42; Simon, 732 F.3d at 273-74; see also Nat'l Ass'n of Home Builders v. Defs. of Wildlife, 551 U.S. 644, 662, 127 S.Ct. 2518, 168 L.Ed.2d 467 (2007) ("While a later enacted statute ... can sometimes operate to amend or even repeal an earlier statutory provision ..., 'repeals by implication are not favored' and will not be presumed unless the 'intention of the legislature to repeal [is] clear and manifest.'" (third alteration in original) (quoting Watt v. Alaska, 451 U.S. 259, 267, 101 S.Ct. 1673, 68 L.Ed.2d 80 (1981))).

I would side with the view of the Third, Seventh, and Eleventh Circuits, at least on the facts of this case. Atlas does not argue that the Bankruptcy Code expressly bars FDCPA remedies. Instead, it contends the statutes are irreconcilable: "[W]hat [the debtors] allege is prohibited by the FDCPA (the filing of a proof of claim with respect to a 'stale' debt) is expressly permitted by the Bankruptcy Code." Appellee's Br. at 34. But this argument is easily answered: Because the Bankruptcy Code does not obligate a creditor to file a proof of claim, a debt collector such as Atlas can comply with both statutes by not filing unscheduled, time-barred proofs of claim. See Johnson, 823 F.3d at 1341-42; Randolph, 368 F.3d at 730.[3]

This conclusion is buttressed by our holding, in a somewhat different posture, that an FDCPA claim may be brought during bankruptcy proceedings. Covert v. LVNV Funding, LLC, 779 F.3d 242, 246-48 (4th Cir. 2015). In Covert, debtors filed suit under the FDCPA and MCDCA after the completion of their bankruptcies, alleging that a creditor had unlawfully filed proofs of claim without a debt-collection license. Id. at 245. We found the claims barred by res judicata because the debtors failed to raise them during the bankruptcy. Id. at 247-48. Because res judicata applies to unraised claims only if they "could have p.537 been adjudicated in an earlier action," id. at 246, we necessarily determined that the debtors "could ... have brought their affirmative claims for damages [under the FDCPA and MCDCA] during the bankruptcy process under Federal Rule of Bankruptcy Procedure 7001(1), which provides that 'a proceeding to recover money or property' may be brought as an adversary action," id. at 248. Similarly, I would hold that the Bankruptcy Code does not preclude or preempt the filing of the FDCPA and MCDCA claims in this case.

III.

Because I believe the debtors state a claim under the FDCPA (and MCDCA), I would reverse and remand for further proceedings.

[1] "A proof of claim is a form filed by a creditor in a bankruptcy proceeding that states the amount the debtor owes to the creditor and the reason for the debt." Covert v. LVNV Funding, LLC, 779 F.3d 242, 244 n.1 (4th Cir. 2015).

[2] Atlas asks the Court to strike any allegation that the loans in this appeal originated with payday lenders. However, the proofs of claim attached to Appellants' complaints indicate that Atlas itself designated the debts "payday." See J.A. 55, 140. Accordingly, we find this fact sufficiently alleged. See Goines v. Valley Cmty. Servs. Bd., 822 F.3d 159, 164-65 (4th Cir.2016) (explaining that on motion to dismiss, courts may consider documents attached to complaint as exhibits).

[3] Dubois additionally alleged that Atlas violated the Maryland Consumer Debt Collection Act (MCDCA). Md. Code Ann., Com. Law § 14-201, et seq. The parties do not analyze the MCDCA separately from the FDCPA. Accordingly, neither do we.

[4] While the parties do not address the issue, it appears that creditors are also parties in interest who may object to a claim filed by another creditor. See, e.g., Adair v. Sherman, 230 F.3d 890, 894 n.3 (7th Cir. 2000) ("Parties in interest include not only the debtor, but anyone who has a legally protected interest that could be affected by a bankruptcy proceeding. Therefore, if one creditor files a potentially fraudulent proof of claim, other creditors have standing to object to the proof of claim." (citation omitted)); In re Varat Enters., Inc., 81 F.3d 1310, 1317 n.8 (4th Cir. 1996) ("All creditors of a debtor are parties in interest.").

[5] Appellants suggest that "by filing proofs of claim on time-barred debt, Atlas is trying to trick debtors into unwittingly reviving the statute [of limitations]." Appellants' Reply Br. 4. Regardless of whether this is Atlas's intent, it is difficult to see how a creditor's filing a proof of claim would constitute acknowledgement of the debt by the debtor, particularly when there is persuasive authority that a debtor does not revive a time-barred debt by listing it in his bankruptcy schedules. See, e.g., Biggs v. Mays, 125 F.2d 693, 697-98 (8th Cir. 1942); In re Povill, 105 F.2d 157, 160 (2d Cir. 1939).

[6] The Eleventh Circuit in Crawford is the only court of appeals to hold that filing a proof of claim on a time-barred debt in a Chapter 13 proceeding violates the FDCPA. 758 F.3d at 1256-57. The Eighth Circuit has "reject[ed] extending the FDCPA to time-barred proofs of claim," Nelson v. Midland Credit Mgmt., Inc., No. 15-2984, 828 F.3d 749, 752, 2016 WL 3672073, at *2 (8th Cir. July 11, 2016), and the Second Circuit has broadly held that "filing a proof of claim in bankruptcy court (even one that is somehow invalid) cannot constitute the sort of abusive debt collection practice proscribed by the FDCPA." Simmons v. Roundup Funding, LLC, 622 F.3d 93, 95 (2d Cir. 2010). Other circuits are presently considering the issue. See, e.g., Owens v. LVNV Funding, LLC, No 14-cv-02083, 2015 WL 1826005 (S.D. Ind. Apr. 21, 2015), appeal docketed, No. 15-2044 (7th Cir. May 13, 2015); Torres v. Asset Acceptance, LLC, 96 F.Supp.3d 541 (E.D. Pa. 2015), appeal docketed, No. 15-2132 (3d Cir. May 13, 2015).

[7] By contrast, raising a statute of limitations defense may defeat a lawsuit to collect a time-barred debt but would not extinguish the debt or necessarily prevent collection activity.

[8] Indeed, if Appellants are correct that trustees are failing to fulfill their statutory duty to examine and object to improper claims, this is surely producing adverse consequences beyond the context of time-barred debts.

[9] As noted above, the FDCPA was enacted in part to protect scrupulous debt collectors from unfair competition. However, bankruptcy creditors are sophisticated entities that may object to improper claims. Thus, we will not invoke the FDCPA solely on their behalf when, as discussed above, there are reasons not to do so on behalf of bankruptcy debtors.

[10] There is no allegation that Atlas filed inaccurate proofs of claim. A debt collector who supplies false dates to obscure a claim's staleness may well violate the FDCPA. However, we have no occasion to consider that issue today.

[11] In light of this decision, we do not reach Atlas's argument that the Bankruptcy Code precludes the FDCPA and preempts the MCDCA from applying to the filing of a proof of claim.

[1] I join the majority in analyzing the FDCPA and MCDCA claims together, as the parties do.

[2] As the debtors concede, their case might be different had they scheduled these debts with the bankruptcy court, an action that might be seen as an invitation to a creditor to file a claim.

[3] For similar reasons, I would hold that the Bankruptcy Code does not preempt the MCDCA.

817 F.3d 131 (2016)

Ricky HENSON; Ian Matthew Glover; Karen Pacouloute, f/k/a Karen Welcome Kuteyi; Paulette House, Plaintiffs-Appellants,
v.
SANTANDER CONSUMER USA, INC., Defendant-Appellee, and Commercial Recovery Systems, Inc.; NCB Management Services, Incorporated, Defendants.
AARP; National Consumer Law Center; National Association of Consumer Advocates; Civil Justice, Inc.; Public Justice Center, Inc.; Maryland Consumer Rights Coalition, Inc.; Attorney General of Maryland, Amici Supporting, Appellants.

No. 15-1187.

United States Court of Appeals, Fourth Circuit.

Argued: December 9, 2015.
Decided: March 23, 2016.

Henson v. Santander Consumer USA, Inc., 817 F. 3d 131 (4th Cir. 2016)

p.133 ARGUED: Cory Lev Zajdel, Z Law, LLC, Reisterstown, Maryland, for Appellants. Kim M. Watterson, Reed Smith LLP, Pittsburgh, Pennsylvania, for Appellee. ON BRIEF: Travis Sabalewski, Robert Luck Jr., Richmond, Virginia, Richard L. Heppner, Reed Smith LLP, Pittsburgh, Pennsylvania, for Appellee. Julie Nepveu, AARP Foundation Litigation, Washington, D.C., for Amicus AARP. Joseph S. Mack, Catherine Gonzalez, Civil Justice, Inc., Baltimore, Maryland; Brian E. Frosh, Attorney General, Office of the Attorney General of Maryland, Baltimore, Maryland, for Amici Attorney General of Maryland, Civil Justice, Inc., Maryland Consumer Rights Coalition, Inc., National Association of Consumer Advocates, National Consumer Law Center and Public Justice Center, Inc.

Before NIEMEYER, DUNCAN, and AGEE, Circuit Judges.

Affirmed by published opinion. Judge NIEMEYER wrote the opinion, in which Judge DUNCAN and Judge AGEE joined.

p.132 NIEMEYER, Circuit Judge:

Four Maryland consumers commenced this action against Santander Consumer USA, Inc., and its agents, alleging that the defendants violated the Fair Debt Collection Practices Act ("FDCPA"), 15 U.S.C. §§ 1692-1692p, by engaging in prohibited collection practices when collecting on the plaintiffs' automobile loans. The loans were originally made by CitiFinancial Auto, and, after the plaintiffs were unable to make payments, CitiFinancial Auto foreclosed on the loans, leaving the plaintiffs obligated to pay deficiencies. CitiFinancial Auto then sold the defaulted loans to Santander as part of an investment bundle of receivables, and Santander thereafter attempted to collect on the loans it had purchased.

The district court granted Santander's motion to dismiss the claims against it under Federal Rule of Civil Procedure 12(b)(6) on the ground that the complaint did not allege facts showing that Santander qualified as a "debt collector" subject to the

FDCPA. The court concluded that the complaint demonstrated that Santander was a consumer finance company that was collecting debts *on its own behalf* as a creditor and that the FDCPA generally does not regulate creditors collecting on debt owed to themselves.

p.134 We affirm. While the FDCPA is a somewhat complex and technical regulation of debt collector practices, we conclude that it generally does not regulate creditors when they collect debt on their own account and that, on the facts alleged by the plaintiffs, Santander became a creditor when it purchased the loans before engaging in the challenged practices.

I

Ricky Henson, Ian Glover, Karen Pacouloute, and Paulette House, Maryland consumers who are the plaintiffs in this action, each signed a retail installment sales contract with CitiFinancial Auto Credit, Inc., CitiFinancial Auto Corp., or CitiFinancial Auto, LTD (collectively, "CitiFinancial Auto") to finance the purchase of an automobile. When the plaintiffs were unable to make the payments required by the contracts and thereby defaulted, CitiFinancial Auto repossessed and sold their vehicles and subsequently informed each plaintiff that he or she owed a deficiency balance.

On December 1, 2011, CitiFinancial Auto sold $3.55 billion in loan receivables, including the plaintiffs' defaulted loans, to Santander, a consumer finance company. The plaintiffs allege that, as part of its business, Santander "acquires defaulted consumer debt . . . for a few cents on the dollar."

Thereafter, Santander and its agents, presumably in an effort to collect more than the few cents on the dollar that it paid for defaulted loans, "began communicating with [the plaintiffs] . . . in an attempt to collect on the alleged debts." And during the course of those communications, Santander and its agents allegedly misrepresented the amount of the debt and their entitlement to collect it.

The plaintiffs commenced this action in November 2012 against Santander and its agents, alleging that they violated the FDCPA in pursuing the debts and in the manner they pursued them. In their complaint, they proposed to represent a class of certain debtors "who were subjected to debt collection efforts by Santander Consumer USA, Inc. on or after December 1, 2011," the date on which Santander purchased the receivables from CitiFinancial Auto.

Santander filed a motion to dismiss the complaint against it under Federal Rule of Civil Procedure 12(b)(6) on the ground that the complaint's allegations did not demonstrate that Santander qualified as a "debt collector," as necessary to trigger liability under the FDCPA, and the district court granted the motion by order dated May 6, 2014. In its supporting opinion, the court noted that the FDCPA applies to "debt collectors," as that term is defined in the Act, but not to "creditors collecting debts in their own names and whose primary business is not debt collection." In reaching its conclusion, the court rejected the plaintiffs' argument that, because the plaintiffs' loans were in default when Santander acquired them from CitiFinancial Auto, Santander qualified as a debt collector under the FDCPA, rather than as a creditor.

The plaintiffs filed this appeal, presenting the single issue of whether, as necessary to state an FDCPA claim, their complaint adequately alleged that Santander was acting as a "debt collector," as that term is defined in 15 U.S.C. § 1692a(6), when it engaged in the collection practices challenged in the suit.

II

In their brief on appeal, the plaintiffs state their position that Santander was a "debt collector," subject to regulation p.135 by the FDCPA, based on the following reasoning:

> The terms "debt collector" and "creditor" are mutually exclusive under the FDCPA. An entity can be either a "debt collector" or a "creditor" in any particular transaction. The determining factor of whether an entity is a "debt collector" or "creditor" in any particular transaction when the entity in question is not the originating lender is *whether the debt was acquired prior to default or after default.* Since Santander acquired [the plaintiffs'] debts from the original lender well after each [plaintiff] defaulted on their debt, Santander's collection activities on these defaulted debts make[ ] it a "debt collector."

(Emphasis added). To make their argument, the plaintiffs rely on their interpretations of 15 U.S.C. §§ 1692a(4) and 1692a(6), which define "creditor" and "debt collector," respectively. Their argument rests on the premise that the FDCPA regulates debt collectors, not creditors, and that the two terms, as used in the Act, are mutually exclusive. *See Bridge v. Ocwen Fed. Bank, FSB,* 681 F.3d 355, 359 (6th Cir.2012); *FTC v. Check Investors, Inc.,* 502 F.3d 159, 173 (3d Cir.2007). Thus, they reason, because § 1692a(4) excludes from the definition of *creditor* "any person to the extent that he receives an assignment or transfer of *a debt in default* solely for the purpose of facilitating collection of such debt for another," such person must of logical necessity be a *debt collector.* Because Santander fits, as they argue, the exclusion from the definition of "creditor," it must therefore be a "debt collector." They claim that this conclusion is fortified by one of the exclusions to the definition of "debt collector." *See* 15 U.S.C. § 1692a(6)(F)(iii) (excluding from the definition of debt collector "any person collecting or attempting to collect any debt. . . owed or due another to the extent such activity . . . concerns a debt which was not *in default* at the time it was obtained" (emphasis added)). At bottom, they maintain that *the default status of debt* determines whether a purchaser of debt, such as Santander, is a debt collector or a creditor.

The plaintiffs' argument, however, contains several interpretational and logical flaws, such that their interpretation of the FDCPA ultimately stands in tension with its plain language. When arguing from the definition of *creditor,* they overlook the fact that the exclusion applies only to a person who receives defaulted debt "solely for the purpose of facilitating collection. . . *for another.*" 15 U.S.C. § 1692a(4) (emphasis added). Similarly, in relying on the exclusion in § 1692a(6)(F)(iii), they fail to address whether Santander fits under any definition of "debt collector" before addressing whether the (F)(iii) exclusion applies.

We conclude that the default status of a debt has no bearing on whether a person qualifies as a debt collector under the threshold definition set forth in 15 U.S.C. § 1692a(6). That determination is ordinarily based on whether a person collects debt *on behalf of others* or *for its own account,* the main exception being when the "principal purpose" of the person's business is to collect debt.

We begin our explanation by noting at a general level that the FDCPA purports to regulate only the conduct of debt collectors, not creditors, generally distinguishing between the two based on whether the person acts in an agency relationship with the person to whom the borrower is indebted. With limited exceptions, a debt collector thus collects debt on behalf of a creditor. A creditor, on the other hand, is a person to whom the debt is owed, and when a creditor collects its p.136 debt for its own account, it is not generally acting as a debt collector.

The FDCPA's definitions of debt collector and creditor bear out this distinction.

The definition of debt collector, which is contained in § 1692a(6), is comprised of two parts. The first part defines the classes of persons that are *included* within the term "debt collector," while the second part defines those classes of persons that are *excluded* from the definition of debt collector. The first part, defining those who are included, provides in relevant part:

> The term "debt collector" means any person [1] who uses any instrumentality of interstate commerce or the mails in any business *the principal purpose of which is the collection of any debts,* or [2] who *regularly collects* or attempts to collect, directly or indirectly, *debts owed or due or asserted to be owed or due another.* Notwithstanding the exclusion provided by clause (F) of the last sentence of this paragraph, the term includes any creditor [3] who, in the process of collecting his own debts, *uses any name other than his own* which would indicate that a third person is collecting or attempting to collect such debts.

15 U.S.C. § 1692a(6) (emphasis added). Stated more simply, this provision defines a debt collector as (1) a person whose *principal purpose* is to collect debts; (2) a person who *regularly* collects debts *owed to another*. or (3) a person who collects *its own debts,* using *a name other than its own* as if it were a debt collector.

The second part of § 1692a(6) defines the classes of persons that are excluded from the definition of debt collector, so that a person who meets one of the definitions of debt collector contained in the first part of § 1692a(6) will not qualify as such if it falls within one of the exclusions. As relevant here, exclusion (F)(iii) provides that "[t]he term [debt collector] does not include . . . any person collecting or attempting to collect any debt owed or due or asserted to be owed or due another to the extent such activity . . . concerns a debt which was not in default at the time it was obtained by such person." 15 U.S.C. § 1692a(6)(F)(iii). To simplify, this exclusion means that a person collecting nondefaulted debts on behalf of others is not a debt collector. This exclusion was intended by Congress to protect those entities that function as loan servicers for debt not in default. *See* S. Rep. No. 95-382, at 3-4 (1977), *as reprinted in* 1977 U.S.C.C.A.N. 1695, 1698 ("[T]he committee does not intend the definition [of debt collector] to cover the activities of . . . *mortgage service companies and others who service outstanding debts for others,* so long as the debts were not in default when taken for servicing" (emphasis added)).

Thus, the overall structure of § 1692a(6) makes clear that when assessing whether a person qualifies as a "debt collector," we must first determine whether the person satisfies one of the statutory definitions given in the main text of § 1692a(6) before considering whether that person falls into one of the exclusions contained in subsections § 1692a(6)(A)-(F). If a person does not satisfy one of the definitions in the main text, the exclusions in subsections § 1692a(6)(A)-(F) do not come into play. *See Davidson v. Capital One Bank (USA), N.A.,* 797 F.3d 1309, 1314 (11th Cir.2015) ("[W]here a person does not fall within subsection (F) or any one of the six statutory exclusions, he is not deemed a 'debt collector' as a matter of course. [Instead], . . . he must satisfy the Act's substantive requirements").

The material distinction between a debt collector and a creditor—at least with respect p.137 to the second definition of "debt collector" provided by § 1692a(6)-is therefore whether a person's regular collection activity is only *for itself* (a creditor) or whether it regularly collects *for others* (a debt collector)—not, as the plaintiffs urge, whether the debt was in default when the person acquired it. *See Heintz v. Jenkins,* 514 U.S. 291, 293, 115 S.Ct. 1489, 131 L.Ed.2d 395 (1995) ("The Act's definition of the term 'debt collector' includes a person 'who regularly collects or attempts to collect, directly or indirectly, debts owed [to] . . . another'" (alteration in original) (quoting § 1692a(6))); *see also Davidson,* 797 F.3d at 1315-16 ("The statutory text is entirely transparent. . . . [A] person must regularly collect or attempt to collect debts *for others* in order to qualify as a 'debt collector' under the second definition of the term"); S. Rep. No. 95-382, at 3 ("The Committee intends the term 'debt collector,' subject to the exclusions discussed below, to cover all *third persons* who regularly collect debts *for others*" (emphasis added)). *But see Bridge,* 681 F.3d at 359; *Ruth v. Triumph P'ships,* 577 F.3d 790, 796-97 (7th Cir.2009); *Check Investors,* 502 F.3d at 173.

With this interpretation of § 1692a(6), we turn to the complaint in this case to assess what it states about Santander. The complaint alleges that the plaintiffs borrowed money from CitiFinancial Auto to purchase automobiles and that, when the plaintiffs went into default on the loans, CitiFinancial Auto repossessed and sold their automobiles, leaving them owing deficiency balances. It also alleges that when the loans were in default but *before* December 1, 2011, Santander was "hired. . . as a servicer to collect" on the loans, presumably on behalf of CitiFinancial Auto.

But the very next paragraph of the complaint alleges that on December 1, 2011, CitiFinancial Auto sold the plaintiffs' loans to Santander. *Only thereafter,* when Santander began collecting from the plaintiffs on the loans that it had purchased, did Santander engage in the conduct that the plaintiffs allege was in violation of the FDCPA. Specifically, the complaint alleges that after December 1, 2011, Santander improperly contacted the borrowers directly, misrepresented the amounts owed, and misrepresented the fact that Santander was entitled to collect on the loans. Importantly, however, the complaint does *not* allege that, when Santander engaged in the allegedly illegal collection practices, it was collecting the debts *on behalf of Citi-Financial Auto.* Rather, it alleges that CitiFinancial Auto had *sold* the loans to Santander, presumably "for a few cents on the dollar," thus leaving Santander to collect on the debts for its own account. And this allegation is consistent with public SEC filings, which reveal that Santander purchased $3.55 billion in loan receivables from CitiFinancial Auto on December 1, 2011, following which Santander presumably attempted to obtain a return by collecting more than a few cents on the dollar through its collection efforts.

Applying these allegations to the definition of debt collector in § 1692a(6), it is apparent that Santander does not fall within the first or third definitions of debt collector. The complaint does not allege, nor do the plaintiffs argue, that Santander's *principal business* was to collect debt, alleging instead that Santander was a consumer finance company. The complaint also does not allege, nor do the plaintiffs contend, that Santander was using a name other than its own in collecting the debts. Thus, to allege that Santander was a debt collector, the complaint is left to satisfy the second definition of debt collector—that Santander regularly collects debts owed to others and was doing so here.

p.138 Yet, the complaint's allegations also do not satisfy this definition because the debts that Santander was collecting were owed to it, Santander, not to another. This is alleged specifically and unambiguously. The complaint asserts that *after* Santander purchased the plaintiffs' debts on December 1, 2011 (and became the entity to which the debts were owed), it engaged in collection efforts that violated the FDCPA. Thus, those collection efforts were pursued *for its own account,* as the loans were then owed to it. Santander was therefore not a person collecting a debt *on behalf of another,* so as to qualify as a debt collector under the second definition, but *on behalf of itself,* making it a creditor.

Because the complaint does not satisfy any definition of debt collector, the analysis ends, and the exclusions from the definition of debt collector, on which the plaintiffs rely, have no significance.

Nonetheless, the plaintiffs argue that the *default status* of a debt is determinative of whether a person who purchased the debt is a debt collector, pointing to exclusion (F)(iii), which *excludes* from the class of persons defined as a debt collector "any person collecting or attempting to collect any debt owed or due. . . another to the extent such activity . . . concerns a debt which was *not in default* at the time it was obtained by such person." 15 U.S.C. § 1692a(6)(F)(iii) (emphasis added). They argue that because that provision excludes persons collecting debts not in default, the definition of debt collector must, by a negative pregnant, necessarily include persons collecting defaulted debts that they did not originate. This logic, however, turns the statutory provision upside down, failing to recognize that the FDCPA defines debt collector by reference to those who are included in the various classes and then excludes, among others, the subset of persons who obtain nondefaulted debt to collect on it for others. As noted earlier, this exclusion was included by Congress to protect mortgage service companies and similar loan servicers who acquire debt not in default and service it for a fee. The exclusion thus does not define "debt collector," but rather identifies a class of persons *excluded* from the definition of "debt collector."

In a similar vein, the plaintiffs argue that the definition of *creditor* supports their position that *the default status* of a debt defines whether a person attempting to collect that debt is a debt collector. In making this argument, they rely on the exclusion to the definition of creditor but, in doing so, the plaintiffs again apply the same kind of upside-down logic that relies on an inaccurate premise and a negative pregnant that does not follow.

The term "creditor" is defined by the FDCPA as "any person who offers or extends credit creating a debt or to whom a debt is owed." 15 U.S.C. § 1692a(4). The definition then excludes "any person to the extent that he receives an assignment or transfer of a debt in default solely for the purpose of facilitating collection of such debt for another." *Id.* The plaintiffs argue that Santander fits the creditor exclusion and therefore must necessarily be a debt collector.

The logic does not follow, mainly because debt collector is defined separately and that definition, rather than some implied definition, is determinative. But the logic is flawed even more fundamentally because the premise that Santander satisfies the exclusion is incorrect. In arguing that Santander satisfies the exclusion, the plaintiffs *recharacterize* the facts they alleged in the complaint, stating in their brief that, "although Santander currently owns [the plaintiffs'] debts, those debts were assigned to Santander after default p.139 and *solely for the purpose of facilitating collection of the debts for CitiFinancial [Auto]*." (Emphasis added). But the facts that the plaintiffs presume in their brief are not the facts of their complaint. The complaint alleges that CitiFinancial Auto *sold* the loans to Santander and that Santander thereafter attempted to collect on them *for its own account.* Santander was, at the time of its allegedly illegal collection conduct, the plaintiffs' creditor, and nothing in the complaint suggests that it was acting on behalf of CitiFinancial Auto. The complaint does allege that *before* Citi-Financial Auto sold the loans to Santander, CitiFinancial Auto had "hired" Santander as a servicer to collect the plaintiffs' defaulted debt. But any conduct that Santander might have carried out as a debt servicer on CitiFinancial Auto's behalf was carried out *before* the debts were *sold* to Santander and *before* Santander engaged in the allegedly illegal collection conduct.

Apart from their argument based on the default status of debt, the plaintiffs also seek to avoid the interpretation of "debt collector" that we make, arguing that the second definition of debt collector in § 1692a(6) includes two separate classes of persons, one of which regularly collects "debts owed or due" and the other of which regularly collects "debts . . . asserted to be owed or due *another*." They argue that Santander fits into the first class of persons, even if it does not fit into the second, because the word "another" applies only to the second. To make this argument, however, the plaintiffs break in two the singular statutory phrase in § 1692a(6), which defines debt collector as including any person who "regularly collects or attempts to collect . . . *debts owed or due or asserted to be owed or due another,*" 15 U.S.C. § 1692a(6) (emphasis added), arguing that the term "another" modifies only the portion of the last phrase, "asserted to be owed or due another." We do not agree. While Congress did break up the definition of debt collector in § 1692a(6), defining several distinct classes of persons who qualify as a debt collector, it did not divide the "regularly collects" phrase. *As the phrase is written,* the word "another" modifies both "owed or due" and "asserted to be owed or due," so that the phrase defines a debt collector as including a person who collects debt due another *or* asserted to be due another. *Cf. Paroline v. United States,* ___ U.S. ___, 134 S.Ct. 1710, 1721, 188 L.Ed.2d 714 (2014) ("When several words are followed by a clause which is applicable as much to the first and other words as to the last, the natural construction of the language demands that the clause be read as applicable to all" (quoting *Porto Rico Ry., Light & Power Co. v. Mor,* 253 U.S. 345, 348, 40 S.Ct. 516, 64 L.Ed. 944 (1920))).

In another attempt to avoid our interpretation, the plaintiffs argue that "debts owed or due another" could refer to debts that were due another either when they were first *incurred* or at the time of the *collection activity*. Thus, according to the plaintiffs, when Santander collected on the debts that it had purchased, it could be seen as having acted to collect the debts of *another* because the loans were originally due to CitiFinancial Auto. This argument, however, is no more persuasive. Insofar as Congress was regulating debt-collector conduct, defining the term "debt collector" to include a person who regularly collects debts owed to another, it had to be referring to debts as they existed *at the time of the conduct* that is subject to regulation. *See Davidson,* 797 F.3d at 1318 ("[O]ur inquiry under § 1692a(6) is not whether Capital One regularly collects on debts *originally* owed or due another and now owed to Capital One; our inquiry is whether Capital One regularly collects on debts owed or due another at the time of collection"); p.140 *see also Schlegel v. Wells Fargo Bank, NA,* 720 F.3d 1204, 1209 (9th Cir. 2013) ("The statute is not susceptible to the [plaintiffs'] interpretation that 'owed or due another' means 'originally owed or due another'").

Finally, the plaintiffs argue that because Santander had, before December 1, 2011, been a debt collector with respect to their loans, it remained a debt collector after it purchased their loans and thereafter collected on them. They suggest that Santander's *status* as a debt collector, generally, made it subject to regulation. As they summarize:

> In order for this Court to hold that Santander is not a "debt collector" with respect to [plaintiffs'] defaulted debts, this Court would have to create a loophole in the FDCPA that allows an entity acting as a "debt collector" while servicing. . . defaulted debts to become a "creditor" simply by purchasing the defaulted debt it was collecting for another.

Again, we reject this argument. Under the plaintiffs' interpretation, a company such as Santander—which, as a consumer finance company, lends money, services loans, collects debt for itself, collects debt for others, and otherwise engages in borrowing and investing its capital—would be subject to the FDCPA for *all* of its collection activities simply because one of its several activities involves the collection of debts for others. Congress did not intend this. Rather, it aimed at *abusive conduct by persons who were acting as debt collectors. See* 15 U.S.C. § 1692(e) ("It is the purpose of this subchapter to eliminate abusive debt collection practices by debt collectors"). It therefore provided that, barring application of one of the exclusions, an entity that "collects or attempts to collect . . . debts owed or due . . . another" on a regular basis qualifies as a debt collector *when it engages in collection activity on behalf of another. Id.* § 1692a(6). But when that same entity acts to collect its own debts, it is acting as a *creditor,* not a *debt collector. See id.* §§ 1692a(4), 1692a(6). Santander is therefore subject to the FDCPA only when acting as a "debt collector" as defined in § 1692a(6). Were it otherwise, every creditor that collects on its own loans and that also engages in the business of regularly collecting debts on behalf of others would be pulled under the regulation of the FDCPA not just when it collects for others, but also when it collects for itself.

At bottom, a valid claim under the FDCPA inherently requires the coming together of all the statutory elements at the time of and in connection with the prohibited conduct. Thus, for example, when a plaintiff claims that a defendant violated § 1692e (prohibiting a "debt collector" from using "any false, deceptive, or misleading misrepresentation or means in connection with the collection of any debt"), he must prove that the defendant was acting as a debt collector, as defined by § 1692a(6), when it engaged in misrepresentations in connection with the collection of debt from the plaintiff.

***

Because the complaint failed to allege facts demonstrating that Santander was acting as a "debt collector," as defined by § 1692a(6), when it was collecting on debts owed by the plaintiffs, we affirm the judgment of the district court.

AFFIRMED

839 F.3d 354 (2016)

Renee L. McCRAY, Plaintiff-Appellant,
v.
FEDERAL HOME LOAN MORTGAGE CORPORATION; Wells Fargo Bank, N.A.; Samuel I. White, P.C.; John E. Driscoll, III; Robert E. Frazier; Jana M. Gantt; Laura D. Harris; Kimberly Lane Bitt; Deena L. Reynolds, Substitute Trustees; John Does, 1-20; Wells Fargo Home Mortgage, d/b/a America's Servicing Company, Defendants-Appellees.

No. 15-1444.

United States Court of Appeals, Fourth Circuit.

Argued: May 10, 2016.
Decided: October 7, 2016.

McCray v. Federal Home Loan Mortg. Corp., 839 F. 3d 354 (4th Cir. 2016)

p.356 Appeal from the United States District Court for the District of Maryland, at Baltimore, George L. Russell, III, District Judge, (1:13-cv-01518-GLR).

Kenzie Marie Rakes, MEYNARDIE & NANNEY, PLLC, Raleigh, North Carolina, for Appellant. Robert Harvey Hillman, SAMUEL I. WHITE, PC, Rockville, Maryland; Michael S. Barranco, TREANOR POPE & HUGHES, P.A., Towson, Maryland, for Appellees.

Before NIEMEYER and WYNN, Circuit Judges, and THOMAS E. JOHNSTON, United States District Judge for the Southern District of West Virginia, sitting by designation.

Affirmed in part, reversed in part, and remanded by published opinion. Judge NIEMEYER wrote the opinion, in which Judge WYNN joined. Judge JOHNSTON wrote a separate opinion concurring in part and dissenting in part.

NIEMEYER, Circuit Judge:

In connection with a $66,500 loan secured by a deed of trust on her house, Renee McCray commenced this action for damages against the Federal Home Loan Mortgage Corporation ("Freddie Mac"); Wells Fargo Bank, N.A., and Well Fargo Home Mortgage (collectively, "Wells Fargo"); Samuel I. White, P.C. ("the White Firm"); John E. Driscoll, III, Robert E. Frazier, Jana M. Gantt, Laura D. Harris, Kimberly Lane Bitt, and Deena L. Reynolds (collectively, "Substitute Trustees"); and John Does, 1-20, alleging that, in the administration of and collection efforts on the loan, the defendants violated the Fair Debt Collection Practices Act ("FDCPA"), 15 U.S.C. § 1692 et seq.; the Truth in Lending Act ("TILA"), id. § 1601 et seq., and the Real Estate Settlement Procedures Act ("RESPA"), 12 U.S.C. § 2601 et seq. The allegations center primarily on the defendants' alleged failure to provide McCray with notices and requested information as purportedly required by these statutes.

On the defendants' motions, the district court dismissed McCray's FDCPA and TILA claims and, following discovery, granted Wells Fargo's motion for summary judgment on her RESPA claim.

On appeal, McCray contends (1) that the district court erred in concluding that the White Firm and the Substitute Trustees, who were members of that firm, were not "debt collectors," as that term is used in the FDCPA; (2) that the court erred in concluding that McCray failed to allege a cause of action under TILA when she alleged that Freddie Mac, as the new owner of her loan, failed to provide her timely notice of the purchase; and (3) that the court erred in concluding that Wells Fargo, as servicer of the loan, was not required to provide McCray with notice when the deed of trust was assigned to it.

For the reasons that follow, we conclude that McCray adequately alleged that the White Firm and the Substitute Trustees were "debt collectors," as that term is used in the FDCPA. Accordingly, we reverse the order of dismissal of her FDCPA claims against them and remand for further proceedings, without suggesting whether or not those defendants violated the FDCPA. As to the TILA claims, we affirm.

I

In October 2005, McCray borrowed $66,500 from American Home Mortgage
p.357 Corporation to refinance her house, giving American Home a 30-year note and a deed of trust on her home in Baltimore City, Maryland, to secure repayment of the note. At some point after McCray executed the loan documents, American Home sold the loan to Freddie Mac, and Wells Fargo was retained to service the loan.

For reasons not clear from the record, after making payments on her mortgage for more than five years, McCray disputed a monthly billing statement in June 2011 and sent Wells Fargo a written request for information about the fees and costs that it was charging and how it was maintaining the escrow account on the loan. Wells Fargo allegedly failed to respond or responded inadequately to her request and her follow-up inquiries.

Again for reasons not clear from the record, McCray stopped making payments on her mortgage after making the April 2012 payment and thereby went into default, and Wells Fargo retained the White Firm to pursue foreclosure. By letter dated September 28, 2012, the White Firm informed McCray that the firm had "been instructed to initiate foreclosure proceedings to foreclose on the mortgage on [her] property." The letter concluded with the statements: "This is an attempt to collect a debt. This is a communication from a debt collector. Any information obtained will be used for that purpose." (Capitalization and emphasis modified). A few days later, the White Firm sent McCray a more detailed notice of intent to foreclose, in which the firm advised McCray that her loan payments were currently "154 days past due" and that the amount required to cure default was $4,282.91. The notice also advised McCray of her various options.

Thereafter, several members of the White Firm were substituted as trustees on the deed of trust to facilitate foreclosure, and in February 2013, the Substitute Trustees filed an order to docket a foreclosure action in the Circuit Court for Baltimore City, which McCray has resisted. That proceeding is still pending.

Shortly after the Substitute Trustees commenced the foreclosure proceeding in state court, McCray commenced this action for damages, challenging the amount of her debt and the manner in which the defendants administered the loan. More particularly, she alleged that the defendants "continu[ed] to collect on an alleged debt without proper validation"; that the defendants did not respond to written requests for information and follow-up requests in a timely manner; that the defendants refused to provide her with all the information that she requested; that she was never given notice of the assignment of her deed of trust to Wells Fargo for purposes of servicing the loan; and that she never received notice of the alleged sale of the loan to Freddie Mac, all with the consequence that the defendants "attempted to collect an alleged debt under false, deceptive, and misleading means and stated an inaccurate character, amount and status of said debt."

Wells Fargo and Freddie Mac filed a motion to dismiss McCray's complaint or, in the alternative, a motion for summary judgment, and the White Firm and the Substitute Trustees filed a motion to dismiss the complaint for failure to state a claim. The district court granted the motions to dismiss McCray's FDCPA and TILA claims and, with respect to her RESPA claim, granted summary judgment.

In dismissing McCray's FDCPA claim against the White Firm and the Substitute Trustees, the district court concluded that McCray had failed to allege sufficiently that they were "debt collectors" under the FDCPA. The court distinguished these defendants' role in initiating foreclosure proceedings p.358 from a role focused on collecting the debt, explaining:

> Even when a communication includes, "This is an attempt to collect a debt," it is not an attempt to collect a debt unless there is an express demand for payment and other "specific information about the debt, including the amount of the debt, the creditor to whom the debt is owed, the procedure for validating the debt, and to whom the debt should be paid." [Blagogee v. Equity Trustees, LLC, No. 1:10-CV-13 (GBL-IDD), 2010 WL 2933963,] at *5-6 [(E.D. Va. July 26, 2010)].

Applying Blagogee to the alleged facts, the court concluded that McCray had failed to "allege any facts indicating that [the White Firm and the Substitute Trustees] were engaged in any attempt to collect her debt."

In dismissing McCray's FDCPA claim against Wells Fargo and Freddie Mac, the district court concluded that those defendants were not subject to liability under the FDCPA because they were "creditors, not debt collectors."

In dismissing McCray's TILA claim against Freddie Mac for failing to provide notice that it had purchased her loan, in violation of 15 U.S.C. § 1641(g), the court noted that the cause of action was not created by Congress until 2009, and the complaint, which described a 2005 loan and its sale to Freddie Mac on an unspecified date, failed to allege that the sale to Freddie Mac occurred after 2009. In addition, the court noted that, while McCray was notified in October 2011 that Freddie Mac was the owner of her loan, she failed to bring her TILA claim until May 23, 2013, beyond TILA's one-year statute of limitations.

In dismissing her TILA claim against Wells Fargo for failing to provide notice that the deed of trust had been assigned to it, the court explained that because Wells Fargo received only a "beneficial interest" as necessary to service the loan and not legal title, the assignment did "not implicate" the notification requirement in § 1641(g).

After discovery on the remaining RESPA claim against Wells Fargo, the district court granted Wells Fargo's motion for summary judgment.

From the district court's final judgment dated March 27, 2015, McCray filed this appeal, presenting three distinct issues, which we now address.

II

McCray contends first that the district court erred in concluding that her complaint failed to allege sufficient facts to establish that the White Firm and the Substitute Trustees were "debt collectors" subject to the FDCPA's regulation. She maintains that the complaint sufficiently alleged these defendants' debt collection role when it alleged that the firm is a "debt collection law firm" that employed the Substitute Trustees, and that the firm sent her a "Notice of Intent to Foreclose" with the statement, "This is an attempt to collect a debt," before initiating a foreclosure proceeding in the name of the Substitute Trustees and on behalf of Wells Fargo and Freddie Mac. She argues that these facts were sufficient to demonstrate that the White Firm and the Substitute Trustees "regularly collect[ed] or attempt[ed] to collect debts, [and] use[d] the mail to send her a letter to attempt to collect a debt," owed or due another, which qualified those defendants as "debt collectors" under the FDCPA, 15 U.S.C. § 1692a(6).

The White Firm and the Substitute Trustees contend that the district court properly concluded that McCray's complaint failed to allege their status as debt p.359 collectors because "McCray failed to plead any facts indicating that [they] had made any demands for payment, or that they in any way communicated deadlines and penalties for McCray's failure to make any payment." (Emphasis added). They argue, "All of the pled actions ... occurred in connection with the enforcement of security interests in real property," rendering them "fundamentally distinct from a debt collection activity covered under the FDCPA." They explain that a foreclosure action in Maryland is not designed "to obtain payment on an underlying debt," but rather serves the more limited role of "terminat[ing] the ownership interests of the mortgagor in the property and ... foreclos[ing] [her] right of redemption by the trustee[s'] sale, so that the property can then be transferred free and clear of the mortgagor's interest by the secured party." They contend, therefore, that "up to the point when the actual collection of money is sought, there has been no debt collection activity undertaken." They also contend that their activity was only "incidental to a bona fide fiduciary obligation" and therefore excluded from regulation by an exception contained in the FDCPA's definition of "debt collector."

The question thus presented is whether the White Firm and the Substitute Trustees, who regularly pursue foreclosure on behalf of creditors, were acting as "debt collectors," as that term is defined by § 1692a(6), when they pursued foreclosure against McCray after she defaulted on her loan.

The FDCPA defines the term "debt collector" to include generally "any person [1] who uses any instrumentality of interstate commerce or the mails in any business the principal purpose of which is the collection of any debts, or [2] who regularly collects or attempts to collect, directly or indirectly, debts owed or due or asserted to be owed or due another." 15 U.S.C. § 1692a(6) (emphasis added). The definition excludes "any person collecting or attempting to collect any debt owed or due or asserted to be owed or due another to the extent such activity ... is incidental to a bona fide fiduciary obligation." Id. § 1692a(6)(F)(i).

The FDCPA's definition of debt collector, however, does not include any requirement that a debt collector be engaged in an activity by which it makes a "demand for payment," as the White Firm and the Substitute Trustees claim. They argue that the notice letters and papers they used to initiate foreclosure proceedings were somehow to be distinguished from letters amounting to actual debt collection efforts, maintaining that foreclosure papers are not an attempt to collect a debt unless, as the district court explained, they contain an "express demand for payment or specific information about her debt." (Internal quotation marks and citation omitted).

As we have previously explained, however, "nothing in [the] language [of the FDCPA] requires that a debt collector's misrepresentation [or other violative actions] be made as part of an express demand for payment or even as part of an action designed to induce the debtor to pay." Powell v. Palisades Acquisition XVI, LLC, 782 F.3d 119, 123 (4th Cir. 2014) (second emphasis added). To the contrary, we concluded that, "to be actionable under... the FDCPA, a debt collector needs only to have used a prohibited practice 'in connection with the collection of any debt' or in an 'attempt to collect any debt.'" Id. at 124; see also Sayyed v. Wolpoff & Abramson, 485 F.3d 226, 229-34 (4th Cir. 2007); Wilson v. Draper & Goldberg, P.L.L.C., 443 F.3d 373, 375-77 (4th Cir. 2006).

In Powell, we held that a law firm's filing of an "assignment of judgment" in a p.360 debt collection action qualified as a debt collection activity that triggered the protections of the FDCPA. 782 F.3d at 120-21. Similarly, in Sayyed, we held that a motion for summary judgment filed in a debt collection action was "subject to the provisions of [the] FDCPA." 485 F.3d at 234. And in Wilson, we held that a law firm that provided notice that it was preparing foreclosure papers and that thereafter initiated foreclosure proceedings could be a debt collector as defined by the FDCPA. 443 F.3d at 374-76. Indeed, Wilson directly controls this case.

In Wilson, a lender had retained a law firm and one of its attorneys "to foreclose on [the plaintiff's] property due to her alleged failure to make mortgage payments." 443 F.3d at 374. The law firm and attorney wrote to the plaintiff "to announce that she was in default on her loan and that they were preparing foreclosure papers." Id. They also sent her a "validation of debt notice" pursuant to the FDCPA, which gave specific information concerning the amount of debt, the identity of the creditor, and the procedures for validating the debt. Id. at 374-75. We concluded that the law firm and the attorney were debt collectors under the FDCPA, holding that "Defendants' foreclosure action was an attempt to collect a 'debt.'" Id. at 378.

Particularly relevant to the defendants' arguments here, in Wilson we explicitly rejected the argument "that foreclosure by a trustee under a deed of trust is not the enforcement of an obligation to pay money or a 'debt,' but is [merely] a termination of the debtor's equity of redemption relating to the debtor's property." 443 F.3d at 376. We explained that the plaintiff's "'debt' remained a 'debt' even after foreclosure proceedings commenced" and that "Defendants' actions surrounding the foreclosure proceeding were attempts to collect that debt." Id. We also noted the consequence if that were not so:

> Defendants' argument, if accepted, would create an enormous loophole in the Act immunizing any debt from coverage if that debt happened to be secured by a real property interest and foreclosure proceedings were used to collect the debt. We see no reason to make an exception to the Act when the debt collector uses foreclosure instead of other methods.

Id.

It is clear from the complaint in this case that the whole reason that the White Firm and its members were retained by Wells Fargo was to attempt, through the process of foreclosure, to collect on the $66,500 loan in default. McCray's complaint alleged that the White Firm is a "debt collection law firm" that mailed her a notice of intent to foreclose, which explicitly stated that it was attempting to collect on her debt, and that then filed a foreclosure action against her property. While her complaint referred to and described in part the notice of intent to foreclose, the defendants included a full copy of an October 2, 2012 notice as an attachment to their motion to dismiss. That notice provided:

> You have missed one or more payments on your mortgage loan or you are otherwise in default. If you do not bring the loan current, otherwise cure the default, or reach an agreement with your mortgage company to avoid foreclosure (such as a loan modification, repayment plan, or other alternative to foreclosure), a foreclosure action may be filed in court as early as 45 days from the date of this notice.

(Emphasis added). The notice also included specific loan information, such as the name of the lender, the date of default, and the total amount required to cure the p.361 default. Finally, the notice included a letter detailing loan mitigation programs, which ended with the statement, "This communication is an attempt to collect a debt."

These facts, construed in the light most favorable to McCray on a motion to dismiss under Rule 12(b)(6), indeed show that the White Firm and its members were seeking repayment of a debt — i.e., attempting to collect on a debt. See 15 U.S.C. § 1692a(6). They stated in their notice to McCray that they were pursuing foreclosure because McCray had "missed one or more payments." They noted that if McCray did not "bring the loan current... such as [by] repayment ..., a foreclosure action may be filed in court." In addition, they provided McCray with the nature of default and the amount necessary to cure the default, concluding that the communication was "an attempt to collect a debt." Thus, all of the defendants' activities were taken in connection with the collection of a debt or in an attempt to collect a debt.

As to the White Firm and Substitute Trustees' argument that their actions in foreclosing on the property were "incidental to [their] fiduciary obligation" and therefore fell within the definitional exception contained in § 1692a(6)(F)(i), we also rejected that argument in Wilson, concluding that foreclosure was "central" to the trustee's fiduciary obligation under the deed of trust. Id. at 377.

The White Firm and the Substitute Trustees argue in the alternative that even if they acted as debt collectors, any violations of the FDCPA that they might have committed were not material. But the district court did not reach this argument, and we decline to address it on appeal.

In sum, we hold that McCray's complaint adequately alleges that the White Firm and the Substitute Trustees were debt collectors and that their actions in pursuing foreclosure constituted a step in collecting debt and thus debt collection activity that is regulated by the FDCPA.

III

McCray also contends that the district court erred in dismissing her claim against Freddie Mac, asserting that Freddie Mac violated TILA, 15 U.S.C. § 1641(g), by failing to give her notice of its purchase of her loan. Section 1641(g) provides that "not later than 30 days after the date on which a mortgage loan is sold or otherwise transferred or assigned to a third party, the creditor that is the new owner or assignee of the debt shall notify the borrower in writing of such transfer." Id. § 1641(g)(1). Congress added this provision to TILA in 2009. See Helping Families Save Their Homes Act of 2009, Pub. L. No. 111-22, § 404(g), 123 Stat. 1632, 1658 (2009).

The district court dismissed this claim against Freddie Mac on the ground that McCray failed to "allege any sale, transfer, or assignment of her loan to Freddie Mac after Congress amended TILA to require notice." The court concluded alternatively that because Wells Fargo informed McCray by a letter dated October 25, 2011, that Freddie Mac was the "investor" on the loan, McCray had notice of her claim as of that time and was therefore barred by the statute's one-year limitations period, see 15 U.S.C. § 1640(e), since she did not file the claim until May 2013.

McCray provides no challenge to the district court's conclusion that she failed to state her claim because she failed to allege the sale of her loan after 2009.[*] p.362 And with respect to the district court's alternative ruling on limitations, she argues that the October 25, 2011 letter was not part of her complaint but was attached to the defendants' motion to dismiss. Because the court ruled on the motion to dismiss without converting the motion to one for summary judgment, she maintains that it erred, failing to give her a reasonable opportunity to present her response. In her affidavit in support of her response, McCray did, however, state that she received a letter from Wells Fargo in December 2011, which again repeated the fact that "[t]he investor/noteholder for this loan is [Freddie Mac]."

Inasmuch as McCray has failed to challenge the district court's ruling that she failed to allege a transaction after the notice requirement was added in 2009, we affirm the district court's decision. See United States ex rel. Ubl v. IIF Data Solutions, 650 F.3d 445, 456 (4th Cir. 2011) ("[T]he failure of a party in its opening brief to challenge an alternate ground for a district court's ruling given by the district court waives that challenge" (quoting Rodriguez v. Hayes, 591 F.3d 1105, 1118 n.6 (9th Cir. 2010))); Sapuppo v. Allstate Floridian Ins. Co., 739 F.3d 678, 680 (11th Cir. 2014) ("When an appellant fails to challenge properly on appeal one of the grounds on which the district court based its judgment, he is deemed to have abandoned any challenge of that ground, and it follows that the judgment is due to be affirmed"). And similarly, because McCray seems to concede that at least as of December 2011, she had notice that Freddie Mac was the owner of her loan, we affirm the district court's alternative conclusion that the claim was barred by TILA's one-year statute of limitations.

IV

Finally, McCray contends that the district court erred in dismissing her claim against Wells Fargo for failing to give her notice of the assignment of the deed of trust to it, in violation of 15 U.S.C. § 1641(g). While the complaint alleges that Wells Fargo was assigned an interest in the deed of trust, the court dismissed McCray's claim because Wells Fargo received only a "beneficial interest, not legal title," in order to service the loan. The court concluded that such a limited assignment does not implicate § 1641(g).

On appeal, McCray concedes that "the statute is usually interpreted to mean that notice is required only when legal title to the debt obligation is transferred." See 12 C.F.R. § 1026.39(a)(1); see also 15 U.S.C. § 1641(g) (providing that, within 30 days after "the date on which a mortgage loan is sold or otherwise transferred," the creditor "that is the new owner or assignee of the debt" must make certain notifications to the borrower). She also does not challenge the district court's conclusion that Wells Fargo received a beneficial interest in the deed of trust in order to service the loan. Rather, she argues that, in addition to receiving a beneficial interest, the court could conclude that Wells Fargo also received an ownership interest based on a line in the deed of trust that reads, "The Note or a partial interest in the Note (together with this Security Instrument) can be sold." (Emphasis added). That statement, however, does not support her claim that the note was in fact sold to Wells Fargo. Instead, it indicates only that the note could be sold. Moreover, the inference that she seeks would be inconsistent with her assertion that Freddie Mac p.363 was in fact the owner and failed to give her timely notice of its ownership.

In short, we conclude that the district court did not err in dismissing this claim.

***

For the foregoing reasons, we conclude that McCray's complaint adequately alleges that the White Firm and the Substitute Trustees were acting as "debt collectors" as that term is defined in the FDCPA. Our conclusion, however, is not to be construed to indicate, one way or the other, whether they, as debt collectors, violated the FDCPA. We also conclude that the district court did not err in dismissing McCray's TILA claims. Accordingly, the judgment of the district court is

AFFIRMED IN PART, REVERSED IN PART, AND REMANDED.

JOHNSTON, District Judge, concurring in part and dissenting in part:

I write separately to dissent only from Part IV of the majority's well-reasoned opinion. In my view, McCray's *pro se* complaint, liberally construed, sufficiently states a TILA claim against Wells Fargo.

McCray sued Wells Fargo under a statutory provision that requires the new owner or assignee of a mortgage loan to notify the borrower, in writing and within 30 days of the transfer of the mortgage loan, of the pertinent details surrounding the transfer and the new owner. McCray alleges that she was not given such notice, a circumstance that understandably made the task of identifying the actual owner of the mortgage loan difficult. That task was further complicated by the fact that in this case, it appears that McCray's debt obligation (as the majority points out, the document whose transfer triggers the § 1641(g) notice provision), was uncoupled and transferred separately from her deed of trust (a document which McCray does not dispute confers only a beneficial interest insufficient on its own to trigger § 1641(g)). In general, the record does not disclose details about the various transfers of McCray's loan documents over the years. What is clear, however, is that Wells Fargo received an interest in the deed of trust in 2012 and noted that interest in the public record. McCray duly alleged Wells Fargo's interest in the operative complaint. With respect to Freddie Mac, on the other hand, McCray had nothing to go on but the representations of the defendants in this case. Notably, her pleading asserts that while the "defendants claim[ ] Freddie Mac is the owner of Plaintiff's Promissory Note," there was nothing in the public record indicating that Freddie Mac had ever received such an interest.

Thus, while McCray's TILA claims are based on the understanding that Wells Fargo owned her deed of trust and Freddie Mac owned her promissory note, her fundamental assertion was that she did not know who owned her note because she had not been provided the requisite notice. She then attempted to cast a wide net by naming both of the entities who appeared to have some interest in her mortgage loan and alleging that neither provided her with any notice of any assignment of either her deed of trust or her promissory note. Given this state of affairs, I find the majority's conclusion that McCray asserted Freddie Mac to be the actual owner of her loan to be an unduly strict reading of McCray's *pro se* complaint.

From McCray's perspective, she knew that her deed of trust had been transferred to Wells Fargo and that the deed could be sold "together" with her note, based on the language of her deed of trust. She had no information about any transfer involving her debt obligation. Given that McCray was unaware of who actually p.364 owned her note — again because she alleges that she was not provided statutorily-required notice of the note's transfer — I would draw the inference that the majority opinion does not. That is that liberally construed, McCray's complaint raises the inference that the deed and the loan were transferred together and that Wells Fargo received an interest in both. Her allegations against Freddie Mac are not inconsistent with that inference because they are equivocal at best and based on incomplete information. If Wells Fargo did not in fact receive an ownership interest, and if Freddie Mac did in fact receive such an interest prior to 2009, discovery will surely reveal those facts. At the pleading stage, however, I would find that McCray has done enough to state a plausible § 1641(g) claim and put the burden on Wells Fargo to produce the relevant documentation.

Finally, I would note the irony of dismissing a claim alleging violation of a notice-giving provision on the basis of its failure to identify, at the pleading stage, the party who failed to provide such notice. The discovery process is well-suited to accomplish this task, and under an appropriately liberal construction, McCray has done enough to open discovery's doors.

Accordingly, I respectfully dissent from the portion of the majority opinion that upholds the district court's dismissal of McCray's TILA claim against Wells Fargo. In all other respects, I am pleased to concur in the majority opinion.

[*] Indeed, in a letter dated January 10, 2012, from Wells Fargo to McCray, which was part of the summary judgment record, Wells Fargo informed McCray that her loan was "sold on the secondary market to Federal Home Loan Mortgage Corporation, known as Freddie Mac, on November 14, 2005."

780 F.3d 227 (2015)

Mounia ELYAZIDI, Plaintiff-Appellant,
v.
SUNTRUST BANK; Mitchell Rubenstein & Associates, P.C., d/b/a Rubenstein and Cogan, Defendants-Appellees.

No. 14-1290.

United States Court of Appeals, Fourth Circuit.

Argued: January 27, 2015.
Decided: March 5, 2015.

Elyazidi v. SunTrust Bank, 780 F. 3d 227 (4th Cir. 2015)

p.229 ARGUED: Ernest P. Francis, Ernest P. Francis, Ltd., Alexandria, Virginia, for Appellant. Ronald S. Canter, Law Offices of Ronald S. Canter, LLC, Rockville, Maryland; John Russell Griffin, Hartman & Egeli, LLP, Annapolis, Maryland, for Appellees. ON BRIEF: Matthew A. Egeli, Hartman & Egeli, LLP, Annapolis, Maryland, for Appellee SunTrust Bank.

Before NIEMEYER, THACKER, and HARRIS, Circuit Judges.

Affirmed by published opinion. Judge THACKER wrote the opinion, in which Judge NIEMEYER and Judge HARRIS joined.

THACKER, Circuit Judge:

p.230Mounia Elyazidi ("Appellant") overdrew her checking account when, despite having only a few hundred dollars in the account, she cut herself a check for nearly $10,000. A debt collector, acting on behalf of the bank, took her to court in Virginia and won. Appellant, not content to pay the judgment and let the matter drop, filed this lawsuit against the bank and its lawyers (collectively, "Appellees"). Her suit alleges that Appellees violated Maryland consumer protection laws, and that the bank's lawyers violated the Fair Debt Collection Practices Act ("FDCPA"). The federal district court dismissed Appellant's suit for failure to state a claim pursuant to Rule 12(b)(6) of the Federal Rules of Civil Procedure. We affirm.

I.

Appellant lives in Fairfax County, Virginia. In September 2010, she opened a checking account with SunTrust Bank ("SunTrust"), a Georgia-based bank with thousands of branches and ATMs across much of the South and along the East Coast. In the course of opening the account, Appellant signed an agreement stating that her banking transactions "shall be governed by the rules and regulations for this account." J.A. 38.[1] Those rules and regulations include a provision addressing the account holder's overdraft liability:

> You are liable for all amounts charged to your Account, whether by offset, overdraft, lien or fees. If we take court action or commence an arbitration proceeding against you to collect such amounts, ... you will also be liable for

> court or arbitration costs, other charges or fees, and attorney's fees up to 25 percent, or an amount as permitted by law, of the amount owed to us.

Id. at 56.

As of September 15, 2010, the account held no more than a few hundred dollars. Nevertheless, Appellant cut herself a check for $9,800.[2] She cashed the check at a SunTrust branch, resulting in a sizeable overdraft.

A.

After its own attempts to collect the money proved unsuccessful, SunTrust hired a Maryland law firm, Mitchell Rubenstein & Associates ("MR & A"),[3] to bring a debt collection suit. MR & A filed suit on SunTrust's behalf in the general district court of Fairfax County, Virginia, on June 12, 2012. Instead of drafting a detailed complaint, MR & A utilized a warrant in debt, a standardized pleading that the Virginia courts make available to creditors.[4] This standardized pleading provides, in relevant part:

> Plaintiff(s) claim that Defendant(s) owe Plaintiff(s) a debt in the sum of p.231 $_____ net of any credits, with interest at _____% from date of _____ until paid,
>
> $_____ costs and $_____ attorney's fees....

J.A. 25. Appellees filled in the blanks to indicate that Appellant owed $9,490.82, plus 6 percent interest; $58 in costs; and $2,372.71 in attorneys' fees.

To support the warrant in debt, Appellees submitted to the court an "Affidavit of Account," in which a SunTrust officer affirmed that "[t]he amount of Nine thousand four hundred ninety and 82/100 dollars ($9,490.82) plus reasonable attorney fees of 25% and the costs of this proceeding is justly due and owing from debt to SunTrust." J.A. 31. In addition, MR & A submitted its own affidavit, dated June 11, 2012, in support of the claim for attorneys' fees. In that document (the "June 2012 Revesman Affidavit"), attorney Cynthia Kaplan Revesman ("Revesman") requested "an award of 25% percent [sic] as a just and reasonable fee, which is equal to or less than the actual arrangement with client in this case." *Id.* at 32. Her affidavit attests that her billable rate was $250 per hour and that she spent approximately one hour preparing the warrant in debt. The affidavit further states that Revesman "will require an additional 3 hours for Court appearances and travel," and that, based on similar cases she has handled during her career, "counsel anticipates at least 20 additional hours in order to satisfy its judgment by execution." *Id.*

Later, in response to a court order, Appellees filed a bill of particulars outlining the allegations against Appellant. Among the exhibits accompanying this filing were two monthly statements for Appellant's checking account. Appellant's social security number appeared on both statements. When, in December 2012, Appellant's attorney complained about the exposure of his client's personal financial information, the judge agreed to have the number redacted.

The general district court entered judgment "in the sum demanded for the plaintiff on the evidence." J.A. 151. Later, at a separate hearing, counsel for SunTrust submitted an updated affidavit supporting the claim for attorneys' fees. In this new affidavit, dated February 27, 2013, Revesman reported that she had expended approximately 13.9 hours on the case. She provided a breakdown of how she spent those hours and, based on that breakdown, calculated a billable amount of $4,025. The court—explaining that "it's been the practice of this Court normally to award less than what [counsel] ask[s] for"—opted to award only $2,372.71 "because I think that ... minimally more than that was spent in this entire matter." *Id.* at 174-75.

B.

Appellant's response to her defeat in the collection suit was to file a complaint against SunTrust and MR & A in circuit court in Montgomery County, Maryland. Her amended complaint asserted seven claims in all, of which five are at issue in this appeal.[5] The first four counts challenged Appellees' efforts to recover attorneys' fees in the Virginia suit:

• Count I accused Appellees of violating the Maryland Consumer Debt Collection Act ("MCDCA"), which bars debt collectors from attempting to "enforce a right with knowledge that the right does not exist," Md.Code Ann., Com. Law § 14-202(8);

p.232 • Count II accused SunTrust of unfair or deceptive conduct in violation of the Maryland Consumer Protection Act ("MCPA"), Md.Code Ann., Com. Law §§ 13-301(1), -408(a);

• Count III accused MR & A of making false representations in violation of the FDCPA, 15 U.S.C. § 1692e(2); and

• Count IV accused MR & A of using "unfair or unconscionable means to" collect a debt that was neither "expressly authorized by the agreement creating the debt [n]or permitted by law," in violation of the FDCPA, 15 U.S.C. § 1692f(1).

Lastly, Appellant sought to recover for the disclosure of her social security number. Specifically:

• Count VI accused MR & A of violating 15 U.S.C. § 1692f by failing to redact Appellant's social security number from the bank statements accompanying the bill of particulars.

Appellees removed the case to the United States District Court for the District of Maryland. There, SunTrust and MR & A separately filed motions to dismiss all claims. Broadly speaking, these motions argued that Appellant's amended complaint did not state a claim. In addition, MR & A argued that the *Rooker-Feldman* doctrine deprived the district court of subject matter jurisdiction over the FDCPA claims in Counts III and IV.

Preliminarily, the district court rejected MR & A's *Rooker-Feldman* argument, reasoning that Counts III and IV were not barred because they do not challenge "the propriety of the [Virginia] court's order granting a fee award." *Elyazidi v. SunTrust Bank*, No. 13-2204, 2014 WL 824129, at *5 (D.Md. Feb. 28, 2014). Having assured itself of its jurisdiction, the court proceeded to dismiss all of Appellant's claims pursuant to Rule 12(b)(6) of the Federal Rules of Civil Procedure.

First, the court concluded that Counts III and IV, brought under the FDCPA, failed because the warrant in debt and accompanying affidavits did nothing more than supply an estimate of the attorneys' fees that would be due at the conclusion of the case, in compliance with Virginia state court procedure. *See Elyazidi,* 2014 WL 824129, at *6. Next, the court explained that Count VI could not survive because the disclosure of Appellant's social security number was, in all likelihood, a mere "oversight that was cured by redaction of the relevant documents." *Id.* at *7.

Finally, the district court acknowledged that, having dismissed all federal claims, it was under no obligation to consider Counts I and II, the state law claims. *See Elyazidi,* 2014 WL 824129, at *7 (citing 28 U.S.C. § 1367(c)(3)). Nevertheless, the court opted to exercise supplemental jurisdiction over those claims "[i]n the interest of judicial economy." *Id.* The court proceeded to dismiss Counts I and II on the ground that the Maryland statutes "have no extraterritorial effect." *Id.* at *8.

II.

On appeal, Appellees renew their argument that the district court lacked subject matter jurisdiction over Counts III and IV. The limits of subject matter jurisdiction pose a "threshold issue" that this court must investigate "before addressing the merits" of Appellant's claims. *Jones v. Am. Postal Workers Union,* 192 F.3d 417, 422 (4th Cir.1999).

Appellees argue that the *Rooker-Feldman* doctrine bars Counts III and IV because these counts—both challenging MR & A's pursuit of attorneys' fees in state court—"are premised on the theory that the state court erred when it awarded SunTrust 25% attorney's fees in the judgment." Appellees' Br. 10. Generally p.233 speaking, the *Rooker-Feldman* doctrine provides that jurisdiction to review state court decisions lies not with the lower federal courts, but "exclusively with superior state courts and, ultimately, the United States Supreme Court." *Friedman's, Inc. v. Dunlap,* 290 F.3d 191, 196 (4th Cir.2002) (internal quotation marks omitted). However, a federal court is not stripped of its jurisdiction simply because the claim challenges conduct that was previously examined in a state court action. Rather, the restriction on the federal district courts' jurisdiction is confined to "cases brought by state-court losers complaining of injuries *caused by state-court judgments* rendered before the district court proceedings commenced and inviting district court review and rejection of those judgments." *Exxon Mobil Corp. v. Saudi Basic Indus. Corp.,* 544 U.S. 280, 284, 125 S.Ct. 1517, 161 L.Ed.2d 454 (2005) (emphasis supplied); *see Davani v. Va. Dep't of Transp.,* 434 F.3d 712, 718-19 (4th Cir.2006).

The instant appeal poses no challenge to the Virginia court's judgment. That judgment reflected a post-trial determination that SunTrust's counsel was entitled to $2,372.71 in fees for the 13.9 hours of work put into the case. Appellant's complaint takes no issue with those figures. Her argument, rather, is that Appellees' *pre-trial* representations were unlawful because they insinuated that she owed money that, to that point, SunTrust's counsel had not yet earned. We hold, therefore, that her claims are independent from the Virginia court's judgment, and that the *Rooker-Feldman* doctrine did not bar the federal district court from hearing them.

III.

We proceed now to the merits of Appellant's arguments in this appeal.

A.

We begin with Counts III and IV, which allege that the Virginia warrant in debt and accompanying affidavits wrongfully represented that Appellant owed $2,372.71 in attorneys' fees—an amount exactly equal to 25 percent of Appellant's debt to SunTrust. Appellant argues that these representations were wrongful in two ways. First, she says, SunTrust's rules and regulations merely *capped* her liability for attorneys' fees at 25 percent. Second, she argues that she could not have owed the full 25 percent at the time Appellees filed the Virginia suit because, to that point, MR & A had not yet performed the hours of work necessary to justify the award. Count III alleges that the firm's statements were false or misleading representations in violation of 15 U.S.C. § 1692e. Count IV condemns the statements as an unfair or unconscionable means of debt collection in violation of § 1692f(1).

The district court dismissed both counts for failure to state a claim. "We review the district court's grant of a motion to dismiss de novo, accepting as true the complaint's factual allegations and drawing all reasonable inferences in favor of the plaintiff." *Warren v. Sessoms & Rogers, P.A.*, 676 F.3d 365, 373 (4th Cir. 2012). To survive a Rule 12(b)(6) motion, the allegations must "advance the plaintiff's claim 'across the line from conceivable to plausible.'" *Walters v. McMahen,* 684 F.3d 435, 439 (4th Cir.2012) (quoting *Bell Atl. Corp. v. Twombly,* 550 U.S. 544, 570, 127 S.Ct. 1955, 167 L.Ed.2d 929 (2007)). Appellant, we conclude, has failed to propel any of her claims across that line.

1.

Pursuant to 15 U.S.C. § 1692e, a debt collector[6] may not "use any false, p.234 deceptive, or misleading representation or means in connection with the collection of any debt." 15 U.S.C. § 1692e. It is unlawful to make a "false representation of (A) the character, amount, or legal status of any debt; or (B) any services rendered or compensation which may be lawfully received by any debt collector for the collection of a debt." *Id.* § 1692e(2). To violate the statute, a representation must be material, *see Warren,* 676 F.3d at 374, which is to say, it must be "important in the sense that [it] could objectively affect the least sophisticated consumer's decisionmaking." *Powell v. Palisades Acquisition XVI, LLC,* 782 F.3d 119, 126, No. 14-1171, 2014 WL 7191354, at *7 (4th Cir. Dec. 18, 2014). Similarly, in assessing whether a debt collector's representation is misleading, we view the representation "from the vantage of the least sophisticated consumer." *Russell v. Absolute Collection Servs., Inc.*, 763 F.3d 385, 394 (4th Cir.2014) (internal quotation marks omitted). Under this standard, we consider how a "naive" consumer would interpret the statement. *United States v. Nat'l Fin. Servs., Inc.*, 98 F.3d 131, 136 (4th Cir. 1996). However, we do not give credit to "bizarre or idiosyncratic interpretations"; we assume "a quotient of reasonableness and ... a basic level of understanding and willingness to read with care." *Id.*

There is no denying that, as a general matter, "litigation activity is subject to the FDCPA." *Sayyed v. Wolpoff & Abramson,* 485 F.3d 226, 231 (4th Cir. 2007); *see Heintz v. Jenkins,* 514 U.S. 291, 293, 299, 115 S.Ct. 1489, 131 L.Ed.2d 395 (1995) (holding that a car loan borrower could pursue FDCPA claims against the lender's counsel for falsely asserting in a letter that the borrower owed money for a particularly broad substitute insurance policy on the car). As always, though, we must view the allegedly false or misleading representations in context. Here, where the debt collector sought no more than applicable law allowed and explained via affidavit that the figure was merely an estimate of an amount counsel expected to earn in the course of the litigation,[7] the representations cannot be considered misleading under 15 U.S.C. § 1692e(2).

The September 2010 agreement—which Appellant signed—authorized SunTrust to request "up to 25 percent" of any "amount owed" to the bank. J.A. 38, 56. Appellees' request for $2,372.71 in attorneys' fees fell within the 25 percent cap. The justification for requesting the maximum amount permissible under contract was supplied in the June 2012 Revesman Affidavit, which detailed the number of hours SunTrust's counsel expected to devote to the suit. The affidavit explained that the bulk of those hours would be spent endeavoring to satisfy the judgment by execution. Though Appellant's complaint alleges that this estimate had no basis in p.235 fact, Appellant's counsel conceded at oral argument that he had no evidence to support this allegation.

It is true that the standardized warrant-in-debt form uses the word "owe," *id.* at 30, suggesting perhaps that the requested attorneys' fees were presently due. This language, however, cannot be read in isolation. Taking the June 2012 Revesman Affidavit into consideration, it is abundantly clear that the prayer for attorneys' fees was an estimate of an amount the debtor would owe at the conclusion of the case. The affidavit clarifies that SunTrust's counsel was simply "*request[ing]* an award of 25% percent [sic] as a just and reasonable fee." J.A. 32 (emphasis supplied). It further explains that SunTrust's counsel had spent one hour on the case to date, and that counsel anticipated spending at least 23 more hours pursuing and executing a judgment in SunTrust's favor. Under the circumstances, any consumer—no matter how sophisticated—should have understood the nature of Appellees' request.

In sum, we hold that Appellees' prayer for attorneys' fees cannot, as a matter of law, be a false, deceptive, or misleading representation under § 1692e. Accordingly, we affirm the district court's judgment that Count III fails to state a claim.

2.

Count IV, alleging a violation of 15 U.S.C. § 1692f(1), fails for similar reasons. Section 1692f condemns the use of "unfair or unconscionable means to collect or attempt to collect any debt," and provides a non-exhaustive list of proscribed conduct. 15 U.S.C. § 1692f. Subsection (1), which Appellant invokes, prohibits "[t]he collection of any amount (including any interest, fee, charge, or expense incidental to the principal obligation) unless such amount is expressly authorized by the agreement creating the debt or permitted by law." *Id.* § 1692f(1).

Appellant's complaint alleges that the request for $2,372.71 in attorneys' fees was unauthorized because "neither the agreement nor applicable law permit recovery of attorney's fees for services not performed." J.A. 15. This argument has no merit. By signing the September 2010 agreement, Appellant agreed that, in the event of a "court action" to recover a debt, she would be contractually liable for "attorney's fees up to 25 percent ... of the amount owed" to the bank. *Id.* at 56. Plainly, this agreement authorized SunTrust to seek attorneys' fees in the Virginia debt collection suit.

Though under Virginia law an award of attorneys' fees must be "reasonable ... under the facts and circumstances of the particular case," *Lee v. Mulford,* 269 Va. 562, 611 S.E.2d 349, 350-51 (2005) (internal quotation marks omitted), it was entirely proper for SunTrust to estimate an appropriate fee within the limits prescribed in the September 2010 agreement. Indeed, the Commonwealth encourages plaintiffs to include such estimates when filling out the standardized warrant-in-debt form, which supplies a blank space for attorneys' fees along with the spaces provided for the alleged debt and court costs. Though we draw "all reasonable inferences" in favor of the plaintiff, *Owens v. Balt. City State's Attorneys Office,* 767 F.3d 379, 388 (4th Cir.2014) (internal quotation marks omitted), the only reasonable inference here is that Appellees sought to enforce their contractual rights in compliance with state court procedure. To claim, as Appellant does, that such activity is unfair or unconscionable under § 1692f(1) is simply not plausible. We hold, therefore, that Count IV fails to state a claim for relief.

B.

We turn now to Count VI, which asserts that MR & A's disclosure of Appellant's p.236 social security number in the bank statements accompanying the bill of particulars constituted an unfair or unconscionable means of debt collection, in violation of 15 U.S.C. § 1692f.

Section 1692f lists eight examples of unfair or unconscionable practices. These practices include: collecting money that is not expressly authorized by an agreement creating the debt, *see* 15 U.S.C. § 1692f(1); accepting a postdated check without properly notifying the drawer of when it will be deposited, or threatening to deposit it before the specified date, *see id.* § 1692f(2), (4); soliciting a postdated check "for the purpose of threatening or instituting criminal prosecution," *id.* § 1692f(3); making collect calls to a debtor without disclosing the "true purpose of the communication," *id.* § 1692f(5); threatening nonjudicial action to dispossess the debtor of property, even though the debt collector has no present right to possess the property or no intention to take possession of it, *see id.* § 1692f(6)(A)-(B); "[c]ommunicating with a consumer regarding a debt by post card," *id.* § 1692f(7); and sending mail to a consumer via envelopes that plainly indicate the sender is a debt collector, *id.* § 1692f(8). What all of these enumerated activities have in common is the capacity to harass the debtor or to pressure her to pay the debt.

No doubt, the public disclosure of one's social security number can be alarming. Here, though, where the lapse occurred in the course of litigation and was easily remedied, the disclosure cannot be considered unfair or unconscionable. While, conceivably, a threat to expose one's social security number might pressure a debtor to pay off a debt, there is no allegation that Appellees ever made such a threat. Appellees simply failed to redact the number before enclosing the bank statements with the bill of particulars, an error the court promptly corrected. Though Appellant characterizes the disclosure here as "a means to extort payment," reasoning that a "consumer will simply pay the debt rather than risk identity theft," J.A. 16-17, her logic is dubious at best. The record here belies her assertion that counsel would "have no alternative but to advise the consumer to pay the debt so that the consumer can avoid identity theft." *Id.* at 17. Appellant was not cowed into paying the debt. Rather, she simply asked the court to redact the identifying information.

In sum, we hold that, as a matter of law, the failure to redact Appellant's social security number before submitting the bank statements to the Virginia court was not an unfair or unconscionable means of debt collection under the FDCPA. The district court was correct in concluding that Count VI does not state a claim for relief, and we affirm the dismissal of that claim.

C.

The final two claims are Maryland state-law claims, both challenging Appellees' attempts to recover attorneys' fees in the Virginia suit. Count I accuses Appellees of violating the MCDCA, which provides that debt collectors may not "[c]laim, attempt, or threaten to enforce a right with knowledge that the right does not exist." Md.Code Ann., Com. Law § 14-202(8). Count II accuses SunTrust, exclusively, of making "false statements or representations that had the capacity, tendency, or effect of misleading consumers," J.A. 14, in violation of the MCPA. *See* Md.Code Ann., Com. Law §§ 13-301(1), -303 (prohibiting "unfair or deceptive trade practice[s]," including the making of any "false, falsely disparaging, or misleading oral or written statement, visual description, or other representation of any kind which has the capacity, tendency, or effect of deceiving or p.237 misleading consumers"). The district court, choosing to exercise supplemental jurisdiction over these claims "[i]n the interest of judicial economy," dismissed the claims on the ground that neither the MCDCA nor the MCPA applies to conduct occurring "entirely" in Virginia. *Elyazidi v. SunTrust Bank,* No. 13-2204, 2014 WL 824129, at *7-8 (D.Md. Feb. 28, 2014).

In Maryland, regulatory statutes are "generally construed as not having extraterritorial effect unless a contrary legislative intent is expressly stated." *Consumer Prot. Div. v. Outdoor World Corp.,* 91 Md.App. 275, 603 A.2d 1376, 1382 (Md. Ct.Spec.App.1992); *see also Chairman of Bd. of Trs. of Emps.' Ret. Sys. v. Waldron,* 285 Md. 175, 401 A.2d 172, 177 (1979) (stating that a Maryland statute prohibiting a state pensioner from accepting paid legal work does not prohibit the pensioner from practicing law outside of Maryland, as the state's General Assembly "has no power to regulate whom our sister jurisdictions may authorize to engage in the practice of law within their borders"); *State ex rel. Gildar v. Kriss,* 191 Md. 568, 62 A.2d 568, 569 (1948) ("Ordinarily a statute is not applicable extraterritorially, but only to acts done within the jurisdiction...."). In *Consumer Protection Division v. Outdoor World Corp.,* a Maryland appellate court concluded that the MCPA was capable of reaching at least some out-of-state activity affecting Maryland residents. Specifically, the court held that a state agency could bring administrative charges under the MCPA against an out-of-state company that allegedly made false representations in mailings to Maryland residents. 603 A.2d at 1382-83. At the same time, though, the court determined that the agency had no authority to regulate "sales practices that occur entirely within other States." *Id.* at 1383. Accordingly, even where the challenged mailings enticed Maryland residents to travel out of state on false pretenses, the MCPA did not govern high-pressure sales tactics the company allegedly employed at those out-of-state locations. *See id.*

In an attempt to frame the challenged activities as in-state conduct, Appellant asks us to note that MR & A's office is in Maryland and that SunTrust has "dozens" of branches there. Appellant's Br. 26; *see also* J.A. 6-7. The critical point, however, is not whether Appellees conduct business in Maryland, but whether some significant portion of the challenged activity occurred there. Here, Appellant was a Virginia resident who incurred a debt in Virginia. The allegedly offensive representations appeared in Virginia court documents, and any harm they might have inflicted could have occurred only in Appellant's home state of Virginia.

We likewise find no significance in Appellant's related argument—raised, in the first instance, on appeal—that "virtually every act that would create liability under the Maryland statutes occurred in Maryland." Appellant's Reply Br. 23. As to this, Appellant would have us note that MR & A prepared all legal documents at its Maryland office; "received" instructions from SunTrust there; and, from that office, "directed the filing" of the documents to the Virginia court. *Id.* These facts do not appear in Appellant's complaint, but even assuming we could infer them from the stated allegations, it would make no difference. The act of sitting in a Maryland office and drafting court documents, or taking phone calls, is not the activity that Appellant seeks to condemn in the case. Her complaint, rather is that she suffered harm when Appellees filed the allegedly offensive documents in a Virginia court and served process on her in Virginia. Appellant cannot use Maryland's p.238 consumer protection laws to gin up a lawsuit contesting this activity.

We hold that the MCDCA and MCPA have no application here. Therefore, Counts I and II fail to state a claim and were properly dismissed by the district court.

IV.

For the foregoing reasons, the judgment of the district court is
AFFIRMED.

[1] Citations to the "J.A." refer to the Joint Appendix filed by the parties in this appeal.

[2] The SunTrust branch cashed the check for this amount. In fact, though, there was a discrepancy between the number figure in the dollar box ("$9,800") and the amount stated in text below the payee line ("Nine thousand and nine hundred 00/100 dollars"). J.A. 214.

[3] The amended complaint in this suit asserts that MR & A does business under the name Rubenstein and Cogan. Court filings in the Virginia debt collection action that preceded this suit likewise refer to the firm as Rubenstein and Cogan.

[4] *See* Va.Code Ann. § 16.1-79 (authorizing civil actions "brought by warrant"); *In re Faruque,* No. 07-13375-SSM, 2009 WL 2211210, at *5 n. 8 (Bankr.E.D.Va. July 20, 2009) (characterizing the warrant in debt as a "simplified form of process" that "does not require a detailed statement of the cause of action").

[5] Two of the claims, Counts V and VII, accused MR & A of engaging in unfair or unconscionable acts in violation of 15 U.S.C. § 1692f. The district court dismissed those counts, and Appellant has not appealed their dismissal.

[6] "It is uncontestable that the FDCPA creates a cause of action against attorneys who act as debt collectors for their false statements about the debt." *Sayyed v. Wolpoff & Abramson,* 485 F.3d 226, 235 (4th Cir.2007); *see also Wilson v. Draper & Goldberg, P.L.L.C.,* 443 F.3d 373, 378 (4th Cir.2006). MR & A does not dispute that it qualifies as a debt collector under the statute.

[7] To be clear, this opinion in no way suggests that a prayer for attorneys' fees can never present an actionable misrepresentation under the FDCPA. Some lower courts have taken that position. *See, e.g., Sayyed v. Wolpoff & Abramson, LLP,* 733 F.Supp.2d 635, 648 (D.Md.2010); *Winn v. Unifund CCR Partners,* No. CV 06-447-TUC-FRZ, 2007 WL 974099, at *3 (D.Ariz. Mar. 30, 2007); *see also Argentieri v. Fisher Landscapes, Inc.,* 15 F.Supp.2d 55, 61-62 (D.Mass.1998) (questioning, but never deciding, whether a prayer for attorneys' fees could ever violate the FDCPA). Today's decision does not reach this issue.

779 F.3d 242 (2015)

Christopher M. COVERT; Thomas E. Haworth; Carol J. Haworth; Kifle Ayele; Dwan L. Brown, Plaintiffs-Appellants,

v.

LVNV FUNDING, LLC; Resurgent Capital Services Limited Partnership; Sherman Originator LLC, Defendants-Appellees.

No. 14-1016.

United States Court of Appeals, Fourth Circuit.

Argued: December 11, 2014.

Decided: March 3, 2015.

Covert v. LVNV Funding, LLC, 779 F. 3d 242 (4th Cir. 2015)

p.244 ARGUED: Laura J. Margulies, Laura Margulies & Associates, LLC, Rockville, Maryland, for Appellants. Ronald S. Canter, Law Offices of Ronald S. Canter, LLC, Rockville, Maryland, for Appellees. ON BRIEF: Lawrence P. Block, Janet M. Nesse, Stinson Leonard Street LLP, Washington, D.C., for Appellants.

Before NIEMEYER, SHEDD, and KEENAN, Circuit Judges.

Affirmed by published opinion. Judge SHEDD wrote the opinion, in which Judge NIEMEYER and Judge KEENAN joined.

SHEDD, Circuit Judge.

Christopher M. Covert, Thomas E. Haworth, Carol J. Haworth, Kifle Ayele, and Dwan L. Brown (collectively "Plaintiffs") each separately filed a petition for individual bankruptcy under Chapter 13 in Maryland in 2008. LVNV Funding, LLC ("LVNV") and its affiliated companies (collectively "Defendants") held an unsecured claim against each Plaintiff and filed proofs of those claims in each proceeding.[1] Each Chapter 13 plan was approved, the Defendants' claims were allowed, and each Plaintiff made payments on these claims. In March 2013, the Plaintiffs filed this putative class action lawsuit in the District of Maryland, alleging that the Defendants had violated the federal Fair Debt Collection Practices Act (FDCPA) and various Maryland laws by filing these proofs of claim without a Maryland debt collection license. The Defendants moved to dismiss and the court granted the motion, finding that the state common law claims were barred by res judicata and that the federal and state statutory claims failed to state a claim because filing a proof of claim does not constitute an act to collect a debt. For the reasons stated below, we affirm the dismissal of all claims, but we do so on res judicata grounds.

I.

In 2008, each Plaintiff filed a petition for individual bankruptcy under Chapter 13 in the Bankruptcy Court for the District of Maryland. LVNV had acquired a defaulted debt against each Plaintiff from Sherman Originator, LLC, and LVNV then filed a proof of unsecured claim based on these debts in each bankruptcy proceeding through its servicer, Resurgent Capital p.245 Services Limited Partnership. The bankruptcy court confirmed a plan in each proceeding that provided for unsecured claims to be paid in *pro rata* amounts. The Defendants' claims were allowed, and they received payments from the Chapter 13 Trustees on these claims. At all relevant times, none of the Defendants was licensed to do business as a debt collection agency in Maryland.

In March 2013, the Plaintiffs filed this lawsuit in the District of Maryland, alleging that the Defendants had violated the FDCPA by filing proofs of claim without a Maryland debt collection license. The FDCPA defines a "debt collector" as "any person . . . who regularly collects or attempts to collect, directly or indirectly, debts owed or due or asserted to be owed or due another." 15 U.S.C. § 1692a(6). Under the FDCPA, debt collectors "may not use any false, deceptive, or misleading representation or means in connection with the collection of any debt," including "[t]he threat to take any action that cannot legally be taken," 15 U.S.C. § 1692e(5). Under the Maryland Code, it is a misdemeanor for a person to "knowingly and willfully do business as a collection agency in the State unless the person has a license." Md.Code Ann., Bus. Reg. § 7-401. The Plaintiffs allege that because the Defendants filed claims in the bankruptcy proceedings without a license, the Defendants were not legally entitled to collect those debts and thus took an "action that cannot legally be taken" in violation of the FDCPA. The Plaintiffs also asked for an injunction deeming the Defendants' proofs of claim invalid and instructing the Defendants to return to the Plaintiffs all money paid pursuant to those claims.[2]

Plaintiff Covert filed several additional Maryland state law claims. Specifically, Covert alleged unjust enrichment, violations of the Maryland Consumer Debt Collection Act (MCDCA), and violations of the Maryland Consumer Protection Act (MCPA).

The Defendants moved under Federal Rule of Civil Procedure 12(b)(6) to dismiss all claims for failure to state a claim upon which relief could be granted. The district court granted the motion. *Covert v. LVNV Funding, LLC,* No. DKC 13-0698, 2013 WL 6490318 (D.Md. Dec. 9, 2013). It held that the Maryland unjust enrichment claim was barred by res judicata, but that the FDCPA, MCDCA, and MCPA claims could not be barred by res judicata absent an adversary proceeding in each bankruptcy action, which had not occurred. Nonetheless, the district court dismissed these statutory claims on the merits because it found that filing a proof of claim is not a "collection activity" within the meaning of those statutes. The Plaintiffs timely appealed.

II.

We review de novo the district court's dismissal of a complaint for failure to state a claim under 12(b)(6). *United States ex rel. Rostholder v. Omnicare, Inc.,* 745 F.3d 694, 700 (4th Cir.2014). Federal law governs the res judicata effect of earlier bankruptcy proceedings. *See Grausz v. Englander,* 321 F.3d 467, 472 (4th Cir. 2003) ("We look to res judicata principles developed in our own case law to determine whether an earlier federal judgment, including the judgment of a bankruptcy p.246 court, bars a claim asserted in a later action.").

"Under *res judicata* principles, a prior judgment between the same parties can preclude subsequent litigation on those matters actually and necessarily resolved in the first adjudication." *In re Varat Enters., Inc.*, 81 F.3d 1310, 1314-15 (4th Cir.1996). As we have applied it, the doctrine of res judicata encompasses two concepts: claim preclusion, which bars later litigation of all claims that were actually adjudicated or that could have been adjudicated in an earlier action, and issue preclusion, which bars later litigation of legal and factual issues that were "actually and necessarily determined" in an earlier action. *Id.* at 1315 (internal citation omitted). Rather than attempting to draw a sharp distinction between these two aspects here, we conduct our analysis under the general res judicata framework, as has been our practice in bankruptcy cases. We have held that a prior bankruptcy judgment has res judicata effect on future litigation when the following three conditions are met:

> 1) [T]he prior judgment was final and on the merits, and rendered by a court of competent jurisdiction in accordance with the requirements of due process; 2) the parties are identical, or in privity, in the two actions; and, 3) the claims in the second matter are based upon the same cause of action involved in the earlier proceeding.

Id. All three requirements are met here.

The first requirement is easily satisfied because confirmation of a bankruptcy plan is a final judgment on the merits. *See, e.g., id.* ("[T]he [bankruptcy plan] confirmation order constitutes a final judgment on the merits with *res judicata* effect."); *In re Linkous,* 990 F.2d 160, 162 (4th Cir.1993) (same). 11 U.S.C. § 1327(a) states the general rule that "[t]he provisions of a confirmed plan bind the debtor and each creditor, whether or not the claim of such creditor is provided for by the plan, and whether or not such creditor has objected to, has accepted, or has rejected the plan." It is this provision that gives plan confirmation the res judicata effect of a final judgment. *Linkous,* 990 F.2d at 162; *see also In re Beard,* 112 B.R. 951, 954 (Bankr.N.D.Ind.1990) ("The Bankruptcy Code gives confirmation a binding effect, through 11 U.S.C. § 1327.").

The second res judicata requirement is also satisfied because both the Plaintiffs and the Defendants in this action were parties to the earlier Chapter 13 plan confirmation proceedings. Self-evidently, each Plaintiff participated in the confirmation proceedings for his own bankruptcy plan. *See Varat,* 81 F.3d at 1316 n. 6 ("A party for the purposes of former adjudication includes one who participates in a . . . plan confirmation proceeding."). Here, the Defendants were also parties to these proceedings because of their financial interest in the amount allotted to satisfy unsecured claims. *See Grausz,* 321 F.3d at 473 ("In the bankruptcy context a party in interest is one who has a pecuniary interest in the distribution of assets to creditors."). *See also In re Snow,* 270 B.R. 38, 40 (D.Md.2001) (holding that both debtor and creditor were parties to Chapter 13 plan confirmation for res judicata purposes).

The third res judicata condition requires that Plaintiffs' claims be "based upon the same cause of action involved in" the plan confirmation proceedings. *Varat,* 81 F.3d at 1315. Although we have said that "no simple test exists to determine whether claims are based on the same cause of action for claim preclusion purposes," *Grausz,* 321 F.3d at 473 (*quoting* p.247 *Pittston Co. v. United States,* 199 F.3d 694, 704 (4th Cir.1999)), generally, "claims are part of the same cause of action when they arise out of the same transaction or series of transactions, or the same core of operative facts," *id.* at 473 (*quoting Varat,* 81 F.3d at 1316).

Applying these principles, it is clear that the Plaintiffs' current claims are based upon the same cause of action as the Defendants' claims in the confirmed bankruptcy plans. To prove his unjust enrichment claim, Covert would have to show that the Defendants had accepted and retained a benefit under inequitable circumstances, *see Hill v. Cross Country Settlements, LLC,* 402 Md. 281, 936 A.2d 343, 351 (2007), because the claim on which he had paid the Defendants was procedurally invalid. Similarly, to establish their claims for reimbursement and injunctive relief, Covert and the other Plaintiffs would have to show that they made payments on claims that are invalid because they were illegally filed. Finally, to succeed on their statutory claims for damages under the FDCPA, MCDCA, and MCPA, the Plaintiffs would need to show that these statutes prohibited the Defendants from filing the proofs of claim. A finding for the Plaintiffs on any of these claims, therefore, would entail a holding that the Defendants' proofs of claim are invalid, which would directly contradict the bankruptcy court's plan confirmation order approving those proofs of claim as legitimate.

We have held, in fact, that even claims that do not directly contradict confirmed orders, but merely "assert rights that are inconsistent with" those orders, are sufficient to satisfy the third res judicata requirement. *Varat,* 81 F.3d at 1317. *See also Grausz,* 321 F.3d at 475 (debtor's malpractice action was precluded by bankruptcy court's prior order which had allowed firm's fees because a successful "malpractice action at this stage could impair rights accorded the . . . firm in the final fee order") (internal citation omitted). Our sister circuits share this view that "once a bankruptcy plan is confirmed, its terms are not subject to collateral attack" through suits that raise claims inconsistent with the confirmed plan. *Adair v. Sherman,* 230 F.3d 890, 894 (7th Cir.2000) (dismissing post-confirmation FDCPA action alleging that creditor had inflated the amount of its claim). *See also, e.g., In re Szostek,* 886 F.2d 1405, 1413 (3d Cir.1989) (creditor could not challenge amount of claim in confirmed plan, even though a hearing to consider a Truth in Lending Act challenge to that claim amount had been scheduled before the plan was confirmed). In sum, because all of the Plaintiffs' claims implicitly ask the district court to reconsider the provisions of the confirmed plans, they are based on the same cause of action as the plan confirmation orders. Accordingly, all three requirements are satisfied and the Plaintiffs' claims are barred by res judicata.

III.

Res judicata bars not only those claims that were actually raised during prior litigation, but also those claims that could have been raised, and the Plaintiffs in this case did indeed have the opportunity to raise their statutory claims for relief under the FDCPA, the MCDCA, and the MCPA during the bankruptcy proceedings. The Plaintiffs, as debtors in their own bankruptcy proceedings, could have objected to LVNV's proofs of claim at the time they were filed on the basis that they violated these consumer protection statutes. *See* 11 U.S.C. § 502(a)-(b)(1) (if a party in interest objects to a proof of claim, the bankruptcy court will hold a hearing and will determine whether the claim is "unenforceable against the debtor p.248. . . under any

. . . applicable law"); *see also Sampson v. Chase Home Finance,* 667 F.Supp.2d 692, 696-97 (S.D.W.V.2009) (plaintiffs' consumer protection challenges to allowed claim were barred by res judicata after plan was confirmed because the challenges could have been raised during the bankruptcy proceedings). The Plaintiffs could also have brought their affirmative claims for damages during the bankruptcy process under Federal Rule of Bankruptcy Procedure 7001(1), which provides that "a proceeding to recover money or property" may be brought as an adversary action. But the Plaintiffs were not free to raise statutory objections after the court had entered its confirmation order when those objections were known or should have been known to them during the bankruptcy proceedings. *See Varat,* 81 F.3d at 1317. *See also U.S. Dept. of Air Force v. Carolina Parachute Corp.,* 907 F.2d 1469, 1473 (4th Cir.1990) (government, as creditor, could not bring post-confirmation statutory challenge to plan's assignment of government's contract with debtor, even though the government had already begun court proceedings to terminate the contract); *Grausz,* 321 F.3d at 474 (res judicata barred debtor's malpractice claim after fee order because "by the time the bankruptcy court entered the final fee order, [debtor] knew or should have known there was a real likelihood that he had a malpractice claim against the firm.").

Here, Plaintiffs do not assert that any information necessary to make out their statutory claims was unavailable to them at the time their plans were confirmed. Accordingly, Plaintiffs should have raised these statutory claims during the plan confirmation hearings, and their failure to do so means that these claims are barred by res judicata.[3] *See Varat,* 81 F.3d at 1317 ("When all of the requirements for claim preclusion are satisfied, the judgment in the first case acts as an absolute bar to the subsequent action with regard to every claim which was actually made . . . and those which might have been presented.").

One of the core purposes of bankruptcy is to collect all of "the debtor's assets for equitable distribution amongst creditors." *Kuehner v. Irving Trust Co.,* 299 U.S. 445, 452, 57 S.Ct. 298, 81 L.Ed. 340 (1937). Were we to hold that proofs of claim are subject to post-confirmation challenge, we would risk undermining this purpose by creating an incentive for debtors to enrich themselves at the expense of their creditors. Debtors would be motivated to refrain from pursuing claims for monetary damages until after a plan has been confirmed in order to obtain additional p.249 post-plan assets that would not be subject to distribution in bankruptcy. The only recourse for creditors in this situation would be to petition the court to revoke the discharge order based on a showing of fraud under 11 U.S.C. § 727(d). In the majority of cases, however, it is unlikely that a showing of fraud could be made, leaving the creditors without a remedy and frustrating bankruptcy's goal of collecting and equitably distributing all of a debtor's assets.

Moreover, allowing these kinds of post-confirmation collateral attacks on a bankruptcy plan's terms would "destroy the finality that bankruptcy confirmation is intended to provide." *Adair,* 230 F.3d at 895. *See also Grausz,* 321 F.3d at 475 (allowing debtor's malpractice action after confirmation of final attorneys' fees order would "undermine a fundamental purpose of the doctrine of res judicata: . . . encouraging reliance on adjudication") (internal citation omitted). Thus, allowing the kinds of post-confirmation actions that the Plaintiffs bring in this case would frustrate two fundamental aims of the bankruptcy process.

IV.

In deciding that these statutory claims were not barred by res judicata, the district court relied on our opinion in *Cen-Pen Corp. v. Hanson,* 58 F.3d 89 (4th Cir.1995). In *Cen-Pen,* we held that a creditor may challenge a plan's treatment of his secured claim as unsecured even after the plan is confirmed, because "Bankruptcy Rule 7001(2) expressly requires initiation of an *adversary proceeding* to determine the validity, priority or extent of a lien." *Id.* at 93 (emphasis in original). We then held that "[i]f an issue must be raised through an adversary proceeding it is not part of the confirmation process and, unless it is actually litigated, confirmation will not have a preclusive effect." *Id.*

Although there is no lien at issue in this case, the district court nevertheless read *Cen-Pen* to create a blanket rule that plan confirmation does not have preclusive effect as to any issue that must have been decided through an adversary process. *Covert,* 2013 WL 6490318 at *5. It then concluded that the Plaintiffs' statutory claims for damages were claims to "recover money or property," and were thus not precluded because Federal Rule of Bankruptcy Procedure 7001(1) requires such claims to be raised in adversary proceedings. *Id.*

This reading of *Cen-Pen* is too broad. First, *Cen-Pen* dealt with the status of *secured* claims following a bankruptcy proceeding, noting "the general rule that liens pass through bankruptcy unaffected." *Id.* at 92. We noted that this rule has statutory support in 11 U.S.C. § 506(d)(2), which states that liens are not voided "due only to the failure of any entity to file a proof of such claim." *Cen-Pen,* 58 F.3d at 93. Here, by contrast, Plaintiffs challenge the legality of the *process* used to collect an *unsecured* claim. There is no analogous rule or statute establishing that claims challenging the filing process pass through bankruptcy unaffected, nor any rule that unsecured claims pass through bankruptcy unaffected. Indeed, the opposite is true. *See* 11 U.S.C. § 1327(c) (stating the general rule that "[e]xcept as otherwise provided in the plan or in the order confirming the plan, the property [that a confirmed plan distributes] is free and clear of any claim or interest of any creditor provided for by the plan.").

Second, our reasoning in *Cen-Pen* was motivated by the need to protect the rights of parties in interest who are not directly involved in a bankruptcy proceeding. In *Cen-Pen,* the party seeking post-confirmation p.250 reinstatement of its secured lien apparently did not participate in the debtors' bankruptcy proceedings at all, and its liens were "nowhere mentioned or otherwise acknowledged" in the debtors' proposed plans. *Cen-Pen,* 58 F.3d at 94. Under such circumstances, we found that a creditor's lien could not be avoided simply because a plan had been confirmed because "[w]here [an adversary proceeding] is required to resolve the disputed rights of third parties, the potential defendant has the right to expect that the proper procedures will be followed." *Id.* at 93 (internal citation omitted). Any such concerns over the notice necessary before altering the rights of third parties are inapplicable here, where the Plaintiffs seeking relief from the confirmation orders are the debtors *themselves,* and they clearly suffered from no lack of notice of the claims against them.

The *Cen-Pen* exception simply does not apply in this case. The Plaintiffs' statutory claims are therefore subject to the normal principles of res judicata, and are thus precluded by the confirmation of the Chapter 13 plans.

V.

For the foregoing reasons, the judgment of the district court is affirmed. *AFFIRMED.*

[1] A proof of claim is a form filed by a creditor in a bankruptcy proceeding that states the amount the debtor owes to the creditor and the reason for the debt.

[2] The Plaintiffs also asserted a claim seeking attorneys' fees and reasonable expenses incurred in litigating this suit. Because a request for expenses and attorneys' fees is not a separate claim, but rather a request for a particular form of relief, this request necessarily fails because the underlying action is barred by res judicata. We therefore adopt the reasoning of the district court dismissing this claim.

[3] We note that the Plaintiffs failed to raise a claim for equitable relief under 11 U.S.C. § 502(j), which states that "[a] claim that has been allowed . . . may be reconsidered for cause," until oral argument in this case. We thus consider this argument waived. *See Equal Rights Center v. Niles Bolton Assocs.*, 602 F.3d 597, 604 n. 4 (4th Cir.2010) (arguments not raised in appellant's opening brief are deemed waived). We also note, however, that the burden of establishing cause for reconsideration under 502(j) rests with the moving party, *In re Starlight Group, LLC,* 515 B.R. 290, 293 (Bankr.E.D.Va.2014), and "the clearest cause for reconsideration is the discovery, subsequent to allowance, of new relevant facts or evidence that could not have been discovered at an earlier stage, or the discovery of clear error in the order of allowance," *In re Gold & Silversmiths, Inc.*, 170 B.R. 538, 545 (Bankr.W.D.N.Y.1994) (quoting Collier on Bankruptcy 14th Ed., ¶ 57.23(3)). Here, the Plaintiffs freely admit that no new relevant facts have come to light since their plans were confirmed, and they allege no clear error in the confirmation order. As a result, they would be unable to meet their burden of establishing cause for reconsideration under § 502(j).

FIFTH CIRCUIT DECISIONS

Trademark Infringement

95 F.4th 951 (2024)

Iris CALOGERO, on her own behalf and on behalf of all others similarly situated; Margie Nell Randolph, individually and on behalf of all others similarly situated, Plaintiffs-Appellants,

v.

SHOWS, CALI & WALSH, L.L.P., a Louisiana limited liability partnership; Mary Catherine Cali; John C. Walsh, Defendants-Appellees.

No. 22-30487.

United States Court of Appeals, Fifth Circuit.

FILED March 15, 2024.

Calogero v. Shows, Cali & Walsh, LLP, 95 F. 4th 951 (5th Cir. 2024)

p.955 Appeal from the United States District Court for the Eastern District of Louisiana USDC No. 2:18-CV-6709.

Margaret E. Woodward (argued), New Orleans, LA, Kirsten Anderson, Southern Poverty Law Center, Tallahassee, FL, Jennifer C. Deasy, New Orleans, LA, Keren E. Gesund, Attorney, LaFleur & Laborde, New Orleans, LA, Crystal McElrath, Attorney, Jamie Bj Rush, Southern Poverty Law Center, Decatur, GA, for Plaintiffs-Appellants.

David Scranton Daly, Esq., Senior Trial Attorney (argued), Frilot, L.L.C., New Orleans, LA, for Defendants-Appellees.

Before Clement, Haynes, and Oldham, Circuit Judges.

Andrew S. Oldham, Circuit Judge:[*]

Widowed octogenarians Iris Calogero and Margie Nell Randolph received dunning letters from a Louisiana law firm named Shows, Cali & Walsh. The widows sued under the Fair Debt Collection Practices Act. The district court granted summary judgment to defendant law firm. We reverse and remand.

p.956 I.

A.

This case centers on the "Road Home" grant program. As we previously described the program:

> In the aftermath of Hurricanes Katrina and Rita's devastation to displaced homeowners whose primary residences were either destroyed or severely damaged, Congress appropriated billions of dollars through the Community Development Block Grant program ("CDBG") of the Department of Housing and Urban Development ("HUD"). In 2006, Louisiana applied for CDBG funds for the Road Home Program ("Road Home") to provide grants for home repair and rebuilding, support affordable rental housing, and offer housing support services. Upon HUD's approval of the largest single housing

> recovery program in the United States, the Louisiana Office of Community Development ("OCD") and Louisiana Recovery Authority ("LRA") were tasked with implementing Road Home.

Calogero v. Shows, Cali & Walsh, L.L.P., 970 F.3d 576, 579 (5th Cir. 2020). OCD in turn outsourced a number of duties to contractors including ICF Emergency Management Services, LLC. ("ICF"). ICF handled individual grant applications, calculated award eligibility, and disbursed funds.

All Road Home grant recipients were required to sign a suite of documents. Breach of any of these agreements could result in demand for repayment by either the federal or state governments. For example, the program required Road Home applicants to disclose repair benefits they previously received. And where Road Home beneficiaries failed to disclose previous repair benefits, the Road Home Grant Agreement authorized the State to recoup duplicative payments.

B.

Calogero and Randolph are Louisiana homeowners. In 2005, their homes were devastated by Hurricane Katrina. That same year, Calogero received repair payments from FEMA and her insurance carrier. Randolph also received an insurance payment in 2005.

In the summer of 2007, both women applied for and received Road Home grants. Allegedly, neither woman disclosed the repair benefits she previously received from FEMA or a private insurance carrier. Calogero received a total Road Home grant of $33,393, which closed on May 11, 2007. ROA.6337, 7126. Randolph received a total Road Home grant of $28,793, which closed on June 30, 2007. ROA.6337, 7126.

On July 3, 2007, FEMA reported to the State of Louisiana its 2005 payments to Calogero. ROA.7814, 6338, 7126. A few weeks later, on August 5, 2007, Calogero's insurance carrier notified the State of its 2005 payments to Calogero. ROA.7814, 7229-30. Shortly thereafter, on October 23, 2007, the State received notice of Randolph's 2005 insurance payment. ROA. 6129, 8097-98. In March 2008, the State's contractor, ICF, noticed the potential double payments to the two women and placed an internal flag on their accounts in the Road Home database. ROA.7837, 7840.

A decade passed.

Then, in 2017, Shows, Cali & Walsh ("SCW") appeared on the scene. The State of Louisiana paid SCW more than $10 million to help recover double payments made in the Road Home program.

On February 9, 2018, SCW sent Calogero a dunning letter. The reference line stated, "Total Grant Funds Repayment Amount Due: $4,598.89." ROA.7929. The letter explained:

> Our client's records indicate that you received more in total insurance proceeds p.957 than the amount used to calculate your Grant award. Since you have not repaid those additional insurance funds to Road Home in accordance with your Road Home Grant Agreement, you have breached your Grant obligations. Those obligations are clearly outlined in your Road Home Grant Agreement.

Ibid. The letter demanded payment in 90 days, or else SCW "may proceed with further action against you, including legal action." *Ibid.* It further stated: "[y]ou may also be responsible for legal interest from judicial demand, court costs, and attorney fees if it is necessary to bring legal action against you." *Ibid.*

Calogero, through counsel, disputed the debt. SCW then sent a more detailed letter. In its second letter, SCW changed the basis of the alleged debt from "insurance proceeds" alone to include FEMA relief and a "30% penalty" for "lack" of flood insurance. ROA.7940-42. The Road Home grants make no mention of a 30% flood insurance-based "penalty." ROA.7721-33. And the second letter cites no basis for assessing Calogero a 30% "penalty." ROA. 7941.

SCW likewise sent Randolph a dunning letter on August 3, 2017, demanding $2,500. It contained no basis for that figure, other than a reference to her Road Home grant from ten years earlier. Like Calogero's letter, it contained a threat to proceed to litigation in 90 days if the debt was not paid. This threat of litigation also included the possibility that Randolph would have to pay attorneys' fees and other litigation costs.

Randolph was "terrified" by SCW's letter and feared that she would lose her house. ROA.7029. She called SCW's office and was told that her only option was to pay the money. Randolph explained that she did not have the money for a lump payment, but the firm agreed to accept monthly payments of $25 if she signed a promissory note. She took that deal for fear that litigation would destroy her financially. She dutifully wrote personal checks for $25, payable to SCW, every month.

C.

Calogero instead sued SCW under the Fair Debt Collection Practices Act ("FDCPA"). The FDCPA regulates the practices of debt collectors like SCW. The FDCPA's text provides in material part:

> A debt collector may not use any false, deceptive, or misleading representation or means in connection with the collection of any debt. Without limiting the general application of the foregoing, the following conduct is a violation of this section:
>
> * * *
>
> (2) The false representation of—
>
> (A) the character, amount, or legal status of any debt; or
>
> (B) any services rendered or compensation which may be lawfully received by any debt collector for the collection of a debt.
>
> * * *
>
> (5) The threat to take any action that cannot legally be taken or that is not intended to be taken.
>
> * * *
>
> (10) The use of any false representation or deceptive means to collect or attempt to collect any debt....

15 U.S.C. § 1692e (emphasis added).

In applying § 1692e, a court must "view the letter from the perspective of an unsophisticated or least sophisticated consumer." *Salinas v. R.A. Rogers, Inc.,* 952 F.3d 680, 683 (5th Cir. 2020) (quotation omitted). Under that standard, "we do not consider the debtor as tied to the very last rung on the intelligence or sophistication ladder." *Ibid.* (quoting *Goswami v. Am.* p.958 *Collections Enter.,* 377 F.3d 488, 495 (5th Cir. 2004)). We have "generally treat[ed]... as a question of law," the application of the unsophisticated-consumer standard. *Manuel v. Merchants & Pro. Bureau, Inc.,* 956 F.3d 822, 826 (5th Cir. 2020) (quoting *Salinas,* 952 F.3d at 683 n.2).

The district court dismissed Calogero's complaint, finding that the Road Home program grants were not debts within the meaning of the FDCPA. *See Calogero,* 970 F.3d at 580. We reversed. *See id.* at 586. On remand, Calogero amended her complaint to add Randolph as a plaintiff. The amended complaint alleged SCW: (1) collected or attempted to collect time-barred debts; (2) failed to itemize the alleged debts; and (3) threatened to assess attorneys' fees without determining whether such a right existed. The parties cross-moved for summary judgment.

The district court granted summary judgment to SCW. It held (1) the alleged debts were not time-barred; (2) the alleged debts did not require itemization, and the dunning letters did not misrepresent those debts in any event; and (3) that SCW could recover attorneys' fees.

Plaintiffs timely appealed. Our review is de novo. *See Playa Vista Conroe v. Ins. Co. of the W.,* 989 F.3d 411, 414 (5th Cir. 2021).

II.

As always, jurisdiction first. *See, e.g., E.T. v. Paxton,* 41 F.4th 709, 714 (5th Cir. 2022). SCW argues that the widows do not have standing to bring this claim because they lack a concrete injury.

The Supreme Court recently reiterated that: "Article III standing requires a concrete injury even in the context of a statutory violation." *TransUnion LLC v. Ramirez,* 594 U.S. 413, 426, 141 S.Ct. 2190, 210 L.Ed.2d 568 (2021) (quoting *Spokeo, Inc. v. Robins,* 578 U.S. 330, 341, 136 S.Ct. 1540, 194 L.Ed.2d 635 (2016)). The Court explained that beyond typical harms like physical and money damages, "intangible harms" may also be cognizable. *Id.* at 425, 141 S.Ct. 2190. But an intangible harm is not concrete for Article III purposes unless it has a "close relationship to a harm traditionally recognized as providing a basis for a lawsuit in American courts." *Ibid.*

In applying *TransUnion,* we must "focus[] on types of harms protected at common law, not the precise point at which those harms become actionable." *Perez v. McCreary, Veselka, Bragg & Allen, P.C.,* 45 F.4th 816, 822 (5th Cir. 2022) (alteration in original) (quoting *Cranor v. 5 Star Nutrition, LLC,* 998 F.3d 686, 693 (5th Cir. 2021)). That inquiry does not look to an exact analog at common law, but rather to harms that are close "in kind, not degree" to those traditionally remedied in American courts. *Ibid.* (quoting *Gadelhak v. AT&T Servs., Inc.,* 950 F.3d 458, 462 (7th Cir. 2020) (Barrett, J.)).

This case is controlled by *Perez.* There we recognized that "emotional distress" is a traditional harm that satisfies *TransUnion*'s concreteness requirement. *Id.* at 824 (citing *TransUnion,* 594 U.S. at 434-37, 141 S.Ct. 2190). And Calogero and Randolph complained of "fear, anxiety, and emotional distress" after receiving "intimidating" and "misleading" dunning letters. ROA.823. Randolph was so "terrified" by SCW's unlawful threat to sue and by the prospect of losing her home that she agreed to make monthly payments on a promissory note. *See* ROA.7028-30. That is a concrete and cognizable harm under Article III. *See Perez*, 45 F.4th at 824.

SCW's only responses border on frivolous. First, SCW selectively quotes *Perez* to omit the passage that explicitly recognizes emotional distress as a concrete injury. *See* Red Br. 21-22. Second, SCW p.959 claims that Calogero did not establish her emotional distress in her original complaint, so she cannot fix that omission later. It is true, subject-matter jurisdiction "depends on the state of things at the time of the action brought." *Mollan v. Torrance,* 22 U.S. (9 Wheat.) 537, 539, 6 L.Ed. 154 (1824). But that just means one plaintiff must have suffered emotional distress at the time the complaint was filed—not that failure to plead that injury in the original complaint forever deprives federal courts of jurisdiction. *Cf. Rockwell Int'l Corp. v. United States,* 549 U.S. 457, 473, 127 S.Ct. 1397, 167 L.Ed.2d 190 (2007) ("The state of things and the originally alleged state of things are not synonymous...."). That is why federal law expressly allows plaintiffs to cure defective allegations of jurisdiction—an allowance that would mean nothing if plaintiffs got only one shot, as SCW says. *See* 28 U.S.C. § 1653. "Thus, when a plaintiff files a complaint in federal court and then voluntarily amends the complaint, courts look to the amended complaint to determine jurisdiction." *Rockwell,* 549 U.S. at 473-74, 127 S.Ct. 1397 (citation omitted).

III.

On the merits, the district court erred in granting summary judgment to SCW. Viewing the facts in the light most favorable to plaintiffs, we hold that a reasonable jury could find that SCW violated the FDCPA in three ways: (A) by misrepresenting the judicial enforceability of the time-barred debts; (B) by mischaracterizing Calogero's debt; and (C) by misrepresenting the availability of attorneys' fees.

A.

We start with the limitations period. Attempting to collect on a time-barred debt does not *per se* violate the FDCPA. *Manuel,* 956 F.3d at 829; *see also Mahmoud v. De Moss Owners Ass'n, Inc.,* 865 F.3d 322, 333 (5th Cir. 2017) (holding it was not a violation of the FDCPA to collect a partially time-barred debt when only a small portion was subject to the statute of limitations); *Holzman v. Malcolm S. Gerald & Assocs., Inc.,* 920 F.3d 1264, 1273-74 (11th Cir. 2019) ("[C]ourts generally have recognized that the FDCPA does not impose a bright-line rule prohibiting debt collectors from attempting to collect on time-barred debt."). But a debt-collector can run afoul of the FDCPA by threatening judicial action while completely failing to mention that a limitations period might affect judicial enforceability. *Manuel,* 956 F.3d at 831 (emphasizing that disclosure of a potential limitations problem "might give a consumer at least some inkling that the debt might be too old to be legally enforceable"). As we have explained:

> When a collection letter creates confusion about a creditor's right to sue, that is illegal. The FDCPA singles out as unlawful the false representation of the

> character, amount, or legal status of any debt. Whether a debt is legally enforceable is a central fact about the character and legal status of that debt. A misrepresentation about the limitations period amounts to a straightforward violation of § 1692e(2)(A).

Daugherty v. Convergent Outsourcing, Inc., 836 F.3d 507, 512 (5th Cir. 2016) (quotation omitted).

The parties argue at length as to *which* limitations period should apply. The plaintiffs' first assert it should be the six-year federal statute of limitations under 28 U.S.C. § 2415(a). Alternatively, plaintiffs point to a five-year prescription period under article 1564 of the Louisiana Civil Code. On the other hand, SCW contends that Louisiana's general ten-year prescription period should apply. *See* La. Civ. Code Ann. art. 3499.

p.960 We need not resolve that dispute, however, because the dunning letters were untimely even under the most liberal, 10-year time window. Thus, no matter which limitations period applies, SCW misrepresented the judicial enforceability of these debts by threatening suit without acknowledging its timeliness problem. We (1) explain that timeliness problem and then (2) reject SCW's counterarguments.

1.

Under article 3499 of the Louisiana Civil Code, "a personal action is subject to a liberative prescription of ten years." This includes contract actions. *Taranto v. Louisiana Citizens Prop. Ins. Corp.*, 62 So. 3d 721, 734 (La. 2011).

Normally, the prescription period begins to run when the injured party has knowledge of the "facts that would entitle him to bring a suit." *Campo v. Correa*, 828 So. 2d 502, 510 (La. 2002). The State of Louisiana emphasizes that this is not an "actual knowledge" requirement; rather, state law imputes "constructive knowledge" of "whatever notice is enough to excite attention and put the injured party on guard and call for inquiry." *Id.* at 510-11. "Such notice is tantamount to knowledge or notice of everything to which a reasonable inquiry may lead." *Id.* at 511. The general rule in a contract action is that a claim accrues (and hence the prescriptive period begins to run) on the date of the breach. *All. Hosp., LLC v. Esquivel*, 322 So. 3d 253, 256 (La. Ct. App. 2021); *see also Richard v. Wal-Mart Stores, Inc.*, 559 F.3d 341, 345 (5th Cir. 2009) (same, applying Louisiana law).

Here, insofar as plaintiffs breached their contracts with the State of Louisiana, the breach occurred when they closed on their Road Home grants. For Calogero that was on May 11, 2007; for Randolph that was on June 30, 2007. On those dates, the women received their respective Road Home payments. And on those dates, the women allegedly failed to disclose duplicative repair payments they received two years earlier in 2005. So from their closing dates in 2007 (May 11 and June 30), both Calogero and Randolph were suable for breaching their Road Home contracts. Neither received a dunning letter until over a decade later in either August 2017 (Randolph) or February 2018 (Calogero).

Moreover, FEMA and Calogero's insurance carrier provided *actual* notice to the State of the allegedly duplicative payments in 2007. FEMA provided its notice on July 3, 2007. And Calogero's insurer provided its notice on August 5, 2007. Thus, as to Calogero, the latest conceivable accrual date for the State's claim was August 5, 2007—the date it received notice of the allegedly duplicative payments. Still, Calogero did not receive a dunning letter until over a decade later, in February 2018. Thus, SCW's dunning letter to Calogero plainly violated the FDCPA. *Manuel,* 956 F.3d at 829; *see also Daugherty,* 836 F.3d at 513.

Randolph's situation is slightly more complicated. (But only slightly.) Her insurer provided notice to the State of Randolph's allegedly duplicative repair benefit on October 23, 2007. If that constituted the accrual date for the State's claim, it might appear that SCW's dunning letter to Randolph —dated August 3, 2017—fell within the 10-year prescriptive period. But it did not. In its dunning letter to Randolph, SCW threatened to sue if not paid in 90 days. That 90 days ran until November 3, 2017—and by that time, Randolph's debt would be barred under any conceivable application of the 10-year prescriptive period. Thus, SCW's threat to Randolph (pay us now, or we will sue you in 90 days) was misleading. *Manuel,* 956 F.3d at 829; *see also Daugherty,* 836 F.3d at 513.

p.961 **2.**

SCW offers two counterarguments.[1] Both are wrong.

First, the firm claims that "the time period in C.C. art. 3499 does not commence to run until the party becomes aware of the breach." Red Br. 45. For this proposition, SCW cites *New Orleans Jazz and Heritage Foundation, Inc. v. Kirksey,* 40 So. 3d 394, 408 (La. Ct. App. 2010). Applying that standard, SCW claims prescription began to run on March 1, 2008, when the State's contractor, using data it already had at its disposal, internally flagged that Calogero and Randolph may have been overpaid. To SCW, "aware" means the date the State's contractor chose to review existing information and put a notification in its database. Red Br. 45.

This is a misstatement of Louisiana law. *New Orleans Jazz* applied the ten-year period in a straightforward breach of contract case, and the court remarked in passing about the date the plaintiff "first became aware" of the alleged breach. 40 So. 3d at 408. It is obvious from the context of those three words that the court was simply describing the facts of its case—not announcing some new, pathbreaking rule that deviates from the well-settled principle of state law that actual notice is not required. The Louisiana Supreme Court could not be clearer on this point. *Campo,* 828 So. 2d at 510-11 (constructive notice sufficient); *see also Hawthorne Land Co. v. Occidental Chem. Corp.,* 431 F.3d 221, 228 (5th Cir. 2005) (similar, applying Louisiana law). A passing description of the facts in an intermediate appellate court decision cannot somehow overrule the State Supreme Court on a point of state law.

Applying the correct, constructive-notice standard required by Louisiana law, we hold the State had constructive notice of plaintiffs' alleged breach of the Road Home contracts at the very latest when FEMA and the insurance carrier provided notice to the State in August and October 2007. SCW can find no support in state law for its contention that a claim does not accrue until a third party actually studied the notices sent to the State and flagged them. Were it otherwise, the State (or any other contractual counterparty) could stick its head in the sand, sleep on its rights, and otherwise delay enforcing a contract indefinitely. That is the exact opposite of the "reasonable inquiry" required by state law. *Campo,* 828 So. 2d at 511.

Second, SCW argues that the Louisiana legislature tolled the normal prescription period, for some undefined length of time, when it supposedly "stay[ed]" OCD's efforts in 2014. *See* Red Br. 46 (citing LA. STAT. ANN. § 49:663.1). But § 49:663.1 does no such thing. It simply directed OCD to develop new, robust procedures for grant payment recovery. *See* §§ 49:663.1(d)-(e). The Legislature's action makes no reference to the judicial enforceability of debts. It says nothing about the prescription period. And SCW offers no authority for inferring that this legislative silence should add some indeterminate amount of time to the prescription period.

p.962 **B.**

Next, SCW mischaracterizes Calogero's debt. The parties argue at length over whether SCW was required to itemize Calogero's debt in its dunning letter. We need not decide whether the FDCPA requires itemization. *Cf. Manuel,* 956 F.3d at 824 (deciding to "leave for another day" the question of whether a certain practice was "misleading as a matter of law"); *Salinas,* 952 F.3d at 684 ("To date, our court has not settled on precise definitions for the FDCPA terms 'deceptive' and 'misleading.'"). That is because Calogero's letter was misleading and easily transgresses our precedent regardless of its failure to itemize.

Take for example our decision in *Goswami.* In that case, a collection letter falsely advised a debtor that the holder of the underlying debt would only accept a 30% write-down of the principal value, and such an offer was only available for a limited time. 377 F.3d at 495. The client had in fact authorized a 50% write-down at any time. *Ibid.* Our court found a violation of the FDCPA because the dunning letter was deceptive on the true value of the write-down. *Id.* at 496; *see also Taylor v. Perrin, Landry, deLaunay & Durand,* 103 F.3d 1232, 1237-38 (5th Cir. 1997) (finding a debt collector's form letter misleading under the FDCPA because it appeared on law firm letterhead, even though no attorney ever participated in the dunning efforts).

SCW's letter stated that Calogero owed $4,598.89 in "insurance proceeds." ROA. 7929. But in reality, it was nowhere close to that figure. When pressed by Calogero's counsel, SCW completely changed that calculation. Upon inspection, most of that $4,598.89 was made up of FEMA benefits. And it included a 30% "penalty" for "lack" of flood insurance. ROA.7941. SCW provided no basis for the "penalty" assessment. *Ibid.* And it is nowhere to be found in the Road Home documents. It is plainly an incomplete and incorrect presentation under 15 U.S.C. § 1692e to represent to a consumer that a debt is for one thing, and then switch justifications completely when pressed by counsel. *Cf. Goswami,* 377 F.3d at 496; *Taylor,* 103 F.3d at 1237-38.

SCW nonetheless contends that the only relevant question is whether Calogero owed the final bottom-line number specified in the dunning letter. If Calogero owed $4,598.89, SCW contends, the rest of the letter is no-harm-no-foul.

We disagree. The FDCPA forbids SCW from *misleading* or *deceiving* debtors. 15 U.S.C. § 1692e. "As the addition of the term 'misleading' confirms, the statute outlaws more than just falsehoods. That is why truth is not always a defense." *Buchanan v. Northland Grp., Inc.,* 776 F.3d 393, 396 (6th Cir. 2015) (quotation omitted). If a debt collector hopes to pressure someone into paying a debt, it cannot demand payments on imaginary debts and then escape the FDCPA's reach by pointing to the bottom line. It instead must present the debt accurately.[2]

C.

Finally, SCW violated the FDCPA by threatening to collect attorneys' fees that it had no lawful basis to recover.

p.963 A debt collector violates the FDCPA when it has "no legal basis" for its demand. *See* 15 U.S.C. § 1692e(5) (banning "[t]he threat to take any action that cannot legally be taken or that is not intended to be taken"). Therefore, the question is whether SCW had a legal basis to threaten plaintiffs with attorneys' fees.

Louisiana law follows the "American Rule," under which courts cannot award attorneys' fees unless authorized by contract or statute. *See, e.g., Maloney v. Oak Builders, Inc.,* 256 La. 85, 235 So. 2d 386, 390 (1970). In interpreting a contractual fee-shifting provision, "[t]he reasonable intention of the parties to a contract is to be sought by examining the words of the contract itself." *Prejean v. Guillory,* 38 So. 3d 274, 279 (La. 2010). And "[w]hen the words of a contract are clear and explicit and lead to no absurd consequences, no further interpretation may be made in search of the parties' intent." *Ibid.* (citation omitted).

This case is governed by the "American Rule," because none of the contracts in the Road Home program authorized the fee shifting that SCW threatened. And SCW points to no statute sanctioning the firm's demands. Yet its dunning letters to Calogero and Randolph threatened that the widows would be "responsible for legal interest from judicial demand, court costs, and attorney fees if it is necessary to bring legal action against you." ROA.7927. That plainly violates § 1692e(5).[3]

SCW nonetheless points to one fee-related document in the Road Home suite of contracts—the Road Home Limited Subrogation/Assignment Agreement ("LSAA"). SCW is correct that the LSAA authorizes the State to recover attorneys' fees. But SCW is incorrect that the LSAA applies to either Calogero or Randolph. The LSAA provides in relevant part:

> [T]o the extent of the grant proceeds awarded or to be awarded to me under the Program, all of my/our claims and future rights to reimbursement and all payments hereafter received or to be received by me/us (a) under any policy of casualty or property damage insurance or flood insurance on the residence, excluding contents ("Residence") described in my/our application....

ROA.7728-29, 7741-42 (emphasis added). Thus, the LSAA allows for recuperation (and fees) only where the grant recipient receives *future* payments *after* signing the Road Home suite of contracts. It provides no fee-shifting remedy against grant recipients like Calogero and Randolph who allegedly received payments *before* signing the LSAA.

A separate document in the Road Home suite of contracts—called the "Grant Agreement"—applies to payments received and not disclosed *before* closing. ROA.7726, 7731. And that instrument authorizes fee-shifting in the tightly circumscribed scenario in which a homeowner sued the Road Home program and suffered an adverse judgment. That obviously has not happened here, so the Grant Agreement does not justify the threat in SCW's dunning letters.

SCW's last remaining counterargument is that it should be able to pick and choose different clauses from the LSAA and the Grant Agreement and then mush them together to demand money from debtors. SCW offers no authority for this proposition,[4] but simply urges this p.964 court to combine the separate instruments into one. We will not. The words of the LSAA are "clear and explicit": fee shifting can occur only for future payments. *Prejean,* 38 So. 3d at 279. SCW does not dispute that clarity.

***

For the foregoing reasons, the district court's judgment is REVERSED, and the case is REMANDED for further proceedings consistent with this opinion.

[*] JUDGE HAYNES concurs in the judgment only.

[1] The district court discussed the equitable doctrine of *contra non valentem,* which it used to toll the prescription period. SCW does not press that argument on appeal. *Cf. Rollins v. Home Depot USA,* 8 F.4th 393, 397 (5th Cir. 2021) (explaining that a party forfeits an argument by failing to adequately brief it). And in any event, *contra non valentem* would likely not apply here, as the Louisiana Supreme Court has warned that it "only applies in exceptional circumstances." *Marin v. Exxon Mobil Corp.,* 48 So. 3d 234, 245 (La. 2010) (quotation omitted). And none of those "exceptional" preconditions are met here. *Ibid.*

[2] The dunning letter SCW sent to Randolph does not contain these same deceptive and misleading flaws. The Randolph letter simply demands payment for $2,500. As to that letter, plaintiffs urge us to hold the letter was deceptive because SCW failed to itemize the $2,500 debt. We need not do so, however, because Randolph's letter was misleading and deceptive both because it unlawfully attempted to recover on a time-barred debt (as discussed in Part III.A, *supra*) and because it unlawfully attempted to recover attorneys' fees (as discussed in Part III.C, *infra*).

[3] The attorneys' fees threat is an independent violation of the FDCPA under 15 U.S.C. § 1692e(5). So even if SCW timely dunned some grant recipients for alleged overpayments, any unlawful threats of attorneys' fees would constitute distinct violations of the FDCPA.

[4] Although not pressed by SCW on appeal, the district court cited *Robinson v. Marks,* 211 La. 452, 30 So. 2d 200, 203 (1947), for the proposition that multiple contracts between the same parties can constitute "one entire and indivisible contract or one transaction." *Ibid.* But the rule from *Robinson* has been partially abrogated by statute. La. Civ. Code Ann. art. 2053 ("[O]ther contracts of a like nature between the same parties" should be used to interpret only "doubtful provisions."). The provisions at issue here are not "doubtful." *Ibid.* And, in any event, SCW forfeited the point by not pressing it. The district court also *sua sponte* raised a theory of fraud against Calogero and Randolph. SCW forfeited that point too by failing to press it on appeal. *Rollins,* 8 F.4th at 397.

45 F.4th 816 (2022)

Mariela PEREZ, on behalf of herself and all others similarly situated, Plaintiff-Appellee,

v.

McCREARY, VESELKA, BRAGG & ALLEN, P.C.; MVBA, L.L.C., formerly known as McCreary, Veselka, Bragg & Allen, L.L.C., Defendants-Appellants.

No. 21-50958.

United States Court of Appeals, Fifth Circuit.

Filed August 15, 2022.

Perez v. McCreary, Veselka, Bragg & Allen, PC, 45 F. 4th 816 (5th Cir. 2022)

Appeal from the United States District Court for the Western District of Texas No. 1:19-CV-724

Brent Allen Devere, Esq., Austin, TX, for Plaintiff-Appellee.

Eugene Xerxes Martin, Esq., Malone Frost Martin, P.L.L.C., Dallas, TX, for Defendants-Appellants.

Before DAVIS, SMITH, and ENGELHARDT, Circuit Judges.

p.820 JERRY E. SMITH, Circuit Judge.

McCreary, Veselka, Bragg & Allen ("MVBA") is a law firm that specializes in collecting debts owed to Texas local governments. In 2019, it sent a letter to Mariela Perez demanding that she pay several hundred dollars in delinquent utility debt that she owed to the City of College Station. But limitations on that debt had run, and the letter did not disclose that fact. So Perez sued MVBA under the Fair Debt Collection Practices Act ("FDCPA"), 15 U.S.C. § 1692e. She also sought to certify a class of Texans with time-barred debt who had received the same form letter. The district court granted that request, and MVBA appealed under Federal Rule of Civil Procedure 23(f).

On appeal, MVBA does not contest Perez's standing. But we have an "independent obligation to assure that standing exists, regardless of whether it is challenged by any of the parties." *Summers v. Earth Island Inst.,* 555 U.S. 488, 499, 129 S.Ct. 1142, 173 L.Ed.2d 1 (2009). Perez has standing only if the letter inflicted an injury with a "close relationship to a harm traditionally recognized as providing a basis for a lawsuit in American courts." *Trans Union LLC v. Ramirez,* ___ U.S. ____, 141 S. Ct. 2190, 2200, 210 L.Ed.2d 568 (2021) (quotation omitted). Because Perez hasn't shown that she has suffered such an injury, we vacate the class-certification order and remand with instruction to dismiss for want of jurisdiction.

I.

When Perez was living in College Station, she incurred $486.57 in utility bills that she did not pay. Later, the city hired MVBA to collect the debt. The firm tried to do so by sending Perez a form letter demanding payment. Notably, her debt had become delinquent four years and one day before MVBA sent its letter. Under Texas law, that meant it was unenforceable. *See* TEX. CIV. PRAC. & REM. CODE § 16.004(a). But the letter failed to mention that fact.

MVBA soon paid a price for its omission. Perez had previously filed FDCPA suits against three other defendants. And when she received the form letter, she sued MVBA, too.

Perez alleged that the firm had violated the FDCPA by making a misrepresentation in connection with an attempt to collect her debts. *See* 15 U.S.C. § 1692e. She also sought to represent a class of Texas consumers who had received the same form letter from MVBA in connection with their time-barred debts. And she requested that she be awarded statutory damages, a declaration that MVBA's debt-collection practices violate the FDCPA, costs, and attorneys' fees.

Importantly for present purposes, Perez's complaint highlighted three injuries that she suffered as a result of MVBA's letter. First, she maintained that the letter "created a significant risk of harm" in that she might have paid her time-barred debts. Second, she claimed that the letter misled and confused her about the enforceability of her debt. Finally, she said that the letter required her to consult an attorney p.821 to determine the enforceability of the debt.

After discovery, Perez moved to certify her class. Both parties also moved for summary judgment. As relevant here, MVBA contended that Perez did not have standing to bring suit because she had not suffered a concrete injury-in-fact under *Spokeo, Inc. v. Robins,* 578 U.S. 330, 136 S.Ct. 1540, 194 L.Ed.2d 635 (2016). While those motions were pending, the Supreme Court decided *TransUnion.* MVBA brought that decision to the attention of the district court in a motion for leave to file supplemental authority that reiterated its position that Perez had not suffered an injury in fact.

One day later, the district court ruled on the three motions. First, it rejected MVBA's claim that Perez lacked standing to bring suit. It held that the violation of Perez's statutory rights under the FDCPA constituted a concrete injury-in-fact because those rights were substantive, not procedural. In the alternative, it maintained that Perez's confusion qualified as a concrete injury-in-fact. And, in a footnote, it distinguished *TransUnion* based on its facts. Second, it held that MVBA's letter had violated the FDCPA but factual disputes concerning an affirmative defense precluded summary judgment. Finally, it certified the proposed class under Rule 23(b)(3).

MVBA sought permission to appeal the class-certification order under Rule 23(f). It received that permission from a motions panel of our court and now appeals.

II.

Federal courts are courts of limited subject matter jurisdiction. Our power to resolve disputes is limited to "Cases" and "Controversies," U.S. Const. art. III, § 2, to prevent us from encroaching on domains properly allocated to the other branches in our system of self-government, *see TransUnion,* 141 S. Ct. at 2203; *Clapper v. Amnesty Int'l USA,* 568 U.S. 398, 408, 133 S.Ct. 1138, 185 L.Ed.2d 264 (2013); *Lujan v. Defs. of Wildlife,* 504 U.S. 555, 560-61, 112 S.Ct. 2130, 119 L.Ed.2d 351 (1992). As relevant for our purposes, a lawsuit is not a "Case[]" or "Controvers[y]" unless the plaintiff can prove that he has standing to bring suit. *Lujan,* 504 U.S. at 560-61, 112 S.Ct. 2130.

That requires the plaintiff to "show (i) that he suffered an injury in fact that is concrete, particularized, and actual or imminent; (ii) that the injury was likely caused by the defendant; and (iii) that the injury would likely be redressed by judicial relief." *TransUnion,* 141 S. Ct. at 2203. Moreover, "standing is not dispensed in gross; rather, plaintiffs must demonstrate standing for each claim that they press and for each form of relief that they seek (for example, injunctive relief and damages)." *Id.* at 2208.

This case involves the first element of standing: the requirement that the plaintiff show he has suffered a concrete injury-in-fact. Last Term, the Supreme Court clarified standing's concrete-injury requirement in *TransUnion.* There, it reiterated that a purported injury is not concrete for purposes of Article III unless it has a "'close relationship' to a harm traditionally recognized as providing a basis for a lawsuit in American courts." *TransUnion,* 141 S. Ct. at 2200 (quoting *Spokeo,* 578 U.S. at 340-41, 136 S.Ct. 1540). That standard doesn't require an "exact duplicate." *Id.* at 2204. But "federal courts" may not "loosen Article III based on contemporary, evolving beliefs about what kinds of suits should be heard in federal courts." *Ibid.*

p.822 Some harms plainly have that "close relationship." Think of "traditional tangible harms, such as physical harms and monetary harms." *Ibid.* But intangible harms can also be concrete. Think of the kind of harms recognized in longstanding tort law or the Constitution itself. *See ibid.* When evaluating whether intangible harms are concrete, Congress's views are also entitled to "due respect." *Ibid.* "Congress may 'elevate to the status of legally cognizable injuries concrete, *de facto* injuries that were previously inadequate in law.'" *Spokeo,* 578 U.S. at 341, 136 S.Ct. 1540 (alteration adopted and quotation omitted).

But "Congress's creation of a statutory prohibition or obligation and a cause of action does not relieve courts of their responsibility to independently decide whether a plaintiff has suffered a concrete harm under Article III." *TransUnion,* 141 S. Ct. at 2205. Any other rule would allow Congress to grant private plaintiffs a personal stake in enforcing regulatory law and ultimately usurp the President's Article II authority to execute the laws. *See id.* at 2206-07 & nn.2-3. And that would aggrandize *our* power by letting us resolve disputes that are not "of a Judiciary Nature." 2 THE RECORDS OF THE FEDERAL CONVENTION OF 1787, at 430 (M. Farrand ed. 1911) (Statement of James Madison).

So *TransUnion* is clear: A plaintiff always needs a concrete injury to bring suit, and injuries are concrete only if they bear a "close relationship" to injuries that courts have traditionally recognized as concrete. But how close is close enough? The Supreme Court hasn't provided an exact formulation. But then-Judge Barrett got it right in *Gadelhak v. AT&T Services Inc.*, 950 F.3d 458, 462 (7th Cir. 2020): "[W]e are meant to look for a 'close relationship' in kind, not degree." After all, Congress's ability to "elevate" harms "to the status of legally cognizable injuries," *TransUnion,* 141 S. Ct. at 2205 (quotation omitted), implies that the level of harm required at common law "does not stake out the limits of [its] power to identify harms deserving a remedy," *Gadelhak,* 950 F.3d at 463.

Picking up on that cue, our court has already recognized that we must "focus[ ] on types of harms protected at common law, not the precise point at which those harms become actionable." *Cranor v. 5 Star Nutrition, L.L.C.,* 998 F.3d 686, 693 (5th Cir. 2021) (quotation omitted). Beyond the Seventh Circuit, many of our sister circuits have done the same.[1] So a plaintiff doesn't need to demonstrate that the level of harm he has suffered would be actionable under a similar, common-law cause of action. But he does need to show that the type of harm he's suffered is similar in kind to a type of harm that the common law has recognized as actionable. If he can't do that, he hasn't suffered a concrete injury and doesn't have standing to bring suit.

III.

That brings us to this case. Before the district court, MVBA claimed that Perez hadn't suffered a concrete injury. It failed to do so on appeal. But we have an obligation to assure ourselves of p.823 jurisdiction—even in "limited" Rule 23(f) interlocutory appeals that typically embrace "only the issue of class certification." *Bertulli v. Indep. Ass'n of Cont'l Pilots,* 242 F.3d 290, 294 (5th Cir. 2001); *see also Flecha v. Medicredit, Inc.,* 946 F.3d 762, 769 (5th Cir. 2020). And in a class action, "federal courts lack jurisdiction if no named plaintiff has standing." *Frank v. Gaos,* ___ U.S. ___, 139 S. Ct. 1041, 1046, 203 L.Ed.2d 404 (2019) (per curiam). Accordingly, we directed the parties to be prepared to discuss at oral argument whether Perez had suffered a concrete injury-in-fact under *TransUnion.*

There, Perez's counsel advanced five theories for holding that Perez had suffered a concrete injury-in-fact. As he had before the district court, he claimed that the violation of Perez's rights under the FDCPA itself qualified as an injury-in-fact. He again pressed three theories of injury that were mentioned in Perez's complaint: that the letter subjected Perez to a material risk of financial harm, that it confused or misled her, and that it required her to waste her time by consulting with an attorney. And he advanced a new theory that the receipt of the unwanted letter was analogous to the tort of intrusion upon seclusion. Perez has failed to meet her burden for all of those theories.

A.

We begin with Perez's request for damages. *First,* Perez claims that the violation of her statutory rights under the FDCPA itself qualifies as a concrete injury. The district court advanced a similar contention, reasoning that Perez's suit related to her substantive right to be free from misleading information instead of a "bare procedural violation" of the FDCPA that would not be cognizable under *Spokeo,* 578 U.S. at 341, 136 S.Ct. 1540.

TransUnion forecloses those theories. It explicitly held that "Article III standing requires a concrete injury even in the context of a statutory violation." 141 S. Ct. at 2205 (quoting *Spokeo,* 578 U.S. at 341, 136 S.Ct. 1540); *see also id.* ("[U]nder Article III, an injury in law is not an injury in fact."). It "reject[s] the proposition that 'a plaintiff automatically satisfies the injury-in-fact requirement whenever a statute grants a person a statutory right and purports to authorize that person to sue to vindicate that right.'"[2] And it emphasizes that a hypothetical lawsuit based only on the violation of an environmental statute "may not proceed because that plaintiff has not suffered any physical, monetary, or cognizable intangible harm traditionally recognized as providing a basis for a lawsuit in American courts." *Id.* at 2206.

Nor is *Spokeo* to the contrary. Granted, that opinion held that a "bare procedural violation" of a statute does not qualify as an injury-in-fact. 578 U.S. at 341, 136 S.Ct. 1540. But *Spokeo* merely cited that as an "example" of a statutory violation that alone would not create an injury-in-fact. *Id.* Again, regardless of whether a statutory right is procedural or substantive, *Spokeo* emphasized that "Article III standing requires a concrete injury even in the context of a statutory violation." *Id.* Its reference to procedural violations merely underscored that conclusion: The "[d]eprivation of a procedural right without some concrete interest that is affected by the deprivation ... is insufficient p.824 to create Article III standing." *Id.* (quoting *Summers,* 555 U.S. at 496, 129 S.Ct. 1142). For Article III purposes, *Spokeo* never distinguished between substantive and procedural statutory rights. Accordingly, Perez's first theory doesn't establish that she has standing to bring suit.

Second, Perez maintains that MVBA's letter subjected her to a material risk of financial harm and that that exposure qualifies as a concrete injury. Specifically, Perez claims that her receipt of the letter subjected her to a risk that she might accidentally pay her time-barred debts.

This theory, too, is foreclosed by *TransUnion.* Remember: A plaintiff always must be able to point to a concrete injury to bring suit. And if a risk hasn't materialized, the plaintiff hasn't yet been injured. *TransUnion* held that merely being subjected to a risk of future harm cannot support a suit for damages. 141 S. Ct. at 2210-11. A plaintiff can sue for damages if the risk materializes or causes a separate injury-in-fact, such as emotional distress. *Id.* But those are suits based on those injuries, not the risk itself. *Id.*

Once again, *Spokeo* doesn't save this theory. That case acknowledged that a "material risk of harm" can "satisfy the requirement of concreteness." 578 U.S. at 341-42, 136 S.Ct. 1540. But *TransUnion* clarified that this language applied to "forward-looking" suits for declaratory or injunctive relief that seek to "prevent the harm from occurring." 141 S. Ct. at 2210-11. A suit for damages demands compensation for injuries that a plaintiff has suffered in the past, so that principle doesn't apply.

True, we have previously held that a plaintiffs "expos[ure] ... to a real risk of financial harm" caused by an FDCPA violation can qualify as a concrete injury-in-fact in a suit for damages. *See Sayles v. Advanced Recovery Sys., Inc.,* 865 F.3d 246, 250 (5th Cir. 2017), *aff'g* 206 F. Supp. 3d 1210 (S.D. Miss. 2016) (awarding damages to the plaintiff). But that case predated *TransUnion* by nearly four years, and we aren't bound by panel opinions that the Supreme Court has "implicitly overruled." *In re Bonvillian Marine Serv., Inc.,* 19 F.4th 787, 792 (5th Cir. 2021) (quotation omitted). One way that can happen is "if a subsequent Supreme Court opinion establishes a rule of law inconsistent with [our] precedent." *Id.* (quotation omitted). *Sayles* can't be squared with *TransUnion,* so *TransUnion* controls. And that means the unmaterialized risk Perez experienced can't support her suit for damages.

Third, Perez says the confusion she experienced from MVBA's letter qualifies as a concrete injury. The district court endorsed that theory, but we disagree.

Perez's argument isn't entirely clear, but we understand her to analogize the confusion she suffered to fraudulent-misrepresentation torts. Such torts make *A* liable for *B*'s pecuniary losses where *A* intentionally misleads *B* and *B* justifiably relies on that misrepresentation. RESTATEMENT (FIRST) OF TORTS §§ 525, 549, 553 (Am. L. INST. 1938).[3] Perez's confusion bears some p.825 similarities to those torts. After all, her confusion is the result of MVBA's allegedly misleading letter, and those torts make tortfeasors liable for similar misrepresentations.

But Perez's problem is that her confusion isn't similar "in kind" to the harm recognized by fraudulent misrepresentation, *Gadelhak,* 950 F.3d at 462, and that's what matters for standing purposes. The nature of the harm recognized by fraudulent misrepresentation is a traditional, *tangible* harm: the "pecuniary loss" the plaintiff sustains.[4] And that means Perez's confusion—which can only be an intangible harm, if it's a harm at all—is necessarily *different* "in kind" from her common-law analog. *Gadelhak,* 950 F.3d at 462. We thus join several of our sister circuits in holding that the state of confusion, absent more, is not a concrete injury under Article III.[5]

Fourth, Perez says the time she wasted by consulting with her lawyer after receiving the letter qualifies as a concrete injury. Absent an allegation that Perez paid her attorney anything for the consultation, we must assume that her purported injury is solely lost time.

Perez doesn't offer a common-law analog to the time-based injury she claims to have suffered. In other words, she has not met her "burden [to] demonstrate[e] that [she has] standing" based on that theory. *TransUnion,* 141 S. Ct. at 2207. After all, how can we decide whether two harms have a "close relationship" if we don't know what one of them is? *Id.* at 2200 (quotation omitted). It is not our job to "conjure up possible theories" that could carry a litigant's burden. *Raley v. Hyundai Motor Co.,* 642 F.3d 1271, 1275 (10th Cir. 2011).

Besides, we are not aware of any tort that makes a person liable for wasting another's time. Although tort plaintiffs can sometimes recover damages for the opportunity costs attributable to the tort, the nature of the underlying harm is different—*e.g.,* physical damage in the case of a personal injury suit. Like at least one of our sister circuits, we are thus skeptical that a time-based injury alone could qualify as a concrete injury. *Cf. Brunett,* 982 F.3d at 1069. Still, we do not conclusively decide whether such injuries are closely related to traditional harms, permitting future parties to develop the question further. We hold only that Perez did not carry her burden to show that a time-based injury could sustain her claims.

Finally, Perez claims that her receipt of an unwanted letter caused her to suffer a concrete injury analogous to the tort of intrusion upon seclusion. Once again, we disagree.

p.826 A person commits the tort of intrusion upon seclusion by "intentionally intrud[ing], physically or otherwise, upon the solitude or seclusion of another or his private affairs or concerns ... if the intrusion would be highly offensive to a reasonable person." RESTATEMENT (SECOND) § 652B. One pattern of liability is for repeated, harassing communications. *See id.* cmt. d; *Gadelhak,* 950 F.3d at 462.

TransUnion explicitly recognized that harms analogous to this tort can qualify as concrete. *See* 141 S. Ct. at 2204 (citing *Gadelhak,* 950 F.3d at 462). Before and after *TransUnion,* many of our sister circuits also held that unwanted communications could cause concrete injuries similar to intrusion upon seclusion or other privacy torts.[6] Since the harms elevated by Congress need only be similar "in kind, not degree," *Gadelhak,* 950 F.3d at 462, it seems to follow that a single unwanted communication could qualify as a concrete injury even though intrusion upon seclusion requires many. So how can we say that Perez's receipt of the letter did not inflict a concrete injury?

The answer is that Congress *didn't* elevate the receipt of a single, unwanted message to the status of a legally cognizable injury in the FDCPA. Perez sued MVBA for violating the statute's antifraud provision. 15 U.S.C. § 1692e. Congress's concern in prohibiting "false, deceptive, or misleading representation[s] or means in connection with the collection of any debt" wasn't consumer privacy. It was the economic harms that consumers suffered due to aggressive and unfair attempts to collect their debts. *See id.* § 1692(a) (finding that "[a]busive debt collection practices contribute to the number of personal bankruptcies, to marital instability, [and] to the loss of jobs").

Congress also expressed concern about "invasions of individual privacy." *Id.* § 1692(a). But it addressed those problems through a *different* section of the FDCPA: the statute's prohibition on harassment and abuse. *Id.* § 1692d. Perez hasn't sued MVBA based on that provision, so she can't bootstrap the harms it recognizes as actionable to demonstrate standing to sue based on a different provision.[7]

Anyway, the FDCPA's harassment provision doesn't recognize that a single unwanted message qualifies as a concrete harm. Instead, its closest analog to an unwanted letter—unwanted telephone calls—must be made "repeatedly or continuously." 15 U.S.C. § 1692d(5). Its general prohibition on actions that "harass, oppress, or abuse" a debtor carries the same connotation. *Id.* § 1692d. Accordingly, even if Congress could elevate a single unwanted message to the status of a concrete injury, it hasn't done so here. Perez does not have standing to bring her suit for damages.

B.

That brings us to Perez's request for a declaratory judgment. Perez asks us to declare that MVBA's debt-collection p.827 practices violate the FDCPA. But Perez must "demonstrate standing" for this "form of relief," too. *TransUnion,* 141 S. Ct. at 2208. Once again, none of her claimed injuries is concrete. Our reasoning is the same except for one of Perez's purported injuries: the risk of financial harm she suffered from MVBA's letter.

As we have previously explained, a risk of injury does not qualify as concrete harm for purposes of a damages claim. But the story is different where a plaintiff requests a "forward-looking" remedy such as an injunction or declaration.

TransUnion, 141 S. Ct. at 2210; *see also City of Austin v. Paxton,* 943 F.3d 993, 1002 (5th Cir. 2019). That's because standing doesn't always require a plaintiff's concrete injury to be "actual"—*i.e.,* an injury that the plaintiff has already sustained. *Lujan,* 504 U.S. at 560, 112 S.Ct. 2130 (quotation omitted). A plaintiff can sometimes show standing by pointing to a concrete injury that is "imminent." *Id.* (quotation omitted). Accordingly, "a material risk of future harm" permits the plaintiff to sue "to prevent the harm from occurring, at least so long as the risk of harm is sufficiently imminent and substantial." *TransUnion,* 141 S. Ct. at 2210.

The problem for Perez is that she doesn't allege that she is *currently* subject to a material risk of financial harm. Instead, she says that she suffered that risk *in the past.* According to her complaint, Perez was confused by MVBA's letter and might have accidentally paid a time-barred debt. But that confusion dissipated once she consulted her attorney. She hasn't alleged facts that show she might receive another misleading letter from MVBA in the future. So she can't point to an "imminent" concrete harm to support her request for forward-looking relief.

Nor can the risk she suffered in the past give her standing to bring suit. We have already explained why that risk does not qualify as a concrete injury under *TransUnion.* But even if that weren't true, forward-looking relief like injunctions and declarations couldn't fix it. And that means Perez's couldn't meet standing's redressability requirement when seeking that relief. *Stringer v. Whitley,* 942 F.3d 715, 720 (5th Cir. 2019). Thus, Perez doesn't have standing to bring a suit for a declaration.

*****

The class-certification order is VACATED, and the case is REMANDED with instruction to dismiss for want of jurisdiction.

[1] *See Krakauer v. Dish Network, LLC,* 925 F.3d 643, 653-54 (4th Cir. 2019); *Golan v. FreeEats.com, Inc.,* 930 F.3d 950, 959 (8th Cir. 2019); *Lupia v. Medicredit, Inc.,* 8 F.4th 1184, 1191 (10th Cir. 2021); *Hunstein v. Preferred Collection & Mgmt. Servs., Inc.,* 17 F.4th 1016, 1024-27 (11th Cir.), *reh'g en banc granted, opinion vacated,* 17 F.4th 1103 (11th Cir. 2021). Two others have also focused on the "character" of the relevant harms. *Melito v. Experian Mktg. Sols., Inc.,* 923 F.3d 85, 92-93 (2d Cir. 2019); *Susinno v. Work Out World Inc.,* 862 F.3d 346, 352 (3d Cir. 2017).

[2] *Id.* (quotation omitted); *see also id.* ("For standing purposes ..., an important difference exists between (i) a plaintiff 's statutory cause of action to sue a defendant over the defendant's violation of federal law, and (ii) a plaintiff's suffering concrete harm because of the defendant's violation of federal law.").

[3] As an originalist matter, it would make the most sense to limit the category of concrete harms to those recognized at the time Article III was ratified. But *TransUnion* relied in part on the twentieth-century *Restatement (First) of Torts* to establish the nature of several types of concrete harms. 141 S. Ct. at 2208-09. Likewise, the Courts of Appeals—including this one—have relied on both the *Restatement (First)* and the *Restatement (Second)* to do the same. *See, e.g., Amrhein v. eClinical Works, LLC,* 954 F.3d 328, 334 (1st Cir. 2020); *Melito,* 923 F.3d at 93; *Susinno,*

862 F.3d at 351; *Krakauer,* 925 F.3d at 653; *Cranor,* 998 F.3d at 691; *Buchholz v. Meyer Njus Tanick, PA,* 946 F.3d 855, 864 (6th Cir. 2020); *Gadelhak,* 950 F.3d at 462; *Braitberg v. Charter Commc'ns, Inc.,* 836 F.3d 925, 930 (8th Cir. 2016); *Van Patten v. Vertical Fitness Grp., LLC,* 847 F.3d 1037, 1043 (9th Cir. 2017); *Lupia,* 8 F.4th at 1191; *Salcedo v. Hanna,* 936 F.3d 1162, 1171 (11th Cir. 2019); *Owner-Operator Indep. Drivers Ass'n, Inc. v. U.S. Dep't of Transp.,* 879 F.3d 339, 345 (D.C. Cir. 2018). So we, too, will rely on the *Restatements.*

[4] RESTATEMENT (FIRST) § 549; *see also id.* § 553 (noting that liability attaches for "the loss caused by the *making* of the gift" (emphasis added)); RESTATEMENT (SECOND) OF TORTS §§ 525, 529 (AM. L. INST. 1977); *cf. Trichell v. Midland Credit Mgmt., Inc.,* 964 F.3d 990, 997-98 (11th Cir. 2020) (holding that the plaintiffs had not suffered a harm similar in kind to fraudulent misrepresentation because they had not suffered actual damages).

[5] *Garland v. Orlans, PC,* 999 F.3d 432, 438 (6th Cir. 2021); *Brunett v. Convergent Outsourcing, Inc.,* 982 F.3d 1067, 1068 (7th Cir. 2020); *see also Trichell,* 964 F.3d at 997-98. The Eighth Circuit also appeared to endorse this holding in *Ojogwu v. Rodenburg Law Firm,* 26 F.4th 457, 463 (8th Cir. 2022).

[6] *Melito,* 923 F.3d at 92-93; *Susinno,* 862 F.3d at 351; *Krakauer,* 925 F.3d at 653; *Gadelhak,* 950 F.3d at 462; *Van Patten,* 847 F.3d at 1042-43; *Lupia,* 8 F.4th at 1191; *Hunstein,* 17 F.4th at 1023-24; *but see Salcedo,* 936 F.3d at 1172. Two circuits—including this one—have also recognized that unwanted communications can inflict a concrete injury analogous to a nuisance or a public nuisance. *Cranor,* 998 F.3d at 692; *Golan,* 930 F.3d at 959.

[7] Other circuits have also rejected the use of privacy-related torts to bootstrap standing when a plaintiff sues a defendant for violating statutory provision that do not involve privacy. *Ward v. Nat'l Patient Acct. Servs. Sols., Inc.,* 9 F.4th 357, 362 (6th Cir. 2021); *cf. Gunn v. Thrasher, Buschmann & Voelkel, P.C.,* 982 F.3d 1069, 1071 (7th Cir. 2020).

989 F.3d 338 (2021)

Zachary FONTANA, Plaintiff-Appellant,
v.
HOVG LLC, doing business as Bay Area Credit Service, L.L.C., Defendant-Appellee.

No. 20-30471.

United States Court of Appeals, Fifth Circuit.

Filed February 26, 2021.

Fontana v. HOVG LLC, 989 F. 3d 338 (5th Cir. 2021)

Appeal from the United States District Court for the Western District of Louisiana USDC No. 3:20-CV-100.

David Patrick Keating, Keating Firm, A.P.L.C., Lafayette, LA, Robert Ramo Amador, Centennial Law Offices, Orcutt, CA, for Plaintiff-Appellant.

Ryan D. Dry, Krebs Farley & Dry, P.L.L.C., Plano, TX, Jane M. Daily, Krebs Farley & Dry, P.L.L.C., New Orleans, LA, for Defendant-Appellee.

Before ELROD, WILLETT, and ENGELHARDT, Circuit Judges.

p.340JENNIFER WALKER ELROD, Circuit Judge.

After a debt collector spoke with Zachary Fontana's sister over the phone, Fontana sued, alleging a violation of the Fair Debt Collection Practices Act's prohibition on communicating with third parties about a consumer's debt. The district court dismissed Fontana's claim, and he now appeals the dismissal. Because the conversation between Fontana's sister and the debt collector was not a "communication" as defined by the statute, we AFFIRM the district court's judgment.

I.

HOVG LLC, which does business as Bay Area Credit Service LLC, operates a debt collection service. In early 2019, a representative of Bay Area Credit Service attempted to call Fontana regarding a consumer debt he allegedly owed. Fontana did not answer, and the representative did not leave a message. Roughly ten minutes later, the representative called Fontana's sister's phone number and had the following conversation:

> Fontana's sister: Hello?
>
> Collector: Hello, good afternoon, my name is Lisa Hayes calling you on a recording line. Am I talking to Zachary Fontana?
>
> Fontana's sister: This is not his number.
>
> Collector: Oh—ah, so do you know him?
>
> Fontana's sister: Who ... where are you from?

Collector: Ok, I'm calling from Bay Area Credit Service. Actually, it's an important personal business matter for him, ok? Can I talk to the spouse?

Fontana's sister: I'm not sure I want to give you his number, so what agency are you with?

Collector: Ok, uh, that is why I'm asking. Can I talk to the spouse so I can discuss about this?

Fontana's sister: This is his sister, and this is not his phone number and I do not live near him, that is why I was going to have him contact you if it was that important.

Collector: It is an important personal business matter for him, ok. I will give you my call back number ma'am. You can provide my number and tell him to call me back.

Fontana's sister: What agency is this with?

Collector: Bay Area Credit Service.

Fontana's sister: Ok, I'll tell him to give you a call.

Collector: Ok, you can see my call back number on your caller ID?

Fontana's sister: Ok, I'll tell him to give you a call.

Collector: Please tell him to call me back on this number.

Fontana's sister: All right.

Fontana's sister contacted Fontana and told him to call the agency back that same day. Fontana, "concerned and harassed by [HOVG's] call to his sister," called a lawyer p.341 immediately. Later that day, he called HOVG back, and HOVG attempted to collect Fontana's medical debt.

In January 2020, Fontana filed a lawsuit in the Western District of Louisiana. HOVG filed a motion to dismiss for failure to state a claim under Federal Rule of Civil Procedure 12(b)(6). The district court dismissed Fontana's claim with prejudice, and Fontana now appeals the dismissal of his lawsuit.

II.

We review a district court's grant of a motion to dismiss *de novo,* "accepting all well-pleaded facts as true and viewing those facts in the light most favorable to the plaintiffs." *Anderson v. Valdez,* 845 F.3d 580, 589 (5th Cir. 2016) (quoting *Dorsey v. Portfolio Equities, Inc.*, 540 F.3d 333, 338 (5th Cir. 2008)). To succeed on a motion to dismiss, the plaintiff's complaint must plead sufficient facts to state a claim for relief if those facts were accepted as true. *Id.* A claim is plausible on its face "when the plaintiff pleads factual content that allows the court to draw the reasonable inference that the defendant is liable for the misconduct alleged." *Id.* (quoting *Ashcroft v. Iqbal,* 556 U.S. 662, 678, 129 S.Ct. 1937, 173 L.Ed.2d 868 (2009)).

The Fair Debt Collection Practices Act provides that debt collectors "may not communicate, in connection with the collection of any debt, with any person other than the consumer" or certain other prescribed parties to the debt "without the prior consent of the consumer." 15 U.S.C. § 1692c(b). Section 1692b provides an exception for debt collectors who communicate with third parties "for the purpose of acquiring location information about the consumer." *Id.* § 1692b. "The term 'location information' means a consumer's place of abode and his telephone number at such place, or his place of employment." *Id.* § 1692a(7).

Even when obtaining location information, a debt collector must follow prescribed protocol. Among other things, the debt collector must "(1) identify himself, state that he is confirming or correcting location information concerning the consumer, and, only if expressly requested, identify his employer; (2) not state that such consumer owes any debt; [and] (3) not communicate with any such person more than once." *Id.* § 1692b(1)-(3).

Fontana alleges that HOVG violated § 1692c(b) when it left a message with his sister and asked her to have Fontana return HOVG's call. According to Fontana, HOVG called Fontana's sister intending to contact Fontana, not merely to confirm his phone number. Rather than explaining that it was looking to update Fontana's contact information, HOVG asked to speak with him. And instead of obtaining location information, HOVG left a message with instructions for Fontana to return its call. Fontana contends that this went beyond the scope of a permissible call for the purposes of obtaining location information. He insists that HOVG communicated with his sister "in connection with the collection of [a] debt" in violation of § 1692c(b).

Before addressing whether that alleged conversation was a permissible call to obtain location information or not, we must first decide a related threshold issue. Because the Act prohibits debt collectors from "communicating" with third parties in connection with the collection of a debt, we need to determine whether the alleged conversation qualifies as a "communication" as defined by the statute.

The Act states that "[t]he term 'communication' means the conveying of information regarding a debt directly or indirectly to any person through any medium." p.342 *Id.* § 1692a(2). Although we have interpreted other definitions in § 1692a, *see, e.g., Hester v. Graham, Bright & Smith, P.C.,* 289 F. App'x 35, 41 (5th Cir. 2008) (deciding whether a party qualifies as a "debt collector" under § 1692a(6)), we have not previously addressed the scope of this definition. However, the text makes it clear that, to be considered a communication, any message or conversation must convey "information regarding a debt." 15 U.S.C. § 1692a(2).

Even taking the pleaded facts in this case in the light most favorable to Fontana, the conversation between HOVG's representative and Fontana's sister did not convey any information regarding a debt, either directly or indirectly. HOVG's representative did not mention Fontana's debt at all and did not directly provide any information about it. Instead, HOVG's representative mentioned "an important personal business matter." That does not even suggest the existence of a debt, much less provide information about it. The closest HOVG's representative came to giving information about a debt was providing the name of the debt collector.

Stating the debt collector's name, however, does not even indirectly convey any information regarding a debt. The smallest piece of information about a debt that a debt collector could potentially convey to a third party is the debt's existence. Therefore, to indirectly convey information regarding a debt, a conversation or message would need to, at the very least, imply that a debt existed. Knowing the name of a debt collector does not imply the existence of a debt. Here, the representative gave the name Bay Area Credit Service. The average consumer likely would not know that Bay Area Credit Service is a debt collection agency. Although the company's name includes the word "Credit," "the word 'credit' refers to a category of financial activities far broader than debt collection" and would not necessarily imply the existence of a debt. *Brown v. Van Ru Credit Corp.*, 804 F.3d 740, 742 (6th Cir. 2015).

Even if the average consumer recognized the company's name and identified it as a debt collector, receiving a phone call from a debt collector does not suggest any information about an underlying debt. Nor does it imply that the person the debt collector wants to speak with owes a debt at all. Debt collectors may call for any number of reasons, including to obtain location information about another individual as contemplated by § 1692b. Or, as the HOVG representative stated here, it could be a matter of personal business that might be separate from the collection of a debt, such as a response to an employment application. Simply knowing the name of the debt collection agency does not imply that a debt exists and so does not indirectly convey information regarding a debt.

Had HOVG provided any additional information beyond its name, the analysis might be different. Even small bits of information can indirectly convey information regarding a debt. For example, in *Hart v. Credit Control, LLC,* the Eleventh Circuit held that a message stating, "This call is from a debt collector" qualified as a "communication" because it "indicated that a debt collector was seeking to speak with [the person] as a part of its efforts to collect a debt." *Hart v. Credit Control, LLC,* 871 F.3d 1255, 1256, 1258 (11th Cir. 2017). By stating the caller's purpose, the debt collector in that case had not directly conveyed any information regarding the underlying debt to be collected. Yet it had indirectly conveyed the information that such a debt existed and implied that the call was in connection with that debt.

p.343 That did not happen in this case. HOVG's representative gave only the agency's name and no other information regarding its business or the true reason for its call. The representative told Fontana's sister that the call was about an "important personal business matter," which, even in the light most favorable to Fontana, does not imply that a debt existed. Without more, simply knowing the name of a debt collector does not indirectly convey information regarding the debt.

We find support for our interpretation in the opinions of our sister circuits that involved similar facts. In one case where a debt collector's voice message included only the name of the debt collector but no information regarding the debt, the Sixth Circuit held that "[t]o convey information regarding a debt, a communication must at a minimum imply the existence of a debt. Otherwise, whatever information is conveyed cannot be understood as 'regarding a debt.'" *Brown,* 804 F.3d at 742. The Seventh and Tenth Circuits have also agreed that "a debt collector's message must at least *imply* the existence of a debt to meet the Act's definition of 'communication.'" *Lavallee v. Med-1 Sols., LLC,* 932 F.3d 1049, 1055 (7th Cir. 2019) (holding that a message that contained only the name of the debt collector was not a "communication" under the Act); *accord Marx v. Gen. Revenue Corp.,* 668 F.3d 1174, 1177 (10th Cir. 2011) (holding that a fax that contained the name of the debt collector and the debtor's account number was not a "communication" because it could not "reasonably be construed to imply a debt").

In this case, HOVG's representative did not convey any information to Fontana's sister that would imply a debt existed. The representative revealed only the name of the debt collector. But conveying information about a debt collector is not the same as conveying information about a debt. Because the conversation between HOVG's representative and Fontana's sister did not even imply the existence of a debt, much less convey information about one, it was not a "communication" as defined by the Act. Fontana has therefore failed to adequately plead facts that suggest a plausible violation of the Fair Debt Collection Practices Act. Accordingly, we do not need to address whether the conversation was made "in connection with the collection of any debt." 15 U.S.C. § 1692c(b).

III.

Because Fontana has failed to plead sufficient facts to establish a violation of the Fair Debt Collection Practices Act, we AFFIRM the district court's judgment.

955 F.3d 453 (2020)

Luis TEJERO, Plaintiff-Appellant,
Michael Jacob Wood; Celetha Chatman; Robert Alan Zimmer, Jr.; Tyler Hickle, Appellants,
v.
PORTFOLIO RECOVERY ASSOCIATES, L.L.C.; Western Surety Company, Defendants-Appellees.

No. 18-50661.

United States Court of Appeals, Fifth Circuit.

Filed April 6, 2020.

Tejero v. Portfolio Recovery Associates, LLC, 955 F. 3d 453 (5th Cir. 2020)

Appeal from the United States District Court for the Western District of Texas.

Ruth A. Kollman, Houston, TX, Robert Zimmer, Esq., Austin, TX, Daniel Brown, Main Street Attorney, L.L.C., Chicago, IL, for Plaintiffs-Appellants.

p.456 Robbie LuAnn Malone, Esq., Jacob Michael Bach, Eugene Xerxes Martin, Esq., Malone Frost Martin, P.L.L.C., Dallas, TX, for Defendants-Appellees.

Before ELROD, WILLETT, and OLDHAM, Circuit Judges.

p.455 ANDREW S. OLDHAM, Circuit Judge:

Luis Tejero sued Portfolio Recovery Associates, L.L.C. under the federal Fair Debt Collection Practices Act and a parallel state law. The parties eventually reached a settlement that forgave Tejero's debt and awarded him $1,000 in damages. As favorable as that result was to the plaintiff, the district court determined that Tejero's attorneys did not settle his lawsuit quickly enough. So the district court sanctioned them. That was an abuse of discretion, so we reverse it. But we disagree with Tejero that the district court is biased against him, so we affirm the denial of his recusal motion.

I.

A.

Portfolio Recovery attempted to recover from Tejero a credit-card debt of approximately $2,100. As a debt collector in Texas, Portfolio Recovery was obligated to comply with the federal Fair Debt Collection Practices Act ("FDCPA") and the Texas Debt Collection Act ("Texas Act"). The former makes it unlawful for a debt collector to "use any false, deceptive, or misleading representation or means in connection with the collection of any debt." 15 U.S.C. § 1692e. That prohibition includes, among other things, communicating "credit information which is known or which should be known to be false, including the failure to communicate that a disputed debt is disputed." *Id.* § 1692e(8). The Texas Act contains a parallel prohibition. *See* TEX. FIN. CODE §§ 392.202(a), 392.301(a)(3).

Tejero says he disputed his credit-card debt in January 2016. Through his attorneys, Tejero sent the following fax to Portfolio Recovery:

> Dear Sir or Madam:
>
> I am writing to you regarding the account referenced above. I refuse to pay this debt.
>
> My monthly expenses exceed my monthly income; as such there is no reason for you to continue contacting me, and the amount you are reporting is not accurate either. If my circumstances should change I will be in touch.
>
> Sincerely,
>
> Luis Tejero

Despite this letter, Portfolio Recovery subsequently informed a consumer agency of the debt without noting that Tejero disputed it.

In June 2016, Tejero sued Portfolio Recovery for violating the FDCPA and the Texas Act. In September of that year, the district court ordered the parties to exchange settlement offers by October 19, 2016. Portfolio Recovery offered to settle the case for $1,101, plus reasonable attorney's fees and costs.[1] Tejero's lawyers neither submitted a written offer nor responded to Portfolio Recovery's offer. Later, during discovery, Tejero acknowledged that $1,000 "would make [him] whole" and conclude the case.

Once discovery ended, the parties cross-moved for summary judgment. The district p.457 court denied Tejero's motion. The district court identified a triable issue regarding whether Tejero validly disputed his credit-card debt in his January 2016 fax to Portfolio Recovery.

On Portfolio Recovery's motion, the district court found no competent evidence to support Tejero's claims for actual damages. Because actual damages are required to state a claim under the Texas Act, the court dismissed that claim. But the court denied the motion with respect to the FDCPA claim. The district court again identified a triable issue regarding whether Tejero "actually disputed the [d]ebt" in the January 2016 letter.

Following these rulings, the parties settled and filed a notice of settlement with the court. Portfolio Recovery agreed to pay Tejero $1,000 and to forgive the underlying debt. The parties left the district court to decide the issue of attorney's fees and costs.

B.

Tejero moved for attorney's fees and costs, seeking a total of $14,731.80. Portfolio Recovery moved to sanction Tejero's lawyers under 28 U.S.C. § 1927 and 15 U.S.C. § 1692k(a)(3), and it requested $13,950.38 in attorney's fees and costs.

Before ruling, Judge Sparks wrote to the disciplinary committee for the Western District of Texas. He listed the FDCPA cases in which Tejero's attorneys had participated. And he accused the lawyers of various ethics violations, including their purported participation in "a scheme to force settlements from debt collectors by abusing the FDCPA."

Then, in April 2018, the district court declined to award Tejero his attorney's fees and costs. Instead, it sanctioned Tejero's attorneys (the "Attorney-Appellants") under 15 U.S.C. § 1692k(a)(3) and Federal Rule of Civil Procedure 11(c), and ordered that they pay Portfolio Recovery's attorney's fees and costs. The court reasoned that Tejero's attorneys acted in bad faith when they: (1) failed to comply with the September 2016 settlement-offer order; (2) continued to litigate the case even after receiving an offer that would make Tejero whole; and (3) drafted the January 2016 debt letter in a manner that would cause the debt collector not to realize that the debt was disputed, so that counsel could engage in a "scheme" to "force settlements from debt collectors by abusing the FDCPA."

C.

Following the sanctions order, Tejero moved to recuse Judge Sparks under 28 U.S.C. §§ 144 and 455. Tejero argued that the judge had "personal knowledge of disputed evidentiary facts" (a disqualifying factor under §§ 144 and 455(b)(1)) because the judge's disciplinary referral made mention of FDCPA lawsuits in which Tejero's attorneys had relied on an identically worded dispute letter. Tejero and his attorneys also said the district court evidenced partiality requiring recusal under § 455(a) by accusing Tejero's counsel of orchestrating a "scheme" to "abuse" the FDCPA.

In a May 2018 order, Judge Ezra (to whom the recusal issue had been assigned) denied Tejero's motion. He found that Judge Sparks was not in possession of extrajudicial knowledge because the disciplinary letter and the sanctions order were both based on information gathered in Judge Sparks's judicial capacity. And, Judge Ezra concluded, Judge Sparks's referrals and rulings did not show sufficient antagonism for a reasonable person to harbor doubts about the judge's impartiality. Tejero and his lawyers timely appealed.

p.458 II.

We first consider the district court's sanctions orders. Our review is for abuse of discretion. *See LSR Consulting, LLC v. Wells Fargo Bank, N.A.*, 835 F.3d 530, 535 (5th Cir. 2016) (standard of review for § 1692k(a)(3) attorney's fee awards); *Snow Ingredients, Inc. v. SnoWizard, Inc.*, 833 F.3d 512, 527 (5th Cir. 2016) (standard of review for Rule 11 sanctions). We find it.

A.

We start with Rule 11, and the district court's procedural misstep: A court may not award attorney's fees *sua sponte* under Rule 11, as it did here. There must first be a Rule 11 motion, or an order to show cause under Rule 11(c)(3). *Brunig v. Clark*, 560 F.3d 292, 298 (5th Cir. 2009). If preserved, this procedural error would have justified reversal. *See Marlin v. Moody Nat'l Bank, N.A.*, 533 F.3d 374, 378-79 (5th Cir. 2008). But Tejero's attorneys raised this point for the first time in their reply brief on appeal, and therefore forfeited the argument. *See United States ex rel. Drummond v. BestCare Lab. Servs., L.L.C.*, 950 F.3d 277, 284 (5th Cir. 2020). We must instead reach the merits.

Rule 11 requires, in relevant part, that "[e]very pleading, written motion, and other paper must be signed by at least one attorney of record in the attorney's name." FED. R. CIV. P. 11(a). The signature required by Rule 11(a) "certifies that to the best of the person's knowledge, information, and belief, formed after an inquiry reasonable under the circumstances," the paper is not sanctionable under Rule 11(b). It follows from the text of Rule 11 that it applies *only* where a person files a paper. *See Cooter & Gell v. Hartmarx Corp.*, 496 U.S. 384, 393, 110 S.Ct. 2447, 110 L.Ed.2d 359 (1990) (Rule 11 "deter[s] baseless *filings* in district court" (emphasis added)); *In re Case*, 937 F.2d 1014, 1022 (5th Cir. 1991) (Rule 11 "ties sanctions to an attorney's signature on a particular pleading or document which is filed with the court"). Rule 11 does not extend to "abusive tactics in litigation in respects other than the signing of papers." *Thomas v. Capital Sec. Servs., Inc.*, 836 F.2d 866, 875 (5th Cir. 1988) (en banc); *see also Chambers v. NASCO, Inc.*, 501 U.S. 32, 41, 111 S.Ct. 2123, 115 L.Ed.2d 27 (1991). That's why a district court should "evaluate[] an attorney's conduct at the time a pleading, motion, or other paper is signed." *Thomas*, 836 F.2d at 874 (quotation omitted).

The district court proffered three reasons for sanctioning the Attorney-Appellants under Rule 11: (1) they failed to make or respond to a settlement offer, in violation of a scheduling order; (2) they continued to litigate even after Tejero indicated that the amount offered by Portfolio Recovery would have made him whole; and (3) the debt letter to Portfolio Recovery was part of a fraudulent scheme to abuse the FDCPA. None is tied to a filing. All are meritless.

1.

The failure to engage in settlement discussions relates to an attorney's litigation tactics, rather than a filing subject to Rule 11. We have previously held that the violation of a discovery order did not justify Rule 11 sanctions because the attorney "had signed no objectionable court papers." *Nat. Gas Pipeline Co. of Am. v. Energy Gathering, Inc.*, 2 F.3d 1397, 1410 (5th Cir. 1993). The same rationale applies to an attorney's violation of an order to exchange settlement offers.

Additionally, the Fifth Circuit and a number of our sister circuits have held that courts do not have the power to compel parties to make settlement offers, and p.459 that the failure to make an offer is not sanctionable. *See Dawson v. United States*, 68 F.3d 886, 897 (5th Cir. 1995) (collecting cases from other circuits). Despite this holding, it is our understanding that it has become common within the Western District of Texas for judges to require parties to exchange settlement offers. *See* Oral Argument at 13:13-28. We take this opportunity to reiterate the rule that has (or at least should have) applied in our Circuit for the last twenty-five years: "[I]f a party is forced to make a settlement offer because of the threat of sanctions, and the offer is accepted, a settlement has been achieved through coercion. Such a result cannot be tolerated." *Dawson*, 68 F.3d at 897.

Here, because the district court lacked the power to order Tejero to make a settlement offer, it was improper to sanction his attorneys for their failure to abide by that order.

2.

The district court's second reason for leveling sanctions relies on Tejero's decision to continue litigating after receiving a $1,101 settlement offer. Again, the decision to reject a settlement offer is not a court filing subject to Rule 11(b). Litigation conduct can trigger sanctions under other statutes. *See, e.g.*, 28 U.S.C. § 1927 (providing for counsel's liability for "multipl[ying] the proceedings in any case unreasonably and vexatiously"); *Thomas*, 836 F.2d at 875. But the district court explicitly ruled out the award of § 1927 sanctions in its April 2018 order.

Perhaps the district court meant to say that the Attorney-Appellants' decision to file a summary judgment motion after discovery and settlement negotiations violated Rule 11. But the district court did not find that the motion was frivolous, which would have been a violation of Rule 11(b)(2). And it did not determine that the attorneys knew or ought to have known that factual contentions or denials in the motion were unsupported by the evidence, in violation of Rule 11(b)(3) and (4). To the contrary, the district court *denied* Portfolio Recovery's cross-motion for summary judgment on the FDCPA claim—which indicates Tejero's position was far from frivolous. In fact, it was so substantial that the district court thought it warranted a trial.

That leaves just one other basis for Rule 11 sanctions: the prohibition against filing motions that are "presented for any improper purpose, such as to harass, cause unnecessary delay, or needlessly increase the cost of litigation." FED. R. CIV. P. 11(b)(1). It's possible that the district court considered the summary judgment motion "improper" because Tejero filed that motion rather than accept the $1,101 settlement offer from Portfolio Recovery, thereby driving up the parties' costs.

If that was the reasoning of the district court, it was clearly wrong. Portfolio Recovery made a Rule 68 offer for $1,101 in October 2016. The deposition at which Tejero indicated that he'd accept $1,000 took place in March 2017. By that time, the $1,101 offer had been withdrawn for over four months. *See* FED R. CIV. P. 68(a)-(b) (providing that an opposing party has fourteen days to accept an offer of judgment; otherwise, the offer is "considered withdrawn"). There is no indication that another offer was on the table when Tejero signed and filed his motion for summary judgment. And that's the only relevant time period for the Rule 11 inquiry. *See Thomas*, 836 F.2d at 874.

Nor is it clear that $1,101 would have made Tejero whole. At the time Portfolio Recovery made the offer, it claimed Tejero's debt was $2,100. So the Rule 68 offer would have covered just over one half of p.460 the purported debt. Moreover, at the time the offer was made—indeed, also at the time the summary judgment motions were filed—Tejero still had a live claim under the Texas Act. And that latter claim carried the potential for exemplary damages.

It's of no moment that Tejero later lost the Texas Act claim. All that matters is that he had a non-frivolous basis to bring it. Nor does it matter that Tejero himself did not understand all of this when answering questions in his deposition. All that matters is that his attorneys did. Under those circumstances, it was entirely reasonable (if risky) for Tejero's attorneys to roll the dice with a motion for summary judgment. *See Nat'l Ass'n of Gov't Emps., Inc. v. Nat'l Fed'n of Fed. Emps.*, 844 F.2d 216, 223 (5th Cir. 1988) ("Failure to compromise a case, ... even pursuant to terms suggested by the court, does not constitute grounds for imposing sanctions...."). In all events, we struggle to think of any instance when the decision to file a summary judgment motion rather than settle would constitute sanctionable conduct.

3.

The district court's final ground for imposing Rule 11 sanctions was the debt-dispute letter. The court considered the letter intentionally unclear—a "bad faith" attempt to use "ambiguously worded" language to "expose[] debt collectors to [FDCPA] liability." The letter also is not a filing or other paper subject to Rule 11. But Tejero incorporated it into his complaint. So at last we're talking about a filing to which Rule 11 *could* apply. Even so, there is no evidence that Tejero filed his complaint in "bad faith."

The phrase "bad faith" does not appear in the Rule. And the district court did not explain precisely which part of Rule 11 it considered violated. The court might have thought that the factual contentions in the letter—the existence of a dispute over the debt—did not "have evidentiary support." FED. R. CIV. P. 11(b)(3). But the district court found elsewhere that an issue of fact "exist[ed] on whether Plaintiff actually disputed the Debt." So lack of evidentiary foundation cannot be the problem here.

A claim that survives summary judgment likewise cannot be frivolous. *See* FED. R. CIV. P. 11(b)(2). The district court itself acknowledged that the dispute letter "expose[d] debt collectors to liability." If a claim has merit, it cannot be frivolous. *See Nat'l Ass'n of Gov't Emps.*, 844 F.2d at 222-23; *cf. Dawson*, 68 F.3d at 896 ("[A] district court's disagreement with the merits of a position ... cannot serve as the basis for sanctions.").

It's also possible the district court thought the claims were brought for an improper purpose—to drum up business for the lawyers and extract attorney's fees from unsuspecting debt collectors. But "[w]hen a complaint is well grounded in fact and warranted by existing law, only under unusual circumstances should the filing of papers constitute sanctionable conduct." *FDIC v. Calhoun*, 34 F.3d 1291, 1300 (5th Cir. 1994) (quotation omitted). And the inquiry into whether an improper purpose or unusual circumstances existed should be based on the objective reasonableness of the filing, not subjective suspicion. *Nat'l Ass'n of Gov't Emps.*, 844 F.2d at 224 ("[P]urely subjective elements should not be reintroduced into the determination concerning 'improper purpose.'"); *see also Snow Ingredients*, 833 F.3d at 528 ("An attorney's conduct is judged under each standard with an objective, not a subjective, standard of reasonableness.").

Here, the district court found the Attorney-Appellants "intentionally" drafted an unclear dispute letter. The relevant part of p.461 the letter reads: "My monthly expenses exceed my monthly income ... and the amount you are reporting is not accurate either." Aside from invoking the word "dispute," we struggle to see how a debtor could dispute a debt more clearly than by writing, "the amount you are reporting is not accurate."

We are not alone on this issue. The Seventh Circuit, and every district court within it to have considered the matter, has concluded that the phrase "the amount reported is not accurate" unambiguously and clearly "dispute[s]" a debt—"[t]here is simply no other way to interpret this language." *Evans v. Portfolio Recovery Assocs. LLC*, 889 F.3d 337, 346 (7th Cir. 2018); *see also ibid.* (listing the district courts that "arrived at the same conclusion"). Another judge within the Western District of Texas agreed, seven months before Judge Sparks sanctioned Tejero's attorneys. *See Jones v. Portfolio Recovery Assocs., LLC*, No. 1:16-cv-572-RP, 2017 WL 7052288, at *4 (W.D. Tex. Aug. 16, 2017).

Granted, the Rule 11 inquiry focuses on the attorney's purpose at the time of the filing. *Snow Ingredients*, 833 F.3d at 528 ("Reasonableness is reviewed according to the 'snapshot' rule, focusing upon the instant the attorney affixes his signature to the document." (quotation omitted)). At the time the Tejero complaint was filed, none of these cases had been decided. But they demonstrate that other courts—and hence other readers, like debt collectors—understand the letter to dispute a debt. And, if anything, the fact no court had found the letter insufficient to dispute a debt should have made the district court here especially reluctant to condemn it.

The district court simply had no basis to ignore the language of the letter and instead infer subjective bad faith based on its view of the attorneys' "inten[t]." Even with the high degree of deference afforded a district court's factual findings, that's reversible error. *Cf. id.* at 529 ("[M]isapplication of Rule 11 can chill counsel's enthusiasm and stifle the creativity of litigants in purs[u]ing novel factual or legal theories, contrary to the intent of its framers." (quotation omitted)).

B.

We now turn to the district court's fee award to Portfolio Recovery under 15 U.S.C. § 1692k(a)(3). That subsection permits a court to "award to the defendant attorney's fees" "[o]n a finding ... that an action under this section was brought in bad faith and for the purpose of harassment." 15 U.S.C. § 1692k(a)(3). We have already expressed disagreement with the court's finding of bad faith. That's a sufficient reason to reverse the § 1692k(a)(3) fee award. But there's another problem: The district court ordered Tejero's *lawyers* to pay it. Section 1692k(a)(3) does not stretch that far.

The American Rule against awarding costs and fees to the prevailing party was well-established by 1796, when the Supreme Court described it as the "general practice of the United States." *Arcambel v. Wiseman*, 3 U.S. (3 Dall.) 306, 306, 1 L.Ed. 613 (1796). Because of the common-law origins of the rule, statutes that alter it "are to be read with a presumption favoring the retention of long-established and familiar legal principles," *Baker Botts L.L.P. v. ASARCO LLC*, 576 U.S. 121, 135 S. Ct. 2158, 2164, 192 L.Ed.2d 208 (2015) (quotation omitted). That's why we "analyze[] a statute's specificity and explicitness in the context of a particular fee request. That a statute is sufficiently specific and explicit to authorize one type of fee award does not make it sufficiently specific and explicit to authorize p.462 another type of fee award." *Gahagan v. U.S. Citizenship & Immigration Servs.*, 911 F.3d 298, 300 (5th Cir. 2018), *cert. denied*, ___ U.S. ___, 140 S. Ct. 449, 205 L.Ed.2d 252 (2019) (mem.).

Accordingly, when a statute awards fees to one party, but does not identify from whom they may be collected, we're reluctant to allow recovery from the other party's counsel. *See, e.g., Monk v. Roadway Express, Inc.*, 599 F.2d 1378, 1383 (5th Cir. 1979) (refusing to read the attorney's fees provisions in 42 U.S.C. §§ 1988 and 2000e-5(k) to "authorize the imposition of attorneys' fees against an unsuccessful party's attorneys"), *aff'd in relevant part sub nom. Roadway Express, Inc. v. Piper,* 447 U.S. 752, 100 S.Ct. 2455, 65 L.Ed.2d 488 (1980); *accord Hyde v. Midland Credit Mgmt., Inc.,* 567 F.3d 1137, 1140-41 (9th Cir. 2009) (noting that "there is a general presumption that an attorney is generally not liable for fees unless that prospect is spelled out," and holding that attorneys are not liable under the FDCPA (quotation omitted)).

Section 1692k(a)(3) says only that "the court may award to the defendant attorney's fees...." It is silent as to whether a plaintiff's attorney may be ordered to pay them. Unlike 28 U.S.C. § 1927 or Rule 11, there is no language that specifically and explicitly permits the courts to depart from the common law and make fee awards against lawyers.[2] Consistent with our interpretation of 42 U.S.C. §§ 1988 and 2000e-5(k) in *Monk,* we hold that 15 U.S.C. § 1692k(a)(3) permits fee awards only against parties, not against their counsel. *Cf. Gahagan,* 911 F.3d at 303 ("The Supreme Court has repeatedly instructed us to apply consistent interpretations to federal fee-shifting statutes.").

The district court was wrong to rely on § 1692k(a)(3) as a basis for sanctioning Tejero's counsel.

C.

While we agree with Tejero that the district court erred in sanctioning his lawyers, we are not prepared to order Portfolio Recovery to pay Tejero's fees and costs. Tejero premised his request on 15 U.S.C. § 1692k(a)(3). That section required Tejero to show that he brought "a[] successful action to enforce [FDCPA] liability." 15 U.S.C. § 1692k(a)(3). Our circuit has not previously decided whether a private settlement renders the action "successful" under § 1692k(a)(3). True, private settlements generally do not suffice for fee-shifting statutes like 42 U.S.C. § 1988(b). *See, e.g., Buckhannon Bd. & Care Home, Inc. v. W. Va. Dep't of Health & Human Res.,* 532 U.S. 598, 605, 121 S.Ct. 1835, 149 L.Ed.2d 855 (2001); *Davis v. Abbott,* 781 F.3d 207, 214 (5th Cir. 2015). But there are textual differences between the FDCPA and § 1988(b). And the district court did not have an opportunity to evaluate them because it erroneously rejected Tejero's fee application on the basis of his purportedly sanctionable conduct. Now that we have corrected that mistake, we leave for the district court's consideration in the first instance the important question of whether Tejero is entitled to fees under the FDCPA. *See Ultra Petroleum Corp. v.* p.463 *Ad Hoc Comm. of Unsecured Creditors of Ultra Res., Inc.* (*In re Ultra Petroleum Corp.*), 943 F.3d 758, 766 (5th Cir. 2019) ("[W]e are a court of review, not of first view." (quotation omitted)).

III.

Finally, Tejero appeals the denial of his recusal motion. Again, our review is for abuse of discretion. *See Henderson v. Dep't of Pub. Safety & Corr.,* 901 F.2d 1288, 1296 (5th Cir. 1990). This time, we don't find it.

Tejero's motion to recuse Judge Sparks relied on 28 U.S.C. §§ 144 and 455. These provisions require recusal if a judge "has a personal bias" concerning a party,

28 U.S.C. §§ 144, 455(b)(1), if "his impartiality might reasonably be questioned," *id.* § 455(a), or if he has "personal knowledge of disputed evidentiary facts concerning the proceeding," *id.* § 455(b)(1).

Sections 144 and 455(b)(1) are governed by the same principles. *Liteky v. United States,* 510 U.S. 540, 548-51, 114 S.Ct. 1147, 127 L.Ed.2d 474 (1994). And because these provisions use the word "party," "[b]ias for or against an attorney, who is not a party, is not enough to require disqualification unless it can also be shown that such a controversy would demonstrate a bias for or against the party itself." *Henderson,* 901 F.2d at 1296. "In order for bias against an attorney to require disqualification of the trial judge, it must be of a continuing and personal nature and not simply bias against the attorney or in favor of another attorney because of his conduct." *Ibid.*

Additionally, the Supreme Court has directed us to consider whether the judge's views are "extrajudicial." *Liteky,* 510 U.S. at 551, 114 S.Ct. 1147. An opinion is not extrajudicial if it was "formed by the judge on the basis of facts introduced or events occurring in the course of the current proceedings, or of prior proceedings." *Id.* at 555, 114 S.Ct. 1147. Non-extrajudicial facts "do not constitute a basis for a bias or partiality motion unless they display a deep-seated favoritism or antagonism that would make fair judgment impossible." *Ibid.* Even the presence of extrajudicial facts, without something more, does not suffice to show bias. *Id.* at 554, 114 S.Ct. 1147.

Finally, when applying § 455(a), a court must determine "whether a reasonable and objective person, knowing all of the facts, would harbor doubts concerning the judge's impartiality." *United States v. Jordan,* 49 F.3d 152, 155 (5th Cir. 1995). Whether the judge is in possession of extrajudicial facts is also relevant to recusal motions under this subsection. *Liteky,* 510 U.S. at 554, 114 S.Ct. 1147.

A.

First, Judge Sparks's alleged bias was not based on extrajudicial knowledge. The Attorney-Appellants make much of the fact that the judge looked beyond the record in *Tejero.* They decry the judge's mention of other FDCPA cases in which the attorneys acted as plaintiff's counsel. But Judge Sparks presided over three of the cases mentioned in the sanctions order and disciplinary referral—*Ozmun v. Portfolio Recovery Assocs., LLC,* No. 1:16-cv-940 (W.D. Tex.); *Palomo v. Portfolio Recovery Assocs., LLC,* No. 1:16-cv-628 (W.D. Tex.); and *Jones v. Midland Funding, LLC.,* No. 1:16-cv-592 (W.D. Tex.). His knowledge of the facts of those cases was not extrajudicial. *See United States v. Reagan,* 725 F.3d 471, 491 (5th Cir. 2013) (holding that information about a party gained from an unrelated trial was not extrajudicial).

The Attorney-Appellants also complain that Judge Sparks included other cases— p.464 including some over which he did not preside—in his letter to the disciplinary committee. But the list took no special effort to compile: It was simply a record generated by the ECF system of every case before the Western District of Texas in which Tejero attorney Ms. Chatman had entered an appearance. And it is evident from the "-SS" suffix to the case numbers that Judge Sparks was assigned to half of them. Again, information about those cases is not extrajudicial. As for the other half, because Judge Sparks's method of compiling the list of cases was evenhanded and well within the normal day-to-day activities of a judge presiding over a similar case, we do not think their inclusion in the list to be problematic. *See ibid.*

("[F]acts learned by a judge in his or her judicial capacity regarding the parties before the court cannot be the basis for disqualification." (quotation omitted)).

The Attorney-Appellants' gripe is not just that Judge Sparks listed these cases, but that he appears to have reviewed the docket of each case (including cases over which he did not preside) to determine whether they were brought under the FDCPA with a similar dispute letter. For that, the Attorney-Appellants have only themselves to blame. In their request for fees, Tejero's attorneys identified a number of other FDCPA cases in which they had participated. The attorneys provided the case names in the hope that the judge would review those cases and conclude that the lawyers' experience justified their billing rates. Judge Sparks did just that—he reviewed the dockets of the Attorney-Appellants' FDCPA cases. Evidently, they do not like what he found. But that does not give the Attorney-Appellants grounds to allege bias.

B.

Given that Judge Sparks did not possess extrajudicial knowledge of Tejero or his attorneys, Tejero bears the burden of showing that the judge "display[ed] a deep-seated favoritism or antagonism that would make fair judgment impossible." *Liteky,* 510 U.S. at 555, 114 S.Ct. 1147. The judge did not. Judge Sparks's categorization of Tejero's claims as part of a "scheme" certainly reveals a degree of distaste towards the attorneys and their frequent resort to claims premised on statutory damages. But "expressions of impatience, dissatisfaction, annoyance, and even anger, that are within the bounds of what imperfect men and women ... sometimes display," do not establish bias. *Id.* at 555-56, 114 S.Ct. 1147.

The judge's ire was clearly directed at Tejero's lawyers, not their client: His April 2018 order and the referral letter set out concerns solely about the *lawyers'* supposedly unprofessional behavior, and it is the lawyers whom he chose to sanction. This reaction stems from the lawyers' conduct, rather than from bias of "a continuing and personal nature," and does not require recusal. *Henderson,* 901 F.2d at 1296.

Further, there is no indication that Judge Sparks harbors a deep-seated antagonism towards Tejero that would make fair judgment impossible. To the contrary, the judge expressed some concern that Tejero was an "unsophisticated debtor[]" who had not been told about the offer of settlement. Again, the record does not reveal improper animus towards Tejero himself.

For these reasons, we affirm Judge Ezra's finding that a "reasonable person, knowing all of the facts and circumstances surrounding this case, would [not] question Judge Sparks's impartiality or fairness to the parties."

***

p.465 The judgment of the district court is REVERSED in part, AFFIRMED in part, and REMANDED for further proceedings.

[1] "There are at least eleven competing terms we could use instead of '[attorney's fees].'" *Gahagan v. U.S. Citizenship & Immigration Servs.,* 911 F.3d 298, 300

n.1 (5th Cir. 2018), *cert. denied,* ___ U.S. ___, 140 S. Ct. 449, 205 L.Ed.2d 252 (2019) (mem.). In keeping with the statute we're interpreting, we'll use the terms "attorney's fee" or "attorney's fees." *See* 15 U.S.C. § 1692k(a)(3) (using both "attorney's fee" and "attorney's fees").

[2] Section 1927 reads:

Any *attorney* or other person admitted to conduct cases in any court of the United States or any Territory thereof who so multiplies the proceedings in any case unreasonably and vexatiously may be required by the court to satisfy *personally* the excess costs, expenses, and attorneys' fees reasonably incurred because of such conduct.

28 U.S.C. § 1927 (emphases added). And Rule 11 permits a court to "impose an appropriate sanction on any attorney, law firm, or party that violated the rule or is responsible for the violation." FED. R. CIV. P. 11(c)(1).

946 F.3d 762 (2020)

Nina FLECHA, on behalf of herself and all others similarly situated, Plaintiff-Appellee,
v.
MEDICREDIT, INCORPORATED; Fidelity and Deposit Company of Maryland, Defendants-Appellants.

No. 18-50551.

United States Court of Appeals, Fifth Circuit.

FILED January 8, 2020.

Flecha v. Medicredit, Inc., 946 F. 3d 762 (5th Cir. 2020)

Appeal from the United States District Court for the Western District of Texas.

Robert Zimmer, Esq., Austin, TX, Michael Jacob Wood, Community Lawyers, L.L.C., Chicago, IL, for Plaintiff-Appellee.

Maura Kathleen Monaghan, Esq., Senior Litigating Attorney, Jacob W. Stahl, Harold W. Williford, Debevoise & Plimpton, L.L.P., New York, NY, Tara Moriarty Kumpf, Esq., Olgetree, Deakins, Nash, Smoak & Stewart, P.C., Austin, TX, Jacob Ward Sparks, Esq., Spencer Fane, L.L.P., Plano, TX, for MEDICREDIT, INCORPORATED Defendant-Appellant.

Scott James Dickenson, Spencer Fane, L.L.P., Saint Louis, MO, Tara Moriarty Kumpf, Esq., Olgetree, Deakins, Nash, Smoak & Stewart, P.C., Austin, TX, Jacob W. Stahl, Harold W. Williford, Debevoise & Plimpton, L.L.P., New York, NY, for FIDELITY AND DEPOSIT COMPANY OF MARYLAND Defendant-Appellant.

Before JONES, HO, and OLDHAM, Circuit Judges.

p.764 JAMES C. HO, Circuit Judge:

As the Supreme Court has repeatedly reminded us, "the class action is 'an exception to the usual rule that litigation is conducted by and on behalf of the individual named parties only.'" *Wal-Mart Stores, Inc. v. Dukes,* 564 U.S. 338, 348, 131 S.Ct. 2541, 180 L.Ed.2d 374 (2011) (quoting *Califano v. Yamasaki,* 442 U.S. 682, 700-1, 99 S.Ct. 2545, 61 L.Ed.2d 176 (1979)). As Rule 23 of the Federal Rules of Civil Procedure makes clear, multiple conditions must be met before a district court may certify a class. The putative class certified here failed to satisfy several of those conditions, including commonality, typicality, and predominance. In addition, the putative class presents substantial questions of Article III standing. Accordingly, p.765 we reverse the class certification order and remand for further proceedings.

I.

Nina Flecha neglected to pay for the medical care she received from Seton Medical Center Hays. To help Seton collect on that debt, Medicredit, Inc., a voluntary debt collection service provider, sent Flecha a series of collection letters—including the one at the heart of this suit. That letter stated:

> Your seriously delinquent Seton Medical Center Hays account remains unpaid despite past requests for payment.
>
> At this time, a determination must be made with our client as to the disposition of your account. Your failure to cooperate in satisfying this debt indicates voluntary resolution is doubtful. However, if it is now your desire to clear your account, you need to promptly remit the balance in full.

The letter concluded: "To discuss payment arrangements call our office."

Flecha never contacted Medicredit. But she did contact Seton and ask if she was eligible for any debt repayment programs. Seton informed her that she could enter into a payment plan if she made an upfront payment—one Flecha could not afford. Over the course of these conversations, Flecha claims she was given the impression that Seton would sue her to collect her debt.

In response to both the letter from Medicredit and her subsequent conversations with Seton, Flecha brought this suit under the Fair Debt Collection Practices Act (FDCPA) against Medicredit (as well as its surety bondholder, Fidelity and Deposit Company of Maryland). Flecha alleged that Medicredit's letter made a false threat of legal action against her, in violation of the FDCPA, because Seton in fact never intended to sue her over her unpaid medical debt.

Flecha sought class certification. She argued that everyone who received the same letter from Medicredit was likewise falsely threatened with legal action that Seton never actually intended to bring, and that everyone was accordingly entitled to statutory damages under the FDCPA. Both Flecha and Medicredit also filed cross-motions for summary judgment.

The district court denied summary judgment. It concluded that questions of fact remained about (1) whether an unsophisticated consumer would construe the Medicredit letter to threaten legal action, and (2) whether Seton intended to take legal action against Flecha.

After disposing of the summary judgment motions, the district court then granted Flecha's motion for class certification and appointed her class representative. The court defined the class as all Texans who had received the same letter from Medicredit that Flecha received:

> [A]ll persons in Texas from whom Medicredit attempted to collect and who received a form collection letter from Medicredit containing these statements:
>
> Your seriously delinquent Seton Medical Center Hays account remains unpaid despite past requests for payment.
>
> At this time, a determination must be made with our client as to the disposition of your account. Your failure to cooperate in satisfying this debt indicates voluntary resolution is doubtful. However, if it is now your desire to clear your account, you need to promptly remit the balance in full.

Flecha estimates that at least 7,650 people in Texas received such a letter.

We granted Medicredit's motion for leave to appeal the class certification order under Rule 23(f).

p.766 II.

In a Rule 23(f) class certification appeal, our analysis must "begin[], of course, with the elements of the underlying cause of action." *Erica P. John Fund, Inc. v. Halliburton Co.,* 563 U.S. 804, 809, 131 S.Ct. 2179, 180 L.Ed.2d 24 (2011). After all, "a court must understand the claims, defenses, relevant facts, and applicable substantive law in order to make a meaningful determination of the certification issues." *Castano v. American Tobacco Co.,* 84 F.3d 734, 744 (5th Cir. 1996). Absent such knowledge, it will be "impossible" for a court to determine, *inter alia,* (1) whether the issues for trial will be individualized or common to all putative class members, (2) whether the issues presented by the class representative will be typical of class members, and (3) whether the common issues at trial will predominate over individualized issues. *Id.* at 745.

The FDCPA prohibits the use of "false, deceptive, or misleading representation[s] or means in connection with the collection of any debt." 15 U.S.C. § 1692e. As relevant here, it specifically forbids debt collectors from making a "threat to take any action ... *that is not intended to be taken.*" 15 U.S.C. § 1692e(5) (emphasis added).

So the question in such suits is not only whether a consumer would perceive a particular statement as threatening legal action, but also whether such a statement is in fact true—that is, whether the creditor does indeed intend to bring suit against the debtor. This element is significant to the class certification question because some creditors may not have a uniform litigation policy when it comes to all debtors. They may instead decide whether to bring suit based on individualized circumstances. And there is no false statement under the FDCPA (or as a matter of common sense) if the threat to bring suit is in fact sincere and true.

III.

"We review class-certification decisions for abuse of discretion.... We review *de novo,* however, whether the district court applied the correct legal standards in determining whether to certify the class." *Gene & Gene LLC v. BioPay LLC,* 541 F.3d 318, 325 (5th Cir. 2008) (citing *Allison v. Citgo Petroleum Corp.,* 151 F.3d 402, 408 (5th Cir. 1998)).

To be certified by a district court, the putative class must first satisfy all four threshold conditions of Rule 23(a)—namely, that "(1) the class is so numerous that joinder of all members is impracticable; (2) there are questions of law or fact common to the class; (3) the claims or defenses of the representative parties are typical of the claims or defenses of the class; and (4) the representative parties will fairly and adequately protect the interests of the class"—conditions commonly known as "numerosity, commonality, typicality, and adequacy of representation." FED. R. CIV. P. 23(a); *Gen. Tel. Co. of the Nw., Inc. v. EEOC,* 446 U.S. 318, 330, 100 S.Ct. 1698, 64 L.Ed.2d 319 (1980).

In addition, Flecha pursued a class under Rule 23(b)(3), which additionally requires "that the questions of law or fact common to class members predominate over any questions affecting only individual members, and that a class action is superior to other available methods for fairly and efficiently adjudicating the controversy" —conditions commonly known as "predominance and superiority." FED. R. CIV. P. 23(b)(3); *Amchem Products, Inc. v. Windsor,* 521 U.S. 591, 615, 117 S.Ct. 2231, 138 L.Ed.2d 689 (1997).

Courts must enforce the requirements of Rule 23 vigorously. As the Supreme Court has made clear, the conditions of Rule 23 "do not set forth a mere pleading standard. A party seeking class p.767 certification must *affirmatively demonstrate* his compliance with the Rule—that is, he must be prepared to prove that there are *in fact* sufficiently numerous parties, common questions of law or fact, etc." *Dukes,* 564 U.S. at 350, 131 S.Ct. 2541 (first emphasis added).

On appeal, Medicredit argues that Flecha failed to meet this exacting standard. It contends that the putative class fails the commonality and typicality requirements of Rule 23(a) as well as the predominance requirement of Rule 23(b)(3). We agree.

To establish liability under the FDCPA, the class must prove not only that Medicredit's letter threatened legal action, but that it did so despite the fact that Seton did not intend to pursue legal action. Yet Flecha failed to provide *any* evidence concerning Seton's intent to sue (or lack thereof)—let alone any evidence of *class-wide* intent. This lack of evidence concerning Seton's class-wide intent is fatal to class certification here.

Under Rule 23(a)(2)'s "commonality" requirement, there must be "questions of law or fact common to the class." As the Supreme Court explained in *Dukes,* commonality requires more than a shared cause of action or common allegation of fact—it requires a common legal contention capable of class-wide resolution:

> Commonality requires the plaintiff to demonstrate that the class members have suffered the same injury. This does not mean merely that they have all suffered a violation of the same provision of law.... Their claims must depend upon a common contention—for example, the assertion of discriminatory bias on the part of the same supervisor. That common contention, moreover, must be of such a nature that it is capable of classwide resolution—which means that determination of its truth or falsity will resolve an issue that is central to the validity of each one of the claims in one stroke.

Id. at 349-50, 131 S.Ct. 2541 (citation and quotations omitted). "What matters to class certification ... is not the raising of common 'questions'—even in droves—but, rather the capacity of a class-wide proceeding to generate *common answers* apt to drive the resolution of the litigation. Dissimilarities within the proposed class are what have the potential to impede the generation of common answers." *Id.* at 350, 131 S.Ct. 2541 (quotations omitted).

The putative Title VII sex discrimination class in *Dukes* failed because the class members "wish[ed] to sue about literally millions of employment decisions at once. Without some glue holding the alleged reasons for all those decisions together, it will be impossible to say that examination of all the class members' claims for relief will produce a common answer to the crucial question *why was I disfavored.*" *Id.* at 352, 131 S.Ct. 2541.

This class fails for similar reasons. Every member of the putative class received the same allegedly threatening letter from Medicredit. But the FDCPA penalizes *empty* threats, not all threats. So the letter alone is insufficient to certify a class. As in *Dukes,* there is no "glue" here "holding the alleged reasons for all those [letters] together"—namely, evidence of a uniform intention by Seton regarding suit. *Id.* So it is likewise "impossible to say that examination of all the class members' claims for relief will produce a common answer to the crucial question" *why was I threatened. Id.*

And that is because the record here is wholly devoid of any evidence of Seton's debt collection practices. Flecha presented no evidence concerning Seton's actual intent to sue—either to sue her or others like her.

p.768 To be sure, her complaint declares that Seton "does not sue consumers for medical debt." But she presented no evidence to that effect to support class certification. She did not depose anyone from Seton. And the deposition testimony from Medicredit indicates that Seton's practices were unknown even to Medicredit.

Rather than require evidentiary support, the district court simply "presume[d] for the purposes of class certification that Medicredit and Seton acted consistently in determining whether to sue the recipient of its letters." But courts must certify class actions based on proof, not presumptions. *See, e.g., Gen. Tel. Co. of Sw. v. Falcon,* 457 U.S. 147, 160, 102 S.Ct. 2364, 72 L.Ed.2d 740 (1982) ("[A]ctual, not presumed, conformance with Rule 23(a) remains [] indispensable."); *Berger v. Compaq Comput. Corp.,* 257 F.3d 475, 481 (5th Cir. 2001) ("The district court unquestionably adopted an incorrect legal standard by stating that '[t]he adequacy of the putative representatives and of plaintiffs' counsel is presumed in the absence of specific proof to the contrary.' This is error; the party seeking certification bears the burden of establishing that *all* requirements of rule 23(a) have been satisfied.").

So Flecha failed to carry her burden to "affirmatively demonstrate" commonality. *Dukes,* 564 U.S. at 350, 131 S.Ct. 2541. She failed to demonstrate that her claim that Medicredit falsely threatened to take legal action against class members is capable of classwide resolution. And so that leaves the class without a common issue.

Her failure to prove commonality also establishes her failure to prove either typicality or predominance. After all, if there is no common issue uniting the putative class, Flecha's claim can't be "typical of the claims or defenses of the class." FED. R. CIV. P. 23(a)(3). *See also Falcon,* 457 U.S. at 157 n.13, 102 S.Ct. 2364 ("The commonality and typicality requirements of Rule 23(a) tend to merge."). Nor can Flecha demonstrate that common issues "predominate over any questions affecting only individual members," when she hasn't even established the existence of a common issue to begin with. FED. R. CIV. P. 23(b)(2).

In sum, the putative class fails under Rule 23 and cannot be certified.

IV.

Because the class fails under Rule 23, there is no need to separately decide whether the class additionally fails under Article III. But the standing issues in this case are real. Countless unnamed class members lack standing.

Our court has not yet decided whether standing must be proven for unnamed class members, in addition to the class representative. *See, e.g., In re Deepwater Horizon,* 785 F.3d 1003, 1018-20 (5th Cir. 2015). But some circuits have held that "no class may be certified that contains members lacking Article III standing." *Denney v. Deutsche Bank AG,* 443 F.3d 253, 264 (2d Cir. 2006).

That is significant, because there are undoubtedly many unnamed class members here who lack the requisite injury to establish Article III standing. After all, the putative class sweeps in "all persons in Texas ... who received a form collection letter" from Medicredit. As a result, the putative class inevitably includes people who received the letter, but ignored it as junk mail or otherwise gave it no meaningful attention—and therefore lack a cognizable injury under Article III.

That said, we do not reach the issue. That is because the Supreme Court has repeatedly instructed that we should first decide whether a proposed class satisfies Rule 23, before deciding whether it satisfies Article III—and that there is no p.769 need to answer the latter question if the class fails under the former. *See Amchem,* 521 U.S. at 612, 117 S.Ct. 2231 ("The class certification issues are dispositive; because their resolution ... is logically antecedent to the existence of any Article III issues, it is appropriate to reach them first."); *Ortiz v. Fibreboard Corp.,* 527 U.S. 815, 831, 119 S.Ct. 2295, 144 L.Ed.2d 715 (1999) ("Ordinarily, of course, this or any other Article III court must be sure of its own jurisdiction before getting to the merits. But the class certification issues are, as they were in *Amchem,* 'logically antecedent' to Article III concerns.") (internal citations omitted); Transcript of Oral Argument at 13, *Ortiz v. Fibreboard Corp.,* 527 U.S. 815, 119 S.Ct. 2295, 144 L.Ed.2d 715 (1999) ("The Court: If you can't certify under [Rule 23](b)(1)(B), all the rest is beside the point."). *See also, e.g., In re Hyundai & Kia Fuel Economy Litig.,* 926 F.3d 539, 565 n.12 (9th Cir. 2019) (declining to address jurisdiction "because the certification issue ... is dispositive"); *Payton v. County of Kane,* 308 F.3d 673, 680 (7th Cir. 2002) (beginning its "analysis with the question of class certification, mindful of the Supreme Court's directive to consider issues of class certification prior to issues of standing").

After all, if there is no class action under Rule 23, then there are no unnamed class members in the suit—and thus no attendant class standing concerns.

To be sure, if it is the *class representative* who presents a standing problem, then *that* standing issue must be addressed first, prior to deciding class certification. After all, if the class representative lacks standing, then there is no Article III suit to begin with—class certification or otherwise. *See, e.g., Rivera v. Wyeth-Ayerst Labs.,* 283 F.3d 315, 319 n.6 (5th Cir. 2002) ("In the instant case, in contrast to *Ortiz* and *Amchem,* the standing question would exist whether Rivera filed her claim alone or as part of a class; class certification did not create the jurisdictional issue."); *Ford v. NYLCare Health Plans,* 301 F.3d 329, 333 (5th Cir. 2002) (same).

But if it is only the unnamed class members who present a standing problem, then we are duty-bound to follow *Amchem* and *Ortiz.* Under those precedents, if there is no class action, then there is no need to analyze the Article III standing of the unnamed members of a non-existent class.

In this case, no one alleges that Flecha herself has an Article III problem. The only issue is whether the unnamed class members have standing. And under *Amchem* and *Ortiz,* that standing issue is "moot," because the class fails under Rule 23. *See, e.g., In re Wellbutrin XL Antitrust Litig.,* 260 F.R.D. 143, 153 (E.D. Penn. 2009) (noting that if "certification of the proposed class was improper, the issue of certain class members' standing would have been moot").

***

The reversal of the class certification order here could mean that legitimate claims will go unheard. This may be a "negative value suit," "in which class members' claims 'would be uneconomical to litigate individually.'" *In re Monumental Life Ins. Co.,* 365 F.3d 408, 411 n.1 (5th Cir. 2004) (quoting *Phillips Petroleum v. Shutts,* 472 U.S. 797, 809, 105 S.Ct. 2965, 86 L.Ed.2d 628 (1985)).

But the Supreme Court has made clear that fear of underenforcement is no justification for class certification. *See, e.g., Am. Exp. Co. v. Italian Colors Rest.,* 570 U.S. 228, 234, 133 S.Ct. 2304, 186 L.Ed.2d 417 (2013) (Rule 23 does not "establish an entitlement to class proceedings for the vindication of statutory rights"). As we have recognized, proof that a particular action is a negative value suit may satisfy p.770 the requirement of superiority under Rule 23(b)(3). *See, e.g., Castano,* 84 F.3d at 748 (noting "[t]he most compelling rationale for finding superiority in a class action—the existence of a negative value suit'"). But superiority is only one of the numerous conditions that must be met before a class may be certified under Rule 23. Proof of a negative value suit may be necessary to prove superiority—but it is not sufficient to warrant class certification under Rule 23(b)(3).[1]

Accordingly, we reverse the class certification order and remand for further proceedings.

ANDREW S. OLDHAM, Circuit Judge, concurring:

I agree with the Court's excellent opinion that the class must be decertified. I also agree with the Court's conclusion that "[c]ountless unnamed class members lack standing." *Ante,* at 768. In my view, that lack of standing is sufficient to decide the case.

I.

Standing is "an essential and unchanging part of the case-or-controversy requirement of Article III." *Lujan v. Defs. of Wildlife,* 504 U.S. 555, 560, 112 S.Ct. 2130, 119 L.Ed.2d 351 (1992). With it, the Constitution empowers us to hear a case before us and decide the relevant issues of law. Without it, we can do nothing but announce the fact and dismiss the case. *See Ex parte McCardle,* 74 U.S. (7 Wall.) 506, 514, 19 L.Ed. 264 (1868). After all, "[h]ypothetical jurisdiction produces nothing more than a hypothetical judgment." *Steel Co. v. Citizens for a Better Env't,* 523 U.S. 83, 101, 118 S.Ct. 1003, 140 L.Ed.2d 210 (1998).

It's unclear to me why these venerable principles would not apply with equal force at the class-certification stage. A plaintiff must show standing at each "successive stage[] of the litigation." *Lujan,* 504 U.S. at 561, 112 S.Ct. 2130; *see also Arizonans for Official English v. Arizona,* 520 U.S. 43, 64-65, 117 S.Ct. 1055, 137 L.Ed.2d 170 (1997). Nothing in Rule 23 could exempt the class-certification stage from this requirement. *See Amchem Prods., Inc. v. Windsor,* 521 U.S. 591, 613, 117 S.Ct. 2231, 138 L.Ed.2d 689 (1997) ("Rule 23's requirements must be interpreted in keeping with Article III constraints...."); FED. R. CIV. P. 82 ("These rules do not extend ... the jurisdiction of the district courts."); *accord Ortiz v. Fibreboard Corp.,* 527 U.S. 815, 831, 119 S.Ct. 2295, 144 L.Ed.2d 715 (1999). If anything, I'd think our standing analysis would be particularly rigorous at this stage, given the transformative nature of the class-certification decision. *Cf. Wal-Mart Stores, Inc. v. Dukes,* 564 U.S. 338, 351, 131 S.Ct. 2541, 180 L.Ed.2d 374 (2011) (noting certification stage requires "rigorous analysis").

Not only can certification change the number of plaintiffs from one to one million, but it also can dramatically change the rights and obligations of the plaintiffs. Class certification is the thing that gives an Article III court the power to "render dispositive judgments" affecting unnamed class members. *Plaut v. Spendthrift Farm, Inc.,* 514 U.S. 211, 219, 115 S.Ct. 1447, 131 p.771 L.Ed.2d 328 (1995) (quotation omitted); *see also Cooper v. Fed. Reserve Bank of Richmond,* 467 U.S. 867, 874, 104 S.Ct. 2794, 81 L.Ed.2d 718 (1984) ("There is of course no dispute that under elementary principles of prior adjudication a judgment in a properly entertained class action is binding on class members in any subsequent litigation."). That means, for example, that a post-certification judgment can prevent unnamed class members from bringing their claims again. *See Taylor v. Sturgell,* 553 U.S. 880, 894, 128 S.Ct. 2161, 171 L.Ed.2d 155 (2008); *Cooper,* 467 U.S. at 874, 104 S.Ct. 2794. It also means we must consider unnamed class members' standing before adjudicating the merits of their claims: "The exercise of judicial power, which can so profoundly affect the lives, liberty, and property of those to whom it extends, is therefore restricted to litigants who can show 'injury in fact' resulting from the action which they seek to have the court adjudicate." *Valley Forge Christian Coll. v. Americans United for Separation of Church & State, Inc.,* 454 U.S. 464, 473, 102 S.Ct. 752, 70 L.Ed.2d 700 (1982).

II.

It's true that the Supreme Court in both *Amchem* and *Ortiz* avoided the Article III standing question. The Court did so, in part, by stating that certification "pertain[s] to statutory standing." *Ortiz,* 527 U.S. at 831, 119 S.Ct. 2295. And at the time, the Court held statutory standing "may properly be treated before Article III standing." *Ibid.* That makes sense where both questions—whether the plaintiffs can sue under Rule 23 and whether the plaintiffs have Article III standing— are jurisdictional.

But the Supreme Court subsequently told us they're not. In *Lexmark Intern., Inc. v. Static Control Components, Inc.,* 572 U.S. 118, 134 S.Ct. 1377, 188 L.Ed.2d 392 (2014), the Court emphasized that the label "statutory standing" is "misleading" because the inquiry "does not implicate subject-matter jurisdiction, *i.e.,* the court's statutory or constitutional power to adjudicate the case." *Id.* at 128 n.4, 134 S.Ct. 1377 (quotation omitted). That suggests it's a *merits* question whether the unnamed class members can sue under Rule 23—not a jurisdictional one. *See id.* at 128, 134 S.Ct. 1377; *Steel Co.,* 523 U.S. at 89, 118 S.Ct. 1003. And if *Steel Co.* teaches us anything, it's that we must do jurisdiction before the merits. That's why our precedent holds that "though the certification inquiry is more straightforward, we must decide standing first, because it determines the court's fundamental power even to hear the suit." *Rivera v. Wyeth-Ayerst Labs,* 283 F.3d 315, 319 & n.6 (5th Cir. 2002).

Article III is just as important in class actions as it is in individual ones. *See Tyson Foods, Inc. v. Bouaphakeo,* ___ U.S. ___, 136 S. Ct. 1036, 1053, 194 L.Ed.2d 124 (2016) (Roberts, C.J., concurring) ("Article III does not give federal courts the power to order relief to any uninjured plaintiff, class action or not."). It's why the Court has reminded us that "[i]n an era of frequent litigation, class actions, sweeping injunctions with prospective effect, and continuing jurisdiction to enforce judicial remedies, courts must be more careful to insist on the formal rules of standing, not less so." *Ariz. Christian Sch. Tuition Org. v. Winn,* 563 U.S. 125, 146, 131 S.Ct. 1436, 179 L.Ed.2d 523 (2011). I'd do so here.

[1] Nor is class certification the only solution to a negative value suit. The ability of prevailing parties to recover attorney fees (as is available here under the FDCPA) may also help solve the problem. *See* 15 U.S.C. § 1692k(a)(3) ("[I]n the case of any successful action to enforce the foregoing liability, the costs of the action, together with a reasonable attorney's fee as determined by the court."); *see also Castano,* 84 F.3d at 748 ("The expense of litigation does not necessarily turn this case into a negative value suit, in part because the prevailing party may recover attorneys' fees under many consumer protection statutes.") (citing *Boggs v. Alto Trailer Sales,* 511 F.2d 114, 118 (5th Cir. 1975)).

952 F.3d 680 (2020)

Marco SALINAS, Plaintiff-Appellant,
v.
R.A. ROGERS, INCORPORATED, Defendant-Appellee.

No. 19-50618.

United States Court of Appeals, Fifth Circuit.

FILED March 12, 2020.

Salinas v. RA Rogers, Inc., 952 F. 3d 680 (5th Cir. 2020)

Appeal from the United States District Court for the Western District of Texas.

Daniel Zemel, Zemel Law, L.L.C., Clifton, NJ, for Plaintiff-Appellant.

Kevin Thomas Crocker, Barron & Newburger, P.C., Austin, TX, for Defendant-Appellee.

Before BARKSDALE, HIGGINSON, and DUNCAN, Circuit Judges.

p.681 STUART KYLE DUNCAN, Circuit Judge.

R.A. Rogers, Inc., a debt collection agency, mailed a collections letter to Appellant Marco Salinas listing the total amount due on his account ($4629.96) and the interest and fees due (both $0.00). The letter also included this statement: "In the event there is interest or other charges accruing on your account, the amount due may be greater than the amount shown above after the date of this notice." In response, Salinas sued R.A. Rogers, alleging the letter was false, deceptive, and misleading in violation of the Fair Debt Collection Practices Act ("FDCPA"), 15 U.S.C. §§ 1692 *et seq.*, because no interest or other charges could actually accrue on his account. The district court granted summary judgment for R.A. Rogers, holding that the letter accurately conveyed what was possible under Texas law—that interest could accrue—and was therefore not false, deceptive, or misleading. We affirm the summary judgment, but based on a more fundamental proposition. The challenged statement in the letter is not false, deceptive or misleading because it merely expresses a common-sense truism about borrowing—*if* interest is accruing on a debt, then the amount due may go up. That simple statement would have been clear even to an unsophisticated borrower thousands of years ago, just as it would be today. We therefore conclude that putting the statement in a dunning letter does not violate the FDCPA.

I.

At some unknown point in the past, Marco Salinas obtained a loan for personal, family, or household use from Security Service Federal Credit Union ("SSFCU"). Apparently, the loan agreement between Salinas and SSFCU was silent as to whether interest or other charges could accrue in the event of default. Salinas eventually did default on the loan, which led to R.A. Rogers sending Salinas an initial dunning letter on September 5, 2017. The letter lists the "Principal Balance" and "Total Amount Due" as $4629.96, and states that the "Interest" and "Fee[s]" are each $0.00. A sentence near the bottom of the letter reads: "In the event there is interest or other charges accruing on your account, the amount due may be greater than the amount shown above after the date of this notice."

On July 16, 2018, Salinas filed suit against R.A. Rogers in federal district court, alleging that the language quoted above is false, deceptive, and misleading in violation of the FDCPA, 15 U.S.C. § 1692e, because (1) R.A. Rogers does not collect interest or other charges on debts related to SSFCU and (2) the agreement between Salinas and SSFCU "does not allow" for p.682 interest to accrue or other charges to be added. Salinas characterized the language as an attempt to "induce payment . . . by scaring him." Contending that R.A. Rogers sent "hundreds if not thousands" of similar letters, Salinas sought certification of a class of "[a]ll consumers within the State of Texas that have received collection letters from Defendant concerning debts from Security Service FCU within one year prior to filing of this complaint which falsely represent to the consumer that interest or other charges may accrue." Salinas requested $1000.00 in statutory damages for himself and each class member, plus attorneys' fees and costs.

The parties stipulated that "R.A. Rogers does not collect interest or other charges on debts referred to it for collection by the creditor, Security Service FCU" and also that "[t]he agreement between Security Service FCU and Salinas is silent as to whether interest or other charges can accrue in the event of default." R.A. Rogers moved for summary judgment, arguing that even on the stipulated facts the letter complies with the FDCPA because it "clearly and unambiguously states the amount of the debt." According to R.A. Rogers, the "plain statement" that the total amount due is $4629.96 and interest and fees are $0.00 "is not undercut by the contingent (but obviously inapplicable rather than 'applicable') language of the [challenged] sentence." R.A. Rogers added that "common sense also dictates that Salinas' claims lack merit."

In granting summary judgment, the district court *sua sponte* detoured to the Texas Finance Code, reasoning that the letter was not false, misleading, or deceptive because "Texas law stipulates that a six percent interest rate may be applied to the principal balance of the loan starting thirty days after payment is due when the obligor has not agreed on an interest rate." *Salinas v. R.A. Rogers, Inc.*, No. SA-18-CV-733-XR, 2019 WL 2465325, at *5 (W.D. Tex. June 13, 2019) (citing TEX. FIN. CODE ANN. § 302.002). The court faulted Salinas for "fail[ing] to produce the loan agreement or any statute or regulation that would absolutely prohibit interest or other charges to accrue on the account following default." *Id.* Given the possibility that SSFCU could, under Texas law, elect to charge interest on the defaulted loan, the district court also held that the letter was "not confusing or unclear on its face" and faulted Salinas further for failing to produce any objective or subjective evidence of confusion. *Id.* Ultimately, the court concluded "[t]here is insufficient evidence in the record to create a triable issue of fact as to whether Defendant's debt collection letter is false, deceptive, or misleading." *Id.* Salinas timely appealed.

II.

We review a summary judgment *de novo*. *Mahmoud v. De Moss Owners Ass'n, Inc.*, 865 F.3d 322, 328 (5th Cir. 2017). "Summary judgment is required 'if the movant shows that there is no genuine dispute as to any material fact and the movant is entitled to judgment as a matter of law.'" *Id.* (quoting FED. R. CIV. P. 56(a)). A genuine dispute of material fact exists "if the evidence is such that a reasonable jury could return a verdict for the nonmoving party." *Anderson v. Liberty Lobby, Inc.*, 477 U.S. 242, 248, 106 S.Ct. 2505, 91 L.Ed.2d 202 (1986). "This court may affirm the district court's grant of summary judgment on any ground supported by the record and presented to the district court." *Mahmoud*, 865 F.3d at 328 (citation omitted).

III.

On appeal, Salinas argues that the district court erred in granting summary p.683 judgment because, given the stipulated facts, the conditional language in R.A. Rogers' letter is misleading, deceptive, and "utterly false," and therefore violates the FDCPA. He also contends that the district court misapplied the summary judgment standard by drawing one or more inferences in R.A. Rogers' favor. We consider each argument in turn.

A.

The FDCPA provides: "A debt collector may not use any false, deceptive, or misleading representation or means in connection with the collection of any debt." 15 U.S.C. § 1692e.[1] Among its nonexclusive list of proscribed practices, the FDCPA prohibits "[t]he false representation of (A) the character, amount, or legal status of any debt; or (B) any services rendered or compensation which may be lawfully received by any debt collector for the collection of a debt." *Id.* § 1692e(2). It is also a violation of the FDCPA to use "any false representation or deceptive means to collect or attempt to collect any debt or to obtain information concerning a consumer." *Id.* § 1692(e)(10). Because Congress "intended the FDCPA to have a broad remedial scope," the FDCPA should "be construed broadly and in favor of the consumer." *Daugherty v. Convergent Outsourcing, Inc.*, 836 F.3d 507, 511 (5th Cir. 2016) (internal quotation marks and citations omitted). We evaluate whether a collection letter violates § 1692e by "view[ing] the letter from the perspective of an 'unsophisticated or least sophisticated consumer.'" *Id.* (quoting *McMurray v. ProCollect, Inc.*, 687 F.3d 665, 669 (5th Cir. 2012)). "At the same time we do not consider the debtor as tied to the very last rung on the intelligence or sophistication ladder." *Goswami v. Am. Collections Enter., Inc.*, 377 F.3d 488, 495 (5th Cir. 2004) (cleaned up).[2]

Salinas argues that the conditional language in the letter—"In the event there is interest or other charges accruing on your account, the amount due may be greater than the amount shown above after the date of this notice"—is false, deceptive, and misleading because under no set of circumstances would Salinas' debt have increased due to interest or other charges while being collected upon by R.A. Rogers. According to Salinas, the letter clearly implied the false proposition that in the absence of prompt payment, interest or other charges could accrue on his account.

To the extent Salinas contends the language in the dunning letter is false, his claim is "downright frivolous." *See Taylor v. Cavalry Inv., L.L.C.*, 365 F.3d 572, 575 (7th Cir. 2004). The language merely expresses a truism: "*In the event* there is interest or other charges accruing on your account, the amount due may be greater than the amount shown above after the date of this notice" (emphasis added). In American legal usage, "in the event" is the equivalent of "if." *See* BRYAN A. GARNER, A DICTIONARY OF MODERN LEGAL USAGE 465 (2d ed. 1995) (observing that "in the event of" and "in the event that" are "unnecessarily prolix" equivalents of "if"). Thus, the letter's statement is no more false than the statement: "If it is raining outside, the ground may be wet"—a proposition as true p.684 in Death Valley as in New Orleans. It matters not whether Salinas' agreement with SSFCU prohibited SSFCU from applying interest or other charges to the debt, because the language at issue does not state that R.A. Rogers or SSFCU would—or even could—collect interest.

A perhaps closer question is whether the language is "deceptive" or "misleading," insofar as Salinas reads it to imply the possibility that interest or other charges may accrue when in fact they cannot. To date, our court has not settled on precise definitions for the FDCPA terms "deceptive" and "misleading." We have previously held that a collection agency's form letter was deceptive and misleading because it appeared on law firm letterhead even though no attorney from the firm ever participated in debt collection efforts. *Taylor v. Perrin, Landry, deLaunay & Durand*, 103 F.3d 1232, 1237 (5th Cir. 1997); *accord Gonzalez*, 577 F.3d at 606-07 (allowing FDCPA claim to proceed where deceptive law firm letter contained disclaimer on back in "legalese"). We have also stated that "a collection letter that is silent as to litigation, but which offers to 'settle' a time-barred debt without acknowledging that such debt is judicially unenforceable, can be sufficiently deceptive or misleading to violate the FDCPA." *Daugherty*, 836 F.3d at 511; *but see Mahmoud*, 865 F.3d at 334 (no FDCPA violation where "only a small portion of the debt may have been time-barred"). On the other hand, we have held non-misleading a collection letter stating—"FULL COLLECTION ACTIVITY WILL CONTINUE UNTIL THIS ACCOUNT IS PAID IN FULL . . . TO AVOID FURTHER COLLECTION ACTIVITY, YOUR STUDENT LOAN MUST BE PAID IN FULL"—because the back of the letter informed the debtor she could contest the debt within 30 days of receiving the collection letter. *Peter v. GC Servs. L.P.*, 310 F.3d 344, 349-50 (5th Cir. 2002); *see* 15 U.S.C. § 1692g(b).

While our court has not yet faced conditional language akin to that in the R.A. Rogers letter, we agree with the district court that the language at issue here is not deceptive or misleading. Reading the letter as a whole, even the least sophisticated consumer would not conclude, as Salinas urges, that absent prompt payment interest and other charges will accrue. Salinas reads the letter as if it literally says "interest and other charges may accrue" on his account, but the letter does not say that. Instead, it warns of a possible outcome— an increase in the amount due—"*in the event*" interest or other charges *are* accruing. Logically speaking, the actual text of the letter does not state or imply that interest or other charges will accrue, or even that they may accrue, on Salinas' account.[3]

An illustration shows the problem with Salinas' reading of the letter. Suppose a traveler boards a flight from El Paso, TX, to Tucson, AZ—a route traversing only desert—and is shown a safety video describing steps to take "*in the event of a water landing.*" Even the least sophisticated traveler would not take the video to imply the plane would be flying over water. No passenger would leap out of his seat in panic, concluding he had boarded the wrong flight. Even a traveler "tied to the very last rung on the intelligence or sophistication ladder" would interpret the video as merely acknowledging the reality that *some* flights, if not this one, fly over water. Admittedly, there might be confusion p.685 in the cabin if the captain announced, "We may be flying over water today," just as there might be confusion if the R.A. Rogers letter announced, "Interest may be accruing on your account." But that is not what the letter said. Instead, the innocuous, boilerplate language merely reiterates what unsophisticated borrowers have collectively experienced for thousands of years: that interest and other charges tend to accrue on *some* debts, and that *if* that occurs, the amount the debtor owes usually goes up.

Indeed, Salinas' argument, if adopted, would lead to absurd results. For example, by Salinas' logic, the letter would be misleading even without the offending sentence since the mere mention of "Interest" and "Fee[s]"—even though currently pegged at "$0.00"—could suggest the possibility that interest or fees may accrue in the future. What is more, the outcome Salinas proposes would force collection agencies to sift through applicable statutes and loan contracts to determine with absolute certainty, for each and every account, whether interest or other charges might possibly accrue, insofar as some debt collectors have been exposed to FDCPA liability for *omitting* statements similar to the one at issue here. *See, e.g., Gill v. Credit Bureau of Carbon Cty.*, No. 14-CV-01888-KMT, 2015 WL 2128465, at *5 (D. Colo. May 5, 2015); *Dragon v. I.C. Sys., Inc.*, 483 F. Supp. 2d 198, 202-03 (D. Conn. 2007); *see also Miller v. McCalla, Raymer, Padrick, Cobb, Nichols, & Clark, L.L.C.*, 214 F.3d 872, 876 (7th Cir. 2000) (prescribing as safe harbor language under FDCPA: "Because of interest, late charges, and other charges that may vary from day to day, the amount due on the day you pay may be greater"); *Avila v. Riexinger & Assocs., LLC*, 817 F.3d 72, 74, 77 (2d Cir. 2016) (holding that "Section 1692e requires debt collectors, when they notify consumers of their account balance, to disclose that the balance may increase due to interest and fees" and adopting *Miller*'s safe harbor language).

To support his position, Salinas relies on cases from other circuits involving conditional language in collection letters. These cases are not controlling and, more importantly, not on point. Many involve language implying the possibility of some ominous event beyond the familiarity of unsophisticated consumers. *See, e.g., Schultz v. Midland Credit Mgmt.*, 905 F.3d 159, 160 (3d Cir. 2018) (conditional language implying collection agency could report debt forgiveness to IRS); *Lox v. CDA, Ltd.*, 689 F.3d 818, 820 (7th Cir. 2012) (conditional language implying debtor could be charged attorneys' fees); *Gonzales v. Arrow Fin. Servs., LLC*, 660 F.3d 1055, 1059-60 (9th Cir. 2011) (conditional language implying settlement of old debts could be reported to credit bureaus); *Ruth v. Triumph P'ships*, 577 F.3d 790, 793 (7th Cir. 2009) (conditional language implying debtor's information could be shared without consent). In contrast, the conditional language at issue here involves a basic concept familiar to even the least sophisticated debtor: that interest and other charges, in the event they are accruing, may lead to an increase in the amount due.

To be sure, some of the cases cited by Salinas do involve statements about interest or other charges. These cases are nevertheless distinguishable because the structure of the offending statements differs from the one at issue here. For example, in *Walker v. Shermeta, Adams, Von Allmen, PC,* 623 F. App'x 764 (6th Cir. 2015), the collections letter stated: "Because of interest and other charges that may accrue, the amount you owe may continue to increase daily." *Id.* at 765. The Sixth Circuit held that, "if Plaintiff can show that interest or charges could never p.686 accrue and therefore the balance owed is truly fixed," then it was at least possible the statement was "materially misleading."[4] *Id.* at 768. But even if the Sixth Circuit had held the statement misleading —which it did not—the differences in grammar would thwart direct comparison. The complex causal sentence in *Walker* included a relative clause ("Because of interest and other charges *that may accrue*") implying that interest may accrue on the debtor's account. In contrast, the sentence at issue in the present case is best described as a "zero" conditional: it expresses a general truth without implying anything about the debtor's actual account. The same distinction applies to the dunning letter in *Boucher v. Fin. Sys. of Green Bay, Inc.,* 880 F.3d 362 (7th Cir. 2018), which stated: "Because of interest, late charges, and other charges that may vary from day to day, the amount due on the day you pay may be greater." *Id.* at 365. Unlike the letters in *Walker* and *Boucher,* the letter Salinas received does not "imply" that interest or other charges will accrue on his account; it merely communicates that Salinas' balance "may" increase "*in the event*" such charges *are* accruing.

In sum, we hold that the language at issue in this case expresses a common-sense truism about borrowing and lending, and does not imply that interest or other charges may actually accrue on the debtor's account. We therefore conclude that R.A. Rogers' dunning letter is not false, misleading, or deceptive in violation of the FDCPA.

B.

Salinas also argues that the district court applied the wrong summary judgment standard because the court drew an inference in R.A. Rogers' favor—the court inferred that R.A. Rogers *would* collect interest based on the fact that (under Texas law) the agency *could* collect interest— and, further, improperly required evidence of "subjective confusion" on the part of Salinas. Because our holding today does not depend on either point, we need not address these arguments.

* * *

The judgment of the district court is AFFIRMED.

[1] The parties agree that Salinas is a "consumer" and R.A. Rogers is a "debt collector" under the FDCPA. *See* 15 U.S.C. § 1692a(3), (6).

[2] Other circuits are split on whether to treat the application of the unsophisticated consumer standard as a question of law or question of fact. *See Gonzalez v. Kay,* 577 F.3d 600, 610 (5th Cir. 2009) (Jolly, J., dissenting). We have not formally picked sides in that debate, but generally treat the issue as a question of law, *see id.* at 609-10, as we do again here.

[3] Moreover, the letter unambiguously states that Salinas owed "$0.00" in "Interest" and "$0.00" in "Fee[s]," further undermining his claim that the letter was misleading or deceptive.

[4] Importantly, the Sixth Circuit did not hold the statement at issue in that case misleading or deceptive. Indeed, it recognized that the letter "tracks the FDCPA requirements for debt collection letters." *Id.* at 768.

956 F.3d 822 (2020)

Silvia MANUEL, Plaintiff-Appellee
v.
MERCHANTS AND PROFESSIONAL BUREAU, INCORPORATED, Defendant-Appellant.

No. 19-50814.

United States Court of Appeals, Fifth Circuit.

FILED April 29, 2020.

Manuel v. Merchants and Professional Bureau, Inc., 956 F. 3d 822 (5th Cir. 2020)

Appeals from the United States District Court for the Western District of Texas.

Brent Allen Devere, Esq., Karen Elisabeth Oprea, Law Office of Oprea & Weber, Austin, TX, for Plaintiff-Appellee.

David C. Sander, Esq., Scanlan, Buckle & Young, P.C., Austin, TX, for Defendant-Appellant.

James Allen Moseley, Esq., Dylan Owen Drummond, Esq., Gray Reed & McGraw, L.L.P., Dallas, TX, for Amicus Curiae.

Before OWEN, Chief Judge, and HIGGINBOTHAM and WILLETT, Circuit Judges.

p.823 PATRICK E. HIGGINBOTHAM, Circuit Judge:

This Fair Debt Collection Practices Act ("FDCPA") appeal concerns the collection of debt too old to be legally enforced under the applicable statute of limitations. In 2016, we held in *Daugherty v. Convergent Outsourcing, Inc.*, that "a collection letter seeking payment on a time-barred debt (without disclosing its unenforceability) but offering a 'settlement' and inviting partial payment (without disclosing the possible pitfalls) could constitute a violation of the FDCPA."[1] Here, the collection letters did p.824 not expressly threaten litigation or offer a settlement. Still, the district court, leaning on *Daugherty* and the out-of-circuit cases it endorsed, held that letters seeking collection of time-barred debt that do not flag the existence and operation of statutes of limitations are misleading as a matter of law. On that basis, it granted Appellee Silvia Manuel partial summary judgment on one of her FDCPA claims. Appellant Merchants and Professional Bureau, Inc. ("Merchants") timely appealed this order. As the letters in question were misleading for more than their mere silence as to the age and time-barred nature of the debt, we leave for another day whether such silence on its own is misleading as a matter of law. We affirm summary judgment on alternate grounds.

I.

A.

Manuel owes Texas Orthopedics, Sports and Rehabilitation Associates ("Texas Orthopedics") a $250 debt for services from December 2010 and January 2011. No payments have been made on the debt, which was transferred to Merchants for collection. Merchants sent Manuel six collection letters in 2011 and, after six years with seemingly no collection effort, it sent four more in 2017. When Merchants sent the 2017 letters, it is undisputed that the four-year Texas statute of limitations barred any lawsuit to collect the debt. At issue here, these letters did not disclose (1) that a lawsuit seeking payment of the debt was time-barred or (2) that any partial payment might defeat a statute-of-limitations defense.

The first letter at issue, dated October 2, 2017, stated in relevant part:

> YOU OWE: TX ORTHOPEDICS, SPORTS, & REHAB
>
> AMOUNT DUE: $250.00
>
> Urgent! Payment has not been received!
>
> In reviewing your account today, we show you still have an unpaid balance due. Please remit your balance due immediately in order to prevent any additional collection efforts, such as personal phone calls.
>
> Payment may be made over the phone, by mail or through our secure website shown above. We report unpaid collection accounts to the three national credit reporting repositories. Check by phone and major credit cards accepted by phone, with no service fees added.

The second, dated October 10, 2017, was written in Spanish and stated in relevant part:

> YOU OWE: TX ORTHOPEDICS, SPORTS, & REHAB
>
> AMOUNT DUE: $250.00
>
> IMPORTANT NOTICE:
>
> Your account is being reevaluated. We must notify you of additional collection efforts, such as phone calls, can be anticipated if you don't pay your account immediately.
>
> Pay this debt now to suspend these efforts. We report statements in collection to the national credit repositories.[2]

The third, dated October 17, 2017, was also written in Spanish and stated in relevant part:

> YOU OWE: TX ORTHOPEDICS, SPORTS, & REHAB
>
> AMOUNT DUE: $250.00
>
> Important Warning
>
> You have only one more opportunity to stop all collection efforts. Make payment arrangements immediately.
>
> Please call our office today to make a complete payment or to make payment arrangements on the balance due. We report to the three national repositories.

p.825 Finally, the fourth, dated October 25, 2017, again written in Spanish, stated:

> YOU OWE: TX ORTHOPEDICS, SPORTS, & REHAB
>
> AMOUNT DUE: $250.00
>
> Account eliminated when it is paid.
>
> Our client has authorized the elimination of this element of your credit history, but we need to receive your complete payment immediately! In most cases this should improve your credit points since this will be eliminated completely from your credit history. As you know, a good credit score is more essential than ever. We will notify all the credit reporting agencies when the bill is paid.
>
> This is a very special offer. Please take advantage of this now.

B.

In March 2018, Manuel sued Merchants and Merchants's surety, Travelers Casualty and Surety Company of America ("Travelers"). Manuel brought claims under the FDCPA, alleging the 2017 letters were false or misleading (15 U.S.C. § 1692e) and unfair or unconscionable (15 U.S.C. § 1692f) for failing to disclose the time-barred nature of the debt. Manuel also brought a claim under the Texas Debt Collection Act based on the same conduct. Manuel argued that the 2017 letters violated the Texas and federal statutes by failing to inform her that the debt was time-barred and thus judicially unenforceable, and that any partial payment could reinstate the statute of limitations. Manuel also contended that the threat to use "additional collection efforts" could induce an unsophisticated consumer to anticipate litigation.

In December 2018, Manuel moved for partial summary judgment on her § 1692e claim. Merchants then filed its own summary judgment motion. With these motions pending, the parties filed a joint stipulation narrowing the case. They stipulated that Manuel dismissed all claims against Travelers, leaving Merchants as the only defendant, and that Manuel dismissed without prejudice her TDCA claim. Finally, they stipulated that Manuel did not seek actual damages, and if she won summary judgment she would receive the maximum $1,000 statutory damages rather than proceed to trial on that issue.

The district court granted summary judgment for Manuel on her § 1692e claim, concluding

> that a debt collection letter that does not inform the consumer that judicial enforcement of the debt is time-barred or that any partial payment on the debt could defeat the otherwise absolute defense of the statute of limitations is a 'false representation of the character, amount, or legal status of any debt' under 15 U.S.C. § 1692e(2)(A) and the use of a 'false representation or deceptive means to collect or attempt to collect any debt' under 15 U.S.C. § 1692e(10).

Since the letters were misleading under § 1692e, and "there is a growing consensus" that a claim under § 1692f is a "backstop" to catch conduct outside that barred by § 1692e and other provisions, the court granted summary judgment to Merchants on Manuel's § 1692f claim. Merchants timely appealed.

II.

This Court reviews a grant of summary judgment de novo, applying the same standard as the district court.[3] Summary judgment is warranted "if the movant shows that there is no genuine dispute as to any material fact and the movant is entitled to judgment as a matter of law."[4] p.826 "This court may affirm the district court's grant of summary judgment on any ground supported by the record and presented to the district court."[5]

III.

A.

The FDCPA's purpose is to "eliminate abusive debt collection practices by debt collectors[.]"[6] Because "Congress ... clearly intended the FDCPA to have a broad remedial scope[,]" it should "be construed broadly and in favor of the consumer."[7] The provisions of § 1692e relied on by Manuel are as follows:

> A debt collector may not use any false, deceptive, or misleading representation or means in connection with the collection of any debt. Without limiting the general application of the foregoing, the following conduct is a violation of this section:
>
> ....
>
> (2) The false representation of—
>
> (A) the character, amount, or legal status of any debt; ....
>
> (5) The threat to take any action that cannot legally be taken or that is not intended to be taken.
>
> ....
>
> (10) The use of any false representation or deceptive means to collect or attempt to collect any debt or to obtain information concerning a consumer.[8]

The parties do not dispute that Merchants is a debt collector as understood by the FDCPA or that Manuel was the object of debt-collection activity arising from a consumer debt. This leaves the sole issue of whether Merchants's letters "use[d] any false, deceptive, or misleading representation or means in connection with the collection of any debt."[9]

"When evaluating whether a collection letter violates § 1692e or § 1692f, a court must view the letter from the perspective of an 'unsophisticated or least sophisticated consumer.'"[10] The unsophisticated consumer is "neither shrewd nor experienced in dealing with creditors[,]" but neither is that consumer "tied to the very last rung on the intelligence or sophistication ladder."[11] While "[w]e have not formally picked sides" in the circuit debate over whether application of the unsophisticated-consumer standard is a question of law or fact, we "generally treat the issue as a question of law, as we do again here."[12]

B.

Our decision in *Daugherty* is central to this appeal. There, a debt collector offered to "settle" the plaintiff's old credit card p.827 debt of roughly $32,000 for a payment of roughly $3,000.[13] We held that "a collection letter that is silent as to litigation, but which offers to 'settle' a timebarred debt without acknowledging that such debt is judicially unenforceable, can be sufficiently deceptive or misleading to violate the FDCPA."[14] In doing so we "agree[d] with the Seventh Circuit's interpretation of the FDCPA in [*McMahon v. LVNV Funding, LLC,*[15]] and with the Sixth Circuit's opinion in [*Buchanan v. Northland Group, Inc,*[16]] insofar as it is consistent with *McMahon.*"[17]

In *McMahon,* the Seventh Circuit noted it is not "automatically improper" to seek payment of old debts, as "some people might consider full debt re-payment a moral obligation, even though the legal remedy for the debt has been extinguished."[18] But the letters at issue, which offered to "settle" time-barred debt that did not state when the debt was incurred and otherwise "contained no hint" that the debt was time-barred, misrepresented the legal status of the debts.[19] The silence as to the debt's age was worsened by the offers of settlement, "since a gullible consumer who made a partial payment would inadvertently have reset the limitations period and made herself vulnerable to a suit on the full amount."[20] The settlement offers thus "reinforced the misleading impression that the debt was legally enforceable."[21] As support, the court pointed to the view of the FTC and CFPB that most consumers do not understand their legal rights regarding time-barred debt.[22] "If p.828 unsophisticated consumers believe either that the settlement offer is their chance to avoid court proceedings where they would be defenseless, or if they believe that the debt is legally enforceable at all, they have been misled[.]"[23]

Finally, *McMahon* sought to dispel the idea that its decision requires additional research by debt collectors. While *McMahon* expected most collectors would know the age and legal enforceability of a debt, it noted that a collector who does not know whether a debt is time-barred could easily "include general language about that possibility."[24]

Our court's most recent FDCPA case regarding old debt is *Mahmoud v. De Moss Owners Association.*[25] In *Mahmoud,* which concerned a foreclosure sale on a condominium unit, the plaintiffs brought FDCPA claims, alleging in part that the attorneys who acted as debt collectors misrepresented the character or legal status of the debt in their collection letters because about 25 percent of the debt was allegedly time-barred.[26] Even assuming that this part of the debt was time-barred, however, we concluded that "[n]o Fifth Circuit authority compels the holding that a nonjudicial foreclosure on a partially time-barred debt can violate FDCPA Sections 1692e or f."[27]

Mahmoud noted *Daugherty* held that collection of old debt "can be" violative, not that it always is, and distinguished *Daugherty* on its facts because: (1) all of the *Daugherty* debt was old while less than 25 percent, at most, of the *Mahmoud* debt was; (2) the application of limitations was unclear as a bar to nonjudicial foreclosure but was undisputed as to the *Daugherty* credit-card debt; and (3) the course of events showed the *Mahmoud* plaintiffs were not misled about what they owed or about the consequence (foreclosure) of nonpayment.[28] *Mahmoud* distinguished *McMahon* and

Buchanan along the same lines—as cases concerning "dubious exercises of collection activity on indisputably and wholly time-barred debt."[29]

Another Seventh Circuit case relying on *McMahon* warrants mention. In *Pantoja v. Portfolio Recovery Associates, LLC,* the collection letter had a settlement offer similar to those in the cases described above.[30] It also stated, "Because of the age of your debt, we will not sue you for it and we will not report it to any credit reporting agency."[31] Even with this warning, the *Pantoja* court affirmed summary judgment granted to the plaintiff because (1) the letter did not warn that partial payment would forfeit any limitations defense and (2) it "deceptively said that [the collector] had chosen not to sue [the plaintiff], rather than saying that the debt was so old that [the collector] could not sue him for the alleged debt."[32] As to the first reason, the court concluded that a collector cannot "lur[e] p.829 debtors away from the statute of limitations without providing an unambiguous warning" but declined to prescribe exact language for debt collectors to use.[33] As to the second, the court found the chosen language to be a "careful and deliberate ambiguity[.]"[34]

The Ninth Circuit, on the other hand, reversed a grant of summary judgment to plaintiffs for a letter with the following warning: "The law limits how long you can be sued on a debt and how long a debt can appear on your credit report. Due to the age of this debt, we will not sue you for it or report payment or non-payment of it to a credit bureau."[35] The second sentence matches the vague warning in *Pantoja,* but the first sentence informs the debtor that there is a statute of limitations. Indeed, *Pantoja* quoted this longer warning, which comes from a 2012 consent decree between the Federal Trade Commission and another debt collector.[36] The *Pantoja* court noted that the effect of omitting the first sentence is that "[t]he reader is left to wonder whether [the collector] has chosen to go easy on this old debt out of the goodness of its heart, or perhaps because it might be difficult to prove the debt, or perhaps for some other reason."[37]

IV.

In assessing the letters at hand, we begin with the following proposition from *McMahon*: "Whether a debt is legally enforceable is a central fact about the character and legal status of that debt. A misrepresentation about that fact thus violates the FDCPA."[38] Collectors do not automatically violate the FDCPA when p.830 seeking collection of time-barred debt.[39] Still, we cannot conclude, as Merchants presses us to, that settlement offers and litigation threats are the only ways debt collectors can mislead unsophisticated consumers regarding old debt. This would place artificial constraints on broad terms—like "deceptive" and "misleading" —under a statute we should construe broadly.[40]

In *Daugherty,* we did not purport to catalogue all the ways collection of time-barred debt can be misleading. Instead, deciding only what was necessary on the facts then before us, we concluded that collectors can misrepresent a debt's legal enforceability by offering to settle the debt at a discount. That is not to say that all settlement offers violate the statute, nor that such offers are the only way to misrepresent the character of old debt. While Merchants's letters do not contain settlement offers, we agree with the district court: Confining *Daugherty* and *McMahon* "to the specifics of the letters involved in those cases does not comport with the broad language of *McMahon*—expressly agreed with by the Fifth Circuit in *Daugherty* —and the edict that the FDCPA 'should therefore be construed broadly and in favor of the consumer.'"

Further, *McMahon* made its basic premise clear: "[A] debt collector violates the FDCPA when it misleads an unsophisticated consumer to believe a time-barred debt is legally enforceable[.]"[41] The *McMahon* letters did so because they did not "g[i]ve a hint" that the debts were time-barred.[42] "Matters may be even worse if the debt collector adds a threat of litigation," and the settlement offer in that case also "[made] things worse," since consumers may unwittingly reset the limitations period, which is "why those offers only reinforced the misleading impression that the debt was legally enforceable."[43]

The question, then, is not whether the letters include a settlement offer or litigation threat but whether, read as a whole, they misrepresent the legal enforceability and character of the debt in violation of 15 U.S.C. § 1692e(2) and (10). In answering this question, the district court went further than was necessary. It concluded that a letter is misleading as a matter of law if it lacks warnings "that judicial enforcement of the debt is time-barred or that any partial payment on the debt could defeat the otherwise absolute defense of the statute of limitations."

We and other circuits have framed our holdings in this area with moderation.[44] So we leave for another day the question of whether a letter seeking collection on time-barred debt is misleading as a matter of law by its mere silence as to the age and legal unenforceability. We do not need to draw that line because the letters at issue do not toe it. Instead, the sum effect of the 2017 letters is at least as misleading as any settlement offer from prior cases.[45]

p.831 Read "as a whole,"[46] several aspects of the 2017 letters from Merchants lead us to this conclusion. First, the letters do not just fail to warn that Texas has a statute of limitations or how that statute may affect the collection methods available to Merchants —the letters do not even state when the debt was incurred. If they had, as the district court noted, they "might give a consumer at least some inkling that the debt might be too old to be legally enforceable." Although we need not hold that all letters without statute-of-limitations warnings are misleading as a matter of law, the complete silence in these letters works in conjunction with their vague language to mislead the unsophisticated consumer that the debt is enforceable.[47]

As for the language itself, although there is no specific settlement offer that would discount Manuel's debt, the letters are rife with characterization of a soon-to-expire special deal or offer:

- "Important Warning."
- "You have only one more opportunity to stop all collection efforts."
- "This is a very special offer. Please take advantage of this now."
- "Our client has authorized the elimination of this element of your credit history but we need to receive your complete payment immediately!"
- "Urgent!"

There is nothing urgent about this old debt, nor are there any details offered to explain the "very special offer," nor are these permissible attempts at "moral suasion."[48]

Further, the letters hint at "additional collection efforts" should Manuel not pay the debt:

- "Please remit your balance due immediately in order to prevent any additional collection efforts, such as personal phone calls."
- "We must notify you of additional collection efforts, such as phone calls, can be anticipated if you don't pay your account immediately. Pay this debt now to suspend these efforts."

The unexplained urgent language and the vague threats of additional but unspecified collection efforts perform a similar role to the settlement offers in *Daugherty* and *McMahon.* The combined effect of the letters' vague language and their silence as to the debt's time-barred nature leaves an unsophisticated consumer with the impression that the debt is enforceable, and that if payment is not levied quickly then adverse collection efforts will follow.[49]

p.832 That consumer does not know the terms of the special offer or why payment is "urgent" after years have passed. And that consumer does not know what collection efforts will follow if payment is withheld. "Where the FDCPA requires clarity, ... ambiguity itself can prove a violation."[50] For the reasons discussed above, we agree with the district court that Merchants's letters are "example[s] of careful and crafted ambiguity."[51] "The only reason to use such carefully ambiguous language is the expectation that at least some unsophisticated debtors will misunderstand and will choose to pay on the ancient, time-barred debts because they fear the consequences of not doing so."[52]

Courts have recognized that the risk of partial payment reviving old debt amplifies the effect of the want of limitations-period warnings. *Daugherty* observed that an "unsophisticated debtor who could not afford the settlement might assume from the letter that at least a partial payment would be advisable" without knowing the risk of restarting the limitations clock.[53] That danger is perhaps reduced but not absent with letters like these. A debtor confronted with an "urgent" letter seeking full payment might also think it advisable to pay some of it.

Thus, these letters seeking collection of time-barred debt, filled with ambiguous offers and threats with no indication that the debt is old, much less that the limitations period has run, misrepresent the legal enforceability of the underlying debt in violation of 15 U.S.C. § 1692e(2) and (10).[54]

V.

The grant of summary judgment to Plaintiff Silvia Manuel is affirmed.

[1] 836 F.3d 507, 513 (5th Cir. 2016).

[2] The quoted text is from the district court's reproduction and translation. The parties do not object to the translated text as analyzed by the district court.

[3] *Cuadra v. Hous. Indep. Sch. Dist.,* 626 F.3d 808, 812 (5th Cir. 2010).

[4] FED. R. CIV. P. 56(a).

[5] *Salinas v. R.A. Rogers, Inc.,* 952 F.3d 680, 682 (5th Cir. 2020).

[6] 15 U.S.C. § 1692(e).

[7] *Daugherty*, 836 F.3d at 511 (5th Cir. 2016) (quoting *Serna v. Law Office of Joseph Onwuteaka, P.C.*, 732 F.3d 440, 445 (5th Cir. 2013) (emphasis omitted)).

[8] 15 U.S.C. § 1692e.

[9] 15 U.S.C. § 1692e.

[10] *Daugherty*, 836 F.3d at 511 (quoting *McMurray v. ProCollect, Inc.*, 687 F.3d 665, 669 (5th Cir. 2012)). We generally refer to the "unsophisticated consumer" and "least sophisticated consumer" standards interchangeably as "unsophisticated consumers." *Id.* at 511 n.2. (citing *Peter v. GC Servs. L.P.*, 310 F.3d 344, 349 n.1 (5th Cir. 2002) (opting not to decide which of the two standards governs because "the difference between the standards is de minimis at most")).

[11] *Id.* (quoting *Goswami v. Am. Collections Enter.*, 377 F.3d 488, 495 (5th Cir. 2004) (cleaned up)).

[12] *Salinas*, 952 F.3d at 683 n.2 (citing *Gonzalez v. Kay*, 577 F.3d 600, 610 (5th Cir. 2009) (Jolly, J., dissenting)) (citation omitted).

[13] *Daugherty*, 836 F.3d at 509.

[14] *Id.* at 511.

[15] 744 F.3d 1010 (7th Cir. 2014).

[16] 776 F.3d 393 (6th Cir. 2015).

[17] *Daugherty*, 836 F.3d at 513. This required a choice between an "apparent conflict" between these circuits and the Third and Eighth Circuits, which had concluded that "[i]n the absence of a threat of litigation or actual litigation, no violation of the FDCPA has occurred when a debt collector attempts to collect on a potentially time-barred debt that is otherwise valid." *Huertas v. Galaxy Asset Mgmt.*, 641 F.3d 28, 33 (3d Cir. 2011) (quoting *Freyermuth v. Credit Bureau Servs., Inc.*, 248 F.3d 767, 771 (8th Cir. 2001)).

Since then, the Eleventh Circuit has joined the approach of *Daugherty, McMahon,* and *Buchanan*. *See Holzman v. Malcolm S. Gerald & Assocs., Inc.*, 920 F.3d 1264, 1267 (11th Cir. 2019) (extending the reasoning of these cases to an offer to "resolve" an account with a "balance reduction"). So has the Third Circuit, cabining its *Huertas* decision to the specific provision it discussed, § 1692e(2)(A), and holding that a letter regarding time-barred debt can mislead even without threatening suit. *See Tatis v. Allied Interstate, LLC*, 882 F.3d 422, 427-30 (3d Cir. 2018); *see also id.* at 429 (endorsing the "considered view" of *Daugherty, McMahon,* and *Buchanan* as "the best interpretation of the FDCPA" and concluding that a "threat of litigation" requirement overly restricts the terms "deceptive" and "misleading").

[18] *McMahon*, 744 F.3d at 1020.

[19] *Id.* at 1013, 1014-15, 1021.

[20] *Id.*

[21] *Id.*

[22] *Id.* (citing Fed. Trade Comm'n, *Repairing a Broken System: Protecting Consumers in Debt Collection Litigation and Arbitration* 26-27 (2010)). In February 2020, the CFPB issued a proposed rule that would require a debt collector "who knows or should know that a debt is time barred when the debt collector makes the initial

communication" to clearly and conspicuously disclose (1) "[t]hat the law limits how long the consumer can be sued for a debt and that, because of the age of the debt, the debt collector will not sue the consumer to collect it" and (2) "[i]f, under applicable law, the debt collector's right to bring a legal action against the consumer can be revived, the fact that revival can occur and the circumstances in which it can occur." *See* Debt Collection Practices (Regulation F) Supplemental Proposal on Time-Barred Debt, 85 FED. REG. 12672 (proposed Feb. 21, 2020).

[23] *McMahon,* 744 F.3d at 1022.

[24] *Id. McMahon* surmised that an original creditor would know the dates, a third-party collector would be able to get that information from the original creditor for whom it was collecting, and a debt purchaser pays different amounts depending on the age of debts and so should know whether debts are time-barred. *Id.*

[25] 865 F.3d 322 (5th Cir. 2017). In March 2020, this Court issued *Salinas v. R.A. Rogers, Inc.,* 952 F.3d 680 (5th Cir. 2020), which cited *Mahmoud* and *Daugherty* but concerned unrelated legal theories under § 1692e.

[26] *Mahmoud,* 865 F.3d at 331.

[27] *Id.* at 332-33.

[28] *Id.* at 333.

[29] *Id.*

[30] 852 F.3d 679, 682 (7th Cir. 2017).

[31] *Id.*

[32] *Id.* at 682-83.

[33] *Id.* at 685-86.

[34] *Id.* at 687.

[35] *Stimpson v. Midland Credit Mgmt., Inc.,* 944 F.3d 1190, 1196 (9th Cir. 2019). *Stimpson* also concluded that "nothing in the FDCPA requires debt collectors to make disclosures that partial payments on debts may revive the statute of limitations in certain states." *Id.* at 1198.

[36] *Pantoja,* 852 F.3d at 686. Similar language crops up repeatedly, including in state laws requiring limitations-period disclosures. Effective September 2019, for debt buyers in Texas, all first collection letters sent on debt for which the limitations period has run must contain one of three variations of the following notice: "THE LAW LIMITS HOW LONG YOU CAN BE SUED ON A DEBT. BECAUSE OF THE AGE OF YOUR DEBT, WE WILL NOT SUE YOU FOR IT. THIS NOTICE IS REQUIRED BY LAW." TEX. FIN. CODE § 392.307 (2019). The precise formulation depends on whether the reporting period for including the debt in a consumer report prepared has expired under the Fair Credit Reporting Act. *See id.* (e)(1)-(3). Texas joins several other jurisdictions in requiring statute-of-limitations disclosures. *See, e.g.,* CAL. CIV. CODE 1788.14(d); CONN. GEN. STAT. 36a-805(a)(14); MASS. CODE REGS., tit. 940, 7.07(24); N.M. ADMIN. CODE 12.2.12.9; N.Y. COMP. CODES R. & RECS., tit. 23, 1.3; N.C. GEN. STAT. XX-XX-XXX(1); 6 VT. CODE R. 031-004-Rule-CF 104.05; W. Va. Code 46a-2-128(f). And almost this exact language has survived legal challenges like Manuel's. *See Stimpson,* 944 F.3d at 1194.

Note, however, that the model forms included in the proposed CFPB disclosure rule would impose even stricter language. *See* Debt Collection Practices (Regulation F) Supplemental Proposal on Time-Barred Debt, 85 FED. REG. 12672 (proposed Feb. 21, 2020). For example, where, like in Texas, an acknowledgement is required to revive old debt, the rule would provide: "The law limits how long you can be sued for a debt. If you do nothing or speak to us about this debt, we will not sue you to collect it. This is because the debt is too old. BUT if you acknowledge in writing that you owe this debt, then we can sue you to collect it." *Id.* at 12682, B-7 Model Form for Time-Barred Debt and Revival Disclosure (Written Acknowledgement).

[37] *Pantoja,* 852 F.3d at 686.

[38] *McMahon,* 744 F.3d at 1020; *see also Daugherty,* 836 F.3d at 513 ("We agree with the Seventh Circuit's interpretation of the FDCPA in *McMahon*[.]").

[39] *See id.* at 509 (noting that "it is not automatically unlawful for a debt collector to seek payment of a time-barred debt"); *see also Holzman v. Malcolm S. Gerald & Assocs., Inc.,* 920 F.3d 1264, 1273-74 (11th Cir. 2019) ("[C]ourts generally have recognized that the FDCPA does not impose a bright-line rule prohibiting debt collectors from attempting to collect on time-barred debt.") (collecting cases).

[40] *See Tatis,* 882 F.3d at 429.

[41] *McMahon,* 744 F.3d at 1020.

[42] *Id.*

[43] *Id.* at 1020-21.

[44] *See Mahmoud,* 865 F.3d at 333 (noting that *Daugherty, McMahon,* and *Buchanan* "qualified their holdings").

[45] Despite Merchants's claim to the contrary, Manuel's summary judgment motion argued that the specific language of the letters would mislead an unsophisticated consumer that the debt is enforceable. There is no reason we may not affirm on this alternate ground. *See TIG Specialty Ins. Co. v. Pinkmonkey.com,* 375 F.3d 365, 369 (5th Cir. 2004).

[46] *Gonzalez v. Kay,* 577 F.3d 600, 607 (5th Cir. 2009).

[47] *See McMahon,* 744 F.3d at 1021 (concluding that the silence as to limitations was worsened by an offer of settlement that reinforced the misleading nature of the letters). In the Seventh Circuit, one circuit and at least two district-court cases have relied on *McMahon* at the summary-judgment stage in finding that debt collection efforts that failed to disclose the time-barred nature of a debt violated the FDCPA as a matter of law. *See Pantoja,* 852 F.3d at 687; *Rawson v. Source Receivables Mgmt., LLC,* 215 F. Supp. 3d 684, 685-86 (N.D. Ill. 2016); *Slick v. Portfolio Recovery Assocs., LLC,* 111 F. Supp. 3d 900, 906 (N.D. Ill. 2015) ("[A] letter that is completely silent on the subject [of the time-barred nature of the debt] is ... misleading.").

[48] *Mahmoud,* 865 F.3d at 333 n.3.

[49] *See Holzman,* 920 F.3d at 1272 ("[B]y urging the debtor to 'take advantage' of the offer, the letter might have caused an unsophisticated consumer to mistakenly believe that the debt was legally enforceable and that he had something to gain by accepting the offer, or to lose by declining it.... [A]n unsophisticated reader might conclude from this language that he is being presented with an ultimatum, and that

failure to make payment within the required time frame would result in negative consequences, such as legal action.").

[50] *Pantoja,* 852 F.3d at 687.

[51] *Id.*

[52] *Id.*

[53] *Daugherty,* 836 F.3d at 512.

[54] *Mahmoud* is no barrier to our holding. This case is factually distinct from *Mahmoud* for the same reasons *Mahmoud* distinguished *Daugherty* and its like cases: the letters in this case "exhibit dubious exercises of collection activity on indisputably and wholly time-barred debt." *See Mahmoud,* 865 F.3d at 333.

908 F.3d 972 (2018)

Crystal DAVIS, Plaintiff-Appellant
v.
CREDIT BUREAU OF THE SOUTH, Defendant-Appellee.

No. 17-41136.

United States Court of Appeals, Fifth Circuit.

FILED November 16, 2018.

Davis v. Credit Bureau of the South, 908 F. 3d 972 (5th Cir. 2018)

Appeal from the United States District Court, for the Eastern District of Texas.

Dennis Dean McCarty, Esq., Carrollton, TX, Jonathan Forrest Raburn, Plano, TX, for Plaintiff-Appellant.

Ralph Scott Bowie, Jr., Bowie & Beresko, A.P.L.C., Shreveport, LA, for Defendant-Appellee.

Before STEWART, Chief Judge, and JONES and ENGELHARDT, Circuit Judges.

p.974 PER CURIAM:

Crystal Davis appeals the district court's denial of her motion for attorney's fees, arguing that an award of reasonable attorney's fees is mandatory for a successful action under the Fair Debt Collection Practices Act. Based on the outrageous facts in this case and the conduct of Davis' attorneys, we AFFIRM.

FACTS AND PROCEEDINGS

Appellant Crystal Davis (Davis) filed a complaint in the Eastern District of Texas alleging that Credit Bureau of the South (CBOTS), a debt collector, violated the Fair Debt Collection Practices Act (FDCPA)[1] and the Texas Debt Collection Act (TDCA)[2] by using the words "credit bureau" in its name, misrepresenting itself as a credit bureau in an attempt to collect a debt. Davis identified two incidents when CBOTS allegedly attempted to unlawfully collect the debt at issue—a 2013 water bill in the amount of $107.29 Davis owed to the City of Shreveport. First, Davis alleged that on August 18, 2015, CBOTS mailed her a collection letter on letterhead "that clearly stated 'Credit Bureau of the South, Inc.'" The second violation Davis alleged involved a recorded phone call she made to CBOTS on September 22, 2015, during which Davis claims CBOTS misrepresented itself as a credit bureau in its collection efforts.

The parties filed cross motions for summary judgment.[3] Following a hearing, the magistrate judge concluded in his Report and Recommendation that "summary judgment evidence establishes that Defendant engaged in debt collection activities while using the term 'credit bureau' in its name, even though it ceased to be a consumer reporting agency years ago." Relying on *McKenzie v. E.A. Uffman & Assocs., Inc.*, 119 F.3d 358 (5th Cir. 1997), the magistrate judge found that these facts "constitute the false representation or implication that [CBOTS] is a consumer reporting agency in violation of the FDCPA," and recommended that Davis be awarded $1,000 in statutory damages. Accepting the magistrate judge's recommendation and finding that CBOTS violated section 1692e(16) of the FDCPA, the district court p.975 granted summary judgment, in part, in favor of Davis and awarded her statutory damages of $1,000.[4] The district court rejected all other claims.[5]

Davis filed a subsequent opposed motion for attorney's fees in the amount of $130,410, pursuant to 15 U.S.C. § 1692k(a)(3).[6] The motion was referred to the magistrate judge, who denied Davis' motion for attorney's fees, finding that the case involved special circumstances that would render an award of attorney's fees unjust:

> It appears that this cause of action was created by counsel for the purpose of generating, in counsel's own words, an "incredibly high" fee request. While Defendant has been found to have committed a violation of the FDCPA, which ordinarily justifies an award of fees as a disincentive to future similar conduct, the Court is even more concerned about disincentivizing the conduct of Plaintiff's counsel.

As further support of his decision, the magistrate judge discussed, *inter alia,* that the collusion between Davis and her counsel essentially created her claim. Additionally, the magistrate judge explained that the court was "stunned" by Davis' request for $130,000 in attorney's fees, noting that there were substantial duplicative and excessive fees charged by Plaintiff's multiple counsel; the case was simple with a Fifth Circuit case on point and was disposed of on summary judgment; and the number of hours (nearly 300 hours), as well as the hourly rate of $450 demanded by Plaintiff's counsel, was "excessive by orders of magnitude."

Davis objected to the magistrate judge's denial of attorney's fees, contending that given the favorable summary judgment ruling and the plain language of the statute, an award of attorney's fees is mandatory. Thus, Davis argued that the magistrate judge erred in denying her mandatory attorney's fees and that his reasoning was flawed. Without providing further written reasons, the district judge overruled Davis' objections to the magistrate judge's denial of attorney's fees, adopting the order as its final judgment. Davis timely appealed.

STANDARD OF REVIEW

We review the district court's denial of attorney's fees for abuse of discretion. *Sw. Bell Tel. Co. v. City of El Paso,* 346 F.3d 541, 550 (5th Cir. 2003). "In evaluating whether the district court abused its discretion to award attorney's fees, this Court reviews the factual findings supporting the grant or denial of attorney's fees for clear error and the conclusions of law underlying the award *de novo.*" *Dearmore v. City of Garland,* 519 F.3d 517, 520 (5th Cir. 2008) (citing *Energy Mgmt. Corp. v. City of Shreveport,* 467 F.3d 471, 482 (5th Cir. 2006)). "A district court abuses its discretion if it bases its decision on an erroneous view of the law or on a clearly erroneous assessment of the evidence." *CenterPoint Energy Hous. Elec. LLC v. Harris Cnty. Toll Rd. Auth.,* 436 F.3d 541, 550 (5th Cir. 2006) (quoting p.976 *Ross v. Marshall,* 426 F.3d 745, 763 (5th Cir. 2005)).

DISCUSSION

According to the FDCPA, "[a] debt collector may not use any false, deceptive, or misleading representation or means in connection with the collection of any debt." 15 U.S.C. § 1692e. Specifically, the Act prohibits the "false representation or implication that a debt collector operates or is employed by a consumer reporting agency...." 15 U.S.C. § 1692e(16). The FDCPA's fee-shifting provision provides that any debt collector who fails to comply "*is liable* ... in the case of any successful [FDCPA] action ... [for] the costs of the action, together with a *reasonable* attorney's fee *as determined by the court.*" 15 U.S.C. § 1692k(a)(3) (emphasis added). This provision evidences Congress' intent to enforce the FDCPA through a "private attorney general" approach. *See Graziano v. Harrison,* 950 F.2d 107, 113 (3d Cir. 1991).

Based on the plain language of the statute, a debt collector who fails to comply with the FDCPA "is liable" for reasonable attorney's fees, which suggests that district courts are denied the discretion to determine whether or not attorney's fees are appropriate. Several circuits have held that the award of attorney's fees to a successful plaintiff in an FDCPA action is mandatory. *See, e.g., Evon v. Law Offices of Sidney Mickell,* 688 F.3d 1015, 1032 (9th Cir. 2012); *Zagorski v. Midwest Billing Servs., Inc.,* 128 F.3d 1164 (7th Cir. 1997); *Emanuel v. Am. Credit Exch.,* 870 F.2d 805, 809 (2d Cir. 1989). Thus, these courts have found it an abuse of discretion to deny attorney's fees to a prevailing debtor as required by the FDCPA. *See, e.g., Zagorski,* 128 F.3d at 1164; *Emanuel,* 870 F.2d at 809.

The Third and Fourth Circuits have recognized an exception to the mandatory attorney's fee under § 1692k, suggesting that the FDCPA permits outright denial in "unusual circumstances." *See Graziano,* 950 F.2d at 114; *Carroll v. Wolpoff & Abramson,* 53 F.3d 626, 628 (4th Cir. 1995). In *Graziano v. Harrison,* the Third Circuit stated that a court may decline to award a prevailing FDCPA plaintiff attorney's fees "only in unusual circumstances... [and] in such circumstances, it should formulate particularized findings of fact and conclusions of law explaining its decision." 950 F.2d at 114. The *Graziano* court provided further insight: "The presence of bad faith conduct on the part of a plaintiff would surely be an unusual circumstance justifying a denial of an attorney's fee. Inability of a losing party to pay the attorney's fee is not a relevant consideration, however." *Id.* at n.13 (citations omitted).

Although neither party cites a Fifth Circuit case that has found special circumstances warranting the denial of attorney's fees in an FDCPA action, we have acknowledged the viability that "special circumstances" can justify a decision not to award fees in similar contexts. For example, while "[p]laintiffs as prevailing parties [under 42 U.S.C. § 1988] ordinarily should recover an attorney's fee," a district court may deny an award of fees if "special circumstances would render such an award unjust." *Romain v. Walters,* 856 F.3d 402, 407 (5th Cir. 2017) (quoting *Hensley v. Eckerhart,* 461 U.S. 424, 429, 103 S.Ct. 1933, 76 L.Ed.2d 40 (1983)); *see also Sanchez v. City of Austin,* 774 F.3d 873, 880 (5th Cir. 2014) ("The special-circumstances exception is a narrow carve-out of the general rule that prevailing civil-rights plaintiffs should be awarded fees."). In *Romain v. Walters,* we noted that our precedent requires an "extremely strong showing of special circumstances to avoid paying attorneys' fees and that the discretion to deny § 1988 fees is ... extremely narrow. p.977... In the absence of special circumstances a district court not merely may but *must* award fees to the prevailing plaintiff." *Romain,* 856 F.3d at 407-08 (internal quotations and citations omitted).

Further, we have narrowly interpreted the FDCPA attorney's fee provision. In *Johnson v. Eaton,* this court held that although plaintiff demonstrated a technical violation of the FDCPA, she was not entitled to attorney's fees because she did not prove actual damages and was not awarded statutory damages, reasoning that the statute required a "successful action to enforce the [claimed] liability." 80 F.3d 148, 151 (5th Cir. 1996). In *Johnson,* the plaintiff won a declaration that the defendant violated the FDCPA, "but was unable to prove any damages, either actual or additional, under the statute." *Johnson,* 80 F.3d at 152. Consequently, this court concluded that plaintiff was not entitled to attorney's fees under the FDCPA for her technical victory and, alternatively, that the most appropriate award of attorney's fees was $0.00: "[E]ven if we did agree with Johnson that she merits an award of a reasonable attorney's fee against White for proving that White violated the FDCPA, we would find that a reasonable attorney's fee in cases where no actual or additional damages were awarded is $0.00." *Id.* (citing *Farrar v. Hobby,* 506 U.S. 103, 120, 113 S.Ct. 566, 121 L.Ed.2d 494 (1992)).

Notwithstanding Davis' award of statutory damages, we conclude that the extreme facts of the instant case justify the district court's denial of attorney's fees. *See Carroll,* 53 F.3d at 628; *Graziano,* 950 F.2d at 114; *see also de Jesus v. Banco Popular de Puerto Rico,* 918 F.2d 232, 234 & n.4 (1st Cir. 1990) (reasoning that because the Truth in Lending Act's "attorney's fees provision is phrased in mandatory, rather than discretionary terms—it is evident that fees may be denied a successful plaintiff only in the most unusual of circumstances" such as bad faith, obdurate conduct, unjust hardship, or other special circumstances). "And even assuming arguendo that some 'reasonable' fee is always required, 15 U.S.C. § 1692k(a)(3), the statutory text does not preclude a court from deciding—consistent with its inherent authority to protect the integrity of its proceedings, *Chambers v. NASCO, Inc.,* 501 U.S. 32, 42-51, 111 S.Ct. 2123, 115 L.Ed.2d 27 (1991)—that a 'reasonable' fee in response to an exorbitant request is a nominal amount approaching zero." *Baylor v. Mitchell Rubenstein & Assocs., P.C.,* 857 F.3d 939, 958 (D.C. Cir. 2017) (Henderson, J., concurring) (collecting appellate cases that have held that a court may punish an intolerably excessive fee request by denying any award at all).

While attorney's fees need not be proportionate to the minimal statutory damages in FDCPA cases, they must nevertheless be reasonable. *See Tolentino v. Friedman,* 46 F.3d 645, 652 (7th Cir. 1995) ("In order to encourage able counsel to undertake FDCPA cases, as congress intended, it is necessary that counsel be awarded fees commensurate with those which they could obtain by taking other types of cases."). The Supreme Court has explained that "the most useful starting point for determining the amount of a reasonable fee is the number of hours reasonably expended on the litigation multiplied by a reasonable hourly rate." *Hensley v. Eckerhart,* 461 U.S. 424, 433, 103 S.Ct. 1933, 76 L.Ed.2d 40 (1983). The district court may increase or decrease the amount of attorney's fees based on a number of factors, including the time and labor required; difficulty of the question; skill needed; amount involved and results obtained; time limitations imposed by the case; and experience, reputation, and ability of the lawyers. *See id.* at 434-37, 103 p.978 S.Ct. 1933; *Johnson v. Ga. Highway Express, Inc.,* 488 F.2d 714, 717-19 (5th Cir. 1974). "The determination of a reasonable attorney's fee is left to the sound discretion of the trial judge." *Weeks v. S. Bell Tel. and Tel. Co.,* 467 F.2d 95, 97 (5th Cir. 1972).

Despite recognizing that a successful FDCPA case ordinarily justifies an award of attorney's fees, the district court declined to award fees in this case based on several thoroughly discussed reasons revolving around the conduct of Davis and her counsel. We agree with the district court's reasoning. As an initial matter, we join the magistrate judge's stunned reaction to Davis' request for $130,000 in attorneys' fees and concur that "the record reflects neither the quality of legal work necessary for the requested hourly billing rate ($450.00 per hour), nor the quantity of work to support the 156.55 hours claimed by Jonathan Raburn and the 133.25 hours claimed by Dennis McCarty." The pleadings filed by McCarty and Raburn, including the brief on appeal, are replete with grammatical errors, formatting issues, and improper citations, and is certainly not the caliber of work warranting such an extraordinary hourly rate.

The record does not suggest that the district court applied the incorrect method in considering Davis' request for attorney's fees. The district court's fee calculus involved a consideration of the number of hours it found reasonable for the type of litigation involved, as well as the "reasonable hourly rate for the services rendered by counsel." This is consistent with the lodestar method that is applied by this circuit. *See Black v. SettlePou, P.C.,* 732 F.3d 492, 502 (5th Cir. 2013) (quoting *Heidtman v. Cnty. of El Paso,* 171 F.3d 1038, 1043 (5th Cir. 1999)).

The magistrate judge appropriately reduced the fee request based on Plaintiff's limited success, emphasizing that Davis failed on the Texas law claim and on the claim for compensatory and exemplary damages under the FDCPA. *See Hensley,* 461 U.S. at 436, 103 S.Ct. 1933 (degree of success obtained is the most critical factor in determining the reasonableness of the award of attorney's fees). The court assessed further reductions based on the unnecessary duplication of efforts by McCarty and Raburn (citing duplications in counsel's time records), *see Walker v. U.S. Dept. of Hous. and Urban Dev.,* 99 F.3d 761, 768 (5th Cir. 1996), finding that the case was not complex enough to require or justify multiple counsel. The court excluded excessive time,[7] considering the simplicity of the claim, that Plaintiff only took one deposition, and that the case was disposed of on summary judgment with Fifth Circuit precedent directly on point. *See Watkins v. Fordice,* 7 F.3d 453, 457 (5th Cir. 1993). Finally, the court found that the $450 hourly rate request "exceeds by half the rate justified by the work performed for Plaintiff in this case."

Despite the district court's failure to assign numerical values to its reductions or "show its work" so to speak, it can be inferred that the district court found that the reasonable attorney's fee owed in this case was $0 (no fee at all). In addition to the aforementioned substantial reductions it discussed, the court "confidently" concluded—albeit with minimal jurisprudential guidance[8]—that the circumstances of p.979 this case constitute "special circumstances" that would render an award of attorney's fees unjust. This was largely based on the district court's finding of bad faith conduct on the part of plaintiff and her counsel: "It appears this cause of action was created by counsel for the purpose of generating, in counsel's own words, an 'incredibly high' fee request."[9] Specifically, in the order denying Davis' motion for attorney fees, the district court concluded that Davis and her counsel colluded in establishing the cause of action and created the appearance that CBOTS, a Louisiana entity, engaged in debt collection activities in Texas.

These factual findings are supported by the record. In her deposition, Davis admits that she called CBOTS and requested that CBOTS mail the water bill to her parents' address in Hallsville, Texas. Davis also testified that she retained Jonathan Raburn in April 2015, a date prior to CBOTS' alleged FDCPA violations, and worked for the Raburn Law Firm in the summer of 2015. At the pretrial hearing, McCarty also admitted that CBOTS mailed the water bill to Davis' parents' house in Texas per Davis' request. This provoked conduct (mailing of the August 18, 2015 "collection letter" to Texas address) is one of only two incidents wherein Davis alleged that CBOTS violated the FDCPA.[10] Notably, there is no mention of other attempts made by CBOTS to collect this debt since CBOTS mailed a statement of the bill to Davis' home in Shreveport in 2013. The magistrate judge expressed his suspicions of Davis and her counsel at the hearing:

> [C]ertainly the appearance is that she had it [the water bill] mailed to Texas for the purpose of generating this cause of action. It just seems suspicious to me that while employed by the law firm she asks for this Shreveport bill to be mailed to Texas and now files a lawsuit based upon that mailing.

Additionally, Davis admits that the phone call she made from Shreveport to CBOTS on September 22, 2015, which was one of at least three calls wherein she asked the same questions, was recorded using the Raburn Law Firm's recorder, and was apparently made in the presence of her attorney, Jonathan Raburn. Raburn's involvement in the recorded phone call—conduct at the center of this case—arguably made him a fact witness, potentially disqualifying him from representing Davis.[11] Although Davis is correct that CBOTS failed to raise the disqualification argument at the district level and thus waives it here, CBOTS nevertheless asserted, and the district court considered, allegations of collusion between Davis and her counsel. Such allegations are relevant to the consideration of the conduct of Davis' counsel and the special circumstances inquiry.

p.980 In the complaint, Davis' counsel misrepresented that Davis was a citizen of Harrison County, Texas, despite the overwhelming evidence that Davis was a citizen of Louisiana: she had a Louisiana driver's license, her vehicle was registered in Louisiana, she was registered to vote in Louisiana, she filed her state and federal income tax returns in Louisiana, and she lived and worked in Louisiana.[12] Counsel maintained this inaccurate representation in the answers to interrogatories and deposition of Davis. At the pretrial conference, the magistrate judge questioned McCarty about the truth of the representation made in the complaint, finding the only indication that Davis was a citizen of Texas was that her parents lived in Texas, which was insufficient to establish citizenship. McCarty conceded to the court that he knew that Davis could only be a citizen in one state, averring that he made a "mischoice of words" and offering to amend the complaint. Despite this admission and his lack of success below, counsel attempts to convince this court that Davis had "dual residency."[13] The record does not support that Davis was a *citizen* of Texas. For these reasons, there is nothing in the record to suggest that the district court's conclusions or ethical concerns are based on an incorrect assessment of the facts.

In exercising its broad discretion in deciding attorney's fees, the district court also considered the purpose of the FDCPA's attorney fee provision, finding that no such incentive was needed here "since her counsel essentially created her claim." Davis was employed by her attorney's law firm, the Raburn Law Firm, and on June 11, 2015—*prior to* the underlying lawsuit—she wrote an article articulating that it was against the law for a debt collector to use the words "Credit Bureau" in its company name, explicitly recognizing the difference between debt collectors and credit bureaus. While Davis' knowledge is not relevant in determining whether a FDCPA violation occurred, it further supports that Davis is not the type of person Congress intended to protect with the attorney fee-shifting provision.

Moreover, as conceded by Davis' counsel at oral argument, there were no actual damages in this case: the record contains no credible evidence of mental anguish and Davis testified that she had not suffered any economic loss. In denying an award of attorney's fees for a technical violation of the FDCPA, without actual or additional damages, this court in *Johnson* stated:

> Reading the FDCPA as requiring attorney's fees to be paid in actions where the plaintiff fails to prove damages, rewards lawyers for bringing suits to stop behavior that, by definition, has caused legal injury to no one. Our interpretation of the statute will require attorneys to look for more than a technical violation of the FDCPA before bringing suit and will deter suits brought only as a means of generating attorney's fees.

Johnson, 80 F.3d at 151. *Contra Pipiles v. Credit Bureau of Lockport, Inc.*, 886 F.2d 22, 28 (2d Cir. 1989) ("Because the FDCPA was violated ... the statute requires the award of costs and a reasonable attorney's fee," without requiring plaintiff to prove actual or additional damages.). While the case *sub judice* is distinguishable because Davis was awarded statutory p.981 damages, *Johnson* is illustrative of our disapproval of utilizing technical violations of the FDCPA solely as a means for generating attorney's fees.

In short, it appears that McCarty and Raburn lost sight of the real party in interest. The magistrate judge condemned the unreasonable attorney's fee request: "Plaintiff's counsel seem to believe that prevailing on a very simple claim under the FDCPA gives rise to a blank check for attorney's fees." The record suggests that McCarty and Raburn—in an attempt to receive an unwarranted and inflated award—impermissibly treated the $130,410 fee request as an "opening bid" in an attempt to negotiate the attorney's fee award. *See Baylor,* 857 F.3d at 959 (Henderson, J., concurring) (persuasively criticizing such tactics in FDCPA cases). "If similar demands become the norm ... they will sow distrust and spawn satellite fee litigation—one of the last things lawyers and judges should be spending their time on." *Id.* at 960.[14] This simply cannot be tolerated. Bottom-line: the FDCPA does not support avaricious efforts of attorneys seeking a windfall. Because grossly excessive attorney's fee requests directly contravene the purpose of the FDCPA, these tactics must be deterred. "Steep overbilling ought to come at a steep price." *Baylor,* 857 F.3d at 960 (Henderson, J., concurring).

Although complete denial of otherwise generally mandatory attorney's fees is a rare and drastic sanction, the outrageous facts in this case suggest that the district court did not abuse its discretion in determining that Davis was not entitled to attorney's fees, or that the reasonable attorney's fee was $0. The district court calculated a reasonable hourly rate to be, at most, $225 (half of the $450 demanded), which can further be reduced based on the poor draftsmanship that permeates the pleadings. The district court cited valid, precedentially-supported reasons for reducing the number of hours and amount of the fee award claimed by Davis' attorneys. Moreover, given the district court's desire to "disincentivize the conduct of Plaintiff's counsel," coupled with an additional, punitive reduction (or outright denial) for McCarty and Raburn's exorbitant fee request, it was not an abuse of discretion for the district court to deny Davis' motion for attorney's fees.

CONCLUSION

Because this case presents special and unusual circumstances justifying the denial of attorney's fees, the judgment of the district court is AFFIRMED.

[1] 15 U.S.C. §§ 1692e(10), (16) and § 1692f.

[2] Tex. Fin. Code § 392.301(a)(8), § 392.304(a)(19), § 392.305.

[3] CBOTS' motion for summary judgment included an alternative motion to transfer venue to the District Court for the Western District of Louisiana, arguing that Davis was a citizen of Louisiana (not a citizen of Texas) and that all relevant events occurred in Louisiana. CBOTS' motions were denied.

[4] Notably, there were no actual damages in this case.

[5] The TDCA claim was rejected by the district court on summary judgment and is not challenged on appeal. Additionally, Davis failed to provide credible record evidence of her claim for mental anguish (or any other actual damages) and, unsurprisingly, explicitly waived her TDCA cause of action and mental anguish claim at the summary judgment hearing/pretrial conference.

[6] In her motion, Davis requested attorneys' fees of $70,447.50 to Jonathan Raburn and $59,962.50 to Dennis McCarty, based on a "reasonable" $450.00 hourly fee.

[7] Raburn and McCarty collectively charged over $8,000 in travel fees alone. Additionally, the fee request included a charge for an attorney-client meeting that occurred on August 13, 2015—a date *prior* to the events Davis alleged in her complaint as the collection efforts that gave rise to her lawsuit (August 18, 2015 and September 22, 2015).

[8] The district court recognized that little jurisprudence exists on what facts constitute "special circumstances" that would render such an award unjust.

[9] The magistrate judge stated, "Indeed, Plaintiff's counsel surprisingly admit in their motion that they 'warned Defendant to take the mediation seriously because the attorney's fees was [sic] going to be incredibly high if it couldn't get resolved,'" threatening $200,000 in attorney's fees.

[10] Moreover, this was the only connection to Texas and provided the sole basis for Davis' claim under the Texas Debt Collection Act.

[11] *See Champaneria v. Brachfeld Law Grp., PC,* 3:12-CV-86, 2013 WL 244899, *3 (S.D. Tex. Jan. 22, 2013) (denying Defendant's disqualification argument made after default judgment was entered because the argument did not reach the merits of the case, and even if successful would only affect one of Champaneria's two attorneys); *McCarty v. Allen L. Adkins & Assocs., PC,* 3:12-CV-3852 (N.D. Tex. Feb. 20, 2013)

(disqualifying Dennis McCarty from representing plaintiff, finding that McCarty was directly involved in the event that prompted the FDCPA suit [a phone call to the debt collector], making him a material witness to the facts underlying the suit).

[12] CBOTS filed a motion for sanctions pursuant to Fed. R. Civ. P. 11 based on this misrepresentation.

[13] *See Wachovia Bank, N.A. v. Schmidt,* 546 U.S. 303, 318, 126 S.Ct. 941, 163 L.Ed.2d 797 (2006) (an individual that resides in more than one state is regarded as a citizen of but one state); *see also Acridge v. Evangelical Lutheran Good Samaritan Soc'y,* 334 F.3d 444, 451 (5th Cir. 2003) ("The general rule is that a person has only one domicile at a particular time.").

[14] Justice Brennan aptly characterized appeals from awards of attorney's fees as "one of the least socially productive types of litigation imaginable." *Hensley,* 461 U.S. at 442, 103 S.Ct. 1933 (Brennan, J., concurring in part and dissenting in part); *see also Carroll,* 53 F.3d at 628 (noting the "systemic costs of such appeals [of requests for attorney's fees] are often disproportionate to the limited benefits achieved by appellate second-guessing of a district court's fee calculation").

865 F.3d 322 (2017)

Ashraf MAHMOUD; Valerie Jackson, Plaintiffs-Appellants,
v.
DE MOSS OWNERS ASSOCIATION, INCORPORATED; Creative Management Company; Frank, Elmore, Lievens, Chesney & Turet, L.L.P.; Kristi A. Slaughter; Khosrow Abtahi, Defendants-Appellees.

No. 15-20618.

United States Court of Appeals, Fifth Circuit.

FILED July 28, 2017.

Mahmoud v. De Moss Owners Association, Inc., 865 F. 3d 322 (5th Cir. 2017)

Appeal from the United States District Court for the Southern District of Texas.

Lindsay Lee Lambert, Esq., Henry A. Jakob, Esq., Lambert & Jakob, P.L.L.C.,, Houston, TX, for Plaintiffs-Appellants.

Valarie J. Eissler, Litchfield Cavo, L.L.P., William L. Van Fleet, Esq., William Samuel Chesney, III, Frank, Elmore, Lievens, Chesney & Turet, L.L.P., Houston, TX, for Defendants-Appellees.

Before JONES, CLEMENT, and HIGGINSON, Circuit Judges.

p.325 EDITH H. JONES, Circuit Judge.

This appeal arises from the 2013 foreclosure sale of appellants Ashraf Mahmoud and Valerie Jackson's condominium unit in Houston, Texas. In 2013, Mahmoud and Jackson filed suit against the condo owners association, the company that manages the day-to-day affairs of the complex, the law firm hired to collect on delinquent homeowner accounts, and the attorney responsible for their account. Appellants alleged common law claims for breach of contract, wrongful foreclosure, negligent misrepresentation, and breach of fiduciary duty, and violations of the Federal Debt Collection Practices Act, Texas Fair Debt Collection Practices Act, and Texas Deceptive Trade Practices Act. 15 U.S.C. §§ 1692c, e, and f; Tex. Fin. Code Ann. p.326 § 392; Tex. Bus. & Com. Code Ann. § 17. The district court granted summary judgment on all claims. We affirm.

I

In 2001, Mahmoud and Jackson purchased condominium unit 806 located at 6606 De Moss Drive, Houston, Texas. The condo is part of De Moss Condominiums, which is run by the De Moss Owners Association (the Association) and governed by the Condominium Declaration (the Declaration) filed in Harris County, Texas in 1981. Paragraph 5.1 of the Declaration requires all owners to pay monthly assessments and grants the Association the power to assess late fees of $5.00 for each late payment, a late fee that was subsequently increased to $25.00. Common assessments include assessments based on non-recurring costs for repairs and improvements to the common areas of the premises. Paragraph 5.9 grants the

Association a lien to secure payment of these assessments. Finally, paragraph 3.10 allows the Association to charge individual owners for repairs to common elements willfully or negligently damaged by an owner or his or her guests.

Creative Management Company (Creative) managed the day-to-day operations of the condo complex. By letter dated August 24, 2012, Creative notified Jackson and Mahmoud that their account was delinquent by $1611.80 and gave them one month to make payment. The letter listed dated and itemized charges, including: a repair from May 2006, a repair from April 2007, a repair from February 2010, maintenance fees from July and August 2012, and an August 2012 late penalty.[1] The letter allowed Jackson and Mahmoud 30 days from receipt to challenge the validity of the debt or the account would be turned over to an agent or an attorney to initiate foreclosure proceedings or to file a lawsuit to recover the total amount due. The Association then turned the collection over to Appellee Kristi Slaughter of Frank, Elmore, Lievens, Chesney & Turet, L.L.P. (Appellee FELCT).

Slaughter sent Mahmoud and Jackson a letter dated October 8, 2012, identifying the balance on the "Resident Transaction Report" maintained by Creative as $2,171.80, and informing Mahmoud and Jackson that the debt was secured by a continuing lien against their condo and failure to pay the total amount within 30 days would result in a nonjudicial foreclosure on the lien. Page one of the letter stated that the balance was secured by a continuing lien against their condominium and that failure to pay the total amount "on or before the expiration of thirty (30) days from and after the date hereof" would result in nonjudicial foreclosure. Page two contained a notice, in all-caps, which included the following warning three times: "UNLESS YOU DISPUTE THE p.327 VALIDITY OF THIS DEBT OR ANY PORTION THEREOF WITHIN THIRTY (30) DAYS AFTER RECEIVING THIS LETTER, WE WILL ASSUME THE DEBT IS VALID." Mahmoud and Jackson never disputed the validity of the debt before filing this lawsuit.

Mahmoud and Jackson sent in three checks covering the three most recent monthly assessments ($750), but not the full amount of the debt owed ($2,171.80). Slaughter responded with two separate letters dated November 12, 2012, advising the owners that their unit would be put up for foreclosure sale and returning the checks. The charging of attorneys' fees and assessments had increased the balance due to $2,796.80. The property was posted for nonjudicial foreclosure on December 4, 2012. Both letters gave Mahmoud and Jackson until December 3 to pay the full amount or submit an Association-approved payment plan proposal.

On November 17, Mahmoud and Jackson sent a letter again including three checks for the most recent monthly assessments and requesting a breakdown of all outstanding fees to set up a payment plan. On November 20, 2012, Slaughter responded with the Resident Transaction Report which included all charges dating back to January 2006, returned the partial payment, and reminded them that they needed to establish an approved payment plan with the Association prior to the foreclosure date. A similar set of letters was exchanged a week later—Mahmoud and Jackson sending partial payment on November 27, 2012 and Slaughter returning it on November 28, 2012. Mahmoud acknowledged receiving Slaughter's November 28 letter and admitted that he did not contact the Association, Creative, or the Association's lawyers about its contents.

Slaughter, with the Association's permission, elected to delay the foreclosure sale and gave Mahmoud and Jackson more time to work out a payment plan. Her letter of December 10 confirms this forbearance until January 10, 2013 to make full payment (now increased to $3,321.80) or work out a payment plan. Once again, Mahmoud and Jackson sent an incomplete payment ($240), which was rejected, and no payment plan was forthcoming. A properly noticed foreclosure sale occurred on February 5, 2013. The amount owed to the Association ($4,861.80) was deducted from the sale price ($18,500) and the remainder deposited in the FELCT trust account ($13,638.20). Slaughter held the funds until receipt of a signed release. FELCT paid the $13,638.20 to Mahmoud and Jackson in February 2014. The new owner conveyed the unit back to Mahmoud and Jackson on June 17, 2014 via warranty deed. Ultimately, Mahmoud and Jackson were never dispossessed of the condo.

Mahmoud and Jackson filed suit on multiple common law and statutory claims and sought partial summary judgment as to liability (not damages) in January 2015. In March and April 2015, the Appellees sought summary judgment as to the claims against them. In September 2015, after hearing oral arguments, the district court issued a 23-page Memorandum Opinion and Order and entered judgment in favor of the Appellees. Mahmoud and Jackson timely appealed.

II

This court must "review the trial court's evidentiary rulings under an abuse of discretion standard." *Curtis v. M&S Petroleum, Inc.*, 174 F.3d 661, 667 (5th Cir. 1999). Evidentiary rulings, however, are also subject to harmless error review, "so even if a district court has abused its discretion, we will not reverse unless the error affected 'the substantial rights of the parties.'" *Heinsohn v. Carabin & Shaw,* p.328 P.C., 832 F.3d 224, 233 (5th Cir. 2016) (quoting *Nunez v. Allstate Ins. Co.*, 604 F.3d 840, 844 (5th Cir. 2010)).

With the record properly defined, this court then reviews a summary judgment de novo. *Wilcox v. Wild Well Control, Inc.*, 794 F.3d 531, 535 (5th Cir. 2015). Summary judgment is required "if the movant shows that there is no genuine dispute as to any material fact and the movant is entitled to judgment as a matter of law." FED. R. CIV. P. 56(a). This court may affirm the district court's grant of summary judgment on any ground supported by the record and presented to the district court. *Hernandez v. Velasquez*, 522 F.3d 556, 560 (5th Cir. 2008).

III

Mahmoud and Jackson's evidentiary objection was that the Certificate of Corporate Resolution regarding the increased late fees was hearsay, conclusory, and lacked foundation. They moved to strike the exhibit. In their motion for summary judgment, Mahmoud and Jackson additionally raised five new objections, all based on lack of foundation. Appellees argued successfully to the district court that the objections were waived.

On appeal, Mahmoud and Jackson contend that the district court did not identify any authority holding that objections to summary judgment evidence not made the first time the evidence is presented to the court are waived. Regardless whether the district court abused its discretion, however, any error was harmless. The issue whether the late fee increase was properly adopted by the Association is not dispositive of any claims, so it did not affect the outcome of the litigation and did not affect their substantial rights. *See Heinsohn,* 832 F.3d at 233.

IV

We consider separately each of the claims asserted by Mahmoud and Jackson. First, they argue that the district court erred in granting summary judgment for three different alleged breaches of the Declaration: that the Condo Defendants charged and demanded excessive late fees, wrongfully included time-barred debt in the assessment lien, and charged and ultimately foreclosed upon repair assessments without giving them notice and an opportunity to be heard. Under Texas law, it is a "strict" and "well established rule" that "a party to a contract who is himself in default cannot maintain a suit for its breach." *Dobbins v. Redden,* 785 S.W.2d 377, 378 (Tex. 1990) (quoting *Gulf Pipe Line Co. v. Nearen,* 135 Tex. 50, 138 S.W.2d 1065, 1068 (Tex. Comm'n App. 1940)).

Mahmoud and Jackson were indisputably in default under the contract. Paragraph 3.11. of the Declaration states: "Each Owner shall comply *strictly* with the provisions of this Declaration, the By-Laws and the decisions and resolutions of the Association adopted pursuant thereto." Paragraph 5.9 provides that "[a]ll sums assessed but unpaid by a Unit Owner for its share of Common Expenses chargeable to its respective Condominium Unit ... shall constitute a lien on such Unit" and expressly gives the Association the right to foreclose on such a lien. Mahmoud and Jackson's failure to pay their balance and to make timely payments on their monthly assessments was a material breach of the Declaration. *See E. Friedman & Assoc., Inc. v. ABC Hotel & Rest. Supply, Inc.,* 412 S.W.3d 561, 565 (Tex. App. 2013) ("One of the considerations in determining whether a breach is material is the extent to which the nonbreaching party will be deprived of the benefit that it could have reasonably anticipated from full performance."). p.329 Mahmoud and Jackson's argument that the Association waived the right to timely payment is incorrect; the Association's election to receive untimely payments, for which a late fee was charged, in no way compromised its contractual rights. Likewise, their performance was not prevented or excused by the Association's allegedly erroneous statements about their balance due; this argument, as the Association points out, conflates performance with cure. Summary judgment on this claim was proper.

V

Mahmoud and Jackson next assert that because of material disputed fact issues, their wrongful foreclosure claim should have gone to trial. "A wrongful-foreclosure claim under Texas law has three elements: (i) a defect in the foreclosure sale proceedings; (ii) a grossly inadequate selling price; and (iii) a causal connection between the defect and the grossly inadequate selling price." *Villarreal v. Wells Fargo Bank, N.A.,* 814 F.3d 763, 767-68 (5th Cir. 2016) (quoting *Miller v. BAC Home Loans Servicing, L.P.,* 726 F.3d 717, 726 (5th Cir. 2013)). Appellants offer no authority—and we have found none—to support the conclusion that an inaccurate balance included in a default notice constitutes a defect in the foreclosure proceedings, they do not allege that the sale price was grossly inadequate, and they never allege any causal connection between the defect and the sale price. Therefore, the district court did not err on this ground for granting summary judgment.

VI

Although they challenge the adverse summary judgment on their claim for negligent misrepresentation, Mahmoud and Jackson failed to cite specific misrepresentations by the Appellees. A cause of action for negligent misrepresentation in Texas requires: "(1) the representation is made by a defendant in the course of his business, or in a transaction in which he has a pecuniary interest; (2) the defendant supplies 'false information' for the guidance of others in their business, (3) the defendant did not exercise reasonable care or competence in obtaining or communicating the information, and (4) the plaintiff suffers pecuniary loss by justifiably relying on the representation." *Fed. Land Bank Ass'n v. Sloane,* 825 S.W.2d 439, 442 (Tex. 1991).

Both the Attorney and Condo Defendants sought and obtained summary judgment on these claims. But, as just noted, it is not clear what representations Mahmoud and Jackson allege were false or misleading, and there is no evidence that Mahmoud and Jackson either entered into or withdrew from any transaction on the basis of any statements made by the Appellees. *See McCamish, Martin, Brown & Loeffler v. F.E. Appling Interests,* 991 S.W.2d 787, 791 (Tex. 1999). Again, the district court did not err.

VII

The most legally plausible arguments asserted by Mahmoud and Jackson concern the summary judgment awarded in favor of the Attorney Defendants on the Fair Debt Collection Practices Act (FDCPA) claims. Specifically, the Appellants contend that the debt collection notices sent by the Attorney Defendants were defective, 15 U.S.C. § 1692g, and the Attorney Defendants unlawfully threatened to sue to recover a time-barred debt, see generally 15 U.S.C. §§ 1692e and f.

The FDCPA, 15 U.S.C. § 1692 et seq., imposes civil liability on "debt collector[s]" for certain prohibited debt collection p.330 practices. The Act regulates interactions between consumer debtors and "debt collector[s]," defined to include any person who "regularly collects ... debts owed or due or asserted to be owed or due another." §§ 1692a(5),(6). Attorneys qualify as debt collectors for purposes of the FDCPA when they regularly engage in consumer debt collection, including but not limited to litigation on behalf of a creditor client. *Heintz v. Jenkins,* 514 U.S. 291, 299, 115 S.Ct. 1489, 1493, 131 L.Ed.2d 395 (1995). There is no serious contention in this case that the Attorney Defendants were not "debt collectors." Nor is there any dispute that condominium association fees may qualify as debts regulated by the FDCPA. § 1692a(5) (debt is defined as "any obligation or alleged obligation of a consumer to pay money arising out of a transaction in which the money ... [is] primarily for personal, family, or household purposes...."); *see Newman v. Boehm,*

Pearlstein & Bright, Ltd., 119 F.3d 477, 481-82 (7th Cir. 1997) (homeowners' assessments are debts within FDCPA because they "directly benefit each household in the development").

A.

As an initial matter, the Attorney Defendants maintain an overarching defense that, when they engaged in enforcing the Association's lien by nonjudicial foreclosure, their actions were exempt from the FDCPA except for § 1692(f)(6), which specifies the circumstances under which a debt collector may take or threaten nonjudicial foreclosures:

> A debt collector may not use unfair or unconscionable means to collect or attempt to collect any debt. Without limiting the general application of the foregoing, the following conduct is a violation of this section: ... (6) Taking or threatening to take any nonjudicial action to effect dispossession or disablement of property if—(A) there is no present right to possession of the property claimed as collateral through an enforceable security interest; (B) there is no present intention to take possession of the property; or (C) the property is exempt by law from such dispossession or disablement.

This broad proposition was, however, rejected by this court in *Kaltenbach v. Richards*, which held that "a party who satisfies § 1692a(6)'s general definition of a 'debt collector' is a debt collector for the purposes of the entire FDCPA even when enforcing security interests." 464 F.3d 524, 529 (5th Cir. 2006). This court did not, however, decide "whether ... enforcement of the security interest ... constituted a 'communication in connection with the collection of any debt' within the meaning of § 1692g," *Id.* at n.5, and we need not address the question in this appeal while addressing each of Mahmoud and Jackson' claims.

B.

Addressing first the Appellants' § 1692g claim, we may assume arguendo that this provision applied to Slaughter's demand letters. The FDCPA requires debt collectors to provide notice that unless the consumer, with thirty days after receipt of the notice, disputes the validity of the debt, or any portion thereof, the debt will be assumed to be valid, § 1692g(a)(3), and no collection activities and communication during the 30-day period may overshadow or be inconsistent with the disclosure of the consumer's right to dispute the debt, § 1692g(b). Courts evaluate any potential deception in debt-related communications under an "unsophisticated" or "least sophisticated" consumer standard. *Taylor v. Perrin, Landry, deLaunay & Durand*, 103 F.3d 1232, 1236 (5th Cir. 1997). "That is, in p.331 determining whether the defendant's actions are deceptive under the FDCPA we must assume that the plaintiff-debtor is neither shrewd nor experienced in dealing with creditors." *Goswami v. Am. Collections Enter., Inc.*, 377 F.3d 488, 495 (5th Cir. 2004).

A fair interpretation of Slaughter's demand letter dated October 8, 2012, pursuant to this stringent standard demonstrates there is no violation of the 30-day rule. "Courts have generally found contradiction or apparent contradiction of the printed § 1692g notice where payment is demanded in a concrete period shorter than the 30-day statutory contest period." *McMurray v. ProCollect, Inc.*, 687 F.3d 665, 670 (5th Cir. 2012) (quoting *Peter v. GC Servs. L.P.*, 310 F.3d 344, 348 (5th Cir. 2002)). We must read the notice in its entirety and then determine if there is a concrete period shorter than is required. Here, the letter stated once on page one that Mahmoud and Jackson needed to pay "on or before the expiration of thirty (30) days from and after the date hereof" or nonjudicial foreclosure would occur. But three times on page two, the letter repeated that "[U]NLESS YOU DISPUTE THE VALIDITY OF THIS DEBT OR ANY PORTION THEREOF WITHIN THIRTY (30) DAYS AFTER RECEIVING THIS LETTER, WE WILL ASSUME THE DEBT IS VALID." This notice does not demand a concrete action period shorter than 30-days from receipt of the letter when read by the least sophisticated consumer.

Reinforcing our conclusion, other circuits have clearly held that if "any confusion created by the ambiguity on the front of the letter dissipates when read in conjunction with the language on the back," then there is no violation. *Jacobson v. Healthcare Fin. Servs., Inc.*, 516 F.3d 85, 93 (2d Cir. 2008) (quoting *McStay v. I.C. Sys., Inc.*, 308 F.3d 188, 191 (2d Cir.2002)). The district court did not err in determining that the notice did not violate § 1692g.

C.

The second set of FDCPA issues raised by Mahmoud and Jackson is that the Attorney Defendants' efforts to collect on allegedly partially time-barred debt violated § 1692e and § 1692f. Concerning § 1692e, they allege violations through "the false representation of" "the character, amount, or legal status of any debt," "[t]he threat to take any action that cannot legally be taken or that is not intended to be taken," and "[t]he use of any false representation or deceptive means to collect or attempt to collect any debt or to obtain information concerning a consumer." 15 U.S.C. § 1692e(2)(A), (5), (10). They claim the Attorney Defendants violated § 1692f by "[t]he collection of any amount (including any interest, fee, charge, or expense incidental to the principal obligation) unless such amount is expressly authorized by the agreement creating the debt or permitted by law." 15 U.S.C. § 1692f(1).

Notably, Mahmoud and Jackson did not take advantage of the verification periods they were offered to challenge any portion of the debt, yet in their lawsuit they contend that any attempt to foreclose based on $541.80 of the original $2,171.80 balance was time-barred. The Texas Property Code clearly states that an association's lien against a unit owner may include: "regular and special assessments, dues, fees, charges, interest, late fees, fines, collection costs, attorney's fees, and any other amount due to the association by the unit owner or levied against the unit by the association." Tex. Prop. Code § 82.113(a). The Declaration declared that assessments against condo owners are "covenants running with the land." Therefore, it is appropriate p.332 to examine the whole debt—repairs, monthly assessments, late fees, collection fees, and attorneys' fees—within the context of the Association's lien.

The threshold question is whether any of the debt is time-barred, specifically the portion that originated with two repairs in 2006 and 2007. Formal, itemized demand notices on the overall obligation for condo fees were sent to the owners beginning in August 2012. The parties do not dispute that Mahmoud and Jackson were in default for their condo payments from and after about mid-2012, and as to those there is no question of limitation. There is, however, no Texas case law identifying the statute of limitations that applies to nonjudicial foreclosure of liens on real property created to ensure the payment of condominium association fees and assessments. We do not rule on this novel issue of Texas law but will assume *arguendo* that limitations barred recovery of this small portion of the debt.[2]

But this preliminary assumption hardly carries the day for Mahmoud and Jackson, as they and the dissent would contend. No Fifth Circuit authority compels the holding p.333 that a nonjudicial foreclosure on a partially time-barred debt can violate FDCPA Sections 1692e or f. In *Castro v. Collecto, Inc.*, 634 F.3d 779, 783 (5th Cir. 2011), this court went only so far as to say that "threatening to sue on time-barred debt *may* well constitute a violation of the FDCPA." *Id.* (emphasis added). This court's more recent decision in *Daugherty v. Convergent Outsourcing, Inc.*, 836 F.3d 507 (5th Cir. 2016) extended *Castro* to the extent it overturned a dismissal on the pleadings and held that "a collection letter that is silent on litigation, but which offers to 'settle' a time-barred debt without acknowledging that such debt is judicially unenforceable, *can be sufficiently deceptive or misleading* to violate the FDCPA." *Id.* (emphasis added). The court holds merely that seeking collection "can be" violative, which is a far cry from implying, especially in the face of the summary judgment materials before us, that every attempt to collect such a debt infringes FDCPA-created rights.

Daugherty, moreover, is factually distinguishable for three significant reasons. First, there was no dispute that plaintiff's credit card debt had aged "over the course of many years;" the debt had been sold to a collection agency. *Id.* at 509. Here, less than 25% of the debt is allegedly time-barred. Second, *Daugherty* was premised on the undisputed assertion that limitations had run as to the entire debt, whereas the application of limitations as a bar to nonjudicial foreclosure here (whether on the whole debt or only the allegedly time-barred portion) is uncertain. Third, *Daugherty* remarks that the debt collector's offer of a discounted "settlement" that invited partial payment, without disclosing pitfalls like the potential renewal of the entire obligation, could be misleading to the unsophisticated consumer. *Id.* at 512-13. Here, Mahmoud and Jackson were not misled about the amounts they owed, three quarters of which were not time-barred, nor were they misled about the potential consequence of nonpayment: non-judicial foreclosure on their condo. That they were not misled is confirmed by the subsequent course of events: the purchaser at foreclosure paid for the condo in an amount fully burdened with the overdue fees and assessments, those amounts were deducted from the purchase price, and a rebate was paid to Mahmoud and Jackson.

For reasons similar to the factual background in *Daugherty*, the other circuits' cases on which the appellants (and dissent) rely exhibit dubious exercises of collection activity on indisputably and wholly time-barred debt. *Buchanan v. Northland Grp., Inc.*, 776 F.3d 393, 397 (6th Cir. 2015); *McMahon v. LVNV Funding, LLC*, 744 F.3d 1010, 1020 (7th Cir. 2014). *But see Huertas v. Galaxy Asset Mgmt.*, 641 F.3d 28, 33 ("[i]n the absence of a threat of litigation or actual litigation, no violation of the FDCPA has occurred when a debt collector attempts to collect on a potentially time-barred debt that is otherwise valid," (quoting *Freyermuth v. Credit Bureau Svces., Inc.*, 248 F.3d 767 (8th Cir. 2001))).[3] Additionally, both cases were decided in appeals from dismissal on the pleadings, and in each one the courts qualified their holdings. Thus,

McMahon states: "We do not hold that it is automatically improper for a debt collector to seek re-payment of time-barred debts; some people might consider p.334 full debt re-payment a moral obligation, even though the legal remedy for the debt has been extinguished." 744 F.3d at 1020. The majority in *Buchanan* concede "[n]or does a 'settlement offer' with respect to a time-barred debt by itself amount to a threat of litigation," 776 F.3d at 397, but "consumers might still be confused about the enforceability of a debt or the pitfalls of partial payment." *Id. at* 400.

To repeat once more, this case is unlike the cases that allowed FDCPA claims to proceed because of (1) its summary judgment posture; (2) the fact that only a small portion of the debt may have been time-barred; and (3) the parties' hot dispute over whether in fact even that small portion was both time-barred and could not be enforced by nonjudicial foreclosure. Without compelling authority, we decline to extend potential FDCPA liability to these circumstances.

It is also important to note that nonjudicial foreclosures on real property are an area traditionally dominated and closely regulated by state law, and federalism concerns are heightened in fields "which the states have traditionally occupied." *Rice v. Santa Fe Elevator Corp.*, 331 U.S. 218, 230, 67 S.Ct. 1146, 91 L.Ed. 1447 (1947).

"When one interpretation of an ambiguous federal statute would create a conflict with state foreclosure law and another plausible interpretation would not, we must adopt the latter interpretation." *Ho,* 840 F.3d at 626. In *Ho,* the Ninth Circuit, quoting the Supreme Court, declined to "'construe federal law in a manner that interferes with [California's] arrangements for conducting' non-judicial foreclosures." *Id.* (quoting *Sheriff,* 136 S.Ct. at 1602). To construe §§ 1692e and f the way Mahmoud and Jackson request would interfere with Texas's carefully articulated arrangements for conducting nonjudicial real property foreclosures by creating causes of action where state law finds no wrongful foreclosure. Moreover, applying these provisions to the debts owed by Mahmoud and Jackson makes no sense, inasmuch as the couple received repeated notices, in compliance with § 1692g as well as state law, and had multiple opportunities short of nonjudicial foreclosure in which to challenge the allegedly time-barred portion.

We do not hold that nonjudicial real property foreclosures in Texas are wholly exempt from the FDCPA; under the facts of this case, however, summary judgment was properly granted on Appellants' §§ 1692e and f claims based on the contention that part of the debts they owed were time-barred.

VIII

Mahmoud and Jackson argue that the district court erred in granting summary judgment to the Attorney Defendants on their claim under the Texas Debt Collection Act (TDCA), Tex. Fin. Code Ann. § 392.304(a)(8), asserting that "the summary judgment proof shows Slaughter's demands and threat of foreclosure were based in part on time-barred debt." They do not identify—nor have we found— any authority that supports the position that attempts to collect time-barred debt violate the TDCA. This argument is therefore forfeited for lack of sufficient briefing. *See* FED. R. APP. P. 28(a)(8)(A).

The Texas Deceptive Trade Practices Act (DTPA) provides that "a consumer" may bring an action for a variety of deceptive business practices listed under the Act. Tex. Bus. & Com. Code Ann. § 17.50(a). The district court held that "[t]he payment of monthly maintenance fees to a condominium association does not constitute a 'purchase' under the DTPA, such that a unit owner, like the plaintiff, p.335 would qualify as a consumer." On appeal, despite the Texas Supreme Court's clear and consistent holdings that "[o]nly a 'consumer' can maintain a cause of action directly under the DTPA," Mahmoud and Jackson do not contend that they are consumers within the statute's meaning. *Crown Life Insurance v. Casteel,* 22 S.W.3d 378, 386 (Tex. 2000); *Cruz v. Andrews Restoration, Inc.,* 364 S.W.3d 817, 822 (Tex. 2012); *Melody Home Mfg. Co. v. Barnes,* 741 S.W.2d 349 (Tex. 1987); *Flenniken v. Longview Bank and Trust Co.,* 661 S.W.2d 705, 706 (Tex. 1983). Therefore, the district court did not err.

IX

Mahmoud and Jackson argue that the district court erred in granting summary judgment on their claim that the Attorney Defendants breached their fiduciary duty when they refused to deliver the excess foreclosure sale proceeds without a release. This claim is meritless. The existence of a fiduciary relationship between the plaintiffs and defendants is a prerequisite to finding a breach of duty. *Jones v. Blume,* 196 S.W.3d 440, 447 (Tex. App.-Dallas 2006, pet. denied). Mahmoud and Jackson cannot establish that the Attorney Defendants owed them a fiduciary duty. Indeed, this court has specifically observed that foreclosure trustees do not owe the party subject to the foreclosure sale a fiduciary duty. *Stephenson v. LeBoeuf,* 16 S.W.3d 829, 837 (Tex. App. 14th 2000).

X

Finally, Mahmoud and Jackson sought declaratory relief "to determine their rights and true obligations under the agreements and statutes governing their ownership of the Property." They make assertions about the obligations created by the Declaration, but there is neither supporting argument nor case law authority. This argument is forfeited for lack of sufficient briefing. *See* FED. R. APP. P. 28(a)(8).

***

For the foregoing reasons, we AFFIRM the district court's judgment.

STEPHEN A. HIGGINSON, Circuit Judge, dissenting in part:

Concerned about the consequences for Texas property owners, I respectfully dissent from the majority opinion's holding that threatening to nonjudicially foreclose to collect the entirety of a debt that is partially time-barred cannot violate the FDCPA. The majority opinion emphasizes that this case is unique because of "its summary judgment posture." But the majority opinion affirms summary judgment based on a "hot dispute"—the applicable statute of limitations, which is a legal question to be decided by the court.

And the majority opinion incorrectly holds that, as matter of law, FDCPA claims must fail when "only a small portion of the debt [sought to be collected] may have been time-barred." I would hold instead that, consistent with the text and spirit of the Act, demanding full repayment of a partially time-barred debt under the threat of foreclosure—implying that the entirety of the debt is legally enforceable —violates the FDCPA. We should reverse and remand for further proceedings on Mahmoud and Jackson's claims under 15 U.S.C. §§ 1692e and 1692f.[1]

p.336 Because the majority opinion presupposes two elements of Mahmoud and Jackson's FDCPA claims—whether the Act applies to foreclosure-related conduct and whether foreclosure on some of the assessments here was time-barred—I begin by analyzing these two issues.

First, foreclosure-related conduct can be "debt collection" subject to FDCPA regulation. The majority opinion "assumes arguendo" this point, but every circuit that has considered the issue has held that foreclosure-related conduct, particularly demand letters that anticipate foreclosure proceedings, can constitute debt collection and therefore can—if false, misleading, deceptive, or unfair—violate the FDCPA.[2]

Second, as I read Texas law, part of the debts the Attorney Defendants tried to collect here were in fact time-barred from foreclosure. Starting with the general rules in Texas, a creditor must sue for payment of debt "not later than four years after the day the cause of action accrues." Tex. Civ. Prac. & Rem. Code § 16.004(a)(3). If the debt arose from an installment contract, the four-year statute of limitations "begins to run against each installment when it comes due." *Palmer v. Palmer,* 831 S.W.2d 479, 480 (Tex. App.-Texarkana 1992, no pet.) (collecting cases). As the Attorney Defendants admit, under Texas law, "the time period within which one must sue to recover a debt ... is also the same period within which one must sue to foreclose upon the lien [securing that debt]." *Hoarel Sign Co. v. Dominion Equity Corp.,* 910 S.W.2d 140, 144 (Tex. App.-Amarillo 1995, writ denied). In other words, a creditor has four years from the date an installment comes due to initiate foreclosure.

Section 16.035 of Texas's Civil Practice and Remedies Code is a statutory exception to these general rules. *See Holy Cross Church of God in Christ v. Wolf,* 44 S.W.3d 562, 566 (Tex. 2001) ("Section 16.0035 modifies the general rule that a claim accrues and limitations begins to run on each installment when it becomes due."). It provides that "[a] sale of real property under a power of sale in a mortgage or deed of trust that creates a real property lien must be made not later than four years after the day the cause of action accrues" and specifies that if the "real property lien" secures an installment contract, the cause of action does not accrue "until the maturity date of the last note, obligation, or installment." Tex. Civ. Prac. & Rem. Code § 16.035(b), (e). But—as the Attorney Defendants readily admit—this exception, which applies only to specially defined "real property liens," does not cover the condo association's contractually created assessment lien. So the general p.337 limitations period still applies.[3] Applying the general rule that the time period for foreclosing on a lien is the same four-year period within which the creditor could have sued to recover the underlying debt, *see Hoarel,* 910 S.W.2d at 144, the statute of limitations for foreclosing to collect the repair assessments levied against Mahmoud and Jackson in 2006 and 2007 expired in 2010 and 2011, well before the Attorney Defendants sent their first demand letter on October 8, 2012.

Nonetheless, the question remains whether threatening to nonjudicially foreclose on a debtor's home to collect partially time-barred debts violates the FDCPA. Mahmoud and Jackson argue that this conduct violates:

- Section 1692e(2), which prohibits "false[ly] represent[ing] ... the character, amount, or legal status of any debt";
- Section 1692e(5), which prohibits "threat[ening] to take any action that cannot legally be taken";
- Section 1692e(10), which prohibits "us[ing] ... false representation[s] or deceptive means to collect or attempt to collect any debt or to obtain information concerning a consumer"; and
- Section 1693f(1), which prohibits "collecti[ng]... any amount ... unless such amount is expressly authorized by the agreement creating the debt or permitted by law."

The majority opinion holds as a matter of law that because "only a small portion of the debt" the Attorney Defendants collected via foreclosure was time-barred, their demand letters cannot violate the FDCPA. This holding contravenes the plain language of the FDCPA and misreads existing Fifth Circuit law.

The FDCPA plainly prohibits a debt collector's using "false, deceptive, or misleading representation[s]" or "unfair or unconscionable means" to collect a debt. §§ 16923, 1692f. There is no authority for the majority opinion's proposition that when collection letters are only *a little bit* false, misleading, or unfair, debt collectors cannot be statutorily liable. "Small" violations of the Act are still violations of the Act. *See, e.g., Haney v. Portfolio Recovery Assocs., LLC,* 837 F.3d 918, 932 (8th Cir. 2016) (finding viable FDCPA claims based on amounts "misstated by $1.29, $1.84, and $0.65" because "there [i]s no *de minimis* exception to FDCPA liability based upon low dollar amounts").[4]

The Act specifically prohibits a debt collector's "threat[ening] to take *any action* that cannot legally be taken." § 1692e(5) (emphasis added). "Action" is simply "the process of doing something; [one's] conduct or behavior." *Action,* Black's Law Dictionary (10th ed. 2014). In other words, the FDCPA prohibits a debt collector from threatening to engage in any process, conduct, or behavior that the debt collector cannot legally engage in. *See generally Huertas v. Galaxy Asset Mgmt.,* 641 F.3d 28 (3d Cir. 2011) ("[T]he FDCPA permits a debt collector to seek voluntary repayment p.338 of the time-barred debt so long as the debt collector does not initiate or threaten *legal action* in connection with its debt collection efforts." (emphasis added)). State law may create varying processes (like judicial or nonjudicial foreclosure) that enable creditors to collect on outstanding debts, and the FDCPA—both written broadly and intended to be read broadly, *see Daugherty,* 836 F.3d at 511—prohibits unlawfully threatening to use any of those processes.

And in *Daugherty v. Convergent Outsourcing, Inc.,* our court held that "a collection letter violates the FDCPA," specifically §§ 1692e(2)(5) and 1692f, "when its statements could mislead an unsophisticated consumer to believe that [the consumer's] time-barred debt is legally enforceable, regardless of whether litigation is threatened." 836 F.3d 507, 509 (5th Cir. 2016). In doing so, we adopted the Sixth Circuit's analysis in *Buchanan v. Northland Group,* in which the court said, "A misrepresentation about the limitations period amounts to a 'straightforward' violation of § 1692e(2)(A)." 776 F.3d 393, 398-99 (6th Cir. 2015). This makes sense: by implying in any way that a time-barred debt is legally enforceable, the debt collector misrepresents "the character ... or legal status" of the debt, which is a separate example of prohibited conduct under the Act, § 1692e(2)(A).[5] And a debt collector's threatening to foreclose and ultimately foreclosing on someone's home to collect a debt certainly implies that the debt is legally enforceable.

Because the Attorney Defendants threatened nonjudicial foreclosure to collect the entirety of a partially time-barred debt, in violation of § 1692e(5), and thus implied that the full amount demanded was legally enforceable, in violation of §§ 1692e(2)(A), (10) and 1692f, I would remand this case for further proceedings.

[1] The letter included a breakdown of the balance:

05/10/2006 09/05 REPAIR 195.00 04/09/2007 PLUMBING REPAIR 346.80 02/16/2010 ROYAL INVESTMENT SVC 575.00 07/01/2012 MAINTENANCE FEES 220.00 08/01/2016 MAINTENANCE FEES 250.00 08/16/2012 LATE PENALTY 25.00 ________ 1,611.80

[2] The linchpin of the dissent is the superficial conclusion that under Texas law, a suit may not be filed to collect a "debt" that accrued more than four years before the instigation of litigation. Tex. Civ. Prac. & Rem. Code Ann. Sec. 16.004(a)(3). Because a lien at common law is "simply an incident of, and inseparable from the debt which it secures," it has been held that "if limitations prevent collection of the debt, the lien becomes unenforceable." *Hoarel Sign Co. v. Dominion Equity Corp.*, 910 S.W.2d 140, 144 (Tex. App. 1995), *writ denied* (May 10, 1996). But the dissent's wading into this uncharted territory is imprudent and inconclusive. First, the intermingling of the obligations to pay ongoing fees and assessments with the continuing lien makes this an unique case under Texas law. Condominium association fees and assessments are governed by a specific section of the Texas Property Code, Sec. 82.113, which prescribes enforcement by nonjudicial foreclosure according to the procedures prescribed for real property liens, Tex. Prop. Code Ch. 52. A four-year statute of limitations governs foreclosures of "real property liens", but the cause of action for foreclosure does not accrue on an installment obligation "until the maturity date of the last note, obligation, or installment." Tex. Civ. Prac. & Rem. Code Ann. Sec. 16.035(b), (e). It is true that Sec. 16.035(g)'s definition of "real property lien" does not appear to cover condominium association fees. The obligation to pay such fees, however, has been described by the Texas Supreme Court as a covenant running with the land and as creating a contractual lien *on the real property*. *But cf. Hoarel Sign Co.*, 910 S.W.2d at 144 (applying common law limitations because the materialmen's lien there derived from improvements "that d[id] not become part of the real estate.)" It is possible that a lacuna exists in Texas's limitations statutes for these types of assessments and fees. *Cf.* Tex.Civ. Prac. & Rem. Code Sec. 16.051 (residual limitations statute excludes actions for foreclose real property).

Second, even if a four-year statute applies, exactly when and how limitations began to run on Mahmoud and Jackson's obligations is unclear. For instance, it has been held that no limitations bar prevents suit by a party to an open account where the defendant did not prescribe and the court accordingly presumes that any payments received should have been applied to the oldest outstanding obligation. *Watson v. Cargill, Inc., Nutrena Div.*, 573 S.W.2d 35 (Tex. Civ. App-Waco, 1978); *Prowell v. Berry-Barnett Gro. Co.*, 462 S.W.2d 53 (Tex. Civ. App.-Waco, 1970) (writ refused). It has also been held, in a suit for partition, where a cotenant makes improvements to or pays expenses for jointly owned property, which benefit the common ownership, the cotenant may recover them irrespective of statutes of limitations so long as the cotenancy continued. *Tapp v. Tapp,* 134 S.W.2d 683 (Tex. Civ. App.-Texarkana 1939). Finally, it has been held that where a deed of trust authorized the trustee to pay taxes and insurance, *i.e.* ongoing costs, on mortgaged property, "the mere fact that the debt was barred [by limitations] does not ... make against the deed of trust lien securing the taxes and insurance subsequently paid." *Burke v. Guilford Mtg. Co.,* 161 S.W.2d 574, 582 (Tex. Civ. App.-Dallas 1942).

[3] We are bound by *Daugherty,* but I agree with the broader principles expressed in *Huertas, Freyermuth,* and in Judge Kethledge's dissent in *Buchanan Grp.*, 776 F.3d at 400-02. In nearly every state, the fact that a debt is time-barred from collection by a lawsuit does not extinguish the obligation. And particularly where a collection letter threatens no legal action, even an unsophisticated debtor knows enough to throw it away. Using moral suasion in these matters is not abusive or overbearing.

[1] As an initial matter, to the best of my review of the record, the Attorney Defendants never actually *moved* for summary judgment on Mahmoud and Jackson's FDCPA claims under §§ 1692e(2), (5), (10), and 1692f. Mahmoud and Jackson alleged distinct violations of the Act, specifically §§ 1692e, 1692f, and 1692g, in their amended complaint. In the Attorney Defendants' motion for summary judgment, they expressly "limit[ed] their arguments in [the FDCPA] section of their Motion to the requirements of § 1692g." The Attorney Defendants never addressed, and thus never asked for summary judgment on, Mahmoud and Jackson's allegations under §§ 1692e and 1692f. If this review of the record is accurate, the district court erred by "grant[ing] summary judgment *sua sponte* on grounds not requested by the moving party" without giving the parties' notice and a reasonable opportunity to respond. *Baker v. Metro. Life Ins. Co.,* 364 F.3d 624, 632 (5th Cir. 2004) (citation omitted); *see* Fed. R. Civ. P. 56(f)(2).

[2] *See, e.g., Glazer v. Chase Home Fin., LLC,* 704 F.3d 453 (6th Cir. 2013); *Reese v. Ellis, Painter, Ratterree & Adams, LLP,* 678 F.3d 1211 (11th Cir. 2012); *Gburek v. Litton Loan Servicing LP,* 614 F.3d 380 (7th Cir. 2010); *Wilson v. Draper & Goldberg, PLLC,* 443 F.3d 373 (4th Cir. 2006); *Piper v. Portnoff Law Assocs., Ltd.,* 396 F.3d 227 (3d Cir. 2005); *Romea v. Heiberger & Assocs.,* 163 F.3d 111 (2d Cir. 1998); *cf. Ho v. ReconTrust Co.,* 858 F.3d 568 (9th Cir. 2016) (explaining that enforcing a security interest and collecting a debt "are not mutually exclusive").

[3] Overlooking the general rules, the Attorney Defendants argue that because condo association liens don't meet the statutory definition of "real property liens," condo association liens must not be subject to *any* statute of limitations—a bizarre proposition that the majority opinion rightfully does not entertain.

[4] The majority opinion's reluctance to reach this conclusion may stem from a misimpression that finding an FDCPA violation based on threats to collect partially time-barred debts would "bar" or somehow undo the foreclosure on the whole debt that has already taken place. I do not suggest, nor do I read the damages provision of the FDCPA to mean, that this would be the appropriate result. *See* § 1692k.

[5] If a debt collector falsely represents the character or legal status of a debt in a demand letter to the debtor, specifically in violation of § 1692e(2)(A), it would seem that the debt collector has also violated the more general example of prohibited conduct in § 1692e(10): "[t]he use of any false representation... to collect or attempt to collect any debt...."

www.ingramcontent.com/pod-product-compliance
Lightning Source LLC
LaVergne TN
LVHW052015200926
848481LV00005B/1498